The Civil War Roster
of Davie County,
North Carolina

The Civil War Roster of Davie County, North Carolina

Biographies of 1,147 Men Before, During and After the Conflict

MARY ALICE M. HASTY *AND*
HAZEL M. WINFREE

Foreword by Jim Rumley

McFarland & Company, Inc., Publishers
Jefferson, North Carolina, and London

To our parents, with wonderful memories:
Annie Clementine Campbell and
George Locke Miller

The present work is a reprint of the illustrated case bound edition of The Civil War Roster of Davie County, North Carolina: Biographies of 1,147 Men Before, During and After the Conflict, *first published in 2009 by McFarland.*

LIBRARY OF CONGRESS CATALOGUING-IN-PUBLICATION DATA

Hasty, Mary Alice.
The Civil War roster of Davie County, North Carolina : biographies of 1,147 men before, during and after the conflict / Mary Alice M. Hasty and Hazel M. Winfree ; foreword by Jim Rumley.
p. cm.
Includes bibliographical references and index.

ISBN 978-0-7864-7159-1
softcover: acid free paper ∞

1. Davie County (N.C.) — Genealogy. 2. Davie County (N.C.) — Biography. 3. Confederate States of America. Army — Registers. 4. United States — History — Civil War, 1861–1865 — Registers. 5. North Carolina — History — Civil War, 1861–1865 — Registers. 6. Veterans — North Carolina — Davie County — Registers. 7. Soldiers — North Carolina — Davie County — Registers. 8. Veterans — North Carolina — Davie County — Biography. 9. Soldiers — North Carolina — Davie County — Biography.   I. Winfree, Hazel M., 1924– II. Title.
F262.D4H37 2012   929'.375669 — dc22   2008052980

BRITISH LIBRARY CATALOGUING DATA ARE AVAILABLE

© 2009 Mary Alice M. Hasty and Hazel M. Winfree. All rights reserved

No part of this book may be reproduced or transmitted in any form or by any means, electronic or mechanical, including photocopying or recording, or by any information storage and retrieval system, without permission in writing from the publisher.

On the cover: Albert Alexander Anderson (courtesy Taylor Slye); background and frame © 2012 Shutterstock

Manufactured in the United States of America

*McFarland & Company, Inc., Publishers
Box 611, Jefferson, North Carolina 28640
www.mcfarlandpub.com*

Acknowledgments

Doris Frye was the librarian of the Martin-Wall History Room of the Davie County Library for thirty years and she was "good at her craft." One day she observed me trying to research whether or not I had any Civil War era ancestors from Davidson County. She strolled over to my table, handed me a green book with white letters which read: *The Civil War Roster of Davidson County*, by Christopher M. Watford, and said "Here! This might help." I flipped it open to the M's and within seconds had found Alexander, Allison, Elias, Felix, Henry J., John A., Levi Franklin and Nicholas Franklin, along with their parents (my great-great-grandparents), Nicholas and Elizabeth Livengood Miller. Christopher Watford had done a lot of research and at that moment I was the beneficiary. What a bonanza! My immediate reaction was to ask Doris if Davie County had such a book. When she shook her head no, I exclaimed, "I can do this! I will make my sister help me; she should be good at history because she was in the first history class Jim Wall taught in Cooleemee back in 1938!"

That was several years ago. Today, Doris has retired and her name heads a list of kind souls who have been so helpful to my sister Hazel and me as we gathered data. Doris always knew where to find what we needed, and best of all, her sense of humor was in sync with ours. We were devastated when she retired, but then Jane McAllister stepped right into her shoes and we were off again. Jane's ideas and technical knowledge are real assets, along with her wonderful sense of humor.

It was impossible to write this book without quoting James Wall's *History of Davie County*, the most comprehensive history of the county. He has no idea how much his encouragement meant to us.

Research in Davie County would be difficult in the extreme except for the work already undertaken by Nancy Murphy, Everette Sain, the Davie County Historical and Genealogical Society and the Davie County Library staff in their transcription and compilation of the *Federal Census of 1860, 1870, 1880*; *Davie County Marriages 1836–1900*; and *Davie County Cemetery Volumes I and II*; as well as the Forsyth County Genealogical Society in preparing *Davie County, N.C. 1850 Federal Census*. We are extremely fortunate in Davie County to have such useful resources and research tools at our fingertips because of these wonderful people.

Thank you to Taylor Slye (and the Anderson clan) who provided the photograph of Albert Alexander Anderson which graces our cover. A.A. fought from Manassas to Appomattox and returned home to Davie County where he lived a long and successful life.

Jeanette Wilson, former custodian of the genealogy room at the Lexington Library, retired recently, but I want her to know how very helpful she was. It was she who introduced me to Robert Driver's book, *Company B, 10th Virginia Cavalry*. He in turn, gave me permission to use all the information, as did Claude Medlin, who had prepared lists of the Davie and Davidson County men who served in that cavalry.

It was in the Lexington Library that my sister and I met Ed and Sue Curtis, who hap-

Acknowledgments

pen to be two of Salisbury's most gracious and best-known historians. Their suggestions and enthusiasm for what we were attempting were genuinely appreciated.

We also wish to convey our gratitude to Jim Rumley, author and historian, for his support and for writing the foreword to this book.

There are four young men in Raleigh who are aware that this book is being written, and no doubt they will be glad when it is finished. They have all answered questions for me when I had nowhere else to turn. "Mike" Coffey is assistant editor to Matthew Brown, who happens to be editor of the series *North Carolina Troops 1861–1865 Roster*. Both men have patiently answered my questions from the beginning. Earl Ijames, archivist in the N.C. Division of Archives and History, was the first of the four to provide advice and assistance, and he was especially helpful with the pension applications. He is also related to the Ijames families in Davie and Forsyth counties. Sion Harrington, Erwin, North Carolina, is military collection archivist, also in the Office of Archives and History in Raleigh. He is also my former neighbor and he is among the kindest and most gracious of men. He is also one of the best former high school history teachers Harnett County ever had. To verify this, just ask the faculty who always signed up for his workshops.

Next, I want to thank my friend Emily Rogers who shares an interest in historical people and places, Civil War cemeteries and correspondence, and who is always willing to help before being asked.

A special "thank you" goes to Marie Roth and Brenda Bailey, cousins who obviously share some of the same creative genes, who not only typed and formatted the manuscript, but worked directly with the publisher to expedite the printing of the book.

Finally, the person who was most inconvenienced by way of relinquishing his dining room table for work space was John Austin Spillman, who tolerated impositions and loss of privacy until new arrangements could be made so two sisters intent on researching the lives of approximately 1,150 men could complete their task. The country ham biscuits and hot coffee, hot tomato soup and grilled sandwiches really hit the spot on those cold winter work days. He can honestly say he has paid his dues. The reward? An autographed copy of *The Civil War Roster of Davie County*!

— Mary Alice M. Hasty

Table of Contents

Acknowledgments   v
Foreword by Jim Rumley   1
Introduction   7

The Davie County Roster   11

Appendix 1: Company Rosters   235
Appendix 2: Townships Covered in the Censuses   247
Appendix 3: Burial Sites of Davie County Confederate Soldiers   249
Appendix 4: Mocksville Monument Names of Men Who Died in the Civil War   255
Appendix 5: Men Who Died in the Civil War Not on the Mocksville Monument   258
Bibliography   259
Index   261

Foreword by Jim Rumley

An attempt to summarize or explain any war immediately runs into the same problem: words. Even what to call a particular war is often in dispute. The Civil War has had many names; for the North it was the "War of the Rebellion"; for the South it was the "War of Northern Aggression." Then there was the compromise, "War Between the States."

Perhaps scholar Michael Walzer termed it best when he identified the problem as the "moral vocabulary of warfare." I call your attack on me a "massacre," and you brand my resistance as "treachery." If you kill me, the act can be justified by claiming I acted in a treacherous manner. As years pass, not only am I no longer around to dispute you — but, more importantly, I am not there to call your acts a massacre. In that case, only you are left to give meaning to my death.

The widows of the South's heroes were especially determined to see that the meaning of their husbands' deaths, in the tens of thousands, would not be left to the interpretation of those who killed them. Today, the struggle for their honor goes on.

The Miller sisters, Mary Alice Hasty and Hazel Winfree, have spent endless hours pouring over books, census tracts and other documents to assure that this precious piece of Davie County history remains a part of public memory. In the course of their research they were able to locate still more Davie soldiers, and more Civil War dead, than had previously been recorded.

While such memory is important for the living, it is even more important for those Southern generations yet to be born. After the present darkness passes future generations will have to study and reconstruct the Southern past, lest their culture vanishes from public memory. This book is more than a log of Confederate soldiers. Its brief biographical sketches give life and humanity to what would otherwise be simply a forgotten list.

In undertaking this important work, Cooleemee's Miller sisters follow in the footsteps of an earlier generation of Southern women who struggled to assure the history of the South would not be lost or misrepresented. The movement to preserve the South's war history began in late 1865 when some women in Winchester, Virginia, met and planned a memorial cemetery for those Confederate soldiers who had fallen in the nearby battles.

In 1866 women in Columbus, Georgia, began holding springtime memorial services for their local Confederate dead. They followed this up with a call for the whole South to organize such events. Today, North Carolina's Confederate Memorial Day ceremonies are still held on May 10th — the anniversary of Stonewall Jackson's death.

From these earliest of activities there grew a movement of Southern women which eventually organized itself into the Daughters of the Confederacy, an organization that remains active today. Their greatest contribution was their grasp that history written in granite or bronze could not be easily gotten rid of. In hundreds of small towns of our region, a solitary Confederate sentinel still stands facing North toward what had been an invading Northern force.

The Secession Crisis

North Carolina and Davie County entered the war only reluctantly. The area had a long history of wrestling with related questions. Planters in the South River section had formed a chapter of the American Colonization Society, which bought freedom for many slaves and paid for black freemen and former slaves to return to Africa, where the society established the colony called Liberia.

Davie County was home to Hinton Rowan Helper who authored *The Impending Crisis of the South: How to Meet It*. The book attacked slavery from the vantage point of the region's non-slaveholding whites and was considered second only to *Uncle Tom's Cabin* in its call for ending slavery. The 1857 volume became a powerful Republican Party tool in the election of Lincoln.

Two out of every three of Davie's citizens opposed the war as late as the winter of 1861. A ballot calling for a statewide convention on secession in February of 1861 had gone down to defeat by a vote of 47,321 against to 46,672 in favor. In Davie County some 754 voted against it while only 263 voted for the convention.

Barely a month after Lincoln's call for troops on April 15, 1861, public opinion changed overnight. North Carolina's Governor Ellis responded that no troops would be sent, adding: "I regard the levy of troops made by the administration for the purpose of subjugating the states of the South, as a violation of the constitution and as a gross usurpation of power."

For a people a mere two generations removed from the founding of the new nation, and the writing of its constitution, the compact had been broken. All the King's horses and all the King's men would not be able to put it together again. North Carolina anti-war leader John A. Gilmer announced, "we are all now one." Powerful unionist Thomas Ruffin declared, "Blood is thicker than water, fight, fight, fight."

On May 20, 1861, a statewide convention met in Raleigh and broke with the Union. Its resolution read: "that the union now subsisting between the state of North Carolina and the other states, under the title of the 'The United States of America' is hereby dissolved, and the state of North Carolina is in full possession and exercise of all those rights of sovereignty which belong and appertain to a free and independent state."

For all practical purposes, the Civil War began on April 12, 1861, with Lincoln's call for troops to attack the South. It would be a war like none that had ever come before or after. It brought more changes to American government and its people than any other single event in American history with the exception of the American Revolution itself.

The two sides facing each other were something of a huge mismatch. The total population of the South stood at a grand total of nine million — of which about one-third were slaves. Facing them just across the Mason and Dixon Line was a population of twenty-three million, placing the odds against the South at roughly five to two.

As far as the means of war, factories and a trained work force were just as important as population numbers. In this regard the South was also far behind. The Yankees had six times the number of factory workers as the South. North Carolina was industrially the weakest of the southern states with only one-hundredth of its population in factories.

North Carolina's population stood at just under one million people, with its 992,622 people. Its African-American population stood at 360,000, with some 30,500 of these holding the status of freemen. From this population the state contributed 125,000 soldiers, a number greater than its entire voting population.

Davie County was typical of the state in as much as it was very rural. Most of its population sweated for a living on small farms raising such staples as corn, wheat, fruits, cattle, hogs and whiskey. Nine out of ten people in ante-bellum Davie County were farmers or laborers and seventy-eight per cent of the white families owned no slaves in 1860. Most white families did their own work, grew what they ate, and made what they wore or used. A typical Davie family produced little surplus for the market and had little or no cash money.

Of the remaining families who did own slaves, fifteen percent of these listed from one to three. For the most part they worked in the fields along with their slave or slaves. Most all lived in log cabins. In Davie County, the true "plantation class," generally measured by ownership of at least twenty slaves, was very small, about seven percent.

By 1861 the population of Davie County was approximately 6,000 souls. Of this number, more than 1,200 men served in the Confederate service, approximately three-fourths of whom were volunteers. Nearly all of Davie County's white families, some 1,173, had one or more members who had gone to war.

The War

> "Join with me in expelling from our firesides the armies which an insane despotism sent amongst us to subjugate us to the iron rule of puritanical New England."
> — *General Arndt M. Stickes*

Describing the two armies that first formed up to fight, a famous German general, Von Moltke, denied it was warfare at all. For him, it was rather a movement of "armed mobs." This may have been a good description at the beginning, but it did not take long to bring about change. Both the Northern and Southern armies were essentially composed of civilians who entered their national service as regiments complete with officers. What made even citizen soldiers so dangerous was their arms. The Civil War was the first major war fought by two armies fully armed with rifles.

It is a remarkable fact that, by and large, rank and file soldiers on both sides pretty much agreed upon the form of government they lived under. Both sides' citizen soldiers believed they were in a struggle over the "first principles" each had inherited as fundamental truths from their revolutionary forefathers.

The war in the South began in a great rush. Young men flocked to arms; in fact, only the shortage of arms reduced the numbers who first stepped forward. Young women sewed flags and presented them as their neighborhood units marched off to war. Part of the rush was due to the belief of many that the war might be over before they had an opportunity to participate. While some may have hated Yankees and were fed up with the constant barrage of propaganda against their homeland, most probably had a strong desire for adventure. As Bell Irvin Wiley writes in his book, *The Life of Johnny Reb*, they were "rarin' for a fight."

Troops from North Carolina suffered the first casualties of the war and they may well have suffered its last. Henry L. Wyatt, from Edgecombe County, was killed in the first battle in June of 1861 at Big Bethal, Virginia. As Robert E. Lee began his last retreat on the way to his surrender at the Appomattox Court House on April 9, 1865, over 50 percent of the troops were Tar Heels, as had been the case of the last two years of the war.

North Carolina's role in the war was also central in ways other than supplying soldiers. It held a key strategic position in regard to food and other supplies for Lee's Army of Northern Virginia. The state's ports and railroads provided the means of acquiring still more supplies from Europe right up to February 1865 when Fort Fisher fell. That Tar Heels entered the war reluctantly was, in the end, no measure of their belief in the Southern Cause.

Men went off to fight as members of companies with names such as the "Davie Greys" and the "Davie Sweepstakes," to name only two. They hailed from small, rural neighborhoods scattered across the Davie countryside.

For the most part, the men filling local Confederate ranks had grown up together. From childhood, these young men grew up as sturdy individuals whose families had been drawn together in the ways of the collective rural small market society. They were linked by the customs of swap-work such as taking in hay or barn and house raisings. Many had hunted or fished together.

As soldiers their backgrounds were reflected in the creation of highly independent units representative of the small democracies from which they had mustered. Such democracies shaped their people from childhood to see themselves as equal with anyone else. From this grew one of the most democratic armies to mass since the classic republics of Greece and Rome.

Officers were elected by the men they would serve over, and in this war, honor and courage were the essential elements to winning election and holding on to their position on the battlefield. Officers literally led their men into battle. It was expected by the men that officers, by example, showed the bravery and courage necessary to face the enemy and stand under fire. The loss of a well-liked officer at a critical stage of a battle could mean the difference between victory and defeat.

In the brief space of this foreword, it is only possible to touch on some highlights of Davie County's Civil War troops. What can be said is that they generally fought or served in either Virginia or on the east coast of North Carolina. While Lee did cross into the north and an important battle was fought in Pennsylvania, most of their service time was spent within southern borders. It is also safe to say most saw some combat, but only a few experienced little combat.

Men from Davie County ended up in many different regiments and one of the largest was the 42nd regiment. Before being sent to Petersburg, Companies E and F of the "Davie Greys" guarded prisoners of war at the Salisbury Prison. This regiment later returned to the eastern part of the state to fight federal forces up and down the coast. They participated in the Battle of Fort Fisher. Following its fall, they participated in at least three battles against Sherman, the last being at Bentonville in March and April of 1865.

The Davie Greys seem to have been organized and largely led by the Clement family; at least five of the eight companies listed in James Wall's *History of Davie County* were. The Clements were joined by leaders such as John Edmunds Brown and William E. Booe. Our knowledge of this unit has been greatly enhanced by the research and writing of Mark Whitman.

Company F, 13th Regiment North Carolina Troops was organized in Mocksville by Jessie A. Clement. The first action for this company came on April 1862 near Williamsburg, Virginia, where they were ambushed. Luck was with them and they escaped with only a couple wounded.

In June of 1862, the unit hooked up with Stonewall Jackson's Valley Army and became part of his famous foot cavalry, known for their ability to cover more miles than was generally considered possible in that day. Rapid movement and surprise allowed Jackson to defeat army after army sent against him.

These Davie Greys would see their fiercest fighting in such battles as Seven Pines, Second Manassas, Harper's Ferry, Antietam and Fredericksburg-in short, most of the major battles of the war. By the time the 13th Regiment joined Lee's retreat from Gettysburg in July of 1863, the ranks of this company had been reduced to just eleven men. As its ranks were refilled, the unit continued fighting as part of Lee's army. On April 9, 1865, those remaining were present at Lee's surrender.

One has only to glance at the granite war monument near Davie's courthouse to fully appreciate the enormous local losses suffered in the Civil War. One cannot help but be struck by the number of names of local men who gave their lives, especially when compared to all other wars in which Davie citizens have fought.

The following documentary record provides both scholars and general readers a great service by adding much information which gives us a sense for what happened to the soldiers who returned home. Many walked home. Many returned to their small farms as cripples, or had suffered so much they could no longer work. As these veterans grew older, many found themselves with little more to support them than a small state war pension.

Of Things Lost

By war's end, the combined Northern and Southern losses totaled some 623,026 dead, from either fighting or hazards of camp life. War dead from all of America's wars to follow have yet to reach this number. If the same percentage of today's population were lost in a war, the toll would reach some six million.

For most of Davie's returning soldiers there was little free time to reflect on what had happened. Most of them certainly believed that the North's riches in men and materials had overwhelmed them. Many concluded that God had not been on their side after all.

That the war ended in the spring meant men could get home in time to plant a crop and hopefully be able to feed their families the following winter. Due to the North's decision to fight a "total war," meaning both civilian population as well as military forces were targets, the state's countryside was destroyed.

In their rush to survive there was one matter that could not but help remain in the forefront of their minds, the terrible loss of life. One in four of the South's white males between the ages of 20 and 40 did not return to the homes or fields of their small neighborhoods. The loss of some 5 percent of the South's productive population, coupled with the destruction of half of its livestock and a drop by 50 percent in food production, meant recovery would be very difficult.

The brave North Carolina troops suffered one-fourth of all battlefield deaths during the war: 20,000 men killed; 23,000 died of disease under field conditions. While Tar Heel deserters numbered 23,000, over one-third of these returned to their units.

For all the dissent against the war recorded in North Carolina, those who fought from Davie County were, for the most part, volunteers. Of the 125,000 North Carolinians who served in the war, seventy-two regiments in all—only 20,000 were drafted.

Jim Rumley is the historian and archivist of the Cooleemee Historical Association and the coordinator of the Southwide Textile Heritage Initiative.

Introduction

For many of us who grew up during World War II, the Civil War did not seem relevant. We read *Gone with the Wind* and we watched the movie, but Clark Gable and Vivian Leigh were larger than life and what was happening on the screen was their story. It seemed to have little to do with us except for the freeing of the slaves, which was of course, a very good thing. We just felt that the Civil War was as passé as hoop skirts and nineteen-inch waistlines. Young people can be indifferent to say the least.

Then it was 1990 and Ken Burns was presenting "The Civil War" on PBS television. Suddenly, there it was in our living rooms and we were mesmerized by the horror, the irony and the tragedy. Americans killed each other until 600,000 men had died. According to the documentary, "there was scarcely a family in the South that did not lose a son or brother or father."

To bring this closer home, Jim Wall states in his *History of Davie County*, that "nearly every Davie County family sent a father, brother, or son to the Civil War; and many sent two or more." On a personal note, my sister and I were stunned to learn that over in Davidson County eight Miller brothers (including our great-grandfather) went away to war and only one brother came home.

In Mocksville, the names of two hundred sixty-two men who died in the Civil War, 1861–1865, are listed on the Memorial Monument on the square. Listed in this book are fifty-five additional names of men who died.

The purpose of this book is to document the life of each of the Davie County men who served during the war by presenting his military history; identifying his parents, their occupations, the years and places of their births; his place and date of birth; his marriages, children, his occupation and his place of burial.

Of course, there will be errors. To illustrate the complexity of accurately compiling a roster, consider there are a minimum of thirty-eight men with the surname Foster who are listed, and eleven of those have first names that begin with the letter "J." Often a man's name will be spelled differently in different decades, or the census enumerators will use a first name in one decade and the middle name in another. Families would often delay naming a new baby. The names of locations would change ("the U.S. Census of Davie County Townships," courtesy of Marie Roth is printed here for your easy reference.) And we learned that information on a tombstone may or may not be correct. Take care to notice the surnames (last names) of step-children; they may use the stepfather's name instead of their own, and as a result may lose their true identity.

Tribute to Alfred "Teen" Blackburn

The Last Body Servant

This information was submitted by Alice G. Brown and Magalene Gaither

It is common knowledge that prosperous men who were slave owners and who fought in the war would often take their

Alfred "Teen" Blackburn (Joel Reese, Iredell County Public Library)

"body servants" with them. These servants usually had been with their masters for years and they played a major role in their welfare. Other men in their units often benefited as well as the servants procured and prepared food, kept living quarters and uniforms clean, polished weapons and tools, nursed their masters when they were sick or wounded, and performed myriad other duties necessary to their welfare and some sense of order. The State of North Carolina began to realize the contributions these servants were making and declared them eligible to receive a Class B Confederate pension of $26.26 per month. This information was taken from *Forgotten Confederates: An Anthology about Black Southerners*, compiled and edited by Charles Kelly Barrow, J.H. Segars and R.B. Rosenburg, Journal of Confederate History series, vol. XIV (Copyright 1995 Southern Heritage Press; Post Office Box 347163, Atlanta, Georgia 30334).

According to the reference work *Civil War in North Carolina*, the last Civil War Veteran to receive a Class B pension in North Carolina was Alfred "Teen" Blackburn, a body servant.

In addition, he was also the last person in Yadkin County to have been a slave. He was also the last surviving Confederate veteran of the Old North State for over nine months, until his death on March 8, 1951, at age 100 years, 10 months and 4 days.

This historic figure chose to make Davie County his home for four years after the war before returning to his lifetime home in Hamptonville in Yadkin County. Because of his brief tenure in Davie County, he became the great-great-grandfather (on his mother's side) of Clyde Sturdivant, Jr., for whom the gymnasium at Central Davie Academy is named.

The Davie County Roster

1. Adams, John F.
Private, Carolina Rangers • Company B, 10th Virginia Cavalry Regiment

John was born March 4, 1840. He enlisted in Davie County on October 29, 1861, at age 21. He was present until July–August of 1863, when he was absent on detached service. He returned in September 1863, and was present until August 1864. He lost his cartridge box on June 23, 1864, and his horse in July. He survived the war and was paroled on May 5, 1865, at Greensboro, North Carolina. He died in Raleigh, North Carolina, in the Confederate Soldiers' Home, on March 14, 1922, and is buried in Oakwood Cemetery, Raleigh, North Carolina.

2. Adams, John Q.
Private, Company G, 7th Regiment • Confederate Cavalry • Company D, 16th Battalion • N.C. Cavalry

John enlisted in Davie County on September 3, 1862, with the rank of Private. He transferred from Company G, 7th Regiment Confederate Cavalry on July 11, 1864, while absent in confinement at Point Lookout, Maryland, as a prisoner of war. He transferred to Fort Delaware, Delaware, on August 15, 1864, where he remained until paroled and exchanged at Venus Point, Savannah River, Georgia, on November 15, 1864.

3. Adams, W. (William)
Private, Company E, 42nd Regiment • N.C. Troops

William was born in Davie County in 1803. Census figures for 1850 list William's age as 47 years. He worked as a farmer and shoemaker prior to enlistment. The place and date of enlistment were not reported. He was hospitalized at Richmond, Virginia, on January 3, 1865, with an unspecified complaint. He died in the hospital at Richmond on January 11, 1865, of "mania." William's name is listed on the Memorial Monument for the Davie County men who died in the Civil War, 1861–1865.

Confederate soldiers "on the square" in Mocksville (Davie County Public Library).

Veterans circa 1900. Left to right: (seated) J.D. Hodges, Jesse Lee Clement and W.H. Clement; (standing) J.L. Glasscock, Simeon Goins, W.P. Ray and Leo A. Sheek (Davie County Public Library).

4. Albea, William
Sergeant • Captain William E. Booe's Partisan Rangers • N.C. Volunteers • Company H, 63rd Regiment • (5th Regiment N.C. Cavalry) • N.C. Troops

William was born in 1827. He enlisted in Davie at age 35, on July 14, 1862, for the war. He mustered in as a Private and was appointed Sergeant, November-December, 1862. He was present or accounted for through 1865.

5. Allen, A.C.
Private • Captain William E. Booe's Partisan Rangers • N.C. Volunteers • Company H, 63rd Regiment • (5th Regiment N.C. Cavalry) • N.C. Troops

A.C. enlisted in Davie County for the war. His name is reported on the muster roll dated September 17, 1862, but the date of enrollment is not given. The claim for the balance of pay due the widow of the deceased soldier was filed by A.C.'s widow on June 30, 1863, stating that he died in Davie County. Date and cause of death were not given. A.C.'s name is listed on the Memorial Monument for the Davie County men who died in the Civil War, 1861–1865.

6. Allen, Abram T.
Private, Company E, 42nd Regiment • N.C. Troops

Abram was born in Davie County in 1841, the son of Batson N. (1818, Davie) and Tabitha Chambers Allen. In 1860 the family lived in Fulton District where Abram worked as a laborer and his father worked as a farmer. Abram enlisted in Davie County at age 21, on March 18, 1862. He was present or accounted for through October 1864. Abram was paroled at Mocksville on June 10, 1865.

7. Allen, B.R.
Private • Captain William E. Booe's Partisan Rangers • N.C. Volunteers • Company H, 63rd Regiment • (5th Regiment N.C. Cavalry) • N.C. Troops

B.R. was born March 12, 1830. He married Dorcas A. (1835) Allen and they resided in the Smith Grove District of Davie County. Their two children were Sarah J. (1858) and William G. (1859). B.R. worked as a farmer prior to enlisting in Davie County, July 14, 1862, for the war. He mustered in as a Corporal, but was reduced to ranks August 1, 1863. He was present or accounted for until paroled at Salisbury, North Carolina, in

May 1865. Dorcas died on May 19, 1908, and B.R. died on June 20, 1911. They are buried in Smith Grove United Methodist Church Cemetery.

8. Allen, Isaac
Private, "Davie Sweep Stakes" • Company G, 4th Regiment • N.C. State Troops

Isaac was born in Davie County in 1840 to Jacob (1790, Lincoln) and Mary Allen (1809, Cabarrus). He worked as a laborer in the Farmington District prior to his enlistment at Camp Pickens, near Manassas, Virginia, September 16, 1861, for the war. He died in hospital at Plains Station, Virginia, October 30, 1861, of "phthisis pulmonalis." Isaac's name is listed on the Memorial Monument for the Davie County men who died in the Civil War, 1861–1865.

9. Allen, J.F.
Private, Company M, 7th Regiment • Confederate Cavalry • Company E, 16th Battalion • N.C. Cavalry

J.F. enlisted in Davie County on September 3, 1862. He was transferred from Company M, 7th Regiment Confederate Cavalry on July 11, 1864, while absent in confinement at Point Lookout, Maryland, as a prisoner of war. He remained there until paroled and exchanged at Venus Point, Savannah River, Georgia, November 15, 1864.

10. Allen, James P.
Private, "Davie Greys" • Company F, 13th Regiment • (3rd Regiment, N.C. Volunteers) • N.C. Troops

James was born in Davie County in 1846 to Jacob (1790, Lincoln) and Mary (1809, Cabarrus) Allen. The family farmed in the Farmington District. James enlisted at Camp Holmes, on September 29, 1864, for the war. He was present or accounted for through October 1864.

11. Allen, Peter
Private, Company D, 42nd Regiment • N.C. Troops

Peter was born in 1825 in Davie County. In 1850 he lived with Anderson and Mary Allen Smith and worked as a laborer. On September 30, 1854, he married Rebecca Tanner (Danner). They had two boys prior to the war: Eli (1859) and Samuel (1861). Peter enlisted for the war in either Rowan or Lenoir County at age 35, on March 20, 1863. He was present or accounted for until he deserted on August 12, 1864. He returned to duty on an unspecified date but was captured at or near Wise's Forks, Kinston, North Carolina, on March 10, 1865. He was confined at Point Lookout, Maryland, on March 16, 1865, and released on June 23, 1865, after taking the Oath of Allegiance. Peter returned to his family in Farmington and resumed his life of farming. He was still there in 1880. Peter is buried in Macedonia Moravian Church Cemetery. No dates are given.

12. Allen, William W.
Private, Company M, 7th Regiment • Confederate Cavalry • Company E, 16th Battalion • N.C. Cavalry

William enlisted in Davie County on September 3, 1862. He was transferred from Company M, 7th Regiment Confederate Cavalry to Company E, 16th Battalion N.C. Cavalry on July 11, 1864. He was present or accounted for through October 1, 1864.

13. Anderson, A.A. (Albert Alexander)
Sergeant, Company B, 21st Regiment • (11th Regiment, N.C. Volunteers) • Sergeant Major, Company A • Field and Staff, First Battalion • N.C. Sharpshooters

Albert was born on September 28, 1842, in Davie County to Richard (1793, Virginia) and

Albert Alexander Anderson (Taylor Slye)

The home of A.A. Anderson. Albert served from First Manassas, July 21, 1861, to Appomattox Courthouse, April 9, 1865. He returned home and fathered nine children (Mohney, *The Historic Architecture of Davie County*).

Sarah Neil Anderson. He was the youngest in a family of eleven. They resided in the Calahaln District where the Anderson clan continued to grow and prosper, providing doctors, dentists, educators and entrepreneurs throughout the county. At age 19, Albert was a schoolteacher. When the war began he resigned that position and joined the Confederacy, mustering in as a Sergeant. He was wounded at the first battle of Manassas, Virginia, on or about July 21, 1861. He returned to duty prior to November 1, 1861, and served with distinction for the rest of the war. He had the privilege to witness Generals Grant and Lee at the signing of the surrender at Appomattox Courthouse on April 9, 1865. He returned home, resumed teaching and married Mary Frances Poindexter on October 23, 1865. He was a successful businessman, owning and operating a tenant farm along with operating a mercantile business with his brothers Charles and John under the name "Anderson Brothers." "Uncle Ab" and "Aunt Fanny" had nine children: Annie Agnes, Robert Poindexter, Zollicofer Nelson, Frances Neil, Benjamin Richard, Martha Frances, Wiley Neil, Holt and Mary Ellen. Albert Anderson died on November 4, 1926; his wife Frances Poindexter Anderson died on January 9, 1942. Both are buried in the Anderson Family Cemetery.

14. Anderson, Andrew Jackson
Sergeant, Company C, 4th Regiment • N.C. State Troops

Andrew was born in Davie County on January 8, 1841, to Richard (1793, Virginia) and Sarah Ann Neil (Virginia) Anderson. They resided in the Calahaln District as one of the most prominent families in the county. Andrew was a student and a merchant prior to enlisting in Iredell County at age 21, on June 7, 1861, for the war. He mustered in as a Corporal and was promoted to Sergeant on September 1, 1861. He was present or accounted for until he was wounded at Seven Pines, Virginia, on May 31, 1862. He died in Davie County on June 19, 1862, and according to family history he died at "2 o'clock A.M. of typhus fever and the consequences of a camp life for twelve months and a wound received in the Battle of Chicomohomony, May 3, 1862." Andrew's name is not presently listed on the Memorial Monument for the Davie County men who died in the Civil War, 1861–1865. Andrew is buried in the Anderson Family Cemetery.

Note: Quote from Anderson Family File, Davie County Library.

15. Anderson, Charles Jefferson
Second Lieutenant, Company F • 77th Regiment, 19th Division • N.C. Militia 1861–1865

Charles J. was born October 17, 1826, in Davie County to Garland (1788, Virginia) and Sarah "Sally" Frost (1796, Davie) Anderson. (Sarah was the granddaughter of John Boone, cousin of Daniel Boone.) Charles was born into one of Davie County's most distinguished and respected families. He married Elizabeth C. Sharpe (1824, North Carolina) on December 4, 1849, and supported his growing family by farming. When the militia was activated he was appointed Second Lieutenant of Company F. He and Elizabeth were the parents of Thomas M. (1850), Garland S. (1852), Charles G. (1854), Mattie (no date), Edwin M. (1857), Henry E. (1859), Molly D. (1864) and Alice C. (1866). Charles died on March 1, 1891. He is buried in the Anderson Family Cemetery in Calahaln.

16. Anderson, Charles S.
Private, "Davie Greys" • Company F, 13th Regiment • (3rd Regiment, N.C. Volunteers) • N.C. Troops

Charles was born in Davie County in 1825. He worked as a farmer prior to marrying Nancy Penry on August 8, 1846. Their children were Sarah E. (1846), Eli W. (1848), Mary H. (1850), Franklin P. (1852), James B. "Thomas" (1853), Emily L. (1855) and Beal I. (1860). In 1860 they lived and farmed in the Calahaln District. Anderson enlisted in Davie County at age 36 on April 26, 1861. He was present or accounted for until he died in hospital at Richmond, Virginia, on June 2, 1862, of "typhoid fever." In 1870 Nancy continued to live and work as a farmer in Calahaln with her three youngest children. Charles's name is listed on the Memorial Monument for the Davie County men who died in the Civil War, 1861–1865.

17. Anderson, Edwin M.
Private, Company E, 42nd Regiment • Sergeant Major, Field and Staff• Third Lieutenant, Company E, 42nd Regiment • N.C. Troops

Edwin was born in Davie County in 1837. He was the son of Garland (1788, Davie) and Sarah (1798, Davie). On December 14, 1857, he and Martha M. Cheshire were married. Their son, Docter J.L. was born in 1859. Edwin was a farmer in the Mocksville District before he enlisted in Davie County at age 25, on March 18, 1862. He mustered in as a Private, was appointed acting Sergeant Major in July-August, 1863, and transferred for temporary duty with the Field and Staff of this regiment. Edwin was promoted to Sergeant Major in November-December, 1863, and assigned to permanent duty with the Field and Staff of this regiment. He was elected Third Lieutenant on March 18, 1864, and transferred back to this company. He was reduced to ranks in May-October, 1864, and was present or accounted for through October 1864. He was paroled at Mocksville on June 7, 1865.

18. Anderson, Dr. John
First Lieutenant, Company F • 77th Regiment, 19th Division • N.C. Militia 1861–1865

John was born April 1, 1837, in Davie County to Richard (1793, Virginia) and Sarah

Dr. Anderson received his medical diploma from the New York City Medical College and interned at Bellevue Hospital in New York City (Taylor Slye).

Dr. Anderson established his medical practice at his home, above, in Calahaln as early as 1877. His office still stands to the rear of this house (Mohney, *The Historic Architecture of Davie County*).

Ann Neil Anderson. They resided in the Calahaln District where they farmed and functioned as an integral part of the county. Prior to the war John was educated at Davie Academy and at the New York City Medical College. After his internship at Bellevue Hospital he returned home where he began his medical practice. He married Tobitha Olivia Turner on July 28, 1862. She died just four months later. He was called to serve in the Home Guard as a Lieutenant and was sent to Fort Fisher, North Carolina, near the end of the war. He married Julia Ellen Blackwell on September 14, 1868, and Tobitha O. was born September 24, 1869. Their other children were Sarah Emily (1-7-73), Mary Jennie (7-31-75), John Richard (10-28-81) and Frederick Anderson (12-11-86). Dr. Anderson continued to live in Calahaln until his death on August 22, 1896. He was initially buried in the Anderson Family Cemetery but was later interred in Oakwood Cemetery in Statesville, North Carolina.

19. Anderson, John T.
Private, Company B, 48th Regiment • N.C. Troops

John was born in 1842 in Davie County to Gairy (Garry) (1786, Edgecomb) and Lucinda Gentle (1815, Davie) Anderson. In 1860 John lived with his mother and his brother Thomas in the Fulton District of Davie, where he worked as a laborer prior to enlisting in Davidson County at age 20, March 6, 1862. He was wounded at or near King's School House, Virginia, on or about June 25, 1862. He died on June 26, of wounds. The place of death was not reported. John's name is not presently listed on the Memorial Monument for the Davie County men who died in the Civil War, 1861–1865.

20. Anderton, William D.
Private, Company F, 42nd Regiment • N.C. Troops

William was born in 1832 in Virginia to William (1795, Virginia) and Elizabeth (1800, Virginia) Anderton. They resided in the Chinquepin District of Davie County where William worked as a laborer prior to enlisting in Davie County at age 28, March 18, 1862. He died "at home" on June 27, 1862. The cause of death was not reported. William's name is listed on the Memorial Monument for the Davie County men who died in the Civil War, 1861–1865.

21. Armsworthy, J.C.
Private, Company E, 42nd Regiment • N.C. Troops

J.C. enlisted in Davie County, for the war, on June 15, 1863. He was present or accounted for through October 1864. No further information.

22. Arnold, Thomas L.
Bugler, William E. Booe's Partisan Rangers • N.C. Volunteers • Company H, 63rd Regiment • (5th Regiment N.C. Cavalry) • N.C. Troops

Thomas enlisted in Davie County at age 20, July 10, 1862, for the war. He mustered in as a Private and was appointed Bugler in November-December, 1863. He was present or accounted for through February 1865.

23. Atham, Horatio
Third Corporal, Carolina Rangers • Company B, 10th Virginia Cavalry Regiment • Company G, 4th N.C. Cavalry

Horatio was born in 1830 in Davie County. In 1850 he lived with his wife Mary (1830, Guilford) and daughter Amanda (1849, Davie) in Davie where he worked as a farmer; Mary A. was born in 1857, followed by Cora in 1865. The family resided with Daniel C. Wallace, a tobacconist, and his wife Caroline, prior to Horatio's enlisting on October 31, 1861. He was present as a Private in 1863. After that date he was absent on detail for a horse or present without a horse until November-December, 1863. He was detailed as a teamster January 1, 1864; by the end of the month he was absent sick with "gonorrhoea" in Charlottesville hospital in Virginia. He returned to duty February 22, 1864, and transferred to Company G where he continued as a teamster. In 1870 Mary and her three daughters lived in the Farmington District but there was no mention of Horatio.

24. Athan, Asbury
Private, "Davie Sweep Stakes" • Company G, 4th Regiment • N.C. State Troops

Asbury was born in 1816 in Davie County where he worked as a laborer. He and his wife, Mary Polly (1815) would have five children prior to his enlisting in Davie on June 4, 1861, for the war: Melissa (1844), Amos A. (1846), Betsy (1849), Carmila (1852) and William F. (1856). Company muster rolls indicate that he was reported absent without leave August 27, 1862; however, other company records indicate he was a prisoner of war who was "confined" September 27, 1862. He was admitted to hospital at Richmond, Virginia, October 9, 1862, and deserted November 7, 1862. He was reported absent without leave until apprehended and returned to duty in May-July, 1863. Records of the Federal Provost Marshal indicate that he was paroled at Appomattox Court House, Virginia, April 9, 1865; however, North Carolina pension records indicate that he was "mortally" wounded at "Winchester in Virginia [and] died in Davie County some eighteen months after the war closed....was wounded in the thigh and died from the effects of the wound." His military record states that he was mortally wounded in Virginia on May 15, 1864. Mary's application for a widow's pension is on file in the State Archives, Raleigh, North Carolina. Asbury's name is listed on the Memorial Monument for the Davie County men who died in the Civil War, 1861–1865.

25. Austin, Asberry
Sergeant, Company E, 42nd Regiment • N.C. Troops

Asberry was born in North Carolina, in 1835. In 1860 he lived in Smith Grove with the R.S. Naylor family where he made a living as a cabinet and wagon-maker. Elizabeth J. Naylor (1838, Davie) and Asberry were married and had a son, Thomas, born in 1861. Asberry enlisted in Davie County at age 27, on March 18, 1862. He mustered in as a Corporal, then was promoted to Sergeant on December 31, 1863. He was present or accounted for through April 26, 1865. He was paroled at Mocksville on June 8, 1865. In 1870 they lived in the Mocksville District where he worked as a carpenter. (In 1850 "Austin and Waggoman" had a cabinet shop where they made and sold wooden articles. This list shows their production for a year: 15 bureaus $250; 4 cupboards $75; 18 coffins $180; 15 bedsteads $75; 1 sideboard $25.)

26. Austin, C.
Drum Major • Field and Staff, 66th Regiment • N.C. Troops

C. enlisted in Davie County but the place and date are not known. He was reported present on the regimental roll dated November 1863. No further records.

27. Austin, Ephraim A.
20th Regiment, Tennessee Volunteers

Eph was born June 3, 1839, in Davie County to Henry R. (1808, Davie) and Elvira (1811, Davie) Gaither Austin. His birth coincided with the completion of the construction of Davie County's first courthouse and jail, which incidentally, were also built by his father. In 1850 and

1860, the census lists the family as living in the hotel in the Town of Mocksville District. Eph's parents are named as "Landlord" and "Landlady" of the hotel. Including the Austin family, there were seventeen occupants in 1860. All were listed as being from North Carolina, with the exception of a silversmith from New York (appropriately named W. Sellers), and a merchant from Prussia by the name of J.A. Rosler. Ephraim was 21 at the time and employed as a clerk. When war was declared he enlisted in the Tennessee Volunteers, and his tombstone in Joppa Cemetery tells the rest of the story:

Eph A. Austin
June 3, 1839   November 28, 1861
In memory of our Soldier Brother
Son of H.R. and Elvira Austin
A member of the 20th Regt.
Of Tennessee Volunteers

Ephraim's name is not presently listed on the Memorial Monument for the Davie County men who died in the Civil War, 1861–1865.

28. Austin, Green B.
Musician, "Davie Sweep Stakes" • Company G, 4th Regiment • N.C. State Troops

Green was born to Berry and Malona Austin in 1840. By 1850 his mother had assumed the role of family provider as a "farmerist" to support her five children. They resided in the Mocksville District prior to Green's enlistment at age 20, June 4, 1861, for the war. He mustered in as a Musician and was present and accounted for until transferred to the regimental band on February 11, 1863. Green married Catherine Hillard in Davie County on October 2, 1867.

29. Austin, James
Private, "Davie Sweep Stakes" • Company G, 4th Regiment • N.C. State Troops

James was born in 1842 to Ransom (1803, Davie) and Sarah (1811, Davie) Austin. They resided in the Fulton District of Davie County prior to James's enlistment at age 20, March 10, 1862, for the war. He died in Davie County on June 2, 1862, of disease. James's name is listed on the Memorial Monument for the Davie County men who died in the Civil War, 1861–1865.

The Davie Hotel was a large two-story log building located where the present Davie Courthouse (2008) stands. Ephraim Austin's parents were the proprietors from the 1850s until Henry R. Austin's death March 11, 1872 (***Davie County Heritage North Carolina 1997***).

Turrentine School parade float on the square. Note the spinning wheel. Circa 1910 (Davie County Public Library).

30. Austin, James C. (Clinton)
Private, Company D, 42nd Regiment • Captain William Howard's Company • N.C. Prison Guards • Musician, 1st Company A, Salisbury Prison Guard • "The Rough and Readys" • Company G, 66th Regiment • N.C. Troops

James was born on September 5, 1835, to Melona (1813, Davie) Austin. He married Barbara C. Gowan on December 24, 1856. They lived in Mocksville where he worked as a blacksmith prior to enlisting in Davie County on February 1, 1862. He initially served in Company D of the 42nd Regiment until he transferred to Howard's Company on or about May 1, 1862. He served as Musician in 1st Company A, Salisbury Prison Guard; then he was transferred to Company G, 66th Regiment on October 2, 1863. He was reported present through August 31, 1864. Several weeks later he was hospitalized at Richmond, Virginia, October 5, 1864. He returned to duty on November 15, 1864, and was paroled at Mocksville on June 3, 1865. He and Barbara remained in Davie County where he worked in a tobacco factory and she was a seamstress. James died on April 22, 1894, and he is buried in Joppa Cemetery.

31. Austin, John
Private, "Davie Sweep Stakes" • Company G, 4th Regiment • N.C. State Troops

John was born in 1844 to Ransom (1803, Davie) and Sarah (1811, Davie) Austin. They resided in the Fulton District of Davie County prior to John's enlistment at age 18, March 10, 1862, for the war. He died in hospital at Richmond, Virginia, June 19, 1862, of "pneumonia." John's name is listed on the Memorial Monument for the Davie County men who died in the Civil War, 1861–1865.

32. Austin, R.M. (Richard)
Private • Captain William E. Booe's Partisan Rangers • N.C. Volunteers • Company H, 63rd Regiment • (5th Regiment N.C. Cavalry) • N.C. Troops

Resided in Davie County and provided L. Clark as his substitute.

33. Austin, William
Private, "Davie Sweep Stakes" • Company G, 4th Regiment • N.C. State Troops

William was born in 1839 to Ransom (1803, Davie) and Sarah (1811, Davie) Austin. They resided in the Fulton District of Davie County prior to William's enlistment at age 22, June 5, 1861, for the war. He was wounded in the left hip at Seven Pines, Virginia, May 31, 1862, and died in hospital at Gordonsville, Virginia, March 26, 1863, of "pneumonia." William's name is listed on the Memorial Monument for the Davie County men who died in the Civil War, 1861–1865.

34. Bagarly, John F.
Private, "Davie Sweep Stakes" • Company G, 4th Regiment • N.C. State Troops

John was born in 1830. He lived in the Liberty District with the Henry Cope family and worked as a trader prior to enlisting at Camp Pickens near Manassas, Virginia, at age 30, August 2, 1861, for the war. He was reported on extra duty as a courier during most of the war and was present or accounted for until paroled at Appomattox Court House, Virginia, April 9, 1865. His parole indicates that he was an "ambulance driver."

35. Bahnson, Charles F.
Captain, Company 6, 2nd Battalion

Charles was born in 1840 in Lancaster, Pennsylvania. His parents moved to Salem where he attended Salem Boys School. He returned to Pennsylvania but joined the Confederate Army, Company 6, 2nd Battalion, September 1861. He was discharged with the rank of Captain. He practiced his profession as optician and jeweler in a small office in Farmington. Charles was a charter member of the Farmington Masonic Lodge and was elected the Grand Lecturer of the Grand Lodge of North Carolina. He married Jane Amanda Johnson, December 12, 1865. Charles' father, Bishop George Frederick Bahnson of Salem, performed the marriage ceremony. By 1880 they were the parents of George W. (1867), Mat-

The home of Charles F. Bahnson and his wife Jane Amanda Johnson. They resided in Farmington where in 1892 Charles published *The North Carolina Lodge Manual* (Mohney, *The Historic Architecture of Davie County*).

tie (1870) and Frank H. (1873). Charles died on February 16, 1911, and is buried in Farmington Community Cemetery. (Courtesy of *The Historic Architecture of Davie County* by Kirk Franklin Mohney, p.133)

36. Bailey, Benjamin (Berry)
Private, Company H, 23rd Regiment • N.C. Troops

Benjamin worked as a shoemaker prior to marrying Sarah Camoline Brooks on June 2, 1861. He enlisted in Iredell County at age 23, August 1, 1862, for the war. He was present or accounted for until wounded at Spotsylvania Court House, Virginia, May 12, 1864. He was reported absent wounded through December 1864 and paroled at Mocksville on June 9, 1865. He was buried in Fork Baptist Church Cemetery in 1904 where 103 years later he would be honored by the Daughters of the Confederacy with the placement of the Iron Cross on his grave.

Benjamin Berry Bailey (Jim Bailey)

37. Bailey, H.H.
Private, Company M, 7th Regiment • Confederate Cavalry • Company E, 16th Battalion • N.C. Cavalry

H.H. enlisted in Davie County on September 3, 1862. He was transferred from Company M, 7th Regiment Confederate Cavalry to Company E, 16th Battalion N.C. Cavalry on July 11, 1864, while absent on detail as a wagoner. He was reported absent on detail through October 1, 1864.

38. Bailey, Henry L.
Private, Company F, 42nd Regiment • N.C. Troops

Henry was born on March 8, 1844, to Wilie (1814, Davie) and Mary (1822, Davie) Bailey. They resided in the Mocksville District of Davie County where he enlisted at age 18, September 3, 1862, for the war. He was present or accounted for until captured at or near Wise's Forks, Kinston, North Carolina, March 10, 1865. He was confined at Point Lookout, Maryland, March 16, 1865, and released at Point Lookout on or about June 24, 1865, after taking the Oath of Allegiance. (North Carolina pension records indicate he was wounded on an unspecified date.) On December 25, 1865, Henry married Nancy (1844) Lowry. They lived in the Calahaln District where they raised their children: Sarah (1866), Parthena E. L. (1869), Dabney W. (1872), Nancy B. (1875) and John R. (1879). Henry died on February 18, 1923, and is buried at Center United Methodist Church Cemetery.

39. Bailey, John K.
Corporal, Company E, 42nd Regiment • N.C. Troops

John was born in 1842 in Davie County. He was the son of Nimrod (1817, Davie) and Nancy (1816, Davie) Bailey. John lived with his parents in the Smith Grove District where he farmed prior to enlisting in Davie County at age 18, on March 18, 1862. He was mustered in as a Private and promoted to Corporal on December 31, 1863. He was present or accounted for until captured near Fort Fisher, North Carolina, on February 16, 1865. John was confined at Point Lookout, Maryland, February 28, 1865, and was released there on May 12, 1865. He was paroled at Mocksville on June 3, 1865. John and M.A. Smith were married on January 21, 1868. In 1870 they lived in the Farmington District where M.A. kept house and John worked "manufacturing/tobacco."

40. Bailey, Lemuel Johnston
Private • Captain William E. Booe's Partisan Rangers • N.C. Volunteers • Company H, 63rd Regiment • (5th Regiment N.C. Cavalry) • N.C. Troops

Lemuel was born in 1846 to Braxton (1809, Davie) and Jane M. (1820, Rowan) Bailey. They resided in the Mocksville District of Davie County where Braxton worked as a merchant. Lemuel enlisted in Davie on September 18, 1863, for the war. He was captured near Madison Court House, Virginia, September 22, 1863, and confined at Old Capitol Prison, Washington, D.C., until transferred to Point Lookout, Maryland, September 26, 1863. He died in hospital at Point Lookout on January 7, 1864, of "febris typhoides" and was buried in the Confederate Cemetery, Point Lookout, Maryland. Lemuel's name is listed on the Memorial Monument for the Davie County men who died in the Civil War, 1861–1865.

41. Bailey, Nathan A.
Private, Carolina Rangers • Company B, 10th Virginia Cavalry Regiment

Nathan was born in 1843 in Davie County to Richmond (1810, Davie) and Eliza (1820, Davie) Bailey. He lived with his parents and worked as a farmhand in the Shady Grove District prior to enlisting in Davie on November 8, 1861. He was present through April 30, 1862, but was captured at White Oak Swamp, Virginia, on August 5, 1862. Nathan was sent to Fort Monroe, Virginia, and then transferred to Fort "Wool," where he was exchanged August 26, 1862. He was present through April 1863, although he had been without a horse since March 3, 1863. He was absent on detail at various times from then until the end of 1864.

42. Bailey, Thomas
Private • Captain William E. Booe's Partisan Rangers • N.C. Volunteers • Company H, 63rd Regiment • (5th Regiment N.C. Cavalry) • N.C. Troops

Thomas was born between 1843 and 1849 to Braxton (1809, Davie) and Jane M. (1820, Rowan) Bailey. They resided in the Mocksville District of Davie County where Braxton worked as a merchant. Thomas's military record begins with his being admitted to hospital at Danville, Virginia, April 2, 1865, with "erysipelas idiopathic," and ends with his being paroled at Mocksville, North Carolina, June 9, 1865. Census records show that Thomas Braxton Bailey attended college at age 21, that he became a lawyer and married Jessie Hall. They are both buried in Rose Cemetery. Jessie died in 1934 and Thomas died in 1916.

43. Bailey, William A.
Private, Carolina Rangers • Company B, 10th Virginia Cavalry Regiment

William A. Bailey, prominent in Davie politics, purchased this property in the last quarter of the nineteenth century. The ruin still reflects the style of its first owner, Hiram Phelps, a prosperous Davie County landowner (Mohney, ***The Historic Architecture of Davie County***).

William was born in 1844 in Davie County to Samuel (1815, Davie) and Sarah (1821, Davie) Wagoner Bailey. He lived with his parents in the Smith Grove District prior to enlisting in Davie on November 8, 1861, at age 16. He was present until he furnished a substitute and was discharged April 26, 1863. He resumed his life in Davie where he married P. Jane Phelps on July 21, 1864. Jane was the widow of Hiram Phelps, with four children of her own: Ida (1857), Hiram (1859), Fallie (1860) and Solomon (1862). William and Jane were the parents of Noah (1865) who died in 1868. In 1880 the family lived in Fulton District where William was classified as a farmer with a retinue of servants. According to Kirk Franklin Mohney's statement in his *Historic Architecture of Davie County, North Carolina*, William was a prominent figure in Davie County politics and he also owned a large farm in excess of 1000 acres near Advance. He served as Davie County Sheriff from 1882 to 1892, and served in the N.C. House of Representatives from 1897 until 1899 and 1911 until 1913. He was a Davie County Commissioner between the years 1902 and 1906. Jane died on January 16, 1891. On February 10, 1892, William married Anna Bailey. Both wives are buried in Advance Methodist Church Cemetery. When the Civil War Veterans' Census of 1890 was taken, William was listed as living in Shady Grove Township, Davie County. He died on August 2, 1914, and is buried in Advance Methodist Church Cemetery also.

44. Bailey, William Hall
Second Lieutenant, Company F, 42nd Regiment • N.C. Troops

William was born June 22, 1843, to Braxton (1809, Davie) and Jane (1820, Rowan) Bailey. They resided in the Mocksville District of Davie County where William worked as a clerk prior to enlisting at age 18, March 18, 1862. He mustered in as First Sergeant, was appointed Second Lieutenant on June 25, 1863, and was present or accounted for through October 1864. He was paroled at Greensboro, North Carolina, on May 1, 1865. He returned to Davie where he resumed working as a dry goods merchant in the Mocksville District. He died on November 21, 1932, and is buried in Rose Cemetery.

45. Baity, F.A. (Francis)
Corporal, Captain William E. Booe's Partisan Rangers • N.C. Volunteers • Company H, 63rd Regiment • (5th Regiment N.C. Cavalry) • N.C. Troops

F.A. (Francis) was born in 1830 in Davie County to Mary T. (1798, Surry) Baity. He worked as a farmer prior to his marriage to Eliza; David N. was born in 1857, followed by Andrew F. in 1861. F.A. enlisted at age 32, July 14, 1862, for the war, mustering in as a Corporal. He was reported as "wounded and taken prisoner June 21, at Upperville, Virginia," on the May–June, 1863, muster roll and as present on the July–August muster rolls. No Federal Provost Marshal records were found relative to his capture or release. He was counted present or accounted for until admitted to hospital at Richmond, Virginia, with a gunshot wound in the right hip on September 22, 1863, and furloughed for 60 days September 30, 1863. He was present or accounted for through December 1864. Upon his return to Davie, F.A. worked as a farmer and a shoemaker. Three more children were born: John Wesley (1870), Laura Belle (1873) and Henry F. (1876). An application for pension submitted by Eliza is on file at the State Archives, Raleigh, North Carolina.

46. Baity, G.A. (George Alex)
Private, Captain William E. Booe's Partisan Rangers • N.C. Volunteers • Company H, 63rd Regiment • (5th Regiment N.C. Cavalry) • N.C. Troops

G.A. was born in 1837. He lived with his mother Mary (1798, Davie), as well as with the David Hill family in Farmington prior to enlisting at age 25, 1862, for the war. He was captured at Ashley's Gap, Virginia, July 20, 1863, and confined at Point Lookout, Maryland, until paroled and exchanged at Aiken's Landing, Virginia, March 5, 1865. On September 19, 1865, he married J.S. Hill (1842, Surry). Her name has been recorded as "Jane" and "Jenetta." In 1870 they were living in the Smith Grove District with their two children, Mary (1866) and George (1869).

47. Baity (Beaty), George W.
Private, Company F, 42nd Regiment • N.C. Troops

George was born in 1832 to Mary (1798, Davie) Baity. On December 23, 1857, he married Abigail Colette. They resided in the Mocksville District of Davie County where George farmed prior to enlisting at age 30, March 18, 1862. He was present or accounted for through October 1864. He was paroled at Mocksville on June 3, 1865. By that time George had become the father of five children; six more would follow: Sarah V. (J.) (1853), John W. D. (1855), Ruth (1859), Charles W. (1860), Nancy E. (1862), Eliza B.

(1866), Susan E. (1868), Amanda A. (1869), George T. (1872), Joseph H. (1873) and Lucienda A. (1875).

48. Baity, J.W.
Private, Company A, 57th Regiment • N.C. Troops

J.W. was born in 1829 in Davie County. In 1850 at age 21, he worked as a laborer and resided in the home of Joseph and Eliza Eaton. On November 19, 1851, Mary Eaton (1833, North Carolina) and J.W. were married. Three children were born to them: Lou W. (1853), Mary E. (1857) and Josephine (1862). They lived in Fulton District where he was a tobacconist. He enlisted at age 33, July 4, 1862, for the war. J.W. was hospitalized at Richmond, Virginia, on or about October 20, 1862, with remittent fever. He died in the hospital at Richmond on or about December 25, 1862, of "variola confluent." After his death Mary and her three daughters lived in Jerusalem District, where Louisa later taught school at age 16. J.W.'s name is not presently listed on the Memorial Monument for the Davie County men who died in the Civil War, 1861–1865.

49. Baity, James D.
Private, Company G, 5th Regiment • N.C. State Troops

James was born in 1832 in Davie County to William (1799, Surry) and Margaret (1798, Surry) Baity. James married Sara C. and their daughter Malinda J. was born in 1859. He worked as a farmer in the Smith Grove District of Davie County prior to enlisting in Northampton County at age 31, August 13, 1862, for the war. He was present or accounted for until captured at Spotsylvania Court House, Virginia, May 12, 1864. He was confined at Point Lookout, Maryland, until transferred to Elmira, New York, August 3, 1864, and released there on June 30, 1865, after taking the Oath of Allegiance. James's brother William served as Corporal in this company.

50. Baity (Beatty), Thomas B.
Private, "Davie Greys" • Company F, 13th Regiment • (3rd Regiment, N.C. Volunteers) • N.C. Troops

Thomas was born in 1838 in Davie County. He lived with his mother Mary (1798, Davie) in the Chinquepin District where he worked as a laborer. On August 6, 1861, at age 26, he enlisted in Davie, for the war. He was present or accounted for until he died in hospital on July 3, 1862, of wounds received in battle near Richmond, Virginia. The date wounded and place of death were not reported. Thomas's name is listed on the Memorial Monument for the Davie County men who died in the Civil War, 1861–1865.

51. Baity, Wiley
Private, Carolina Rangers • Company B, 10th Virginia Cavalry Regiment

Wiley was born in Davie County in 1827 to William (1799, Surry) and Margaret (1798, Davie) Baity. They lived in the Smith Grove District where they worked as millers. Wiley enlisted in Davie on October 29, 1861, at age 34. He was present until May 8, 1863, when he was listed absent on detail and with no horse from July 1, 1863. He was present from November 1863 through April 1, 1864, and absent sick January 27, 1865. He was paroled in Salisbury, North Carolina, in May 1865.

52. Baity, William J.
Private, Company E, 4th Regiment • Corporal, Company G, 5th Regiment • N.C. State Troops

William was born in 1829 in Davie County to William (1799, Surry) and Margaret (1798, Davie) Baity. He married Sarah Elisabeth Tyson, November 13, 1850. They had two daughters: Martha (1855) and Julia (1858). William worked as a miller in the Smith Grove District of Davie County prior to enlisting in Wake County at age 33, July 15, 1862, for the war. He was transferred to Company G, 5th Regiment, N.C. State Troops on July 5, 1863, with the rank of Private. He was promoted to Corporal on November 1, 1863, and was present or accounted for until he was wounded at Spotsylvania Court House, Virginia, May 9, 1864. He was hospitalized at Lynchburg, Virginia, where he died of his wounds. The date of his death was not reported. Sarah's application for a widow's pension is on file in the State Archives, Raleigh, North Carolina. However, the application was denied by the commission because her real estate taxes were based on assets of $1200, which exceeded the value allowed. William's name is not presently listed on the Memorial Monument for the Davie County men who died in the Civil War, 1861–1865.

53. Baker, Thomas J.
Private, "Davie Sweep Stakes" • Company G, 4th Regiment • N.C. State Troops

Thomas was born to Thomas J. Baker, Sr.

(1813, Virginia), and Elizabeth (1817, North Carolina); he resided in Davie County where he enlisted at age 19, June 4, 1861, for the war. He was reported on detached duty with the Balloon Corps from June 20, 1862, through December 1862, and wounded in the right thigh and captured at Winchester, Virginia, September 19, 1864. He was hospitalized at Baltimore, Maryland, and then transferred to Point Lookout, Maryland, October 25, 1864, where he was paroled and transferred to Venus Point, Savannah River, Georgia, November 15, 1864, for exchange. He was paroled at Salisbury, North Carolina, in 1865. Upon returning to Davie County, Thomas married Margaret E. Blackwelder, October 29, 1865. By 1880 they had become the parents of five children: Wiley M. (1868), Sarah J. (1869), Virginia B. (1871), Marion H. (1873) and Susan E. (1878).

54. Baker, Thomas J. (Jefferson)
Private, Company E, 42nd Regiment • N.C. Troops

Thomas was born in 1820 in Virginia. By 1850. he resided in Davie County and was by occupation a farmer. Thomas married Elizabeth (1817, Davie) and they resided in Chinquepin with their four children: Elener (Ellen) (1845), Nancy (1846), Solomon (1850) and Mary R. (1854). Thomas enlisted at age 42, on March 18, 1862. He was present or accounted for until captured at or near Sugar Loaf, near Fort Fisher, North Carolina, on or about February 11, 1865. He was confined at Point Lookout, Maryland, on February 28, 1865, and later released at Point Lookout on May 12, 1865. Thomas returned home to Davie and resumed his life in the Clarksville District as a farmer.

55. Barlow, John J.
Private, "Davie Sweep Stakes" • Company G, 4th Regiment • N.C. State Troops

John was born in Davie County in 1825. He worked as a laborer in the Farmington area, married Sarah (1834, North Carolina) and had four children by 1860: Nancy E. (1852), Sarah L. (1855), James F. (1857) and Thomas (1860). On June 4, 1861, he enlisted for the war; on May 31, 1862, he was killed at Seven Pines, Virginia. John's name is listed on the Memorial Monument for the Davie County men who died in the Civil War, 1861–1865.

56. Barlow, Wiley
Private, Company E, 42nd Regiment • N.C. Troops

Wiley was born in 1830 in Davie County to James (1801, Davie) and Nancy (1799, Davie) Barlow. He and his father were farmers. He married Nancy M. Alexander on December 16, 1857. They were the parents of five children: Mary E. (1858), William A. (1861), Calob A. (1864), Fannie V. (1867) and Sallie A. (1869). Wiley enlisted in Davie County on March 18, 1862, at age 34. He was present or accounted for until he was wounded in an unspecified action on July 10, 1864. He was reported wounded through October 1864. He returned to duty prior to March 10, 1865, when he was captured at or near Wise's Forks, Kinston, North Carolina. He was confined at Point Lookout, Maryland, on March 16, 1865, and released there on June 23, 1865, after taking the Oath of Allegiance. He returned home to his family and resumed his life as a farmer in the Farmington District.

57. Barnes, W.J.
Private • Captain William E. Booe's Partisan Rangers • N.C. Volunteers • Company H, 63rd Regiment • (5th Regiment N.C. Cavalry) • N.C. Troops

W. (William) J. was born in 1813 in Virginia. He lived with his two sons Andrew (1833, Virginia) and William (1836, Virginia) in Davie County, where he worked as a farmer prior to enlisting in Davie at age 52, July 12, 1862, for the war as a substitute for Wiley Shores. He was sent to the hospital May–June, 1863, where he was detailed as a nurse. He was captured near Madison Court House, Virginia, September 22, 1863, and confined at Old Capitol Prison, Washington, D.C., until transferred to Point Lookout, Maryland, September 26, 1863. On August 16, 1864, he was transferred to Elmira, New York, where he remained until paroled and exchanged at Venus Point, Savannah River, Georgia, November 15, 1864.

58. Barneycastle, Jabus A.
Private, Company M, 7th Regiment • Confederate Cavalry • Company E, 16th Battalion • N.C. Cavalry

Jabus enlisted in Davie County on September 3, 1862. He transferred from Company M, 7th Regiment Confederate Cavalry to Company E, 16th Battalion N.C. Cavalry on July 11, 1864. He was present or accounted for through October 1864.

59. Barneycastle, James
Private, Company E, 42nd Regiment • N.C. Troops

James was born in 1844 in Davie County, the son of Levi (1813, Davie) and Hanna Elrod Barneycastle. In 1860 the family lived in the Mocksville District where they were farmers. James enlisted in Davie County at age 20, on April 11, 1862. He was present or accounted for until wounded at or near Petersburg, Virginia, in June 1864. He returned to duty on September 20, 1864. He was present or accounted for through January 20, 1865. James was paroled at Mocksville on June 7, 1865.

60. Barneycastle, P.F. (Pleasant Franklin)
Private, Company E, 42nd Regiment • N.C. Troops

P.F. was born in 1846 in Davie County to Levi (1813, Davie) and Hanna Elrod Barneycastle. In 1860 the family lived in the District of Mocksville where they worked as farmers. On April 6, 1864, P. F. enlisted for the war. He was present or accounted for through October 1864, and paroled at Mocksville on June 6, 1865.

61. Barnhart, George E. (Ephraim)
Private • Captain William E. Booe's Partisan Rangers • N.C. Volunteers • Company H, 63rd Regiment • (5th Regiment N.C. Cavalry) • N.C. Troops

George was born February 11, 1839. He married Elizabeth (1839) S. Kenly on September 10, 1857. They resided in the Fulton District where he farmed prior to enlisting at age 23, July 15, 1862, for the war. He was present or accounted for through November 1864, and paroled at Salisbury, North Carolina, in 1865. After the war he resumed his life as a farmer in the Jerusalem District where he and Elizabeth raised nine children: Mary J. (1858), William L. (1860), Charles E. (1863), Elizabeth S. (1866), Amelia L. (1869), Anne B. (1871), John F. (1873), Columbus F. (1875) and James F. (1877). George died on January 11, 1911, and is buried in Concord United Methodist Church Cemetery.

62. Barrouth, Henry F.
Private, Company G, 7th Regiment • Confederate Cavalry • Company D, 16th Battalion • N.C. Cavalry

Henry enlisted in Davie County on September 3, 1862, with the rank of Private. He transferred from Company G, 7th Regiment Confederate Cavalry on July 11, 1864. He was captured at Fort Harrison, Virginia, September 30, 1864, and confined at Point Lookout, Maryland, until paroled and exchanged at Boulware's Wharf, James River, Virginia, March 19, 1865.

63. Baxter, John W.
Sergeant, Company D, 42nd Regiment • Captain William Howard's Company • N.C. Prison Guards • Private, 1st Company A, Salisbury Prison Guard • Corporal, "The Rough and Readys" • Company G, 66th Regiment • N.C. Troops

John was born in 1836 in Davie County to Henry (1809, Iredell) and Elizabeth (1809, Iredell) Baxter. John lived with his family in the Mocksville District of Davie where his father farmed and he worked as a laborer prior to enlisting at age 26 on February 1, 1862. He mustered in as a Sergeant in Company D of the 42nd where he served briefly before transferring to Howard's Company on or about May 1, 1862. He served as Private in 1st Company A, Salisbury Prison Guard before transferring to Company G of the 66th on October 2, 1863. He was promoted to Corporal in January–February, 1864, and was present through April 30, 1864. On August 25, 1864, he was sent to the brigade infirmary and hospitalized at Richmond, Virginia, on an unspecified date. He was furloughed on September 26, 1864, and died at home on October 5, 1864. The cause of death was not reported. John's name is not presently listed on the Memorial Monument for the Davie County men who died in the Civil War, 1861–1865.

64. Beauchamp, John W.
Private, "Davie Sweep Stakes" • Company G, 4th Regiment • N.C. State Troops

John was the son of Anderson Beauchamp (Andrew Veacham) (1813, Davie). They resided in the Smith Grove area of Davie County, where John enlisted at age 20, June 4, 1861, for the war. He was wounded at Seven Pines, Virginia, May 31, 1862. While recuperating, he married Mary E. Miller, August 11, 1862, in Davie. He rejoined the company prior to January 1, 1863, was wounded during the battle at Chancellorsville, Virginia, May 3, 1863, and died on June 20, 1863, of wounds. Place of death is not known. John's name is listed on the Memorial Monument for the Davie County men who died in the Civil War, 1861–1865.

65. Beck, A.M. (Andrew)
Private, Company M, 7th Regiment • Confederate Cavalry • Company E, 16th Battalion • N.C. Cavalry

Andrew was born in 1818 in Davie County. He married Juley Thomas on September 23, 1840, and they lived in the Mocksville District where he farmed for a living. Their children were William H. (1845), Eady Elizabeth (1846), Sally T. (1847), Thomas J. (1849), Nancy M. (1851), Maria C. (1853), Thursa (1857) and John (1862). Andrew enlisted in Davie County on December 2, 1862, with the rank of Private. He transferred from Company M, 7th Regiment Confederate Cavalry to Company E, 16th Battalion N.C. Cavalry on July 11, 1864. He was present or accounted for through October 1864, and paroled at Salisbury, North Carolina, in 1865. After the war the family lived in Calahaln where Andrew resumed farming. Andrew is buried in Zion Chapel United Methodist Church Cemetery. No dates are given on his tombstone.

66. Beck, Henry
Private, Company A, 57th Regiment • N.C. Troops

Henry was born in 1831 in Davie County, the son of Richmond (1808, Davidson) who was a chair maker, and Sarah (1798, Davie). Henry resided in the Liberty District where he worked as a manufacturer and tobacconist. He married Amanda J. Baity (1840, North Carolina) prior to his enlistment in Rowan County on July 4, 1862, for the war. He was reported present though October 31, 1862, but was hospitalized at Richmond, Virginia, on November 25, 1862, with typhoid fever, then transferred to the hospital at Farmville, Virginia, on December 20, 1862, with "local paralysis." He was discharged from service at Farmville on January 8, 1863, by reason of "paralysis of left arm." Henry took the Oath of Allegiance at Salisbury, North Carolina, on June 2, 1865. The family continued to live and farm in the Jerusalem District. Henry and Amanda were the parents of seven children: Mary C. (1862), William Hewston (1864), Sarah E. (1867), John W. (1871), Albert O. (1873), David E. (1876) and Frances E. (1878). Henry died in 1907 and is buried in the Jerusalem Baptist Church Cemetery (Tatum Family Cemetery).

67. Beck, J.P.
Corporal, Company M, 7th Regiment • Confederate Cavalry • Company E, 16th Battalion • N.C. Cavalry

J.P. enlisted in Davie County on September 3, 1862. He transferred from Company M, 7th Regiment Confederate Cavalry on July 11, 1864, to Company E, 16th Regiment N.C. Cavalry. He was present or accounted for through October 1864. He was paroled at Salisbury, North Carolina, in 1865.

68. Beck, J.W. (John)
Private, Company A, 57th Regiment • N.C. Troops

J.W. was born in 1839, the son of Richmond (1808, Davidson) and Sarah (1798, Davie). He resided and worked as a farmer in Davie County. J.W. married Sarah E.J. Godby on June 20, 1858, and their son Beal S. was born in 1859. J.W. enlisted in Rowan County at age 23, on July 4, 1862, for the war. He was reported present through October 31, 1863, but was captured on November 7, 1863, at Rappahannock Station, Virginia, then sent to Washington, D.C. He was confined at Point Lookout, Maryland, on March 16, 1864, and was received at City Point, Virginia, on March 20, 1864, for exchange. He was reported absent without leave from May 20 through September 6, 1864, then reported absent on a surgeon's certificate in September 1864–February 1865. J.W. was paroled at Mocksville on June 9, 1865.

69. Beck, Little W.
Private, "Davie Sweep Stakes" • Company G, 4th Regiment • N.C. State Troops

Little was born in 1843 to Richmond (1808, Davidson) and Sarah (1798, Davie) Beck. Richmond was a chair maker and Sarah was a housekeeper. Little resided in Davie County where he enlisted at age 18, June 4, 1861, for the war. He was wounded and captured at Chancellorsville, Virginia, May 3, 1863, and confined at Washington, D.C., until paroled and transferred to City Point, Virginia, May 10, 1863, for exchange. The company muster roll dated April 30–August 31, 1863, states that he "deserted May 21, 1863, at a camp near Fredericksburg, Virginia." However, records of the Federal Provost Marshal indicate he was captured at Madison, Virginia, March 3, 1864, and confined at Old Capitol Prison, Washington, until released March 22, 1864, after taking the Oath of Amnesty. Little married Annie M. Beck and their son, Alson was born in 1868.

70. Beck, St. Leger
Private, Company M, 7th Regiment • Confederate Cavalry • Company E, 16th Battalion • N.C. Cavalry

St. Leger was born in Davie County in 1835, the son of David (1809, Davie) and Mary (1815, Virginia) Beck. He married Sarah A. Smith on

December 15, 1858, and they lived and farmed in the Mocksville District. St. Leger enlisted in Davie County on September 3, 1862, with the rank of Private. On July 11, 1864, he was transferred from Company M, 7th Regiment Confederate Cavalry to Company E, 16th Battalion N.C. Cavalry, while absent detailed as a blacksmith. He remained absent on detail through October 1864, and was paroled at Salisbury, North Carolina, in 1865. After the war he returned to Davie County and farmed in the Calahaln District. He married again, this time to Elizabeth Parish on March 18, 1885. He died on November 30, 1910, and is buried in Zion Chapel United Methodist Church Cemetery.

71. Beck, William
Private, "Davie Greys" • Company F, 13th Regiment • (3rd Regiment, N.C. Volunteers) • N.C. Troops

William resided in Davidson County and enlisted at Camp Holmes, on February 24, 1864, for the war. He was present or accounted for until captured at Sutherland's Station, Virginia, on or about April 3, 1865. He was confined at Point Lookout, Maryland, until hospitalized at Washington, D.C., July 24, 1865, and died on July 25, 1865, of "chronic diarrhoea and scurvy." Federal hospital records give his age as 30. William's name is listed on the Memorial Monument for the Davie County men who died in the Civil War, 1861–1865.

72. Beck, William H.
Private, "Davie Sweep Stakes" • Company G, 4th Regiment • N.C. State Troops

William was born in 1845 in Davie County to Andrew M. (1818, Davie) and Julia (1818, Davie) Thomas Beck. William worked as a farmer prior to enlisting at age 20, 1861, for the war. He was wounded in the right leg at Seven Pines, Virginia, May 31, 1862. He was discharged June 17, 1862, by reason of disability, following the amputation of the leg. He returned home to Davie where he worked as a shoemaker. He married Margaret M.A. (1844) Russel on January 26, 1864; their children were Wiley (1865), Henry (1867), Sally (1869), Andrew J.A. (1873), Julie (1875) and Noah J.L. (1877).

73. Beck, William P.
Private, "Davie Sweep Stakes" • Company G, 4th Regiment • N.C. State Troops

William was born in Davie County in 1838 to David (1809, Davie) and Mary (1815, Virginia) Beck. He married Rachel Whitaker in Davie County on October 12, 1858. He worked as a farmer in the Mocksville area prior to enlisting at age 23, June 17, 1861, for the war. William was recorded present and accounted for until he was captured at Burkeville, Virginia, April 6, 1865, confined at Newport News, Virginia, and released June 30, 1865, after taking the Oath of Allegiance. William returned to the Calahaln area of Davie County where he farmed and raised his family. He and Rachel would have three children by 1870: Cenethie T. (1863), Mary R. (1866) and David (1869).

74. Beeman, Richmond S.
Private, "Davie Sweep Stakes" • Company G, 4th Regiment • N.C. State Troops

Richmond was born in 1844 in Davie County. He lived with his mother, Louisa D. Little Beeman Booe, and his stepfather, John C. Booe. At age 18, on June 4, 1861, Richmond enlisted for the war. He died at Martinsville, West Virginia, July 1, 1863, of disease. Richmond's name is listed as "Richard" on the Memorial Monument for the Davie County men who died in the Civil War, 1861–1865.

75. Beeman, T.A. (Thomas)
Private, Company H, 63rd Regiment • (5th Regiment N.C. Cavalry) • Company G, 4th Regiment • N.C. State Troops

Thomas was born in 1829, the son of Elizabeth (1809, Davie) Beeman. He worked as a laborer prior to enlisting in Davie County at age 33, July 10, 1862, for the war. He was detailed as a wagoner and ambulance driver from November 1862 through August 1863, and was present or accounted for until he "deserted April 1, 1864." The muster roll for July–August, 1864, reports him as a "deserter." On November 26, 1864, he was transferred to Company G, 4th Regiment, N.C. State Troops, and paroled at Appomattox Court House, Virginia, April 9, 1865.

76. Bell, N.R.
Private, "Davie Greys" • Company F, 13th Regiment • (3rd Regiment, N.C. Volunteers) • N.C. Troops

N.R. enlisted at Camp Vance on January 25, 1864, for the war. He was present or accounted for until he died in hospital at Gordonsville, Virginia, April 15, 1864. The cause of death was not reported. N.R.'s name is listed on the Memorial Monument for the Davie County men who died in the Civil War, 1861–1865.

77. Bently, A. (Abner)
Private, "Davie Sweep Stakes" • Company G, 4th Regiment • N.C. State Troops

Abner was born in 1839 in North Carolina. In 1860 he was a laborer living in the Smith Grove District, married to Mary J. Bentley, with a son, John H. (1859). Abner enlisted in Davie County at age 23, March 12, 1862, for the war. He died in the hospital at Richmond, Virginia, June 25, 1862, of "diarrhoea acute and syphlis." Abner's name is listed on the Memorial Monument for the Davie County men who died in the Civil War, 1861–1865.

78. Berryman, Alfred S.
Private, "Davie Sweep Stakes" • Company G, 4th Regiment • N.C. State Troops

Alfred was born in 1830 in Davie County where he resided as a farmer prior to enlisting at age 31, 1861, for the war. He was discharged January 3, 1863, by reason of "sencoma." In 1870 Alfred was living with Sarah Berryman, age 19, in the Fulton District of Davie, where he continued to farm.

79. Berryman, James M.
Private, Company F, 42nd Regiment • N.C. Troops

James was born in 1840. He enlisted in Davie County at age 22, March 24, 1862. He was present or accounted for until killed at or near Cold Harbor, Virginia, on or about June 5, 1864. James's name is listed on the Memorial Monument for the Davie County men who died in the Civil War, 1861–1865.

80. Bessent, Daniel D.
Private, "Davie Greys" • Company F, 13th Regiment • (3rd Regiment, N.C. Volunteers) • N.C. Troops

Daniel was born in 1843 in Davie County. He was the son of Calton W. (1814, Davie) and Rebekah Click (1823, Davie) Bessent. His father was a Baptist minister. In 1860, at age 16, he was working as a laborer, still at home with his parents in Liberty District. On April 26, 1861, he was a tobacconist who enlisted in Davie County for the war. He was present or accounted for until killed at Chancellorsville, Virginia, on May 3, 1863. Daniel is buried in Jerusalem Baptist Church Cemetery. His tombstone contradicts military data:

Battle of Wilderness
Fredericksburg Campaign
1843/1862

Daniel's name is listed on the Memorial Monument for the Davie County men who died in the Civil War, 1861–1865.

81. Bingham, G.M. (George)
Sergeant, Company M, 7th Regiment • Confederate Cavalry • Company E, 16th Battalion • N.C. Cavalry

G.M. was born in Cumberland County in 1825. He was the son of Lemuel (1795, Massachusetts) and Jane (1797, Rowan) Bingham. At age 25 he lived with his parents and worked as an apothecary in Mocksville District; at the time of his enlistment he was working as a clerk. George enlisted with the rank of Sergeant, in Davie County, on December 19, 1862. He was transferred from Company M, 7th Regiment Confederate Cavalry on July 11, 1864, to Company E, 16th Battalion N.C. Cavalry. He was present or accounted for through October 1, 1864, and paroled at Appomattox Court House, Virginia, April 9, 1865. George returned to Mocksville where he eventually became Clerk of Superior Court. He boarded at the hotel run by Elvira Austin.

82. Bingham, Gustavus Adolphus
First Lieutenant, Carolina Rangers • Company B, 10th Virginia Cavalry Regiment

Gustavus was born in 1830 in Rowan County to Lemuel (1795, Massachusetts) and Jane (1797, Rowan). His father was a "Clerk and Master" and Gustavus was a bookkeeper prior to enlisting in Davie on October 29, 1861. He enlisted as a Third Lieutenant, was promoted to Second Lieutenant on January 13, 1863, and commanded the dismounted men of the regiment known as "Company Q" on May 13, 1863. He received the rank of First Lieutenant on September 26, 1863. He was absent on leave January 25–31, 1865, and was paid February 27, 1865, after which there was no further military record. Gustavus and T.E. Neely were married in Davie County, April 30, 1867.

83. Binkley, J.W.
Private, Company G, 7th Regiment • Confederate Cavalry • Company D, 16th Battalion • N.C. Cavalry

J.W. enlisted in Davie County on September 3, 1862, with the rank of Private. He transferred from Company G, 7th Regiment Confederate Cavalry on July 11, 1864, while absent "detailed with artillery." He was absent on detail through August 1864, and present or accounted for through October 1, 1864.

84. Binkley, James H.
Private, Company E, 42nd Regiment • N.C. Troops

James was born in 1827 in Davie County. In 1850 he was 24 years old, a laborer living with the Mary Baity family. On August 20, 1854, he married Margaret I. Baity (1834, Davie). James and Margaret moved to the Smith Grove District where he became a farmer. At age 35, on March 18, 1862, he enlisted in Davie County. James was present or accounted for through February 17, 1865. By 1870, James and Margaret Isabella had moved to the Fulton District where he continued to farm for a living. There were no children.

85. Black, Daniel L.
Private, Company G, 7th Regiment • Confederate Cavalry • Company D, 16th Battalion • N.C. Cavalry

Daniel enlisted in Davie County on September 3, 1862, with the rank of Private. He transferred from Company G, 7th Regiment Confederate Cavalry on July 11, 1864, while absent in confinement at Point Lookout, Maryland, as a prisoner of war. He was transferred to Elmira, New York, on August 15, 1864, where he died of "chronic diarrhoea" on September 26, 1864. Daniel's name is listed on the Memorial Monument for the Davie County men who died in the Civil War, 1861–1865.

86. Black, Samuel F.
Private, Company G, 7th Regiment • Confederate Cavalry • Company D, 16th Battalion • N.C. Cavalry

Samuel enlisted in Davie County on September 3, 1862, with the rank of Private. He transferred from Company G, 7th Regiment Confederate Cavalry on July 11, 1864, while in confinement at Point Lookout, Maryland, as a prisoner of war. He was transferred to Elmira, New York, on August 15, 1864, where he remained until paroled and exchanged on February 13, 1865. He was admitted to the hospital at Richmond, Virginia, February 22, 1865, and furloughed.

87. Blackburn, James A.
Private, Company G, 7th Regiment • Confederate Cavalry • Company D, 16th Battalion • N.C. Cavalry

James enlisted in Davie County on September 3, 1862, with the rank of Private. He transferred from Company G of the 7th Regiment to Company D of the 16th Battalion on July 11, 1864. He was present or accounted for through October 1864.

88. Blackburn, John
Private, Company G, 7th Regiment • Confederate Cavalry • Company D, 16th Battalion • N.C. Cavalry

John was transferred from Company G, 7th Regiment Confederate Cavalry on July 11, 1864. He was captured at Fort Harrison, Virginia, on September 30, 1864, and confined at Point Lookout, Maryland, where he died of "chronic diarrhoea" on May 8, 1865. John's name is listed on the Memorial Monument for the Davie County men who died in the Civil War, 1861–1865.

89. Blackwelder, Daniel E.
Private, "Davie Sweep Stakes" • Company G, 4th Regiment • N.C. State Troops

Daniel was born in 1839. He resided in Davie County where he enlisted at age 26, July 1, 1861, for the war. He was reported absent without leave on May 21, 1863, but rejoined the company in October 1863. He was killed at Spotsylvania Court House, Virginia, May 19, 1864. Daniel's name is listed on the Memorial Monument for the Davie County men who died in the Civil War, 1861–1865.

90. Blackwood, John B.
Private, "Davie Greys" • Company F, 13th Regiment • (3rd Regiment, N.C. Volunteers) • N.C. Troops

John was born in 1843. He was the son of John Smith of Ijames (1799) and Temy Blackwood (1819, Davie). John B. was a farmer in the Farmington District until he enlisted in Davie County at age 18 on May 21, 1861. He was present or accounted for until he was wounded in the left hand at Gaines' Mill, Virginia, June 27, 1862. He rejoined the company in November–December, 1862, and was present or accounted for through April 28, 1864; he was, however, reported absent sick or absent on detail during most of that period. He retired to the Invalid Corps on April 29, 1864, by reason of the wounds he had received in 1862. John B. married Mariah (Ann M.) Tutirow [sic] (1838) on December 26, 1867. Records show that he continued to farm in the Calahaln District in 1870 and 1880.

91. Boger, Moses
Private, Company F, 42nd Regiment • N.C. Troops

Moses was born in 1825. He married Sarah M. (1826, Davie) Tutterow on January 24, 1849. They resided in the Mocksville District of Davie County where Moses worked as a farmer prior to enlisting on October 5, 1863, for the war. Moses and Sarah were the parents of William (1850), Franklin (1852), Jacob (1855), John (1856), Thomas S. (1858), Nathan D. (1862) and Moses A. (1864). He was present or accounted for until he died in hospital at Petersburg, Virginia, June 9, 1864, of "diarrhoea acute." Moses' name is listed on the Memorial Monument for the Davie County men who died in the Civil War, 1861–1865.

92. Boger, Paul
Private, Company F, 42nd Regiment • N.C. Troops

Paul was born in 1829 in Rowan County. He married Jane Taylor (1824) on December 9, 1850. They farmed in the Mocksville District of Davie County and began what would become a family of eleven children: Thomas H. (1851), James L. (1853), John W. F. (1855), Nathan D. (1857), Lewis S. (1860), Daniel B. (1862), Sarah E. (1863), Robert L. (1866), Wiley A. (1869), Calvin B. (1871) and Lulu V. (1876). Paul enlisted on December 18, 1862, for the war. He was present or accounted for until captured at or near Wise's Forks, Kinston, North Carolina, on March 8, 1865. He was confined at Point Lookout, Maryland, March 16, 1865, and released at Point Lookout on June 24, 1865, after taking the Oath of Allegiance. Following the war he farmed in the Calahaln District. After the death of his wife, Jane, in 1887, he married Vira (1859) Taylor on January 15, 1889. Paul died on May 3, 1895, and is buried at Union Chapel United Methodist Church Cemetery.

93. Bolds (Boles) (Bowles), James L.
Private, Company F, 42nd Regiment • N.C. Troops

James was born May 4, 1828. He worked as a farmer in the Mocksville District, married Jusha (Jerusha) (1830), and together they raised five children: John C. (1851), Frances (1855), Lovey B. (1858), Mary (1862) and Cornelia (1866). James enlisted in Davie County at age 28, March 18, 1862. He was present or accounted for through October 1864. He was paroled at Greensboro, North Carolina, on May 1, 1865, and returned home to resume his life in the Mocksville District. He died on April 12, 1909, and is buried in the Center United Methodist Church Cemetery.

94. Boles (Bowles), James D.
Private, "Davie Greys" • Company F, 13th Regiment • (3rd Regiment, N.C. Volunteers) • N.C. Troops

James was born in 1833. He resided in Davie County and was a farmer prior to enlisting in Davie at age 28, on April 26, 1861. James was present or accounted for until hospitalized at Richmond, Virginia, on August 29, 1862, with a wound of the hand; however, the place and date where he was wounded were not reported. He was absent wounded, absent sick, or absent on detail until he was captured at Hanover Junction, Virginia, on May 23, 1864. James was confined at Point Lookout, Maryland, until he was transferred to Cox's Landing, on the James River, Virginia, where he was received on February 14–15, 1865, for exchange. He was paroled at Salisbury, North Carolina, in 1865. On February 21, 1866, he married Martha E. Gowens. In 1880 James was living in Jerusalem District and working as a distiller. He was about 47 years of age.

95. Boner, Jacob
Private, Company G, 7th Regiment • Confederate Cavalry • Company D, 16th Battalion • N.C. Cavalry

Jacob transferred from Company G of the 7th Regiment to Company D of the 16th Battalion on July 11, 1864. He was present or accounted for through October 1864.

96. Booe, Alexander Martin
Captain, Company L, 77th Regiment, 19th Division • N.C. Militia 1861–1865

A.M. was born in 1821 in Davie County. He married Sarah Anne J. (1824, Davie) Clement on December 18, 1844. In 1850 he served as "D. Sheriff" in Davie; his household consisted of his wife Sarah and their son, George, born August 22, 1847. Also living there were James and Jacob Booe and Wilie Champlin. These three young men were classified as laborers. George was followed by five more siblings: Philip H. (1854), Sarah C. (Sallie) (1858), Maggie H. (1861), Alice (1864) and Ruth (1868). A.M. was a farmer and a leader as well; at age 43 he was Captain of Company L, and his was one of the first militia companies to be "called out." It was also one of the last. By April 14, 1865, Colonel Booe's Home Guards "were still under arms at Lexington," North Carolina, (according to Clark, Walter, ed. Vol. IV). Following the war, A.M. resumed his life as a farmer and patriarch. The household in Mocksville consisted of thirteen residents in 1870—eight of them being family with the rest being servants or boarders. Alexander Martin Booe died on March 26, 1895. He is buried in Rose Cemetery with his wife Sarah and several of their children.

97. Booe, G.W.
Private • William E. Booe's Partisan Rangers • N.C. Volunteers • Company H, 63rd Regiment • (5th Regiment N.C. Cavalry) • N.C. Troops

G.W. enlisted in Davie County on July 12, 1862, for the war. He was captured at Hagerstown, Maryland, July 12, 1863, and confined at Point Lookout, Maryland, until paroled and exchanged at City Point, Virginia, on March 6, 1864. He was present or accounted for through December 1864, and paroled at Salisbury, North Carolina, in 1865.

98. Booe, George W.
Private, "Davie Greys" • Company F, 13th Regiment • (3rd Regiment, N.C. Volunteers) • N.C. Troops

George resided in Davie County and was by occupation a farmer prior to enlisting in Davie County at age 19, April 26, 1861. He was present or accounted for until wounded in the left arm and captured at South Mountain, Maryland, September 14, 1862. He was exchanged at Aiken's Landing, James River, Virginia, on or about October 12, 1862. He rejoined the company in November–December, 1862, and was present or accounted for until wounded in the hip at Chancellorsville, Virginia, May 3, 1863. He rejoined the company in November–December, 1863, and was present or accounted for until wounded at or near Spotsylvania Court House, Virginia, May 21, 1864. He rejoined the company in July–August, 1864, and was present or accounted for until captured at Hatcher's Run, Virginia, April 2, 1865. He was confined at Point Lookout, Maryland, until released on June 23, 1865, after taking the Oath of Allegiance.

99. Booe, George W.
Sergeant, "Davie Greys" • Company F, 13th Regiment • (3rd Regiment, N.C. Volunteers) • N.C. Troops

George resided in Davie County and was by occupation a student prior to enlisting in Davie County at age 19, April 26, 1861. He mustered in as a Corporal and was promoted to Sergeant on April 28, 1862. He was present or accounted for until transferred to Company H, 63rd Regiment N.C. Troops (5th Regiment N.C. Cavalry), on or about October 31, 1862.

100. Booe, Marshall N. (Ney)
Private, Company F, 42nd Regiment • N.C. Troops

Marshall was born about 1826 in Davie County to Daniel (1781, Davie) and Mary (1784, Virginia) Booe. In 1860 he lived in the Mocksville District where he was listed as Martin Ney Booe in the census. He was a farmer prior to enlisting in Davie at age 36, March 27, 1862. He was present or accounted for until discharged on November 14, 1862, by reason of "phthisis."

101. Booe, William E.
Captain, William E. Booe's Partisan Rangers • N.C. Volunteers • Company H, 63rd Regiment • (5th Regiment N.C. Cavalry) • N.C. Troops

William was born in Davie County in 1827. He married Jane (1837, Davie) Holman on March 24, 1852. They resided in the Mocksville District of Davie where he worked as a trader. When war was declared eight volunteer companies quickly formed, one of which was Company H, later assigned to the 63rd Regiment on September 1, 1862, with William being appointed Captain to rank from the same date. The company was known as Captain William E. Booe's Partisan Rangers, North Carolina Volunteers. On June 3, 1863, he was wounded in the left shoulder at Upperville, Virginia. He was present or accounted for until he resigned July 20, 1864, and was retired to the Invalid Corps on July 26, 1864. He was detailed to light duty on September 27, 1864.

102. Booe, William H.
Private, William E. Booe's Partisan Rangers • N.C. Volunteers • Company H, 63rd Regiment • (5th Regiment N.C. Cavalry) • N.C. Troops

William was born in 1842. He enlisted in Davie County at age 21, July 15, 1862, for the war. He was present or accounted for through August 1864. He was transferred to the 47th Regiment, N.C. Troops on October 5, 1864, but it appears that the order was not carried out as he was paroled at Salisbury, North Carolina, as a member of this company and regiment. He returned to Davie where he married (Nancy) Emaline Granger on December 20, 1866. Their children were David M. (1868), Sarah (1870), Laura (1872) and Mary M. (1875).

103. Booe, William M.
Private, Company F, 42nd Regiment • N.C. Troops

William was born in 1844 in Davie County to Ransom (1820, Davie) and Emelene (1816, Davie) Glascock Booe. They lived in the Calahaln District where he enlisted in Davie at age 18, March 18, 1862. He was present or accounted for through October 1864. He was paroled at Salisbury, North Carolina, on May 30, 1865. North Carolina pension records indicate he was wounded at New Bern on March 10, 1865.

104. Bowden, John O.
Private, "Davie Sweep Stakes" • Company G, 4th Regiment • N.C. State Troops

John was born in Davie County in 1842 to Caleb (1816, Davie) and Mary (1821, Davie) Bowden. Prior to his enlistment the family lived in the Smith Grove District. John enlisted in Davie County at age 20, June 4, 1861, for the war. He was killed at Seven Pines, Virginia, May 31, 1862. John's name is listed on the Memorial Monument for the Davie County men who died in the Civil War, 1861–1865.

105. Bowden, S.W. (Shadrick)
Private • Captain William E. Booe's Partisan Rangers • N.C. Volunteers • Company H, 63rd Regiment • (5th Regiment N.C. Cavalry) • N.C. Troops

Shadrick W. was born February 15, 1844, in Davie County. He resided with his parents, Caleb (1816, Davie) and Mary (1821, Davie) in the Smith Grove District of Davie where he enlisted at age 18, July 15, 1862, for the war. He was captured at Upperville, Virginia, June 21, 1863, and confined at Old Capitol Prison, Washington, D.C., until paroled and exchanged at City Point, Virginia, June 30, 1863. He was

Shadrick W. Bowden back row center, served with Captain William E. Booe's Partisan Rangers. His brothers, from left: seated Asbury and Alexander; standing, Columbia, and Watson (Alice Faye Clontz and Terry P. Smith).

Shadrick W. Bowden with his son Grady Caleb, daughter Hazel Luna Bowden, wife Clarissa (Clara) Plott Bowden, infant Nell Bowden Smith, Aunt "Manth" King and Ray Bowden (Alice Faye Clontz and Terry P. Smith).

present or accounted for through August 1864, and paroled in Salisbury, North Carolina, in 1865. He married Jennetta (1843) Hartman, July 23, 1868. Their children were Enoch M. (1872), Zollie M. (1874), Mosley (1875), John (1877), Caleb (1880), Nannie V. (1884) and Mary F. (1887). After Jennetta's death September 5, 1896, Shaderick married Clearissy Plott on June 12, 1898, and they had three sons and three daughters. The two wives and Shaderick W. are all buried in Bethlehem United Methodist Church Cemetery. Shaderick died on March 29, 1930.

Shadrick W. Bowden wore this badge to the N.C. Reunion of the U.C.V., on August 12, 1912 (Alice Faye Clontz and Terry P. Smith).

106. Bowers, Eli W.
Private, Company G, 7th Regiment • Confederate Cavalry • Company D, 16th Battalion • N.C. Cavalry

Eli transferred from Company G, 7th Regiment Confederate Cavalry to Company D, 16th Battalion N.C. Cavalry on July 11, 1864. He was present or accounted for through October 1864. He was paroled at Greensboro, North Carolina, on May 8, 1865.

107. Bowles, B.F.
Private, Company F, 42nd Regiment • N.C. Troops

B.F. was born in 1823 in North Carolina. He married Mary Jarvis on January 26, 1853, in Davie County where they resided in the Farmington District. He was a mechanic. The place and date of enlistment were not reported. He was captured at or near Wise's Forks, Kinston, North Carolina, on March 10, 1865, and confined at Point Lookout, Maryland, March 16, 1865. He was released at Point Lookout on May 12, 1865.

108. Bowles, Benjamin T.
Private, Carolina Rangers • Company B, 10th Virginia Cavalry Regiment

Benjamin was born circa 1814 in North Carolina. He farmed in Farmington, married Amanda E. and fathered four children: Mary L. (1847), William (Mitchell) (1849), Margaret (1851) and Laura (1858). Then the war began and Benjamin, age 45, enlisted in Davie County on October 29, 1861. He was present through April 30, 1862, but apparently had been discharged for being overage on March 1, 1862. So he reenlisted at an unknown place and time. Things did not go well after that. He was admitted to Richmond hospital with neuralgia on December 28, 1862, transferred to Danville hospital January 8, 1863, was absent sick through December 1863, absent without leave January 3, 1864, absent sick with "Feb. Intermitt" in Richmond hospital June 19, 1864, and furloughed for 30 days August 4, 1864. He was reported absent without leave January 27, 1865, and was paroled at Salisbury, North Carolina, May 1865. During his war years he had fathered Martin (1862) and Leonard (1864), followed by Lela (1866). At age 53, Benjamin was at home with his family in the Mocksville District of Davie County.

109. Bowles, Erwin L.
Private, Carolina Rangers • Company B, 10th Virginia Cavalry Regiment

Erwin was born circa 1818 in North Carolina. He worked as a farm hand in the Smith Grove District of Davie County, married Eliza (1822, North Carolina) and had a son, Robert (1847). He enlisted in Davie on March 18, 1862, at age 41. He was present even though he was "dismounted" after April 1863. His absences were documented; he was absent on detail from May through December of 1863. He was issued clothing July 9, 1864, and was paroled at Salisbury, North Carolina, in May 1865.

110. Bowles, G.W.
Private, Company F, 42nd Regiment • N.C. Troops

George W. was born in 1826 in North Carolina. He married Clementine (1833) and they were the parents of Mary (1856), Charles (1863), Sarah (1865) and an infant (1870). He was a farmer prior to enlisting; the place and date of enlistment were not reported. He was captured near Wise's Forks, Kinston, North Carolina, on March 10, 1865, confined at Point Lookout, Maryland, March 16, 1865, and released at Point Lookout on May 12, 1865. He returned to the Mocksville District of Davie. He died in 1910 and is buried at Oak Grove United Methodist Church Cemetery.

111. Bowles, William J.
Private, Carolina Rangers • Company B, 10th Virginia Cavalry Regiment • McGregor's Battery • Virginia Horse Artillery

William was born circa 1842 in North Carolina. He worked as a farm laborer and lived with the Richard W. Griffeth family in the Mocksville District of Davie County where he enlisted on October 29, 1861. He was either present or absent on detail through December 1863. On April 1, 1864, he was listed as absent without leave and on July 8, 1864, he was listed as "deserter on rolls." William was court-martialed October 31, 1864, and transferred to McGregor's Battery, Virginia Horse Artillery on November 7, 1864. William and his wife Prudence, both age 28, are listed in the 1870 census and again in 1880. He worked as a laborer in the Clarksville District of Davie County. William's tombstone in Bear Creek Baptist Church Cemetery reads: William J. Bowles, 1840–1914.

112. Boyd, James S. (Sam'l)
Private, "Davie Greys" • Company F, 13th Regiment • (3rd Regiment, N.C. Volunteers) • N.C. Troops

James was born in Randolph County in 1838. He resided in Davie County with the E.P. Casey family where E.P. worked as a blacksmith in the Calahaln District and James worked as a farmer or blacksmith. He enlisted in Davie at age 23, April 26, 1861. He was present or accounted for until killed at Gaines' Mill, Virginia, June 27, 1862. James's name is listed on the Memorial Monument for the Davie County men who died in the Civil War, 1861–1865.

113. Boyer, John
Private, Company G, 7th Regiment • Confederate Cavalry • Company D, 16th Battalion • N.C. Cavalry

John transferred from Company G, 7th Regiment Confederate Cavalry to Company D, 16th Battalion N.C. Cavalry on July 11, 1864. He was present or accounted for through October 1, 1864.

114. Bracken, John W.
Private, Company F, 42nd Regiment • N.C. Troops

John was born March 25, 1841, to Rutherford and Elizabeth (1820, Robeson) M. Bracken. He worked as a laborer and resided with the Chas. Hunter family in the Chinquepin District prior to enlisting at age 20, March 24, 1862. He was present or accounted for through October 1864, and paroled at Mocksville on June 3, 1865. He returned to the Jerusalem District of Davie and married Mary (1845) Graves on December 25, 1866. They would have two children: William G. (1870) and David L. (1872). John lived in the Clarksville District of Davie in 1880. On December 17, 1885, he married Elizabeth C. (1848) Graves. John died on July 8, 1905, and is buried at Chestnut Grove United Methodist Church Cemetery.

115. Bracken, Thomas H.
Private • Captain William E. Booe's Partisan Rangers • N.C. Volunteers • Company H, 63rd Regiment • (5th Regiment N.C. Cavalry) • N.C. Troops

Thomas was born in 1813 in Davie County. In the 1850s, he worked as a farmer and he lived with his mother Mary (1794, Davie) Bracken, and his two young children, March (1844, Ashe) and John (1845, Ashe). By 1862 he had married Sarah A. (1828, North Carolina), and they had become the parents of four children: Eliza J. (1855), Melvina E. (1857), Sarah M. (1859) and Thomas H. (1861). They resided in the Mocksville District of Davie where he enlisted September 3, 1862, for the war as a substitute for W. F. McMahan. He was wounded and captured at Upperville, Virginia, June 21, 1863, and reported as "absent wounded left arm" on the September–October, 1863, muster roll. No Federal Provost Marshal records relative to his capture and release were found. He was present or accounted for until he retired to the Invalid Corps October 15, 1864, and was assigned to light duty at Richmond, Virginia, November 24, 1864. His disability was reported as "permanent" on February 3, 1865. He married Nancy Jane Revis on March 25, 1866. They resided in the Clarksville District where he continued to farm.

116. Bracken, William H.
Private, Company F, 42nd Regiment • N.C. Troops

William was born in 1844 to Rutherford (1823, Davie) and Elizabeth (1820, Robeson) Bracken. They resided in the Chinquepin District of Davie County where William enlisted at age 18, March 24, 1862. He was present or accounted for through October 1864, and paroled at Mocksville on June 7, 1865. He returned to Davie where he worked as a laborer in the Farmington District. He married E.J. (1855) Green on December 31, 1871.

117. Brackin, John
Private • Captain William E. Booe's Partisan Rangers • N.C. Volunteers • Company H, 63rd Regiment • (5th Regiment N.C. Cavalry) • N.C. Troops

John was born in 1845 in Ashe County. He was the son of Thomas H. (1813, Davie) Bracken, who also served in Company H, 63rd Regiment. They resided in the Mocksville District of Davie County where he enlisted at age 17, July 15, 1862, for the war as a substitute for Abner Glasscock. He was detailed as a nurse for the wounded at Middleburg, Virginia, May–June, 1863, and was present or accounted for through August 1864. He became a casualty himself with a gunshot wound to his left little finger and was admitted to the hospital at Danville, Virginia, on April 3, 1865. After being furloughed for thirty days on April 9, 1865, he was paroled at Salisbury, North Carolina. John married Sallie (Sarah) Stanly on April 3, 1870; Sarah's daughter Elizabeth (1861) Stanly lived with them. John married his second wife, Ellen Elizabeth McDaniel, on December 3, 1879. They resided in the Mocksville District where he farmed and they raised two children: Jesse C. (1872) and James M. (1874). Elizabeth received a widow's pension until her death December 10, 1936.

118. Branden, W.F.
Private, Company G, 7th Regiment • Confederate Cavalry • Company D, 16th Battalion • N.C. Cavalry

W.F. enlisted in Davie County on September 3, 1862, with the rank of Private. He transferred from Company G, 7th Regiment Confederate Cavalry to Company D, 16th Battalion N.C. Cavalry on July 11, 1864. He was captured at Fort Harrison, Virginia, September 30, 1864, and confined at Point Lookout, Maryland, where he remained until paroled and exchanged at Boulware's Wharf, James River, Virginia, on March 19, 1865.

119. Brandon, J.C.
Private • Captain William E. Booe's Partisan Rangers • N.C. Volunteers • Company H, 63rd Regiment • (5th Regiment N.C. Cavalry) • N.C. Troops

J.C. enlisted in Davie County at age 29, July 10, 1862, for the war. He was captured at Hagerstown, Maryland, July 12, 1863, and confined at Point Lookout, Maryland, until paroled and exchanged at City Point, Virginia, March 20, 1864. He was present or accounted for through February 1865.

120. Brandon, Joshua
Private • Captain William E. Booe's Partisan Rangers • N.C. Volunteers • Company H, 63rd Regiment • (5th Regiment N.C. Cavalry) • N.C. Troops

Joshua enlisted in Davie County at age 25, July 10, 1862, for the war. He was present or accounted for through February 1865.

121. Brandon, Thomas
Private, Company G, 7th Regiment • Confederate Cavalry • Company D, 16th Battalion • N.C. Cavalry

Thomas transferred from Company G, 7th Regiment Confederate Cavalry to Company D, 16th Battalion N.C. Cavalry on July 11, 1865. He was captured on the Weldon Railroad, Virginia, September 2, 1864, and confined at Point Lookout, Maryland, where he remained until paroled and exchanged at Boulware's Wharf, James River, Virginia, on January 21, 1865. He was reported as present on a roll of detachment of paroled and exchanged prisoners at Camp Lee, near Richmond, Virginia, dated January 26, 1865.

122. Brandon, W.A.
Private • Captain William E. Booe's Partisan Rangers • N.C. Volunteers • Company H, 63rd Regiment • (5th Regiment N.C. Cavalry) • N.C. Troops

W.A. enlisted in Davie County at age 21, July 10, 1862, for the war. He was captured at Hanover Court House, Virginia, May 31, 1864, and confined at Point Lookout, Maryland, until transferred to Elmira, New York, July 12, 1864. He was paroled at Elmira, March 10, 1865, and exchanged at Boulware's Wharf, James River, Virginia, March 15, 1865.

123. Brewbaker, Richard P.
Private, Carolina Rangers • Company B, 10th Virginia Cavalry Regiment

Richard was born circa 1836. He enlisted in Davie County on October 29, 1861, at age 25. He was present although he was without a horse April 25–30, 1863, and again present until wounded in action at Upperville, June 21, 1863, and again present until he was detailed as a teamster at Brigade Headquarters in January and July of 1864. He was issued clothing on September 30, 1864, and was without a horse on January 27, 1865.

124. Brewer, Hubbard L.
Private, Company G, 7th Regiment • Confederate Cavalry • Company D, 16th Battalion • N.C. Cavalry

Hubbard enlisted in Davie County on September 3, 1862, with the rank of Private. He transferred from Company G, 7th Regiment Confederate Cavalry to Company D, 16th Battalion N.C. Cavalry on July 11, 1864. He was killed at Burgess' Mill, Virginia, on October 27, 1864. Hubbard's name is listed on the Memorial Monument for the Davie County men who died in the Civil War, 1861–1865.

125. Brindle (Brintle), Robert R.
Private, Company D, 42nd Regiment • N.C. Troops

Robert was born in 1810 in Virginia, the son of Elizabeth Brintle (1775, Davie). Robert married Nancy Brintle who was born in 1812 in Brunswick County. The couple had five children: Thomas (1835), Elizabeth (1838), John (1840), James (1846) and Mary (1849). Robert enlisted at age 45 in Rowan County, on or about March 4, 1862. He was present or accounted for until he died in the hospital at Richmond, Virginia, on September 4, 1864, of "dysentery chronic." Robert's name is listed on the Memorial Monument for the Davie County men who died in the Civil War, 1861–1865.

126. Brinegar, M.
Private • Captain William E. Booe's Partisan Rangers • N.C. Volunteers • Company H, 63rd Regiment • (5th Regiment N.C. Cavalry) • N.C. Troops

Milton was born in 1845 in Davie County. He was the son of Thomas Hampton (1816, Davie) and Elizabeth (1827, Davie) Brinegar. They resided in the Smith Grove District of Davie where he enlisted April 1, 1864, for the war. He was captured at Hanover Court House, Virginia, May 31, 1864, and confined at Point Lookout, Maryland, until transferred to Elmira, New York, July 12, 1864. He died at Elmira on August 24, 1864, of "chronic diarrhoea." Milton's name is listed on the Memorial Monument for the Davie County men who died in the Civil War, 1861–1865.

127. Briniger (Brinager) (Brinegan), John
Private, "Davie Greys" • Company F, 13th Regiment • (3rd Regiment, N.C. Volunteers) • N.C. Troops

John was born in Davie County in 1843 to John (1805, Davie) and Ann (1805, Davie) Brinegar. In 1860, at age 18, he was a laborer living in the Fulton District. At age 19, on August 6, 1861, he enlisted in Davie County for the war. John was present or accounted for until he was hospitalized at Richmond, Virginia, on June 10, 1862. The place and date of his being wounded were not reported. John rejoined the company prior to November 1, 1862, and was present or accounted for until he died on November 4, 1863. The place and cause of death were not reported. John's name is listed on the Memorial Monument for the Davie County men who died in the Civil War, 1861–1865.

128. Brinkley, James
Private, Company E, 42nd Regiment • N.C. Troops

James enlisted in Davie County on August 17, 1862, for the war. He was present or accounted for until May–August, 1864, when he was reported absent wounded. The place and date wounded were not reported. James was reported absent wounded or absent sick through October 1864. He was paroled at Greensboro, North Carolina, on May 19, 1865.

129. Brinkley, John F.
Sergeant, Company H, 57th Regiment • N.C. Troops

John was born in Surry County in 1837. In 1850, at age 13, he lived with the John Hall family in Davie County. John married Margaret J. Otrich (1842) on February 24, 1859, and they settled in the Mocksville District where he worked as a laborer. On July 4, 1862, at age 25, he enlisted in Davie County, for the war. He mustered in as a Private. John was hospitalized at Richmond, Virginia, on December 17, 1862, with bronchitis; he returned to duty on February 14, 1863, was promoted to Sergeant in March–May, 1863, and was reported present through October 31, 1863, but was captured at Rappahannock Station, Virginia, on November 7, 1863. John was confined at Point Lookout, Maryland, November 11, 1863, where he was paroled on February 24, 1865. He was received at Aiken's Landing, James River, Virginia, on or about February 25–28 or March 2–3, 1865, for exchange. He was hospitalized at Richmond on March 4, 1865, with "scorbutus." John died in hospital at Richmond on March 19, 1865. John's name is not presently listed on the Memorial Monument for the Davie County men who died in the Civil War, 1861–1865.

130. Brock, J.N. (James)
Private, Carolina Rangers • Company B, 10th Virginia Cavalry Regiment

J.N. was born December 6, 1810, in Davie County. His first wife died prior to 1850, leaving him with John (1836), Enoch (1838), Thomas

(1839), Sarah E. (1842) and James (1844). He married Margaret A. (1818, Virginia) Chinn on November 22, 1854; their children were Moses (1856), Joseph (1857) and Emma (1862). They lived in the Farmington District of Davie where J.N. worked as a farmer. As luck would have it, Stoneman and his raiders bivouacked only one-half mile away from the farm when they swept through the state. The story goes that the Brock family gathered all the hams, cattle and most of the chickens and hid them in a secluded, wooded area, leaving a few chickens at the house to be taken by the invaders. Moses Brock (later to become the grandfather of present-day John T. Brock) recalled sitting on the gatepost to watch the soldiers march by; there is also a restored slave cabin on the property. His enlistment date is not listed, but he was in Richmond hospital June 10–30, 1864, and paroled in Mocksville on June 9, 1865. His son, Thomas M. Brock, also served in this company. James is buried in Olive Branch Cemetery in Davie County. His tombstone states that he was the son of Enoch and Sarah Brock and that he died on June 12 (17), 1886.

131. Brock, J.W.
Corporal, Company A, 57th Regiment • N.C. Troops

J.W. was born in 1834 in Davie County, the son of James Brock (1811, Davie). He resided in Fulton District and made his living as a farmer. On December 8, 1858, he married Sarah L. Ward (1839, Davie). They were the parents of a daughter, Ann (1859). At age 26, on July 4, 1862, he enlisted in Rowan County for the war. He mustered in as a Private, then was hospitalized at Richmond, Virginia, on or about August 31, 1862. He was promoted to Corporal prior to September 1, 1862. He was reported in hospital at Richmond on October 3, 1862, with rubeola, later returning to duty on November 4, 1862. Again, he was sent to hospital at Richmond on December 31, 1862, and returned on or about March 13, 1863. J.W. was reported missing at Gettysburg, Pennsylvania, on July 2, 1863. He was captured on or about July 5, 1863, and was confined at Fort Delaware, Delaware, then later transferred to Point Lookout, Maryland, on October 20, 1863, where he died on July 13, 1864; the cause of death was not reported. J.W.'s name is listed on the Memorial Monument for the Davie County men who died in the Civil War, 1861–1865.

132. Brock, James V.
Third Lieutenant, Company E, 42nd Regiment • N.C. Troops

James was born in 1843 in Davie to James (1811, Davie) and Margaret A. (1818, Virginia) Brock. They lived in Farmington District where his father farmed. James enlisted in Davie County at age 19, March 18, 1862. He mustered in as a Private, was promoted to Corporal on August 1, 1862, promoted to First Sergeant in January–February, 1864, and elected Third Lieutenant on July 31, 1864. He was present or accounted for through October 1864. He was held in high esteem by his commanding officers who praised him as "a brave officer and a sterling man."

133. Brock, L.E. (Levin)
Private • Captain William E. Booe's Partisan Rangers • N.C. Volunteers • Company H, 63rd Regiment • (5th Regiment N.C. Cavalry) • N.C. Troops

Levin was born either May 16, 1843 or May 11, 1849, in Davie County to Nathaniel T. (1813, Davie) and Clarisa E. (1816, Davie) Smith Brock. The family lived in the Farmington District where his father worked as a farmer and Levin worked as a laborer prior to enlisting at age 18, July 18, 1862, for the war. He was captured at Hagerstown, Maryland, July 12, 1863, and confined at Point Lookout, Maryland, until paroled and exchanged at City Point, Virginia, on September 27, 1863. He was present or accounted for through August 1864, when he was reported as "wounded August 21, 1864." He was paroled at Salisbury, North Carolina, in 1865, and returned to Farmington where he farmed until his death June 19, 1871. He is buried in Olive Branch Cemetery.

134. Brock, Noah Monroe
First Lieutenant, Carolina Rangers • Company B, 10th Virginia Cavalry Regiment

Noah was born August 14, 1836, in Davie County to William B. (1800, Currituck) and Frances (1807, Davie) Brock. They farmed in the Farmington District of Davie County where Noah enlisted October 29, 1861, as a Second Sergeant. He was promoted to Second Lieutenant May 20, 1863, and was wounded in action in a battle at Shepherdstown on July 18, 1863. He returned to duty in September 1863, and was present until April 1, 1864. He was promoted to First Lieutenant on July 18, 1864, and was absent commanding dismounted men at Stoney Creek, October 13 to November 30, 1864. He was present for the surrender of General Lee at Appomattox Court House on April 9, 1865. He returned to Mocksville where he was paroled June 9, 1865. He married Emily in 1866; William was born in 1867 and Sallie in 1869. The family moved to Indiana in 1873. He died in Darlington, Indiana, June 10, 1942. An application for a Civil War pension is on file at the State Archives, Raleigh, North Carolina.

135. Brock, Richard Emmerson
Second Lieutenant, Company B, 77th Regiment, 19th Division • N.C. Militia 1861–1865 • First Sergeant, Company E, 42nd Regiment • N.C. Troops

Richard was born July 18, 1840, in Davie County to Nathaniel T. (1813, Davie) and Clarisa E. (1816, Davie) Smith Brock. They lived in the Farmington District where they farmed. Richard served in both the militia and in the North Carolina Troops but the militia date of service is not known, although he was selected as Second Lieutenant of Company B. He enlisted in Company E, 42nd Regiment as a Corporal at age 21, on April 1, 1862. He was promoted to Sergeant on December 31, 1863, and to First Sergeant on July 31, 1864. He was present or accounted for until wounded at or near Bermuda Hundred, Virginia, on or about May 21, 1864. He returned to duty September–October, 1864. He was present or accounted for through December 22, 1864. Richard and Mary A. Howell were married March 24, 1868. By 1880 they were the parents of Willie E. (1869), Matthew L. (1872) and Josephine (1876). Sarah Howell, Mary's mother, also made her home with them. Richard died on May 31, 1889, and is buried in Farmington Community Cemetery.

136. Brock, Thomas M.
Private, Carolina Rangers • Company B, 10th Virginia Cavalry Regiment

Thomas was born April 30, 1839, in Davie County, the son of J. N. (1810, North Carolina) and Margaret A. Chinn (1818, Virginia) Brock. They farmed in the Farmington District where Thomas enlisted at age 22, on October 29, 1861. He was present or accounted for throughout his tour of duty. His absences were due to sickness, serving on other details and being wounded in both thighs at Reams' Station on August 25, 1864; he was sent to Raleigh hospital August 28, 1864, and furloughed for sixty days on September 22, 1864. His last recorded roll call present was January 27, 1865. His father also served in this company. Marriage records show that Thomas married C. Brunt Buley on March 20, 1866, but census records list her name as Bulah C. By 1880 they were the parents of Victor Z. (1868), Mariah E. (1870), James W. (1873), Edgar H. (1876) and Moses (1878). Thomas died on May 22, 1920, and is buried in Farmington Community Cemetery.

Note: There is a "Thomas M. Brock" listed on the Memorial Monument located on Court Square, Mocksville.

137. Brock, William F.
First Corporal, Carolina Rangers • Company B, 10th Virginia Cavalry Regiment

William was born circa 1835 in Davie County to William B. (1800, Currituck) and Frances (1807, Davie) Brock. They farmed in the Farmington District where William married Martha J. (1839, Davie) Ferebee on February 17, 1858. Their son Francis was born in 1859. William enlisted in Davie County on October 29, 1861, at age 26. He was present through April 30, 1862, but died in Richmond hospital August 10, 1862, of typhoid fever contracted on the battlefield at Gaines' Mills, Virginia. Martha's application for a widow's pension is on file at the State Archives, Raleigh, North Carolina. William's name is listed on the Memorial Monument for the Davie County men who died in the Civil War, 1861–1865.

138. Brogden, John W.
Private, Company E, 42nd Regiment • N.C. Troops

John was born in 1844 in Davie County. He was the son of Thomas (1812, Surry) and Nancy (1821, Iredell). In 1860 he was a farm worker who lived with the D.N. Cain family in the Chinquepin District. At age 18, on March 18, 1862, he enlisted in Davie County. John was present or accounted for through October 1864. (North Carolina pension records indicate he was wounded near Smithfield on an unspecified date.) By 1870 he had married Mary (1844, North Carolina) and they were the parents of two children: America (1865) and Samuel (1869), and were living in the Jerusalem District where John worked as a farm laborer.

139. Brown, Burton
Private, "The Rough and Readys" • Company G, 66th Regiment • N.C. Troops

Burton was born in 1825 in North Carolina. In 1860 he lived with his wife, Hetty C. (1825, North Carolina) and their three children, Margaret E. (1850), Sarah L. (1853) and John W. (1858), in the Town of Mocksville, where he worked as a blacksmith. He enlisted with the rank of Private near Richmond, Virginia, October 29, 1864, for the war. He was wounded in the right side at Bentonville on March 19, 1865, and paroled at Mocksville on June 2, 1865. A daughter, Minty C. (Catharine M.) had been born in 1864. In 1880 Burton continued to reside with his family in Mocksville and to continue his work as a blacksmith. He died on November 24, 1910, and is buried in Joppa Cemetery.

140. Brown, J. Frank
Private • Captain William E. Booe's Partisan Rangers • N.C. Volunteers • Company H, 63rd Regiment • (5th Regiment N.C. Cavalry) • N.C. Troops

Frank enlisted in Davie County April 1, 1864, for the war. He was present or accounted for through August 1864, captured in Amelia County, Virginia, April 3, 1865, and confined at Hart's Island, New York Harbor until released after taking the Oath of Allegiance on June 21, 1865.

141. Brown, John Edmunds
Adjutant, 7th N.C. Regiment • N.C. State Troops • Colonel, 42nd Regiment • N.C. Troops

"Colonel Brown was born in Caswell County in 1830, and was educated at Hampden-Sidney College, Virginia. He read law under Judge Richmond Pearson and began practice at Charlotte, North Carolina. Upon the outbreak of the Civil War, he enlisted in the Seventh North Carolina Regiment, of which he was adjutant. He next became Lieutenant-Colonel of the Forty-second North Carolina, but in reality he was Colonel of the regiment almost from its organization though he was not commissioned as Colonel until January 1864. Colonel Brown possessed many of the qualities of a great soldier. His troops were drilled until they had attained the utmost proficiency in the manual of arms and when ordered to execute a difficult maneuver at a critical moment, they never faltered nor blundered ... every man in the regiment loved him and would have followed him anywhere. On or about May 20, 1864, he was wounded at or near Bermuda Hundred, Virginia, when he was struck on the head by a minié-ball, making a gash some two inches long. The Colonel was knocked down and temporarily stunned, but he remained on the field upwards of an hour afterward." He returned to duty prior to August 31, 1864, and was paroled at Greensboro, North Carolina, on May 1, 1865. Another item of interest is that Colonel Brown and General Stonewall Jackson married sisters. The above information was written by Major Thomas J. Brown of the Forty-second for publication in Walter Clark's great five-volume set, *Histories of the Several Regiments and Battalions from North Carolina in the Great War 1861–1865*. Colonel Brown was the second of three brothers, the oldest of whom was Dr. W.C. Brown, the Surgeon of the Regiment. The third brother was T.J. Brown, Major of the Forty-second and the writer of most of this article.

142. Brown, Rufus D.
Second Lieutenant, "Davie Sweep Stakes" • Company G, 4th Regiment • N.C. State Troops

Rufus was born to Thomas (1808, Davie) and Margaret Brown (1810, Davie). They resided in Davie County where Rufus worked as a merchant prior to enlisting at age 23, June 4, 1861, for the war. He mustered in as a Sergeant, then was appointed Second Lieutenant to rank from May 28, 1862. He was wounded at Sharpsburg, Maryland, on September 17, 1862. He resigned February 25, 1863, by reason of chronic diarrhoea and debility. His resignation was accepted on March 16, 1863. Rufus married Sally I. Gibbs on October 20, 1868, and a son, George, was born in 1869. Rufus and his brother William became very successful tobacco product manufacturers. William served as First Lieutenant in the militia. The following information was reported in *The Republican* by Miss Mary Wiley in her column, "Mostly Local," June 1949: "In 1878 the largest tobacco factory in Winston was that of Brown and Brother. It was built of brick, five floors high, in length 132 feet, in width 50 feet. This factory, manufacturing plug, twist, and smoking tobacco was situated on Church Street between Fourth and Fifth. It had the distinction of being the only tobacco factory in North Carolina heated by steam. The brick factory of P. H. Hanes and Company, Chestnut Street, second door north of Second Street, three and one-half stories high, 110 feet by 45, was the second largest tobacco factory in 1878. The R.J. Reynolds factory of brick and wood, three and one-half stories, 95 feet long, 38 wide, on Chestnut Street, second door north of

First Street, was the third largest. At this time Brown and Brother (William L. and Rufus D.) employed 200 hands; P.H. Hanes 85 to 100; R.J. Reynolds 75."

143. Brown, Thomas J. (Jeff)
Lieutenant, Company G, 4th Regiment • Captain, Company E, 42nd Regiment • Major, Field and Staff, 42nd Regiment • N.C. Troops

Jeff was born circa 1835 to John E. and Elizabeth Brown. His family moved from Caswell County to Davie County where his mother owned Prospect Plantation along Dutchman Creek at Horse Shoe Neck on the Yadkin River. When the war began, Jeff was working as a merchant and living in the hotel in Mocksville (H.R. Austin, Landlord). He enlisted in Company G of the 4th Regiment at age 26 and was appointed Second Lieutenant to rank from May 16, 1861. He was appointed Captain of Company E, 42nd Regiment on March 21, 1862, and appointed Major on January 7, 1864, and transferred to the Field and Staff where he served until he was paroled at Greensboro, North Carolina, on May 1, 1865. He returned to Davie County where he married Delphine Hall of Alabama, on October 14, 1868. They lived for a while with his sister-in-law, Ann P. Brown, widow of his oldest brother, Dr. William Carter Brown, who died during the war. Major Brown farmed in Davie, but not for long. He crossed the Yadkin River to Winston-Salem, North Carolina, where he had the "distinction of opening the first flue-cured leaf market in 1872." (Article in *Journal-Sentinel*, April 23, 1872.)

144. Brown, William
Private, Company D, 42nd Regiment • N.C. Troops

William was born in 1839 in North Carolina. He resided in Iredell County, but made his home with Burton and Hetty Brown, prior to enlisting in Davie County at age 21, February 2, 1862. Both Burton and William were "Smiths" in Mocksville. William was present or accounted for until he died at Lynchburg, Virginia, on August 28, 1862, of "pneumonia typhoides." William's name is not presently listed on the Memorial Monument for the Davie County men who died in the Civil War, 1861–1865.

145. Brown, William
Sergeant, 1st Company A, Salisbury Prison Guard • "The Rough and Readys" • Company G, 66th Regiment • N.C. Troops

William served as Sergeant in the Salisbury Prison Guard prior to transferring to Company G of the 66th on October 2, 1863. He was reported present through February 29, 1864; three days later he was hospitalized at Richmond, Virginia, March 3, 1864, with pneumonia. He was confined at Castle Thunder Prison, Richmond, on April 15, 1864. The reason he was confined was not reported. He returned to duty prior to May 1, 1864, but was back in the hospital in Richmond on June 11, 1864, with dropsy. This cycle continued, alternating between prison and the hospital. He was sent to Castle Thunder Prison on August 25, 1864; in the hospital at Richmond on September 2, 1864, with acute diarrhoea; sent to Castle Thunder Prison on September 19, 1864; returned to duty subsequent to October 31, 1864. He was captured near Kinston on March 8, 1865, and confined at Point Lookout, Maryland, on March 16, 1865, and released there on June 23, 1865, after taking the Oath of Allegiance.

146. Brown, Dr. William Carter
Captain, Company J, 77th Regiment, 19th Division • N.C. Militia 1861–1865 • Surgeon, Field and Staff, 42nd Regiment • N.C. Troops

William was born December 16, 1828, in Caswell County to John E. and Elizabeth Brown. His mother moved from Caswell to Davie County where she owned Prospect Plantation, located along Dutchman Creek at Horse Shoe Neck on the Yadkin River. William was the eldest of three brothers who would serve together in the Field and Staff of the 42nd Regiment. He married Ann P. Carter on May 4, 1852, in Davie County and they settled in the Fulton District where he worked as a physician, farmer and tobacco manufacturer. Their children were John (1853), Lutitia (1856), Frank (1858), William (1860), Elizabeth (1862) and Ann (1864). When it became evident that war would be inevitable, he served as Captain to Company J of the militia and later was appointed Surgeon of the 42nd Regiment on April 22, 1862. His service to the young soldiers was described in Clark's *Regiments*, Volume II, page 805: "Capable and skillful, he performed his duties well, many times exposing his life for the men. When a large part of the regiment was sick with measles at Petersburg, he attended them day and night. So great was the strain and the exposure that his health was wrecked." He died in Davie County on July 25, 1863, of "congestion of the brain." William is buried in Rose Cemetery. His name is not presently listed on the Memorial Monument for the Davie County men who died in the Civil War, 1861–1865.

147. Brown, William L.
First Lieutenant, Regiment Assistant Surgeon • 77th Regiment, 19th Division • N.C. Militia 1861–1865

William was born in 1831 in Davie County to Thomas (1808, Davie) and Margaret (1810, Davie) Brown. William spent his early years helping his father on the farm and reading medicine under Dr. J.F. Martin in Mocksville. According to an article written by Hugh Larew, October 10, 1963, Dr. Brown received his "formal training in the Medical Department of the University of New York, at that time the leading medical college in the country." He received his degree in 1857 and interned aboard the Trans-Atlantic steamship between New York and Liverpool for one year. He returned home and by 1860 he was practicing medicine and was in business with his brother Rufus. "In 1878, their tobacco plant was the largest in the city of Winston, having 200 employees compared with the 75 employees of R.J. Reynolds. Brown Brothers later merged into the R.J. Reynolds Tobacco Company ... the popular brand of Reynolds' chewing tobacco, Brown's Mule, was named for the little mule owned by Thomas Brown of Mocksville." When the militia was activated he was appointed First Lieutenant. He also married Mary Eliza Chinn on December 1, 1863. They had three sons and ten daughters. William and his brother Rufus moved their tobacco business across the Yadkin River to Winston-Salem, North Carolina, where, in 1878, they owned the largest tobacco factory in the city. They were known by the trade name Brown and Brother. (Rufus served as a Second Lieutenant in Company G, 4th Regiment.)

148. Bryan, Dr. Talliafero Jay
Regimental Surgeon, 77th Regiment, 19th Division • N.C. Militia 1861–1865

Talliafero was born in 1820 in Davie County. In 1850 he resided in the hotel run by Robert F. Johnson in Mocksville, where Allen Harbin also lodged. Both men were to become leaders of the militia. Talliafero married Margaret T. Luckey on September 24, 1851; their children were Lella (1852), Sara (1857) and Frank (1861). In 1860 the family lived in the Town of Mocksville where Talliafero served as physician. When the militia was activated he served as Regimental Surgeon.

149. Burgess, Thomas
Private, Company M, 7th Regiment • Confederate Cavalry • Company E, 16th Battalion • N.C. Troops

Thomas was born in 1842 in Davie County, the son of Moses (1799, Davie) Burgess. In 1860 Thomas and his older brother John worked as laborers in the Mocksville District prior to Thomas's enlistment as a Private on September 3, 1862. He was transferred from Company M, 7th Regiment Confederate Cavalry on July 11, 1864, to Company E, 16th Battalion N.C. Cavalry. He was present or accounted for through October 1, 1864.

150. Burgis (Burgess), John M.
Private, Company D, 42nd Regiment • N.C. Troops

John was born in 1838 in Davie County. He was the son of Moses Burgess (1799, Davie). As a young man, John and his brother Thomas made their home with the M. Bean family in the Mocksville District where they worked as laborers prior to John's enlistment on February 1, 1862, in Davie County. No further records.

151. Burk, James W.
Sergeant, "Davie Sweep Stakes" • Company G, 4th Regiment • N.C. State Troops

James resided in Davie County where he en-

Dr. William L. Brown (Hugh Larew)

listed at age 26, June 17, 1861, for the war. He mustered in as a Private and was promoted to Corporal in March–April, 1863. During the battle at Chancellorsville, Virginia, May 3, 1863, he was wounded in the thigh, but rejoined the company in September–October, 1863. On December 1, 1863, he was promoted to Sergeant. He was present or accounted for through August 1864.

152. Burton, Daniel P.
Private, "Davie Greys" • Company F, 13th Regiment • (3rd Regiment, N.C. Volunteers) • N.C. Troops

Daniel was born in Virginia in 1833. In 1860 at age 23, he was living in Fulton District with the J.M. and Agnes Burton family and was working as an overseer. He enlisted in Davie County at age 24, on July 4, 1861. He was present or accounted for until he was paroled at Appomattox Court House, Virginia, on April 9, 1865. He was paroled again at Salisbury, North Carolina, on May 25, 1865. Daniel had married Nancy T. Motley on January 18, 1864. They would have two children by 1870: Robert (1865) and Mary (1869). In 1870 the family was living in the Jerusalem District; by 1880 they were back in the Fulton District where Daniel continued to farm. Daniel died on March 19, 1892, and is buried in Jerusalem Baptist Church Cemetery.

153. Burton, James M.
First Sergeant, 1st Company A, Salisbury Prison Guard • "The Rough and Readys" • Company G, 66th Regiment • N.C. Troops

James was born in 1824 in North Carolina. In 1860 he lived in the Fulton District of Davie County with his wife Agnes (1832, North Carolina) where he worked as a farmer prior to enlisting. James served as First Sergeant in 1st Company A, Salisbury Prison Guard prior to transferring to Company G of the 66th on October 2, 1863. He mustered in as First Sergeant but was reduced to the rank of Sergeant in March–April, 1864. He was killed near Hair's House, Virginia, August 12, 1864. James's name is not presently listed on the Memorial Monument for the Davie County men who died in the Civil War, 1861–1865.

154. Butler, Thomas S.
Private, "Davie Greys" • Company F, 13th Regiment • (3rd Regiment, N.C. Volunteers) • N.C. Troops

Thomas was born in Davie County in 1840. He was the son of Elizabeth Butler (1815, Davie) and stepfather William (1818, Davie) Spry. In 1860 he lived in the Fulton District and worked as a teacher and a tobacconist. At age 21, on April 26, 1861, he enlisted in Davie County. He was present or accounted for until wounded at Chancellorsville, Virginia, on May 3, 1863. He rejoined the company prior to July 14, 1863, when he was captured at Falling Waters, Maryland. He was confined at Baltimore, Maryland, and Point Lookout, Maryland, until he was paroled and transferred to City Point, Virginia, where he was received on March 6, 1864, for exchange. He rejoined the company in May–June, 1864, and was present or accounted for until captured on the South Side Railroad, Virginia, April 3, 1865. Again he was confined at Point Lookout until released on June 23, 1865, after taking the Oath of Allegiance. Upon returning home, he married Lucy Jane Dedman on August 12, 1866. They would have one child by 1870, a daughter named Sarah. They lived in the Jerusalem District where Thomas worked as a store clerk. In 1880 he added farming to his occupation. He was 41 years of age. His application for a pension is on file in the State Archives, Raleigh, North Carolina. Thomas is buried in Concord United Methodist Church Cemetery. No dates are given.

155. Byerly, Hiram
Corporal • Captain William E. Booe's Partisan Rangers • N.C. Volunteers • Company H, 63rd Regiment • (5th Regiment N.C. Cavalry) • N.C. Troops

Hiram was born October 25, 1831. He married Eliza (1829, North Carolina) and they would have four children prior to the beginning of the war: Sarah A. (1852), Frances (1857), Susan E. (1859) and Alice (1861). At age 32, on July 8, 1862, Hiram enlisted for the war. He mustered in as a Private and on August 1, 1863, was appointed Corporal. He was wounded in action June 6, 1864, and reported as absent wounded on July–August, 1864, muster roll. He was issued clothing October 17, 1864. After the war the family increased with the births of Nathaniel (1866), Martha (1868) and Thomas (1870). They resided in the Fulton District of Davie. Eliza died on October 8, 1901; Hiram died on June 22, 1911. They are buried in the Elbaville United Methodist Church Cemetery.

156. Cain, Anderson H.
Private, "Davie Sweep Stakes" • Company G, 4th Regiment • N.C. State Troops

Anderson was born in 1838 to William

(1805, Davie) and Emily (1811, Davie) Cain. They lived in the Chinquepin District where Anderson worked as a teacher prior to enlisting at age 23, June 11, 1861, for the war. He was killed at Seven Pines, Virginia, May 31, 1862. Anderson's name is listed on the Memorial Monument for the Davie County men who died in the Civil War, 1861–1865.

157. Cain, Daniel H.
Private, Company F, 42nd Regiment • N.C. Troops

Daniel was born in 1827 to Samuel (1798, Davie) and Elizabeth (1802, Davie) Cain. He lived in the Chinquepin District of Davie where he married Adeline Steelman (1834) on April 14, 1854. They were the parents of J.W. (1856) and Sarah M. (1858). Daniel worked as a farmer prior to enlisting. The place and date of his enlistment were not reported. He died in hospital at Wilmington on February 16, 1865, of "phthisis." Daniel's name is listed on the Memorial Monument for the Davie County men who died in the Civil War, 1861–1865.

158. Cain, Daniel J.
Second Lieutenant, "Davie Sweep Stakes" • Company G, 4th Regiment • N.C. State Troops

Daniel was born in 1831 to Samuel (1798, Davie) and Elizabeth (1802, Davie) Cain. He worked as a clerk and resided in Davie with John W. and Mary L. Hudson prior to enlisting on June 4, 1861, at age 30, for the war. He mustered in as First Sergeant but was appointed Second Lieutenant to rank from April 19, 1862. He died on June 5, 1862, from wounds received at Seven Pines, Virginia, May 31, 1862. Daniel's name is listed on the Memorial Monument for the Davie County men who died in the Civil War, 1861–1865.

159. Cain, James H. (Harrison)
Confederate States Navy

James was born in Davie County on April 14, 1845, to Daniel W. (1812, Davie) and Temperance (1814, Virginia) Cain. He lived in Cana District and later moved to Mocksville. According to his obituary, he first joined the Home Guards during the War Between The States, but he later enlisted in the Confederate Navy at age 18. He was a crew member on the Confederate ship the ram *Albemarle*, an early iron-plated wooden ship that patrolled the North Carolina coast, especially the mouth of the Roanoke River. The following episode is filed in the Cain Family file drawer in Davie County Library: The ship carried a 60-man crew and was commissioned in April 1864. Two days later she got in a "scrap," sunk [*sic*] the federal ship *Smithfield*, and forced three other Federal ships to withdraw. The Federal Navy went to work devising a plan to destroy the *Albemarle*, using a small very shallow draft boat. On the night of October 27, 1864, the Federal ship with a torpedo secured to the front of a long pole, went over the *Albemarle*'s protective logs and exploded against her side, causing the ram to sink in about eight feet of water. Of the 60 men aboard the *Albemarle*, two were killed by the explosion, fifty-six were captured and two escaped. Of the two escapees, one was the ram's gunner and the other was James Harrison Cain. These two escapees rigged a torpedo and blew up the *Albemarle*'s gun room, which remained above water. "If we could not save her we were determined the enemy would not have her." The two men swam ashore in the dark of the night with a few personal items, including Cain's muzzle-loading six shot revolver. Shortly after the war ended, James married Elizabeth Frost of Cana, on August 18, 1869. Their children were, by 1880, Walter B. (1869), Effey E. (1872), Richard B. (1874), Nany M. (1875), Emily

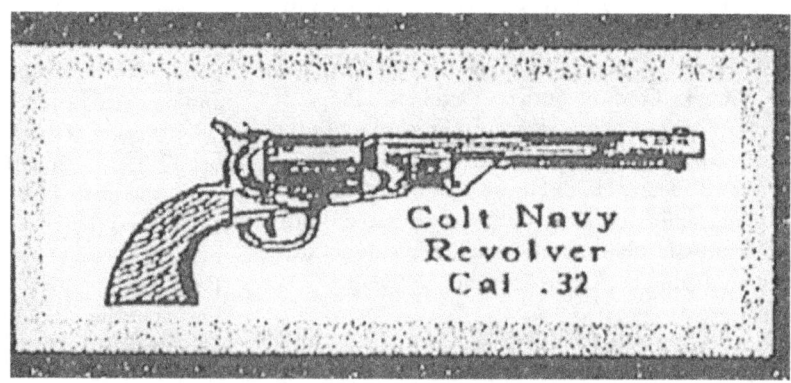

A depiction of the Colt Navy Revolver that James Harrison Cain carried when he jumped from the ram *Albemarle* (Davie County Public Library).

Q. (1876) and Margaret L. (1878). James died on August 28, 1932. He is buried in Eaton's Baptist Church Cemetery.

160. Cain, John L.
Private • Captain William E. Booe's Partisan Rangers • N.C. Volunteers • Company H, 63rd Regiment • (5th Regiment N.C. Cavalry) • N.C. Troops

John was born in 1825 in Davie County. He worked as a farmer and he married Sarah A. (1833, Davie) Kurfees on July 17, 1850. He enlisted in Davie County, April 1, 1864, for the war, while absent without leave from Company D, 1st Regiment Arkansas Infantry. The July–August, 1864, muster roll carries the remark: "Deserter from 1st Arkansas Regiment. Returned through Provost Marshal."

161. Cain, Patrick A.
Private, 1st Company A, Salisbury Prison Guard • Company G, 66th Regiment • N.C. Troops

Patrick served as Private in 1st Company A, Salisbury Prison Guard prior to transferring to Company A of the 66th on October 2, 1863. He was hospitalized at Wilmington on November 7, 1863, with acute dysentery, and returned to duty on January 9, 1864. He was furloughed a week later on January 15, 1864. In March–April, 1864, he returned to duty. He was reported sick in the infirmary from July 25 through August 31, 1864. He returned to duty in September–October, 1864, then was hospitalized in Wilmington on January 23, 1865, with catarrhs. He returned to duty on February 3, 1865, and was hospitalized on February 23, 1865, with debilitas. He was furloughed on March 3, 1865, and paroled at Mocksville on June 3, 1865.

162. Cain, Richard (Richmond) F.
First Lieutenant, Company L, 77th Regiment, 19th Division • N.C. Militia 1861–1865

Richard was born in 1836 in Davie County to William (1805, Davie) and Emily (1811, Davie) Cain. When the war began, Richard was working as a clerk in Mocksville and was boarding with P.R. and Mary Martin, who were merchants. R.F. was appointed a First Lieutenant in Company L of the militia. He married Leonora S. Taylor on October 22, 1863, and by 1870 they were dry goods merchants with two small children: Frank T. (1867) and Pauline (1870).

163. Cain, William F.
Private, Company F, 42nd Regiment • N.C. Troops

William was born in 1835 to Samuel (1798, Davie) and Elizabeth (1802, Davie) Cain. He married Lydia M. Baitey on February 3, 1859. Their son Rufus A. was born in 1860. They resided in the Chinquepin District of Davie where William worked as a farmer prior to enlisting at age 27, March 18, 1862. He died in hospital at Lynchburg, Virginia, July 11, 1862. The cause of death was not reported. William's name is listed on the Memorial Monument for the Davie County men who died in the Civil War, 1861–1865.

164. Cain, William G.
Private, "Davie Sweep Stakes" • Company G, 4th Regiment • N.C. State Troops

William was born on October 8, 1843, the son of Patrick H. and Susan Cain. He resided in Davie County where he enlisted at age 18, June 4, 1861, for the war. He was wounded at Seven Pines, Virginia, May 31, 1862. He rejoined the company in January–April, 1863, and was present or accounted for until admitted to hospital at Richmond, Virginia, June 24, 1863, with a gunshot wound of the "right molar bone." The place and date of receiving the wound were not reported. He was reported absent sick or absent without leave until admitted to hospital at Richmond on March 31, 1865, with a gunshot wound of the left arm. Place and date wounded were not reported. He was captured in the hospital at Richmond on April 3, 1865, and confined at Libbey Prison, Richmond, until transferred to Newport News, Virginia, April 23, 1865. He was released there on June 30, 1865, after taking the Oath of Allegiance. He returned home to the Clarksville District where he worked as a farm laborer. He married Betty Harris, age 33, October 18, 1896. William died on September 22, 1897, and is buried in Bear Creek Baptist Church Cemetery.

165. Call, Burke (Birch)
Private, Carolina Rangers • Company B, 10th Virginia Cavalry Regiment

Burke was born in Davie County circa 1826. He married Mary Holmes on May 19, 1845, and they settled in the Shady Grove District where their children were born: Elizabeth (1847), Nancy (1848), Sarah (1850), Albert F. (1854) and Susan L. (1856). Burke was a carpenter prior to enlisting March 24, 1862, at age 35. He was documented as being present through February 1863, but had to deal with having no horse, being absent on horse detail and then being detailed as a teamster through 1864. He was paroled at Mocksville, North Carolina, on June 9, 1865.

166. Call, David
Corporal, Company M, 7th Regiment • Confederate Cavalry • Company E, 16th Battalion • N.C. Cavalry

David was born in Davie County in 1836 to Sarah (1802, Davie) Call. His brother Berry was head of the household in 1860 when they lived in Smith Grove District, where David married Elizabeth Call on August 25 of the same year. He enlisted as a Corporal on September 3, 1862, in Davie County. On July 11, 1864, he was transferred from Company M, 7th Regiment Confederate Cavalry to Company E, 16th Battalion N.C. Cavalry. He was present or accounted for through October 1, 1864, and paroled at Salisbury, North Carolina, in 1865. He returned to Davie where he farmed in Fulton District. He and Elizabeth had three children: Sarah (1860), Lewis (1862) and Mary B. (1865).

167. Call, Henry
Sergeant, Company M, 7th Regiment • Confederate Cavalry • Company E, 16th Battalion • N.C. Cavalry

Henry was born in Davie County in 1840. He worked as a laborer in the Fulton District prior to enlisting on December 24, 1862, in Davie County, with the rank of Sergeant. On July 11, 1864, he was transferred from Company M, 7th Regiment Confederate Cavalry to Company E, 16th Battalion N.C. Cavalry, while sick on furlough through October 1864. He was paroled at Salisbury, North Carolina, in 1865.

168. Call, Henry G.
Private, Company H, 57th Regiment • N.C. Troops

Henry was born in Davie County in 1843, the son of John (1800, Davie) and Margaret (1808, Davie) Call. He was a laborer living in the Fulton District where at age 19, on July 4, 1862, he enlisted for the war. He was hospitalized at Richmond, Virginia, on September 25, 1862, with measles. After returning to duty on December 9, 1862, he was captured at Chancellorsville, Virginia, on May 3–4, 1863. He was confined at Fort Delaware, Delaware, on or about May 7, 1863, then paroled there and transferred to City Point, Virginia, where he was received on May 23, 1863, for exchange. He was hospitalized at Petersburg, Virginia, on or about May 23, 1863, with pneumonia, where he died on May 30, 1863, of "febris continua communis." Henry's name is listed on the Memorial Monument for the Davie County men who died in the Civil War, 1861–1865.

169. Call, John
Private, Company G, 5th Regiment • N.C. State Troops

John was born in 1828 in Rowan County. He was a farmer in the Smith Grove District of Davie County where he lived with his wife, Sarah A. (1836, Davie), prior to enlisting in Northampton County at age 34, August 13, 1862, for the war. He died in Davie County on March 29, 1863, of "pneumonia." John's name is not presently listed on the Memorial Monument for the Davie County men who died in the Civil War, 1861–1865.

170. Call, Murphy G.
Private, Company E, 42nd Regiment • N.C. Troops

Murphy was born in 1835 and resided in Davie County. He was a farmer in the Smith Grove District when he enlisted at age 27, on March 18, 1862. He was present or accounted for until captured at or near Wise's Forks, Kinston, North Carolina, March 10, 1865. He was confined at Point Lookout, Maryland, March 16, 1865, and released there June 26, 1865, after taking the Oath of Allegiance. Shortly after enlisting, Murphy had married Martha E. Ellis (1835, North Carolina) on December 23, 1862; their son Willis was born in 1867. After the war the family lived in the Farmington District where Martha died in early 1870. Murphy then married Sallie E. Sanders on April 11, 1875; Mary was born in 1879, followed by Buford O. on September 24, 1880. Buford died on March 4, 1913. Sallie (Sarah) died on December 15, 1916, and Murphy died on November 19, 1919. They are buried in Smith Grove United Methodist Church Cemetery.

171. Call, Nathan F.
Private, Company M, 7th Regiment • Confederate Cavalry • Company E, 16th Battalion • N.C. Cavalry

Nathan was born in 1845 in Davie County, the son of John (1800, Davie) and Margaret (1808, Davie) Call. He worked as a laborer in the Fulton District where his father farmed, prior to enlisting with the rank of Private. He was transferred from Company M, 7th Regiment Confederate Cavalry to Company E, 16th Battalion N.C. Cavalry on July 11, 1864. He was present or accounted for through October 1, 1864, and paroled at Salisbury, North Carolina, May 23, 1865. He returned home to marry Mary Call on October 20, 1867.

172. Call, W.H. (Will)
First Sergeant, Company G, 7th Regiment • Confederate Cavalry • Company D, 16th Battalion • N.C. Cavalry

W.H. enlisted as a First Sergeant on September 3, 1862, in Davie County. He transferred from Company G, 7th Regiment Confederate Cavalry on July 11, 1864. He was present or accounted for through October 1, 1864. He was paroled at Appomattox Court House, Virginia, on April 9, 1865.

173. Campbell, Arthur N. (Neely)
First Lieutenant • Captain William E. Booe's Partisan Rangers • N.C. Volunteers • Company H, 63rd Regiment • (5th Regiment N.C. Cavalry) • N.C. Troops

Arthur was born in 1844 to George (1827, Davie) and Ann (1822, Davie) Campbell. They resided in Davie where he enlisted at age 18, July 7, 1862, for the war. He mustered in as Sergeant and was reduced to ranks November–December, 1862. He was promoted to Sergeant May–June, 1863, to First Sergeant July–August, 1863, was present or accounted for on company muster rolls through August 1864, elected Third Lieutenant February 1, 1865, and appointed Second Lieutenant February 15, 1865, to rank from February 1, 1865. He was promoted to First Lieutenant February 15, 1865, to rank from February 2, 1865. No further records.

174. Campbell, Benjamin Frank
Private, Company F, 42nd Regiment • N.C. Troops

Benjamin resided in Davie County where he enlisted at age 28, on April 1, 1862. He was present or accounted for until hospitalized at Richmond, Virginia, October 6, 1864, with a gunshot wound to the left leg. The place and date where he was wounded were not reported. He was furloughed for thirty days on October 21, 1864. "On one occasion (during the siege of Petersburg, Virginia), a loaded shell fell into the trenches — Campbell caught it up immediately and threw it outside, before it could explode, thereby saving the lives of a number of his comrades. On another occasion, he threw water upon a shell for a like purpose." Clark's *Regiments*, Volume V, page 15. The Salem *People's Press* of June 30, 1864, indicates he was wounded June 1–15, 1864.) Reported by Colonel Jno. E. Brown, Forty-second North Carolina Regiment.

175. Campbell, George W.
Private, "Davie Greys" • Company F, 13th Regiment • (3rd Regiment, N.C. Volunteers) • N.C. Troops

George was born in Davie County in 1817. He married Sarah Ann Locke on July 12, 1842. Their five children were Arther [sic] Neely (1844), Amanda T. (Mary) (1847), Laura P. (1849), Elizabeth A. (1851) and Charley (1856). George worked as a carpenter and a farmer in the Mocksville District prior to enlisting in Davie at age 42, August 6, 1861. He was present or accounted for until discharged at Camp Gregg, Virginia, May 9, 1863, by reason of "being over forty years of age."

176. Campbell, Thomas B.
Private, "Davie Sweep Stakes" • Company G, 4th Regiment • N.C. State Troops

Thomas was born in 1832. He worked as a farmer in the Calahaln District, was married to Jane E., and they had a son, John M. (1859). Thomas enlisted at age 31, March 13, 1862, for the war. He was reported present or absent on detail as a teamster until October 19, 1864, when he was captured at Strasburg, Virginia. He was confined at Point Lookout, Maryland, until released June 24, 1865, after taking the Oath of Allegiance. Thomas returned to Davie County and resumed family life. Three more children were born: William B. (1865), Mary E. (1867) and Shafner C. (1869). In 1870 at age 38, Thomas farmed in the Calahaln District. On December 24, 1890, at age 53, Thomas married Delia Anderson, age 37.

177. Canter (Carter), Pleasant H.
Private, Company E, 42nd Regiment • N.C. Troops

Pleasant was born in Davie County in 1843. He was the son of Azariah (1808, Davie) and Edith (1815, Davie). In 1860 the family lived in the Smith Grove District where Azariah worked as a shoemaker and Pleasant was a laborer. He enlisted at age 18, in Davie County, on March 18, 1862. He was present or accounted for through October 1864, and paroled at Mocksville on June 3, 1865. Francis [sic] King and Pleasant were married October 12, 1865. In 1870 they moved to Farmington District where Pleasant worked as a shoemaker and farm laborer and where he and Sarah F. raised their five children: Sallie (1868), Azariah (1870), Lee (1872), Minerva (1874) and Celia (1880).

178. Canter, William M.
Private, Company E. 42nd Regiment • N.C. Troops

William enlisted at age 22, on March 18, 1862. He was present or accounted for until wounded near Petersburg, Virginia, on May 19, 1864. He returned to duty in September–October, 1864, and was paroled at Mocksville on June 3, 1865.

179. Carter, Abraham (Abram H.)
Private, Company D, 42nd Regiment • Captain William Howard's Company • N.C. Prison Guards • 1st Company A, Salisbury Prison Guard • "The Rough and Readys" • Company G, 66th Regiment • N.C. Troops

Abraham was born in 1841 in North Carolina, to A. (1797, North Carolina) and Nancy (1815, North Carolina) Carter. He lived with his family in the Fulton District of Davie County where he worked as a laborer prior to enlisting January 28, 1862, in Company D, 42nd Regiment. On or about May 2, 1862, he transferred to Captain William Howard's Company, N.C. Prison Guards, and served in 1st Company A, Salisbury Prison Guard, before transferring to Company G of the 66th Regiment on October 2, 1863. He was reported sick at home in Davie County through February 29, 1864. He returned to duty in March–April, 1864, but was reported sick at home from July 31 through October 31, 1864. On February 21, 1865, he was hospitalized at Greensboro, North Carolina, with intermittent fever and transferred to another hospital two days later. He was paroled at Mocksville on or about June 2, 1865. Note: He was about 21 years of age in 1863. North Carolina pension records indicate that he was "disabled" on an unspecified date when a horse fell on him and injured his hip and ruptured his belly. Abraham resumed his life as a farmer in Davie. He married Emily E. (1841, North Carolina) Garwood, March 7, 1867. They had four children: William R. (1868), Sarah F. (1870), Bessie J. (1874) and Henry J. (1878). In 1880 Abram [sic] was working in a tobacco factory and Emily was keeping house. Four years later, Abraham married Nancy Ann (1858) Johnson on August 24, 1884. Abraham lived to be 76 years of age. He is buried in Fork Baptist Church Cemetery.

180. Carter, Darius (Davis)
Second Lieutenant • Company C, 77th Regiment, 19th Division • N.C. Militia 1861–1865

David married Sarah Ann Garwood in Davie County on February 15, 1859. The following year they were farming in Fulton with a two-month-old son who had not yet been named. This was the period in which the various companies of the militia were formed. David was named Second Lieutenant of Company C. Another son was born in 1863. The boys' names were Charles and John W., in that order. The father's name does not appear with the family census after 1860.

181. Carter, J.H. (Hinson)
Private • Captain William E. Booe's Partisan Rangers • N.C. Volunteers • Company H, 63rd Regiment • (5th Regiment N.C. Cavalry) • N.C. Troops

Hinson was born in 1841 in Davie County. His father, J.A. Carter (1811, North Carolina) was a mechanic. They resided in the Shady Grove District of Davie where Hinson enlisted at age 21, July 15, 1862, for the war. He was present or accounted for through August 1864, and paroled at Salisbury, North Carolina, in 1865. Two years later he married Amanda (1849) Lard on March 10, 1867. Their children were William (1868), George (1871), John (1874), Charlie (1875) and Louanah (1878). In 1880 the family lived in the Farmington District where Hinson continued to farm. He died in 1886 and is buried in Advance United Methodist Church Cemetery.

182. Carter, William
Private, Company D, 42nd Regiment • Captain William Howard's Company • N.C. Prison Guards • 1st Company A, Salisbury Prison Guard • Private, "The Rough and Readys" • Company G, 66th Regiment • N.C. Troops

William resided in Davie County and enlisted there on January 29, 1862. He was transferred to Captain William Howard's Company, N.C. Prison Guards, on or about May 1, 1862. William previously served as Private in 1st Company A, Salisbury Prison Guard. He was transferred to Company G of the 66th on October 2, 1863. He was reported present through April 30, 1864. He was killed at Hair's House, Virginia, on July 10, 1864. William's name is not presently listed on the Memorial Monument for the Davie County men who died in the Civil War, 1861–1865.

183. Carter (Canter), William Anderson
Second Lieutenant • Company G, 77th Regiment, 19th Division • N.C. Militia 1861–1865

William served as Second Lieutenant of the 77th Regiment, 19th Division, N.C. Militia 1861–1865.

184. Carter, William C.
Private, "Davie Sweep Stakes" • Company G, 4th Regiment • N.C. State Troops

William was born in 1836. He resided in Davie County where he enlisted at age 25, June 15, 1861, for the war. He died at Camp Pickens, near Manassas, Virginia, September 21, 1861. Cause of death was not reported. William's name is listed on the Memorial Monument for the Davie County men who died in the Civil War, 1861–1865.

185. Cartner, James F.
Private, "Davie Greys" • Company F, 13th Regiment • (3rd Regiment, N.C. Volunteers) • N.C. Troops

James was born in 1841. His parents were John (1814, Rowan) and Sarah (1818, Iredell) Cartner. They resided in the Calahaln District where James worked as a farmer prior to enlisting at age 19, August 6, 1861. He was present or accounted for until he died in hospital at Richmond, Virginia, June 28, 1862, of "typhoid fever." His name is listed on the Memorial Monument for the Davie County men who died in the Civil War, 1861–1865.

186. Cartner, John
Private, Company L, 17th Regiment • (2nd Organization) • N.C. Troops

John was born in Davie County in 1834, the son of James (1807, Rowan) and Sarah (1806, Rowan) Cartner. John worked as a laborer in the Chinquepin District where he and Martha M. Smith were married on December 25, 1860. John enlisted on April 11, 1863, at Camp Holmes, for the war. He was present or accounted for through October 1864. He returned to Chinquepin where he resumed farming and where he and Emily raised their six children: Emily E. (1862), John W. (1864), James W. (1866), Samuel (1868), Mary M. (1872) and Rufus W. (1874). John died on March 6, 1905, and is buried in Bear Creek Church Cemetery.

187. Casey, E. Perry
Private • Captain William E. Booe's Partisan Rangers • N.C. Volunteers • Company H, 63rd Regiment • (5th Regiment N.C. Cavalry) • N.C. Troops

Perry was born in 1833. He married Camila Coon (1830, Davie) on June 30, 1857. They resided in the Calahaln District of Davie where he worked as a blacksmith prior to enlisting on July 15, 1862, for the war. He was detailed as a blacksmith November–December, 1862, until he was captured at Hagerstown, Maryland, July 12, 1863, and confined at Point Lookout, Maryland. He was paroled and exchanged at City Point, Virginia, March 6, 1864, and was present or accounted for through February 1865. He was paroled at Salisbury, North Carolina, the same year, and returned to his home in Calahaln. Perry and Camila were the parents of nine children: Sarah J. (1858), James M. (1859) who was blind, Terry R. (1861), John D. (1863), Emma D. (1865), Tobatha A. (1867), Mattie E. (Mary) (1869), Elizabeth E. B. (1872) and Oscar L. (1873). Perry was buried at Center Methodist Church Cemetery in 1913.

188. Casey, Ephraim C.
Private, Company D, 42nd Regiment • N.C. Troops

Ephraim was born in 1838 in Davie County. He was the son of Daniel Casey (1791, Davie) and Matilda (1818, Davie). While living in the Chinquepin District of Davie, Ephraim worked as a laborer. At age 18, Ephraim enlisted in Rowan County on March 26, 1862. He was listed as a deserter in July–August, 1862, but returned to duty prior to January 1, 1863. He was present or accounted for through October 1864, and was paroled at Mocksville on June 3, 1865. On June 11, 1867, Eliza Jane Livengood and Ephraim were married. They lived and worked in the Clarksville District where they raised their children: Samuel W. (1869), Plutina B. (1872), Martha E. (1874), Nancy (1876), Tilly (1878) and Minerva (1879). In 1880 the family moved to Farmington, where Ephraim continued to work as a farm laborer.

189. Caton, Alfred (Alpha)
Private, Carolina Rangers • Company B, 10th Virginia Cavalry Regiment

Alfred was born in 1835 in Davie County to Elizabeth (1796, Davie) Caton. He married Mary Elizabeth Bailey on February 8, 1854. They farmed in the Shady Grove District where he enlisted on April 5, 1862. He was present or accounted for throughout his enlistment. His absences were for sickness and being detailed as an ambulance driver; he also was without a horse in 1863 and 1864. He was issued clothing on September 30, 1864, and again on December 31, 1864. After that there were no further records. Alfred returned home to his growing family, a total of eight children by 1880: Junius (1855), Sarah J. (1860), Lou (1862), Samuel (1866), Victoria

(1871), Joseph L. (1873), Etta (1875) and Minnie (1879). Alfred is buried at Advance United Methodist Church Cemetery. His tombstone lists Alfred Caton, Company B, 10th Virginia Cavalry, CSA. No dates are given.

190. Caton, Green (Greenberry)
Private, Company E, 42nd Regiment • N.C. Troops

Green was born in 1827 and was a farmer most of his life. He enlisted in Davie County on March 18, 1862, at age 38, and was present or accounted for through October 1864. He was paroled at Greensboro, North Carolina, on May 1, 1865. On April 2, 1878, Green and Sallie (Sarah) Chambers were married; he was 51 years old; she was 35. In 1880 they lived in Fulton District where Green made a living by farming.

191. Caton, Orrell
Private, Company E, 42nd Regiment • N.C. Troops

Orrell was born in Davie County in 1838, the son of Elizabeth Caton (1796, Davie). In 1860 he was a laborer living in Shady Grove with his wife, Mary Wood, whom he had married on June 14, 1857. Orrell enlisted in Davie County at age 23, on March 18, 1862. He was present or accounted for through October 1864. Orrell married his second wife, Sarah Wood on June 1, 1865. In 1870 he was a farmer in Fulton District where he lived with Sarah and their children: Lula Lee (1866), Burgess (1868), Maggie (1870), Cornelia (1872), William (1875), Della May (1878) and Junie E. (1884). Orrell died in 1886. He is buried in Advance United Methodist Church Cemetery. Sarah's application for a widow's pension is on file at the State Archives, Raleigh, North Carolina.

192. Caudle, F. Marion
Private, Company G, 7th Regiment • Confederate Cavalry • Company D, 16th Battalion • N.C. Cavalry

Marion was born in Davie County in 1835, the son of Catharine (1795, Davie) Caudle. He enlisted in Davie on November 7, 1863, with the rank of Private, and transferred from Company G, 7th Regiment Confederate Cavalry to Company D, 16th Battalion N.C. Cavalry on July 11, 1864. He was present or accounted for through October 1, 1864, and paroled at Salisbury, North Carolina, on July 10, 1865.

193. Chaffin, Alexander W.
Private, "Davie Sweep Stakes" • Company G, 4th Regiment • N.C. State Troops

Alexander was born in 1838 to Nathan S. (1819) and Elizabeth Baker. Nathan was a farmer and Baptist minister who lived in the Chinquepin District and later married Elvira Glascock, June 30, 1845. Alexander was a student living with his father and step-mother until he enlisted at age 22, June 14, 1861, for the war. He was killed at Seven Pines, Virginia, May 31, 1862. Alexander's name is listed on the Memorial Monument for the Davie County men who died in the Civil War, 1861–1865.

194. Chaffin, Charles Stanley
Private, Company E, 42nd Regiment • N.C. Troops

Charles was born in 1846 in Davie County. He was the son of William O. (1807, Davie) a schoolteacher, and Lydia (1814, Davie) Chaffin. In 1860 Charles was a student attending school in the Mocksville District. He enlisted in Davie County on February 16, 1864, for the war. He was present or accounted for through October 1864. He was paroled at Mocksville on June 7, 1865. No further information.

195. Chaffin, Martin Rowan
First Lieutenant • Company B, 77th Regiment, 19th Division • N.C. Militia 1861–1865

Martin was born November 5, 1828, in Davie County. In 1850 he boarded with the Baxter Clegg family and worked as a laborer. Ten years later he had become a constable for the county, had a wife and small son and was head of his household. He had married Mary Frances McClannon, September 5, 1858, and Frank R. had been born in 1859. When the militia was activated M.R. was appointed First Lieutenant of Company B. On January 15, 1865, he married again, this time to Emeline F. Brock, born November 1838. Their five children were Anna B. (1866), Nathan T. (1867), William B. (1870), Jesse B. (1875) and Corrine (1879). He served the county as Deputy Sheriff, and was appointed to the U.S. Commissions. Martin died on December 8, 1925. He is buried in Rose Cemetery.

196. Chaffin, Nathan M.D.
Private, "Davie Sweep Stakes" • Company G, 4th Regiment • N.C. State Troops

Nathan was born in 1839 to Archibald H. (1803, Davie) and Jemima (1813, Davie) Chaffin. Archibald was a schoolteacher. In 1860 Nathan lived with the William Clark family in the Fulton District where he worked as a laborer. He enlisted at age 22, June 4, 1861, for the war and died at

Camp Pickens, near Manassas, Virginia, November 24, 1861, of "febris typhoides." Nathan's name is listed on the Memorial Monument for the Davie County men who died in the Civil War, 1861–1865.

197. Chambers, Martin
Private, Company E, 42nd Regiment • N.C. Troops

Martin was born in 1837 in Davie County. He was the son of Patterson (1804, Guilford) and Phebee (1815, Davie). In 1860 he was a laborer in the Shady Grove District. Martin enlisted in Davie County at age 23, on March 18, 1862. He was present or accounted for until wounded at or near Petersburg, Virginia, on May 21, 1864. He was reported absent wounded through October 1864. In 1870 he was listed in the Fulton District as a farmer.

198. Chambers, Peter
Private, Company E, 42nd Regiment • N.C. Troops

Peter was born in North Carolina in 1842, the son of Patterson (1804, Guilford) and Phebe (1815, Davie) Chambers. In 1860 he was a laborer living in the Shady Grove District. At age 21, on March 18, 1862, he enlisted in Davie County. Peter was present or accounted for through December 8, 1864. He was paroled at Mocksville on June 7, 1865. In 1870 he was a farmer in the Fulton District, living with Elizabeth Cornatzer, age 75. Peter died in 1907 and is buried in Advance United Methodist Church Cemetery. His tombstone states that he was a "Union Republican."

199. Chandler, Solomon
Private, "Davie Greys" • Company F, 13th Regiment • (3rd Regiment, N.C. Volunteers) • N.C. Troops

Solomon enlisted at Camp Holmes, on November 21, 1863, for the war. He died on December 2, 1863. The place and cause of death were not reported. Solomon's name is listed on the Memorial Monument for the Davie County men who died in the Civil War, 1861–1865.

200. Chaplin, Alexander (James)
Private, "Davie Greys" • Company F, 13th Regiment • (3rd Regiment, N.C. Volunteers) • N.C. Troops

Alexander was born in Davie County November 2, 1824. By 1850 he was a trader, had married Mary Ann (1826, Davie) and settled in the Fulton District. Alexander and Mary Ann had one daughter, Eliza, born on May 22, 1849. At age 33, on April 26, 1861, he enlisted in Davie County. He was present or accounted for until discharged near Richmond, Virginia, on July 26, 1862, under the provisions of the conscript act. He returned to Fulton where he worked as a farmer. Alexander died on May 21, 1913, and is buried at Fork Baptist Church Cemetery. Mary Ann died on May 5, 1892. Daughter Eliza died on September 2, 1935.

201. Chaplin, Jesse
Private • Captain William E. Booe's Partisan Rangers • N.C. Volunteers • Company H, 63rd Regiment • (5th Regiment N.C. Cavalry) • N.C. Troops

Jesse enlisted in Davie County on March 15, 1863, for the war. He was captured at Madison Court House, Virginia, on September 22, 1863, and confined at Old Capitol Prison, Washington, D.C., until transferred to Point Lookout, Maryland, September 25, 1863. He died at Point Lookout, Maryland on April 17, 1864, of "dysentery" and was buried in the Confederate Cemetery, same place. Jesse's name is listed on the Memorial Monument for the Davie County men who died in the Civil War, 1861–1865.

202. Chaplin, John
Private, Company E, 42nd Regiment • N.C. Troops

John was born in 1841 in Currituck, North Carolina. He was the son of Solomon (1816, Davie) who was a farmer and Mary (1824, Davie) Chaplin. In 1860 he was a laborer living in the Fulton District. At age 21, on March 18, 1862, he enlisted in Davie. He was present or accounted for through October 1864.

203. Charles, Francis W.
Private, Company F, 42nd Regiment • N.C. Troops

Francis was born in 1845 in North Carolina. He was the son of J.T. (1815, North Carolina) and Eliza (1816, North Carolina) Charles, who lived in Davie County. Francis resided there until he enlisted for the war at age 18, on April 18, 1863. He was present or accounted for until hospitalized at Petersburg, Virginia, June 23, 1864, with a gunshot wound. Francis returned to duty in September–October, 1864. He was captured at or near Wise's Forks, Kinston, North Carolina, on March 10, 1865, and was released at Point Lookout, Maryland, on June 24, 1865, after taking the Oath of Allegiance. In 1880 he was a merchant living with the John N. Charles family. Francis was the brother of William F. Charles who also served in this company.

204. Charles, John N. (Newton)
Private, "Davie Sweep Stakes" • Company G, 4th Regiment • N.C. State Troops

John was born to J.T. (1815, North Carolina) and Eliza (1816, North Carolina) Charles in April 1837. He was living at home as a student when he enlisted at age 20, June 4, 1861, for the war. He was wounded at Seven Pines, Virginia, May 31, 1862. He rejoined the company prior to September 17, 1862, when he was captured at Sharpsburg, Maryland. He was paroled September 27, 1862, then reported absent through April 1863, but was reported absent on detached service as Assistant Tithe Collector in Davie County from May–August, 1863, through August 1864. In 1870 John was living with the Thomas Bessent family in the Jerusalem District where he worked as a merchant. He married Sarah (Sallie) Bessent on January 24, 1871. Their children were John C. (1873), Eliza R. (1875), Robert P. (1876) and Margaret E. (1877). Sallie died in 1915 and John died in 1931. Both are buried in the Jerusalem Baptist Church Cemetery.

205. Charles, William F.
Private, Company F, 42nd Regiment • N.C. Troops

William was born in 1839 to J.T. (1815, North Carolina) and Eliza (1816, North Carolina) Charles. William enlisted in Davie County at age 22, March 18, 1862, for the war. He died at Lynchburg, Virginia, August 6, 1862. The cause of death was not reported. William was the brother of Francis W. Charles who also served in this company. William's name is listed on the Memorial Monument for the Davie County men who died in the Civil War, 1861–1865

206. Cheshire, F.A. (Francis)
Private, Company M, 7th Regiment • Confederate Cavalry • Company E, 16th Battalion • N.C. Cavalry

Francis was born in Davie County in 1834, to Thomas (1804, Davidson) and Sarah (1809, Davidson) Cheshire. In 1860 he worked as a laborer on the farm of Asbury and Elizabeth Gaither in the Chinquepin District of Davie. Francis enlisted on September 3, 1862, in Davie with the rank of Private. On July 11, 1864, he was transferred from Company M, 7th Regiment Confederate Cavalry to Company E, 16th Battalion N.C. Cavalry. He was present or accounted for through October 1, 1864.

207. Cheshire, John A.
Private, Company G, 5th Regiment • N.C. State Troops

John was born October 27, 1837, in Davie County, to John (1793, Davie) and Temperance (1795, Davie) Cheshire. He married Mary J. Stonestreet on November 22, 1860; they resided in the Mocksville District of Davie where he worked as a farmer prior to enlisting at age 25, August 13, 1862, for the war. He was present or accounted for until wounded in the "third finger of the left hand" at Chancellorsville, Virginia, May 3, 1863, and finger was amputated. He was reported absent wounded through February 1864, then detailed as a nurse at Richmond, Virginia, from March 1, 1864, through January 21, 1865. He was paroled at Salisbury, North Carolina, in April–May, 1865. John resumed his life as a "farmer/crippled" in the Mocksville area where he and Mary had four children by 1880: Minnie (1866), Maggie B. (1871), William H. (1877) and Rupert P. (1880). He died on February 22, 1916. John and Mary are buried at Union Chapel United Methodist Church Cemetery.

208. Cheshire, Jonathan Wesley
Sergeant, Company K, 57th Regiment • N.C. Troops

Jonathan was born into a prosperous Davie County family in 1836. His parents were Tennison (1791, Rowan) and Barbara Mock (1795, Davie) Cheshire. Tennison died in 1854 and Jonathan was the chief recipient of his father's estate. He married Paulina Neely on February 25, 1857; they had three children: Arthur Neely Cheshire, Baxter Clegg Cheshire and Della Cheshire. Jonathan enlisted in Rowan County on July 8, 1862, for the war. He mustered in as a Private and was promoted to Sergeant by January 24, 1863. He was reported present through May 11, 1863, appointed acting Ordnance Sergeant on or about May 22, 1863, and was transferred to the Field and Staff of this regiment. He was on duty as acting regimental Ordnance Sergeant through December 31, 1863. The military record states that he died of disease and that the place and date were not reported. Family tradition says that he was killed and buried in Lynchburg, Virginia. Jonathan's name is listed on the Memorial Monument for the Davie County men who died in the Civil War, 1861–1865. (See photograph, page 53.)

209. Cheshire, Richard (Richmond) B.
Private, Company G, 5th Regiment • N.C. State Troops

Richard was born in 1840 in Davie County

The Tennison Cheshire House. Jonathan Cheshire's father, Tennison, was one of Davie County's largest slaveholders; he also owned over 1600 acres of Davie County in the 1850s (Mohney, *The Historic Architecture of Davie County*).

to John (1793, Davie) and Temperance (1795, Davie) Cheshire. Richard lived with his parents in the Mocksville District prior to enlisting in Northampton County at age 19, on August 13, 1862, for the war. He was present or accounted for until he died in camp on February 29, 1864. The cause of death was not reported. Richard's brother John A. also served in this company. Richard's name is not presently listed on the Memorial Monument for the Davie County men who died in the Civil War, 1861–1865.

210. Chick (Click), John Nicholas
Second Lieutenant • Company A, 77th Regiment, 19th Division • N.C. Militia 1861–1865

John served as a Second Lieutenant of Company A. Although he is listed as "Chick," the correct surname is probably "Click."

211. Church, William
Private, "Davie Greys" • Company F, 13th Regiment • (3rd Regiment, N.C. Volunteers) • N.C. Troops

William resided in Wilkes County and enlisted at Camp Vance on March 14, 1864, for the war. He deserted on May 24, 1864, but was reported sick in hospital on the company muster roll dated July–August, 1864. He died in hospital at Richmond, Virginia, on September 5, 1864, of "colitis acuta." William's name is listed on the Memorial Monument for the Davie County men who died in the Civil War, 1861–1865.

212. Clark, Edward M.
Sergeant, Company F, 42nd Regiment • N.C. Troops

Edward was born in 1841. He enlisted in Davie County at age 21, on March 25, 1862. He was mustered in as a Corporal and promoted to Sergeant in May–June, 1863. He was present or accounted for through October 1864, and was paroled at Greensboro, North Carolina, on May 1, 1865.

213. Clark, L. (Louis)
Private • Captain William E. Booe's Partisan Rangers • N.C. Volunteers • Company H, 63rd Regiment • (5th Regiment N.C. Cavalry) • N.C. Troops

In 1860 Louis lived in the household of T.J. Deadmon. They resided in the Liberty District of

Davie County where Louis enlisted at age 16, July 15, 1862, for the war, as a substitute for R. M. Austin. He was reported as wounded and captured at Upperville, Virginia, June 21, 1863, but no Federal Provost Marshal records relative to his capture were found. On July 2, 1863, he was admitted to hospital at Staunton, Virginia, with a gunshot wound. He was present or accounted for until he retired to the Invalid Corps on August 10, 1864, and was declared as "totally disqualified" by the Medical Examining Board on February 15, 1865.

214. Clark, William Albea
First Lieutenant • Company K, 77th Regiment, 19th Division • N.C. Militia 1861–1865

William was born September 15, 1836, in Davie County. When the militia was activated he was appointed First Lieutenant of Company K. His first marriage was to Cornelia V. Williams on May 27, 1862, but it ended with her untimely death on June 21, 1864. Cornelia is buried in the Dr. Francis Rush Williams Family Cemetery. William's second marriage, at age 30, was to Nancy E. Furches on January 18, 1866. Their children were Sallie E. (1867), M. Louisa (1868) and Dora (1871). They lived and farmed in the Farmington District of Davie where William was a member of the Masonic Lodge. He died on July 16, 1885, and is buried in Olive Branch Cemetery.

215. Clary, James
Private, "Davie Sweep Stakes" • Company G, 4th Regiment • N.C. State Troops

James was born in 1840. He resided with the Thomas Furches family in the Farmington District of Davie County prior to enlisting at age 21, June 5, 1861, for the war. He was mortally wounded at Chancellorsville, Virginia, May 3, 1863. The place and date of death were not reported. James's name is listed on the Memorial Monument for the Davie County men who died in the Civil War, 1861–1865.

216. Clary, William
Private, "Davie Sweep Stakes" • Company G, 4th Regiment • N.C. State Troops

William was born in 1842 to William (1815, North Carolina) Clary. His step-mother was Martha (1830, Virginia). They resided in the Mocksville District of Davie County where William worked as a laborer prior to enlisting at Camp Pickens, near Manassas, Virginia, August 9, 1861, for the war. He was wounded in both thighs at Gettysburg, Pennsylvania, July 3, 1863, and captured at Gettysburg or at Waterloo, Pennsylvania, July 3–5, 1863. He was confined at Fort Delaware, Delaware, until transferred to Point Lookout, Maryland, October 15–18, 1863. He was paroled at Point Lookout and transferred to Cox's Wharf, James River, Virginia, where he was received October 15, 1864, for exchange. On April 9, 1865, he was paroled at Appomattox Court House, Virginia.

217. Clement, Baxter Clegg
Captain, Company M, 7th Regiment • Confederate Cavalry • Company E, 16th Battalion • N.C. Cavalry

Baxter was born January 5, 1841, in Davie County, to Jesse A. (1808, Davie) and Melinda (1810, Davie) Nail Clement. Although he was born into a prosperous family, his father demanded that his children maintain a high work ethic, and so Baxter "worked in the fields with the slaves and at every other task his father found need to impose." According to an article written by his daughter dated November 14, 1963, Baxter was in charge of a covered wagon train in Florida in 1861, no doubt delivering the tobacco products, cotton and wheat brokered by his father, when war was declared. He returned home to find that his father had raised a company of volunteers from Davie, Forsyth and Davidson counties, and was serving, at age 53, as Captain of Company F, 13th Regiment. However, his father, Jesse, was not re-elected in April 1862, and so became a part of Company G, 7th Regiment Confederate Cavalry, until he was transferred to Company D, 16th Battalion as Captain. Baxter, in turn, was commissioned Captain in 1862 and served as Commanding Officer of Company M, 7th Regiment Confederate Cavalry, until he was transferred to Company E, 16th Battalion N.C. Cavalry, July 11, 1864. Baxter's younger brother, Jesse Lee Clement, age 17, served in his company and they were indeed comrades-in-arms. James Wall tells in his *History of Davie County* how the Clement brothers participated in a raid against the Yankees on September 16, 1864, to successfully rustle "2,468 head of beef to feed the starving Confederate Armies at Petersburg." This was a huge morale booster but the war was already winding to a close and it ended with General Lee's surrender on April 9, 1865. The Clement brothers, however, were not there to see it. Both had been captured at Hatcher's Run, Virginia, on April 1, 1865. Baxter was confined at Johnson's Island, Ohio, where he remained until released after taking the Oath of Allegiance on June 18, 1865, and Jesse Lee was shipped to New York State. Baxter returned home to "read medicine" with his older brother, Dr. William Clement, in Rover, Arkansas, and to attend the University of Louisiana for his medical training. He eventually returned to North Carolina and established a medical practice in Rowan County. He married Lina Barber, moved to Mocksville where he continued his profession, and parented three children: Linda, Jesse Frank and Baxter Clegg Clement, Jr. He died on July 19, 1927, in the Clement homestead where he was born. He is buried in Clement Family Cemetery.

218. Clement, Jesse A.
Captain, "Davie Greys" • Company F, 13th Regiment • (3rd Regiment, N.C. Volunteers) • Company G, 7th Regiment • Confederate Cavalry • Company D, 16th Battalion • N.C. Cavalry

Jesse was born in Rowan County, December 6, 1808, to Henry and Elizabeth Winkler Clement. He and several of his siblings would become leaders in the early development of Davie County; his brother John Clement of Rowan County served in the House of Commons in 1836, where he presented a petition to establish Davie County. (Details are presented in James Wall's *History of Davie County*, page 109.) Jesse quickly became a prominent citizen whose influence was widely felt. He served in the N.C. House of Commons in 1838–1839 and was always alert to any new investment opportunity. By the time he married in 1828 he had constructed what would be recognized as one of the area's most significant houses. It was placed on the National Register of Historic Places in 1979. Today it serves as a bed and breakfast inn known as Clement Plantation House. Jesse married Melinda (1810, Davie) Nail on January 1, 1828. By 1850 there were seven children in the household: Sally (1828), Martha (1833), William (1839), Baxter (1841), Laura (1844), Jesse (1847) and Charles (1849). Jesse operated two plantations, a tannery and did a brokerage business in manufactured plug tobacco, cotton and wheat which were shipped by wagon train to Columbia and other points south. Imme-

Jesse A. Clement was a prominent and well-respected citizen of Mocksville. His house, built in 1828, was placed on the National Register of Historic Places in 1979. When war began in 1861, Clement men raised their own companies (later merging with other units) and fought until the Armistice was signed April 9, 1865 (Mohney, *The Historic Architecture of Davie County*).

diately after war was declared, Jesse, at age 53, became Captain of the first company organized in Davie County, Company F, 13th Regiment. This was his company and the men saw some of the worst fighting of the war and had many losses. He was defeated for re-election when the regiment reorganized on April 26, 1862. He then joined Company G, 7th Regiment Confederate Cavalry, until he was transferred to Company D, 16th Battalion as Captain, and was present or accounted for through October 1, 1864. He submitted his resignation on December 1, 1864, and it was officially accepted December 16, 1864. He died on May 7, 1876, and is buried in the Clement Family Cemetery.

219. Clement, Jesse Lee
Private, Company M, 7th Regiment • Confederate Cavalry • Company E, 16th Battalion • N.C. Cavalry

Jesse Lee was born in Davie County, March 26, 1847, to Jesse A. (1808, Davie) and Melinda (1810, Davie) Nail. Jesse was a young man whose family played a major, if not the lead role in providing military leaders from Davie County to serve in the Civil War. His father, brother and cousins were captains whose integrity and force of character were as noteworthy as their military leadership. Private Jesse Lee had the good fortune to serve under his older brother Captain Baxter Clegg and no doubt their shared experiences provided many fireside discussions for the rest of their lives. Two examples are the cattle rustling episode James Wall provides in his *History of Davie County*, and the unfortunate incident of their capture by the Yankees on April 1, 1865, just nine days before the surrender at Appomattox. Jesse came home to live a very long life in Mocksville where he was one of its "most highly esteemed citizens," to use a quote from the "Davie Record" dated March 29, 1934. Jesse married Lettie Lindsay on December 14, 1881. Their children were Jesse Lee (1882), Elizabeth Gray (1886), Charles Hargrave (1889), Laura (1892), Martha Lindsay (1895), William Norman (1897) and Milinda Gray (1900). Jesse Lee died on August 1, 1934, and is buried in the Clement Family Cemetery.

220. Clement, John H. (Henry)
First Lieutenant, Company F, 42nd Regiment • N.C. Troops

John was born in 1828 in Davie County to Godfrey (1789) and Elizabeth Brown (1803,

The home of John Henry Clement, who is described in Clark's *Regiments* as "a courageous and capable officer" (Mohney, *The Historic Architecture of Davie County*).

Davie) Clement. His father died four years later, leaving John and two younger sisters, with their mother. He was listed as head of the household in 1860 prior to enlisting in Rowan County. He was appointed Second Lieutenant on or about March 21, 1862, and promoted to First Lieutenant on June 22, 1863. He was present or accounted for through October 1864 and paroled at Greensboro, North Carolina, on May 1, 1865. He resumed farm life, married Mary Emily Foster on November 14, 1878, and they were the parents of Mary L. in 1880. He is mentioned in Clark's *Regiments* as being "a courageous and capable officer. He occupied a prominent position in Davie County, having served in the State Senate for a number of terms." John Henry Clement died in 1917 and is buried in Clement Family Cemetery.

221. Clement, Wiley Adam
Second Lieutenant, Company F, 13th Regiment • (3rd Regiment, N.C. Volunteers) • Captain, Company F, 42nd Regiment • N.C. Troops

Wiley was born May 16, 1846, in Davie County, the youngest child of John (1795) and Nancy (1799, Davie) Bailey Clement. His father died when Wiley was five, but he had four older brothers who were excellent role models and a mother who was quite capable of managing 16 slaves and a plantation. The family lived in the Liberty District of Davie. Wiley was a student prior to enlisting in Davie at age 21; he was elected to serve as Second Lieutenant, Company F, 13th Regiment, N.C. Troops, to rank from May 5, 1861. He was present or accounted for until he resigned on March 21, 1862, by reason of having raised his own company. He was appointed Captain of Company F, 42nd Regiment to rank from March 21, 1862. (One of Wiley's older brothers was Major William Bailey Clement "Dart," Company B, 10th Virginia Cavalry.) Wiley was present or accounted for through October 1864, and paroled at Greensboro, North Carolina, on May 1, 1865. (The Salem *People's Press* of June 30, 1864, indicates he was wounded in action June 1–15, 1864.) He was commended in Clark's *Regiments* as being "a fine officer and did his duty well." Volume II, page 806. He returned home to Davie County where he married Nancy Cornelia Parker on October 21, 1875. Their two sons in 1880 were Hugh (1877) and Ray (1880). Wiley had also be-

The home of Wiley A. Clement. After serving as a Second Lieutenant in Company F, 13th Regiment, for a year, Wiley resigned to form his own Company F, 42nd Regiment, which he served as Captain (Mohney, *The Historic Architecture of Davie County*).

come "Clerk of F. Court." He died on June 24, 1901, and is buried in Clement Family Cemetery.

222. Clement, William Bailey (Dart)
Captain, Carolina Rangers • Major, Company B, 10th Virginia Cavalry Regiment

"Dart" Clement was born in Davie County on February 3, 1835, to John (1795) and Nancy Bailey (1799, Davie) Clement. When he was 23, Dart went to Texas to make a lot of money. In a letter written in "Austin City, Texas," dated November 24, 1858, he describes part of his trip and his urgency: "I staid [sic] in New Orleans two days. I put up at a private boarding house and there was a child buried the morning I arrived, which had died there with yellow fever. I was urged not to go to the city, as soon as I did, but I was so anxious to get out here, to try and make some money, that I did not pay any attention." Several days later he had reached Texas and was with some of his business associates, and his impatience was growing: "I like Texas very well but I haven't seen any money growing on trees yet." Apparently his venture was a success. When Davie County men were gathering at "Camp Liberty" Church, south of Mocksville, October 25, 1861, "Dart" was there to organize and finance their enlistment into Company B, known as the North Carolina Rangers, later to become a part of the 10th Virginia Cavalry. Following the accepted procedure of the time, the men then voted unanimously to accept him as their commanding officer and they remained together until the end. There is a wonderful collection of personal correspondence between "Dart" and Mattie K. Martin, his future wife, which serves as a window through which we can observe both the public and private lives of two individuals caught up in the age-old conflict between love and war. The datelines of "Dart's" letters serve as a chronology of many of the major battles both won and lost. The letters were a conduit through which news of local men wounded, dead or alive could be shared with their families. Against the backdrop of carnage, bravery and deprivation, "Dart" and Mattie managed to marry in Mocksville on March 18, 1863; their son William was born December 19, 1863. Captain Clement was elected Major on September 25,

William Bailey Clement and Mattie K. Martin, were married March 18, 1863, in Mocksville, North Carolina. These paintings are believed to be their wedding portraits (Cheryl Clement and Glen Clement).

1863. General W. H. F. Lee recommended that "Dart" be promoted to Colonel of the 7th North Carolina Cavalry on March 1, 1865, but it was never acted on because of the end of the war. To quote from James Wall's *History of Davie County*, page 173, "This cavalry company fought at Seven Pines, Gaines' Mill, Cold Harbor, Malvern Hill, Second Manassas, Antietam, Fredericksburg and Gettysburg. Once it was under fire eighteen of twenty-two consecutive days. It reached Gettysburg on July 2, 1863, the second day of the battle, and was in Hampton's Charge on July 3. In the closing weeks of the war, it fell back with Lee toward Appomattox but did not surrender — the men took their horses and just returned home." "Dart" was paroled in Salisbury, North Carolina, on May 1, 1865. He returned to his family, built a house on Daniel Road south of Mocksville, and became a farmer, according to the Davie County census of 1870 and 1880. During the latter part of his life he was an invalid and lived in Mocksville where he died on January 14, 1895. He is buried in Clement Family Cemetery. The name on his tombstone reads:

Col. Wm. B. Clement
10th Virginia Cavalry CSA
1861–1865
February 3, 1835. January 12, 1896

Mattie and William K. are buried there as well.

223. Click, Daniel W.
Private, "Davie Greys" • Company F, 13th Regiment • (3rd Regiment, N.C. Volunteers) • N.C. Troops

Daniel was born in 1840 in Davie County. He was the son of Henry H. Click (1808, Davie). He worked as a tobacconist or constable prior to enlisting in Davie County at age 21, on April 26, 1861. He was present or accounted for until he died in the hospital at Richmond, Virginia, on July 10, 1862, of "typhoid fever." Daniel's name is listed on the Memorial Monument for the Davie County men who died in the Civil War, 1861–1865.

224. Click, Michael
Private, Company E, 42nd Regiment • N.C. Troops

Michael was born in Davie County in 1832. His parents were Michael (1783) and Sarah (1792, Davie) Click. Michael married Milly J. Snider on March 23, 1854. In 1860 they were living in the Liberty District, when he enlisted in Davie County on March 18, 1862. He was present or accounted for through October 1864. He was paroled at Salisbury on May 22, 1865, and took the Oath of Allegiance at Salisbury, North Carolina, on June 3, 1865. Milly and Michael were parents of five children: John F. (1856), Godfrey (1857), Dewit C. (1860), Charles (1863), Sarah (1865) and also a grandson, William (1872). In 1870 the family lived in the Jerusalem District where they farmed. On December 24, 1879, Michael married Sarah C. Daniel (1833, North Carolina).

225. Click, W.H.
Private • Captain William E. Booe's Partisan Rangers • N.C. Volunteers • Company H, 63rd Regiment • (5th Regiment N.C. Cavalry) • N.C. Troops

W.H. was born in North Carolina circa 1847. In 1860 at age 13, he lived with the B.R. Eaton family in the Smith Grove District of Davie County, where he enlisted September 18, 1863, for the war. He was captured at Weldon Railroad, August 21, 1864, and confined at Point Lookout, Maryland, until paroled and exchanged at Boulware's Wharf, James River, Virginia, March 16, 1865.

226. Clifford, A.M.
Private, Company M, 7th Regiment • Confederate Cavalry • Company E, 16th Battalion • N.C. Cavalry

A.M. was born in 1829 in Davie County to Susannah (1797, Davie) Clifford. He married Martha E. (1833, North Carolina) and they were parents to four children prior to the war: Frances N. (1854), Alice G. (1855), John W. (1857) and Thidosia E. (1859). They farmed in the Mocksville District where A.M. enlisted September 3, 1862. He was transferred from Company M, 7th Regiment Confederate Cavalry on July 11, 1864. Federal Provost Marshal records show that he was received by the Provost Marshal General, in Washington, D.C., as a "deserter from the enemy" on March 29, 1865, from the Provost Marshal, Army of the Potomac. He took the Oath of Allegiance and was provided transportation to Green County, Illinois.

227. Clifford, Franklin A.
Private, Company F, 42nd Regiment • N.C. Troops

Franklin was born in 1845 in Davie County, to James G. (1816, Davie) and Rebecca (1818) Clifford. They resided in the Chinquepin District of Davie where he worked as a laborer prior to enlisting. The place and date of enlistment were not reported. Franklin was captured at or near Wise's Forks, Kinston, North Carolina, on March 10, 1865, confined at Point Lookout, Maryland, March 16, 1865, and he was released on June 24, 1865, from Point Lookout after taking the Oath of Allegiance. He married Louesa Ellen Wiseman on February 22, 1866, and settled in the Clarksville District of Davie where he was a farmer. Their children were Lillian E. (1867), Joseph W. (1869), Annetta (1871), Becky G. (1875), James O. (1877) and Dora Lee (1879).

228. Clifford, John H.
Private, Company F, 42nd Regiment • N.C. Troops

John was born in 1840 in Davie to Ahira (1811, Davie) and Roseannah (1815, Davie) Clifford. They lived in the Chinquepin District where his father was a farmer and John worked as a laborer. He enlisted in Davie County at age 22, on March 18, 1862. He was present or accounted for until May–June, 1863, when he was reported absent wounded; the place and date were not reported. Prior to November 1863, he returned to duty. He was present or accounted for until detailed in the Quartermaster Department at Salisbury, North Carolina, on March 20, 1864, because of disability. He was absent on detail at Salisbury through October 1864. He retired to the Invalid Corps on December 19, 1864, and later was paroled at Mocksville on June 3, 1865.

229. Clifford, Joseph C.
Private, Company G, 5th Regiment • N.C. State Troops

Joseph was born in 1840 in Davie County to James G. (1816, Davie) and Rebecca Coker (1818) Clifford. They resided in the Chinquepin District where Joseph worked as a laborer prior to enlisting in Northampton County at age 22, August 13, 1862, for the war. He was present or accounted for until killed at Gettysburg, Pennsylvania, July 1, 1863. Joseph's parents are buried at Eaton's Baptist Church Cemetery in Davie County. Joseph's name is not presently listed on the Memorial Monument for the Davie County men who died in the Civil War, 1861–1865.

James Gray Clifford built this house in the 1850s. Three of his four sons were drafted into the Confederate Army despite the fact they were Union sympathizers (Mohney, ***The Historic Architecture of Davie County***).

230. Clifford, William C.
Private, Company G, 5th Regiment • N.C. State Troops

William was born in 1843 in Davie County to James (1816, Davie) and Rebecca (1818, Davie) Coker Clifford. They lived in the Chinquepin District of Davie where William worked as a laborer prior to enlisting in Northampton County at age 19, on August 13, 1862, for the war. He was present or accounted for until captured at Spotsylvania Court House, Virginia, May 12, 1864. He was confined at Point Lookout, Maryland, until transferred to Elmira, New York, on August 3, 1864. He died at Elmira on May 12, 1865, of "chronic diarrhoea." William's brother Joseph also served in this company. William's name is not presently listed on the Memorial Monument for the Davie County men who died in the Civil War, 1861–1865.

231. Cline, Henry
Private, Company G, 7th Regiment • Confederate Cavalry • Company D, 16th Battalion • N.C. Cavalry

Henry enlisted in Davie County on September 3, 1862, with the rank of Private. He transferred from Company G, 7th Regiment Confederate Cavalry to Company D, 16th Battalion N.C. Cavalry on July 11, 1864, while absent without leave. He was reported on the muster roll dated October 1, 1864, as "absent without leave since October 1862."

232. Cloninger, Alonzo
Private, 2nd Company B, 42nd Regiment • N.C. Troops • Company F, 13th Regiment, "Davie Greys" • (3rd Regiment, N.C. Volunteers) • N.C. Troops

Alonzo was born in 1845 in Catawba County and resided in Rowan County where he enlisted at age 17, on January 22, 1862. He was present or accounted for until transferred to Company F, 13th Regiment, N.C. Troops (3rd Regiment N.C. Volunteers), on February 18, 1863. Alonzo was killed at Chancellorsville, Virginia, on May 3, 1863. Alonzo's name is listed on the Memorial Monument for the Davie County men who died in the Civil War, 1861–1865.

233. Clouse, L.A.
Sergeant, Company E, 42nd Regiment • Musician, Regimental Band • Field and Staff, 42nd Regiment • N.C. Troops

Leander was born in Davie County in 1843. He was the son of Enoch (1821, Davidson) and Julia (1824, Davidson). Leander was 18 years old and a student in Smith Grove, when he married Ann M. Naylor on December 12, 1860. He enlisted in Davie County at age 20, on March 18, 1862, and was mustered in as a Sergeant. Leander was present or accounted for until appointed Musician on or about December 31, 1863, and transferred to the regimental band. He was present or accounted for through January 3, 1865. He was paroled at Mocksville on or about June 9, 1865. Leander and Ann were the parents of four children: L.A. (1862), E.B. (1864), Julia (1867) and Laura (1869). After the war, Leander and his family lived and farmed in Farmington. He is buried in Smith Grove United Methodist Church Cemetery. No dates are given.

234. Clouse, William
Captain • Company E, 77th Regiment, 19th Division • N.C. Militia 1861–1865

William was born in 1816 in Davidson County. He and his wife, Nancy (1821, Davidson) moved to Davie County where they farmed and raised their children in the Farmington District. Their children were Catherine J. (1843), Joseph N. (1845), Cintha Loueza (1847), John A. (1849), Martha A. (1853), Mary E. (1860) and Clauda (1865). William served as Captain of Company E and resumed his life as a farmer when the war ended.

235. Codie (Cody), Godfrey
Private, Company G, 5th Regiment • N.C. State Troops

Godfrey was born in 1843 in Davie County to John (1817, Randolph) and Leah (1818, Cabarrus) Cody. In 1860 Godfrey boarded with the C. H. Bessent family in the Liberty District where he worked as a laborer. He enlisted in Northampton County at age 19, on August 13, 1862, for the war. He was present or accounted for until killed at Spotsylvania Court House, Virginia, May 9, 1864. Godfrey's name is not presently listed on the Memorial Monument for the Davie County men who died in the Civil War, 1861–1865.

236. Collett, Ezekiel
Private, Company F, 42nd Regiment • N.C. Troops

Ezekiel was born in 1840 in North Carolina, to Charles (1815, North Carolina) and Eliza (1816, North Carolina) Collett. They resided in the Mocksville District where Ezekiel enlisted at age 22, March 18, 1862. He was present or accounted for until March–April, 1863, when he was reported absent wounded. The place and date were not reported. In July–October of 1863, he returned to duty. He was present or accounted for through October 1864. On June 3, 1865, he was paroled in Mocksville. Ezekiel returned home where he married Sarah L. Grimes (1846, North Carolina) on August 19, 1866. They raised their children, Fidella A. (1869), Thomas (1870) and Juna A. (1872) in the Clarksville District of Davie County. Ezekiel died on November 8, 1882, and is buried in Eaton's Baptist Church Cemetery.

237. Collette, Benjamin F.
Private, Company G, 5th Regiment • N.C. State Troops

Benjamin was born on August 8, 1841, in North Carolina, to Charles (1815, North Carolina) and Eliza (1816, North Carolina) Collet [*sic*]. He worked as a laborer in the Mocksville District of Davie County prior to enlisting in Northampton County on August 13, 1862, at age 21, for the war. He was present or accounted for until wounded in the right leg and captured at Gettysburg, Pennsylvania, July 1–3, 1863. He was hospitalized at Gettysburg and Davids Island, New York Harbor, until transferred to City Point, Virginia, where he was received October 28, 1863, for exchange. He was reported absent wounded through February 1864, and reported on sick furlough through December 1864. He was paroled at Salisbury, North Carolina, in April–May, 1865. He was certainly back home by May 2, 1865, the day he married Sally Hunter. Their children were John (1868), Sam'l (1869), Susan (1872), Julia A. (1875) and Mary (1879). They resided in the Clarksville District where Benjamin supported his family by farming. He died in 1885 and is buried in Eaton's Baptist Church Cemetery.

238. Collette, Robert W.
Private, Company G, 5th Regiment • N.C. State Troops

Robert was born in 1838. He married Sarah M. (1838) Clifford on November 15, 1860, in Davie County where he worked as a laborer. They were residing in the Mocksville District when he enlisted in Northampton County at age 25, August 13, 1862, for the war. He was present or accounted for until he was wounded in the foot at Chancellorsville, Virginia, May 1–2, 1863. He was reported absent wounded until November 14, 1863, when he was reported absent without leave. He rejoined the company in March–April, 1864,

Three Collette brothers: Ezekiel, Benjamin and Robert lived and worked here before enlisting for the war. Robert died two months before the war ended (Mohney, *The Historic Architecture of Davie County*).

Collette Barn (Mohney, *The Historic Architecture of Davie County*)

and was present or accounted for until captured at Spotsylvania Court House, Virginia, May 9–12, 1864. After being confined at Point Lookout, Maryland, he was transferred to Elmira, New York, August 3, 1864, where he died on February 18, 1865, of "chronic diarrhoea." Sarah's application for a widow's pension is on file in the State Archives, Raleigh, North Carolina; her request was approved. Robert's name is not presently listed on the Memorial Monument for the Davie County men who died in the Civil War, 1861–1865.

239. Conner, J.C.
Private, Company G, 7th Regiment • Confederate Cavalry • Company D, 16th Battalion • N.C. Cavalry

J.C. transferred from Company G, 7th Regiment Confederate Cavalry to Company D, 16th Battalion N.C. Cavalry on July 11, 1864. He was present or accounted for through October 1, 1864.

240. Conrad, P.J. (Phillip)
Private • Captain William E. Booe's Partisan Rangers • N.C. Volunteers • Company H, 63rd Regiment • (5th Regiment N.C. Cavalry) • N.C. Troops

Phillip was born circa 1829 in Orange County, Virginia. He established his residence in Davie County where he farmed and where he married Susan Dwiggins on March 8, 1857. By the time he enlisted on July 23, 1862, for the war, they were the parents of James M. (1858) and Sarah A. (1859). Phillip died on August 21, 1863. His name is listed on the Memorial Monument for the Davie County men who died in the Civil War, 1861–1865.

241. Cook, George B.
Private, Company E, 42nd Regiment • N.C. Troops

George was born in Davie County in 1845. He was the son of Harrison (1813, Davie) and Ann (1821, Davie) Cook. In 1860 at age 14, George was a laborer living in the Chinquepin District. On September 11, 1864, he enlisted in Davie County, for the war; he was 19 years old. He was present or accounted for through October 1864. George was paroled at Mocksville on June 7, 1865. George and his wife Martha Hines (1845) had three children: Merta (1868), Mary J. (1870) and George L. (1879). In 1880 they were farmers in the Clarksville District. (See photograph on page 64.)

242. Cook, James
Private, "Davie Sweep Stakes" • Company G, 4th Regiment • N.C. State Troops

James was born to Harrison (1813, Davie) and Anna Baity (1821, Davie) Cook in 1844. James's father worked as a farmer / tanner in the Chinquepin District. James enlisted in Davie County at age 18, March 10, 1862, for the war. He

After serving in the war, George Cook came home, married Martha Hines and raised three children in this house (Mohney, *The Historic Architecture of Davie County*).

was killed at Seven Pines, Virginia, May 31, 1862. James's name is listed on the Memorial Monument for the Davie County men who died in the Civil War, 1861–1865.

243. Cook, Lemuel Blick
Second Lieutenant • Company E, 77th Regiment, 19th Division • N.C. Militia 1861–1865

Lemuel was born December 22, 1824, in Stokes County. He moved to the Farmington District of Davie County where he worked as a farmer and a millwright. On April 17, 1849, he married Susannah (1825, Davie) Sheek Mock, widow of Henry Mock and mother of two small children: William Mock (1846) and Margaret Mock (1848). Both children were born in Virginia. Lemuel and Susannah would have six or seven children by 1880: Mary (1850), Emily (1855), Icy Ann (1858), George L. (1861), Dan'l J. (1863), Henry L. (1867) and Bob. When war was imminent and the militia was activated Lemuel was appointed Second Lieutenant of Company E. The family remained in the Farmington District. Lemuel died on June 2, 1896, and is buried in Macedonia Moravian Church Cemetery. Susannah died on February 10, 1922, at age 96!

244. Coon, Benjamin G.
Second Lieutenant, Company B, 15th Regiment • N.C. Troops

Benjamin was born in 1844 in Davie County. He was the son of Jacob A. and Sarah P. Jones (1816, Davie). He resided in Davie County and enlisted in Union County at age 19, on May 3, 1861. He mustered in as a Corporal and was present or accounted for until wounded at Lee's Mill, Virginia, on April 16, 1862. Benjamin returned to duty prior to January 1, 1863, and was promoted to Corporal on March 4, 1863, followed by promotion to First Sergeant on June 4, 1863. He was present or accounted for until wounded in the right thigh at Bristoe Station, Virginia, on October 14, 1863. Benjamin returned to duty on January 26, 1864, and was appointed Second Lieutenant on April 2, 1864. He was present or accounted for until he retired to the Invalid Corps about November 29, 1864.

245. Cope, Andrew
Private, Company D, 42nd Regiment • N.C. Troops

Andrew was born in 1825 in Davie County. In 1850 he lived in Davie County with his brother Thomas, where they farmed. By 1860 both had married and Andrew and his new bride "Nealey" A. Austin (married December 13, 1859) continued to live with Thomas and his family. At that time Andrew was 32 years old and Cornelia was 17. Andrew enlisted in Lenoir County at age 38, on September 28, 1863, for the war. He died in the hospital at Wilmington, on December 4, 1863, of "pneumonia." In 1870 Cornelia continued live in Farmington with three children in the household: William T. (1860), Charity (1866) and George W. (1870). Cornelia is buried in Macedonia Moravian Church Cemetery. She died on January 3, 1921. Andrew's name is listed on the Memorial Monument for the Davie County men who died in the Civil War, 1861–1865.

246. Cope, Frederick T.
Private, Company A, 57th Regiment • N.C. Troops

Frederick was born in 1836 in Davie County. He was the son of Henry (1813, Davie) and Nancy (1810, Davie). The family lived in the Liberty District of Davie where Frederick worked as a laborer. On December 23, 1860, he and Mary J. Foster were married. At age 26, on July 4, 1862, he enlisted in Davie, for the war. He was reported sick at home in July–September, 1862, but was reported absent without leave on October 27, 1862. He returned to duty in November–December, 1862, and was reported present January–October, 1863. He was captured at Rappahannock Station, Virginia, November 7, 1863, sent to Washington, D.C., and confined at Point Lookout, Maryland, on November 11, 1863. Four months later Frederick was paroled on March 16, 1864, and received at City Point, Virginia, on March 20, 1864, for exchange. Two months later he was reported absent without leave May 20, 1864 through February 28, 1865. On an unspecified date in 1865, he took the Oath of Allegiance at Salisbury, North Carolina. (North Carolina Pension records indicate that he was wounded at Fredericksburg, Virginia, December 13, 1862.) Frederick and Mary had four children: Sarah E. (1862), Nancy J. (1864), Martha (1866) and Samuel L. (1868). Frederick married a second time to Mary McDaniel on May 25, 1871. Their children were William (1873), Ada (1874) and Daniel M. (1880). Frederick's application for a pension is on file at the State Archives, Raleigh, North Carolina.

247. Cope, John
Private, Company A, 42nd Regiment • N.C. Troops

John was born in Davie County on November 22, 1843, to Enoch (1818, Davie) and Elizabeth (1824, Rowan) Cope. Enoch was a farmer. John enlisted in Davidson County at age 18, November 26, 1861. He was present or accounted for through October 1864, and paroled at Salisbury, North Carolina, on May 16, 1865. (The Salem *People's Press* of June 30, 1864, indicates that he was wounded in action June 1–15, 1864.) John died on February 19, 1924, and is buried in Legion Memorial Park Cemetery.

248. Cope, P. Jacob
Private, Carolina Rangers • Company B, 10th Virginia Cavalry Regiment

Jacob was born January 13, 1842, in Davie County to Enoch (1818, Davie) and Elizabeth (1824, Rowan) Foster Cope. He worked as a farmhand in the Mocksville District prior to enlisting on October 29, 1861, at age 19. He was present and accounted for throughout his service, with absences for detached service, on detail as a teamster and sick with camp itch in Charlottesville hospital on April 13–22, 1864. Probably his greatest frustration was having to serve without a horse for long periods of time. He returned to Fulton District in Davie County; he married Elizabeth Cansas on January 14, 1868. Their children were Charlie M. (1872), Jessie A. (1874), Samuel (1876), Candiss (1878) and Mary J. (1880). Jacob died on October 29, 1916, and is buried in Fork Baptist Church Cemetery.

249. Cope, William G.
Private, Company E, 42nd Regiment • N.C. Troops

William was born in 1845 in Davie County to Henry (1814, Davie) and Nancy (1808, Davie) Cope. In 1860 he was 15 years old, and working as a laborer in Liberty District. William enlisted in Davie County on September 21, 1863, for the war. He died in the hospital at Wilmington on December 5, 1863, of "dysenteria acuta." William's name is listed on the Memorial Monument for the Davie County men who died in the Civil War, 1861–1865.

250. Cornatser (Cornatzer), Jacob C.
Private, Company D, 42nd Regiment • Captain William Howard's Company • N.C. Prison Guards

Jacob was born in 1826 in Davie County. He and his wife, Lucinda (Cynthia) (1826) made their home in the Smith Grove District of Davie where they farmed and raised a growing family prior to the war. Jacob enlisted in Davie County on February 28, 1862. He transferred to Howard's Prison Guards on or about May 1, 1862. Following the war the family made their home in the Fulton District where they continued to farm. Their children were Anderson (1849), Daniel (1851), Mary (1851), Albert (1853), George (1855), William Lillington (1858), Jacob (1861), Lindsay (1864) and Pinkston (1866). Jacob C. died in 1910 and is buried in Cornatzer Baptist Church Cemetery.

251. Cranfield, Hanes
Private, Company F, 42nd Regiment • N.C. Troops

Hanes was born in 1841 in Davie County. He was the son of Jabin (1803, Surry) and Sarah (1812, Davie) Cranfield. Hanes lived with his parents in the Chinquepin District of the county. He enlisted at age 20, on March 18, 1862. He was present or accounted for through October 1864. He was killed in March of 1865. The place of death was not reported. Hanes's name is listed on the Memorial Monument for the Davie County men who died in the Civil War, 1861–1865.

252. Cranfield, Henry
Private, Company F, 42nd Regiment • N.C. Troops

Henry enlisted in Davie County at age 22, March 24, 1862. He was present or accounted for through October 1864.

253. Cranfield, Jackson Lewis (Louis)
Private, "Davie Sweep Stakes" • Company G, 4th Regiment • N.C. State Troops

Jackson was born in 1840. In 1860 "Louis" Cranfield, age 21, was working as a laborer and living with the N.S. Chaffin family in the Chinquepin District of Davie County. On June 14, 1861, he enlisted at age 21, for the war. He was present or accounted for until wounded in the right hip and ileum and captured at Winchester, Virginia, September 19, 1864. He died in hospital at Winchester on September 27, 1864, of "hemorrhage." Jackson's name is listed on the Memorial Monument for the Davie County men who died in the Civil War, 1861–1865.

254. Cranfield, James L.
Private, "Davie Sweep Stakes" • Company G, 4th Regiment • N.C. State Troops

James was born in Davie County where he resided prior to enlisting in Davie County at age 21, July 8, 1861, for the war. He died in hospital at White Sulphur Springs, West Virginia, February 27, 1863, of "diarrhoea chronica." James's name is listed on the Memorial Monument for the Davie County men who died in the Civil War, 1861–1865.

255. Cranfield, William H.
Private, Company E, 42nd Regiment • N.C. Troops

William was born in 1843 in Davie County. He was the son of Jonathan (1815, Davie) and Sarah (1826, Davie). At age 18, on March 18, 1862, William enlisted in Davie County. He was present or accounted for until he was captured at or near Sugar Loaf, near Fort Fisher, on or about February 11, 1865. He was confined at Point Lookout, Maryland, February 28, 1865, and released at Point Lookout on May 13, 1865, and paroled at Mocksville on June 3, 1865. William H. and S.J. Allen were married on March 13, 1866.

256. Cranfill, Gideon
Private, "Davie Sweep Stakes" • Company G, 4th Regiment • N.C. State Troops

Gideon was born in 1831. He resided in Davie County and enlisted at age 31, August 18, 1862, for the war. He died in hospital at Winchester, Virginia, October 13–15, 1862, of "measles." Gideon's name is listed on the Memorial Monument for the Davie County men who died in the Civil War, 1861–1865.

257. Cranfill, Jonathan
Private, "Davie Sweep Stakes" • Company G, 4th Regiment • N.C. State Troops

Jonathan was born in 1841. He lived with his father John (1810) and his stepmother Elizabeth Bowles (1833) in the Chinquepin District of Davie County prior to enlisting at age 20, July 5, 1861, for the war. He was present or accounted for until paroled at Appomattox Court House, Virginia, April 9, 1865.

258. Craver, David Lindsey
Private, Company F, 42nd Regiment • Musician, Regimental Band • Field and Staff, 42nd Regiment • N.C. Troops

David enlisted in Davie County at age 19, on March 18, 1862. He was present or accounted for until appointed Musician in November–December, 1863, and transferred to the regimental band. He was present or accounted for through August 1864.

259. Crews, William P.
Private, Company G, 7th Regiment • Confederate Cavalry • Company D, 16th Battalion • N.C. Cavalry

William transferred from Company G, 7th Regiment Confederate Cavalry to Company D, 16th Battalion N.C. Cavalry on July 11, 1864. He was present or accounted for through October 1, 1864.

260. Crump, James Adderson
Captain • Company A, 77th Regiment, 19th Division • N.C. Militia 1861–1865

James was born March 10, 1822, to Rowland (1791) and Sarah (1798, North Carolina) Crump. He served as Captain of Company A during the war. By 1870 he had married Elizabeth (1843) Hearne and they were living with his mother in the Mocksville District of Davie County where James farmed. In 1880 he and Elizabeth lived in Jerusalem District with two servants and four children. The children were Mary (Minnie) (1869), Sally L. (1872), Samuel B. (1874) and John P. (1879). Elizabeth died on January 26, 1919; James died on June 21, 1904. They are buried in Crump Family Cemetery.

261. Crump, Pleasant John
Second Lieutenant • Company A, 77th Regiment, 19th Division • N.C. Militia 1861–1865

Pleasant was born August 27, 1823, to Rowland (1791, Montgomery) and Sarah Campbell (1798, Davidson) Crump. They farmed in the Liberty District of Davie County where Pleasant was appointed Second Lieutenant of Company A when the militia was activated. Both his parents and Pleasant are buried in the Crump Family Cemetery in Davie County. Pleasant died on April 20, 1867.

262. Cunningham, F.M. (Francis)
Private, "Davie Sweep Stakes" • Company G, 4th Regiment • N.C. State Troops

Francis was born in 1837 in Davie County to Samuel (1814) and Nancy (1809) Cunningham. His father worked as a shoemaker. Francis married Margaret Gaither on June 15, 1855, in Davie County where they resided when he enlisted at age 24, March 12, 1862, for the war. He was wounded in the arm at Chancellorsville, Virginia, May 3, 1863, and died in hospital at Richmond, Virginia, June 1, 1863, of wounds. Francis was one of five brothers who served in the war. They were George H., Rubin, Samuel and Thomas. Francis's name is listed on the Memorial Monument for the Davie County men who died in the Civil War, 1861–1865.

263. Cunningham, George H.
Private, "Davie Sweep Stakes" • Company G, 4th Regiment • N.C. State Troops

George was born in 1839 in Davie County to Samuel (1814) and Nancy (1809) Cunningham. His father was a shoemaker. George lived in Davie County where he enlisted at age 22, June 14, 1861, for the war. He was present or accounted for until killed at Gettysburg, Pennsylvania, July 1–3, 1863. George was one of five brothers who served in the war. They were F.M., Rubin, Samuel and Thomas. George's name is listed on the Memorial Monument for the Davie County men who died in the Civil War, 1861–1865.

264. Cunningham, Rubin W.
Private, "Davie Sweep Stakes" • Company G, 4th Regiment • N.C. State Troops

Rubin was born in 1844 in Davie County to Samuel (1814) and Nancy (1809) Cunningham. His father worked as a shoemaker. Rubin enlisted at age 18, March 12, 1862, for the war. He was reported discharged in January 1863, and his name does not appear on company muster rolls of later date. He married Nancy Gaither on December 20, 1863, in the Mocksville District of Davie County, where they resided. He was paroled at Salisbury, North Carolina in 1865; the exact date is not reported. No further records. Rubin was one of five brothers who served in the war. They were George H., Samuel, F.M. and Thomas.

265. Cunningham, Samuel M.
Private, "Davie Sweep Stakes" • Company G, 4th Regiment • N.C. State Troops

Samuel was born in 1839 in Davie County to Samuel (1814) and Nancy (1809) Cunningham. His father was a shoemaker. Samuel married Elviney Reavis (1839, North Carolina) October 12, 1859. Their daughter Sarah was born in 1861. They resided in the Calahaln District prior to Samuel's enlistment at age 22, June 14, 1861, for the war. He was wounded at Gaines' Mill, Virginia, June 27, 1862, rejoined the company in January–April, 1863, and was wounded at Chancellorsville, Virginia, May 3, 1863. He was reported absent wounded until September 8, 1863, when he was reported absent without leave and reported "in arrest" prior to January 1, 1864. He was detailed for duty as a nurse in hospital at Richmond, Virginia, April 25, 1864. Hospital records indicate that he was suffering from gunshot wounds of both legs. He returned to duty October 10, 1864, and was paroled at Appomattox Court House, Virginia, April 9, 1865. Samuel returned to the Clarksville District of Davie County where he resumed his life as a farmer. Both he and Elviney are buried at Bear Creek Baptist Church Cemetery. Samuel was one of five brothers who served in the war. They were F.M., George, Rubin and Thomas.

266. Cunningham, Thomas M.
Private, "Davie Sweep Stakes" • Company G, 4th Regiment • N.C. State Troops

Thomas was born in 1843 in Davie County to Samuel (1814) and Nancy (1809) Cunningham. His father worked as a shoemaker. Thomas lived in the Mocksville District prior to his enlistment at age 19, June 14, 1861, for the war. He was present or accounted for until killed in battle near Richmond, Virginia, June 3, 1864. Thomas was one of five brothers who served in the war. They were F.M., George, Rubin and Samuel. Thomas's name is listed on the Memorial Monument for the Davie County men who died in the Civil War, 1861–1865.

267. Cuthrell, James N.
Private, Company E, 42nd Regiment • N.C. Troops

James was born in 1828 in Davie County, to Sarah (1809, Davie) Cuthrell. In 1850 James was listed as head of the household and a cabinetmaker. William Fulford, age 23 and a constable, was their boarder. By 1860 James had married Nancy and they were the parents of four small daughters: Martha J. (1852), Sarah E. (1854), Mary L. (1856) and Nancy S. (1858). James's mother Sarah continued to live with them. On August 1, 1863, James enlisted in Lenoir County, for the war. He was present or accounted for through August 1864, and then ordered transferred to Company G, 2nd Regiment Confederate Engineer Troops, on an unspecified date; however, before the transfer could be carried out he died in the hospital at Greensboro on October 13, 1864, of "diarrhoea chronic." The 1870 census reveals that another daughter, Emma (1862), had been born probably just before James enlisted. Nancy, by 1870, age 39, was head of the household, all the daughters were still at home, and even their grandmother was still with them. There was one boarder, Samuel Jarvis, age 26, who was a merchant.

268. Daniel, William Harrison
Private, Company D, 42nd Regiment • N.C. Troops

William was born in Davie County in 1837. He was the son of Anderson (1818, Davie) and Susan (1824, Davie) Daniel. On November 20, 1857, he married Jane Lagle (1838, Davie) and they resided in the Liberty District where William worked as a laborer. William enlisted at age 25 in Rowan County, on or about March 1, 1862. He was present or accounted for until he deserted on July 18, 1864. He returned to duty on September 23, 1864, was captured at or near Wise's Forks, Kinston, North Carolina, on March 10, 1865, and was confined at Point Lookout, Maryland, on March 16, 1865. William was released at Point Lookout on May 13, 1865, after taking the Oath of Allegiance. (North Carolina pension records indicate that he was wounded in 1863.) By 1870 the family had moved to the Jerusalem District where William worked as a farmer and a shoemaker. Their children were Virginia (1860), Samantha Elizabeth (1864), Henry (1868), Amos N. (1869), William E. (1870), Lovice Jane (1875) and Lula C. (1879).

269. Daniel, Wilson C.
Captain, Company J, 77th Regiment, 19th Brigade • N.C. Militia 1861–1865 • Private, Company E, 42nd Regiment • N.C. Troops

Wilson was born March 9, 1824, in Virginia, to John and Mary Daniel. They moved to Davie County in the 1830s where Wilson married Mary Earnest on January 1, 1846. Their children were Columbus Bryant (1849), Toliver Chestine (1850) and Goshen Parker (1853). Mary Earnest died on March 15, 1857, and Wilson married Mary Keller on September 22, 1857. They lived in the Mocksville District of Davie where Wilson made his living as a farmer. He was also active in county affairs. He was listed in court records as a commissioner in Davie County in October 1843, and was documented as participating in several legal transactions. When the militia mobilized, Wilson served as Captain of Company J, Liberty Company, after being promoted from Second Lieutenant. When the Home Guard was created by the act of July 1863, the militia ceased to exist except for the officers over the age of 45. Two months later, on September 30, 1863, Wilson enlisted as a Private in Company E of the 42nd Regiment. He was present or accounted for through October 1864. He was captured at Salisbury on April

Wilson C. Daniel served as a commissioner in Davie County in 1843, a Captain of the militia when it mobilized and a Private in Company E of the 42nd Regiment in 1863, after the Home Guard was created (Clark's *Regiments*).

12, 1865, and confined at Louisville, Kentucky, on May 1, 1865. On May 4, he was transferred to Camp Chase, Ohio, and was released there on June 13, 1865, after taking the Oath of Allegiance. (Records of the Federal Provost Marshal dated June 1865, give his age as 44.) Wilson returned to his farm and family in Davie County. He died only three years later on December 26, 1868. He is buried between his two wives in Liberty United Methodist Church Cemetery.

270. Daniels (Dannel), William L.
Private, Company E, 42nd Regiment • N.C. Troops

William was born in 1846 in Davie County. He was the son of Wilson (1822, Davie) and Sabrina B. (1826, Davie) Willson Daniels. In 1860 William lived with his parents in the Mocksville District. On April 15, 1864, he enlisted in Davie for the war. William was wounded at or near Petersburg, Virginia, on or about July 30, 1864. He was reported absent wounded through October 1864, and was paroled at Mocksville on June 10, 1865.

271. Danner, Eli
Private, "Davie Greys" • Company F, 13th Regiment • (3rd Regiment, N.C. Volunteers) • N.C. Troops

Eli was born in 1839 in either Davie or Surry County. His father was Jacob (1795, Surry) and his mother was Sarah (1794, Surry). Eli worked as a farmer prior to enlisting in Davie County at age 22, on August 6, 1861. He was present or accounted for until wounded at Chancellorsville, Virginia, on May 3, 1863. He rejoined the company in July–August, 1863, and was present or accounted for until wounded in the right thigh at Petersburg, Virginia, on June 22, 1864. He was reported absent wounded until retired on February 8, 1865, by reason of wounds received at Petersburg, and then paroled at Salisbury, North Carolina, in 1865. Eli married Delia Slater on January 23, 1864.

272. Danner, Frederick (M)
Company E, 42nd Regiment • N.C. Troops

Frederick was born in 1821 or 1829 in Surry County. He was the son of Jacob and Sallie. Jacob was a blacksmith in the Farmington Community. In 1850 Frederick lived in Davie County, Farmington District, with the Elliott Walker family, probably as an apprentice shoemaker, since that was Mr. Walker's occupation. Frederick married Elizabeth Reavis and Noah was born in 1851 followed by Richmond (1853), Luvina (1856), Martha E. (1860), Edy E. (1861), Fred E. (1865), Jacob A. (1867) and Jennie (1874). North Carolina pension records indicate that Frederick served in Company E, 42nd Regiment but there is no further record available at the present time. Following the war the family lived in the Clarksville District where he worked as a farmer and lived to be 92 years old, according to his tombstone at Bear Creek Baptist Church Cemetery.

273. Danner, Samuel
Private, Company F, 42nd Regiment • N.C. Troops

Samuel was born in 1840. He married Nancy Emaline Granger on March 12, 1860. They resided in the Farmington District where he worked as a laborer. He enlisted at age 22, on March 24, 1862, and was present or accounted for through June 1863. He deserted on an unspecified date, was apprehended on or about October 14, 1863, and was reported absent under arrest through October 1864. He returned to duty prior to March 10, 1865, when he was captured at or near Wise's Forks, Kinston, North Carolina. After being confined at Point Lookout, Maryland, March 16, 1865, he was released there on June 11, 1865, where he took the Oath of Allegiance.

274. Davis, Franklin (J.F.)
Private, "Davie Greys" • Company F, 13th Regiment • (3rd Regiment, N.C. Volunteers) • N.C. Troops

Franklin was born in Randolph County in 1836. He resided in Davie County where he worked as a farmer in the Mocksville District. On January 10, 1858, Franklin married Amanda A. Clary (1828). In 1860, Thomas, age 8, lived with them. At age 23, on August 6, 1861, Franklin enlisted in Davie County. He was present or accounted for until he died in hospital at Richmond, Virginia, on June 30, 1862, of "febris typhoides" and/or "intermittent fever." Amanda's application to the widow's pension fund is on file at the State Archives, Raleigh, North Carolina. It was approved. Franklin's name is listed on the Memorial Monument for the Davie County men who died in the Civil War, 1861–1865.

275. Davis, Joseph N.
Private, Carolina Rangers • Company B, 10th Virginia Cavalry Regiment

Joseph enlisted in Davie County at age 16 on October 27, 1861. He was present June 23, 1864, and absent on detached service July 8, 1864. He was issued clothing in September and December, 1864, and paroled in Richmond on April 17, 1865.

276. Davis, Mercer J.
First Lieutenant, Company E, 42nd Regiment • N.C. Troops

M.J. Davis is documented in *North Carolina Troops*, Clark's *Regiments* and in Moore's *Roster* as a Second Lieutenant who was promoted to First Lieutenant and served the company for an unspecified period.

277. Davis, Samuel A.
Private, "Davie Sweep Stakes" • Company G, 4th Regiment • N.C. State Troops

Samuel was born in 1827. In 1860 he worked as a blacksmith and lived in the Chinquepin District with Sarah (1833) and their three children: Thomas (1855), John W. (1856) and Pleasant A. (1860). Samuel had previously lived in Yadkin County. He enlisted in Davie County at age 34, June 5, 1861, for the war. He was present or accounted for through August 1864. In 1870 Samuel lived in the Farmington District with Susan (1845) and an additional child, William (1867). He made his living as a blacksmith.

278. Davis, Samuel C.
Second Lieutenant, "Davie Sweep Stakes" • Company G, 4th Regiment • N.C. State Troops

Samuel was born in 1839. He resided in Davie County where he enlisted at age 22, and was appointed Second Lieutenant to rank from May 16, 1861. He resigned April 2, 1862. The reason for his resignation was not reported.

279. Davis, Silas
Private, "Davie Sweep Stakes" • Company G, 4th Regiment • N.C. State Troops

Silas was born about 1840. He resided in Davie County where he married Eliza Jane Perry on October 10, 1860. He enlisted at age 21, June 4, 1861, for the war. He was wounded at Chancellorsville, Virginia, May 3, 1863, and reported absent wounded or absent sick through December 1863. He rejoined the company prior to May 12, 1864, when he was wounded in the hand at Spotsylvania Court House, Virginia. He retired to the Invalid Corps on February 25, 1865, was admitted to hospital in Richmond, Virginia, February 26, 1865, and was returned to duty March 29, 1865. He was paroled at Salisbury, North Carolina, on an unspecified date in 1865.

280. Davis, William
Private, "Davie Sweep Stakes" • Company G, 4th Regiment • N.C. State Troops

William was born in 1834. He was married to Peneller (1833) and they had four children: Mahala (1852), Thomas (1854), Mary J. (1856) and James (1857). They resided in the Shady Grove District of Davie County where he enlisted at age 27, June 4, 1861, for the war. On October 9, 1862, he was admitted to hospital at Chancellorsville, Virginia, with a shell wound, place and date wounded not reported. He returned to duty December 28, 1862, and was wounded at Chancellorsville, Virginia, May 3, 1863. After rejoining the company in November–December, 1863, he was present or accounted for until wounded in the hip at Cold Harbor, Virginia, about May 30, 1864, and reported absent wounded through August 1864. He was paroled at Salisbury, North Carolina, on an unspecified date in 1865.

281. Davis, William E.
Private, Company M, 7th Regiment • Confederate Cavalry • Company E, 16th Battalion • N.C. Cavalry

William was born in North Carolina. He was transferred from Company M, 7th Regiment Confederate Cavalry on July 11, 1864. He was present or accounted for through October 1, 1864. He was paroled on May 4, 1865, at Goldsboro, North Carolina.

282. Dayvault (Daywalt), Solomon M.
Private, Company F, 42nd Regiment • N.C. Troops

Solomon was born in 1827 in Davie County. At age 20 he married Mary L. (1827, Davie) Safret and they settled in the Hunting Creek District of Davie where he farmed. Their two daughters were Sarah (1849) and Lea R. (1856). Solomon enlisted in Davie at age 34, March 24, 1862. He was present or accounted for until wounded in the face at or near Bermuda Hundred, Virginia, on May 10, 1864. He was hospitalized at Petersburg, Virginia, and was furloughed for sixty days on June 8, 1864. He died at Petersburg prior to November 4, 1864, of his wounds. Solomon has a tombstone at St. Matthew's Lutheran Church Cemetery which reads "Solomon M. Daywalt 1827/1865." Solomon's name is listed on the Memorial Monument for the Davie County men who died in the Civil War, 1861–1865.

283. Dayvault (Davalt), William M.
Sergeant, Company F, 42nd Regiment • N.C. Troops

William was born in 1829 in Davie County. At age 20 he served as one of seven apprentices to Richmond Nail, who was a carpenter with a wife, six children and three slaves. William married Rebecca P. (1838, North Carolina) Smoot on October 9, 1856. They established their home in Hunting Creek where they farmed and raised nine children: David P. (1857), Alexander S. (1860), Temperance V. (1862), Lula E. (1866), James F. (1869), Mica (1872), William A. (1874), Mary R. (1877) and Johnie A. (1879). William enlisted in Davie County at age 32, March 24, 1862. He mustered in as a Sergeant and was present or accounted for through October 1864. He returned home after the war and resumed his life as a farmer, assisted by his sons.

284. Daywalt, Alfred J. (Alford Davalt)
Private, "Davie Greys" • Company F, 13th Regiment • (3rd Regiment, N.C. Volunteers) • N.C. Troops

Alfred was born June 14, 1842. He resided in Davie County where he worked as a farmer prior to enlisting at age 20, on August 6, 1861. He was present or accounted for until wounded in the

This log dwelling was built for Alfred Daywalt. He served four years in Company F, 13th Regiment, returned home and eventually fathered six sons (Mohney, *The Historic Architecture of Davie County*).

Alfred J. Daywalt (Tommy and Helen Daywalt)

breast at Gettysburg, Pennsylvania, July 1, 1863. He rejoined the company in November–December, 1863, and was present or accounted for until paroled at Appomattox Court House, Virginia, April 9, 1865. Upon returning home, he resumed his life in Davie and married Vashti M. Prather, January 26, 1868. A son, David, was born in 1870, and Vashti died on August 1, 1870. Alfred then married Nancy Melinda Beck, October 27, 1870, and became the father of five more sons: James L. (1871), John A. (1873), William T. (1875), Robin G. (1877) and Joe W. (1879). Alfred continued to farm in the Calahaln District. He died on April 1, 1909, and is buried in St. Matthews Lutheran Church Cemetery.

285. Deadman, Haley
Second Lieutenant • Company J, 77th Regiment, 19th Division • N.C. Militia 1861–1865

Haley was born in 1823 in Davie County. He married Elizabeth A. (1826, Davie) Click on October 21, 1852, and they settled in the Jerusalem District where Haley supported his family by farming. When the militia was activated Haley was appointed Second Lieutenant of Company J. By 1880 at least twelve children had lived in the household: John S. Deadman (1855), George D. Deadman(1857), Thomas J. G. (1858), Sarah E. Deadman (1860), J. F. Click (1847), Martha A. Click (1850), Frances A. Click (1852), Nancy Deadman (1862), Mary Deadman (1864), Rebecca Deadman (1867), Joseph R. L. Deadman (1870) and Hailey Deadman (1873). Hailey died on May 9, 1906, and is buried in the Tatum Family Cemetery, which is part of Jerusalem Baptist Church Cemetery.

286. Deadman (Debnam), James Anderson
Private, Company H, 57th Regiment • N.C. Troops

James was born in North Carolina in 1830. He was a farmer, living in the Liberty District, when he married Pauline Van Eaton on February 9, 1854. James and Pauline were the parents of three children before he joined the Army. They were Samuel R. (1855), John F. (1857) and George W. (1859). James enlisted in Rowan County at age 28, on July 4, 1862, for the war. He was reported present through December 1862, but was hospitalized at Richmond, Virginia, on February 27, 1863, with typhoid fever. James died in the hospital at Richmond on March 3, 1863, of "pneumonia." James's name is not presently listed on the Memorial Monument for the Davie County men who died in the Civil War, 1861–1865.

287. Deadman, James R.
Private, Company A, 42nd Regiment • Private, Company F, 42nd Regiment • N.C. Troops

James was born in Davie County in 1844 to William (1812, Davie) and Sarah (1822, Davie) Deadman. James enlisted in Rowan County at age 17, on January 19, 1862. He was apparently discharged in May–June, 1862. He enlisted as a Private in Company F of the same regiment on July 15, 1863, in Lenoir County. He was present or accounted for until wounded at or near Bermuda Hundred, Virginia, on or about May 20, 1864. He returned to duty on or about October 31, 1864. He was captured at or near Wise's Forks, Kinston, North Carolina, on March 10, 1865, and was confined at Point Lookout, Maryland, on March 16, 1865. He was released on June 12, 1865, after taking the Oath of Allegiance. After the war,

James married Martha A. Click on August 7, 1866. They had a family of five children: William (1867), John F. (1869), Dewit R. (1873), Thomas G. (1875) and Sarah E. (1878). James farmed in Jerusalem District following the war. He was a twin brother to Thomas H. who also served in Company F of the 42nd Regiment.

288. Deadman, Thomas H.
Private, Company F, 13th Regiment • (3rd Regiment, N.C. Volunteers) • Private, Company F, 42nd Regiment • N.C. Troops

Thomas was born in 1844 in Davie County. He was the son of William H. (1812, Davie) and Sarah (1822, Davie) Deadman, and the twin brother of James R. He was a student living in Liberty District when he enlisted at age 17, on August 6, 1861, in Davie County. Thomas was present or accounted for until he was discharged November 10, 1862, under the provisions of the Conscript Act. He then enlisted in Lenoir County on July 15, 1863, for the war. His first enlistment was in Company F, 13th Regiment; the second enlistment was in Company F, 42nd Regiment. He was present or accounted for until May–August, 1864, when he was reported absent wounded; the place and date were not reported. Thomas returned home where he married Eliza C. Foster on August 4, 1864. He returned to duty in September–October, 1864, was captured at or near Wise's Forks, Kinston, North Carolina, on March 10, 1865, and confined at Point Lookout, Maryland, on March 16, 1865, where he was released on June 12, 1865, after taking the Oath of Allegiance.

289. Deaver, Nathan
Private, Carolina Rangers • Company B, 10th Virginia Cavalry Regiment

Nathan was born in 1819 in Davie County. He married Ader [sic] Nelson on January 1, 1845, and worked as a painter to support her and their two boys, John (1846) and Thomas (1849). David P. Nelson, age 23, Nathan's brother-in-law, also lived with the family. They resided in the Mocksville District where Nathan enlisted on October 29, 1861, at age 42. He was present through April 30, 1862, and then his life became a struggle of sickness and sadness until he was discharged in November 1863. He was first sick with nephritis and stricture in Petersburg hospital June 10, 1862; he returned to duty July 31, 1862. He was again sick with kidney disease in Richmond hospital on September 10, 1862. For the next seven months his life appeared routine, even to being without a horse during that time. But he was sick on May 10, 1863, and sick with chronic diarrhoea in Richmond hospital on November 9, 1863, and discharged later in the month. It should be noted that Nathan's health decline coincided with the death of his son John who died before his eighth birthday on May 23, 1862, and is buried in Joppa Cemetery.

290. Dedman, W.A.
Private • Captain William E. Booe's Partisan Rangers • N.C. Volunteers • Company H, 63rd Regiment • (5th Regiment N.C. Cavalry) • N.C. Troops

William was born on April 24, 1830, in Davie County. In 1850 he lived with the Jesse Deadmond [sic] family where he worked as a farmer prior to marrying Anna Deadmen [sic] on November 16, 1852. By 1860 they had four children: Lucy (1850), Daniel (1853), Jesse (1856) and Mary A. (1859). They lived in the Liberty District of Davie where he enlisted at age 32, July 16, 1862, for the war. He was present or accounted for through August 1864, being "absent on sick furlough" from November–December, 1862, through August 1864. He was paroled at Salisbury, North Carolina, May 16, 1865. William returned to Davie County where he worked as a farmer in the Jerusalem District. Four more children were added to the family: Sarah (1864), William C. (1866), Louisa (1869) and Loutitia A. (1872). William died on February 19, 1879, and is buried in Liberty United Methodist Church Cemetery.

291. Dedmon, D.M. (Daniel)
Private • Captain William E. Booe's Partisan Rangers • N.C. Volunteers • Company H, 63rd Regiment • (5th Regiment N.C. Cavalry) • N.C. Troops

D.M. was born in 1833 to Jesse (1808, North Carolina) and Hannah (1811, North Carolina) Dedman [sic]. They lived in the Liberty District of Davie where Jesse worked as a smith and Daniel farmed. On July 16, 1862, at age 29, Daniel enlisted for the war. He was present or accounted for through February 1863 when he was reported as "absent on sick furlough." A claim for balance of pay due to deceased soldier was filed April 7, 1864. The date, place or cause of death were not given. D.M.'s name is listed on the Memorial Monument for the Davie County men who died in the Civil War, 1861–1865.

292. Dingler, James
Private, "Davie Greys" • Company F, 13th Regiment • (3rd Regiment, N.C. Volunteers) • N.C. Troops

James was born in 1830 in North Carolina. On April 15, 1852, he married Mary A. Hendricks; he was 22 years of age and she was 24. In 1860 at age 30, he lived with Mary (1825, North Carolina) Emmerson in the Mocksville District. James made his living as a shoemaker prior to enlisting in Davie at age 31, April 26, 1861. He was present or accounted for until discharged on July 26, 1862, under the provisions of the Conscript Act.

293. Dismuks, Richard L.
Sergeant, "Davie Sweep Stakes" • Company G, 4th Regiment • N.C. State Troops

Richard was born in Rowan County in 1844. He lived in Davie County with his stepfather Samuel (1818, Rowan), a carriage maker, and his mother Martha (1825, Iredell) Rosebrugh [sic]. Richard enlisted in Davie County at age 18, June 4, 1861, for the war. He mustered in as a Private and was promoted to Sergeant on October 1, 1861. He was killed at Seven Pines, Virginia, May 31, 1862. Richard's name is listed on the Memorial Monument for the Davie County men who died in the Civil War, 1861–1865.

294. Divire (Dwire), Daniel
Corporal, "Davie Greys" • Company F, 13th Regiment • (3rd Regiment, N.C. Volunteers) • N.C. Troops

Daniel was born December 31, 1830, in Davidson County. He was the son of Gideon (1802, Davidson) and Mary (1801, Guilford) Dwire. By 1860 they lived and farmed in the Fulton District of Davie County where Daniel enlisted on April 26, 1861, at age 27. He mustered in as a Private and was promoted to Corporal on July 1, 1864. He was present or accounted for until he was paroled at Appomattox Court House, Virginia, April 9, 1865. Daniel married Hettie Richardson in Davie County on March 21, 1871. They had three children: Mary E. (1873), John F. (1875) and Jesse (1879). In 1880 Daniel was a farmer living in Mocksville. His application for pension is on file at the State Archives, Raleigh, North Carolina. He died on June 7, 1910, and is buried in Concord Methodist Church Cemetery.

295. Dixon (Dixson), William
Private, Company G, 5th Regiment • N.C. State Troops

William was born in 1831 in North Carolina. In 1860 he lived with his wife Rebecca (1838) and daughter Elisabeth C. (1859) in the Farmington District of Davie County. He worked as a farmer prior to enlisting in Northampton County at age 35, on August 13, 1862, for the war. He was present or accounted for until wounded in the right leg at Gettysburg, Pennsylvania, July 1, 1863. His leg was amputated and he died in hospital at Gettysburg on July 19, 1863. William's name is not presently listed on the Memorial Monument for the Davie County men who died in the Civil War, 1861–1865.

296. Dobbins, Alfred M.C.
Private, "Davie Greys" • Company F, 13th Regiment • (3rd Regiment, N.C. Volunteers) • N.C. Troops

Alfred resided in Davie County and was by occupation a doctor prior to enlisting in Davie County at age 32, April 26, 1861. He was present or accounted for until he was reported absent wounded in May–June, 1862; however, the battle in which he was wounded was not reported. Alfred was elected Third Lieutenant on October 7, 1862, and rejoined the company prior to November 1, 1862. He was "cashiered by sentence of court martial" on or about March 20, 1863, and was reduced to ranks. He deserted to the enemy near Fredericksburg, Virginia, May 2–4, 1863, and took the Oath of Allegiance on May 4, 1863.

297. Douthit, Edward J.
Private, "Davie Sweep Stakes" • Company G, 4th Regiment • N.C. State Troops

Edward was born in 1839 in Surry County, to Stephen (1809, Davie) and Matilda L. (1824, Stokes) Douthit. He resided in the Farmington area of Davie County where he enlisted at age 22, June 4, 1861, for the war. He was wounded at Seven Pines, Virginia, May 31, 1862. He rejoined the company prior to January 1, 1863, and was present or accounted for until captured at Spotsylvania Court House, Virginia, on or about May 20, 1864. He was confined at Point Lookout, Maryland, until he was transferred to Elmira, New York, July 3, 1864. After taking the Oath of Allegiance, he was released on June 30, 1865. Back in Davie County, Edward married Martha F. Perry on May 18, 1868, and they became the parents of five children: Mamie (1870), Jimmy (1872), Robert (1874), Sena (1876) and Johnnie (1879).

298. Douthit, J.M.
Private, Company K, 57th Regiment • N.C. Troops

J.M. resided in Davie County and enlisted in Rowan County on July 7, 1862, for the war. He died in the hospital at Richmond, Virginia, on October 29, 1862, of "typhoid pneumonia." J.M.'s name is not presently listed on the Memorial Monument for the Davie County men who died in the Civil War, 1861–1865.

299. Dowdy (Doudy), James
Private, "Davie Sweep Stakes" • Company G, 4th Regiment • N.C. State Troops

James was born in 1839 in Davie County. In 1850 he lived with James and Elizabeth Etchisson; in 1860 he lived in the Farmington District with Mary (1810, Currituck) Doudy, who worked as a domestic in the household of S.S. and Jane S. Ward. James enlisted at age 20, June 4, 1861, for the war. He was killed at Seven Pines, Virginia, May 31, 1862. James's name is listed on the Memorial Monument for the Davie County men who died in the Civil War, 1861–1865.

300. Drake, William D.
Private, Company F, 42nd Regiment • N.C. Troops

William was born in 1833 in North Carolina. He married Catharine Leach (1837, Davie) on December 30, 1858. They lived in the Mocksville District where he enlisted at age 29, March 26, 1862. He was present or accounted for until May 20, 1864, when he was wounded near Bermuda Hundred, Virginia. William died on May 21, 1864, of those wounds. The place of death was not reported. He and Catharine had one daughter, Cidney T., born in 1859. William's name is listed on the Memorial Monument for the Davie County men who died in the Civil War, 1861–1865.

301. Driver, John E.
Second Lieutenant, "Davie Greys" • Company F, 13th Regiment • (3rd Regiment, N.C. Volunteers) • N.C. Troops

John was born in North Carolina in 1838. He resided in the Fulton District of Davie County and was a tobacconist by occupation prior to enlisting in Davie at age 23, April 26, 1861. He was promoted to Sergeant from an unspecified rank on June 1, 1861. He was elected Second Lieutenant on April 26, 1862. John was present or accounted for until wounded in the left arm at Williamsburg, Virginia, on May 5, 1862. He resigned August 4, 1862, by reason of wounds resulting in "paralysis of the fingers." His resignation was accepted on or about August 22, 1862. He returned to Davie County where he married Amanda A. Gatton (1835, North Carolina).

302. Dulin, William M.
Sergeant, Company E, 42nd Regiment • Musician, Regimental Band • Field and Staff, 42nd Regiment • N.C. Troops

William was born in Davie County in 1834. In 1860 he was a student-clerk while living with W.C. and Mary Parks in the Shady Grove District. William enlisted in Davie County at age 28, on March 18, 1862. He mustered in as Sergeant and was present or accounted for until appointed Musician on December 31, 1863, and transferred to the regimental band. He was present or accounted for through August 1864. He was paroled at Mocksville on June 3, 1865.

303. Dwiggins, D.H.
Private • Captain William E. Booe's Partisan Rangers • N.C. Volunteers • Company H, 63rd Regiment • (5th Regiment N.C. Cavalry) • N.C. Troops

Daniel was born on March 9, 1835, to Ashley (1805, Davie) and Nancy (1820, Davie) Dwiggins. He married Louisa and worked in the Mocksville District as a farmer. Their first child John H. was born in 1859, followed by Mary L.J. in 1861. He enlisted in Davie County at age 27, July 15, 1862, for the war. He was present or accounted for through October 1864 and paroled at Salisbury, North Carolina, in 1865. Five more children were born by 1880: Lydia A.J. (1863), Charles V. (1867), Sarah D.A. (1872), Joel R.G. (1874) and Ossey M. (1880). They lived in the Calahaln District where Daniel continued to farm. He died on August 20, 1916, and is buried at Center United Methodist Church Cemetery.

304. Dwiggins, James Patterson
Private • Captain William E. Booe's Partisan Rangers • N.C. Volunteers • Company H, 63rd Regiment • (5th Regiment N.C. Cavalry) • N.C. Troops

James was born in 1840 in Davie County to Ashley (1805, Davie) and Nancy (1820, Davie) Dwiggins, who were farmers. In 1860 James lived with Joel and Ursula Penry at their home in Mocksville. On January 5, 1860, James and Sarah P. Leach (1841, North Carolina) were married. Their first child, John H., was born in 1861. James enlisted in Davie County on July 15, 1862, at age 22. He was present or accounted for through October 1864, and was paroled in 1865. He and Sarah would have four more children: Mary C.

(1863), William J.F. (1865), Sarah L. (1868) and James A. (1873). Both James and Sarah died in 1927 and are buried at Center United Methodist Church Cemetery.

305. Dwire, H.X. (Henry)
First Sergeant, Company E, 42nd Regiment • Quartermaster Sergeant, Field and Staff, 42nd Regiment • N.C. Troops

Henry was born in Davidson County in 1834. He was the son of Gideon (1802, Davidson) and Mary (1801, Guilford) Dwyer. He and his father both worked as farmers; at age 28, he enlisted in Davie County, on March 18, 1862. He mustered in as First Sergeant and was present or accounted for until promoted to Quartermaster Sergeant on December 31, 1863, and transferred to the Field and Staff of this regiment. He was present or accounted for through August 1864 and was paroled at Greensboro, North Carolina, on May 1, 1865. Henry and Mary M. Hanes were married on January 11, 1866. After the war, he became a merchant in Farmington where he lived with his wife and children, Minnie (1868) and Alexander (1869).

306. Dwire (Dwyer), John F.
Private, Company M, 7th Regiment • Confederate Cavalry • Company E, 16th Battalion • N.C. Cavalry

John was born in 1843 in Davidson County to Gideon (1802, Davidson) and Mary (1801, Guilford) Dwyer. He lived with his parents in the Fulton District of Davie County where he worked as a laborer prior to enlisting on December 20, 1862, with the rank of Private. He was transferred from Company M, 7th Regiment Confederate Cavalry to Company E, 16th Battalion N.C. Cavalry on July 11, 1864. He was present or accounted for through October 1, 1864. Following the war, John made his home with his older brother H.X. in Farmington District where he worked as a huckster.

307. Dyson, David Linsey
First Lieutenant, Company G, 77th Regiment, 19th Division • N.C. Militia 1861–1865

David was born May 19, 1827, in Davie County. In 1850 he worked as a laborer on the farm of Greenbury and Edith Dyson. He married Emeline (Ruthy E.) Martin on August 15, 1850, and they made their home on a farm in Calahaln. When the militia was activated David was appointed First Lieutenant. He and Emeline remained in Calahaln at least through 1880. David died on August 17, 1893, and Emeline died on October 22, 1906. They are both buried in Salem United Methodist Church Cemetery.

308. Dyson, W.L. (William)
Private, Company M, 7th Regiment • Confederate Cavalry • Company E, 16th Battalion • N.C. Cavalry

William enlisted in Davie County on September 3, 1862, with the rank of Private. He was transferred from Company M, 7th Regiment Confederate Cavalry to Company E, 16th Battalion N.C. Cavalry on July 11, 1864. He was present or accounted for through October 1, 1864. He was paroled at Salisbury, North Carolina, in 1865.

309. Eaton, B.F. (Benjamin)
Private • Captain William E. Booe's Partisan Rangers • N.C. Volunteers • Company H, 63rd Regiment • (5th Regiment N.C. Cavalry) • N.C. Troops

Benjamin was born in Davie County in 1816. On March 1, 1838, he married Lucinda (1813, Davie) Tatum. They lived and farmed in the Farmington District where their eight children were born prior to the war: Samuel W. (1840), Joseph C. (1841), Elizabeth J. (1843), Martha L. (1844), Sarah A. (1846), Mary A.L. (1848), Josephine V. (1850) and Ezra Filmore (1852). Benjamin enlisted in Davie County on April 1, 1864, for the war. He was wounded in action on June 24, 1864, and retired to the Invalid Corps on November 2, 1864. He was assigned to light duty at Richmond, Virginia, on January 25, 1865. He was transferred to Salisbury, North Carolina, on February 24, 1865. He returned to Farmington and his family following the end of the war. His son Joseph C. also served in this company; Joseph died of typhoid fever October 31, 1863.

310. Eaton, J.C.
Private, Company D, 42nd Regiment • Captain William E. Booe's Partisan Rangers • N.C. Volunteers • Company H, 63rd Regiment • (5th Regiment N.C. Cavalry) • N.C. Troops

J.C. was born in 1841 in Davie County to Benjamin and Lucinda Eaton. They lived in the Farmington District of Davie where J.C. was a student when he enlisted on July 15, 1862, for the war. He was captured near Hagerstown, Maryland, July 12, 1863, and confined at Point Lookout, Maryland, where he died on October 31, 1863, of "typhoid fever" and was buried in the Confederate Cemetery there. Joseph's name is listed on the Memorial Monument for the Davie County men who died in the Civil War, 1861–1865.

311. Eccles (Eckles), John C.
Private, "Davie Greys" • Company F, 13th Regiment • (3rd Regiment, N.C. Volunteers) • N.C. Troops

John enlisted at Camp Holmes, on February 20, 1864, for the war. He was present or accounted for until wounded and captured at Wilderness, Virginia, on May 6, 1864. He was confined at Point Lookout, Maryland, until transferred to Elmira, New York, July 25, 1864, where he died on March 13, 1865, of "inflammation of lungs." Records of the Federal Provost Marshal give his age as 43 years. John's name is listed on the Memorial Monument for the Davie County men who died in the Civil War, 1861–1865.

312. Eckerson (Etchisson), Andrew Eno
Second Lieutenant, Company M • 77th Regiment, 19th Division • N.C. Militia 1861–1865

Andrew was born in 1824 in Davie County. He married Mary (1824, Davie) Godbey on June 14, 1845. They lived in the Chinquepin District of Davie where he farmed prior to the war. When the militia was activated he was appointed Second Lieutenant of Company M and in 1862 his first-born child, William C. Perry Etchison, age 16, enlisted in Company F of the 42nd Regiment. The family later moved to the Clarksville District where Andrew continued to farm. The children, in addition to Perry, were Mary F. (1850), Elvira (1852), Hettie R. (1855), Louisa (1859) and Amanda (1863).

313. Ellis, E.F. (Enoch)
Private • Captain William E. Booe's Partisan Rangers • N.C. Volunteers • Company H, 63rd Regiment • (5th Regiment N.C. Cavalry) • N.C. Troops

Enoch was born in Davie County in 1839. He was the son of Isaac W. Ellis (1808, Davie) and Temperance Ellis (1809, Davie) who were farmers in the Farmington District. Enoch was also a farmer when he enlisted for the war at age 24, on July 15, 1862. He died in the hospital at Garysburg, North Carolina, on November 16, 1862, of "typhoid." E.F.'s name is listed on the Memorial Monument for the Davie County men who died in the Civil War, 1861–1865.

314. Ellis, Ezekiel P.
Private, Company G, 7th Regiment • Confederate Cavalry • Company D, 16th Battalion • N.C. Cavalry

Ezekial transferred from Company G, 7th Regiment Confederate Cavalry to Company D, 16th Battalion N.C. Cavalry on July 11, 1864, while absent in confinement at Point Lookout, Maryland, as a prisoner of war. He was transferred to Elmira, New York, August 15, 1864, where he remained until sent to James River, Virginia, for exchange on February 20, 1865. The date and place of exchange were not given, but he was admitted to a hospital at Richmond, Virginia, on March 3, 1865.

315. Ellis, James M.
Private, Company M, 7th Regiment • Confederate Cavalry • Company E, 16th Battalion • N.C. Cavalry

James was born in 1829 in Davie County, the son of Isham P. (1805, Davie) and Elizabeth (1807, Davidson) Ellis. Prior to enlisting on September 3, 1862, James lived with his parents and worked as a farmer in the Mocksville District. He was transferred from Company M, 7th Regiment Confederate Cavalry to Company E, 16th Battalion N.C. Cavalry on July 11, 1864, while absent in confinement at Point Lookout, Maryland, as a prisoner of war, where he died on August 17, 1864. James's name is listed on the Memorial Monument for the Davie County men who died in the Civil War, 1861–1865.

316. Ellis, Nathaniel B.
Fourth Corporal, Company B, Carolina Rangers • 10th Virginia Cavalry Regiment

Nathaniel was born in 1840 in Davie County to Jeremiah (1803, Davie) and Mary (1814, Davie) Ellis. He worked as a farmhand in the Smith Grove District of Davie prior to enlisting October 29, 1861, at age 20. He served as a Private through April 30, 1862, and was present as Fourth Corporal on January 5, 1863. He was killed in action at Brandy Station June 9, 1863. He was the brother of Wiley R. Ellis who also served in this company. Nathaniel's name is listed on the Memorial Monument for the Davie County men who died in the Civil War, 1861–1865.

317. Ellis, Thomas Nelson
Private, "Davie Greys" • Company F, 13th Regiment • (3rd Regiment, N.C. Volunteers) • N.C. Troops

Thomas was born to Isham (1805, Davie) and Elizabeth (1807, Davie) Ellis in 1842. He resided in Davie where he enlisted at age 19, August 6, 1861. He was present or accounted for until wounded at Chancellorsville, Virginia, May 3,

1863. He rejoined the company in July–August, 1863, and was present or accounted for until captured at Reams' Station, Virginia, August 25, 1864. He was confined at Point Lookout, Maryland, until paroled and transferred to Cox's Landing, James River, Virginia, where he was received February 14–15, 1865, for exchange. He was paroled at Mocksville on June 9, 1865. He resumed life as a farmer after the war and on November 22, 1866, he and Mary C. McClamrock were married. A daughter, Lula, was born in 1869, followed by Bettie (1872), Maggie L. (1873), John M. (1876), James (1877) and an infant daughter (unnamed) in 1880. The family continued to live in the Mocksville area and Thomas continued to farm; in 1880 he was still a young man, 37 years of age, when he died on November 10. He is buried in Smith Grove United Methodist Church Cemetery.

318. Ellis, Wiley Jones
Private, Company M, 7th Regiment • Confederate Cavalry • Company E, 16th Battalion • N.C. Cavalry

Wiley was born in 1822 in North Carolina. He married Frances and by 1860 they were the parents of Isabella (1851) and W.J. (1859). They were a farm family in Smith Grove when Wiley enlisted in Company M, 7th Regiment Confederate Cavalry. On July 11, 1864, he was transferred to Company E, 16th Battalion N.C. Cavalry. On August 18, 1864, he deserted and surrendered to Federal troops near Petersburg, Virginia. He was confined at Elmira, New York, where he died four months later on December 30, 1864. Wiley's name is listed on the Memorial Monument for the Davie County men who died in the Civil War, 1861–1865.

319. Ellis, Wiley R.
Private, Company B, Carolina Rangers • 10th Virginia Cavalry Regiment

Wiley was born in 1846 in Davie County to Jeremiah (1803, Davie) and Mary (1814, Davie) Ellis. He was a student, age 14, in the Smith Grove District of Davie when the war started. He enlisted in 1864 and was issued clothing on September 30 and December 31, 1864. He was captured at Burkesville on April 13, 1865, and sent to Point Lookout, where he was released June 26, 1865. He was described as being 5'7" tall, with fair complexion, hazel eyes and light brown hair. He returned home to Davie where he farmed with his father and was an agent for U.S.S. and Gugger; married Salie [*sic*] F. and by 1880 was the father of an infant daughter, Sallie Sue (1880). They lived in Fulton District; he is listed in the Confederate Veteran's Census of 1890. He died on September 11, 1899, and is buried in Elbaville United Methodist Church Cemetery. He was the brother of Nathaniel B. Ellis who also served in this company.

320. Ellis, William A.
Private, Company A, 42nd Regiment • N.C. Troops

William was born April 5, 1826, in Davie County to Rebecca (1804, South Carolina) Ellis. By 1850 William's father had died and he and his brother Samuel supported the family, his mother and two sisters, by farming. By 1860 William was farming to support his wife Hannah and their three children: Frank N. (1854), Laura P. (1857) and Buley E. (1859). Emma was born in 1861. On March 17, 1862, William enlisted in Rowan County. He was 31. He was present or accounted for until captured at or near Battery Anderson, near Fort Fisher, December 25, 1864. He was confined near Fort Monroe, Virginia, on December 27, 1864, and transferred to Point Lookout, Maryland, four days later. He was discharged at Point Lookout on May 12, 1865. His tombstone at Smith Grove United Methodist Church Cemetery, states that he died on June 4, 1865. Family legend says that he was so emaciated from starvation that when he arrived at home and saw the apple trees in bloom, he stated he would be dead before the apples could form. His prediction came true.

321. Ellis, William J.
First Lieutenant, Company E, 42nd Regiment • N.C. Troops

William was born in 1835 in Davie County to Jeremiah B. (1803, Davidson) and Mary (1814, Davie) Ellis. Jeremiah was a successful land dealer and by 1858 William was becoming successful in his own right. He enlisted in Davie County on May 10, 1862, with the rank of Third Lieutenant; he was promoted to First Lieutenant in July 1864, and was present and accounted for through October 1864. William was paroled at Greensboro, North Carolina, on May 1, 1865. According to his Commanding Officer, Major Thomas J. Brown, he was "a gallant soldier;" he returned home, served a term in the N.C. House of Representatives (1887–1889), and became a tobacco manufacturer and Assistant Postmaster in Winston-Salem, North Carolina. William and his wife

William J. Ellis probably completed this structure just before joining Company E, 42nd Regiment as a Third Lieutenant, on May 10, 1862. From 1887 to 1889 he served one term in the North Carolina House of Representatives (Mohney, *The Historic Architecture of Davie County*).

Dorothy A. were the parents of Elizabeth G. (1859), L. A. E. (1861), Willie B. (1863), Thomas J. (1864), C. W. (1870), Mary R. (1873) and Robert Lee (1874).

322. Ellis, William R.
Private, Company D, 42nd Regiment • N.C. Troops

William was born May 22, 1821, in Davie County where he worked as a cooper. He married Amanda E. Catton on February 27, 1849, and they settled in the Smith Grove area where he farmed. They had two daughters: Allice (Emma) (1857) and Mary (1860). William enlisted in Rowan County at age 35, on March 24, 1862. He died on July 1, 1862; the place and cause of death were not reported. The military records indicate that the year of death was 1862, but his tombstone indicates that he died in 1865. He is buried in the Ellis Family Cemetery in Davie County. William's name is listed on the Memorial Monument for the Davie County men who died in the Civil War, 1861–1865.

323. Ellison, Donalson
Private, "Davie Greys" • Company F, 13th Regiment • (3rd Regiment, N.C. Volunteers) • N.C. Troops

Donalson was born in 1843. He resided in Davie County where he worked as a farmer prior to enlisting in Davie County at age 18, June 18, 1861. He was present or accounted for until he died in hospital at Richmond, Virginia, August 12, 1862, of disease. Donalson's name is listed on the Memorial Monument for the Davie County men who died in the Civil War, 1861–1865.

324. Etcherson (Etchisson), Alexander H.
Private, Company E, 42nd Regiment • N.C. Troops

Alexander was born in 1840 in Davie County. He was the son of Daniel (1805, Davie) and Rebecca (1815, Virginia) Etchisson. The family lived in the Farmington District where his father worked as a farmer/tanner and Alexander worked as a laborer prior to his enlistment on March 18, 1862, at age 22, for the war. On January 7, 1863, Alexander married Martha A.C. Lee. He was present or accounted for until he deserted to the enemy on or about July 31, 1864, and was sent to Philadelphia, Pennsylvania. No further records.

325. Etcherson, Edmond (Edward)
Private • Captain William E. Booe's Partisan Rangers • N.C. Volunteers • Company H, 63rd Regiment • (5th Regiment N.C. Cavalry) • N.C. Troops

Edmund was born in 1829 in Davie County to Lucket (1804, Davie) and Nancy (1804, Davie) Etcherson. Edmund married Elizabeth Jane Beauchamp, September 19, 1854. They lived in the Smith Grove District of Davie where Edmund worked as wagoner prior to the war. They also had four children by 1860: Mary (1854), William (1856), John (1858) and Nancey (1860). Edmund enlisted in Davie County at age 33, July 12, 1862, for the war. He was present or accounted for through December 1864, and paroled at Salisbury, North Carolina, in 1865. In 1870 the family was situated in Farmington where they farmed. Their numbers had increased by four: Sarah (1862), Martha (1864), Emma (1868) and Laura (1869).

Edmond (Edward) Etcherson worked as a waggoner prior to the war (Sooter, Brenda Etchison. *Etchison Family Roots*).

326. Etcherson (Etchisson), James W.
Private, "Davie Sweep Stakes" • Company G, 4th Regiment • N.C. State Troops

James was born in 1841 in Davie County. At age nine he lived with Andrew E. (1825, Davie) and Mary (1824, Davie) Etchisson; in 1860 he was a farm laborer living with M. and Edney Fulford in the Mocksville District. James enlisted in Davie County at age 20, June 5, 1861, for the war. He was present or accounted for through December 1861, and was reported "sick in quarters" on company muster roll dated April 30–June 30, 1862. He died prior to November 23, 1862. The place, date and cause of death were not reported. James's name is listed on the Memorial Monument for the Davie County men who died in the Civil War, 1861–1865.

327. Etchison, C.H. (Caswell)
Private, Company A, 57th Regiment • N.C. Troops

C.H. was born in Davie County in 1834. He was a farmer in the Farmington District where on March 1, 1860, he married Lou (Louisa) C. Ferebee (1841, Davie). They had two daughters, Robena (1860) and Harriet (1861). C.H. enlisted in Rowan County at age 28, on July 4, 1862. He was hospitalized at Richmond, Virginia, on October 10, 1862, with rubeola, but returned to duty on November 4, 1862. He was again hospitalized at Richmond on January 28, 1863. He returned to duty on February 21, 1863, and again reported present through October 31, 1863. He was captured at Rappahannock Station, Virginia, on November 7, 1863. C.H. was confined at Point Lookout, Maryland, on November 11, 1863. He was paroled at Point Lookout on March 20, 1864, for exchange. He returned to duty subsequent to April 30, 1864. He was captured at Fisher's Hill, Virginia, on September 22, 1864, sent to Harpers Ferry, West Virginia, and confined at Point Lookout, Maryland, on October 3, 1864. He was paroled at Point Lookout on or about February 13, 1865. He was received at Cox's Wharf, James River, Virginia, on February 14–15, 1865, for exchange. He was reported in camp near Richmond on February 19, 1865. No further records. He survived the war. Afterward, two more daughters, Sarah (1866) and Lavenia (1868) were born. C.H. is buried in Eaton's Baptist Church Cemetery, but no dates are given on the tombstone.

328. Etchison, Giles B.
Private, Company D, 42nd Regiment • N.C. Troops

Giles was born in 1838 in Davie County. He was the son of Lucket (Lucky) (1804, Davie) and Nancy (1809, Davie) Etchison. In 1860 he was living in the Mocksville District where he worked as a farmer and where Giles's entire family lived with the H.A. Mock family. On January 2, 1862, Giles and Sarah Hendrix were married. A short time later, at age 22, he enlisted in Rowan County on March 24, 1862. He was present or accounted for until he deserted on June 1, 1863. Giles was reported under arrest in September–October, 1863, but he returned to duty in November–December, 1863. He was present or accounted for until captured at or near Wise's Forks, Kinston, North Carolina, on March 10, 1865. He was confined at Point Lookout, Maryland, on March 16, 1865, and was released at Point Lookout on June 17, 1865, after taking the Oath of Allegiance. Giles and Sarah became the parents of two girls: Nancy (1864) and Julia (1866). In 1870 Sarah and her daughters were living in the Farmington District with Richmond Hendrix and Sarah Howard. In 1880 Sarah, Nancy and Julia were living in the Farmington District with Sarah listed as the head of the household.

329. Etchison, Shadrach M.
Second Corporal, Company B, Carolina Rangers • 10th Virginia Cavalry Regiment

Shadrach was born in 1837 in Davie County to Daniel (1805, Davie) and Rebecca (1815, Virginia) Etchisson. He married Perlina K. Smith on September 24, 1857. In 1860 they farmed in the Farmington District of Davie, where Shadrack [*sic*] enlisted on October 29, 1861, at age 24. He was present through April 30, 1862. He died in January 1863. Shadrach's name is listed on the Memorial Monument for the Davie County men who died in the Civil War, 1861–1865. Perlina's application for a widow's pension is on file in the State Archives, Raleigh, North Carolina.

330. Etchison, W.C. Perry
Private, Company F, 42nd Regiment • N.C. Troops

Perry was born in 1846 in Davie County to Andrew E. (1825, Davie) and Mary (1824, Davie) Etchison. He enlisted in Davie County at age 16, on March 18, 1862. He was present or accounted for until he deserted on December 17, 1862. In March–April, 1863, he returned to duty. He was present or accounted for until he deserted on August 9, 1863. Perry was apprehended on September 18, 1863, and was reported under arrest until February 27, 1864, when he returned to duty. He was present or accounted for until he deserted again on or about August 10, 1864. On September 22, 1864, he returned to duty and was placed under arrest and sentenced to be shot for desertion; however, his sentence was suspended or annulled, and he was paroled at Mocksville on June 7, 1865. Somehow during all the upheaval, he had managed to marry Nancy L. Parker (1840, North Carolina) on January 3, 1865. The couple had two daughters: Sarah L. (1867) and Hetty L.B. (1871). They lived in the Clarksville District for awhile where Perry worked as a farm laborer. He died on March 14, 1923, and is buried in Rose Cemetery in Mocksville. So are his wife and daughters. The execution order of 1865 overshadowed reality and the following rumor evolved: Perry deserted, came home, was accosted on a path by Captain Clement and a contingent of men. He was shot where he stood by Captain Clement and that his body was left where it fell, and Perry's sixteen-year-old son found his body and buried him where he lay. (Remember, Perry was only nineteen years of age at the time.)

Unfortunately for his descendants, the good news of Perry's life was never told. To remedy this

W.C. Perry Etchison, his daughter Sarah, and wife Nancy; daughter Hetty had died at age 8 in 1880 (Gwynn Meroney).

the authors contacted Louise Stroud, who had lived in Davie County ninety plus years and possessed a flawless memory. She had fond memories, as a girl of five or six watching a white haired W.C. Perry Etchison, Mocksville's only policeman, doing his evenng rounds in the square and lighting the kerosene lamps.

331. Evans, Thomas
Private, Company F, 42nd Regiment • N.C. Troops

Thomas was born in 1832 in North Carolina. He and his wife Elizabeth (1841, North Carolina) lived in Davie County where he did farm work. Thomas enlisted in Davie at age 30, on March 18, 1862. He was present or accounted for until September 7, 1864, when he was reported absent wounded. The date and place were not reported. He was detailed for guard duty at Charlotte on October 25, 1864, through December 1864. Thomas was hospitalized at Richmond, Virginia, March 18, 1865, with an unspecified complaint and was transferred on March 19, 1865. (The Salem *People's Press* of June 30, 1864, states he was wounded June 1–15, 1864.) In 1870 he and Elizabeth were farmers in the Farmington District.

332. Evans, William
Private, Company G, 5th Regiment • N.C. State Troops

William was born in 1838 in Davie County. He lived with his mother, Winney (1795, Virginia) in the Calahaln District where he worked as a farmer. He married Mary Granger on December 12, 1858, and James D. was born in 1859. William enlisted in Northampton County at age 24, August 13, 1862, for the war. He died in camp near Fredericksburg, Virginia, on or about February 28, 1863, of disease. William's name is not presently listed on the Memorial Monument for the Davie County men who died in the Civil War, 1861–1865.

333. Faircloth, J.D. (Jacob)
Private • Captain William E. Booe's Partisan Rangers • N.C. Volunteers • Company H, 63rd Regiment • (5th Regiment N.C. Cavalry) • N.C. Troops

J.D. was born in 1841 in Davie County. His father, Thomas (1818, North Carolina), operated a distillery and farmed. J.D. enlisted in Davie County at age 18, July 12, 1862, for the war. He was present or accounted for through August 1864, when he was reported as on "sick furlough." After the war he returned home to Fulton District where he farmed with his father. J.D. married Mary Smith on September 12, 1871. They moved to Farmington, along with their son Samuel (1866), where they continued to farm. J.D. married Bettie Bell Tysinger on August 6, 1893. He died on December 11, 1897, and is buried in Bethlehem United Methodist Church Cemetery.

334. Farrington, Romulus
Private, "Davie Sweep Stakes" • Company G, 4th Regiment • N.C. State Troops

Romulus resided in Davie County where he enlisted at age 22, June 4, 1861, for the war. He was present or accounted for until he deserted at Hanover Junction, Virginia, May 21, 1864.

335. Felker, George
Second Lieutenant • Company G, 77th Regiment, 19th Division • N.C. Militia 1861–1865

George was born May 6, 1827, in North Carolina. He married Leah (1833, Cabarrus) Saferit on December 16, 1852, and they lived in the Calahaln District of Davie County, where he farmed. They would have two children: Henry W. (1855) and Mary J. (1857). After Leah's death on August 7, 1863, George married Sarah E. (1833, North Carolina). Their children were Margaret (1864), Laura E. (1867), John W. (1868), William R.K. (1872) and Albert L.F. (1878). George had served as Second Lieutenant of Company G of the militia when it had been activated. After a long life of 82 years, he died on January 25, 1910, and is buried in St. Matthew's Lutheran Church Cemetery.

336. Ferebee, Joseph H.
Private, Company B, Carolina Rangers • 10th Virginia Cavalry Regiment

Joseph was born in 1843 in Davie County to Thomas (1809, Davie) and Catharine (1818, Davie) Ferebee. He worked as a farmhand in the Farmington District of Davie prior to enlisting there on October 29, 1861, at age 18. He was present or accounted for until April 1, 1864. He was wounded in his left arm on June 23, 1864, was admitted to Richmond hospital on June 26, and furloughed for 60 days on August 30, 1864, and reported back. On March 22, 1865, he was transferred to the Invalid Corps, and assigned to the Army of Northern Virginia on March 24, 1865. He was paroled in Mocksville, North Carolina, on June 9, 1865.

337. Ferebee, S. (Samuel T.)
Private • Captain William E. Booe's Partisan Rangers • N.C. Volunteers • Company H, 63rd Regiment • (5th Regiment N.C. Cavalry) • N.C. Troops

Samuel was born in 1845 in Davie County to Peter (1805, Currituck) and Sousan Lunn (1808, Currituck) Ferebee. He worked as a laborer on the family farm run by his mother after his father's death in 1848. He enlisted in Davie County on April 1, 1863, for the war. He was wounded in Hagerstown, Maryland, on July 6, 1863, and killed in action September 22, 1863. Samuel's name is listed on the Memorial Monument for the Davie County men who died in the Civil War, 1861–1865.

338. Ferebee, W.H. (William)
Corporal • Captain William E. Booe's Partisan Rangers • N.C. Volunteers • Company H, 63rd Regiment • (5th Regiment N.C. Cavalry) • N.C. Troops

William was born in Davie County on October 23, 1835, to Susan Lunn (1808, Currituck) and Peter Ferebee (1805, Currituck). They lived in the Farmington District. On December 13, 1860, William and Mary A. Hill (1839, Surry) were married. Their first child was a son, David (1862). William enlisted for the war at age 27, on June 12, 1862, and was appointed Corporal on August 1, 1863. He was captured near Madison Court House, Virginia, on September 22, 1863, and confined at Old Capitol Prison, Washington, D.C., until he was transferred to Point Lookout, Maryland, on September 26, 1863. He was later transferred to Elmira, New York, on August 16, 1864, where he remained until paroled after the war and exchanged at Boulware's Wharf, James River, Virginia, March 15, 1865. William returned to farming and his family, which later included daughters Mary (1866) and Nancy in (1869). W.H. Ferebee died on January 14, 1907, and is buried in Wesley Chapel United Methodist Church Cemetery.

339. Ferrell, E.L.
Private, Company B, 57th Regiment • N.C. Troops

E.L. resided in Davie County and enlisted in Rowan County at age 18, on July 4, 1862, for the war. He was reported absent without leave in September 1862–April 1863. He returned to duty in May–August, 1863, then was captured at Rappahannock Station, Virginia, on November 7, 1863. He was sent to Washington, D.C., confined at Point Lookout, Maryland, on November 11, 1863, and paroled there on March 16, 1864. He was received at City Point, Virginia, on March 20, 1864, for exchange and returned to duty prior to August 17, 1864. He was wounded in the right arm at Winchester, Virginia, and hospitalized at Kernstown, Virginia. He was reported absent wounded through February 28, 1865, but he survived the war.

340. Ferribee, Thomas M.
Private, Company F, 42nd Regiment • N.C. Troops

Thomas was born in Davie County in 1841. He was the son of Susan (1811, Currituck). Thomas enlisted in Davie at age 21 on or about March 15, 1862. He was present or accounted for until wounded in the left arm at or near Wise's Forks, Kinston, North Carolina, on March 10, 1865, and was released from the hospital on April 27, 1865. Thomas married Sarah R. (1842, North Carolina) Horn on September 27, 1865. Their four children were Mary (1869), John C. (1870), Robert S. (1874) and Marvin (1879). The family lived and farmed in the Farmington District.

341. Fleming, S.F.
Sergeant • Captain William E. Booe's Partisan Rangers • N.C. Volunteers • Company H, 63rd Regiment • (5th Regiment N.C. Cavalry) • N.C. Troops

Samuel married Pheebee E. Brunt on March 30, 1859. He enlisted in Davie County at age 27, July 9, 1862, for the war. He mustered in as Sergeant. He was both wounded and captured at Middleburg, Virginia, on June 17, 1863, and exchanged on June 30, 1863. Samuel was wounded at Ground Squirrel Church, Virginia, May 11, 1864, and again on the Weldon Railroad on August 21, 1864. He was present or accounted for through February 1865.

342. Fletcher, Mathew
Private, "Davie Greys" • Company F, 13th Regiment • (3rd Regiment, N.C. Volunteers) • N.C. Troops

Mathew was born in 1839. He resided in Davie or Wilkes County and was by occupation a farmer prior to enlisting in Davie County at age 22, on April 26, 1861. He was present or accounted for until captured at Gill's Mill, Virginia, April 6, 1865. He was confined at Point Lookout, Maryland, until released on June 26, 1865, after taking the Oath of Allegiance.

343. Foard, John B.
Private • Captain William E. Booe's Partisan Rangers • N.C. Volunteers • Company H, 63rd Regiment • (5th Regiment N.C. Cavalry) • N.C. Troops

John B. was the son of J. Cicero (1812, Davidson) and Sarah (1823, Rowan) Foard. In 1860 the family lived in the Liberty District where they were farmers and John was a laborer. On March 15, 1863, John B. enlisted for the war. He was present or accounted for through December 1864, and paroled at Salisbury, North Carolina, on May 2, 1865.

344. Foote, L.R. (Luther)
Private, Company E, 42nd Regiment • N.C. Troops

Luther was born in North Carolina, in 1834. He was a farmer in the Chinquepin District of Davie County when he married Nancy J. Cain (1842, Davie) on August 30, 1859. On March 18, 1862, at age 23, he enlisted in Davie County. He was present or accounted for until discharged on or about September 26, 1863, by reason of "chronic rheumatism." In 1870 he was again a farm laborer but in the Clarksville District. Luther and Nancy had seven children: A. Jasper (1862), Ada L. (1867), Ella (1869), Mary E. (1872), Nina (1874), Henry (1877) and Narcissus (1879). L.R. died in 1898 and is buried in Bear Creek Baptist Church Cemetery.

345. Foster, A. (Anderson) F.
Private, Company G, 5th Regiment • N.C. State Troops

Anderson F. Foster married Ann Mariah Butler in Davie County on September 18, 1861. He enlisted in Northampton County at age 24, on August 13, 1862, for the war. He died at Middletown, Virginia, November 27, 1862, of disease. Ann M. then married Jacob Spry on January 7, 1868, in Davie County. Anderson's name is not presently listed on the Memorial Monument for the Davie County men who died in the Civil War, 1861–1865.

346. Foster, A.M. (Azariah)
Third Lieutenant, Company D, 42nd Regiment • N.C. Troops

Azariah was born in 1838 in Davie County, the son of Tiglman [sic] (1801, Davie) and Frances (1810, Davie). On August 30, 1859, he married Sarah C. (Caroline) Snider (1839, Davie). In 1860 "Az" lived with Sarah in Liberty District where he worked as a carpenter. At age 24, on or about January 28, 1862, he enlisted in Davie County. He mustered in as a Private and was promoted to Corporal in March–April, 1864. He was ordered transferred to Company G, 2nd Regiment, Confederate Engineer Troops, in the summer of 1864; however, he was appointed Third Lieutenant on August 13, 1864, and the transfer was cancelled. He was present or accounted for through October 1864. Azariah was paroled at Salisbury, North Carolina, on an unspecified date in 1865. After the war he and Sarah lived in Jerusalem District where he resumed his work as a carpenter. Azariah died in 1904. He is buried in Fork Baptist Church Cemetery.

347. Foster, Albert N.
Private • Company F, 42nd Regiment • N.C. Troops

Albert resided in Davie County where he was born in 1847 to James (1794, Davie) and Sarah (1804, Davie) Foster. The place and date of enlistment were not reported. He was captured at or near Wise's Forks, Kinston, North Carolina, on March 10, 1865, and confined at Point Lookout, Maryland, on March 16, 1865. After taking the Oath of Allegiance, he was released from Point Lookout on June 11, 1865. After the war he married Eliza Parks on June 5, 1873, and they settled in the Fulton District. Albert died on February 29, 1920. He is buried in the Fork Baptist Church Cemetery.

348. Foster, Anderson
Private, Company B, Carolina Rangers • 10th Virginia Cavalry Regiment

Anderson was born in 1838 in Davie County to Samuel (1800, Davie) and Naomi (1807, Davie) Foster. By 1860 his father had died and Anderson and his two brothers helped their mother on the farm. They lived in the Mocksville District of Davie where he enlisted on October 29, 1861, at age 21. He was present or accounted for through January 5, 1863. Unfortunately, he was wounded in action in the left thigh during the battle at Brandy Station, June 9, 1863. On July 3, 1863, he was furloughed to Mocksville, North Carolina, for thirty days, through August 1863. He was then absent sick from September 1863 to April 1, 1864. Finally, he was retired by the Medical Board on August 30, 1864, and paroled at Salisbury, North Carolina, May 20, 1865.

349. Foster, Anderson E.
Private, Company B, Carolina Rangers • 10th Virginia Cavalry Regiment

Anderson was born in 1837 in North Carolina, to James A. (1782, Virginia) Foster. Anderson and his wife Eliza (1840, North Carolina) lived in the Liberty District of Davie County where he worked as a laborer prior to his enlisting on October 29, 1861, at age 25. He was present or accounted for throughout his tour of duty. He was without a horse on July 7, 1863, when he went on detached service, but received clothing on September 30 and December 31, 1864. On January 27, 1865, he was again without a horse. He was paroled in Salisbury, North Carolina, May 20, 1865. In 1870 he lived alone in the Fulton District of Davie County where he supported himself by farming.

350. Foster, Andrew J.
Private, Company H, 57th Regiment • N.C. Troops

Andrew was born in 1830 in Davie County. He was the son of Daniel (1788, Davie) and Mary (1797, Davie) Foster. He and Sarah A. Dwire (1835) were married on February 27, 1859, and lived on a farm in the Fulton District. At age 29, on July 4, 1862, he enlisted in Davie for the war. He was hospitalized at Richmond, Virginia, on October 21, 1862, with typhoid fever and was furloughed for thirty days on November 20, 1862. Andrew was reported absent without leave on February 28, 1863, but returned to duty prior to May 11, 1863. He was reported on detail as a teamster through December 1863, and in March–August, 1864. He rejoined the company in September–October, 1864, and was reported present in November 1864–February 1865. Andrew was captured at Fort Stedman, Virginia, on March 25, 1865, and was confined at Point Lookout, Maryland, on March 28, 1865. He was released there on June 26, 1865, after taking the Oath of Allegiance. Andrew and Sarah had three children: Alice (1860), Henry (1867) and Cora May (1871). After the war Andrew returned to farming in the Jerusalem District. He died in 1918 and is buried in the Concord United Methodist Church Cemetery.

351. Foster, Archibald
Private, Company M, 7th Regiment • Confederate Cavalry • Company E, 16th Battalion • N.C. Cavalry

Archibald enlisted in Davie County on December 20, 1862, with the rank of Private. He was transferred from Company M, 7th Regiment Confederate Cavalry to Company E, 16th Battalion N.C. Cavalry on July 11, 1864. He was present or accounted for through October 1, 1864, and paroled at Salisbury, North Carolina, May 24, 1865.

352. Foster, Azanah L.
Private, Company D, 42nd Regiment • N.C. Troops

Azanah resided in Davie County and enlisted in Rowan County at age 22, on April 18, 1862, for the war. He was present or accounted for through August 1862. Azanah died prior to January 1, 1863. Place and cause of death were not reported. Azanah's name is listed on the Memorial Monument for the Davie County men who died in the Civil War, 1861–1865.

353. Foster, Benjamin L.
Private, Company E, 42nd Regiment • N.C. Troops

Benjamin was born in 1826 in Davie County. Early records show that he was 22 years old in 1850, and that he was a farmer. On September 30, 1847, he married Emeline (1828, Davie) Riley. They lived in the Mocksville District where he enlisted on March 18, 1862, at age 35. He was present or accounted for through October 1864. Benjamin was paroled at Mocksville on June 7, 1865. In 1870 he was again a farmer in the Mocksville District and the father of six children: Elizabeth (1849), Sarah E. (1851), Lovy J. (1854), Martha V. (1857), Laura (1863) and Florence (1866). Benjamin died in 1910 and is buried in Smith Grove United Methodist Church Cemetery.

354. Foster, Coleman
Private, Company E, 42nd Regiment • N.C. Troops

Coleman was born in Davie County in 1822, the son of Elizabeth (1810, Davie). He made his living as a farmer. On April 16, 1851, he married Minerva Call and settled in the Fulton District. Coleman enlisted for the war on October 2, 1863. He was present or accounted for through October 1864 and was paroled at Salisbury, North Carolina, on May 30, 1865. Minerva and Coleman were the parents of eight children: George (1854), Mary J. (1856), Sarah E. (1858), Nancy (1861), Martha (1863), Emma (1867), Eliza (1868) and Lewis (1871). In 1870 and 1880 the family lived and farmed in the Fulton District. Coleman died in 1903 and is buried in the Fork Baptist Church Cemetery. (See photograph on page 86.)

355. Foster, Franklin (Francis) A.
Musician, Company E, 42nd Regiment • N.C. Troops

Coleman Foster House (Mohney, *The Historic Architecture of Davie County*)

Franklin was born in 1835 in Davie County to Welden (1801, Virginia) and Zelphia (1806, Currituck) Foster. They resided in the Farmington District where Franklin farmed with his father prior to marrying Mary (1846, North Carolina). Their first child, Caroline, was born in 1861 just as war began. Franklin enlisted in Davie County on August 26, 1863, for the war. He mustered in as a Musician and was present or accounted for through November 8, 1864. He was paroled at Salisbury, North Carolina, on an unspecified date in 1865. His next child Laura was born in 1865, followed by Frank (1867) and Matthew (1868). Franklin died on March 26, 1905; Mary died on January 22, 1927. Both are buried in Wesley Chapel United Methodist Church Cemetery.

356. Foster, George
Captain, "Davie Greys" • Company F, 13th Regiment • (3rd Regiment, N.C. Volunteers) • N.C. Troops

George was born June 1, 1834. He was the son of Samuel (1800, Davie) and Naomi (1807, Davie) Foster. He married Ruth Ann Booe, May 20, 1856, and settled in the Mocksville District where he worked as a farmer. Their children were

George Foster enlisted April 26, 1861, with the rank of Corporal, and was elected Captain April 26, 1862 (Tom Foster).

William A. (1857) and Samuel A. (1860). George enlisted in Davie County at age 26, on April 26, 1861. He mustered in as a Corporal and was elected Captain to rank from April 26, 1862. George was present or accounted for until he resigned on May 11, 1863, by reason of "rheumatism." His resignation was accepted on or about June 5, 1863. Alicia (1864) and Thomas (1867) were born shortly thereafter. George continued his work as a farmer in the Mocksville area until his death in 1876. Ruth and the children lived in the John and Jane Foster household in the Mocksville area following his death. George is buried in Bethel United Methodist Church Cemetery. His tombstone reads: George Foster, June 1, 1834–November 16, 1876.

357. Foster, H.W. (Henderson)
Private • Captain William E. Booe's Partisan Rangers • N.C. Volunteers • Company H, 63rd Regiment • (5th Regiment N.C. Cavalry) • N.C. Troops

Henderson was born in 1829 in Davie County. He married Loueza V. Foster (1829, Davie) and they lived in the Chinquepin District where their children Blackston (1848) and Laura L. (1858) were born. Henderson enlisted in Davie County at age 34 on July 10, 1862, for the war. He was present or accounted for through October 1862.

358. Foster, Henry
Private, "Davie Greys" • Company F, 13th Regiment • (3rd Regiment, N.C. Volunteers) • N.C. Troops

Henry was born in 1832 in Surry County. He was the son of Elijah (1797, Virginia) and Love (1791, Currituck) Foster. In 1850 at age 19, he was a farmer. On March 6, 1854, he married Camilla (Carmela) Foster. Prior to the war they had two children: Sarah Frances (1855) and Ella (Olley) (1858). They resided in Davie County where Henry enlisted at age 30, July 16, 1862. He was present or accounted for until paroled at Appomattox Court House, Virginia, April 9, 1865. Henry returned home to the Fulton District where he resumed his life as a farmer. Their additional children were Emiline (1861), Mary (1863), Noah B. (1865), John G. (1868) and Henry N. (1870). Henry is buried in Foster Family Cemetery #2. His tombstone reads: Henry Naylor Foster, Confederate 1832–1875. His wife is buried there also: Comila Cornatzer Foster, February 2, 1929 [sic]/February 8, 1927 (note: 1829).

359. Foster, Henry
Private, Company B, Carolina Rangers • 10th Virginia Cavalry Regiment

Henry was born April 10, 1830, in Davie County. He lived in the Fulton District of Davie where he enlisted on December 20, 1862. He was absent sick on January 2, 1863. On June 7, 1863, he was wounded in his right knee and was in Richmond hospital on July 20, 1863. He deserted August 8, 1863, and was absent without leave November 12, 1863. After that he was present through August 1864, received clothing September 30, and again on December 31, 1864. He was paroled in Salisbury, North Carolina, on May 20, 1865.

360. Foster, Henry C.
Sergeant, "Davie Greys" • Company F, 13th Regiment • (3rd Regiment, N.C. Volunteers) • N.C. Troops

Henry was born in 1841 to William (1806, Davie) and Matilda (1816, Davie). In 1860 he was a farmer-laborer in Mocksville where he enlisted in Davie at age 18, on April 26, 1861. He mustered in as a Private and was present or accounted for until wounded at Gaines' Mill, Virginia, on June 27, 1862. He rejoined the company prior to March 1, 1863, and was promoted to Sergeant on April 17, 1863. Henry was present or accounted for until wounded at Chancellorsville, Virginia, May 3, 1863. He rejoined the company in July–August, 1863, and was reduced to ranks prior to September 1, 1863, when he was reappointed Sergeant. He was present or accounted for until paroled at Appomattox Court House, Virginia, April 9, 1865. In 1870 he was again a farmer in Fulton District where he married Mary A. Hendrix on January 22, 1871. Henry's application for a pension is on file at the State Archives, Raleigh, North Carolina.

361. Foster, Jacob
Private, "Davie Greys" • Company F, 13th Regiment • (3rd Regiment, N.C. Volunteers) • N.C. Troops

Jacob was born in 1838 in Davie County. He was a farmer, the son of Samuel (1800, Davie) and Naomi (1807, Davie) Foster. In 1860 at age 22, he was living in the Mocksville District where he enlisted for the war on April 26, 1861. He was present or accounted for until wounded in battle near Richmond, Virginia, in May–June, 1862. The battle in which he was wounded was not reported. He rejoined the company prior to November 1, 1862, and was present or accounted for until wounded and captured at or near Fredericksburg, Virginia, May 3, 1863, for exchange.

He rejoined the company prior to July 1, 1863, and was present or accounted for until captured at Hatcher's Run, Virginia, on April 2, 1865. He was confined at Point Lookout, Maryland, until released on June 26, 1865, after taking the Oath of Allegiance. He returned home and lived with his mother, Naomi, and worked as a farmer until he married Catherine Sain (widow of William Sain), April 2, 1871, and became stepfather to her daughter, Julia (1861).

362. Foster, James A.
Private, Company D, 42nd Regiment • N.C. Troops

James resided in Davie County and enlisted in Rowan or Davie at age 19, on January 31, 1862. He was present or accounted for until he died in the hospital at Petersburg, Virginia, of "typhoid fever" on October 26, 1862. James's name is listed on the Memorial Monument for the Davie County men who died in the Civil War, 1861–1865.

363. Foster, James H.W.
Private, Company E, 42nd Regiment • N.C. Troops

James enlisted in Davie County on October 4, 1864, for the war. He was present or accounted for until he died in the hospital at Richmond, Virginia, on January 19, 1865. The cause of death was not reported. James's name is listed on the Memorial Monument for the Davie County men who died in the Civil War, 1861–1865.

364. Foster, James M.
Private, Company D, 42nd Regiment • N.C. Troops

James was born in 1825 in Davie County. In 1850 he was living with the Issac Foster family; both he and Issac were wagon-makers. They resided in Davie where James married Eliza Allen, August 18, 1851. By 1860 he and Eliza were living the Shady Grove District with five children. James enlisted in Rowan County at age 37, on April 18, 1862, for the war. He was present or accounted for through October 1864. He was paroled at Mocksville on June 2, 1865. In 1870 the family was located in Farmington where James still worked as a wagon-maker. Their children were: Mary(1853), George (1854), Elizabeth (1856), Dorcas (1857), Samuel (1858), Thomas (1860), John (1863) and Nancey (1866).

365. Foster, Jesse N.
Private, Company D, 42nd Regiment • Captain William Howard's Company, N.C. Prison Guards •

Jesse Nathan Foster (Gwynn Meroney)

Corporal, 1st Company A, Salisbury Prison Guard • "The Rough and Readys" • Company G, 66th Regiment • N.C. Troops

Jesse was born in 1841 in Davie County to Jesse (1790, Davie) and Mary (1808, Davie) Foster. They farmed in the Liberty District prior to the war. Jesse Jr. enlisted at age 21 in Davie County on January 29, 1862, as a Private; on or about May 1, 1862, he transferred from Company D of the 42nd to Captain William Howard's Company. He served as Corporal in 1st Company A, Salisbury Prison Guard until he transferred to Company G of the 66th on October 2, 1863. He was reported present through December 31, 1863, and reported on detached duty at Wilmington in January–February, 1864. He was reduced to ranks in January–February, 1864. He reported present in March–August, 1864, and reported sick in the hospital from September 27 through October 31, 1864. He was paroled at Salisbury, North Carolina, on May 24, 1865. J.N. and Mary Ann M. Parker were married December 13, 1866. Jesse Jr. [*sic*] was born in 1867, followed by Mary (1870), William A. (1872), Emily J. (1877) and Daniel W. (1879). The family lived in the Jerusalem District of Davie following the war. Jesse N. died in 1915 and is buried in Concord United Methodist Church Cemetery.

366. Foster, John
Private, Company M, 7th Regiment • Confederate Cavalry • Company E, 16th Battalion • N.C. Cavalry

John enlisted in Davie County on December 20, 1862, with the rank of Private. He was transferred from Company M, 7th Regiment Confederate Cavalry to Company E, 16th Battalion N.C. Cavalry on July 11, 1864. He was present or accounted for through October 1, 1864.

367. Foster, John B.
Fourth Sergeant, Company B, Carolina Rangers • 10th Virginia Cavalry Regiment

John was born in 1831 in Davie County to Giles (1805, Davie) and Sarah (1807, Davie) Foster. They lived in the Fulton District of Davie where his father farmed and John worked as a carpenter; it was an extensive household of nine children where the additional four sons were laborers and the older girls were domestics. John enlisted in Davie County on October 29, 1861, at age 30, as a Private. His presence or absence was not stated through April 30, 1862; he was present as a Second Corporal on January 1863 and appointed Fourth Sergeant on January 24, 1863. After that his attendance was routine, except for a brief absence on horse detail on September 10, 1863. John was paroled in Burkesville, Virginia, on April 14–17, 1865. He returned home where he married Ellen, age 20, in 1870. His brother Richmond H. Foster also served in this company.

368. Foster, John E.
Private, Company D, 42nd Regiment • N.C. Troops

John was born in 1839, the son of James (1791, Davie) and Sarah (1802, Davie) Foster. On February 22, 1859, he and Elizabeth Carter (1835) were married. John enlisted in Davie County on January 29, 1862. He died on May 12, 1862. The place and cause of death were not reported. John's name is listed on the Memorial Monument for the Davie County men who died in the Civil War, 1861–1865. John's tombstone lists date of death as March 16, 1862. He is buried in Fork Baptist Church Cemetery.

369. Foster, John M.
Private, Company F, 42nd Regiment • N.C. Troops

John was born in Davie County in 1838. On January 20, 1859, he married A. Orrell from

John Marshall Foster's house is said to have been built in the late 1860s (Mohney, *The Historic Architecture of Davie County*).

Forsyth County. He enlisted in Davie at age 24, March 24, 1862. He was present or accounted for until he was injured in the left thigh "by fall of a tree" near Kinston on or about March 8, 1865. He was captured on April 13, 1865, while in the hospital at Raleigh. John was paroled on an unspecified date.

370. Foster, John M.
Private, Company B, Carolina Rangers • 10th Virginia Cavalry Regiment

John was born in 1842 in Davie County to Berry (1810, Davie) and Mary (1814, Davie) Foster. They farmed in the Smith Grove District of Davie where John enlisted on October 29, 1861, at age 18. His presence or absence was not documented through April 30, 1862. After that he was present on record or absent on horse detail through September 1863. He was captured at Brandy Station on October 11, 1863, and sent to Old Capitol Prison, then transferred to Point Lookout where he was exchanged September 22, 1864, and admitted to Richmond hospital the same day. Six days later he was furloughed to Salisbury, North Carolina. He returned to Davie County where he moved to the Calahaln District and married Julie E. Their son Berry was born in 1868. John died on February 17, 1901, and is buried in Salem United Methodist Church Cemetery. Julie died on May 1, 1913.

371. Foster, John W.
Musician, "Davie Sweep Stakes" • Company G, 4th Regiment • N.C. State Troops

John was born in 1841 to Welden (1801, Virginia) and Zelphia (1806, Currituck) Foster. They resided in the Farmington District where John worked as a laborer prior to enlisting at age 20, June 4, 1861, for the war. He mustered in as a Private but was promoted to Musician prior to September 1, 1861. He was present or accounted for through February 1862. No further records.

372. Foster, K.R. (Kerr)
Private • Captain William E. Booe's Partisan Rangers • N.C. Volunteers • Company H, 63rd Regiment • (5th Regiment N.C. Cavalry) • N.C. Troops

K.R. was born in 1842 in Davie County to Giles (1805, Davie), who was a farmer, and Sarah (1807, Davie) Foster. K.R. was a laborer in the Fulton District when he enlisted in Davie County at age 20, July 11, 1862, for the war. He was present or accounted for through October 1862 on the company muster rolls. He was discharged November 22, 1862. In 1870 he was a farmer living in the Fulton District.

373. Foster, Richmond Henry
Private, Company B, Carolina Rangers • 10th Virginia Cavalry Regiment

Richmond was born in 1840 in Davie County to Giles (1805, Davie) and Sarah (1807, Davie) Foster. They farmed in Fulton District where Richmond enlisted on November 11, 1861. He was documented present, except for two absences on horse detail, throughout his tenure. He was paroled at Salisbury, North Carolina, on May 20, 1865. He returned to Davie where he farmed in the Fulton District and married Fanny. His brother was John B. Foster who also served in this company.

374. Foster, Robert
Private, Company E, 42nd Regiment • N.C. Troops

Robert was born in 1834 in Davie County, the son of Giles (1805, Davie) and Sarah (1807, Davie) Foster. Giles was a farmer and Robert worked as a laborer while living in the Fulton District. He enlisted for the war on July 22, 1862, in Davie County. He died in the hospital at Weldon on February 26, 1863, of "typhoid fever." Robert's name is listed on the Memorial Monument for the Davie County men who died in the Civil War, 1861–1865.

375. Foster, Samuel
Private, Company G, 7th Regiment • Confederate Cavalry • Company D, 16th Battalion • N.C. Cavalry

Samuel was born in 1820 in Davie County. He married Candis Caudle on March 29, 1844. According to page 148 in *The Historic Architecture of Davie County*, he and his brother are said to have built houses on adjoining tracts of land in Fulton District. Samuel and Candice were the parents of Elizabeth (1845), Amanda (1846), Obediah (1848), Benjamin (1850) and Ann (1853). Samuel enlisted November 7, 1863, in Davie County, with the rank of Private. He transferred from Company G, 7th Regiment Confederate Cavalry to Company D, 16th Battalion N.C. Cavalry on July 11, 1864. He was captured at Fort Harrison, Virginia, on September 30, 1864, and confined at Point Lookout, Maryland, where he remained until paroled and exchanged at Boulware's Wharf, James River, Virginia, on March 19, 1865. (See photograph on page 91.)

Samuel Foster is said to have built this house in the 1850s (Mohney, *The Historic Architecture of Davie County*).

376. Foster, Samuel
Private, "Davie Greys" • Company F, 13th Regiment • (3rd Regiment, N.C. Volunteers) • N.C. Troops

Samuel was born in 1843 in Davie County. He was the son of Samuel (1800, Davie) and Naomi (1807, Davie) Foster, and the brother of Jacob, who also served in this company. At age 18, Samuel was a farmer in the Mocksville District. He enlisted on April 26, 1861, in Davie, and was present or accounted for until wounded in the thigh at Gaines' Mill, Virginia, June 27, 1862. He was reported absent wounded until September–October, 1864, when he rejoined the company. He retired to the Invalid Corp on November 2, 1864. Samuel returned home to marry Mary A. (1851, North Carolina). Their two children were Minnie L. (1873) and George H. (1880). In 1870 Samuel was a farmer in Jerusalem District. In 1880 he and his family lived with John P. Granger, his wife Mary E., and their children in the Mocksville area. Samuel is buried in Bethel United Methodist Church Cemetery. The tombstone reads: Samuel Foster, Company F, N.C. Infantry, C.S.A. (no dates given).

377. Foster, Samuel L.
Private, Company D, 42nd Regiment • N.C. Troops

Samuel was born in 1843 in Davie County. He was the son of James (1791, Davie) and Sarah (1802, Davie) Foster. He enlisted in Davie County on February 1, 1862. He died on May 10, 1862. The place and cause of death were not reported. He was the brother of John E. Foster. Samuel's name is listed on the Memorial Monument for the Davie County men who died in the Civil War, 1861–1865. Samuel is buried in Fork Baptist Church Cemetery. His tombstone indicates that he died on March 12, 1862.

378. Foster, Samuel Mc.
Private, Company D, 42nd Regiment • N.C. Troops

Samuel was born in 1844. He resided in Davie County and enlisted in Rowan County at age 19, on September 28, 1863, for the war. He was present or accounted for through October 1864.

379. Foster, Thomas
Private, Company E, 42nd Regiment • N.C. Troops

Thomas was born in Davie County and was by occupation a farmer prior to enlisting in Davie County at age 25, on March 18, 1862. He was present or accounted for until captured at Cold Harbor, Virginia, on June 1–3, 1864. He was confined at Point Lookout, Maryland, June 11, 1864, then transferred to Elmira, New York, where he arrived on July 17, 1864. Thomas died at Elmira on June 12, 1865, of "chronic diarrhoea." Thomas's name is listed on the Memorial Monument for the Davie County men who died in the Civil War, 1861–1865.

380. Foster, William H.
Private, Company E, 42nd Regiment • N.C. Troops

William was born October 4, 1831. Shortly before enlisting for the war, William married Martha M. Laird (1843, Davie). He enlisted in Davie County on December 4, 1862, for the war. He was present or accounted for until November–December, 1863, when he was reported absent without leave. No further military information is known. William eventually resumed his life in Davie County where he remained until his death. In 1870 he was a farm laborer in Fulton District. William and Martha were the parents of four children: Phoebe Jane (1863), Susan F. (1867), William T. (1876) and James F. (1879). William died in 1900 and is buried in Fork Baptist Church Cemetery. Martha died in 1896 and is also buried there.

381. Foster, William M.
Private, Company E, 42nd Regiment • N.C. Troops

W.M. was born in 1823 in Davie County. In 1850 he worked as a wagon-maker and was married to Lydia; they had a small son, Henery (1849). Lydia died and William married Emeline Potts on January 12, 1854. Their children were Brandon (Brainard) (1855), Zenas D. (1857), Weldon E. (1862), William S. (1865) and Emily J. (1867). W.M. enlisted in Davie County at age 30, on July 10, 1862, for the war. He was present or accounted for until he "deserted April 1, 1864." He was reported as a deserter on the July–August, 1864, muster roll. He was paroled at Salisbury, North Carolina, in 1865. No dates are given for his death but W.M. is buried in Bethlehem United Methodist Church Cemetery.

382. Foster, William M.
Private • Captain William E. Booe's Partisan Rangers • N.C. Volunteers • Company H, 63rd Regiment • (5th Regiment N.C. Cavalry) • N.C. Troops

William enlisted in Davie County at age 39, March 18, 1862. He was present or accounted for through October 1864, and paroled at Salisbury, North Carolina, on June 1, 1865. He is buried in New Union United Methodist Church Cemetery.

383. Fraley, Henry L.
Private, Company B, Carolina Rangers • 10th Virginia Cavalry Regiment

Henry was born in 1846 in Davie County to George A. (1813, Davidson) and Mary (1811, Virginia) Fraley. He enlisted in Davie County on December 1, 1863, at age 17. He was present through April 1, 1864, then absent wounded May 1, 1864, until October 1, 1864. He served on a horse detail July 8, 1864, and received clothing in September and December 1864. He was captured at Ford's Depot on April 3, 1865, and sent to Point Lookout where he was released June 12, 1865. He returned home to Davie where he married Amanda Jane Sain/Lain on August 5, 1866.

384. Fraley, John H.
Private, 1st Company A, Salisbury Prison Guard • "The Rough and Readys" • Company G, 66th Regiment • N.C. Troops

John was born in 1842 in Rowan County to Jesse E. (1815, Rowan) and Nancy (1817, Rowan) Fraly [*sic*]. By 1860 they were living in the Fulton District of Davie County where his father farmed and John worked as a laborer prior to enlisting. He served as a Private in 1st Company A, Salisbury Prison Guard and transferred to Company G of the 66th on October 2, 1863. He was reported present through December 31, 1863. He was reported on detail in the quartermaster department at Salisbury from February 14 until October 14, 1864, when he rejoined the company. On December 27, 1864, he was hospitalized at Wilmington with intermittent fever. He returned to duty on January 14, 1865, but was hospitalized again two days later, January 16, 1865, with catarrh. He returned to duty on January 23, 1865, and was paroled at Salisbury, North Carolina, on May 1, 1865. He took the Oath of Allegiance there on May 31, 1865.

385. Fraley, John T.
Second Lieutenant, "Guilford Guards" • Second Company E, 2nd Regiment • N.C. State Troops

John was born in 1842 in Rowan County to Jesse E. (1815, Rowan) and Nancy (1817, Rowan) Fraley. He resided as a farmer in Davie County,

Fulton District, prior to enlisting in Guilford County at age 19, July 26, 1861, for the war. He mustered in as a Private and was appointed Corporal on December 1, 1861, then promoted to Sergeant on April 19, 1862, and Second Lieutenant to rank from September 23, 1862. He was present or accounted for until he died of wounds received in battle at Spotsylvania Court House, Virginia, on May 15, 1864. John's name is not presently listed on the Memorial Monument for the Davie County men who died in the Civil War, 1861–1865.

386. Fraley, Milas J.
Private, "Guilford Guards" • Second Company E, 2nd Regiment • N.C. State Troops

Milas was born in 1839 in Rowan County to Jesse E. (1815, Rowan) and Nancy (1817, Rowan) Fraley. He was a student and farmer in the Fulton District of Davie County prior to enlisting at age 23, on September 1, 1862, for the war. He died in camp near Fredericksburg, Virginia, on March 17, 1863. Milas's name is not presently listed on the Memorial Monument for the Davie County men who died in the Civil War, 1861–1865.

387. Fray (Frey), Benjamin F.
Private, Company G, 5th Regiment • N.C. State Troops

Benjamin was born in 1842 to A. Frey (1813, North Carolina) and Cintha (1818, North Carolina). They resided in the Farmington District prior to his enlistment in Northampton County at age 20, August 13, 1862, for the war. He died at Guinea Depot, Virginia, January 21, 1863, of disease. Benjamin's name is not presently listed on the Memorial Monument for the Davie County men who died in the Civil War, 1861–1865.

388. Frost, Calvin E.
Private, Company G, 5th Regiment • N.C. State Troops

Calvin was born in 1840 in Davie County to Samuel (1791, Davie) and Jane (1801, Rowan) Frost. In 1860 he worked as a laborer in the Mocksville District where he lived with his parents prior to enlisting in Northampton County at age 22, on August 13, 1862, for the war. He died in the hospital at Mount Jackson, Virginia, on November 10, 1862, of "febris typhoides." Calvin's name is not presently listed on the Memorial Monument for the Davie County men who died in the Civil War, 1861–1865.

389. Frost, Eberneza (Ebenezer)
Second Lieutenant • Company K, 77th Regiment, 19th Division • N.C. Militia 1861–1865

Eberneza was born February 4, 1840, in Davie County, to Isaac N. (1799, Davie) and Mary (1810, Davie) Frost. They farmed in the Chinquepin District of Davie prior to the war. When the militia was activated, Eberneza was appointed Second Lieutenant of Company K. On November 15, 1864, he married Maria Tabitha (1839, Davie) Eaton. They moved to the Clarksville District of Davie where they apparently lived busy but quite comfortable lives. They had no children but Tabitha's niece, Josephine Baity, was her housekeeper and there were two indentured servants (bound) to work in the home and in the tobacco factory, along with two of Eberneza's brothers, Benjamin and John C., one to work on the farm and one to work as a tobacco trader. Ebenezer died on October 4, 1903, and is buried in Eaton's Baptist Church Cemetery. Elizabeth died on October 27, 1909.

390. Frost, J.F. (James)
Private • Captain William E. Booe's Partisan Rangers • N.C. Volunteers • Company H, 63rd Regiment • (5th Regiment N.C. Cavalry) • N.C. Troops

James was born in North Carolina, in 1839. He worked as a laborer and lived in the Chinquepin District with the H. Critz family when he enlisted on July 11, 1862, for the war. He was present or accounted for through August 1864, being detailed as a teamster from September–October, 1863, through August 1864. He was issued clothing September 26, 1864. James was paroled at Salisbury, North Carolina, in 1865. He returned to Clarksville and farmed for the rest of his life. He married Elizabeth Cordelia and they became the parents of seven children: James S. (1869), Horace D. (1871), Henry M. (1873), Mary B. (1874), William F. (1876), Frances C. (1879) and "Frost, not named" (1880). James died on March 12, 1913. He is buried in Bear Creek Baptist Church Cemetery.

391. Frost, James D. (Commissary Sergeant)
Private, Company F, 42nd Regiment • N.C. Troops

James enlisted in Rowan County at age 26, on May 16, 1862, for the war. He was assigned to temporary duty as Acting Quartermaster Sergeant during September–December 1862, and transferred to the Field and Staff of this regiment. He rejoined the company in January–February 1863, and was present or accounted for until he was promoted to Commissary Sergeant in November–December 1863, and assigned to permanent duty with the Field and Staff of this regiment.

392. Frost, William A.
Private, Company B, Carolina Rangers • 10th Virginia Cavalry Regiment

William was born October 28, 1844, in Davie County to Isaac N. (1799, Davie) and Mary (1810, Davie) Frost. They farmed in the Clarksville District of Davie where William enlisted on October 29, 1861, at age 18. He was present through April 30, 1862, and died on July 23, 1862. His name is listed on the Memorial Monument for the Davie County men who died in the Civil War, 1861–1865. William is buried in Frost Family Cemetery. His cemetery marker reads: Died in the Confederate Service in Richmond, Virginia, July 23, 1862.

393. Fry, Albert W.
Private, Company E, 42nd Regiment • N.C. Troops

Albert enlisted in Davie County on August 26, 1863, for the war. He was present or accounted for through April 1864. He was wounded near Petersburg, Virginia, on an unspecified date. Albert died in hospital at Richmond, Virginia, on August 1–3, 1864, of wounds. Albert's name is listed on the Memorial Monument for the Davie County men who died in the Civil War, 1861–1865.

394. Fry, George W.
Private • Captain William E. Booe's Partisan Rangers • N.C. Volunteers • Company H, 63rd Regiment • (5th Regiment N.C. Cavalry) • N.C. Troops

George was born in 1841 in Davie County to David (1809, Davidson) and Sarah (1816, Davie) Frost. His father was a miller in the Shady Grove District and George was a farmer when he enlisted in Davie County at age 21, on July 8, 1862, for the war. He was wounded and captured at Upperville, Virginia, June 21, 1863, and confined at Old Capitol Prison, Washington, D.C., until paroled and exchanged at City Point, Virginia, June 30, 1863. He was present or accounted for through December 1864. George returned home, married Roxana Shaver on January 25, 1866, and settled in Fulton District where he worked again as a miller. By 1880 there were five children: Mary F. (1868), Clara (1869), George (1875), Lula (1876) and Samuel (1880). Roxanna died in 1887 and George W. died in 1906. Both are buried in Fulton United Methodist Church Cemetery.

395. Fry, James
Private, Company E, 42nd Regiment • N.C. Troops

James enlisted in Davie County on April 15, 1864, for the war. He was present or accounted for until he deserted on August 10, 1864.

396. Fry, William
Corporal, Company F, 7th Regiment • N.C. State Troops

William was born in 1838 in Davie County. He resided in Caldwell County where he worked as a farmer prior to enlisting in Alamance County at age 23, June 22, 1861, for the war. He mustered in as a Private and was present or accounted for until wounded at Fredericksburg, Virginia, December 13, 1862. He rejoined the company in March–April, 1863, was promoted to Corporal on September 1, 1864, present or accounted for through October 1864, and was paroled at Greensboro, North Carolina, on May 1, 1865.

397. Furches, John M.
Private, "Davie Sweep Stakes" • Company G, 4th Regiment • N.C. State Troops • Company G/M, 7th Regiment • Confederate Cavalry • Company E, 16th Battalion • N.C. Cavalry

John was born February 24, 1838, to Stephen L. (1805, Davie) and Mary (1815, Davie) Furches. He was a student in his early years, later working as a clerk in Farmington. John enlisted in Company G, 4th Regiment, for the war, at age 23, June 11, 1861. He was present or accounted for until he was transferred to either Company G or Company M, 7th Regiment, Confederate Cavalry on September 5, 1863. He was transferred to Company E, 16th Battalion N.C. Cavalry on July 11, 1864. He was present or accounted for through October 1, 1864. John lived with his mother in Farmington after the war and died on March 22, 1901. He is buried in Eaton's Baptist Church Cemetery. John served with his bothers, Thomas and William.

398. Furches, Lewis Alexander
Private, Company A, 57th Regiment • N.C. Troops

Lewis was born in 1832 in Davie County to Thomas (1800, Davie) and Elizabeth (1809, Davie). Lewis married Mary Ann (1837, North Carolina) prior to 1860. He enlisted in Rowan

Lewis Alexander Furches built this house soon after his marriage to Mary Ann Eaton on December 8, 1858 (Mohney, *The Historic Architecture of Davie County*).

County at age 29, July 4, 1862, for the war. He was reported present through October 1862, wounded in the breast at Fredericksburg, Virginia, December 13, 1862, hospitalized at Richmond, Virginia, and furloughed for forty days on or about February 13, 1863. He was reported absent wounded or absent on furlough until January 18, 1864, when he was reported absent without leave. He returned to duty in September–October, 1864, and was reported present but on duty at division headquarters in November–December, 1864. He rejoined the company in January–February, 1865, and surrendered at Appomattox Court House, Virginia, April 9, 1865. In the meantime, Lewis and Mary Ann had become parents to Samuel (1860), Bettie (1863), Sallie (1865) and Mattie (1867). Mary Ann died on February 16, 1871. Lewis then married Martha T. Eaton (1840) and they had three sons: Lewis (1872), Thomas (1875) and Daniel (1878). Martha died on June 2, 1881. Lewis was a farmer in the Farmington area. He died on January 5, 1906, and is buried in Eaton's Baptist Church Cemetery.

399. Furches, Samuel W.
Private, "Davie Greys" • Company F, 13th Regiment • (3rd Regiment, N.C. Volunteers) • N.C. Troops

Samuel was born in 1836 in Davie County. He resided with his parents Thomas (1800, Davie) and Elizabeth (1809, Davie) Furches, prior to enlisting in Davie at age 25, August 6, 1861. He was present or accounted for until captured at Frederick, Maryland, September 12, 1862. He was confined at Fort Delaware, Delaware, until transferred to Aiken's Landing, James River, Virginia, October 2, 1862, for exchange. He was declared exchanged at Aiken's Landing on November 10, 1862. Prior to March 1, 1863, Samuel rejoined the company and was wounded in the right hand and right wrist at Chancellorsville, Virginia, May 3, 1863. He rejoined the company on March–April, 1864, but was retired to the Invalid Corps on April 20, 1864, and was paroled at Mocksville on June 9, 1865. By 1880 S.W. was a farmer, married to Mary L. and living in the Clarksville District with five children: William T. (1871), Milton Z. (1872), Flora A. (1874), Charles V. (1875) and Millard S. (1879).

400. Furches, Thomas G.
Private, Company M, 7th Regiment • Confederate Cavalry • Company E, 16th Battalion • N.C. Cavalry

Thomas was born in 1836 in Davie County to Stephen L. (1805, Davie) and Mary (1815, Davie) Furches. In 1860 the family farmed in the Farmington District. On September 3, 1862, Thomas enlisted with the rank of Private on July 11, 1864; he was transferred from Company M, 7th Regiment Confederate Cavalry to Company E, 16th Battalion N.C. Cavalry. He was present or accounted for through October 1, 1864. Thomas served in this company with his brothers, John and William.

401. Furches, Thomas W. (H.)
Private, "Davie Greys" • Company F, 13th Regiment • (3rd Regiment, N.C. Volunteers) • N.C. Troops

Thomas was born March 9, 1840, in Davie County to Thomas (1798, Davie) and Elizabeth (1808, Davie). They resided and farmed in the Farmington District of Davie where Thomas enlisted at age 22, August 6, 1861. He was present or accounted for until wounded and captured at Williamsburg, Virginia, May 5, 1862. He was hospitalized at Washington, D.C., until transferred to Old Capitol Prison, Washington, June 11, 1862, then exchanged at Aiken's Landing, James River, Virginia, August 5, 1862. He rejoined the company prior to March 1, 1863, and was killed at Chancellorsville, Virginia, May 3, 1863. He is buried at Eaton's Baptist Church Cemetery. Thomas's name is listed on the Memorial Monument for the Davie County men who died in the Civil War, 1861–1865.

402. Furches, W.F. (William)
Third Sergeant, Company M, 7th Regiment • Confederate Cavalry • Company E, 16th Battalion • N.C. Cavalry

William was born in 1840 in Davie County to Stephen L. (1805, Davie) and Mary (1815, Davie) Furches. Prior to the war he lived with his parents in Farmington District where he worked as a laborer. He enlisted in Davie County on September 3, 1862, with the rank of Third Sergeant. He was transferred from Company M, 7th Regiment Confederate Cavalry to Company E, 16th Battalion N.C. Cavalry on July 11, 1864. He was present or accounted for through October 1, 1864, and paroled at Appomattox Court House, Virginia, April 9, 1865. He returned home, married Lou Howell on December 25, 1877, and by 1880, at age 40, was head of an extended family which included John D. (1880), his mother (who was blind), Virginia (1855), Sarah L. (1862) granddaughter, and Henry (1863) grandson. William lived until 1918. He is buried in Eaton's Baptist Church Cemetery. William served in this company with his brothers, John and Thomas.

403. Gabard, William
Private, Company E, 42nd Regiment • N.C. Troops

William was born in 1845. In 1860 he lived with the W.F. Miller family in the Fulton District, where he worked as a laborer. He enlisted in Davie County at age 17, on March 18, 1862. He was reported absent without leave on June 30, 1862. William returned to duty prior to September 1, 1862, and was present or accounted for until wounded in an unspecified action on August 20, 1864. He was reported absent wounded through October 1864.

404. Gaither, David
Private, Company M, 7th Regiment • Confederate Cavalry • Company E, 16th Battalion • N.C. Cavalry

In 1860 David lived in the Calahaln District of Davie County, on the farm of Emely [*sic*] Gaither, where he worked as a laborer. He enlisted in Davie on September 3, 1862, with the rank of Private. On July 11, 1864, he was transferred from Company M, 7th Regiment Confederate Cavalry to Company E, 16th Battalion N.C. Cavalry, while absent without leave. He was reported as such through October 1, 1864. He was paroled at Salisbury, North Carolina, in 1865, and returned to Davie County, Clarksville District, where he lived with the Andrew Etchison family as a "boarder and trader."

405. Gaither, George W.
Private, Company H, 57th Regiment • N.C. Troops

George was born on October 27, 1832, in Davie County. He was the son of Basil (1808, Davie) and Eleanor (1812, Davie). He worked as a miller in the Mocksville District. George enlisted at age 32, on July 4, 1862, for the war. He was hospitalized at Richmond, Virginia, on October 3, 1862, with typhoid fever, but returned to duty on October 12, 1862. He was hospitalized again at Richmond on November 9, 1862, but again returned to duty on November 27, 1862. He was then hospitalized at Richmond on April 28, 1863, with pleuritis, and transferred to the hospital at Danville, Virginia, on May 8, 1863. He returned to duty prior to September 1, 1863, and was detailed as an ambulance driver, but was reported absent on detail on surviving company muster rolls through April 30, 1864. George rejoined the company in May–August, 1864, and was captured at Cedar Creek, Virginia, on October 19, 1864, and confined at Point Lookout, Maryland, on October 25, 1864. He was paroled there on March 28, 1865, and received at Boulware's Wharf, James River, Virginia, on March 30, 1865, for the exchange. On January 7, 1869, he and Mary A. Wilson were married. They had three daughters: Mary E. (1870), Maggie E. (1873) and Sarah J. (1879). George died in 1891. He is buried in Oak Grove United Methodist Church Cemetery.

406. Gaither, Greenberry
Private, Company M, 7th Regiment • Confederate Cavalry • Company E, 16th Battalion • N.C. Cavalry

Greenberry was born May 2, 1831, in North Carolina. In 1860 he lived with his wife Mary E. (1833, Virginia) in the Calahaln District of Davie, with their daughter Melissa A.E.V. (1858). He enlisted on September 3, 1862, with the rank of Private. On July 11, 1864, he was transferred from Company M, 7th Regiment Confederate Cavalry to Company E, 16th Battalion N.C. Cavalry. He was present or accounted for through October 1, 1864, but had the very bad luck to be captured at Petersburg, Virginia, just six days before the surrender was signed on April 9, 1865. He was confined at Point Lookout, Maryland, until released after taking the Oath of Allegiance on June 27, 1865. He returned to his family and farm life in Davie; two sons were added: Richard (1861) and John (1867). Greenberry died on December 26, 1915, and is buried in Society Baptist Church Cemetery.

407. Gaither, James M.
Private, Company H, 57th Regiment • N.C. Troops

James was born in 1834, the son of Basil (1808, Davie) and Elenor [sic] (1812, Davie). He was also the brother of George W. Gaither of this company. James was a farmer who lived in the Mocksville District and on July 4, 1862, at age 30, he enlisted for the war. He was reported present or accounted for through February 28, 1863. He was hospitalized at Richmond, Virginia, on April 25, 1863, with pneumonia. He was then transferred to the hospital at Danville, Virginia, on May 8, 1863. He returned to duty on June 12, 1863, where he was detailed as a teamster prior to September 1, 1863, and on surviving company muster rolls through April 30, 1864. He then rejoined the company in May–August, 1864, and was captured at Cedar Creek, Virginia, on October 19, 1864. James was confined at Point Lookout, Maryland, on October 25, 1864, and released there on June 16, 1865, after taking the Oath of Allegiance. James returned to farming but he was crippled. He died in 1886 and is buried in Oak Grove United Methodist Church Cemetery.

408. Gaither, Lemuel G.
First Lieutenant, Company G, 7th Regiment • Confederate Cavalry • Company D, 16th Battalion • N.C. Cavalry

Lemuel was born in 1838 in Davie County to Ephraim (1809, Davie) and Sarah (1812, Rowan) Gaither. He was part of a prosperous, productive farm enterprise with nineteen slaves. The family of eight also shared their home with two boarders, both music teachers. Lemuel enlisted in Company G, 7th Regiment, Confederate Cavalry and transferred to Company D, 16th Battalion N.C. Cavalry on July 11, 1864. He was present or accounted for through October 1, 1864, and paroled in Salisbury, North Carolina, in 1865. Lemuel returned home where his father had become Register of Deeds and where Lemuel became a merchant and manufacturer. He married Sallie L., and by 1880 they were the parents of Essie (1875) and Carrie (1877). He died in 1913 and is buried in Rose Cemetery. Sallie's application for a pension is on file in the State Archives, Raleigh, North Carolina.

409. Gaither, Wiley
Private, Company G, 5th Regiment • N.C. State Troops

Wiley was born in 1827 in Iredell County to Sarah (1805, Iredell) Gaither. They resided in Davie County where he worked as a farmer in 1850. He married Margaret C. Campbell. He enlisted in Northampton County at age 35, August 13, 1862, for the war. He was present or accounted for until he deserted in May 1863. He rejoined the company in September–October, 1863, and was present or accounted for until wounded in the neck and captured at Spotsylvania Court House, Virginia, May 9, 1864. He died on or about May 9, 1864. The place of death was not reported. Margaret's application for a widow's pension is on file at the State Archives, Raleigh, North Carolina; her application was approved. Letters are also on file in Davie County Library, Mocksville. Wiley's name is not presently listed on the Memorial Monument for the Davie County men who died in the Civil War, 1861–1865.

410. Gaither, William H.
Private, "Davie Sweep Stakes" • Company G, 4th Regiment • N.C. State Troops

William was born in 1840 in Davie County to Ephraim (1809) and Sarah Hall (1812, Rowan) Gaither. He enlisted at age 21, June 4, 1861, for the war. He was present or accounted for until killed at Chancellorsville, Virginia, May 3, 1863. Both of William's parents are buried in Joppa Cemetery. William's name is listed on the Memorial Monument for the Davie County men who died in the Civil War, 1861–1865.

411. Gaither, Zadock L.
Private, Company F, 42nd Regiment • N.C. Troops • Company M, 7th Regiment • Confederate Cavalry • Company E, 16th Battalion • N.C. Cavalry

Zadock was born in North Carolina, in 1841. He lived alone in the Chinquepin District of Davie County until he married Simantha [sic] M. Clifford on September 20, 1860. Zadock enlisted in Company F, 42nd Regiment as a Private, on April 5, 1862. He was present or accounted for until transferred to Company M, 7th Regiment Confederate Cavalry, November 26, 1862. On July 11, 1864, he was transferred to Company E, 16th Battalion N.C. Cavalry. He was present or accounted for through October 11, 1864, and paroled at Salisbury, North Carolina, in 1865.

412. Garwood (Garrawood), David T.
Private, Company E, 42nd Regiment • N.C. Troops

David was born in 1835 in Davie County. He was the son of John (1799, Davie) and Zelah (1805, Davie) Garwood. In 1860 he lived with the S. Baily family in Fulton while working as a laborer. David enlisted at age 25, on March 18, 1862, in Davie. He was present or accounted for through October 1864. He was paroled at Salisbury, North Carolina, on May 22, 1865. (North Carolina pension records indicate he was wounded at Kinston on March 25, 1864.) David married Margaret Foster on January 2, 1866; their daughter, Eliza J. was born in 1866. His second wife was Jane Veach who married David on December 30, 1869; they had two boys: John F. (1870) and William W. (1873). He married his third wife Mary E. Sheets, on September 21, 1876. David continued to farm in the Fulton District. He died on February 24, 1916, and is buried in Advance United Methodist Church Cemetery.

413. Garwood, Lewis B. (Burton)
Private, Company B, Carolina Rangers • 10th Virginia Cavalry Regiment • Company B, 42nd N.C. Infantry

Burton was born in 1843 in Davie County to John (1799, Davie) and Zelah (1805, Davie) Garriwood [sic]. They were farming in Davie when Lewis enlisted on November 18, 1861, at age 16. He was captured at White Oak Swamp on August 5, 1862, and sent to Fort Wool where he was exchanged November 10, 1862. He was present until March 4, 1863, when he was absent on detail; he was absent without leave in May and June and when arrested he was absent two more months. On October 18, 1863, he was sick in Richmond hospital with gonorrhea. He was sent to Castle Thunder on October 29, 1863, and was present until sent to Richmond hospital with "Orchitis" on April 1, 1864. He returned to duty on April 10, 1864, and lost his spurs June 23, 1864. He transferred to Company B, 42nd Infantry on July 29, 1864, and was paroled in Salisbury, North Carolina, on May 22, 1865. Burt married Mary (Elizabeth?) and they lived in the Fulton District where they farmed and raised their children: John (1864), Robert (1867), Mary J. (1871), Sarah F. (1873), Lula Bell (1875) and George W. (1877).

414. Garwood, Robert
Private, Company E, 42nd Regiment • N.C. Troops

Robert was born in 1839 in Davie County. He was the son of John (1799, Davie) and Zelah (1805, Davie) Garriwood [sic]. Robert was also the brother of David Garwood of this company. Robert married Mary Walls on February 4, 1862. He enlisted in Davie County at age 23, on March 18, 1862. He was present or accounted for until killed in an unspecified action on September 1, 1864. Robert's name is listed on the Memorial Monument for the Davie County men who died in the Civil War, 1861–1865.

415. Gatton, Franklin
Private, "Davie Greys" • Company F, 13th Regiment • (3rd Regiment, N.C. Volunteers) • N.C. Troops

Franklin was born in 1840 in Davie County to Henderson (1805, Davie) and Martha (1810, Iredell). Henderson worked as a blacksmith and lived in the Calahaln District and Franklin worked as a laborer. On April 26, 1861, he enlisted in Davie at age 21. He was present or accounted for until wounded at Chancellorsville, Virginia, May 3, 1863. He rejoined the company in November–December, 1863, and died in the hospital at Gordonsville, Virginia, on January 14, 1864, of "pneumonia." Franklin's name is listed on the Memorial Monument for the Davie County men who died in the Civil War, 1861–1865.

416. Gatton, Harrison
Private, "Davie Greys" • Company F, 13th Regiment • (3rd Regiment, N.C. Volunteers) • N.C. Troops

Harrison was born in 1840 in Davie County. In 1850 he lived with Matilda (1790, Delaware) and Mariam (1820, Davie). He was a farmer prior to enlisting in Davie at age 21, April 26, 1861. He was present or accounted for until wounded at Chancellorsville, Virginia, May 3, 1863. He rejoined the company in September–October, 1863, and was present or accounted for until paroled at Appomattox Court House, Virginia, April 9, 1865. He was paroled again in Mocksville on June 9, 1865. Harrison and Temperance F. Grimes had married in Davie County, December 29, 1863. After the war he resumed family life and by 1870, they were the parents of Pearson (1867) and Ida (1869). In 1880 the family lived in Calahaln where Harrison worked as a "Stiller."

417. Gatton, James
Private, Company D, 42nd Regiment • N.C. Troops

James resided in Davie County and enlisted in Rowan County at age 30, March 26, 1862. He died on May 31–June 1, 1862. The place and cause of death were not reported. James's name is listed on the Memorial Monument for the Davie County men who died in the Civil War, 1861–1865.

418. Gatton, Pleasant
Private, Company F, 42nd Regiment • N.C. Troops

Pleasant was born in 1831 in North Carolina. In 1860 he was married to Amanda (1835, North Carolina) and was farming in the Chinquepin District. At age 31 he enlisted in Davie County on March 24, 1862. Pleasant was present or accounted for until killed near Bermuda Hundred, Virginia, on May 20, 1864. Pleasant Gatton's name is listed on the Memorial Monument for the Davie County men who died in the Civil War, 1861–1865.

419. Gaugh, John
Private • Captain William E. Booe's Partisan Rangers • N.C. Volunteers • Company H, 63rd Regiment • (5th Regiment N.C. Cavalry) • N.C. Troops

John enlisted in Davie County on July 30, 1862, for the war. He was captured at Hagerstown, Maryland, July 12, 1863, and confined at Point Lookout, Maryland, until paroled and exchanged at City Point, Virginia, March 20, 1864. He was reported as a deserter on the August 1864 muster roll.

420. Gentle, Jordan M.
Private, Company D, 42nd Regiment • N.C. Troops

Jordan enlisted in Davie County at age 22, January 30, 1862. He was present or accounted for through June 30, 1862. He was listed as a deserter who was in the hospital at Richmond, Virginia, in July–August, 1862. No further records.

421. Gheen (Ghean), William
Private, Company E, 42nd Regiment • N.C. Troops

William was born in Davie County in 1846. He was the son of James (1817, Davie) and Temperance (1821, Davie) Ghean [sic]. He enlisted in Davie on April 15, 1864, for the war. He was reported in prison at Petersburg, Virginia, under charges of deserting during May–October, 1864. He was paroled at Greensboro, North Carolina, on an unspecified date in 1865.

422. Glasscock, Abner
Private • Captain William E. Booe's Partisan Rangers • N.C. Volunteers • Company H, 63rd Regiment • (5th Regiment N.C. Cavalry) • N.C. Troops

Abner was born in Davie County in 1829, to James (1788, Davie) and Sarah (1792, Davie) Glasscock. The family farmed in the Chinquepin District when the war began and Abner, age 30, furnished John Bracken as his substitute.

423. Gobble, Henry C.
Private, 1st Company A, Salisbury Prison Guard • "The Rough and Readys" • Company G, 66th Regiment • N.C. Troops

Henry was born in 1842. He served as a Private in 1st Company A, until he transferred to Company G of the 66th on October 2, 1863. He was reported present through October 31, 1864. There were no further records. He survived the war. Henry and Margaret C. Davis were married in Davie County on October 2, 1866. Florence was born in 1868, followed by John W.B. (1869), Sarah C. (1872), Mary E. (1874) and Henry (1878). In 1880 the family lived in the Jerusalem District of Davie County where Henry worked as a farmer.

424. Gowan, Richard W.
Private, Company E, 42nd Regiment • N.C. Troops

Richard was born in Davie County where he resided prior to enlisting in Davie on January 20, 1863, for the war. He was present or accounted for until wounded near Petersburg, Virginia, on or about July 14–15, 1864. Richard was reported absent wounded through October 1864. He was paroled at Mocksville on June 3, 1865.

425. Gowen, Simeon C.
Private, Company E, 42nd Regiment • N.C. Troops

Simeon was born in 1847 in Davie County. He was a farmer when he enlisted at age 17, in Davie on July 1, 1864, for the war. He was present or accounted for through October 1864, and was paroled at Mocksville on June 3, 1865. Lucy Ann (1839) Bowles and Simeon were married on May 20, 1866. She and Simeon would be parents of four children: Mary (1867), William T. (1869), Maggie M. (1872) and Alice O. (1875). The family farmed in the Mocksville and Fulton Districts of Davie. Simeon died in 1933 and is buried in Center United Methodist Church Cemetery.

426. Granger, James F.
Private, Company F, 42nd Regiment • N.C. Troops

James was born in 1840 in North Carolina. At age 15 he lived in the Fulton District with J.R. Parker and sister, Rebeca [sic] Parker, where he worked as a laborer. He enlisted at age 18 on March 24, 1862. He was present or accounted for until he was wounded at Cold Harbor, Virginia, on or about June 1–3, 1864, and returned to duty on September 1, 1864. He was captured at Salisbury on April 12, 1865, and confined at Louisville, Kentucky, on May 1, 1865. He was transferred to Camp Chase, Ohio, on May 4, 1865, and released there on June 13, 1865, after taking the Oath of Allegiance. James married Catharine (1840, Davie) Shives on June 16, 1867. In 1870 they lived in Jerusalem District with two additional members of the household, America Granger (1860) and his sister Martha J. Granger (1855). James provided for his family by farming. He died on January 28, 1907, and is buried in Liberty United Methodist Church Cemetery. Catharine's application for a Civil War pension is on file at the State Archives, Raleigh, North Carolina.

427. Granger, James M.
Private, Company E, 42nd Regiment • N.C. Troops

James was born in 1837 in Davie County. He was living in the Smith Grove District when he married (Nancy) Jane Foster (1840, North Carolina) on August 17, 1859. James was a carpenter prior to enlisting in Davie at age 25, on March 18, 1862. He was present or accounted for until he died in the hospital at Wilmington on January 11, 1864, of "febris typhoides." James's name is listed on the Memorial Monument for the Davie County men who died in the Civil War, 1861–1865.

428. Granger, John Peter
Private • Company F, 42nd Regiment • N.C. Troops

John Peter was born in Iredell County in 1843. He was the son of John F. (1814, Virginia) and Elizabeth (1815, Rowan) Granger. He enlisted in Davie County at age 18, on March 18, 1862. He was present or accounted for through October 1864 and was paroled at Mocksville on June 6, 1865. On December 13, 1868, he married Mary E. Wellmon (1850, North Carolina). In 1870 they lived in the Farmington District where Mary, age 19, was "keeping house" and where Peter worked as a jobber. By 1880 they had moved to Mocksville with their two daughters, Lula F. (1871) and Mary E. (1880).

429. Granger, M.L. (Moses Lee)
Private, Company G, 5th Regiment • N.C. State Troops

M.L. was born in 1838. He married Elizabeth Casey on December 25, 1859; their children were Mary E. (1853) and Marion (1861). The family lived in the Calahaln District prior to M.L.'s enlisting in Northampton County at age 24, August 13, 1862, for the war. He was "sent to hospital" on September 24, 1862. Company muster rolls indicate that he died prior to January 1, 1864. The place, cause and exact date of death were not reported. M.L.'s name is not presently listed on the Memorial Monument for the Davie County men who died in the Civil War, 1861–1865.

430. Granger, W. Burton
Private, Company F, 42nd Regiment • N.C. Troops

Burton was born in 1845 in North Carolina, to William and Leah Granger. He enlisted in Davie County at age 18, on March 18, 1862. He was present or accounted for through October 1864. On December 26, 1867, Burton married Mary F. Leach. They settled in the Mocksville District where they farmed. Mary died on June 4, 1916, and Burton died on May 24, 1926. He is buried in the Center United Methodist Church Cemetery.

431. Grant, A.T.
Private, Company A, 57th Regiment • N.C. Troops

A.T. was born in Virginia in 1837. He resided in Davie County and married Rebecca Parker (1836, Virginia) on November 11, 1860. A.T. enlisted at age 24, on July 4, 1862, in Rowan County, for the war. He was reported present through May 31, 1863. He served as a hospital clerk and surgeon's orderly during much of that period. He was reported present on surviving company muster rolls through December 31, 1864. A.T. was captured at Hatcher's Run, Virginia, on February 6, 1865, confined at Point Lookout, Maryland, on February 9, 1865, then released there on June 16, 1865, after taking the Oath of Allegiance. Rebecca and A.T. were the parents of five children: Annie P. (1866), Ada R. (1869), Sallie V. (1871), Robinson S. (1874) and John T. (1876). A.T. served for many years as Clerk of Superior Court of Davie County. He died in 1927 and is buried in Rose Cemetery, Mocksville.

432. Graves, Albert N.
Private, Company E, 42nd Regiment • N.C. Troops

Albert was born in Davie County on April 6, 1845. In 1860 he lived in the Fulton District with his parents, Jeremiah (1824, Davie) and Mary Elizabeth (1824, Davie) Graves. At age 19, on August 10, 1864, he enlisted in Davie County for the war. He was present or accounted for until he was captured at or near Wise's Forks, Kinston, North Carolina, on March 10, 1865. He was confined at Point Lookout, Maryland, on March 16, 1865, and was released there on June 27, 1865, after taking the Oath of Allegiance. Albert's father, Jeremiah, also served in this company. After Albert returned from the war, he lived with his parents in the Jerusalem District, where he farmed with his brothers and father. Albert's application for a pension is on file at the State Archives, Raleigh, North Carolina. He died in 1925 and is buried in Liberty United Methodist Church Cemetery.

433. Graves, Andrew J.
Private, Company D, 42nd Regiment • N.C. Troops

Andrew enlisted in Davie County on February 2, 1862. No further records.

434. Graves, Daniel
Private, Company D, 42nd Regiment • Captain William Howard's Company, N.C. Prison Guards • 1st Company A, Salisbury Prison Guard • "The Rough and Readys" • Company G, 66th Regiment • N.C. Troops

Daniel was born in 1824 in Davie County. In 1850 he lived on the farm of David and Sarah Graves where he worked as a farmer. On May 14, 1855, he married Marja I. Stonestreet. Their daughter Sarah E. was born in 1858, in the Mocksville District of Davie where Daniel farmed prior to enlisting there on January 31, 1862. He was transferred to Captain William Howard's Company, N.C. Prison Guards, on or about May 1, 1862. He served as a Private in 1st Company A, Salisbury Prison Guard, then transferred to Company G of the 66th on October 2, 1863. He was reported present through April 30, 1864, and was reported killed at Cold Harbor, Virginia, a month later, June 3, 1864. Daniel's name is not presently listed on the Memorial Monument for the Davie County men who died in the Civil War, 1861–1865.

435. Graves, George F.
Private, Company E, 42nd Regiment • N.C. Troops

George was born in Davie County in 1830, the son of Elizabeth (1797, Davie). He was a farmer in Liberty District when he married Nancy Foster on April 18, 1855. Two years later, he married Amanda Feezer (1829) on January 19, 1858. He was still farming in Liberty prior to enlisting in Davie at the age of 30, on March 24, 1862. He was present or accounted for through October 1864. George was paroled at Salisbury on May 23, 1865. Amanda and George were the parents of four children: Henry J. (1859), Peter G. (1860), George (1862) and John F. (1865). In 1880 they were farming in Jerusalem District. George died in 1903; he is buried in Fork Baptist Church Cemetery. Amanda's application for a pension is on file at the State Archives, Raleigh, North Carolina.

436. Graves, Jacob B.
Private, Company G, 5th Regiment • N.C. State Troops

Jacob was born in 1827 in Davie County. He enlisted in Northampton County at age 35, August 13, 1862, for the war. He was present or accounted for until he deserted in May 1863. He rejoined the company in September–October, 1863, but was reported "in arrest under charge of desertion" in November–December, 1863. He returned to duty prior to March 1, 1864, and was present or accounted for until captured at Spotsylvania Court House, Virginia, on May 12, 1864. He was confined at Point Lookout, Maryland, until transferred to Elmira, New York, August 3,

1864. He died there on December 2, 1864, of "hospital gangrene." Jacob's name is not presently listed on the Memorial Monument for the Davie County men who died in the Civil War, 1861–1865.

437. Graves, Jeremiah
Private, Company E, 42nd Regiment • N.C. Troops

Jeremiah was born in 1820 in Davie County. He was a farmer all his life except for the time he took off to fight in the war. His record states that he enlisted at age 46, March 18, 1862, that he was present or accounted for through October 1864, and that he was paroled at Salisbury, North Carolina, on May 22, 1865. He married three times and fathered ten children. He married Mary Elizabeth Graves on March 20, 1845; Margaret Sutton on September 3, 1850; and (Mary) Polly Hillard on April 16, 1877. The children were Albert (who also served in this company) (1846), Mary (1848), Jesse (1849), Eliza M. (1853), Elizabeth (1855), Ann G. (1859), Thomas (1861), Alice (1863), Catharine (1867) and Martha (1871). The census figures show some puzzling contradictions. Jeremiah is buried in Liberty United Methodist Church Cemetery. His tombstone indicates that he served in the war but no dates are given. It is also probable that there is an error on Mary Elizabeth Graves' tombstone; her date of death is shown as 1877. Perhaps it should be 1847.

438. Graves, John Ellis
Private, Company E, 42nd Regiment • N.C. Troops

John was born in 1827 and resided in Davie where he was a farmer in the Smith Grove District. He married Ethel (Ellen) Mason (1832, North Carolina) on January 21, 1851; their two daughters were Martha J. (1858) and Mary (1860). John enlisted in Davie County, at age 35, on March 18, 1862. He was present or accounted for until he died in the hospital at Weldon on February 27, 1863, of "chronic diarrhoea." Following John's death, Ellen and their daughters lived in the Farmington District of Davie. Ellen's pension application is on file in the State Archives, Raleigh, North Carolina. John's name is listed on the Memorial Monument for the Davie County men who died in the Civil War, 1861–1865.

439. Graves, John Franklin
Private, Company E, 42nd Regiment • N.C. Troops

John was born in 1836 in Davie County. He lived in the Mocksville District with the Chivans and Catherine Spry family. John made a living working as a carpenter; on August 26, 1857, he and Sarah C. (1837) Wishawn (Wishorn) were married. John was married again on January 1, 1860, to Lucinda (1832) Smith. While living in the Mocksville District, John enlisted in Davie County at age 26, on March 18, 1862. He was present or accounted for until captured at or near Cold Harbor, Virginia, on June 1–3, 1864. He was confined at Point Lookout, Maryland, on June 11, 1864, then transferred to Elmira, New York, where he arrived on July 17, 1864. He was paroled at Elmira on March 2, 1865, and transferred to the James River, Virginia, for exchange. He was paroled at Salisbury, North Carolina, on an unspecified date in 1865. John returned home to Davie where he supported his family as a "miller of corn." He and Lucinda had three children: Charles F. (1861), Gannon F. (1863) and Minnie Z. (1867). His pension application is on file at the State Archives, Raleigh, North Carolina.

440. Graves, John W. (H.)
Private, "Davie Greys" • Company F, 13th Regiment • (3rd Regiment, N.C. Volunteers) • N.C. Troops

John was born in 1844 in Davie County. He resided with his parents Wilson (1812, Davie) and Caroline Booe (1817, Davie) Graves in the Mocksville District where he worked as a farmer prior to enlisting in Davie County at age 19, August 6, 1861. He was present or accounted for until wounded in the left hand at Fredericksburg, Virginia, December 13, 1862. His left hand was amputated. He was reported absent wounded or absent on detail as a guard until discharged at Petersburg, Virginia, December 8, 1864, by reason of wounds received at Fredericksburg. John died three years after returning home, July 8, 1868. He is buried in Booe-Hunter-Powell Family Cemetery.

441. Graves, Nathan
Private, Company E, 42nd Regiment • N.C. Troops

Nathan was born in 1827 in Davie County. He was a farmer in the Mocksville District when he married Rebecca Booe on November 27, 1844. They were the parents of William T. (1848), Mary L. (1850), Sarah L. (1852), Nancy E. (1855), Milton G. (1857), Nathan M. (1858) and Martha (1862). Nathan enlisted in Davie County on March 18, 1862. He was present or accounted for until July–August, 1862, when he was reported absent without leave. Nathan was reported absent sick during November 1862–April 1863 and during July–October, 1863. He was reported absent without leave during November–December, 1863, and was paroled at Mocksville on June 3, 1865. Nathan married for the second time on August 24, 1873, to Mary Cline Gordon (1849). Their children were: Laura (1874) and Charles (1878). Ellen Gordon (1868), was Nathan's stepdaughter. In 1870 Nathan was no longer farming but was a cooper living in the Clarksville District.

442. Graves, William H.
Private, Company E, 42nd Regiment • N.C. Troops

William was born in 1843 in Davie County. He and his older brother John lived with the Chivans and Catharine Spry family in the Mocksville District. William worked as a laborer prior to enlisting in Davie at age 19, on or about March 15, 1862. He was present or accounted for through October 1864 and paroled at Salisbury, North Carolina, on May 22, 1865. He had married Mary Ann Banks on July 12, 1864. After the war they settled in the Jerusalem District of Davie where William worked as a farm laborer. Their children were Ida (1866) and William (1869).

443. Gray, G.F. (George F.)
Private, "Davie Greys" • Company F, 13th Regiment • (3rd Regiment, N.C. Volunteers) • N.C. Troops

G.F. was born in 1846 in Davie County. He was the son of Thomas (1815, Currituck) and Eliza (1824, Davie). The family lived in the Fulton District of Davie in 1860 when G.F. was 14 years old. The place and date of his enlistment were not reported and the first listing of his name in this company is dated December 1, 1864. He was paroled at Appomattox Court House, Virginia, four months later on April 9, 1865.

444. Gray, Thomas
Private, Company F, 42nd Regiment • N.C. Troops

Thomas was born in 1844 in Davie County. He made his home with James (1798, Virginia) Gray, probably his father, and worked as a laborer in the Calahaln District prior to enlisting at age 18, March 18, 1862. He was present or accounted for until captured at or near Wise's Forks, Kinston, North Carolina, on March 9, 1865. He was confined at Point Lookout, Maryland, on March 16, 1865, and released there on June 27, 1865, after taking the Oath of Allegiance. North Carolina pension records indicate that he was wounded in an unspecified engagement in 1865. Thomas returned home where he and his father farmed and where Thomas married Elizabeth Dyson on October 23, 1870. In 1880 they continued to live in Calahaln with their two children, Mary E.B. (1867) and Thomas A. (1875). Elizabeth's pension application is on file in the State Archives, Raleigh, North Carolina. Thomas's tombstone at Society Baptist Church Cemetery is inconclusive. It reads:

Thomas Gray
Co. F, 421N.C., C.S.A.

(Perhaps this should be Co. F, 42nd Regiment N.C. Troops, C.S.A.)

No dates given.

445. Green, George E.
Corporal, Company E, 42nd Regiment • N.C. Troops

George was born in 1844, the son of Washington (1810, North Carolina) and Nancy (1813, North Carolina) Green. He lived in the Smith Grove District with his parents where he was an apprentice to his father who was a carpenter. George enlisted in Davie County at age 18, on May 19, 1862, for the war. He mustered in as a Private and was promoted to Corporal in January–February, 1864. He was present or accounted for until he died in the hospital at Richmond, Virginia, on December 19, 1864. The cause of death was not reported. He is buried in the Advance United Methodist Church Cemetery. George's name is listed on the Memorial Monument for the Davie County men who died in the Civil War, 1861–1865.

446. Griffin, Noah J. (G.)
Private, 1st Company A, Salisbury Prison Guard • "The Rough and Readys" • Company G, 66th Regiment • N.C. Troops

Noah was born in 1835 in North Carolina. In 1860 he lived in the Town of Mocksville, in Davie County, with his wife Margaret (1838, North Carolina) and son Thomas H. (1859). He worked as a blacksmith prior to enlisting as a Corporal in 1st Company A. He transferred to Company G of the 66th on October 2, 1863. He mustered in as a Corporal but was reduced to ranks in January–February, 1864. He was reported present through April 30, 1864, then reported sick at home in June–August, 1864. He returned to duty in September–October, 1864. He was captured at Fort Fisher on January 15, 1865, confined at Point

Lookout, Maryland, January 22, 1865, and released at Point Lookout on May 13, 1865, after taking the Oath of Allegiance.

447. Griffin, Samuel C.
Musician, 1st Company A, Salisbury Prison Guard • "The Rough and Readys" • Company G, 66th Regiment • N.C. Troops

Samuel was born in 1839 in North Carolina. He made his home in the Town of Mocksville, with Macage (1805, North Carolina) and Charlotte Griffin. Samuel worked as a carpenter prior to enlisting in 1st Company A, as a Musician (Drummer). He transferred to Company G of the 66th on October 2, 1863. He was hospitalized at Wilmington on November 3, 1863, with chronic bronchitis. He returned to duty November 19, 1863. He was reported absent at Wilmington in January–February, 1864. He rejoined the company in March–April, 1864, and transferred to the regimental band prior to August 31, 1864.

448. Griffin (Griffon), William T.
Sergeant, Company D, 42nd Regiment • Captain William Howard's Company • N.C. Prison Guards • 1st Company A, Salisbury Prison Guard • "The Rough and Readys" • Company G, 66th Regiment • N.C. Troops

William was born in 1828 in Randolph County. In 1850 he lived in Davie County where he worked as a carriage maker and where he married Marie L. Call (1835, Davie), January 20, 1853. They resided in Mocksville and started their family with the birth of Charles in 1856, who was followed by seven other siblings: Alice (1861), Adolphus (1863), Edgars (1866), Lula (1868), Sallie K. (1871), Walter W. (1874) and Carrie B. (1878). William enlisted in Davie County on January 31, 1862, with the rank of Sergeant. He transferred to Captain William Howard's Company on or about May 1, 1862. He served as Sergeant in 1st Company A before being transferred to Company G of the 66th on October 2, 1863. He was reported present through April 30, 1864. He was hospitalized at Petersburg, Virginia, June 24, 1864, with a gunshot wound; the place and date he was wounded were not reported. On June 29, 1864, he was transferred to the hospital at Richmond, Virginia, then reported absent wounded or absent sick through October 31, 1864. He was hospitalized at Raleigh on March 1, 1865, with debilitas. He returned to duty on March 6, 1865, and took the Oath of Allegiance at Mocksville on June 3, 1865. William resumed his occupation as a carriage workman, but in 1880 he served the county as the jailer in Mocksville. He died on September 4, 1888, and is buried in Joppa Cemetery.

449. Griffith, Charles Franklin
First Lieutenant • Company E, 77th Regiment, 19th Division • N.C. Militia 1861–1865

Charles was born March 22, 1825, in Rowan County. In 1850 he and his wife Sarah lived on a farm in Davie County and owned two slaves. Charles was 21 at that time and Sarah was 17. By 1860 two sons had been added to the family: John F. (1852) and William W. (1854). When the militia was activated Charles was appointed First Lieutenant of Company E. The boys were too young to serve, so they survived. The family remained in Farmington and Charles lived to be almost 101 years of age. Both he and Sarah are buried in Macedonia Moravian Church Cemetery. Charles died on February 22, 1926, and Sarah died on January 3, 1906. (See two photographs on page 105.)

450. Grimes, Noah B.
Corporal, Company F, 42nd Regiment • N.C. Troops

Noah was born in 1838 in Davie County to John (1812, Davie) and Eliza (1815, Davie) Grimes. They resided in the Farmington District where his father worked as a farmer and Noah was a laborer prior to enlisting at age 24, March 25, 1862, with the rank of Private. He was promoted to Corporal in May–August, 1864, and was present or accounted for through October 1864. He was killed near Kinston in March 1865. Noah's name is listed on the Memorial Monument for the Davie County men who died in the Civil War, 1861–1865.

451. Grimes, William A.
Private, Company G, 5th Regiment • N.C. State Troops

William was born in 1843 in Davie County. He was a farmer prior to enlisting in Northampton County at age 19, August 13, 1862, for the war. He died in hospital at Guinea Depot, Virginia, May 5, 1863. Cause of death was not reported. There is an application from Martin County for a widow's pension on file at the State Archives, Raleigh, North Carolina. William's name is not presently listed on the Memorial Monument for the Davie County men who died in the Civil War, 1861–1865.

Top: C.F. Griffith completed construction of his house in 1852 (Natalie S. Cash). *Bottom:* Griffith built this house in the 1850s and lived there until his death in 1926, at age 101 (Mohney, *The Historic Architecture of Davie County*).

452. Guffy, Carson A.
Second Lieutenant, "Davie Sweep Stakes" • Company G, 4th Regiment • N.C. State Troops

Carson was born in 1839 in Rowan County to Henry (1801, Davie) and Elizabeth (1809, Iredell) Guffy. He lived and worked as a farm laborer in the Calahaln District of Davie County prior to enlisting at age 22, June 4, 1861, for the war. He mustered in as a Corporal, was promoted to First Sergeant on March 1, 1863, and appointed to Second Lieutenant on May 18, 1864. He was paroled at Appomattox Court House, Virginia, April 9, 1865. In 1870 at age 30 he was living in the Calahaln District. His brother Samuel also served in this company.

453. Guffy, Samuel M.
Private, "Davie Sweep Stakes" • Company G, 4th Regiment • Hospital Steward, Field and Staff, 4th Regiment • N.C. State Troops

Samuel was born in 1833 in Rowan County to Henry (1801, Davie) and Elizabeth (1809, Iredell) Guffy. He resided in Davie County where he enlisted at age 28, June 11, 1861, for the war. He was reported on duty as a nurse or as an acting Hospital Steward on November 14, 1863, and transferred to the Field and Staff of this regiment. Samuel died on September 15, 1867, and is buried in Society Baptist Church Cemetery in Davie County. His tombstone reads: S.M. (Dr.) Guffy.

454. Gullet, Joseph T. (Thomas)
Private, Company H, 57th Regiment • N.C. Troops

Joseph was born in 1846. He was the son of Richmond (1808, Davie) and Mary (1820, Rowan) Gullett. He resided in Davie and enlisted in Rowan County at age 16, on July 4, 1862, for the war as a substitute for William L. Carson. He was reported present through February 28, 1863, then hospitalized at Richmond, Virginia, on March 28, 1863, with pneumonia. He was transferred to Salisbury, North Carolina, on or about April 22, 1863, and returned to duty subsequent to May 11, 1863. He was captured at Gettysburg, Pennsylvania, on or about July 5, 1863, then confined at Fort Delaware, Delaware, on or about July 10, 1863. Joseph was transferred to Point Lookout, Maryland, on October 22, 1863, before he was hospitalized on December 19, 1863, with "chronic diarrhoea." Joseph died at Point Lookout on January 12, 1864. Joseph's name is not presently listed on the Memorial Monument for the Davie County men who died in the Civil War, 1861–1865.

455. Gullet, William
Private, Company M, 7th Regiment • Confederate Cavalry • Company E, 16th Battalion • N.C. Cavalry

William enlisted in Davie County on September 3, 1862, with the rank of Private. On July 11, 1864, he was transferred from Company M, 7th Regiment Confederate Cavalry to Company E, 16th Battalion N.C. Cavalry. He was present or accounted for through October 1, 1864.

456. Hagie (Hajhe) (Hagy), Davidson
Private, "Davie Sweep Stakes" • Company G, 7th Regiment • N.C. State Troops

Davidson was born in 1836 in Davie County to John (1812, Davidson) and Lorena (1818, Davidson) Hagie. He lived in the Shady Grove District of Davie County prior to enlisting at age 25, June 4, 1861, for the war. He was wounded in the shoulder at Seven Pines, Virginia, May 31, 1862. He was reported absent wounded until discharged at Richmond, Virginia, March 21, 1863, by reason of wounds.

457. Haire, Perry
Corporal, Company F, 7th Regiment • N.C. State Troops

Perry was born in 1823 in Iredell County. He resided in Davie where he worked as a carpenter prior to enlisting in Rowan County at age 38, June 29, 1861, for the war. He mustered in as a Private and was promoted to Corporal prior to September 1, 1861. He was present or accounted for until captured at Hanover Court House, Virginia, May 27, 1862. He was held prisoner at Fort Columbus, New York Harbor, until exchanged at Aiken's Landing, James River, Virginia, August 5, 1862. He rejoined the company prior to December 13, 1862, when he was killed at Fredericksburg, Virginia. Perry's name is not presently listed on the Memorial Monument for the Davie County men who died in the Civil War, 1861–1865.

458. Hairston, Peter Wilson

Peter was born in Virginia in 1819 to Samuel (1788, Virginia) and Agnes John Peter Wilson Hairston (1801, Virginia). The family was part of a dynasty that began in 1729 when the first Peter Hairston (ca. 1695, Scotland) arrived in America. Their land holdings were scattered across the South; in Henry County, Virginia, alone, the family owned over 200,000 acres, and in 1851 Samuel was being referred to as the richest man in Virginia. In Davie County, North Carolina, as

This Anglo-Grecian Villa, built in the shape of a Greek Cross, was constructed on Cooleemee Plantation in Davie County over the course of three years (1853–1855). It was commissioned by Peter Wilson Hairston (1819–1886) and today is listed in the National Register of Historic Places (Mohney, *The Historic Architecture of Davie County*).

a part of this wealth, Peter W. Hairston inherited Cooleemee Hill, a plantation of approximately 4,200 acres, along with hundreds of slaves. He married Columbia Lafayette Stuart on November 7, 1849. Their children were Samuel (1850–1867) and Elizabeth (1852–1865). Sadly, Columbia died in childbirth on August 2, 1857. The baby also died. Columbia's brother, James, became famous as General J.E.B. Stuart when the Civil War began. Peter Wilson Hairston and Fanny Caldwell were married June 22, 1859, in St. Luke's Church, Salisbury. Agnes, their first child, was born in August 1860. When war began eight months later, Peter left his young wife at home to confront plantation problems totally unfamiliar to her, while he volunteered to serve as Aide, with the rank of Major, to his kinsman General J.E.B. Stuart. After five months, however, Peter returned home with a letter of commendation for his services, and tackled the myriad problems of running a huge plantation during wartime. It wasn't until after the Battle of Gettysburg in July 1863 that he was finally able to shift the responsibility to Colonel Tiernan Brien, a former member of General Stuart's staff who was recovering from an unknown disability and who was making his temporary home with the Hairstons. Peter was once again able to offer his services as a volunteer aide, this time to Major General Jubal A. Early, another kinsman. He continued in that position until the General, fighting against impossible odds, was relieved of his command March 30, 1865. The source of this write-up is *The Cooleemee Plantation and Its People*, by Peter W. Hairston, 1913–2007.

459. Hall, Ferdinand E. (Eugene)
Corporal, "Davie Sweep Stakes" • Company G, 4th Regiment • N.C. State Troops

Ferdinand was born in Forsyth or Stokes County to John (1807, Pennsylvania) and Mary E. (1818, Stokes) Hall. The family lived in the Farmington District where John worked as a shoemaker. Ferdinand enlisted at age 20, June 4, 1861, for the war, mustering in as a Private. He was wounded at Seven Pines, Virginia, May 31, 1862, rejoined the company in October–December, 1862, and was promoted to Corporal. Ferdinand was killed at Chancellorsville, Virginia, May 3, 1863. He is buried at Macedonia Moravian Church Cemetery in Davie County along with his brother Henry and parents. Ferdinand's name is listed on the Memorial Monument for the Davie County men who died in the Civil War, 1861–1865.

460. Hall, George W.
Sergeant, Company F, 66th Regiment • Musician, Field and Staff, 66th Regiment • N.C. Troops

George was born in 1831 in Ashe County to John (1797, Rowan) and Elizabeth (1812, Davie) Hall. In 1850 George lived with his parents and six siblings in Davie County where his father supported his family working as a blacksmith and George worked as a laborer. He married Rebecca C. Howell, September 11, 1854. When the war began George served as Sergeant in Company F of the 66th Regiment. He was detailed for duty with the regimental band in March–April, 1864, and was appointed Musician and assigned to permanent duty with the regimental band in May–August, 1864. He was reported present on August 31, 1864, and reported absent without leave on March 16, 1865. No further records.

461. Hall, Henry H. (F.)
Private, "Davie Sweep Stakes" • Company G, 4th Regiment • N.C. State Troops

Henry was born in 1842 in Stokes County to John (1807, Pennsylvania) and Mary E. (1818, Stokes) Hall. They lived in the Farmington District of Davie County where Henry enlisted with his brother Ferdinand, at age 18, June 4, 1861, for the war. He mustered in as a Private. He died at Camp Pickens, near Manassas, Virginia, September 5, 1861. The cause of death was not reported. He is buried at Macedonia Moravian Church Cemetery in Davie County, along with his brother Samuel and parents. Henry's name is listed on the Memorial Monument for the Davie County men who died in the Civil War, 1861–1865.

462. Hamilton, William M.
Private, 2nd Company B, 42nd Regiment • N.C. Troops

William was born in 1835 in Davie County. In 1850 as a young boy, he lived with John and Rhoda Foster. On August 23, 1860, he married Catherine Thompson (1843, North Carolina). William resided in Davie, but enlisted in Rowan County at age 27, on March 1, 1862. He was present or accounted for until captured near Fort Fisher on January 15, 1865. William was confined at or near Fort Monroe, Virginia, on or about January 25, 1865. He was transferred to Fort Delaware, Delaware, where he arrived on February 11, 1865. He was later released at Fort Delaware on June 19, 1865, after taking the Oath of Allegiance. In 1870 he lived in the Jerusalem District, where he worked as a farm laborer. He and Catherine were the parents of seven children: John (1862), Mary E. (1865), William T. (1867), Charles H. (1869), Henry J. (1872), H. Bell (1874) and Ida L. (1878). Census figures for 1880 show the family living in the Calahaln District.

463. Hammond (Hammons), Bryant W. (Briant)
Private, Company E, 42nd Regiment • N.C. Troops

Bryant was born in Davie County in 1832 to William (1783, Mecklenburg) and Nancy (1799, Mecklenburg) Hammond. They resided in the Chinquepin District where Bryant worked as a laborer with his father. Bryant married Rachel Revis on March 27, 1854. Their two children were Mary (1856) and William (1859). When the war began Bryant enlisted in Davie at age 30, March 18, 1862. He was present or accounted for through October 1864 and paroled at Mocksville on June 7, 1865.

464. Hanes (Hains), George A.
Private, Company E, 42nd Regiment • N.C. Troops

George was born in 1844 in Davie County to Alexander M. (1809, Davie) and Jane (1812, Davie) Hanes. He lived with his parents in the Fulton District where his father was a tanner and he was a farmer. He enlisted in Davie County on April 15, 1864, for the war. He was killed at Cold Harbor, Virginia, on or about June 3, 1864. (*Clark's Regiments* indicates he was 18 years old at the time of his death.) George is buried in Fulton United Methodist Church Cemetery. His tombstone states that he was killed near Gaines' Mill, Virginia, June 2, 1864. George's name is listed on the Memorial Monument for the Davie County men who died in the Civil War, 1861–1865.

465. Hanes, Harrison Henry
Private, "Davie Sweep Stakes" • Company G, 4th Regiment • N.C. State Troops

Harrison was born in 1841 in Davidson County. He lived with Enos (1808, Davie) and Nancy Phillips (1800, Virginia) James, in the Mocksville District of Davie County. He enlisted in Wake County at age 20, June 15, 1861, for the war. He was wounded at Seven Pines, Virginia, May 31, 1862, and was reported absent wounded through December 1862. During his absence he married Nancy Williams on September 4, 1862. On February 25, 1863, he furnished L.B. King as his substitute. Nancy and Harrison would become the parents of six children: Sallie (1864), Martha (1865), John (1866), Mary Bet (1869), Nancy (1871) and Beulah (1873). They lived in the Farmington District of Davie during the 1870s and 1880s. On January 31, 1884, at age 43, Harrison married Nancy E. Foster, age 35. Their only child was George Clifford Hanes, born January 19, 1887, and died on February 1, 1969. Harrison died on April 30, 1923, and is buried in Smith Grove United Methodist Church Cemetery.

466. Hanes, Jacob H.
Corporal, "Davie Sweep Stakes" • Company G, 4th Regiment • N.C. State Troops

Jacob was born in Davie County, April 3, 1840, to Alexander M. (1809, Davie) and Jane March (1812, Davie) Hanes. They resided in the Shady Grove District of Davie where Jacob enlisted at age 21, June 4, 1861, for the war. He mustered in as a Private and was absent on detached service as a Provost Guard at Gordonsville, Virginia, from December 20, 1861, through April 1863. He was promoted to Corporal on October 1, 1863. He was present or accounted for until killed at Spotsylvania Court House, Virginia, May 12, 1864. Jacob is buried in Fulton United Methodist Church Cemetery. His name is listed on the Memorial Monument for the Davie County men who died in the Civil War, 1861–1865.

467. Hanes, John H.
Sergeant, Company B, 48th Regiment • N.C. Troops

John was born in 1838 in Davie County. He lived with Mary A. (1800, Davie) Hanes in the Shady Grove District of Davie where he enlisted at age 23, March 24, 1862. He mustered in as a Sergeant but was discharged on April 28, 1862, by reason of "imperfect vision." He returned home to Davie County and on November 14, 1865, married Lou C. Clouse. Their children were George A. (1869), Lola (1874) and Lewis (1879). In 1880 the family lived and farmed in Fulton District. John died on February 18, 1915, and is buried in Fulton Methodist Church Cemetery.

468. Hanes, John P.
Private • Captain William E. Booe's Partisan Rangers • N.C. Volunteers • Company H, 63rd Regiment • (5th Regiment N.C. Cavalry) • N.C. Troops

John was born in Davidson County in 1843. He was the son of Enos, a farmer (1808, Davie) and Nancy (1800, Virginia). In 1860 John and his brother Harrison lived in Mocksville where he enlisted at age 19, on July 18, 1862, for the war. He was present or accounted for through August 1864. He was admitted to the hospital at Raleigh, North Carolina, on January 23, 1865, with "onychia" and returned to duty February 27, 1865. John was paroled at Mocksville, North Carolina, June 9, 1865. After the war John returned home and married Hester Ann Young on October 14, 1866. The family farmed in Farmington. Hester Ann and John became the parents of seven children: Rachel (1867), Charles (1869), Sallie (1871), John M. (1873), Mary B. (1875), Valley (1877) and Harrison (1879).

469. Hanes, Pleasant Henderson
Private, Company E, 16th Battalion • N.C. Cavalry

Pleasant was born in 1845 in Davie County to Alexander M. (1809, Davie) and Jane (1812, Davie) Hanes. The family lived in the Shady Grove District of Davie prior to the war; Pleasant traveled to Richmond, Virginia, in 1864 where he enlisted for the war and was paroled at Appomattox Court House, Virginia, on April 9, 1865. His father had died in 1861 and Pleasant returned to live with his mother and make his living as a "huckster" in the Farmington District.

470. Hanes (Hains), Spencer Joseph
Captain, Company E, 42nd Regiment • N.C. Troops

Spencer was born in 1837 in Davie County to Alexander M. (1809, Davie) and Jane (1812, Davie) Hanes. Spencer made his home with his parents in the Fulton District where his father was a tanner and he was a farmer. He was appointed Second Lieutenant on May 10, 1862, the date the company was officially mustered in, for three years or the duration of the war. He was present or accounted for until wounded in the chest, back and/or neck at or near Petersburg, Virginia, July 9,

1864; he was promoted to Captain the next day and was reported absent wounded through December 31, 1864. Major Thom. J. Brown writes in *Clark's Regiments* that Spencer was "an efficient and brave officer." (Confederate hospital records dated July–August, 1864, give his age as 29.) Spencer married Mary J. Clement on September 19, 1865. Their children were Sallie A. (1867), John C. (1869) and Jacob F. (1871). Spencer died on April 9, 1879. He is buried in Fulton United Methodist Church Cemetery. His tombstone states that "He died from the effects of wounds received at a salient near the crater in the works in the defense of his country, July 1864."

Captain and Mrs. Spencer Joseph Hanes. Photograph was taken just prior to his death in 1879 (Davie County Public Library).

471. Hanes, William P.
Sergeant, "Davie Sweep Stakes" • Company G, 4th Regiment • Private, Company C, 48th Regiment • N.C. Troops

William was born in 1840 in Davie County. He lived with Mary A. (1800, Davie) Hanes in the Shady Grove District of Davie where he enlisted at age 21, June 4, 1861, for the war. He mustered in as a Corporal. On September 17, 1862, he was wounded at Sharpsburg, Maryland. Prior to January 1, 1863, he was promoted to Sergeant and rejoined the company in March–April, 1863. He was present or accounted for until he transferred to Company C, 48th Regiment, N.C. Troops, on November 11, 1863, in exchange for Private William R. Moose. William R. mustered in as a Private, Company C, 48th Regiment. He was reported present in March–April and September–October, 1864. He surrendered at Appomattox Court House, Virginia, April 9, 1865. He returned home to Davie where he married Sallie E. Jones, May 8, 1867. Their children were Willie L. (1868), Mary Ellen (1870), Sallie E. (1874) and Joseph G. (1878).

472. Harbin, Allen Alexander
Major, Mocksville Rifles • Colonel, 77th Regiment, 19th Division • N.C. Militia 1861–1865

Allen was born on December 23, 1830, in Davie County, to Caswell (1798, Davie) and Elizabeth Smoot (1805) Harbin. Sadly, Elizabeth died just three days later, at age 25. In 1850 Allen and his father lived in a boarding house in Mocksville operated by Robert F. Johnston; Allen, age 19, was a student and his father was a "Clerk C.C." The other boarders were young men with varied professions: doctor, lawyer, carpenter, merchant, founder and clerk. No doubt dinnertime was an interesting and informative time as they settled in for the evening. Allen married Emma J. Brown on Sunday night, December 28, 1856, in the Presbyterian Church in Mocksville. The Reverend Jesse Rankin performed the ceremony. Allen's father had died only 3 months earlier. By 1860 Allen had assumed the duties of "C.C. Clerk," like his father before him, and he and "Ema J" were living next door to her family. She was a schoolteacher as well as a housewife. The time was 1860 and Allen had been chosen to serve as a Major in the Mocksville Rifles Militia; when war actually began he was given the rank of Colonel and the duties of commanding officer of the 77th Regiment, 19th Division. Following the war Allen and Emma lived in the hotel operated by her brother, Rufus D. Brown. Rufus and another brother William L. did business as Brown and Brother and were leaders in all phases of manufacturing tobacco products. Emma died on June 30, 1901, and Allen died on October 24, 1905. They are buried in Joppa Cemetery along with their parents.

473. Harbin, James H.
Private, Company E, 42nd Regiment • N.C. Troops

James was born in 1841 in Davie County to James B. (1804, Davie) and Casandra (1820, Surry) Harbin. His father was a carpenter and James worked as a laborer in his early years. He was a farmer prior to enlisting in Davie County at age 21, March 18, 1862. He was present or accounted for through October 1864. He served as a teamster during much of the war. He was paroled at Greensboro, North Carolina, on May 1, 1865. In 1870 James worked as a farmer in the Farmington District of Davie and he was the father of a year-old daughter, Ossola. There is no record of her mother.

474. Harding, Green Berry (Patterson)
Sergeant, Company I, 28th Regiment • N.C. Troops

Green Berry was the son of William and Jane Elizabeth Speer Harding. On March 8, 1862, at age 18, he enlisted in Yadkin County with the rank of Private. Three months later, on or about June 27, 1862, he was wounded at Gaines' Mill, Virginia; he would be wounded three more times.

Green Berry Harding was wounded four times before he retired December 28, 1864, by reason of disability (Harvey Harding).

He was wounded at Fredericksburg, Virginia, on or about December 13, 1862. He returned to duty prior to March 1, 1863, and was promoted to Sergeant in March 1863–October 1864. He was wounded at Gettysburg, Pennsylvania, July 1–3, 1863, and returned to duty at an unspecified date. Finally, he was wounded at Gravel Hill, Virginia, on July 28, 1864, when he was "shot in the shoulder by a Yankee Cavalry Pistol. He lay where he fell overnight. When the Burial Detail was gathering bodies for burial next day they noticed that Green Berry was alive. They took him the six miles to the James River and across the river to Ft. Darling on Drewry's Bluff. They dressed the wound and sent him to the Troops Hospital in Richmond. He recuperated there until he was able to travel." He retired from service on December 28, 1864, by reason of disability, and made his home one mile west of Farmington. Green Berry and all his siblings were educated. Following the war he and his wife Elizabeth Steelman Harding continued that tradition; all their children were sent to college to become educators, dentists, lawyers and doctors. Their son Asbury practiced medicine in Yadkin County and then in Mocksville where he had a long and distinguished career. Green Berry and Elizabeth owned property that is today known as the Farmington Drag Strip and there is also a Mocksville street bearing the Harding name; a restored cabin and various Civil War artifacts remain in the family. He died in 1932 and Elizabeth died in 1935. Both are buried in Farmington Community Cemetery.

475. Hargrave, John H.
Private, Company M, 7th Regiment • Confederate Cavalry • Company E, 16th Battalion • N.C. Cavalry

John transferred from Company M, 7th Regiment Confederate Cavalry to Company E, 16th Battalion N.C. Cavalry on July 11, 1864. He was present or accounted for through October 1864.

476. Harper, C.E. (Cannon)
Third Lieutenant, Field and Staff • Company G, 7th Regiment • Confederate Cavalry • Company D, 16th Battalion • N.C. Cavalry

C.E. was born in 1826 in Stokes County. In 1850 he made his home in Davie County with the family of Elisha and Mary Harper. He worked as a stiller prior to the war. He enlisted in Davie County and served as a Third Lieutenant in Company G until he was transferred to Company D,

16th Battalion on July 11, 1864. He was captured at Peebles Farm, Virginia, September 30, 1864, and confined at Fort Delaware, Delaware, where he remained until released after taking the Oath of Allegiance on June 17, 1865.

477. Harper, George W.
Private, Company G, 7th Regiment • Confederate Cavalry • Company D, 16th Battalion • N.C. Cavalry

George transferred from Company G, 7th Regiment Confederate Cavalry to Company D, 16th Battalion N.C. Cavalry on July 11, 1864, while absent in confinement at Point Lookout, Maryland, as a prisoner of war. He remained at Point Lookout until paroled and exchanged at Varina, Virginia, September 22, 1864.

478. Harper, J.L. (John)
Third Sergeant, Field and Staff • Company G, 7th Regiment • Confederate Cavalry • Company D, 16th Battalion • N.C. Cavalry

J.L. was born in Davie County in 1841 to Elisha (1817, Stokes) and Mary Harper. He enlisted in Davie on September 3, 1862, and was given the rank of Third Sergeant, Field and Staff. He transferred from Company G, 7th Regiment Confederate Cavalry to Company D, 16th Battalion N.C. Cavalry on July 11, 1864. He was present or accounted for through October 1, 1864.

479. Harper, John R.
Private, Company G, 7th Regiment • Confederate Cavalry • Company D, 16th Battalion • N.C. Cavalry

John enlisted in Davie County on September 3, 1862, with the rank of Private. He transferred from Company G, 7th Regiment Confederate Cavalry to Company D, 16th Battalion N.C. Cavalry on July 11, 1864. He was captured at Fort Harrison, Virginia, on September 30, 1864, and confined at Point Lookout, Maryland, where he died of "chronic diarrhoea" on April 1, 1865. John's name is listed on the Memorial Monument for the Davie County men who died in the Civil War, 1861–1865.

480. Harris, John W.
Private, "Davie Greys" • Company F, 13th Regiment • (3rd Regiment, N.C. Volunteers) • N.C. Troops

John was born in Wilkes County in 1839. He moved to Davie County and became a farmer prior to enlisting for the war at age 22, April 26, 1861. He was present or accounted for until wounded in the left thigh and captured at Gettysburg, Pennsylvania, July 1–4, 1863. He was hospitalized at Davids Island, New York Harbor, until paroled and transferred to City Point, Virginia, where he was received on September 8, 1863, for exchange. He was reported absent or wounded or absent sick until he rejoined the company in September–October, 1864. John returned to Davie when he married Ann Wagoner on January 17, 1871; in 1880 they were living in Jerusalem District where John was a crippled farmer. John and Ann were the parents of four sons: John C. (1872), Augustus (1877), James A. (1879) and Henry M. (1880).

481. Harris, Williamson G.
Private, Company B, 46th Regiment • N.C. Troops

Williamson was born in 1816 in Davie County. In 1850 he was married to Sarah (1824, Davie) and was the father of three small children: Eliza (1847), John (1848) and Charles (1849). He worked as a carpenter. In 1860 Williamson was married to Mary A. (1833, North Carolina) and there were three more children: Sarah (1852), Fannie (1857) and Peter (1859). They lived in the Liberty District and Williamson worked as a mechanic. He enlisted in Rowan County at age 48, March 28, 1862, as a substitute. He was present or accounted for until wounded in the hip at Bristoe Station, Virginia, October 14, 1863. He was detailed for conscript duty at Salisbury, February 15, 1864, and retired to the Invalid Corps on August 1, 1864, presumably by reason of disability from wounds. In 1870 Williamson was back in Davie County working as a mechanic and residing in the Mocksville District. One more child, Robbins (1869), had joined the family. On February 12, 1885, Williamson, age 65, married Lucinda Mason, age 22.

482. Harrison, Richard
Private, "Davie Greys" • Company F, 13th Regiment • (3rd Regiment, N.C. Volunteers) • N.C. Troops

Richard was born in Davie or Surry County and resided in Davie where he was a farmer prior to enlisting at age 17 on April 26, 1861. He was present or accounted for until discharged at Camp Ruffin, Virginia, on March 2, 1862, by reason of "epilepsy." Richard R. Harrison married Jane Sprye on April 21, 1862, in Davie County.

483. Hartman, Enoch
Private, Company G, 5th Regiment • N.C. State Troops

Enoch was born January 5, 1841, in North Carolina. He enlisted in Northampton County at age 21 on August 13, 1862, for the war. Company muster rolls indicate that he deserted near Fredericksburg, Virginia, December 29, 1862, but was later "discharged by civil authority by decision of the Supreme Court of North Carolina." A roll of deserters dated December 29, 1863, states that he claimed to have been discharged by a decision of Judge R.M. Pearson of the N.C. Supreme Court and was now serving in the home guard of his district. Enoch married Nancy Elizabeth Beauchamp in Davie County on September 16, 1869. They settled in Fulton District where he worked as a farmer and died on April 2, 1880. Their children were Eli (1871), Edward (1873), Thomas (1874) and Fallie (1876). Enoch is buried in Advance United Methodist Church Cemetery.

484. Hartman, G.A. (George)
Private • Captain William E. Booe's Partisan Rangers • N.C. Volunteers • Company H, 63rd Regiment • (5th Regiment N.C. Cavalry) • N.C. Troops

George was born in 1830 in Cabarrus County to Charles (1789, Cabarrus) and Elizabeth (1798, Cabarrus) Hartman. By 1850 the family had moved to Davie County where George married Elizabeth Etchison on November 18, 1852. Their son Charles was born in 1856. After Elizabeth's death, George lived with his deceased wife's parents. His second wife was Sarah A. Williams who married George on February 6, 1862. They lived and farmed in the Farmington District when George enlisted at age 34 on July 18, 1863, for the war. He was present or accounted for through October 1864. Their daughter Mary Betty was born in 1864 and Patti was born in 1875. They continued to live in the Farmington District where George died on December 25, 1891. He is buried in Farmington Community Cemetery.

485. Haskins (Hoskins), James F.
Private, "Davie Sweep Stakes" • Company G, 4th Regiment • N.C. State Troops

James was born July 19, 1824, in North Carolina. He married Mary A. Gibbs (1833, North Carolina) on April 11, 1854. In 1860 they lived in the Smith Grove District where his occupation was given as "steam doctor." He enlisted in Davie County at age 29, June 5, 1861, for the war. He was discharged at Camp Pickens near Manassas, Virginia, February 27, 1862. The reason for the discharge was not reported. He resumed family life in Farmington with the births of daughter Mary (1866) and son Joseph (1871). His occupations were listed as "physician" in 1870 and "farmer" in 1880. He died on October 22, 1886, and is buried in Smith Grove United Methodist Church Cemetery.

486. Hauser, Philip A.
Private, Company G, 7th Regiment • Confederate Cavalry • Company D, 16th Battalion • N.C. Cavalry

Philip enlisted in Davie County on September 3, 1862, with the rank of Private. He transferred from Company G, 7th Regiment Confederate Cavalry to Company D, 16th Battalion N.C. Cavalry on July 11, 1864. He was present or accounted for through October 1, 1864. He was reported on a roll of prisoners of war at Point Lookout, Maryland, as "captured near Petersburg, Virginia, October 27, 1864." No further records.

487. Hauser, Wiley
Private, Company G, 7th Regiment • Confederate Cavalry • Company D, 16th Battalion • N.C. Cavalry

Wiley enlisted in Davie County on September 3, 1862, with the rank of Private. He transferred from Company G, 7th Regiment, Confederate Cavalry to Company D, 16th Battalion N.C. Cavalry on July 11, 1864, while absent "detailed with artillery." He was present or accounted for through October 1, 1864, being absent on detail through August 1864.

488. Heinrich, George
First Sergeant, Company B, Carolina Rangers • 10th Virginia Cavalry Regiment

George was born circa 1833. He enlisted in Davie County on October 29, 1861, at age 28. He was present or accounted for until captured at White Oak Swamp on August 5, 1862. He was sent to Fort Wool and exchanged on November 10, 1862. He resumed his duties but "lost" his horse on July 5, 1863. He was present serving on horse details and twice received clothing before he was recaptured at Ford's Depot on April 3, 1865, and sent to Point Lookout where he was released June 14, 1865. His record states that he was a resident of Davie County, North Carolina.

489. Helfer, A.Y. (Amos Young)
Private, Company E, 42nd Regiment • N.C. Troops

Amos was born in 1836 in Davie County to Samuel (1808, Davie) and Sarah A. (1807, Davie) Helpher [sic]. His father was a shoemaker and Amos worked as a laborer in the Chinquepin District of Davie. He married Rebecca A. Holmes on

December 24, 1856; their daughter Sarah J. was born in 1858. Four years later Amos enlisted in Davie County at age 26 on March 18, 1862. He was present or accounted for until May–August, 1864, when he was reported absent wounded. The place and date were not reported. He returned to duty on October 28, 1864. There were no further records until A.Y., age 64, married Sarah Grimes, age 54, on January 3, 1900. Then nine months later he married once more, this time to M.E. Miller, age 37, on September 16, 1900.

490. Helfer, Pleasant E.
Private, Company E, 42nd Regiment • N.C. Troops

Pleasant was born in 1834 in Davie County to Samuel (1808, Davie) and Sarah A. (1807, Davie) Helpher [sic]. His father worked as a shoemaker and Pleasant worked as a farmer. During the 1850s Pleasant married Susan (1825, North Carolina); their two children were John F. (1856) and Sarah E. (1860). He enlisted in Davie County at age 28 on March 18, 1862. His brother Amos enlisted in this company on the same date. Pleasant was present or accounted for until November–December, 1862, when he was reported "in guard house." The reason he was confined was not reported. He returned to duty in January–February, 1863. He was present or accounted for until he deserted on September 8, 1863. Note: He may have served later as a Private in Company K of this regiment.

491. Helfer, S.F. (Samuel)
Private, Company E, 42nd Regiment • N.C. Troops

S.F. was born in 1840 in Davie County to Samuel (1808, Davie) and Sarah A. (1807, Davie) Helpher [sic]. His father worked as a shoemaker and S.F. was a laborer in the Chinquepin District of Davie in 1860. He enlisted in Davie on August 12, 1862, for the war. His brothers Amos and Pleasant also served in this company. S.F. died in hospital at Wilson on November 16, 1862. The cause of death was not reported. His name is listed on the Memorial Monument for the Davie County men who died in the Civil War, 1861–1865.

492. Hellard, Joe
Private, Company A, 57th Regiment • N.C. Troops

Joe was born in 1832 in Davie County. He resided with his mother, Susannah (1795, Rowan) in Davie where he worked as a farmer. On November 23, 1856, Joseph married Sarah Brinegar and by 1860 they had three children: Mary E. (1857), Susana (1859) and "Baby girl" (1860). At age 30 on July 4, 1862, Joe enlisted in Rowan County for the war. His brother Thomas enlisted at the same time in the same company. Joe was hospitalized at Richmond, Virginia, October 29, 1862, with chronic diarrhoea. He was furloughed for sixty days on November 28, 1862, and died at home in Davie County on January 4, 1863, of "typhoid pneumonia and diarrhoea." Joe's name is listed as "J. Hillard" on the Memorial Monument for the Davie County men who died in the Civil War, 1861–1865.

493. Hellard (Hillard), Thomas
Private, Company A, 57th Regiment • N.C. Troops

Thomas was born in 1830 in Davie County. He resided with his mother, Susannah (1795, Rowan) in Davie where he worked as a farmer and blacksmith. He enlisted in Rowan County at age 33, July 4, 1862, for the war. He was reported present through May 11, 1863, but was killed at Gettysburg, Pennsylvania, July 2, 1863. His brother Joe enlisted at the same time in the same company. Thomas's name is not presently listed on the Memorial Monument for the Davie County men who died in the Civil War, 1861–1865.

494. Hellard (Hillard), William
Private, Company E, 42nd Regiment • N.C. Troops

William was born in Davie County in 1820. He married Nancy Bailey on May 20, 1843. By 1860 he was a farmer living in the Liberty District with seven children: Margaret (1844), John (1847), Susannah (1847), Sarah (1849), Emily (1853), Franklin (1855) and George (1859). He enlisted in Davie at age 42, March 18, 1862. He was present or accounted for through August 1862. He was dropped from the rolls of the company prior to January 1, 1863. He took the Oath of Allegiance at Salisbury, North Carolina, on June 1, 1865.

495. Hellard, William Henry
Private, Company B, Carolina Rangers • 10th Virginia Cavalry Regiment

William was born in 1844 in Davie County to James (1823, Davie) and Mary (1824, Davie) Hillard [sic]. They farmed in Fulton District where William enlisted March 1, 1864. He was present on July 8, 1864, received clothing on September 30 and December 31, 1864, and was paroled at Salisbury, North Carolina, on May 15, 1865.

496. Hendricks, James M.
Third Corporal, Company B, Carolina Rangers • 10th Virginia Cavalry Regiment

James was born in 1839 in Davie County to William (1815, Davie) and Sallie (1817, Davie) Hendrix [sic]. They lived in the Fulton District of Davie where James worked as a farmhand prior to enlisting on November 8, 1861, at age 23 as a Private. He was present during roll check and accounted for when absent on horse detail on September 10, 1863, and on July 8, 1864. He received his appointment to Third Corporal on November 1, 1863. He was allotted clothing in October and December, 1864. He was paroled in Mocksville on June 9, 1865. He later returned to Davie where he married Lucy J. and they lived in Fulton District where James worked as a whiskey dealer and they raised their children: Georgianna (1869), William A. (1871) and Alexander P. (1873).

497. Hendricks, Jesse A.
Private, Company B, Carolina Rangers • 10th Virginia Cavalry Regiment

Jesse was born in Davie County circa 1826. (The 1850 census shows a date of 1822.) He married Mariah C. Jones on July 22, 1847, and they lived in Liberty District where he worked as a blacksmith. They were the parents of six children before the Civil War began: William (1848), Thomas (1850), Mary (1852), Lilla (1854), Lula (1856) and Julia (1858). Jesse A. (Jr.) was born in 1867 following the war. Jesse Sr. enlisted in Davie County on December 14, 1861, at age 39. He was present or accounted for throughout his service. His skills as a blacksmith were utilized when he was appointed Regimental Blacksmith. He was retired to the Invalid Corps by the Medical Board on July 16, 1864. He became blind in his later years; an application by his wife Mariah for a pension was filed at the State Archives, Raleigh, North Carolina. Jesse's son William also served in this company.

498. Hendricks, Nalke
Private, Company E, 42nd Regiment • N.C. Troops

Nalke resided in Davie County. The place and date of enlistment were not reported. He was captured at or near Wise's Forks, Kinston, North Carolina, on March 10, 1865. He was confined at Point Lookout, Maryland, on March 16, 1865, and released there on June 27, 1865, after taking the Oath of Allegiance.

499. Hendricks, William
Private, Company B, Carolina Rangers • 10th Virginia Cavalry Regiment

William was born in 1848 in Davie County to Jesse A. (1826, Davie) and Mariah C. (1828, Davie) Jones Hendricks. They lived in Liberty District where William's father was a blacksmith. They served in this company together but William's place and date of enlistment are not known. He was absent sick on May 26, 1864, and furloughed for 60 days. He was wounded in the back and was absent from May 1 through October 1, 1864. There were no further records. William was back in Davie living with his parents and working as a blacksmith in 1870.

500. Hendricks, William A.
Private, "Davie Sweep Stakes" • Company G, 4th Regiment • N.C. State Troops

William was born in 1842. He lived in the Smith Grove District of Davie with his mother Mary (1822, North Carolina), where he worked as a farmer prior to enlisting at age 19, June 4, 1861, for the war. He was present or accounted for until wounded in the left arm at Chancellorsville, Virginia, May 1–3, 1863. He was reported absent wounded until he retired on or about March 21, 1865, by reason of "loss of use of hand" as a result of wounds received at Chancellorsville. He returned to the Farmington District of Davie where he married Mahala (1847) and had two children: John A. (1869) and Mary J. (1870).

501. Hendrix, C. (William Coston)
Private • Captain William E. Booe's Partisan Rangers • N.C. Volunteers • Company H, 63rd Regiment • (5th Regiment N.C. Cavalry) • N.C. Troops

William Coston was born May 4, 1835. He married Mary E. Williams in Davie County on January 25, 1860, and they lived in the Smith Grove District where he worked as a farmer. On November 3, 1862, Coston enlisted in Northampton County for the war. He was reported present for the September–October, 1862, muster roll. There were no further records. However, in later life Mary filed an application for a pension after 1901. Both Coston and Mary are buried in the Smith Grove United Methodist Church Cemetery. He died on September 27, 1898; she died on November 5, 1930.

502. Hendrix, F.M. (Francis Monroe)
Private • Captain William E. Booe's Partisan Rangers • N.C. Volunteers • Company H, 63rd Regiment • (5th Regiment N.C. Cavalry) • N.C. Troops

Francis Monroe Hendrix inherited this house and 200 acres of land as his parents' only surviving son; he also served as postmaster at Nestor from 1887 to 1891 (Mohney, *The Historic Architecture of Davie County*).

Francis was born in 1838 in Davie County to John (1785) and Lydia (1800, Surry) Hendrix. He married Martha Redman on October 19, 1858, and they settled in the Chinquepin District. Two daughters, Laura J. (1859) and Mary E. (1861) were born there. Francis was a farmer prior to enlisting at age 24 in Davie County on July 10, 1862, for the war. He was captured near Hagerstown, Maryland, on July 12, 1863, and confined at Point Lookout, Maryland, until paroled and exchanged at City Point, Virginia, on March 20, 1864. He was present or accounted for through 1864. After the war the family settled in Clarksville. Eight more children were born: John H. (1865), Melvin J. (1867), Joanna (1869), Louisa B. (1871), Cora F. (1873), Katie (1875), Lydia C. (1876) and Francis D. (1878). F.M. died on November 28, 1920, and is buried in Hendricks Family Cemetery.

503. Hendrix, Jehu (John)
Private, "Davie Greys" • Company F, 13th Regiment • (3rd Regiment, N.C. Volunteers) • N.C. Troops

Jehu was born in 1826 in Davie County. He married Laurena Foster on February 1, 1860; he was 34 and she was 17. They lived in the Smith Grove District where he worked as a farmer. Jehu enlisted in Davie at age 36, July 16, 1862, for the war. He was present or accounted for until captured at Amelia Court House, Virginia, April 5, 1865, and confined at Point Lookout, Maryland, until released on June 27, 1865, after taking the Oath of Allegiance. In 1870 "John" and "Louvenia" lived in the Fulton District with their three children: Sarah (1863), Mary E. (1867) and Emma J. (1869).

504. Hendrix, John H.
Private, Company G, 5th Regiment • Company E, 4th Regiment • N.C. State Troops

John was born in 1845 in Anson County to Mary (1815, Anson) Hendrix. They moved to Davie County in the Smith Grove District where John and his older brother Allen worked as laborers and Mary worked as a seamstress. At age 17 John enlisted in Northampton County on August 13, 1862, for the war. He was captured at Gettysburg, Pennsylvania, July 1–5, 1863, and was confined at Davids Island, New York Harbor, until paroled on August 24, 1863, and transferred to City Point, Virginia, for exchange. He transferred to Company E, 4th Regiment, N.C. State Troops, July 20, 1863, was captured at Winchester, Virginia, September 19, 1864, and confined at Point Lookout, Maryland, until released June 27, 1865, after taking the Oath of Allegiance.

505. Hendrix, N.G. (Ningey)
Private, Company E, 42nd Regiment • Moore's Roster

N.G. was born in Davie County on July 17, 1827, the son of Anderson Hendricks [*sic*] (1785, Orange). In 1860 he farmed in the Fulton District. N.G. enlisted in Davie County on March 18, 1862, for the war. Elizabeth J. Williams married Ningey on January 5, 1860. Their four children were Milton (1862), Charles (1864), Isaac (1866) and Mary (1868). N.G. continued to live and farm in the Fulton District. He died on November 19, 1913, and is buried in Fork Baptist Church Cemetery.

506. Hendrix, Stephen
Private, Company E, 42nd Regiment • N.C. Troops

Stephen was born in Davie County in 1844, the son of Henry (1820, Davie) and Elizabeth (1824, Davie) Hendricks. He lived in the Mocksville District in 1860 where he worked as a laborer. He enlisted in Davie County at age 18 on March 18, 1862. He was present or accounted for until he died in the hospital at Lynchburg, Virginia, on August 19, 1862, of "typhoid fever." Stephen's name is listed on the Memorial Monument for the Davie County men who died in the Civil War, 1861–1865.

507. Hendrix, W.G. (Walter) (Walker)
Private, Company E, 42nd Regiment • N.C. Troops

W.G. was born in 1840 in Davie County. He was the son of Zadock (1815, Davie) and Edith Howard Hendrix. In 1860 he lived in the Shady Grove District and worked as a laborer. At age 21 on or about March 14, 1862, he enlisted in Davie County. He was present or accounted for until captured at or near Wise's Forks, Kinston, North Carolina, on March 10, 1865. W.G. was confined at Point Lookout, Maryland, on March 16, 1865, and released at Point Lookout on May 13, 1865.

508. Hendren, Arthur N. (Neely)
First Sergeant, "Davie Greys" • Company F, 13th Regiment • (3rd Regiment, N.C. Volunteers) • N.C. Troops

Arthur was born in 1838 in Davie County. He was the son of Denton (1816, Davie) and Sarah Rinshaw (1817, Davie) Hendren. On September 11, 1856, he married Sarah (Sallie) Ann Warren (1837, North Carolina). Arthur worked as a farmer in the Mocksville District prior to enlisting at age 23, April 26, 1861. At that time he was the father of two children: James Denton (1858) and Jane (1860). He mustered in as a Musician and was present or accounted for until captured at Sharpsburg, Maryland, on or about September 17, 1862. He was paroled September 20, 1862, and rejoined the company in November–December, 1862. On May 1, 1864, Arthur was promoted to First Sergeant and was present or accounted for until paroled at Appomattox Court House, Virginia, April 9, 1865. He returned to Jerusalem Township in Davie where he farmed. Two more children were born by 1870: Garland (1865) and William (1869).

509. Hendron (Hendren), Denton
Captain • Company F, 77th Regiment, 19th Division • N.C. Militia 1861–1865

Denton was born in 1817 in Davie County. He married Sarah Ann Rinshaw (1817, Davie), raised seven children and farmed for a living in the Mocksville District of Davie. His children were Arthur (1837), Rebecca (1839), Margaret (1844), Mary (1848), Linville T. (1850), Eugenia (1850) and Emma D. (1856). He served as Captain of Company F of the 77th Regiment when the militia was activated. Following the war he moved his family to the Calahaln District where he continued to farm. Sara [*sic*] died in 1878 and Denton died on February 4, 1880. They are buried in Liberty United Methodist Church Cemetery.

510. Hepler, Benjamin F.
Private, "Davie Greys" • Company F, 13th Regiment • (3rd Regiment, N.C. Volunteers) • N.C. Troops

Benjamin was born in 1848. He resided in Davidson County and enlisted in Guilford County at age 17, March 13, 1863, for the war. He was present or accounted for until wounded in the hip at Chancellorsville, Virginia, May 3, 1863. He was reported absent wounded or absent sick until he rejoined the company in March–April, 1864. He was killed at or near Cold Harbor, Virginia, June 1, 1864. Although Benjamin lived in Davidson County, his name is listed on the Memorial Monument for the Davie County men who died in the Civil War, 1861–1865.

511. Hightower, Anderson E.
Private, Company H, 63rd Regiment (5th Regiment, N.C. Cavalry) • N.C. Troops • Company G, 4th Regiment • N.C. State Troops

Anderson was born in 1833. He resided in the Mocksville District with his mother Sarah Hightower and worked as a house carpenter. He married Jane (1840, Davie) Carter on February 11,

1858, and had two children: Nathan (1858) and William (1859). On July 15, 1862, he enlisted in Davie for the war. He was present or accounted for until he transferred to Company G, 4th Regiment, N.C. State Troops, on November 26, 1864; however, records of Company G do not substantiate that he served. No further records. Upon returning home to Davie, Anderson worked as a huckster and as a carpenter. He and Jane also added six more children to the family: Sarah (1863), Henry Giles (1868), Monroe (1871), Ellis (1873), Melissa (1876) and Caldonia (1880).

512. Hill, B. (Benton)
Private • Captain William E. Booe's Partisan Rangers • N.C. Volunteers • Company H, 63rd Regiment • (5th Regiment N.C. Cavalry) • N.C. Troops

B. Hill was born in 1838 in North Carolina. In 1860 he lived with the Abe Pruett family on a farm in the Chinquepin District where he was a miller. He enlisted in Davie County for the war on July 15, 1862. He was present or accounted for through February 1863.

513. Hill, David Franklin
Private, "Davie Sweep Stakes" • Company G, 4th Regiment • N.C. State Troops

David was born in 1840 in Davie County. In 1850 he lived with the John Casel family in Davie where he enlisted at age 21, June 5, 1861, for the war. He died in the hospital in Warrenton, Virginia, December 17, 1861, of "pneumonia typhoides." David's name is listed on the Memorial Monument for the Davie County men who died in the Civil War, 1861–1865

514. Hill, George W.
Private, Company H, 57th Regiment • N.C. Troops

George was born in 1835. He resided in Davie County and was by occupation a mechanic before enlisting in Davie County at age 28 on July 4, 1862. He was reported present through February 28, 1863. George was hospitalized at Richmond, Virginia, on May 6, 1863, with "pneumonia" and died on May 16, 1863. He was married to Lutisha (1844, North Carolina). George's name is listed on the Memorial Monument for the Davie County men who died in the Civil War, 1861–1865.

515. Hinkle, George W.
Private, "Davie Greys" • Company F, 13th Regiment • (3rd Regiment, N.C. Volunteers) • N.C. Troops

George was the son of Mary N. Hinkle (1803, Virginia). He was born in 1842 in Davie County. In 1860 at age 18 he was a farmer in the Mocksville District, where on August 6, 1861, he enlisted for the war. He was present or accounted for until he was wounded and captured at Gettysburg, Pennsylvania, on July 1–4, 1863. George was hospitalized at Davids Island, New York Harbor, until paroled and transferred to City Point, Virginia, where he was received September 8, 1863, for exchange. He rejoined the company in May–June, 1864, and was present or accounted for until captured at the Appomattox River, Virginia, April 3, 1865. He was confined at Hart's Island, New York Harbor, until released on June 19, 1865, after taking the Oath of Allegiance. On January 30, 1868, George married Mary A. Foster Seaford who had four children: William Seford [*sic*] (1855), Elizabeth Seford [*sic*] (1857), Robert Seford [*sic*] (1859) and Emily Seford [*sic*] (1862). Mary and George had a daughter Susannah M. (1869), followed by Jesse A. (1874) and Pinkney R. (1878). In 1870 George was a farm laborer living in Jerusalem District. By 1880 he was a farmer in Calahaln. George's application for a pension is on file in the State Archives, Raleigh, North Carolina.

516. Hobb, Julius (Junius)
Sergeant, "Davie Greys" • Company F, 13th Regiment • (3rd Regiment, N.C. Volunteers) • N.C. Troops

Julius was born in Davie County in 1839. He was the son of Milton (1807, Guilford) and Irena Foster Hobbs. His father was a physician. In 1860 Julius was a laborer living in the Fulton District. At age 22 on April 26, 1861, he enlisted for the war. He was mustered in as a Private and promoted to Sergeant on April 28, 1862. He was present or accounted for until he died in hospital at Charlottesville, Virginia, on December 9, 1862, of "pneumonia." Julius's name is listed on the Memorial Monument for the Davie County men who died in the Civil War, 1861–1865.

517. Hobson, James M.
First Lieutenant, "Guilford Guards" • Second Company E, 2nd Regiment • N.C. State Troops

James was born in 1840 in Rockingham County to Samuel (1802, Virginia) and Ann Hobson (1811, Rockingham). He resided as a student in Davie County, Liberty Township prior to enlisting in Guilford County at age 21, July 26, 1861, for the war. He was mustered in as a Private then was elected Second Lieutenant on February 3,

1862, and appointed to rank from date of election. He was promoted to First Lieutenant to rank from June 21, 1862, and wounded at Chancellorsville, Virginia, May 3, 1863. He was present or accounted for until captured at Spotsylvania Court House, Virginia, on May 8, 1864, then confined at Point Lookout, Maryland, until transferred to Fort Delaware, Delaware, June 23, 1864. He was forwarded to Hilton Head, South Carolina, August 20, 1864, then transferred to Fort Pulaski, Georgia, in October 1864. In December 1864 he was transferred back to Hilton Head then to Fort Delaware on March 12, 1865, where he was released after taking the Oath of Allegiance on June 10, 1865.

518. Hobson, John M.
Second Lieutenant, "Guilford Guards" • Second Company E, 2nd Regiment • N.C. State Troops

John was born September 25, 1842, in Rockingham County to Samuel (1802, Virginia) and Ann Hobson (1811, Rockingham). He resided as a student with his family on their prosperous Davie County farm in Liberty Township, prior to enlisting in Guilford County on July 24, 1861. He mustered in as First Sergeant, and was appointed Second Lieutenant to rank from April 19, 1862. He was wounded at Chancellorsville, Virginia, May 3, 1863, and returned to duty July 5, 1863. Company muster records through October 1864 show him present or accounted for. He was captured at Petersburg, Virginia, April 2, 1865, and confined at Old Capitol Prison, Washington, D.C., until transferred to Johnson's Island, Ohio, April 9, 1865. He was released after taking the Oath of Allegiance on June 18, 1865. John died on March 10, 1878, and is buried in the Hobson Family Cemetery.

519. Hobson, Samuel Morehead
First Lieutenant, Company A, 77th Regiment, 19th Division • N.C. Militia 1861–1865

Samuel was born February 15, 1832, to Samuel Augustus (1802, Virginia) and Ann Morehead (1811, Rockingham) Hobson. He was born into a distinguished and highly respected family. His mother was the sister of Governor John Motley Morehead. Their ancestors were Revolutionary War patriots and military heroes (Congressional Medal of Honor, etc.). When the Civil War began, Samuel lived in the Liberty District where he made his living as a tobacconist. The militia was activated and he was appointed First Lieutenant of Company A. By 1870 he had relocated to Jerusalem District. He died on December 10, 1917, at age 85 and is buried in the Hobson Family Cemetery.

520. Hobson, W. Henry
Sergeant • Captain William E. Booe's Partisan Rangers • N.C. Volunteers • Company H, 63rd Regiment • (5th Regiment N.C. Cavalry) • N.C. Troops

Henry was born on August 13, 1844, in Rockingham County, the son of Samuel (1802, Virginia) and Ann (1811, Rockingham) Morehead Hobson. The family moved to Davie County in the late 1840s and settled in the Liberty District where Henry was a student prior to enlisting on April 15, 1863, for the war. He mustered in as a Private. He was wounded and captured at Upperville, Virginia, June 21, 1863, and confined at Old Capitol Prison, Washington, D.C., until paroled and exchanged at City Point, Virginia, June 30, 1863. Henry was promoted to Sergeant on August 1, 1863, and wounded in action in the left thigh on September 22, 1863. He was furloughed for forty days October 5, 1863, present or accounted for through February 1865 and paroled at Salisbury, North Carolina, on May 16, 1865. He returned home to become a tobacco trader in Jerusalem. He married E.O. (Ossie) Morris on February 14, 1877, and they had two children: John M. (1878) and Ossie Ola (1879). Ossie Ola died in 1880 and John M. died in 1887. Henry was "U.S. Deputy Collector" in 1880. He lived to be 84 years old, long out-living his wife and children. He died on March 6, 1929, and is buried in the Hobson Family Cemetery.

521. Hodges, John D.
Private • Captain William E. Booe's Partisan Rangers • N.C. Volunteers • Company H, 63rd Regiment • (5th Regiment N.C. Cavalry) • N.C. Troops

John was born October 11, 1844, in Davie County. He was the son of Joseph W. (1817, Virginia) and Mary Ann M. (1818, Davie) Click Hodges. By 1860 John's father had died and John had assumed the responsibility of helping his mother tend to the farm in the Liberty District. He enlisted April 15, 1863, for the war. He was captured near Hagerstown, Maryland, July 12, 1863, paroled at the hospital in Baltimore, Maryland, and exchanged at City Point, Virginia, September 27, 1863. He was present or accounted for through December 1864. He was captured again at Dinwiddie Court House, Virginia, on March

30, 1865, and confined at Point Lookout, Maryland, until released after taking the Oath of Allegiance, June 27, 1865. James W. Wall writes in his *History of Davie County* that "After serving in the Civil War, Hodges returned to his farm home in Augusta and then attended Trinity College (Duke) and graduated from Yale University in 1874. He began a fifty-two year career in education as a teacher and administrator in Union County, served as teacher and administrator in Raleigh and New Bern, and in the early 1880s was professor of Greek at Trinity College." He returned home to Davie County where he married Sallie A. Thompson, age 21, on January 9, 1896. Their children were John D., Jr., Paul Eustace, Mary, Sarah and Ruth. He became county superintendent of schools in July 1900, and remained a prominent influence for education until his death on January 4, 1936. He is buried in Concord United Methodist Church Cemetery. Professor Hodges had served as a Private in the Civil War, but during his long life he rose through the ranks of the N.C. Division United Confederate Veterans to become Brigadier General of that organization.

John D. Hodges (Davie County Public Library)

522. Hodges, Joseph
Private, "Davie Greys" • Company F, 13th Regiment • (3rd Regiment, N.C. Volunteers) • N.C. Troops

Joseph was born in 1835 in Davie County (or Virginia), to David (1810, Virginia) and Elizabeth (1808, Virginia). In 1860 the family lived in the Farmington District of Davie. Joseph and his wife Jane, lived beside his parents prior to his enlisting at age 26, August 6, 1861, in Davie. He was present or accounted for until wounded at Fredericksburg, Virginia, on or about December 13, 1862. He rejoined the company prior to January 1, 1863, and was present or accounted for until killed at Chancellorsville, Virginia, May 3, 1863. Joseph's name is listed on the Memorial Monument for the Davie County men who died in the Civil War, 1861–1865. (See second photograph on page 121.)

From dashing Private of Company H, 63rd Regiment, to Brigadier General of the N.C. Division United Confederate Veterans, Professor Hodges proved himself to be a man of many talents. At the time of his death, January 4, 1936, he was the oldest living alumnus of Duke University (Davie County Public Library).

523. Holder, A.A.
Private, Company G, 7th Regiment • Confederate Cavalry • Company D, 16th Battalion • N.C. Cavalry

A.A. enlisted in Davie County on September 3, 1862, with the rank of Private. He transferred from Company G, 7th Regiment Confed-

John D. Hodges' house has been carefully restored (John and Deborah Osborne).

erate Cavalry to Company D, 16th Battalion N.C. Cavalry on July 11, 1864, while absent "detailed with artillery." He remained on detail through August 1864 and was reported as present on September–October, 1864, muster roll. He was paroled at Appomattox Court House, Virginia, on April 9, 1865.

524. Holder, Hosea L.
Private, Company E, 42nd Regiment • N.C. Troops

Hosea was born in 1825. He enlisted in Davie County at age 37, on or about March 17, 1862. He was present or accounted for until killed near Petersburg, Virginia, June 17, 1864. Hosea's name is listed on the Memorial Monument for the Davie County men who died in the Civil War, 1861–1865.

525. Holder, Jacob
Private, Company G, 7th Regiment • Confederate Cavalry • Company D, 16th Battalion • N.C. Cavalry

Jacob transferred from Company G, 7th Regiment Confederate Cavalry on July 11, 1864, while absent in confinement at Point Lookout, Maryland, as a prisoner of war. He transferred to Elmira, New York, on August 15, 1864. He was paroled at Elmira on October 11, 1864, and "died on November 5, 1864, at Fort Monroe, Virginia." Jacob's name is listed on the Memorial Monument for the Davie County men who died in the Civil War, 1861–1865.

526. Holder, Sowell
Private, Company G, 7th Regiment • Confederate Cavalry • Company D, 16th Battalion • N.C. Cavalry

Sowell enlisted in Davie County on September 3, 1862, with the rank of Private. He transferred from Company G, 7th Regiment Confederate Cavalry to Company D, 16th Battalion N.C. Cavalry on July 11, 1864. He was present or accounted for through October 1, 1864.

527. Holder, William
Private, Company D, 42nd Regiment • N.C. Troops

William was born in Stokes County but resided in Davie County. He was the son of Joseph (1785, Stokes) and Mary (1795, Davie) Holder. Susan Etcheson and William were married on September 28, 1854, and settled in Smith Grove where William worked as a laborer. He enlisted in Rowan County at age 25, on March 24, 1862. He was present or accounted for through February 1863 but was dropped from the rolls of the company in March–April, 1863. The reason he was dropped was not reported. He was hospitalized at Wilmington on January 18, 1865, with herpes, then paroled at Mocksville on June 6, 1865. Susan and William were the parents of six children: James Francis (1850), Philip M. (1859), Elizabeth (1861), Dollie (1866), William (1874) and Mary (1877). They moved to the Farmington District in 1870 and William was still working there as a farmhand in 1880.

528. Holdman (Holman), Thomas
Private, Company G, 5th Regiment • N.C. State Troops

Thomas was born about 1835. His father was Samuel (1800, Davie) Holman [sic], a farmer who resided in the Mocksville District of Davie County. Thomas married Sarah F. Owens on October 8, 1859; they were the parents of Mary A.E. (1858). He was a farmer prior to enlisting in Northampton County at age 28, August 13, 1862, for the war. He died in hospital at Richmond, Virginia, January 14, 1863, of "variola." Thomas's name is not presently listed on the Memorial Monument for the Davie County men who died in the Civil War, 1861–1865.

529. Holeman (Holman), James S.
Private, Company A, 46th Regiment • N.C. Troops

James was born in 1833 in either Ohio or Davie County. He lived with Lydia (1777, Davie) and worked as a laborer prior to marrying Rachal Campbell (1839) in Davie on February 19, 1854. He enlisted in Davie County at age 39, April 13, 1863, for the war. He was present or accounted for until he surrendered at Appomattox Court House, Virginia, April 9, 1865. His daughter, Martha E., was born in 1866. The family continued to live in Davie in the Clarksville District. James died on August 17, 1883, and is buried in Bear Creek Baptist Church Cemetery.

530. Holman, Henry Clay
Second Lieutenant • Company M, 77th Regiment, 19th Division • N.C. Militia 1861–1865

Henry was born April 26, 1840, in Davie County to Isaac (1800, Davie) and Mary E. (1819, South Carolina) Holman. Apparently Isaac was a successful farmer and distiller. Prior to the war the family lived in the Shady Grove area where Henry was a student. When the war was imminent he was appointed Second Lieutenant of Company M of the militia. On December 3, 1861, he married Sarah E. Ward, and by 1870 they were living in the Clarksville District with three children: Walter (1865), Mary V. (1857) and Maud (1870). Henry switched from farmer to merchant and added four more children by 1880: Ernest P. (1872), Gertrude E. (1875), Herbert C. (1877) and a son who was not yet named born in 1879. Henry died on November 19, 1915, and is buried in Union Chapel United Methodist Church Cemetery.

531. Holman, J.B.
Private, Company H, 57th Regiment • N.C. Troops

J.B. enlisted in Davie County on July 8, 1862, for the war. No further records. J.B. is buried in Society Baptist Church Cemetery. His dates are February 17, 1839 to July 24, 1904.

532. Holman, Jacob B.
Private • Captain William E. Booe's Partisan Rangers • N.C. Volunteers • Company H, 63rd Regiment • (5th Regiment N.C. Cavalry) • N.C. Troops

Jacob was born in Davie County in 1835, the son of Andrew B. (1805, Davie) and Sarah (1812, Davie) Holman. His father died in 1856 so Jacob assumed the farm duties along with his mother. He enlisted in Davie County at age 27, on July 8, 1862, for the war. He married Heneretta L. Powell on September 1, 1863, but there was little time for a personal life. He was captured near Beaver Dam, Virginia, until transferred to Point Lookout, Maryland, on May 17, 1864. He was moved to Elmira, New York, August 15, 1864, where he died on January 3, 1865, of "chronic diarrhea" and was buried in Woodlawn National Cemetery in Elmira. Jacob's daughter, Frances, was born during this time; Heneretta worked as a seamstress to support herself and her daughter. Frances married A.J. Anderson in Davie County on June 13, 1889. Jacob's name is listed on the Memorial Monument for the Davie County men who died in the Civil War, 1861–1865.

533. Holt, Robert A.
Private, "Davie Greys" • Company F, 13th Regiment • (3rd Regiment, N.C. Volunteers) • N.C. Troops

Robert was born in 1837 in North Carolina. He was a farmer and tanner in 1860 living in the Mocksville District with the J.D. Vick family. At age 22, on April 26, 1861, he enlisted in Davie County, for the war. He was present or accounted for until wounded in the left foot and captured at Gettysburg, Pennsylvania, on July 1–4, 1863. He was hospitalized at Davids Island, New York Harbor, until paroled and transferred to City Point,

Virginia, where he was received October 28, 1863, for exchange. He was reported absent wounded or absent sick until retired to the Invalid Corps on August 13, 1864.

534. Hood, William
Private, Company D, 42nd Regiment • N.C. Troops

William was born in North Carolina, in 1834. On April 23, 1856, he married Mary Daner (1839, North Carolina). In 1860 they were living in the Farmington District where William worked as a farmer. He enlisted in Rowan County at age 30, on April 8, 1862. He was present or accounted for until he deserted on June 1, 1863. He was reported present but under arrest in September–October, 1863. He returned to duty in November–December, 1863. He was present or accounted for through October 1864. He was paroled at Mocksville on June 7, 1865. No further information.

535. Hoose (House), William (J.W.?)
Private, Company F, 42nd Regiment • N.C. Troops

William was born in 1844 in Rowan County. He made his home with Jacob and Mary E. Clement Eaton in the Liberty District of Davie County. William enlisted in Davie at age 18, March 24, 1862. He was present or accounted for until killed near Petersburg, Virginia, June 17, 1864. William's name is listed on the Memorial Monument for the Davie County men who died in the Civil War, 1861–1865.

536. Horn, Enoch
Private, Company F, 42nd Regiment • N.C. Troops

Enoch was born in 1838 in North Carolina. On August 7, 1859, he married Rebecca N. Tutterow (1840, North Carolina). In 1860 he was a farmer in the Calahaln District. At age 24, on May 14, 1862, he enlisted in Davie County for the war. Enoch was present or accounted for through October 1864. He was paroled at Mocksville on June 3, 1865, and returned to farming in the Calahaln District where he died on February 3, 1886. He is buried in Center United Methodist Church Cemetery.

537. Horn, John J.
Private, Company F, 42nd Regiment • N.C. Troops

John was born in 1843 in North Carolina, and lived with Moses (1802, North Carolina) and Kesekiah (1800, North Carolina) Horn. He grew up in the Calahaln District. He enlisted in Davie County at age 19, for the war. He was present or accounted for until he died in the hospital at Lynchburg, Virginia, on October 8, 1862, of "scarlatina." John's name is listed on the Memorial Monument for the Davie County men who died in the Civil War, 1861–1865.

538. Horn, Levi (Louis) G.(iles)
Private, Company G, 5th Regiment • N.C. State Troops

Louis was born in 1834 in Davie County. He married Easter (Etta) H. Campbell on March 9, 1858, and they were parents to Everett Gaston (1859) and L. Giles (1860). They lived in the Calahaln District where Louis farmed prior to his enlisting in Northampton County at age 29, August 13, 1862, for the war. He died in the hospital at Richmond, Virginia, on or about May 20, 1863, of "measles." Easter H. Horne's application for a widow's pension is on file at the State Archives, Raleigh, North Carolina. The application was approved. Louis's name is listed on the Memorial Monument as "Lewis G." Horn.

539. Horn, Thomas
Private • Captain William E. Booe's Partisan Rangers • N.C. Volunteers • Company H, 63rd Regiment • (5th Regiment N.C. Cavalry) • N.C. Troops

Thomas was born in Davie County in 1829, to Lewis (1794, Davie) and Mary (1805, Surry) Horn. He worked as a clerk in Farmington and lived with the G.W. Johnson family prior to enlisting on July 1, 1862, for the war. He was present or accounted for through February 1865. Following the end of the war he returned home to the Farmington District where he lived with his wife Mary (1840, North Carolina) and their two children: Falton (1866) and Nannie (1868).

540. Horn, William Pinkney
Private, Company F, 42nd Regiment • N.C. Troops

William was born in 1830 in Davie County. On August 21, 1854, he married Elizabeth Owens (1838). He worked as a carpenter in Calahaln prior to enlisting in Davie on May 19, 1864, for the war. He was present or accounted for through April 14, 1865. William Pinkney was paroled at Mocksville on June 7, 1865. He and Elizabeth had five children: Mary L. (1858), Cynthia (1860), Emily (1862), Richard R. (1866) and Minnie P. (1869). Pinkney Horn is buried at Society Baptist Church Cemetery. No dates given.

541. Horne, Stephen W.
Sergeant, Company F, 42nd Regiment • N.C. Troops

Stephen was born in 1837 in Davie County,

the son of Lewis (1794, Delaware) and Mary (1805, Surry) Horn. On September 16, 1858, he married Temperance Longwirth. Stephen enlisted in Davie County at age 24, March 18, 1862. He mustered in as a Sergeant and was present or accounted for through October 1864. He was paroled at Greensboro, North Carolina, on May 1, 1865. He would have four children by his second wife Mary J. They were Francis (1868), Walter (1870), Lewis F. (1871) and Leonidas (1874). They raised their children in the Farmington District. Stephen died on November 9, 1923, and is buried in the Farmington Community Cemetery.

542. House, David A.
Private, 2nd Company B, 42nd Regiment • N.C. Troops

David was born in Davie County in 1835. He resided in either Davie or Iredell County and was by occupation a farmer. He married Mary (1840, North Carolina) and they had three children: Mary (1862), John (1864) and Ann (1870). David enlisted in Rowan County at age 36, on July 1, 1862, for the war. He was present or accounted for until wounded in the middle toe of the right foot near Petersburg, Virginia, on August 16, 1864. His toe was amputated and he was absent wounded through October 1864. He was paroled at Salisbury, North Carolina, on May 16, 1865, where he took the Oath of Allegiance on June 5, 1865. David returned to his family and farming in the Jerusalem District of Davie County.

543. House, John W.
Private, Company F, 13th Regiment • (3rd Regiment, N.C. Volunteers) • 2nd Company B, 42nd Regiment • N.C. Troops

John was born in 1844 in Davie County. In his early years, he lived with the John N. Jaybird family, and in 1860 he lived with Jake and Mary C. Eaton in the Liberty District, where he worked as a laborer. At age 20, he enlisted on April 26, 1861. He was present or accounted for until transferred to Company B, 42nd Regiment, N.C. Troops, on April 22, 1863. He was present or accounted for through October 1864. John was paroled at Salisbury, North Carolina, on May 16, 1865. North Carolina pension records indicate he was wounded at Malvern Hill, Virginia, in July 1863. John married Elizabeth and after a long life together he died in 1909. She died in 1923. Both are buried in Legion Memorial Park in Cooleemee, North Carolina.

544. Howard, B.S. (Benjamin)
Private • Captain William E. Booe's Partisan Rangers • N.C. Volunteers • Company H, 63rd Regiment • (5th Regiment N.C. Cavalry) • N.C. Troops

Benjamin was born in 1833 in Davie County, to Sally (1795, Davie) Howard. In 1850 he was the oldest of four children living with their mother. His first marriage was to Martha Matilda James on February 25, 1857. They farmed in the Smith Grove area and their children were Sarah E. (1858), Thomas K. (1860), Mary Belle (1862), Nancy C. (1864) and Caremea (1869). Benjamin enlisted in Davie County at age 30, July 18, 1862, for the war. He was present or accounted for until transferred to the 47th Regiment, N.C. Troops, on October 5, 1864. Benjamin lived on a farm in Farmington when he married his second wife, Nancy E. James, on July 6, 1873. Their children were Jenid (1874), Mattie (1876) and William (1879). Benjamin died on July 24, 1913; he is buried at Bethlehem United Methodist Church Cemetery.

545. Howard, Joseph Bryant
Private • Captain William E. Booe's Partisan Rangers • N.C. Volunteers • Company H, 63rd Regiment • (5th Regiment N.C. Cavalry) • N.C. Troops

Joseph was born in 1830 in Davie County, to William (1785, Davie) and Elenor (1796, Ran-

Joseph Bryant Howard was wounded August 7, 1864, and spent the rest of 1864 either in the hospital or trying to recover (Alvin Howard).

dolph). He worked as a farmer in the Fulton District when he enlisted at age 33, July 18, 1862, for the war. He was present or accounted for on company muster rolls through August 1864 when he was reported with the remark: "Wounded 7 August. At Naval Hospital." He was admitted to the hospital at Richmond, Virginia, October 10, 1864, and furloughed for 60 days, November 11, 1864. Joseph married Mary (1835, North Carolina) and their three children were James M. (1857), Thomas L. (1860) and Nancy J. (1862). He remained in Fulton District where he was listed in 1880 with his wife "Polly" and their daughter Nancy. Joseph died on February 2, 1902, and is buried in Smith Grove United Methodist Church Cemetery.

546. Howard, Cornelius
Private, Company F, 42nd Regiment • N.C. Troops

Cornelius was born in Davie County in 1816. On April 7, 1838, he married Loucinda (1821, Davie) Howard. Cornelius enlisted in Davie County at age 47, on March 18, 1862. He was present or accounted for through February 22, 1865. In 1870 Loucinda and Cornelius were living and farming in the Fulton District with their nine children: William (1839), Sarah (1841), Rachel (1842), Louiza (1846), Emeline (1849), Henry (1851), Mary E. (1853), George W. (1856) and Maria (1860).

547. Howard, Harrison H. (Henry)
Corporal, "Davie Greys" • Company F, 13th Regiment • (3rd Regiment, N.C. Volunteers) • N.C. Troops

Harrison was born in 1841 in Davie County, to Robert (1805, North Carolina) and Matilda Call (1812, North Carolina) Howard. His father was a shoemaker, and Harrison was a printer prior to enlisting in Davie at age 20, April 26, 1861. He mustered in as a Private and was present or accounted for until wounded in the right arm at Chancellorsville, Virginia, May 3, 1863. He rejoined the company in July–August, 1863, and was promoted to Corporal on September 1, 1863. He was present or accounted for until captured at Wilderness, Virginia, May 6, 1864, and confined at Point Lookout, Maryland, until transferred to Elmira, New York, August 10, 1864, where he died on February 13, 1865, of "variola." Harrison's name is listed on the Memorial Monument for the Davie County men who died in the Civil War, 1861–1865.

548. Howard, Joseph
Private, Company F, 42nd Regiment • N.C. Troops

Joseph was born in 1819 in Davie County. By 1860 he and his wife Eliza had become parents to eight children: Manerva (1843), Samuel (1845), Tabitha (Delia) (1847), Henry (1849), Spencer (1852), Thomas (1854), Sarah J. (1855) and Mary L. (1858). On March 18, 1862, at age 43, Joseph enlisted in Davie County. He was present or accounted for through February 20, 1865. The family had lived in the Smith Grove District prior to the war. Upon Joseph's return they farmed in the Farmington and Fulton Districts. Joseph died on November 20, 1907. He is buried in Advance United Methodist Church Cemetery. His tombstone attests to his military service.

549. Howard, Morgan G.
Private, Company E, 42nd Regiment • N.C. Troops

Morgan was born in 1831 in Davie County, the son of Philip (1798, Davie) and Sarah (1800, Davie) Howard. His father was a wagoner and Morgan was a laborer. He married Sarah Ann Foster on December 18, 1856, and farmed in the Liberty District prior to enlisting in Davie County at age 32, on April 24, 1862, for the war. He was present or accounted for through October 1864. He took the Oath of Allegiance at Salisbury, North Carolina, on June 2, 1865. Sarah Ann and Morgan had nine children: Mary J. (1857), William F. (1859), David (1861), Henry (1864), Victoria (1866), DeWitt (1870), Ugene G. (1873), Samuel (1879) and Sarah E. (1879).

550. Howard, Nathan
Private, Company E, 42nd Regiment • N.C. Troops

Nathan was born in 1843 (1839) in Davie County to Sally (1795, Davie) Howard. By 1860 he had married Sarah (1840, North Carolina) and was working as a laborer in the Farmington District. He enlisted on March 18, 1862, and was present or accounted for until killed at Petersburg, Virginia, June 17, 1864. Nathan's name is listed on the Memorial Monument for the Davie County men who died in the Civil War, 1861–1865.

551. Howard, Philip G.
Private, Company E, 42nd Regiment • N.C. Troops

Philip was born in 1838 in Davie County. He was the son of Philip (1798, Davie) and Sarah (1800, Davie) Howard. In 1860 he was working as a wagoner while living with his parents in the Liberty District. He enlisted in Davie County at age 24, on April 24, 1862, for the war. Philip was present or accounted for through October 1864. He was paroled at Salisbury, North Carolina, on May 24, 1865.

552. Howard, Robert
Private, Company D, 42nd Regiment • N.C. Troops

Robert was born in Davie County in 1805. He married Matilda Call (1812, North Carolina) on August 8, 1837. Robert made his living as a shoemaker. He enlisted in Rowan County or Davie County at age 56 on January 30, 1862. He was present or accounted for until December 10, 1862, when he was detailed for duty as a shoemaker in Salisbury, North Carolina. He was reported absent on detail at Salisbury through October 1864. Robert retired from service on January 5, 1865; the reason was not reported. In 1870 at age 62, Robert and Matilda lived in Mocksville with their two sons, William (1839) and Henry (1841), a printer. On October 28, 1879, Robert married Caroline Bullybough, and along with her son Frank (1865), they moved to Farmington where he continued his work as a shoemaker at age 75.

553. Howard, Samuel B.
Private, Company F, 42nd Regiment • N.C. Troops

Samuel B. was born in 1845 in Davie County. He was the son of Joseph (1819, Davie) and Eliza (1819, Davie) Howard. Samuel enlisted in Davie County at age 20, on April 15, 1864, for the war. Samuel's father also served in this company. He was present or accounted for through January 20, 1865. (North Carolina pension records indicate he was wounded at Petersburg, Virginia, in July 1864 or on August 15, 1864.) Ellen Bradford (1854) married Samuel on January 15, 1879. Carrie was born in 1880, in the Fulton District of Davie where they lived and farmed.

554. Howard, Samuel B.
Private • Captain William E. Booe's Partisan Rangers • N.C. Volunteers • Company H, 63rd Regiment • (5th Regiment N.C. Cavalry) • N.C. Troops

Samuel was born in Davie County in 1835 to William (1785, Davie) and Elenor (1796, Randolph) Howard. He lived in Fulton District where he married Mary Jane Call (1840) on June 9, 1861. Samuel enlisted in Davie County at age 25, July 18, 1862, for the war. He was present or accounted for through September 1864, and was paroled at Mocksville, North Carolina, on June 9, 1865. Samuel was a farmer living in Fulton in 1870. Mary and Samuel were the parents of six children: LaFayette (1859), Rush (P.R.) (1864), Emma (1868), Alice (1872), Charlie (1874) and Zachariah (1877). Samuel died on December 20, 1917. He is buried in Smith Grove United Methodist Church Cemetery.

555. Howard, Wilson
Private, Company E, 42nd Regiment • N.C. Troops

Wilson was born in 1816 in Davie County. He married Mary Owens on February 2, 1844. He was a farmer prior to enlisting in Davie County at age 46, on March 25, 1862. He was present or accounted for until discharged on February 27, 1864. The reason for the discharge was not reported. Wilson and Mary were the parents of five children: Sarah (1845), Lewis (1849), John (1850), Malinda (1852) and Samuel (1856). Following his discharge Wilson returned to his family and to farming in the Fulton District.

556. Howell, Alexander Charles
Private, Company F, 42nd Regiment • N.C. Troops

Alexander was born in Davie County in 1844, the son of George (1813, Davie) and Nancy Hall (1827, Davie) Howell. They farmed in the Farmington District. Alexander enlisted in Davie at age 18, on March 18, 1862. He was present or accounted for through October 1864 and paroled at Mocksville on June 7, 1865. In 1870 at age 26, Alexander was living at home with his family in the Farmington District.

557. Howell, John C.
Second Lieutenant • Captain William E. Booe's Partisan Rangers • N.C. Volunteers • Company H, 63rd Regiment • (5th Regiment N.C. Cavalry) • N.C. Troops

John was born December 14, 1832, in Davie County. He married Ester E. Naylor on May 4, 1862, and two months later enlisted in Davie, July 15, 1862, for the war. John was appointed Second Lieutenant to rank from September 1, 1862. He submitted his resignation December 10, 1862, by reason of his health and it was officially accepted December 20, 1862. In 1863 he and Ester became parents of Ida Jane; Bertie was born in 1865. John died on March 31, 1915. Ester died on February 17, 1893. Both are buried in Eaton's Baptist Church Cemetery.

558. Howell, Joseph H.
Second Lieutenant • Captain William E. Booe's Partisan Rangers • N.C. Volunteers • Company H,

63rd Regiment • (5th Regiment N.C. Cavalry) • N.C. Troops

Joseph enlisted in Davie County on July 9, 1862, for the war. He mustered in as Sergeant and was promoted to First Sergeant on November–December, 1862. He was elected Second Lieutenant, March 2, 1863, captured near Hagerstown, Maryland, July 12, 1863, and confined at Point Lookout, Maryland, until paroled and exchanged at City Point, Virginia, March 20, 1864. He was reported as "absent without leave" on July–August, 1864, muster roll. The inspection report dated September 25, 1864, carries the remark: "Absent without leave since July 18, 1864. Dropped from service November 24, 1864."

559. Hunt (Hunter), Henry H.
Private, 1st Company A, Salisbury Prison Guard • "The Rough and Readys" • Company G, 66th Regiment • N.C. Troops

Henry was born in 1841 in Davie County to Charles (1808, Davie) and Elizabeth (1817, Davie) Hunter. They lived in the Chinquepin District of Davie where his father was a farmer and Henry was a laborer. Henry enlisted as a Private in 1st Company A prior to transferring to Company G of the 66th on October 2, 1863. He was reported present through April 30, 1864. He was hospitalized at Richmond, Virginia, August 22, 1864, with an unspecified complaint, furloughed on or about August 29, 1864, and reported sick at home through October 31, 1864. He was paroled at Greensboro, North Carolina, on May 29, 1865. He returned home to Mocksville where he married S.E. Graves on June 16, 1865.

560. Hunt, John W.
Rank unknown • "The Rough and Readys" • Company G, 66th Regiment • N.C. Troops

North Carolina pension records indicate that he served in this company. Survived the war.

561. Hunter, Henry H.
Private, Company F, 42nd Regiment • N.C. Troops

Henry enlisted in Davie County at age 19, March 19, 1862. He was present or accounted for through November 24, 1864.

562. Hunter, John W.
Private, "Davie Greys" • Company F, 13th Regiment • (3rd Regiment, N.C. Volunteers) • N.C. Troops

John was born in 1836 in Davie County. He was the son of Charles (1808, Davie) and Elizabeth (1817, Davie). In 1860 they lived in the Chinquepin District where Charles was a farmer and John, age 23, was a constable. On August 6, 1861, John enlisted in Davie. He was present or accounted for until wounded in the arm, leg and side at Chancellorsville, Virginia, May 3, 1863. He was reported absent wounded or absent on detail as a guard until he rejoined the company in March–April, 1864, and then retired to the Invalid Corps on April 30, 1864. He was paroled at Salisbury, North Carolina, in 1865. He resumed his life in Davie County and married Mary E. Smith on August 29, 1871. A daughter, Clara B., was born in 1873. In 1880 the family lived in the Clarksville District where John worked as a farmer. He died on April 26, 1885, and is buried at Eaton's Baptist Church Cemetery.

563. Hunter, Samuel
Private, Company F, 42nd Regiment • N.C. Troops

Samuel enlisted in Davie County on April 15, 1864, for the war. He was present or accounted for through November 1, 1864. No further records available.

564. Hutchins, Andrew J.
Private • Captain William E. Booe's Partisan Rangers • N.C. Volunteers • Company H, 63rd Regiment • (5th Regiment N.C. Cavalry) • N.C. Troops

Andrew was born in 1834 in Surry County. By 1850 he lived and worked as a laborer on the farm of Alexander Hartman in Davie County. He married Paulina M. Ferebee on December 8, 1856, and they settled in the Farmington District where he enlisted at age 28, on July 15, 1862, for the war. He was present or accounted for through September 1864 and paroled at Salisbury, North Carolina, in 1865. Andrew returned to his home and his growing family. By 1880 there were ten children: Martha E. (1858), Sousan E. (1860), Andrew J. (1862), Samuel F. (1864), Sarah (1867), William R. (1871), Mary L. (1873), Thomas A. (1873), Oscar G. (1876) and an infant (1880). A.J. died on April 3, 1911. He is buried in Wesley Chapel United Methodist Church Cemetery.

565. Idol, A. Jackson
Corporal, Company G, 7th Regiment • Confederate Cavalry • Company D, 16th Battalion • N.C. Cavalry

Jackson enlisted in Davie County on September 3, 1862, with the rank of Corporal, later promoted to Sergeant. He transferred from Company G, 7th Regiment Confederate Cavalry to Company D, 16th Battalion N.C. Cavalry on

July 11, 1864. He was reported on the muster roll of September 1–October 1, 1864, as "captured by the enemy" September 30, 1864. No further records.

566. Ijames, B.G. (Basil) (Boswell)
Private, Captain William E. Booe's Partisan Rangers • N.C. Volunteers • Company H, 63rd Regiment • (5th Regiment N.C. Cavalry) • N.C. Troops

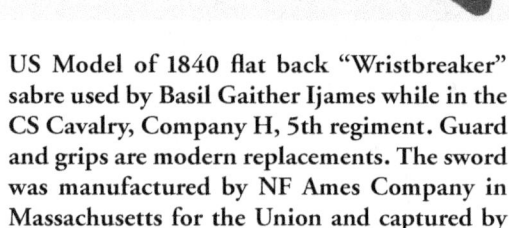

Basil G. Ijames (Melinda Evans)

B.G. was born in 1845 in Davie County to Beal (1809, Davie) and Rachel (1814, Davie) Ijames. They lived on a farm in the Calahaln District when B.G. enlisted on September 18, 1863, for the war. He was present or accounted for through February 1865. He returned home to help his father farm, but established his own farm in Jerusalem Township when he married Dovie A. Brown on December 12, 1871. Their children were Franklin S. (1872), Ossie C. (1874), Maggie V. (1877) and Amelia B. (1879). B.G. died in 1924 and is buried in Center United Methodist Church Cemetery. His brother Beal also served in this company.

US Model of 1840 flat back "Wristbreaker" sabre used by Basil Gaither Ijames while in the CS Cavalry, Company H, 5th regiment. Guard and grips are modern replacements. The sword was manufactured by NF Ames Company in Massachusetts for the Union and captured by Jeb Stuart's troops (Melinda Evans).

567. Ijames, B.R. (Beal)
Private, Captain William E. Booe's Partisan Rangers • N.C. Volunteers • Company H, 63rd Regiment • (5th Regiment N.C. Cavalry) • N.C. Troops

Beal was born October 24, 1837, in Davie County to Beal (1809, Davie) and Rachel (1814, Davie) Ijames. He worked as a farm laborer along with his brothers Matthew and B.G. on the family farm owned by his father, Beal Sr. They lived in Calahaln District where Beal Jr. married Matilda J. Coon on December 20, 1860. Their children were John N. (1862), Alice (1865), Robert M. (1869) and Josephine (1873). Beal enlisted in Davie County at age 24, July 15, 1862, for the war. He was present or accounted for through February 1865, and was paroled at Salisbury, North Carolina, in 1865. He returned home to Davie County and Calahaln, and later moved to Jerusalem District. He died November 8, 1898, and is buried in Center United Methodist Church Cemetery. His brother Basil also served in this company.

568. Ijames (Ijmes) (Ijams), Henry H.
Private, "Davie Sweep Stakes" • Company G, 4th Regiment • N.C. State Troops

Henry was born in 1841 to James (1810, Davie) and Nancy (1819, Davie) Ijames. They lived in the Chinquepin District where Henry worked as a laborer prior to enlisting at age 20, on July 2, 1861, for the war. According to Davie County marriage records, Henry married Mary Jane Anderson two days later July 4, 1861. Company rolls indicate he was wounded at Seven Pines, Virginia, May 31, 1862, and died in the hospital at Richmond, Virginia, on an unspecified date; however, medical records indicate he was admitted to the hospital at Richmond on May 31, 1862, with "typhoid" and died July 28, 1862. No further records. Henry's name is listed on the Memorial Monument for the Davie County men who died in the Civil War, 1861–1865.

569. Ijames, John F.
Private, "Davie Sweep Stakes" • Company G, 4th Regiment • N.C. State Troops

John enlisted in Davie County on March 10, 1862, for the war. He was reported "sick in quarters" through June 1862. No further records.

570. Ijames, John W.
Private, "Davie Sweep Stakes" • Company G, 4th Regiment • N.C. State Troops

John enlisted in Davie County on July 1, 1861, for the war. He died March 8, 1862, of "febris typhus." The place of death is not known. John's name is listed on the Memorial Monument for the Davie County men who died in the Civil War, 1861–1865.

571. Ijams (Ijames), James D.
Sergeant, "Davie Greys" • Company F, 13th Regiment • (3rd Regiment, N.C. Volunteers) • N.C. Troops

James was born in Davie County in 1841, to Beal (1809, Davie) and Rachel (1814, Davie) Ijames. He resided in Davie County and worked as a farmer prior to enlisting at age 20, April 26, 1861. He married Mary E. Coon on November 19, 1861. James mustered in as a Corporal and was present or accounted for until captured at Williamsburg, Virginia, on or about May 6, 1862. He was exchanged and rejoined the company prior to November 1, 1862. He was present or accounted for until wounded at Chancellorsville, Virginia, May 3, 1863. He rejoined the company in July–August, 1863, and was promoted to Sergeant on September 1, 1863. He was present or accounted for until paroled at Appomattox Court House, Virginia, April 9, 1865. By 1870 the family lived and farmed in Calahaln, then in the Jerusalem District in 1880. By then, the family had grown to seven children: Clare A. (1864), James Garland (1866), Beal S. (1866), Bell (Adelia) (1870), Cora L. (1873), George F. (1876) and Emma M. (1879). James is buried in Center United Methodist Church Cemetery. Mary's application for a widow's pension is on file at the State Archives, Raleigh, North Carolina.

572. Ijams, James M.
Private, Company G, 5th Regiment • N.C. State Troops

James was born in 1843 in North Carolina to James (1800, North Carolina) and Nancy (1821, North Carolina) Ijams. They resided in the Chinquepin District of Davie County where James worked as a laborer prior to enlisting in Northampton County at age 19, on August 13, 1862, for the war. He was present or accounted for until captured at Gettysburg, Pennsylvania, July 3–4, 1863. He was confined at Fort McHenry, Maryland, and at Fort Delaware, Delaware, until transferred to Point Lookout, Maryland, October 15–18, 1863. He was paroled at Point Lookout on February 18, 1865, and transferred to Boulware's Wharf, James River, Virginia, for exchange. He was paroled at Salisbury, North Carolina, in 1865.

573. Ijams, Matthew N.
Corporal, "Davie Greys" • Company F, 13th Regiment • (3rd Regiment, N.C. Volunteers) • N.C. Troops

Matthew was born in 1842 in Davie County. He was the son of Beal (1809, Davie) and Rachel (1814, Davie) Ijames, and the brother of James D. Ijames of this company. In 1860 he was a farm laborer living in Calahaln. On August 6, 1861, he enlisted in Davie County for the war. Matthew mustered in as a Private. He was present or accounted for until he was wounded and captured at Williamsburg, Virginia, on or about May 6, 1862. He was hospitalized at Washington, D.C., until transferred to Old Capitol Prison, Washington, June 27, 1862. He transferred to Aiken's Landing, James River, Virginia, where he was received August 5, 1862, for exchange. After rejoining the company prior to November 1, 1862, he was promoted to Corporal on December 6, 1862. He was present or accounted for until captured at Falling Waters, Maryland, July 14, 1863. He was confined at Point Lookout, Maryland, until paroled and transferred to City Point, Virginia, where he was received March 20, 1864, for exchange. He rejoined the company in May–June, 1864, and was present or accounted for through

October 1864, until paroled at Salisbury, North Carolina, in 1865.

574. Inscore, Lewis
Private, Company F, 42nd Regiment • N.C. Troops

Lewis was born in North Carolina in 1821. In 1860 he was a house carpenter living in the Mocksville District with his wife Margaret E. Inscore and their three children: John H. (1845), James H. (1846) and Martin (1856). He enlisted in Davie County at age 41, on March 18, 1862. He deserted on June 8, 1862. No further information.

575. Jackson, Daniel H.
Private, Captain William E. Booe's Partisan Rangers • N.C. Volunteers • Company H, 63rd Regiment • (5th Regiment N.C. Cavalry) • N.C. Troops

Daniel was born in 1834 in North Carolina. He married Mary C. Hall on October 21, 1856, and they settled in the Chinquepin District of Davie County where he worked as a laborer. Their children were Phillip (1857), Cornelia (1859) and John (1862). Daniel enlisted in Davie County on July 18, 1862, for the war. He was present or accounted for through February 1863. The information regarding the death of Private Jackson is not available presently, but his name is listed on the Memorial Monument for the Davie County men who died in the Civil War, 1861–1865.

576. Jacobs, (Gacop), John
Private, Company D, 42nd Regiment • N.C. Troops

John was born in 1842 in North Carolina. As a young man he worked as a farm laborer in the Farmington District, and lived with Jesse and Martha J. Lasiter. He enlisted in Rowan County at age 25, on March 18, 1862. John died in the hospital at Petersburg, Virginia, on September 10, 1862, of "febris typhoides." John's name is listed on the Memorial Monument for the Davie County men who died in the Civil War, 1861–1865.

577. James, J.F. (James)
Private, "Davie Sweep Stakes" • Company G, 4th Regiment • N.C. State Troops

James was born in 1844. He resided in Davie County prior to enlisting at age 18, March 10, 1862, for the war. He died in camp near Richmond, Virginia, on July 18, 1862. Cause of death was not reported. James's name is listed on the Memorial Monument for the Davie County men who died in the Civil War, 1861–1865.

578. James, J.W.
Private, "Davie Sweep Stakes" • Company G, 4th Regiment • N.C. State Troops

J.W. was born in 1843. He resided in Davie County where he enlisted at age 18, July 1, 1861, for the war. He died prior to June 23, 1863. The place, exact date and cause of death were not reported. No further records. J.W.'s name is listed on the Memorial Monument for the Davie County men who died in the Civil War, 1861–1865.

579. James, John R.
Private, Company D, 42nd Regiment • N.C. Troops

John was born in Davie County in 1845 to Annen (1794, Davie) and Sarah (1804, Davie) James. John's father was a farmer in Smith Grove, and John worked as a laborer. The place and date of John's enlistment were not reported. He was captured at or near Wise's Forks, Kinston, North Carolina, on March 10, 1865, and was confined at Point Lookout, Maryland, on March 16, 1865. He was released at Point Lookout on June 28, 1865, after taking the Oath of Allegiance. He returned to the Farmington District of Davie County where he resumed his life as a farmer. He also assumed a new role as a husband and father. He married Mary (1844) Burton on June 22, 1878, and Sarah E. was born in 1880.

580. James, Julius
Private, Captain William E. Booe's Partisan Rangers • N.C. Volunteers • Company H, 63rd Regiment • (5th Regiment N.C. Cavalry) • N.C. Troops

Julius was born in 1846 in Davie County to William (1819, Surry) A. and Sarah A. (1825, Person) Rich James. His father's occupation was "Potter," and the family remained in the Farmington District throughout the war and afterward. Julius enlisted in Davie County April 1, 1864, for the war. He was present or accounted for through August 1864. He returned home and married Sarah A. Rich on August 14, 1866. Their children were W.H. (1869), Vashti (1875) and Joseph (1877).

581. James, Thomas A.
Private, Company E, 42nd Regiment • N.C. Troops

Thomas was the son of Annen (1794, Davie) and Sarah (1804) James, who were farmers. Thomas was born in 1840 in Davie County. In 1860 he was a laborer living in the Smith Grove District. He enlisted in Davie County at age 27, on March 18, 1862. He was present or accounted for until wounded in battle at Camp Wingfield near Edenton, North Carolina, on or about March 23, 1863, and died on or about March 25, 1863. The place of death was not reported. Thomas's name is listed on the Memorial Monument for the Davie County men who died in the Civil War, 1861–1865.

582. James, W. (William) Asberry
Private, Company D, 42nd Regiment • N.C. Troops

Asberry was born in 1825 in Davie County. He was the son of Annen (1794, Davie) and Sarah (1804, Davie) James. He made his living as a farmer, and on April 19, 1853, he married Lydia Etchison. They made their home in Farmington but Asberry enlisted in Rowan County at age 38 for the war. He was present or accounted for through October 1864, and was paroled at Appomattox Court House, Virginia, on April 9, 1865. Lydia and Asberry were the parents of six children: Julia (1854), Nathan W. (1857), Rhoda (1866), Nancy (1868), Rosa M. (1873) and Mary C. (1877). After the war, he returned to farming again in Farmington. Asberry died in 1902 and is buried in Bethlehem United Methodist Church Cemetery. He lived to be 78 years and 29 days old.

583. Jarvis, Jonathan
Private, Company F, 42nd Regiment • N.C. Troops

Jonathan was born in 1818 in Davie County. He married Rachel (1826, Davidson) Owen on May 14, 1848. Their two children were Henry G. (1849) and Jesse F. (1852). When Rachel died, he married Sarah Ann Painter on July 5, 1859. They lived in the Smith Grove District where he worked as a laborer prior to enlisting in Davie County at age 44, on March 24, 1862. He was present or accounted for until he died in the hospital at Richmond, Virginia, on or about August 27, 1864, of disease. Jonathan's name is listed on the Memorial Monument for the Davie County men who died in the Civil War, 1861–1865.

584. Jenkins, Addison
Private, Company D, 42nd Regiment • N.C. Troops

Addison resided in Davie County and enlisted in Rowan County at age 27, March 18, 1862. He deserted prior to September 1, 1862. No further information available.

585. Johnson, B.S. (Burton)
Private, Company H, 23rd Regiment • N.C. Troops

Burton was born in 1840 in North Carolina. On July 25, 1859, he married Elizabeth F. Elum (1843, North Carolina). In 1860 he and Elizabeth lived and farmed in the Calahaln District. On August 1, 1862, he enlisted in Iredell County, for the war. He was present or accounted for until he was paroled at Appomattox Court House, Virginia, on April 9, 1865. Burton served as a teamster during most of the war.

586. Johnson, Baker A.
Private, Company F, 42nd Regiment • N.C. Troops

Baker was born in 1844. He married Ellen Revis in Davie County on December 25, 1861. He enlisted in Davie County at age 18, on March 22, 1862. He was present or accounted for until he was reported absent wounded in May–August, 1864. The place and date were not reported. He returned to duty in September–October, 1864, and was present or accounted for through October 1864. There is no further record except that Ellen (Elender) gave birth to Bettie Johnson in 1866, and the two of them lived with her mother, Edy Revis, in 1870.

587. Johnson, General W.
Private, Company E, 42nd Regiment • N.C. Troops

General was born in 1823. He and Temperance (1822, North Carolina) were married and raising a family in the Fulton District prior to the war. At age 39 he enlisted in Davie County on March 18, 1862. He was present or accounted for through October 1864; however, he was reported absent on detached service as a shoemaker, nurse and cook during much of that period. General returned to his family and farming in the Fulton District. Temperance and General were the parents of seven children: Elizabeth (1844), Winney (1846), Emeline (1848), Jane (1852), Andrew (1856), Nancy A. (1858) and Amanda (1860).

588. Johnson, James Mullis
First Lieutenant, Regiment Assistant Commissary • 77th Regiment, 19th Division • N.C. Militia 1861–1865

James was born October 6, 1824, in Davidson County. By 1850 he had moved to Davie County and married Sarah R. (1828, Surry). Victoria was born in 1848, followed by Eugene (1853), Mary C. (1857), Sarah E. (1860), James M. (1862) and William L. (1865). James worked as a merchant and farmer to support his growing family. When the militia was activated, he was commissioned First Lieutenant. The family lived in the town of Mocksville until they relocated to Farmington prior to 1880. Daughter Sarah was a music teacher; James and Willie were students, and there were four farm hands and one nurse living with them. James's second wife was Rachel Ann Smith. They married August 25, 1879. He died September 8, 1892, and is buried in Farmington Community Cemetery.

589. Johnson, S.W. (Samuel)
First Lieutenant, Company M, 7th Regiment • Confederate Cavalry • Company E, 16th Battalion • N.C. Cavalry

S.W. was born in Davie County in 1839. He lived with J.M. and Sarah Johnson next door to the Mocksville Hotel. In 1862 Samuel enlisted in Company M in Davie County and was commissioned First Lieutenant. He was transferred to Company E, 16th Battalion N.C. Cavalry on July 11, 1864, and was killed in action October 27, 1864. Samuel's name is listed on the Memorial Monument for the Davie County men who died in the Civil War, 1861–1865.

590. Johnson, William Gaston
Corporal, Company F, 42nd Regiment • N.C. Troops

William was born in Davie County on April 23, 1845, the son of George W. (1810,

Interior view of William Gaston Johnson home (Mohney, *The Historic Architecture of Davie County*).

The home of William Gaston Johnson. The George Wesley Johnson family played a prominent role in the development of Farmington in the 1800s (Mohney, *The Historic Architecture of Davie County*).

Davidson) and Martha W. (1816, Davie) Taylor Johnson. His father maintained a large household in the Farmington District where he worked as a merchant. William enlisted in Davie County on June 15, 1863, for the war. He mustered in as a Private and was promoted to Corporal on December 4, 1863. He was present or accounted for through October 1864, and paroled at Greensboro, North Carolina, on May 1, 1865. William entered the University of Pennsylvania in 1870 and was licensed to practice medicine in North Carolina in 1873. He married Emma C. Miller (1851–1917) on February 18, 1875, and they raised three children: Bertha (no dates given), Spencer (no dates given) and Wesley (1883). William, his parents, wife and children are all buried in Farmington Community Cemetery. His tombstone reads "William G. Johnson, M.D." The date of death was October 14, 1911.

591. Jones, Ebed
Private, Company F, 42nd Regiment • N.C. Troops

Ebed was born in 1830 in North Carolina. In 1860 he was a farmer who lived in the Chinquepin District of Davie County. He enlisted there at age 32, on March 18, 1862. Ebed was present or accounted for until he was captured at or near Wise's Forks, Kinston, North Carolina, on March 10, 1865. He was confined at Point Lookout, Maryland, March 16, 1865, and was later released at Point Lookout on May 15, 1865.

592. Jones, Emory W.
Private, Company G, 7th Regiment • Confederate Cavalry • Company D, 16th Battalion • N.C. Cavalry

Emory enlisted in Davie County on September 3, 1862. He was transferred from Company G, 7th Regiment Confederate Cavalry to Company D, 16th Battalion N.C. Cavalry on July 11, 1864, while absent "detailed with artillery." He was absent detailed through August 1864, and present or accounted for through October 1864.

593. Jones, Henry T.
Private, Captain William E. Booe's Partisan Rangers • N.C. Volunteers • Company H, 63rd Regiment • (5th Regiment N.C. Cavalry) • N.C. Troops

Henry enlisted in Davie County on July 18, 1862, for the war. He was killed in action at Upperville, Virginia, June 21, 1863. Henry's name is listed on the Memorial Monument for the Davie County men who died in the Civil War, 1861–1865.

594. Jones, John
Private, Company M, 7th Regiment • Confederate Cavalry • Company E, 16th Battalion • N.C. Cavalry

John enlisted in Davie County on September 3, 1862, with the rank of Private. He was transferred from Company M, 7th Regiment Confederate Cavalry to Company E, 16th Battalion N.C. Cavalry on July 11, 1864. He was present or accounted for through October 1, 1864, and paroled at Salisbury, North Carolina, in 1865.

595. Jones, Madison
Private, Company F, 13th Regiment • (3rd Regiment, N.C. Volunteers) • N.C. Troops

Madison enlisted at Camp Holmes near Raleigh on December 12, 1863, for the war. He was discharged in January–February, 1864. The reason he was discharged was not reported.

596. Jones, Martin
Private, Company D, 42nd Regiment • N.C. Troops

Martin was born in North Carolina in 1838. He worked as a laborer in the Mocksville District where he lived with his brother and sister prior to enlisting in Davie County or Rowan County at age 24, on January 29, 1862. He was present or accounted for until July 18, 1864, when he deserted, but he returned to duty on September 22, 1864. He was paroled at Salisbury, North Carolina, on May 19, 1865. Martin married Caroline and they had two children: William (1867) and Julia (1868). In 1870 they were farming in the Jerusalem District.

597. Jones, Matthew (Mathew)
Private, Company G, 5th Regiment • N.C. State Troops

Matthew was born in 1836 in North Carolina. In 1860 he and his brother Martin resided with S.E. Jones, seamstress, in the Mocksville District of Davie County. He enlisted in Northampton County at age 26, on August 13, 1862, for the war. He was present or accounted for until he deserted in May 1863. He rejoined the company prior to September 1, 1863, and was present or accounted for until wounded in the left arm at Spotsylvania Court House, Virginia, May 19, 1864. The arm was amputated. He took the Oath of Allegiance at Salisbury, North Carolina, on May 25, 1865.

598. Jones, Samuel A.
Private, "Davie Sweep Stakes" • Company G, 4th Regiment • N.C. State Troops

Samuel was born in 1846 to W.G. (1822,

North Carolina) and Martha (1830, North Carolina) Jones. They lived in the Mocksville District of Davie County where he enlisted at age 16, March 17, 1862, for the war. He was wounded at Seven Pines, Virginia, May 31, 1862, and died at Richmond, Virginia, June 20–21, 1862, of wounds. Samuel's name is listed on the Memorial Monument for the Davie County men who died in the Civil War, 1861–1865.

599. Jones, Thomas J.
Private, Company B, Carolina Rangers • 10th Virginia Cavalry Regiment

Thomas was born in 1842 in Davie County to James (1821, Davie) and Sarah (1816, Davie) Jones. His father worked as a "stiller." Thomas enlisted in Davie County on October 29, 1861, at age 19. He was present until December 23, 1862, when he was absent sick in Richmond hospital. He returned to duty but was present in arrest January and February 1863, then "court-martialed June 3, 1863, no horse June 1–15, 1863." He was then either present or absent on detached service through August 1864. He received clothing in September and December 1864. There is no further military information. Thomas returned to Davie County where he married Nancy C. Drake on December 21, 1865.

600. Jones, W. Albert
Private, Company G, 7th Regiment • Confederate Cavalry • Company D, 16th Battalion • N.C. Cavalry

Albert enlisted in Davie County on September 3, 1862. He was transferred from Company G, 7th Regiment Confederate Cavalry to Company D, 16th Battalion N.C. Cavalry on July 11, 1864, while absent "detailed with artillery." He was absent detailed through August 1864 and present or accounted for through October 1, 1864.

601. Jones, Wifey A.G.
First Lieutenant, Company H • 77th Regiment, 19th Division • N.C. Militia 1861–1865

Wifey was born October 5, 1829, in Davie County. In 1850 he boarded with the Joseph Rich family, and was apparently an apprentice to learn the craft of wagon-making, since that happened to be Mr. Rich's occupation. Wilie was unmarried at the time. That changed July 10, 1853, when he wed Eliza B.D. Hoskins, who also happened to board with Mr. Rich. She became a homemaker. She and W.A. had two children: John H. (1858) and Clara J. (Chloe) (1859), by the time he had received his commission as First Lieutenant, Company H, of the North Carolina Militia. Their other children were William J. (1864), Robert (1865), Sarah E. (1867) and Oliver F. (1870). In 1880 the family lived in Fulton District. Wiley died July 3, 1895, and is buried in Advance United Methodist Church Cemetery.

602. Jones, William B.
2nd Lieutenant, "Davie Sweep Stakes" • Company G, 4th Regiment • N.C. State Troops

William was born in Davie County to Basil G. and Mary Jones on May 6, 1831. He enlisted at age 30, June 4, 1861, for the war. He mustered in as Sergeant; he was appointed Third Lieutenant on June 22, 1862, and promoted to 2nd Lieutenant on March 16, 1863. He was reported absent on detached service as a Provost Guard at Gordonsville, Virginia, from December 6, 1861, through October 1863. After being reported absent sick during much of 1864, he was admitted to the hospital at Richmond, Virginia, February 25, 1865, with "rheumatis acuta" and returned to duty March 31, 1865. In 1870 at age 39 he was serving Mocksville as deputy sheriff. Ten years later he was a crippled farmer living with his sister Emma. He died May 13, 1887, and is buried at Joppa Cemetery.

603. Jordan, Eli
Private, "Davie Sweep Stakes" • Company G, 4th Regiment • N.C. State Troops

Eli was born in 1837. He married Jane Parker on July 9, 1857. They resided in Davie County where he enlisted at age 23, June 4, 1861, for the war. He was captured at Seven Pines, Virginia, May 31–June 2, 1862, and confined at Fort Delaware, Delaware, until exchanged at Aiken's Landing, James River, Virginia, August 5, 1862. He was reported absent without leave or absent sick until he rejoined the company in November–December, 1863. He was present or accounted for until captured at Petersburg, Virginia, April 3, 1865, and confined at Hart's Island, New York Harbor, until released June 19–20, 1865, after taking the Oath of Allegiance. He returned to Davie County after the war and resumed his life as a farmer. Eli and Jane were the parents of George (1863), Robert L. (1872) and Mary J. (1876). At age 47 he and his family were living in the Jerusalem District.

604. Jordan, Gurney
Private, "Davie Sweep Stakes" • Company G, 4th Regiment • N.C. State Troops

Gurney was born in 1840. He married Casina (1842, North Carolina) and in 1860 he worked as a laborer in the Mocksville District where he enlisted at age 21, March 6, 1862, for the war. He was present or accounted for until he died in the hospital at Lynchburg, Virginia, on March 3, 1863. The cause of death was not reported. Gurney's name is listed on the Memorial Monument for the Davie County men who died in the Civil War, 1861–1865.

605. Jordan, Jonathan
Private, "Davie Sweep Stakes" • Company G, 4th Regiment • N.C. State Troops

Jonathan was born in 1839. On November 29, 1857, he married Mary Shives in Davie County where he enlisted at age 22, June 4, 1861, for the war. He was killed at Seven Pines, Virginia, May 31, 1862. Jonathan's name is listed on the Memorial Monument for the Davie County men who died in the Civil War, 1861–1865.

606. Jordan, William C.
Private, "Davie Sweep Stakes" • Company G, 4th Regiment • N.C. State Troops

William was born in 1835. He resided in Davie County where he enlisted at age 26, June 5, 1861, for the war. He was discharged at Richmond, Virginia, January 14, 1862. The reason for the discharge was not reported. He returned home to Davie County where he married Sarah Shives, February 4, 1862.

607. Kees, John
Private, Captain William E. Booe's Partisan Rangers • N.C. Volunteers • Company H, 63rd Regiment • (5th Regiment N.C. Cavalry) • N.C. Troops

John enlisted in Davie County on April 15, 1863, for the war. He was killed in action at Upperville, Virginia, on July 21, 1863. John's name is listed on the Memorial Monument for the Davie County men who died in the Civil War, 1861–1865.

608. Keller, Fraley Thomas
Private, Company A, 57th Regiment • N.C. Troops

Fraley was born in Davie County in 1832. He was the son of Henry (1800, Davie) and Susanna (1799, Virginia). Fraley married Q.P. (Quintella) Butler on April 21, 1858. They lived in the Mocksville District where they were farmers. On July 4, 1862, at age 30, Fraley enlisted in Rowan County for the war. He was reported present through October 31, 1862, then was sent to the hospital at Richmond, Virginia, on December 15, 1862, (apparently suffering from debilitas). He was transferred to the hospital at Danville, Virginia, on April 23, 1863, and then returned to duty in January–April, 1864. He was captured near Washington, D.C., on July 12, 1864, and was confined at Old Capitol Prison, Washington, on July 13, 1864. Fraley was transferred to Elmira, New York, where he arrived on July 25, 1864, and was paroled there on March 2, 1865, and transferred for exchange. No further records. Fraley and Quintella had four children: Laura Q. (1859), Virginia (1866), James (1868) and William T. (1875). After the war, Fraley was a farmer in the Jerusalem District, and later a carpenter boarding with the John P. Kurfees family in the Calahaln District.

609. Keller, John D.
Private, Company F, 42nd Regiment • 2nd Regiment Confederate Engineer Troops

John was born in 1824 in Davie County. He was a cabinet maker by trade. On January 4, 1849, he married Rebecah [sic] E. (1826, Davie) Leach. Their children were Mary E. (1849), Louisa S. (1852), Richard L. (1856) and Andrew P. (1858). By 1860 they were living in the Mocksville District where he had become a farmer. John enlisted in Davie County on December 18, 1862, for the war. He was present or accounted for until he was transferred to the 2nd Regiment Confederate Engineer Troops on August 27, 1864. Census figures for 1870 show him and his family farming in the Calahaln District of Davie County.

610. Keller, Joseph
Private, Company E, 42nd Regiment • N.C. Troops

Joseph was born in 1825 in Davie County. He was a farmer all his life. On August 6, 1846, he married Mehetable Keller from Davie County. Prior to the war they were farmers in the Mocksville District. At age 35, on March 18, 1862, he enlisted in Davie County. He was present or accounted for through October 1864. He was paroled at Mocksville on June 7, 1865. (North Carolina pension records indicate he was wounded near Petersburg, Virginia, in April 1864.) Joseph and Mehetable were the parents of seven children: Alexander (1850), Wm. M. (1855), Sarah C. (1857), Thomas J. (1858), Julia A. (1860), Mary

J. (1863) and John (1873). He is buried in Center United Methodist Church Cemetery. No dates are given. Hettie's application for a pension is on file at the State Archives, Raleigh, North Carolina.

611. Kelly, Albert Calvin
First Lieutenant, Company L • 77th Regiment, 19th Division • N.C. Militia 1861–1865

Albert was born December 10, 1840, in Davie County to Colonel William F. (1796) and Sarah A. (1807, Davie) Kelly. Albert was born into an old pioneer family that had furnished men for battle in wars dating back to the time that settlement of the area had begun. He was a student when the militia was activated and he was commissioned First Lieutenant of Company L. After the war he continued to live with his mother in the Mocksville District and to work as a trader. He died on October 11, 1918, and is buried in Joppa Cemetery.

612. Kelly, James Addison
First Lieutenant, Regiment Assistant Quartermaster • 77th Regiment, 19th Division • N.C. Militia 1861–1865

James was born on September 9, 1832, in Davie County to Colonel William F. and Sarah A. (1807, Davie) Kelly. He was one of seven sons born into a prosperous and influential family. Among many noteworthy contributions by the father, Colonel Kelly, was the drawing of plans for the Presbyterian Church built in 1840 in Mocksville, according to an article by Mary J. Heitman filed in the Davie County Library. At age 17, James worked as a clerk and in 1860 he was a trader in the town of Mocksville. When the militia mobilized he was commissioned a First Lieutenant and served as Regiment Assistant Quartermaster. He continued to live with his mother after the war, working as a farmer in the Mocksville District. After his marriage to Mary E. Austin on November 30, 1873, they moved to Jerusalem District where he continued to farm. Around the same time, they became owners of the Kelly Hotel in Mocksville, according to information from the Davie Enterprise Record, April 12, 1979. Their children were James F. (1875), Mary (1876) and Elvira (1879). James died on February 17, 1901. He is buried in Joppa Cemetery.

613. Kelly, John
Private, "Davie Sweep Stakes" • Company G, 4th Regiment • N.C. State Troops

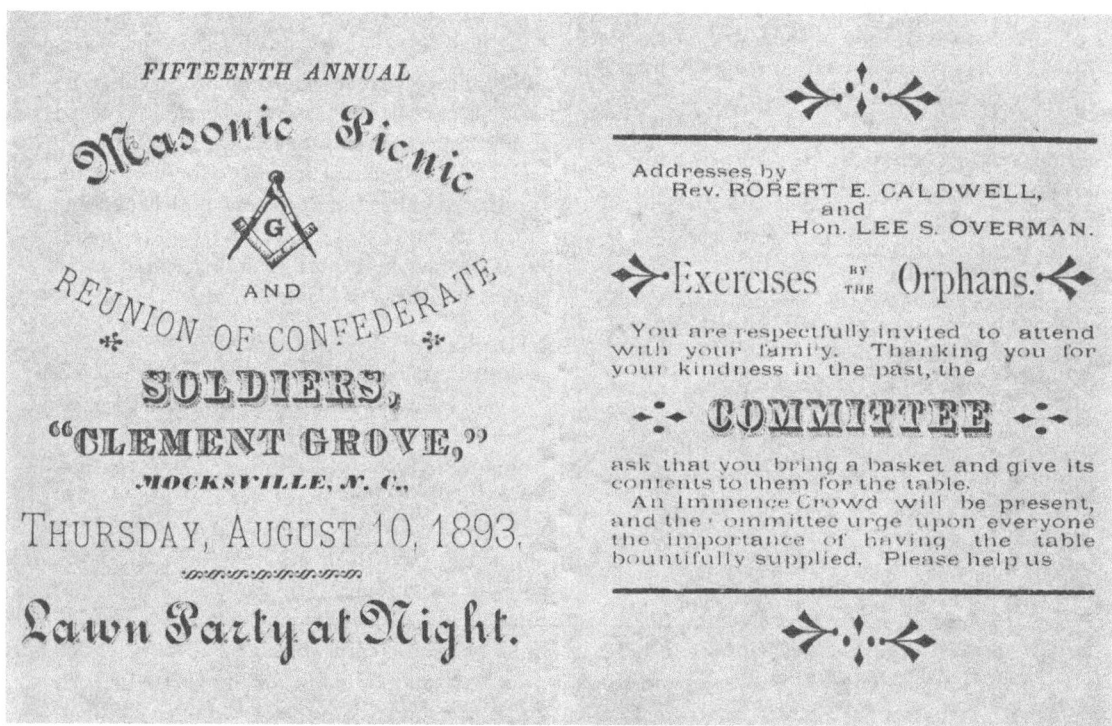

The 15th Annual Masonic Picnic brochure (Davie County Public Library).

Governor Aycock, known as our "Education Governor," addresses his attentive audience at the Masonic Picnic, Clement Grove, in Mocksville, circa early 1900s (Davie County Public Library).

John was born in 1828 in Rowan County (Davie County was formed in 1836 from Rowan County) to Colonel William F. (1795) and Sarah A. (1807, Davie) Kelly. He was the eldest of ten children: seven sons and three daughters, and he was from one of the major pioneering families of the area. They owned extensive property in 1850, including twenty-seven slaves. John resided in Davie County where he by occupation was a clerk prior to enlisting in Davie County at age 33, June 5, 1861, for the war. There is an article (*Davie County Enterprise Record* dated April 12, 1979) in the Davie County Public Library that states he "died in the Confederate Army during the war," but the military record states that he was discharged February 10, 1862, by reason of "disability."

614. Kelly, Samuel A. (Abner)
Captain, "Davie Sweep Stakes" • Company G, 4th Regiment • N.C. State Troops

Samuel was born in 1838 to Colonel William F. and Sarah A. (1807, Davie) Kelly. They resided in the Mocksville District of Davie County where he was a student prior to enlisting at age 23. He was appointed First Lieutenant to rank from May 16, 1861, and was promoted to Captain to rank from February 14, 1863. He was wounded at Chancellorsville, Virginia, May 3, 1863, rejoined the company prior to September 1, 1863, and was present or accounted for until wounded at Spotsylvania Court House, Virginia, May 12, 1864. He was reported absent wounded through August 1864, but rejoined the company prior to September 19, 1864, when he was wounded and captured at Winchester, Virginia. He was confined at Fort Delaware, Delaware, until he was released on June 4, 1865, after taking the Oath of Allegiance. Samuel returned home where he married Edy Johnston on December 31, 1868. In 1870 he served as sheriff. Records indicate that he and his wife, Margaret C. lived with his daughters Margaret S. (1877) and Sallie Y. (1879) in the Jerusalem District where Samuel was described as being a "farmer/crippled" in the 1880 census.

615. Kelly, William Frohock
Colonel, "Mocksville Rifles" Militia • Captain, "Davie Sweep Stakes" • Company G, 4th Regiment • N.C. State Troops

William was born June 6, 1837, in Davie County to Colonel William F. and Sarah A. (1807, Davie) Kelly. Tensions were high in the 1850s with the fear that hostilities would lead to war. Davie County began preparations to protect the citizens by forming two militia companies. One of these was the "Mocksville Rifles" commanded by William F. Kelly, a Colonel at age 21, and Major A.A. Harbin, according to James W. Wall in his *History of Davie County*. When war began, the company known as the "Davie Sweep Stakes" was organized in Davie County and was enlisted at Mocksville on June 4, 1861. William was appointed Captain to rank from May 16, 1861. He was present or accounted for until he resigned after the battle of Fredericksburg on February 5, 1863, because "two Junior officers have been promoted over me to the positions of Lieutenant Colonel and Major under whom it is disagreeable in the extreme for me to serve." (*N.C. Troops*, Volume IV, page 75.) He returned to Davie County and lived alone in Jerusalem District, where he farmed. On November 28, 1876, he married Leila Imogene Bryan and by 1880 they were the parents of William (1878) and Laura (1879). They had moved to the Farmington District where they farmed. William died March 11, 1900, and is buried in Joppa Cemetery.

616. Kepley, Burgess (Burgeons)
Private, Company H, 57th Regiment • N.C. Troops

Burgess was born in 1837 in North Carolina. He lived in the Liberty District and worked as a farm laborer. He was married to Mary Jane and they had a daughter, Cornelia Jane (1860). At age 29, on July 4, 1862, he enlisted in Davie County for the war. He was hospitalized at Richmond, Virginia, on October 10, 1862, with typhoid fever and furloughed on November 6, 1862. He returned to duty prior to May 11, 1863, and was reported absent with leave from May 17 through October 31, 1863. Then he was reported absent without leave on December 1, 1863, but later returned to duty in May–August, 1864. Burgess was reported absent sick from October 1 through December 31, 1864. He was reported present or accounted for in January–February, 1865. No further military records. In 1870 he was farming in Jerusalem with Mary and their four additional children: Lucy (1862), William (1865), James (1867) and Nancy (1869).

617. Kerfees, John Peter
Private, Company F, 42nd Regiment • N.C. Troops

John was born in 1826 in Rowan County to Caleb F. (1786, Germany) and Catherine (1847)

John P. Kurfees' home where he farmed and raised his family (Mohney, *The Historic Architecture of Davie County*).

Kurfees. He lived with his parents in Davie County where they farmed. On January 16, 1852, John married Mary Roberts. Over the next twenty-three years they would have ten children: Sarah A. (1853), Mary C. (1855), Marshal C. (1856), Marlin J. (1859), Barbara J. (1865), James F. (1867), John W. (1869), Jesse L. (1871), Washington N. (1873) and Francis M. (1876). In 1860 the family resided in the Mocksville District where he enlisted on December 18, 1862, for the war. He was present or accounted for until hospitalized at Raleigh, North Carolina, on March 11, 1865, with a gunshot wound of the left lung. The place and date were not reported. He was furloughed for sixty days on March 23, 1865. John resumed his life in Davie County in the Calahaln District where he continued to farm. He died on June 15, 1898, and is buried in Center United Methodist Church Cemetery. (His parents are buried in the Renshaw-Kurfees Family Cemetery. *Davie County Cemeteries*, Volume II, page 464).

618. Kerfuse, J.R. (James)
Private, Captain William E. Booe's Partisan Rangers • N.C. Volunteers • Company H, 63rd Regiment • (5th Regiment N.C. Cavalry) • N.C. Troops

James was born December 17, 1837, in Davie County to Caleb S. (1819, Rowan) and Mary (1815, Davie). They farmed in the Mocksville District where James married Sarah A. Hayse on January 17, 1861. He enlisted in Davie County at age 25, July 17, 1862, for the war. He was captured near Hanover Court House, Virginia, on May 31, 1864, and confined at Elmira, New York, until paroled and exchanged at Boulware's Wharf, James River, Virginia, March 15, 1865. He returned to Davie County and his family. The children were Charles F. (1862), William F. (1864), Mary E. (1868), Neely (1871), Jesse L. (1874) and Dovey B. (1877). He died on April 10, 1915, and is buried in Center United Methodist Church Cemetery.

619. Kesler, Henry P.
Private, Company F, 42nd Regiment • N.C. Troops

Henry was born in 1840 in North Carolina to Peter (1793, North Carolina) and Morinda (1806, North Carolina) Kestler [*sic*]. Henry was a farmer, and his father was a carpenter in the Calahaln District. Henry enlisted in Davie County at age 22, on March 24, 1862. His brother Madison Kesler also served in this company. Henry was present or accounted for through October 1864. In December 1864 he was killed. The place of death was not reported. Henry's name is listed on the Memorial Monument for the Davie County men who died in the Civil War, 1861–1865.

The home of James R. Kerfuse (Kurfees) (Mohney, *The Historic Architecture of Davie County*).

620. Kesler, M.F. (Madison)
Private, Company F, 42nd Regiment • N.C. Troops

M.F. was born April 24, 1844, in North Carolina to Peter (1793, North Carolina) and Morinda (1806, North Carolina) Kestler [*sic*]. They resided in the Calahaln District where his father was a carpenter and Madisson [*sic*] was a farmer. The place and date of his enlistment were not reported. He was captured at or near Wise's Forks, Kinston, North Carolina, on March 10, 1865, confined at Point Lookout, Maryland, March 16, 1865, and released on or about July 13, 1865, after taking the Oath of Allegiance. His brother Henry also served in this company. He returned home to his family in Calahaln where he worked as a farmer and horse trader. Madison died July 18, 1916, and is buried in Salem United Methodist Church Cemetery. His name is written as Madison "Mat" Kestler.

621. Kesler, William Richard
Private, Company F, 42nd Regiment • N.C. Troops

William was born March 12, 1827. On March 24, 1862, at age 35, he enlisted in Davie County. He was present or accounted for through October 1864. North Carolina pension records indicate he was wounded near Richmond, Virginia, in 1864. At age 50 he married Nancy Louisa Richardson Tutterow, age 32, on May 25, 1876. She had a young son, David Tuterow [*sic*]. William and Louisa are buried in Zion Chapel United Methodist Church Cemetery. William died on February 12, 1906. Nancy L. died July 14, 1912.

622. Kindley, J.D.
Private, Company A, 42nd Regiment • N.C. Troops

J.D. was born in 1848 in North Carolina to John (1807, North Carolina) and Amelia (1807, North Carolina) Kindley. He resided in Davie County but the place and date of his enlistment were not reported. He was paroled at Salisbury, North Carolina, on May 24, 1865, and took the Oath of Allegiance there on June 1, 1865. He married Louisa (1848, North Carolina) prior to 1870, and they settled on a farm in the Jerusalem District.

623. King, Anderson
Private, Company E, 42nd Regiment • N.C. Troops

Anderson was born in 1830 in Davie County, the son of Thomas (1810, Davie) King. They were farm laborers in the Shady Grove District. Anderson married twice prior to the war: to Sarah Penny on August 12, 1853, and to Margaret J. Alexander on July 31, 1856. He and Margaret were parents to Victoria (1859), James (1861) and John (1868). Anderson enlisted in Davie County at age 32, on March 18, 1862. He was present or accounted for until he was killed at Wise's Forks, Kinston, North Carolina, or at Gum Swamp on or about March 10, 1865. Margaret's application for a pension is on file at the State Archives, Raleigh, North Carolina. Anderson's name is listed on the Memorial Monument for the Davie County men who died in the Civil War, 1861–1865.

624. King, Calvin
Private, Company E, 42nd Regiment • N.C. Troops

Calvin was born in 1844 in Davie County. He was the son of Thomas (1810, Davie) and Mary Whitecar (1820, Davie) King. His father was a farmer in the Shady Grove District; Calvin worked as a laborer. At age 18, on March 18, 1862, Calvin enlisted in Davie County. He was present or accounted for through October 1864. Calvin was paroled at Mocksville on June 9, 1865.

625. King, L.B.
Private, "Davie Sweep Stakes" • Company G, 4th Regiment • N.C. State Troops

L.B. was born in 1847 to Thomas (1810, Davie) and Mary (1820, Davie) King. They resided in the Smith Grove District of Davie County. L.B. enlisted at Fredericksburg, Virginia, at age 16, February 25, 1863, for the war as a substitute for Harrison H. Hanes. L.B. died in the hospital at Richmond, Virginia, June 15, 1863, of "febris typhoides." L.B.'s name is listed on the Memorial Monument for the Davie County men who died in the Civil War, 1861–1865.

626. King, William A.
Private, Company E, 42nd Regiment • N.C. Troops

William enlisted in Davie County at age 32, March 18, 1862. He was present or accounted for until wounded in battle at Camp Wingfield, near Edenton, North Carolina, on or about March 21, 1863. He returned to duty in May–June, 1863. He was present or accounted for through October 1864, and was paroled at Mocksville on June 7, 1865.

627. Kinyoun (Kinyon) (Kinymon), David Williams
Captain, Company M • 77th Regiment, 19th Division • N.C. Militia 1861–1865

David was born in 1830 in Davie County to James (1804, Currituck) and Mary (1802, Davie) Kinymon. He farmed with his father and brother Lemuel prior to marrying Jane C. Howell on March 19, 1858. Their son James W. was born in 1859, and in 1860 David was practicing medicine in Chinquepin. He was appointed Captain of Company M when the militia was activated. Two more sons were born: John V. (1862) and Samuel C. (Lemuel) (1865). At the end of the war the family lived in the Clarksville District where David continued his medical practice. Another son, Joel J., was born in 1874.

628. Kluttz, Green C.
Private, Company A, 57th Regiment • Company K, 57th Regiment • N.C. Troops

Green was born in 1833 in North Carolina. On May 13, 1860, he married Martha M. (1826, North Carolina) Glasscock. They resided in Chinquepin where he worked as a "smith" prior to enlisting in Rowan County at age 27, on July 4, 1862, for the war. He was transferred to Company K on or about July 17, 1862, and was wounded in the leg at Fredericksburg, Virginia, on December 13, 1862. He was hospitalized at Richmond, Virginia, where he died on January 31, 1863, of "variola" and "gangrene." Green's name is not presently listed on the Memorial Monument for the Davie County men who died in the Civil War, 1861–1865.

629. Kurfees (Kerfeece) (Kerfoose), Caleb W.
Private, "Davie Greys" • Company F, 13th Regiment • (3rd Regiment, N.C. Volunteers) • N.C. Troops

Caleb was born in 1842 in Davie County to Martin (1817, Rowan) and Hannah (1824, Davie) Kurfees. Caleb was a farmer in the Calahaln District of Davie County in 1860. On February 21, 1861, he married Melinda Boid [sic] and on August 6, 1861, he enlisted in Davie County. He was present or accounted for until he died in the hospital at Richmond, Virginia, on June 3, 1862, of "continued fever." Caleb's name is listed on the Memorial Monument for the Davie County men who died in the Civil War, 1861–1865.

630. Kurfees (Kerfoose) (Kerfeese), Franklin J.
Private, "Davie Greys" • Company F, 13th Regiment • (3rd Regiment, N.C. Volunteers) • N.C. Troops

Franklin was the son of Martin Kerfoose [sic] (1817, Rowan) and Hannah (1824, Davie). (His name is shown as James F. Kerfeese in both the marriage record and Davie County census.) He resided in Davie County where he worked as a farmer. On September 2, 1858, Franklin and Martha J. Warren were married. Their son, John L. Kerfeece [sic] was born in 1859. On April 26, 1861, Franklin enlisted in Davie County and was present or accounted for until wounded at South Mountain, Maryland, September 14, 1862. He died September 17 or 18, 1862, of wounds. The place of death was not reported. Franklin's name is listed on the Memorial Monument for the Davie County men who died in the Civil War, 1861–1865.

631. Kurfees (Kerfoose) (Chalmus), Zedock C.
Private, "Davie Greys" • Company F, 13th Regiment • (3rd Regiment, N.C. Volunteers) • N.C. Troops

Zedock was born in 1842 in Davie County to C.S. (Caleb) (1819, Rowan) and Mary (1815, Davie). In 1860 they lived in the Mocksville District where Zedock worked as a laborer. At age 18, on August 6, 1861, he enlisted in Davie County and was present or accounted for until wounded at Chancellorsville, Virginia, on May 3, 1863. He rejoined the company in July–August, 1863, and was present or accounted for until paroled at Appomattox Court House, Virginia, April 9, 1865. Zedock and Mariah (Maria) E. Keller were married on December 2, 1869. They lived in the Calahaln District where he worked as a trader. Their children were Claudius (1871), Robert G. (1872) and Adolphus C. (1878). In 1880 Zedock was farming in Calahaln. He died in 1921 and is buried in Center United Methodist Church Cemetery. Mariah's application for a pension is on file in the State Archives, Raleigh, North Carolina.

632. Lagle, Henry E.
Private, Company E, 42nd Regiment • N.C. Troops

Henry was born in Davie County in 1838. In 1850, at age twelve, he lived with the Anderson Daniel family. In 1860 he worked as a farmer and laborer in the Liberty District while living with the W.A. Deadmon family. Henry married Sarah Turrentine on January 16, 1861, shortly before he enlisted in Davie County at age 24, on March 18, 1862. He was present or accounted for until reported absent wounded in May–August, 1864; the place and date were not reported. He returned to duty in September–October, 1864.

Henry was paroled at Salisbury, North Carolina, on May 16, 1865, and took the Oath of Allegiance there on June 5, 1865. (North Carolina pension records indicate he was wounded at Bermuda Hundred, Virginia, in June 1863.) Following the end of the war, the family lived in the Jerusalem District of Davie County where Henry worked as a laborer. Sarah and Henry were the parents of three children: William (1862), John (1864) and Maggie (1866). Henry's application for a soldier's pension is on file at the State Archives, Raleigh, North Carolina.

633. Lakey, Ellis
Private, Captain William E. Booe's Partisan Rangers • N.C. Volunteers • Company H, 63rd Regiment • (5th Regiment N.C. Cavalry) • N.C. Troops

Ellis was born in 1829; his wife Elizabeth was born January 7, 1834, in North Carolina. Their children were Mary E. (1859), John (1868) and Henry (1854). Ellis enlisted in Davie County on July 18, 1862, for the war. He was wounded and captured at Upperville, Virginia, June 21, 1863, and confined at Old Capitol Prison, Washington, D.C., until paroled and exchanged at City Point, Virginia, on June 30, 1863. He was present or accounted for through February 1865, and paroled at Salisbury, North Carolina, a short time later. Ellis, Elizabeth and their three children were farming in Farmington District in 1880. No dates are available for his death; he is buried in Wesley Chapel United Methodist Church Cemetery.

634. Lane, John H.
Private, "Davie Sweep Stakes" • Company G, 4th Regiment • N.C. State Troops

John was born in 1839 in Davie County to William D. (1819, Rowan) and Sarah Hillard (1819, Rowan) Lane. They lived in the Fulton District where William D. worked as a wagon maker and overseer and John worked as a "smith" prior to John's enlisting in Wake County at age 22, June 15, 1861, for the war. He was reported on detail as a teamster during much of the war and was present or accounted for until January 20, 1865, when he was detailed for duty in the Quartermaster Department by reason of "chronic ulcer of right leg." He was detailed for hospital duty at Salisbury, North Carolina, on March 25, 1865. John was the brother of William A. Lane of this company.

635. Lane, William A.
Private, "Davie Sweep Stakes" • Company G, 4th Regiment • N.C. State Troops

William was born in 1844 to William D. (1819, Rowan) and Sarah Hillard (1819, Rowan) Lane. They resided in the Fulton District of Davie County where William enlisted at age 18, March 17, 1862, for the war. He was wounded at Seven Pines, Virginia, May 31, 1862, and died at Richmond, Virginia, on or about June 24, 1862. William was the brother of John H. Lane of this company. William's name is listed on the Memorial Monument for the Davie County men who died in the Civil War, 1861–1865.

636. Lapish, George
Private, Company F, 42nd Regiment • N.C. Troops

George was born in 1822 in Davie County. He worked as a blacksmith. On September 13, 1845, he married Elizabeth Shives (1822, Cabarrus) and they made their home in the Calahaln District of the county. Their children were John (1845), Elvina (1848), George C. (1853), Rowan (1855) and Sarah E. (1857). On March 24, 1862, George enlisted in Davie County at age 40. His son, John A. Lapish, served in this company as a substitute for his father. There are no further military records. After the war George married Palina A. Williams on February 1, 1877. George married Julia Ann Turner on February 13, 1889.

637. Lapish, John A.
Private, Company F, 42nd Regiment • N.C. Troops

John was born in 1845 to George (1822, Davie) and Elizabeth (1822, Cabarrus) Lapish. They lived in the Calahaln District of Davie County where his father worked as a blacksmith and John worked as a farmer. John enlisted at Lynchburg, Virginia, on June 15, 1862, for the war as a substitute for his father. He was present or accounted for until wounded in the foot at or near Petersburg, Virginia, May 10 or May 15, 1864. He returned to duty on February 3, 1865, and retired to the Invalid Corps two weeks later. His retirement papers, dated February 1865, give his age as 20. John returned home and resumed his life as a farmer. In 1870 he is listed as living with Sarah (1842, North Carolina) and four children: Elizah (1858), John (1860), Sally (1862) and Lena (1868). However, marriage records indicate that he married (Margaret) Jane Thomas, March 10, 1867. Margaret and John are recorded in the 1880 census with two children at home: Malisa L.

(1871) and a stepson, John E. Thomas (1862). John A. Lapish is buried in Salem United Methodist Church Cemetery. No dates are given.

638. Langley, C.A.
Private, Captain William E. Booe's Partisan Rangers • N.C. Volunteers • Company H, 63rd Regiment • (5th Regiment N.C. Cavalry) • N.C. Troops

C.A. was born in 1827 in North Carolina. He married Malinda and they had a son, John H. (1858). Prior to the war the family lived in the Farmington District where C.A. worked as a laborer. He enlisted in Davie County at age 24, on July 18, 1862, for the war. He was captured at Madison Court House, Virginia, on September 22, 1863, and confined at Old Capitol Prison in Washington, D.C., until transferred to Point Lookout, Maryland, September 26, 1863. He was transferred to Elmira, New York, August 16, 1864, where he remained until paroled and exchanged at Venus Point, Savannah River, Georgia, on November 15, 1864.

639. Langley, Pleasant
Private, Company E, 42nd Regiment • N.C. Troops

Pleasant was born in 1844 in North Carolina to Charles (1797, North Carolina) and Nancy (1797, North Carolina) Langley. He worked as a laborer in the Farmington District of Davie County prior to enlisting there at age 18, on March 18, 1862. He was present or accounted for until he was wounded near Petersburg, Virginia, on July 9, 1864. He was reported absent wounded through October 1864, and paroled at Mocksville on June 7, 1865. Pleasant married Zilvia (Zilpha) Alexander on July 30, 1865. Their children were Laura (1866), Mary E. (1868), Kelong (1870), Sally (1872), Eliza (1875) and Vallie (1877). In 1880, the family farmed in Fulton District.

640. Lard (Laird), George W.
Private, Company E, 42nd Regiment • N.C. Troops

George was born in 1814 in Davie County. He married Anne (Anna) (1817, Davie) Gullet on June 10, 1837, and began a family that would consist of seven daughters: Mary (1839), Aney (1841), Martha (1843), Julia (1848), Amanda (1850), Carmilia (1852) and Lou E. (1856). George was a farmer prior to enlisting in Davie at age 48, on March 18, 1862. He was present or accounted for until he was killed near Petersburg, Virginia, on June 17, 1864. George's name is listed on the Memorial Monument for the Davie County men who died in the Civil War, 1861–1865.

641. Lard (Laird), Levi (Levy)
Private, Company E, 42nd Regiment • N.C. Troops

Levi was born in 1821 in Davie County to Margaret (1800, Davie) Laird. He married Susannah F. (1820, Davie) Foster on October 30, 1851. Their children were Berry Elizabeth (1854), John H.H. (1856), Jas. A. (1857), Eliphat (1862) and Ann (1864). Levi was a farm laborer in the Fulton District prior to enlisting in Davie County at age 42, on March 18, 1862. He was present or accounted for through February 23, 1865. He returned home to his family and farming in the Fulton District. He died in 1874 and was buried in Fork Baptist Church Cemetery. His tombstone states that he served in this company. Susanna died on August 7, 1901.

642. Lard (Laird), Samuel
Private, Company E, 42nd Regiment • N.C. Troops

Samuel was born in 1828 in Davie County to Margaret (1800, Davie) Laird. He married E. (Louiser) Foster on December 19, 1857. Their children were Melinda (1859), Charles (1860) and Adelia (1867). The family lived with the E. Foster family in the Fulton District where Samuel worked as a laborer prior to enlisting in Davie County on August 10, 1863, for the war. He was present or accounted for through February 22, 1865. He returned to Fulton from the war and resumed his life as a farmer. He also married again, this time to Martha Hampton on February 1, 1872.

643. Lashmit, John W.
Private, Company E, 42nd Regiment • N.C. Troops

John was born in 1834 in North Carolina. In 1860 he worked as a carpenter in the Smith Grove District where he lived with the Washington Green family. He enlisted in Davie County at age 28, March 24, 1862. He was present or accounted for through October 1864. No further information.

644. Lassiter, Ethadra W.
Private, "Davie Greys" • Company F, 13th Regiment • (3rd Regiment, N.C. Volunteers) • N.C. Troops

Ethadra resided in Davie County where he enlisted at age 35 on March 26, 1863, for the war. He deserted on April 29, 1863. He was reported absent in arrest on company muster roll dated

March–April, 1864, and reported absent in confinement on company muster rolls dated May–October, 1864. He was paroled at Mocksville on June 9, 1865.

645. Lassiter, J. (Jesse)
Private, Captain William E. Booe's Partisan Rangers • N.C. Volunteers • Company H, 63rd Regiment • (5th Regiment N.C. Cavalry) • N.C. Troops

Jesse was born in 1838 in North Carolina. He married Martha J. (1837, North Carolina) and they had three children: Amos G. (1856), Sarah E. (1858) and James E. (1859). They lived in the Farmington District where Jesse farmed prior to enlisting in Davie County on July 16, 1862, for the war. He was present or accounted for through August 1864. He was paroled at Mocksville June 9, 1865.

646. Latham, David Hampton
Private, Company F, 42nd Regiment • N.C. Troops

David Hampton Latham was born in Davie County in 1840 to Maria Latham (1820, Davie). In 1860 Hampton was a laborer living in the Farmington District. He enlisted at age 18, on or about March 15, 1862, in Davie County. He was present or accounted for through October 1864. On July 4, 1867, he married Elizabeth Ann Robertson. In 1870 the family lived in the Farmington District where he was a farm laborer. Elizabeth and Hampton had a daughter, Mary (1870).

647. Latham, James M., Sr.
Private, Company F, 42nd Regiment • N.C. Troops

James was born on October 29, 1833, in Davie County. On March 21, 1860, he married Nancy E. Ferebee (Davie, 1842). They resided in Farmington District where he was a farmer. James enlisted in Davie County at age 28, March 25, 1862. He was present or accounted for through October 1864. Later he was paroled at Mocksville on June 6, 1865. (The Salem *People's Press* of June 30, 1864, indicates he was wounded June 1–15, 1864.) Nancy and James would have eight children: William C. (1862), Burges (1866), Thomas (1869), Benjamin F. (1870), James F. (1872), Elizabeth (1874), John (1876) and Minnie (1879). In 1880 the family lived in the Clarksville District of Davie County. James M. Latham died on January 22, 1918, and is buried in Wesley Chapel United Methodist Church Cemetery.

648. Latham, Jeremiah M.
Private, "Davie Sweep Stakes" • Company G, 4th Regiment • N.C. State Troops

Jeremiah was born in 1838 to James (1807, Davie) and Cassey (1807, Davie) Latham. They resided in the Mocksville District of Davie County where Jeremiah worked as a laborer prior to enlisting at age 22, June 4, 1861, for the war. He died in Davie County on June 9, 1862, of disease. Jeremiah's name is listed on the Memorial Monument for the Davie County men who died in the Civil War, 1861–1865.

649. Latham, Samuel B.
Second Sergeant, Company G, 7th Regiment • Confederate Cavalry • Company D, 16th Battalion • N.C. Cavalry

Samuel was born in 1839 in Davie County to James (1807, Davie) and Cassey (1808, Davie) Latham. In 1860 he lived with his parents in the Mocksville District of Davie County where he worked as a laborer. He enlisted in Davie County on September 3, 1862, as a Second Sergeant. He was transferred from Company G, 7th Regiment Confederate Cavalry to Company D, 16th Battalion N.C. Cavalry on July 11, 1864. He was captured at Fort Harrison, Virginia, on September 30, 1864, and confined at Point Lookout, Maryland, where he remained until paroled and exchanged at Cox's Landing, James River, Virginia, February 14–15, 1865. He was paroled at Salisbury, North Carolina, in 1865. He returned to Davie County where he worked as a trader in 1870.

650. Lazenby, John Tilman
Private, Company F, 42nd Regiment • N.C. Troops

John Tilman was born in North Carolina in 1830. On October 13, 1853, he married Catherine S. Seaford (1827, North Carolina). In 1860 they lived in Calahaln where Tilman was a farm laborer. He enlisted in Davie County at age 32, on March 18, 1862, and was present or accounted for through October 1864. The family remained in Davie County. Tilman was the father of five children: John P. (1851), Samuel (1855), Mary E. (1858), Sarah J. (1860) and Thomas W. (1866).

651. Leach, David
Private, "Davie Greys" • Company F, 13th Regiment • (3rd Regiment, N.C. Volunteers) • N.C. Troops

David was born in 1836 in Davie County. In 1850 he lived with his mother, Mary (1812,

Rowan) Leach and worked as a laborer. He married M. (Mellina) Green Warren (1842) on September 15, 1859. They lived in the Mocksville District of Davie County where he enlisted at age 25, August 6, 1861. He was present or accounted for until wounded at Chancellorsville, Virginia, May 3, 1863. David rejoined the company in September–October, 1863, and was present or accounted for until wounded in action on October 6, 1864, and continued to be reported absent wounded through October 1864. He returned home where he resumed his life as a farmer and where he and Mellina would have five children by 1880: Meeky Ann (1865), Maggie L. (1867), James L. (1870), Cora Bell (1874) and Liza S. (1880). David died on February 5, 1892, and is buried at Center United Methodist Church Cemetery.

652. Leach, James Franklin
Private, Company F, 42nd Regiment • N.C. Troops

James was born in 1844 in Davie County. He was the son of Mary Leach (1812, Rowan). At age 16, he was a farm laborer living in the Mocksville District where he enlisted on March 18, 1862. He was present or accounted for until he was killed at Cold Harbor, Virginia, on June 1, 1864. James's name is listed on the Memorial Monument for the Davie County men who died in the Civil War, 1861–1865.

653. Leach, John
Sergeant, "Davie Greys" • Company F, 13th Regiment • (3rd Regiment, N.C. Volunteers) • N.C. Troops

John was born in 1831 in Davie County. He was the son of Mary (1812, Rowan) and the brother of David Leach, who also served in this company. John married Mary F. Warren on July 31, 1856. He worked as a farmer prior to enlisting in Davie County at age 30, August 6, 1861. He mustered in as a Private and was promoted to Sergeant on January 2, 1863. He was present or accounted for until wounded in the right thigh at Chancellorsville, Virginia, May 3, 1863. He died in the hospital at Richmond, Virginia, August 22, 1863, of wounds. John's name is not presently listed on the Memorial Monument for the Davie County men who died in the Civil War, 1861–1865.

654. Leach, John W.
Private, "Davie Greys" • Company F, 13th Regiment • (3rd Regiment, N.C. Volunteers) • N.C. Troops

John W. was born in Davie County in 1839, the son of Zadock (1817, Davie) and Malvina (1819, Davie). He was a farmer residing in Calahaln prior to enlisting at age 22, on August 6, 1861. He was present or accounted for until he was killed at Sharpsburg, Maryland, September 17, 1862. John's name is listed on the Memorial Monument for the Davie County men who died in the Civil War, 1861–1865.

655. Ledford, John A.
Private, Company G, 7th Regiment • Confederate Cavalry • Company D, 16th Battalion • N.C. Cavalry

John enlisted in Davie County on September 3, 1862. He transferred from Company G, 7th Regiment Confederate Cavalry to Company D, 16th Battalion N.C. Cavalry on July 11, 1864, and was present or accounted for through October 1864, as a wagoner.

656. Lee, Henry Jackson
Second Lieutenant, Company E • 77th Regiment, 19th Division • N.C. Militia 1861–1865

Henry was born December 15, 1831, in Davie County to Edward Lee (1802, Davie). They were lifelong farmers in the Farmington District of Davie County. When the militia was activated Henry was appointed Second Lieutenant of Company E. His marriage to Elizabeth (1840, North Carolina) was followed by the birth of Ellen M. in 1862. They continued to live in the Farmington District as their family increased. Ellen was followed by Addie L. (1864), Wm. H. (1866), Robert (1874) and Johnny (1879). Henry died March 13, 1916, and is buried in Macedonia Moravian Church Cemetery.

657. Lenard, Mathias
Second Lieutenant, Company H • 77th Regiment, 19th Division • N.C. Militia 1861–1865

Mathias was born in 1830 in North Carolina. By 1860 he had established himself as an "overseer," had married Ellen (1835, North Carolina) and was father to Wm. H. (1852), Elizabeth D. (1854), Philop (1857) and Mary A. (1859). When war seemed inevitable and the militia was activated, Mathias was appointed Second Lieutenant of Company H. The family was located in the Smith Grove District.

658. Leonard (Lenard), Emanuel
Private, "Davie Greys" • Company F, 13th Regiment • (3rd Regiment, N.C. Volunteers) • N.C. Troops

Emanuel was born in 1833 in North Carolina. He was a farmer, living alone in the Fulton District, prior to enlisting in Davie County on

April 26, 1861. He was present or accounted for until he was killed at Gettysburg, Pennsylvania, July 1, 1863. Emanuel's name is listed on the Memorial Monument for the Davie County men who died in the Civil War, 1861–1865.

659. Leonard, Jacob
Private, Company H, 57th Regiment • N.C. Troops

Jacob was born in 1838 in North Carolina. He was a farmer who resided in Davie County where he and Christina C. Wagner were married on June 28, 1857. The couple settled in the Fulton District with their son Sam A. (1858) and daughter Martha E. (1859). On July 4, 1862, at age 24, Jacob enlisted for the war. He was present or accounted for through May 11, 1863, then reported absent without leave from May 17 through October 31, 1863. He was reported present but under arrest in November–December, 1863, and court-martialed on or about January 19, 1864. Jacob was hospitalized at Richmond, Virginia, April 7, 1864, with intermittent fever, then transferred to Castle Thunder Prison, Richmond, on April 15, 1864. He returned to duty prior to May 1, 1864, and was captured at the North Anna River, Virginia, on or about May 23, 1864. He was confined at Point Lookout, Maryland, on May 30, 1864, and was paroled there on or about March 14, 1865. He was received at Boulware's Wharf, James River, Virginia, on March 16, 1865, for exchange. He was paroled at Salisbury, North Carolina, on May 24, 1865.

660. Leonard, Jesse
Private, Company D, 42nd Regiment • N.C. Troops

Jesse was born in 1840 in North Carolina. He resided in Davie County where he worked as a farmer in the Fulton District. By 1860 Jesse and his wife Christina (1839, North Carolina) were the parents of Sam A. (1858) and Martha E. (1859). He traveled to Rowan County to enlist in this company at age 22, March 26, 1862. He was present or accounted for until he became another victim of "febris typhoides." He died in the hospital at Petersburg, Virginia, on September 7, 1862. Jesse's name is listed on the Memorial Monument for the Davie County men who died in the Civil War, 1861–1865.

661. Leslie (Lesley), F. (Franklin) M.
Private, 1st Company A, Salisbury Carolina Prison Guard • "The Rough and Readys" • Company G, 66th Regiment • N.C. Troops

Franklin was born in 1844 in Davie County to Levi H. (1819, Iredell) and Lucinda Hughes (1820, Davie) Lesley. His father worked as a carriage maker and served as an officer for the Town of Mocksville. Franklin enlisted as a Private in 1st Company A and transferred to Company G of the 66th on October 2, 1863. He was reported absent sick in Davie County on October 31, 1863, but reported for duty in November–December, 1863. He was present or accounted for through October 31, 1864. He took the Oath of Allegiance at Mocksville on June 3, 1865. Franklin lived with his mother and his sister Mary T. in Mocksville after the war. He was employed as a gun smith.

662. Lewis, William
Private, Captain William E. Booe's Partisan Rangers • N.C. Volunteers • Company H, 63rd Regiment • (5th Regiment N.C. Cavalry) • N.C. Troops

William enlisted in Davie County at age 27, July 6, 1862, for the war. His name was reported on the muster roll dated September 17, 1862. No further records.

663. Linster, McAfee
Private, Company E, 42nd Regiment • N.C. Troops

McAfee was a laborer who was born in 1826 in Rowan County. In 1850 he lived with John and Tabitha Ford where he worked as a laborer. He enlisted in Davie County at age 34, on or about March 13, 1862. He was present or accounted for through October 1864, and was paroled at Salisbury, North Carolina, on June 3, 1865.

664. Linville, John F.
Private, Company F, 42nd Regiment • N.C. Troops

John was born in 1837 in North Carolina. He and his wife Rebecca had a son James in 1857. They resided in Davie County where John enlisted at age 25 on March 24, 1862. He was present or accounted for until he was wounded at Petersburg, Virginia, in August 1864. John returned to duty September–October, 1864, but was captured at or near Wise's Forks, Kinston, North Carolina, on March 10, 1865. He was confined at Point Lookout, Maryland, March 16, 1865, and released at Point Lookout on June 28, 1865, after taking the Oath of Allegiance. In 1870 the family lived in the Farmington District.

665. Little, Daniel M.
Private, Company A, 57th Regiment • N.C. Troops

Daniel was born in Davie County in 1839, the son of Mathias (1811, Davie) and Leah (1816,

Davie). Daniel worked as a laborer, living in the Liberty District with his parents. At age 24, on July 4, 1862, he enlisted in Rowan County for the war. He was reported absent sick at Salisbury, North Carolina, on August 12, 1862, then absent without leave on October 27, 1862. He returned to duty prior to November 1, 1862, when he was reported present or accounted for through February 28, 1863. Daniel was wounded in the abdomen at Chancellorsville, Virginia, on May 4, 1863; he died on or about May 5, 1863, of wounds. The place of death was not reported. Daniel's name is listed on the Memorial Monument for the Davie County men who died in the Civil War, 1861–1865.

666. Little, Robert A.
Private, "Davie Greys" • Company F, 13th Regiment • (3rd Regiment, N.C. Volunteers) • N.C. Troops

Robert was born in 1840 in Davie County. In 1860 he lived with the John Livengood family in the Liberty District and worked as a laborer. He enlisted in Davie County at age 21 on April 26, 1861. He was present or accounted for until wounded near Richmond, Virginia, in March–June, 1862. He rejoined the company prior to November 1, 1862, and was present or accounted for until wounded at Chancellorsville, Virginia, May 3, 1863. He rejoined the company in January–February, 1864, and was present or accounted for until wounded in the right thigh and right shoulder at Wilderness, Virginia, May 5, 1864. He died in the hospital at Charlottesville, Virginia, on May 13, 1864, of "secondary hemorrhage." Robert's name is listed on the Memorial Monument for the Davie County men who died in the Civil War, 1861–1865.

667. Little, Dr. Samuel Winfield
Major, 77th Regiment, 19th Brigade • N.C. Militia 1861–1865

Winfield was born December 20, 1828, in Davie County to Mary Cain (1805, Davie) and Samuel (1799) Little. His father died on April 20, 1830, and his mother married Samuel Holman on September 8, 1839. S. Winfield made his home with his mother and stepfather in the Chinquepin District where he served as a physician. When the militia was activated, Winfield became a physician for the unit. He died July 9, 1913, and is buried in Bear Creek Baptist Church Cemetery.

668. Livengood, Dan E.
Private, Company E, 42nd Regiment • N.C. Troops

Daniel was born September 9, 1833, in Davidson County to John (1804, Davidson) and Catherine (1809, Davidson) Livinggood. By 1850 the family had moved across the Yadkin River into Davie County, Fulton District. Daniel married C.M. (Catherine Martha) Cain on March 13, 1856. Their children were John S.H. (1857) and Amanda (1860). Daniel enlisted in Davie County at age 27, on or about March 18, 1862. He was present or accounted for through December 1863; however, he was reported absent sick during most of that period. He was reported absent without leave in January–February, 1864. After the war the family lived in the Jerusalem District of Davie County where Daniel resumed his livelihood of farming. He died May 1, 1911, and was buried in Jerusalem Baptist Church Cemetery.

669. Livengood, Daniel G.
Private, Company D, 42nd Regiment • N.C. Troops

Daniel resided in Davie County and enlisted in Rowan County at age 22, March 18, 1862. He was present or accounted for through October 1864. He was paroled at Mocksville on June 3, 1865.

670. Livengood, John N.
Private, Company D, 42nd Regiment • N.C. Troops

John was born in North Carolina in 1842. He was the son of George (1811, North Carolina) and Margaret (1813, North Carolina) Livengood. John's father was a cooper, and John worked as a laborer in the Chinquepin District of Davie County. On December 29, 1861, he married Mary S. Stone and enlisted in Rowan County at age 23, on March 18, 1862. He was present or accounted for through October 1864. He was paroled at Mocksville on June 3, 1865.

671. Livingood, David
Private, Company B, Carolina Rangers • 10th Virginia Cavalry Regiment

David was born in 1838 in Davidson County to John (1804, Davidson) and Catharine (1809, Davidson) Livingood. He worked as a farmhand prior to enlisting in the Liberty District on October 29, 1861, at age 23. His presence or absence after that time was "not stated through April 30, 1862." There was no further record. David returned home and married Amanda A. Cain on October 4, 1866. Their son Willie S. was born in 1869. They lived in Jerusalem District where David continued to farm. Amanda died on August 7, 1873, and three years later, February 24, 1876, David married Fannie E. Harris, age 25. Their children were Mary B. (1877) and Charles (1880).

672. Logan, Isaac
Private, Company B, Carolina Rangers • 10th Virginia Cavalry Regiment

Isaac was born in 1841 in North Carolina to W. (1804, North Carolina) and Mary (1822, North Carolina) Logan. Isaac worked as a farmhand in the Farmington District of Davie County prior to enlisting on March 18, 1862, at age 18. He was present through May 6, 1862. He died in Richmond hospital on August 23, 1862. Isaac's name is listed on the Memorial Monument for the Davie County men who died in the Civil War, 1861–1865.

673. Long, L.W.
Private, Company M, 7th Regiment • Confederate Cavalry • Company E, 16th Battalion • N.C. Cavalry

L.W. enlisted in Davie County on August 3, 1863, with the rank of Private. He was transferred from Company M, 7th Regiment Confederate Cavalry to Company E, 16th Battalion N.C. Cavalry on July 11, 1864. He was present or accounted for through October 1, 1864. He was admitted to the hospital at Raleigh, North Carolina, on February 3, 1865, with "pneumonia" and furloughed for sixty days February 20, 1865.

674. Longworth, Samuel
Private, Company D, 53rd Regiment • N.C. Troops

Samuel was born in 1830 in Davie County. At age 18 he was an apprentice to John Taylor, a cabinet maker. He lived with Febe (1815, North Carolina) prior to enlisting at age 32, October 10, 1862, in Davie County for the war. He was present or accounted for on surviving company muster rolls through April 1864. He was wounded in the left arm at Cold Harbor, Virginia, on June 1, 1864, and hospitalized at Petersburg, Virginia. Samuel returned to duty prior to September 19, 1864, when he was killed at Winchester, Virginia. Samuel's name is not presently listed on the Memorial Monument for the Davie County men who died in the Civil War, 1861–1865.

675. Lookabill, William H.
Private, Company I, 9th Regiment • N.C. State Troops

William resided in Davie County and enlisted in Cabarrus County at age 25, March 16, 1863, for the war. He deserted near Culpeper Court House, Virginia, November 10, 1863, and was captured on the Rapidan River, Virginia, by Federal troops and confined at Fort Delaware, Delaware, until released after taking the Oath of Allegiance, May 11, 1865.

676. Lowery, D.L. (Dabney)
Corporal, Company M, 7th Regiment • Confederate Cavalry • Company E, 16th Battalion • N.C. Cavalry

Dabney was born in Virginia on November 29, 1838, to Richard (1799, Virginia) and Nancy B. (1803, Virginia) Lowery. He enlisted in Davie County on September 3, 1862, with the rank of Private, later promoted to Corporal. He was transferred from Company M, 7th Regiment Confederate Cavalry to Company E, 16th Battalion N.C. Cavalry on July 11, 1864. He was present or accounted for through October 1, 1864. After the war Dabney worked as a farmer in Calahaln on his mother's farm. He married Mary T. Blackwell on May 18, 1875, and due to a decline in his health became a storekeeper and distiller. A daughter, Mary E.L. (1878) rounded out the household. Despite being crippled, Dabney lived until July 10, 1917. He is buried at Salem United Methodist Church Cemetery.

677. Lowery, John T.T.
First Sergeant, Company M, 7th Regiment • Confederate Cavalry • Company E, 16th Battalion • N.C. Cavalry

John was born to Richard (1799, Virginia) and Nancy R. (1802, Virginia) Lowery. Prior to the war he worked as a farm manager in Calahaln District, but at age 25, on September 3, 1862, he enlisted in Davie County as a Private. He had been promoted to First Sergeant by July 11, 1864, when he was transferred from Company M, 7th Regiment Confederate Cavalry to Company E, 16th Battalion N.C. Cavalry. He was present or accounted for through October 1, 1864. He married Susan M. Furches on February 26, 1866, and they settled in Farmington District. Their children were Dabner (1866), Watson (1878) and Nancy (1880). John died on August 11, 1882, and is buried in Zion Chapel United Methodist Church Cemetery (formerly known as Hickory Grove Methodist Church).

678. Lunn, Benjamin Franklin
Captain, Company K • 77th Regiment, 19th Division • N.C. Militia 1861–1865

Benjamin was born in 1823 in North Carolina. He married Louisa J. Miller, daughter of the Rev. Thomas and Nancy Young Miller, on April 27, 1850. Their children were Leonidas (Leander) (1852) and Ann E. (1854). The family lived in the Farmington District of Davie County where he was appointed Captain of Company K when the militia was activated. Following the war he resumed farming. Louisa died in 1877 and B.F. married Melvina R. Smith on July 15, 1879. Melvina's six children were Lelia Smith (1859), Minnie Smith (1860), Harmon Smith (1862), Willie Smith (1864), Camilla Smith (1864) and Mary L. Smith (1872). B.F. died on August 17, 1896, and is buried in Olive Branch Cemetery.

679. Lunn, John T.
Private, Captain William E. Booe's Partisan Rangers • N.C. Volunteers • Company H, 63rd Regiment • (5th Regiment N.C. Cavalry) • N.C. Troops

John was born in 1844 in Davie County to John (1813, Currituck) and Sarah (1812, Davie) Lunn. The family lived in the Farmington District of Davie County. John was a student prior to enlisting at age 19, July 12, 1862, for the war. He was captured at Brentsville Court House, Virginia, September 20, 1863, and confined at Old Capitol Prison, Washington, D.C., until transferred to Point Lookout, Maryland, September 26, 1863. He was transferred to Aiken's Landing, Virginia, for exchange on September 18, 1864. The roll of paroled prisoners of war carries the remark: "Died September 1864." John's name is listed on the Memorial Monument for the Davie County men who died in the Civil War, 1861–1865.

680. Lynch, William
Private, "Davie Sweep Stakes" • Company G, 4th Regiment • N.C. State Troops

William was born in Davie County where he resided prior to enlisting at age 18, March 8, 1862, for the war. He died on June 19, 1862. The place and cause of death were not reported. William's name is listed on the Memorial Monument for the Davie County men who died in the Civil War, 1861–1865.

681. Lyons, Richard J.
Private, Company E, 42nd Regiment • N.C. Troops

Richard was born in Davidson County in 1844. He was the son of Joel (1800, Virginia) and Nancy (1811, Virginia) Lyons. In 1860 he worked as a laborer in Smith Grove. He enlisted in Davie County at age 19, on March 18, 1862. He was present or accounted for through October 1864. In 1870 he was a farmer living with the Hillery Baily family in the Mocksville District.

682. Madison, Harrison
Private, Captain William E. Booe's Partisan Rangers • N.C. Volunteers • Company H, 63rd Regiment • (5th Regiment N.C. Cavalry) • N.C. Troops

Harrison enlisted in Davie County on July 18, 1862, for the war. He was present and accounted for until transferred to Company D of this regiment on September 13, 1862, and was present or accounted for through August 1864.

683. Madra (Maddre) (Mady), William H.
Private, "Davie Greys" • Company F, 13th Regiment • (3rd Regiment, N.C. Volunteers) • N.C. Troops

William was born in 1848 in Rowan County. He was the son of William S. Madre, a shoemaker (1808, Missouri). In 1860 at age 19, he was a laborer in the Farmington District who lived with the C.F. Griffith family. William enlisted for the war in Davie County at age 21, on April 26, 1861. He was present or accounted for until he was killed at Gaines' Mill, Virginia, on June 27, 1862. William's name is listed on the Memorial Monument for the Davie County men who died in the Civil War, 1861–1865.

684. Manning, Benjamin F.
Private, Company E, 42nd Regiment • N.C. Troops

Benjamin enlisted in Davie County on March 18, 1862. He was present or accounted for through October 1864.

685. March, H. Giles
Private, Company M, 7th Regiment • Confederate Cavalry • Company E, 16th Battalion • N.C. Cavalry

Giles was born in 1825 in Davie County. He married Delitha Potts, January 1, 1850, and they lived with Elizabeth Potts, who was probably her mother. Giles's second marriage was to Elizabeth Luticia Stewart on March 16, 1860. The children were Obadiah (1856), Alice V. (1861), Dollie (1862) and Jennie (1864). Giles supported his family by farming, but on September 18, 1863, he enlisted in Davie County with the rank of Private. He was transferred from Company M, 7th Regiment Confederate Cavalry to Company E, 16th Battalion N.C. Cavalry on July 11, 1864. He was present or accounted for through October 1,

1864. He returned to farming in Fulton District when the war ended.

686. Markland (Marklin), Matthew
Second Lieutenant, Company D • 77th Regiment, 19th Division • N.C. Militia 1861–1865

Matthew was born in 1830 (1839?) in Davie County to Mary (1797, Davie) Marklin. He married Ann Zimmerman (1836, North Carolina) on March 24, 1852, and Melvin G. was born in 1857. Matthew worked as a farmer in the Smith Grove District when the militia was activated and he was appointed Second Lieutenant of Company D. The war years were busy years at home also; the family increased by three: Julius (1861), Jackson (1863) and Sallie (1865). Matthew moved his family to Fulton District where they remained, at least into the 1880s. He died on February 24, 1903, and is buried at Elbaville United Methodist Church Cemetery.

687. Marlin, Joel P.
Private, 1st Company A, Salisbury Prison Guard • Corporal, "The Rough and Readys" • Company G, 66th Regiment • N.C. Troops

Joel was born in 1844 in Davie County to John M. (1811, Rowan) and Anna (1810, Davie) Penery Marlin. Joel served as a Private in 1st Company A until he transferred to Company G of the 66th on October 2, 1863. He mustered in as a Private. He was present or accounted for through April 30, 1864. On June 18, 1864, he was hospitalized with a gunshot wound, reported in the hospital at Richmond, Virginia, July 1, 1864, and reported sick at home from July 30 through August 31, 1864. He returned to duty and was promoted to Corporal in September–October, 1864. No further records. Both of Joel's parents are buried in Liberty United Methodist Church Cemetery.

688. Marlin, John L.
Private, "Davie Greys" • Company F, 13th Regiment • (3rd Regiment, N.C. Volunteers) • N.C. Troops

John was born in 1843 in Davie County. He was the son of Malinda Marlin (1812, Davie). He was a farmer prior to enlisting in Davie County at age 18, on April 26, 1861. He was present or accounted for until he died in the hospital at Richmond, Virginia, on or about July 20, 1862, of disease. John's name is listed on the Memorial Monument for the Davie County men who died in the Civil War, 1861–1865.

689. Marlow (Marler), George Washington
Private, Company F, 42nd Regiment • N.C. Troops

George was born in Davie County in 1827 to William (1796, Davie) and Patience (1808, Virginia) Marlow. He married E.L. Cain (Elizabeth) on October 11, 1858. In 1860 their household included two young children: Asbury Brogden (1850) and Mary A. Brogden (1860). George enlisted in Davie County at age 34, March 18, 1862. He was present or accounted for until discharged on May 30, 1863, by reason of disability. He was paroled at Mocksville on June 7, 1865. George returned to his family and farming. The family continued to increase with the births of Emily L. (1862), Martha M. (1864) and Patience E. (1868).

690. Marshall (Marshel), George W. (Wesley)
Private, Company E, 42nd Regiment • N.C. Troops

George was born circa 1833 in Iredell County to Elizabeth (1807, North Carolina) Marshel [*sic*]. He enlisted in Davie County at age 25, March 18, 1862. He died in the hospital at Lynchburg, Virginia, June 15–19, 1862. The cause of death was not reported. George's name is listed on the Memorial Monument for the Davie County men who died in the Civil War, 1861–1865.

691. Martin, Benjamin J.
Private, "Davie Sweep Stakes" • Company G, 4th Regiment • N.C. State Troops

Benjamin was born in 1839 in Davie County. He resided in the home of John and Mehatabel Martin as a young boy. At age 21 he resided in the household of Elisha Gibs in the Shady Grove District. He enlisted in Davie County at age 22, June 4, 1861, for the war. He was wounded in the left shoulder at Chancellorsville, Virginia, May 3, 1863, and died at Mocksville on July 9, 1863, of wounds. Benjamin's name is listed on the Memorial Monument for the Davie County men who died in the Civil War, 1861–1865.

692. Martin, David W. (William)
Private, "Davie Greys" • Company F, 13th Regiment • (3rd Regiment, N.C. Volunteers) • N.C. Troops

David was born in Davie County in 1840. He was the son of Elijah (1817) and Edith (1817, Davie). In 1860 David was a laborer, 21 years old, living in the Mocksville District. On April 26, 1861, he enlisted in Davie County for the war. David was present or accounted for until he was killed at Gaines' Mill, Virginia, on June 27, 1862. David's name is listed on the Memorial Monument for the Davie County men who died in the Civil War, 1861–1865.

693. Martin, Giles (John G.)
Private, Company M, 7th Regiment • Confederate Cavalry • Private, Company E, 16th Battalion • N.C. Cavalry

Giles was born in 1825 in Davie County. He married Mehetabel Wellman, August 19, 1845. They would have four children before 1860: John M. (1848), James L. (1851), Mary O. (1853) and Dewit C. (1856). They resided in the Mocksville District of Davie County where Giles worked as a farmer prior to enlisting in Company M, 7th Regiment Confederate Cavalry. He was transferred to Company E, 16th Battalion N.C. Cavalry on July 11, 1864, and was present or accounted for through October 1, 1864. In 1880 at age 55, he was a farmer living in the Farmington District with his family. He is buried in the Smith Grove United Methodist Church Cemetery; his tombstone reads: Jiles Martin, Company C., 16 N.C. Cav. CSA. No dates are given.

694. Martin, James C.
Private, Company D, 42nd Regiment • Captain William Howard's Company • N.C. Prison Guard • 1st Company A, Salisbury Prison Guard • "The Rough and Readys" • Company G, 66th Regiment

James was born October 8, 1842, in Davie County to William (1804, Davie) and Anna (1808, Iredell) Martin. In 1860 the family lived in the Calahaln District where his father was a wagon and cabinet maker and James was a farm laborer. On February 3, 1862, he enlisted in Davie County in Company D of the 42nd but transferred three months later to Captain Howard's Company, on or about May 1, 1862. He served as a Private in 1st Company A, Salisbury Prison Guard until he transferred to Company G of the 66th on October 2, 1863. He was admitted to the hospital in Wilmington on November 27, 1863, with remittent fever. He returned to duty on February 13, 1864, and was counted present through October 31, 1864. No further records. He survived the war. James is buried in Salem United Methodist Church Cemetery in Davie County. He died on August 3, 1915.

695. Martin, Pleasant Rowan
Second Lieutenant, Company L • 77th Regiment, 19th Division • N.C. Militia 1861–1865

Pleasant was born in 1834 in Davie County. He was probably the son of Elijah (1817, Davie) and the stepson of Edith Welman Richardson Martin. He married Mary A. (1840, Davie) Wyatt, on August 11, 1857. In 1860 at age 26, he worked as a merchant in the Mocksville District. The militia was activated and he was appointed Second Lieutenant of Company L. In 1870 he continued to work as a dry goods merchant and to raise his family. His children were Jessie V. (1860), Thomas F. (1867) and William (1868).

696. Mason, Franklin
Captain, Company G • 77th Regiment, 19th Division • N.C. Militia 1861–1865

Mason was born November 9, 1827, in North Carolina. He married Suan T. Curant April 2, 1844, but she apparently died soon after. He then married Drusilla [*sic*]. Dorcas A., the first of ten children, was born in 1850, followed by Elizabeth C. (1852), William B. (1855), John B. (1857), Perry H. (1860), Ortina B. (1862), Ida V. (1864), Mary E.O. (1866) and twins James A.H. and Sarah M. (1870). Franklin farmed in the Calahaln District and was appointed Captain of Company G when the militia was activated. He died March 24, 1913, and is buried in Society Baptist Church Cemetery.

697. Mason, Grief G. (P.)
Corporal, "Davie Greys" • Company F, 13th Regiment • (3rd Regiment, N.C. Volunteers) • N.C. Troops

Grief was born in 1841, either in Caswell County or in Virginia. His parents were Grief G. (1810, Virginia) and Jane (1810, Virginia) Mason. In 1860 he was a tobacconist prior to enlisting in Davie County at age 21, on April 26, 1861. Grief was mustered in as a Private and promoted to Corporal on June 1, 1861. He was present or accounted for until killed at Wilderness, Virginia, on May 5, 1864, "while gallantly carrying the Regimental Colors." Grief's name is listed on the Memorial Monument for the Davie County men who died in the Civil War, 1861–1865.

698. Massey, Daniel (David)
Private, Company E, 42nd Regiment • N.C. Troops

Daniel was born in 1833 in Davie County to William (1813, Davie) and Penelope (1814, Camden) Massey. Like so many of his contemporaries, he was the son of a farmer who would remain a lifelong farmer except for the three years he spent in the military during the war. He married Susanah Orrel on August 16, 1856; their two children were John W.L. (1859) and Nancy (1860). They lived in the Shady Grove District of Davie County prior to Daniel's enlisting at age 29, March 18, 1862. He was present or accounted for until captured at or near Cold Harbor, Virginia, June 1–3, 1864. He was confined at Point Lookout, Maryland, June 11, 1864, and transferred to Elmira, New York, where he arrived on July 17, 1864. He was paroled there and transferred to James River, Virginia, February 20, 1865, for exchange. He was hospitalized at Richmond, Virginia, March 3, 1865, with an unspecified complaint and transferred on March 4, 1865. When the war ended he returned home to Davie County and a new life. He married Mariah Jane Kerry on August 29, 1869, and his family increased with the addition of four stepchildren: Lucinda Curry [sic] (1851), Sandy Curry [sic] (1853), Andrew F. Curry [sic] (1859) and Jane Curry [sic] (1863).

699. Massey, Thomas G.
Private, Company E, 42nd Regiment • N.C. Troops

Thomas was born in 1840 in Davie County. He was the son of William (1813, Davie) and Penelope E. (1814) Massey. He was also the brother of Daniel W. Massey of this company. He worked as a laborer in Smith Grove District prior to enlisting at age 22, on March 18, 1862. A few days later, on March 23, 1862, he married Minerva (1846) L. (Louisa) Howard. Thomas was present or accounted for until wounded in the right leg at or near Bermuda Hundred, Virginia, on May 21, 1864. He was reported absent wounded until January 27, 1865, when he was retired by reason of disability from wounds and was paroled at Mocksville on June 10, 1865. Thomas and Minerva were the parents of six children: Ida (1866), Sarah E. (1868), William C. (1869), Thomas P. (1871), Mary F. (1875) and Calvin S. (1879). He remained in Davie County where he worked as a farmer in the Fulton District. He is buried in Advance Baptist Church Cemetery. Loueza's [sic] application for a pension is on file at the State Archives, Raleigh, North Carolina.

700. May, F.L.
Private, Captain William E. Booe's Partisan Rangers • N.C. Volunteers • Company H, 63rd Regiment • (5th Regiment N.C. Cavalry) • N.C. Troops

F.L. enlisted in Davie County at age 20, July 18, 1862, for the war. He was captured at Catletts Station, Virginia, on October 14, 1863, and confined at Old Capitol Prison, Washington, D.C., until transferred to Point Lookout, Maryland, on October 27, 1863. He remained there until paroled and exchanged at Venus Point, Savannah River, Georgia, November 15, 1864.

701. May, Urban C.
Private, "Davie Greys" • Company F, 13th Regiment • (3rd Regiment, N.C. Volunteers) • N.C. Troops

Urban was born in 1843. He resided in Davie County where he enlisted at age 19, August 4, 1862, for the war. He was present or accounted for until wounded and captured at Gettysburg, Pennsylvania, on July 1–5, 1863. He was hospitalized at David's Island, New York Harbor, until transferred to Fort Wood, Bedloe's Island, New York Harbor, on or about October 24, 1863. He was released at Point Lookout, Maryland, on January 23, 1864, after taking the Oath of Allegiance and joining the U.S. service. The unit to which he was assigned was not reported.

702. May, William F.
Private, Company D, 42nd Regiment • N.C. Troops

William was born in 1837 in Davie County to Daniel L. (1815, Davie) and Elizabeth (1819, Davie) May. His father was a cabinet maker and William was a farmer and blacksmith in the Chinquepin District of Davie County. On November 30, 1859, Martha Cranfield and William were married. Their son Samuel W. was born in 1861. At age 25, on March 4, 1862, William enlisted in Rowan County. He was present or accounted for until captured at or near Wise's Forks, Kinston, North Carolina, on March 10, 1865. He was confined at Point Lookout, Maryland, on March 16, 1865, and released there on May 14, 1865, after taking the Oath of Allegiance. William returned to his wife and son and resumed his work as a blacksmith in the Chinquepin District.

703. McBride, J.A. (John)
Private, Company G, 7th Regiment • Confederate Cavalry • Company D, 16th Battalion • N.C. Cavalry

John enlisted in Davie County on September 3, 1862, with the rank of Private. He was transferred from Company G, 7th Regiment Confederate Cavalry to Company D, 16th Battalion N.C. Cavalry on July 11, 1864. He was wounded in action in the left leg on October 27, 1864, causing an amputation. He died on October 28, 1864. John's name is listed on the Memorial Monument for the Davie County men who died in the Civil War, 1861–1865.

704. McCarter, Thomas
Private, "Davie Greys" • Company F, 13th Regiment • (3rd Regiment, N.C. Volunteers) • N.C. Troops

Thomas was born in 1842. He resided in Davie County where he worked as a farmer prior to enlisting at age 19, April 26, 1861. He was present or accounted for until he died in the hospital at Richmond, Virginia, on or about June 5, 1862, of "typhoid fever." Thomas's name is listed on the Memorial Monument for the Davie County men who died in the Civil War, 1861–1865.

705. McClammar, R. (Robert Reece)
Private, Captain William E. Booe's Partisan Rangers • N.C. Volunteers • Company H, 63rd Regiment • (5th Regiment N.C. Cavalry) • N.C. Troops

Rease [sic] was born in 1839 in Davie County to Sarah (1800, Davie) McCamroch [sic]. They lived in the Farmington District of Davie County where Rease worked as a laborer prior to enlisting there on July 18, 1862, for the war. He was present or accounted for through December 1864. His brother Martin also served in this company. He returned from the war and settled in the Mocksville District where he lived and farmed with his brother John and his family. Robert R. married Margaret T. Bowles on February 10, 1887. He died on April 15, 1920, and is buried in Eaton's Baptist Church Cemetery.

706. McClammer (McCamroch), M. (James Martin)
Private, Captain William E. Booe's Partisan Rangers • N.C. Volunteers • Company H, 63rd Regiment • (5th Regiment N.C. Cavalry) • N.C. Troops

Martin was born December 9, 1830, in Davie County to Sarah (1800, Davie). He worked as a farmer in Farmington District along with his brother, prior to enlisting in Davie County on July 18, 1862, for the war. He was discharged August 20, 1863. His brother Robert Reece McClammar [sic] also served in this company. Martin returned to Farmington District where he married Louisa Elizabeth Barneycastle on January 25, 1866. He died on June 13, 1874, and is buried in Smith Grove United Methodist Church Cemetery. Louisa married Wesley Williams on July 5, 1877.

707. McClammoch, John
Private, Company B, Carolina Rangers • 10th Virginia Cavalry Regiment

John was born in 1832 in Davie County to Sarah McCamroch [sic]. He, along with two brothers, Thomas and Martin, supported the family working as laborers. By 1860 they were farmers in the Farmington District where John enlisted October 29, 1861, at age 25. He was present or accounted for throughout his tenure. He lost his horse on April 28, 1863, was dispatched on horse detail September–October, 1863, and detailed as a teamster on November 12, 1864. He was paroled at Mocksville on June 9, 1865. Upon returning home he married Caroline Gray on February 15, 1867, and they settled in Mocksville. Their children were William (1867), Rufus (1869), Thomas J. (1872), John R. (1877), Albert M. (1878) and an infant (1880). John died May 29, 1895 and is buried in Smith Grove United Methodist Church Cemetery.

708. McClamrock (McClamma), Julius Lawrence
Private, Company M, 7th Regiment • Confederate Cavalry • Company E, 16th Battalion • N.C. Cavalry

Julius was born in 1841. He was the son of James (1810, Davie) and Frances (1820, Davie) McClamrock. Julius was a student in the Mocksville District prior to enlisting. He was a member of Company M, 7th Regiment Confederate Cavalry but was transferred to the 16th Battalion on July 11, 1864. He was present or accounted for through October 1, 1864. Julius married Sarah Ellen Foster on February 18, 1869. Their children were James (1871), Rufus S. (1873), William L. (1875), John (1877) and an infant (1879). In 1880 he farmed in the Mocksville District.

709. McClamrock, Lucius Milton
Private, Company M, 7th Regiment • Confederate Cavalry • Company E, 16th Battalion • N.C. Cavalry

Lucius was born in 1843 in Davie County to James (1810, Davie) and Frances (1820, Davie) McClamroch [sic]. The family farmed in the Mocksville District prior to the war. On September 3, 1862, Lucius enlisted in Davie County with the rank of Private. On July 11, 1864, he was transferred from Company M, 7th Regiment Confederate Cavalry to Company E, 16th Battalion N.C. Cavalry while absent in confinement at Point Lookout, Maryland, as a prisoner of war. He was transferred to Elmira, New York, August 15, 1864, where he remained until released after taking the Oath of Allegiance on June 23, 1865. He came home, married L.J. Foster on February 25, 1869, and had four children to survive: Charles B. (1870), Calvin J. (1873), Dorcas J. (1876) and Albert M. (1876). Lucius lived to be 81; he died on February 3, 1921, and is buried in Oak Grove United Methodist Church Cemetery.

710. McClannan (Clanen), J.W. (John)
Private, Captain William E. Booe's Partisan Rangers • N.C. Volunteers • Company H, 63rd Regiment • (5th Regiment N.C. Cavalry) • N.C. Troops

John was born June 3, 1842, in Davie County to Matilda (1817, Surry) McClannan. He worked as a laborer prior to enlisting in Davie County at age 19 on July 16, 1862, for the war. He was present or accounted for through February 1865, and was paroled in Salisbury, North Carolina. John's brother William also served in this company. John returned to his home in Farmington District where he remained. He married Martha C. Jackson on May 20, 1883. He died on February 27, 1916, and was buried in Wesley Chapel United Methodist Church Cemetery.

711. McClannon, W.H. (William)
Private, Captain William E. Booe's Partisan Rangers • N.C. Volunteers • Company H, 63rd Regiment • (5th Regiment N.C. Cavalry) • N.C. Troops

William was born in Davie County on July 8, 1844, to Matilda (1817, Surry) McClannan. They lived in the Farmington District of Davie County where he enlisted on April 1, 1864, for the war. He was present or accounted for through September 1864. His brother John also served in this company. Following the war, William returned home where he farmed with his brother. On January 29, 1876, William married Sarah A. White. Their son David was born May 7, 1877; sadly, he died on October 8, 1888. W.H. lived to be 78 years old; he died on February 12, 1924. He and his family are buried at Wesley Chapel United Methodist Church Cemetery.

712. McClenan (McClanen), Mathew A.
Corporal, "Davie Greys" • Company F, 13th Regiment • (3rd Regiment, N.C. Volunteers) • N.C. Troops

Mathew was born in 1839 in Davie County to Mary McClanen (1814, Halifax). In 1860 they lived with the M.R. Chaffin (Constable) family in the Farmington District of Davie County. On August 6, 1861, at age 22, Mathew enlisted as a Private and was promoted to Corporal on April 28, 1862. He was present or accounted for until wounded in the thigh and hand at or near Malvern Hill, Virginia, on or about June 30, 1862. He was hospitalized at Richmond, Virginia, where he died on July 27, 1862, of wounds. Mathew's name is listed on the Memorial Monument for the Davie County men who died in the Civil War, 1861–1865.

713. McCracken, William A.
Private, "Davie Sweep Stakes" • Company G, 4th Regiment • N.C. State Troops

William was born in 1841 to Isaac (1795, Davie) and Rose (1810, Davie) McCracken. They resided in Davie County where William enlisted at age 20, on July 1, 1861, for the war. He was wounded at Seven Pines, Virginia, on May 31, 1862, rejoined the company in July–December, 1862, and was present or accounted for until wounded at Chancellorsville, Virginia, May 3, 1863. He died at Richmond, Virginia, prior to November 6, 1863. The cause and exact date of death were not reported. William's name is listed on the Memorial Monument for the Davie County men who died in the Civil War, 1861–1865.

714. McDaniel, Alfred A.
Private, Company F, 42nd Regiment • N.C. Troops

Alfred was born in 1837 in Mecklenburg County, Virginia, to Letha A. McDaniel (1818, Virginia). He was a farmer until he enlisted in Davie County at age 23, on March 18, 1862. He

Alfred C. McDaniel (Jim Rumley)

was present or accounted for until he was discharged on June 17, 1863, by reason of "dyspepsia and extensive hypertrophy of the liver." On November 26, 1857, Alfred married Sarah (1837, North Carolina) Williams. They were the parents of ten children: Henry W. (1858), William T. (1861), James (1863), Nathan (1864), Isabel (1866), Douthit (1868), Benjamin F. (1871), Temperance E. (1874), Doctor J.H. (1877) and Minie (1879). The family continued to live in the Calahaln District.

715. McDaniel (McDannel), Benjamin L. (Lewis)
Private, Company F, 42nd Regiment • N.C. Troops

Benjamin was born in 1829 in Virginia. He resided in Davie County where he married Mary Keller (1828, North Carolina) on February 17, 1849. They settled in the Calahaln District of Davie County and raised a family of five children: Susan G. (1850), Henry T. (1851), Robert L. (1853), Claibon (1855) and Laura L. (1858). Benjamin worked as a farmer prior to enlisting in Davie County on December 2, 1863, for the war. He was present or accounted for until he was captured at or near Wise's Forks, Kinston, North Carolina, on March 10, 1865. He was confined at Point Lookout, Maryland, on March 16, 1865. He was released there on June 29, 1865, after taking the Oath of Allegiance. Benjamin is buried in Salem United Methodist Church Cemetery. There are no dates given.

716. McDaniel, Elias
Private, Company E, 42nd Regiment • N.C. Troops

Elias was born in 1843. He was the son of Allen (1805, Davie) and Rebecca (1820, Davie) McDaniel. Allen worked as a cooper. Elias worked as a laborer in the Shady Grove District when he was 16 years old. On March 18, 1862, at age 17, he enlisted in Davie County. Elias was present or accounted for through October 1864. He was paroled at Mocksville on June 7, 1865. Eliza Cornatzer and Elias were married on January 28, 1870, and she and her two children settled with Elias in Fulton District. He was stepfather to John Cornatzer (1855) and Alice J. Cornatzer (1857). On July 6, 1882, Elias married Luvenia Gullet. Although there is a discrepancy in the dates, it is believed that both Elias and Luvenia are buried in the Cornatzer United Methodist Church Cemetery.

717. McDaniel, George
Private, Company M, 7th Regiment • Confederate Cavalry • Company E, 16th Battalion • N.C. Cavalry

George enlisted in Davie County on September 3, 1862, with the rank of Private. He was transferred from Company M, 7th Regiment Confederate Cavalry to Company E, 16th Battalion N.C. Cavalry on July 11, 1864. He was present or accounted for through October 1, 1864, and paroled at Salisbury, North Carolina, in 1865.

718. McDaniel, George W.
Private, Company E, 42nd Regiment • N.C. Troops

George was born in Davie County in 1842 to Allen (1805, Davie) and Rebecca (1820, Davie) McDaniel. George was a brother of Elias McDaniel who also served in this company. George worked as a farmer in the Fulton District of Davie County prior to enlisting at age 22, on March 18, 1862. He was present or accounted for through October 1864, and was paroled at Mocksville on June 7, 1865. He married M. America Parks on March 10, 1867. She was the widow of William Parks, also of this company, who had died during the war. America had two young children from her first marriage: Charles Parks (1861) and Ellen Parks (1863). In 1880 the family farmed in Fulton and there was a new addition, a daughter, age four months, still unnamed. George died on April 8, 1919, and is buried in Fork Baptist Church Cemetery.

719. McDaniel (McDannel), John G.
Private, Company H, 57th Regiment • N.C. Troops

John was born in 1846. He resided in Davie County and enlisted in Rowan County at age 16, on July 4, 1862, for the war, as a substitute for John Baily of Salisbury, North Carolina. He was hospitalized at Richmond, Virginia, on or about September 29, 1862, then returned to duty on October 10, 1862. John was reported present through May 11, 1863, and reported sick in the hospital from June 16–October 31, 1863. He was reported absent without leave in November–December, 1863, and March–April, 1864. Company muster rolls dated April 30, 1864–February 28, 1865, indicate that he was captured at Gettysburg, Pennsylvania, on July 3, 1863; however, records of the Federal Provost Marshal do not substantiate that report. No further records.

720. McDaniel, Nace
Private, Company E, 42nd Regiment • N.C. Troops

Nace enlisted in Davie County at age 20, on

March 18, 1862. He was present or accounted for until wounded in action in June 1864. He died in the hospital at Richmond, Virginia, on September 1, 1864. The cause of death was not reported. Nace's name is listed as "Mace" on the Memorial Monument for the Davie County men who died in the Civil War, 1861–1865.

721. McDaniel, Nathan
Private, "Davie Sweep Stakes" • Company G, 4th Regiment • N.C. State Troops

Nathan resided in Davie County where he enlisted at age 20, June 15, 1861, for the war. He was present or accounted for until he deserted from camp near Fredericksburg, Virginia, May 21, 1863. After rejoining the company on October 1, 1863, he was reported "in confinement" through December 1863. His name appears on a court-martial record dated January 27, 1864. He was confined at E.D.M. Prison, Richmond, Virginia, until released in May 1864, when he was pardoned by President Jefferson Davis after volunteering to serve in the Winder Legion for the defense of Richmond against the Sheridan raid. He deserted to the enemy at Rosersville, Maryland, July 9, 1864. He was confined at Old Capitol Prison, Washington, D.C., until transferred to Elmira, New York, July 23, 1864, and released at Elmira on May 29, 1865, after taking the Oath of Allegiance.

722. McDaniel, W.H. (William Howard)
Private, Company G, 5th Regiment • N.C. State Troops

W.H. enlisted in Northampton County at age 32, August 13, 1862, for the war. He was present or accounted for until captured at Gettysburg, Pennsylvania, July 1–3, 1863. He was confined at Fort Delaware, Delaware, until transferred to Point Lookout, Maryland, October 15–18, 1863, where he was paroled a year later on October 11, 1864. He was transferred to Cox's Landing, James River, Virginia, for exchange. W.H. rejoined his company at an unspecified date and was paroled at Mocksville on June 9, 1865.

723. McDaniel, William
Private, Company M, 7th Regiment • Confederate Cavalry • Company E, 16th Battalion • N.C. Cavalry

William enlisted in Davie County on September 3, 1862. He was transferred from Company M, 7th Regiment Confederate Cavalry to Company E, 16th Battalion N.C. Cavalry on July 11, 1864. He was present or accounted for through October 1, 1864, and paroled at Salisbury, North Carolina, in 1865.

724. McDonald, James
Private, "Davie Greys" • Company F, 13th Regiment • (3rd Regiment, N.C. Volunteers) • N.C. Troops

James was born in 1842. He resided in Davie County where he enlisted at age 19, August 6, 1861. He was present or accounted for until killed at Gettysburg, Pennsylvania, on July 1, 1863. The Roll of Honor indicates he was wounded "three different times ... without leaving the field" at Chancellorsville, Virginia, May 1–3, 1863, and was "brave in all the battles." James's name is listed on the Memorial Monument for the Davie County men who died in the Civil War, 1861–1865.

725. McElroy, William J.
Private, "Davie Sweep Stakes" • Company G, 4th Regiment • N.C. State Troops

William was born in 1816. He married Rachel C. Oakes, July 29, 1841, in Davie County where they resided. He enlisted at age 45, June 4, 1861, for the war. He was present or accounted for through June 1862. No further records. Rachel is buried at Bethlehem United Methodist Church Cemetery along with an infant son and an infant daughter. She was born in 1820 and died on August 29, 1850.

726. McGill, John A.
Private, Company F, 42nd Regiment • N.C. Troops

John was born in 1821 in North Carolina. In 1860 he and his wife Sallie (1820, North Carolina) and their three children lived in the Farmington District of Davie County. Their children were Mary (1849), Wm. (1851) and Louiza (1854). John worked as a laborer prior to enlisting in Davie County on December 18, 1862, for the war. He was present or accounted for through October 1864.

727. McGuire, James
Captain, Regiment Assistant Surgeon • 77th Regiment, 19th Division • N.C. Militia 1861–1865

James was born April 29, 1829, in Davie County to Sarah McGuire (1795, Davie). According to James W. Wall in his *History of Davie County*, McGuire graduated from the Mocksville Academy and taught school there in the early 1850s. He read medicine under Dr. J.F. Martin of Mocksville and graduated from New York Uni-

THE STATE OF NORTH CAROLINA

To James McGuire of Davie County, Greeting:

We, reposing special trust and confidence in your patriotism, valor and military skill, do hereby commission you Surgeon with of the assimilated rank of Captain of the 77 Regiment, of the 19 Brigade, North-Carolina Militia, and we do hereby vest you with the authority appertaining to said office, to the end that you may promptly and diligently perform its duties, as prescribed by law; in the discharge of which all officers and soldiers under your command are required to yield you obedience.

In Witness Whereof, HENRY T. CLARK, Speaker of the Senate, ex-officio OUR GOVERNOR, CAPTAIN-GENERAL AND COMMANDER-IN-CHIEF, hath signed these presents, and caused our Great Seal to be affixed thereto.

Done at our City of RALEIGH, on the 10th day of March in the year of our Lord, one thousand eight hundred and sixty-one, and in the Eighty-sixth year of our Independence.

Henry T. Clark

By the Governor.

J Cowper
Private Secretary.

Commission of James McGuire to be Surgeon of the 77th Regiment of the 19th Brigade with the rank of Captain (Davie County Public Library).

Dr. and Mrs. James McGuire (Davie County Public Library)

versity Medical College in 1857. He returned home to Mocksville where he married Jane E. Eccles on July 13, 1859. He practiced medicine for more than forty years, served as the first County Superintendent of Health and was county treasurer from 1882 to 1898. Dr. McGuire died August 21, 1909. He is buried in Joppa Cemetery.

728. McGuire, Timothy
Private, Company F, 42nd Regiment • N.C. Troops

Timothy was born in 1820 in Davie County where he made his living as a farmer. On May 31, 1842, he married Eliza Ann Roberts (1820, Davie). Tim and Eliza Ann were the parents of ten children: Sarah (1839), William (1841), Elenor (1846), Forest B. (1849), Milly A. (1848), Thomas G. (1851), James M. (1853), John M. (1857), Sarah J. (1860) and Edward (1866). When the war began, Timothy enlisted in Davie County at age 42, on or about March 18, 1862. He was present or accounted for through October 1864. Following the war, Timothy and his family resumed their lives in Calahaln where he continued to farm.

729. McGuire, William F.
Sergeant, "Davie Greys" • Company F, 13th Regiment • (3rd Regiment, N.C. Volunteers) • N.C. Troops

William was born in 1843 in Davie County to Timothy (1820, Davie) and Eliza A. Roberts (1820, Davie) McGuire. They farmed in the Mocksville District prior to William's enlisting in Davie County at age 18, April 26, 1861. He mustered in as a Private and was promoted to Corporal on January 2, 1863. He was present or accounted for until wounded at Chancellorsville, Virginia, May 1–3, 1863. He rejoined the company prior to July 1, 1863, and was wounded at Gettysburg, Pennsylvania, July 1–3, 1863. He rejoined the company prior to September 1, 1863, when he was promoted to Sergeant. He was present or accounted for until captured at Reams' Station, Virginia, on August 24–25, 1864, and confined at Point Lookout, Maryland, until paroled and transferred to Boulware's and Cox's Wharf, James River, Virginia, where he was received February 20–21, 1865, for exchange. William returned to Davie County where he married Safrona J. Warren on March 22, 1865.

730. McKaughan, Isiah S.
Private, Company G, 7th Regiment • Confederate Cavalry • Company D, 16th Battalion • N.C. Cavalry

Isiah transferred from Company G, 7th Regiment Confederate Cavalry to Company D, 16th Battalion N.C. Cavalry on July 11, 1864. He was present or accounted for through October 1, 1864.

731. McKaughan, J.H.
Sergeant, Company G, 7th Regiment • Confederate Cavalry • Company D, 16th Battalion • N.C. Cavalry

J.H. enlisted in Davie County on September 3, 1862, with the rank of Private, then was promoted to Sergeant. He was transferred from Company G, 7th Regiment Confederate Cavalry to Company D, 16th Battalion N.C. Cavalry on July 11, 1864. He was present or accounted for through October 1, 1864, and paroled at Greensboro, North Carolina, on May 16, 1865.

732. McKaughan, Richard H.
Private, Company G, 7th Regiment • Confederate Cavalry • Company D, 16th Battalion • N.C. Cavalry

Richard was transferred from Company G, 7th Regiment Confederate Cavalry to Company D, 16th Battalion N.C. Cavalry on July 11, 1864. He was present or accounted for through October 1, 1864. He was captured in Dinwiddie County, Virginia, April 1, 1865, and confined at Hart's Island, New York Harbor, until released after taking the Oath of Allegiance, June 18, 1865.

733. McKaughan, William J.
Corporal, Company G, 7th Regiment • Confederate Cavalry • Company D, 16th Battalion • N.C. Cavalry

William enlisted in Davie County on September 3, 1862, as a Corporal. He was transferred from Company G, 7th Regiment Confederate Cavalry to Company D, 16th Battalion N.C. Cavalry on July 11, 1864. He was present or accounted for through October 1, 1864, and paroled at Greensboro, North Carolina, on May 13, 1865.

734. Miller, Henry
Private, Company B, Carolina Rangers • 10th Virginia Cavalry Regiment

Henry was born in 1842 in Davie County to Jacob (1816, Davidson) and Mary (1821, Davie) Miller. His father was an overseer and Henry was a farmhand in the Smith Grove District prior to enlisting on November 8, 1861, at age 18. He was present or accounted for through May 6, 1862. There is no further record.

735. Miller, Henry
Private, Captain William E. Booe's Partisan Rangers • N.C. Volunteers • Company H, 63rd Regiment • (5th Regiment N.C. Cavalry) • N.C. Troops

Henry enlisted in Davie County at age 20, July 15, 1862, for the war. He was wounded and reported "captured at Upperville, Virginia, June 21, 1863," on May–June, 1863, muster roll and as "present" on July–August, 1863, muster roll. No Federal Provost Marshal records relative to his capture or release were found. He was admitted to the hospital at Richmond, Virginia, July 23, 1863, with a wound of the leg and returned to duty August 17, 1863. He was present or accounted for through November 1864.

736. Miller, Jacob C.
Private, Company E, 42nd Regiment • N.C. Troops

Jacob was born in 1819 in Surry County. He apparently moved to Davie County early in life since he married Polly Miller (1819, Davie) on December 1, 1842. (Note: Polly is listed as "Mary" in the census.) Jacob worked as a farmer in the Mocksville District and was the father of nine children before he enlisted: William (1844), John H. (1845), Mary (1847), Sarah (1848), Alfred L. (1853), Daniel M. (1855), Louisa M. (1856), Luther S. (1858) and Foster (1861). Jacob enlisted in Davie County at age 43, March 18, 1862. He was present or accounted for until discharged on May 30, 1863, by reason of disability. (He may have served later as Private in Company A, 4th Regiment N.C. Senior Reserves.) He returned to his family and farming; he died September 16, 1873, and is buried in Smith Grove United Methodist Church Cemetery.

737. Miller, James L.
Private, 1st Company A, Salisbury Prison Guard • "The Rough and Readys" • Company G, 66th Regiment • N.C. Troops

James served as a Private in 1st Company A, Salisbury Prison Guard until he transferred on October 2, 1863, to Company G of the 66th. He was reported present through October 31, 1864. On December 10, 1864, he was hospitalized at Richmond, Virginia. The reason he was hospitalized was not reported. He returned to duty on December 16, 1864, and was paroled at Salisbury, North Carolina, on May 29, 1865.

738. Miller, James W.
Private, "Davie Greys" • Company F, 13th Regiment • (3rd Regiment, N.C. Volunteers) • Company F, 42nd Regiment • N.C. Troops

James was born in 1844 in Davie County to Jacob (1816, Davidson) and Mary (1820, Davie) Miller. Jacob was an overseer. They resided in Davie County where James enlisted at age 17, on August 6, 1861. He was present or accounted for until he was wounded at South Mountain, Maryland, on or about September 14, 1862. He was discharged in November–December, 1862. The reason for the discharge was not reported. On August 3, 1863, James enlisted in Company F of the 42nd Regiment, for the war. He was present or accounted for through October 1864. He was paroled at Greensboro, North Carolina, on May 1, 1865. James married Bulah W. Smith on July 10, 1866, in Davie County. Their daughter Mary Bet was born in 1870. The family lived in the Farmington District where James worked as a farm laborer. Bulah died November 13, 1871, and is buried in Smith Grove Baptist Church Cemetery.

739. Miller, John E.
Private, Company E, 42nd Regiment • N.C. Troops

John was born in 1840 (1835?) in Davie County to Johnathan (1811, Davidson) Miller. John farmed in the Farmington District prior to enlisting at age 22, on March 18, 1862. He was present or accounted for through October 1864, and took the Oath of Allegiance at Salisbury, North Carolina, on June 10, 1865. He resumed his life as a farmer, married Margaret J. Allen on December 13, 1866, and raised six children: Charles (1868), James W. (1869), Sally (1871), Lonna (1873), Bertie (1876) and Paul (1879). Both John and Margaret died in 1920, within fourteen days of each other, according to their tombstones at Macedonia Moravian Church Cemetery.

740. Miller, John F.
Private, Company E, 42nd Regiment • N.C. Troops

John enlisted in Davie County on September 15, 1864, for the war. He was present or accounted for through October 1864. No further information.

741. Miller, John H.
Private, Company E, 42nd Regiment • N.C. Troops

John was born in 1845 in Davie County to Jacob C. (1809, Surry) and Mary (1819, Davie) Miller. His father was a farmer and John was a laborer in the Mocksville District prior to enlisting in Davie County at age 18, on June 9, 1863, for the war. He was present or accounted for through October 1864, and paroled at Mocksville on June 9, 1865. At age 27 he married Allice Willson, age 20, on January 8, 1873.

742. Miller, John R.
Private, Company G, 7th Regiment • Confederate Cavalry • Company D, 16th Battalion • N.C. Cavalry

John transferred from Company G, 7th Regiment Confederate Cavalry to Company D, 16th Battalion N.C. Cavalry on July 11, 1864. He was captured at Fort Harrison, Virginia, on September 30, 1864, and confined at Point Lookout, Maryland, until "released June 29, 1865."

743. Millraney, J.H.
Private, Company G, 7th Regiment • Confederate Cavalry • Company D, 16th Battalion • N.C. Cavalry

J. H. enlisted in Davie County on September 3, 1862, as a Private. He was transferred from Company G, 7th Regiment Confederate Cavalry to Company D, 16th Battalion N.C. Cavalry on July 11, 1864, while absent "detailed as blacksmith." He was also absent on detail through August 1864. He was present or accounted for through October 1, 1864.

744. Minor, C. (Calvin)
Private, Captain William E. Booe's Partisan Rangers • N.C. Volunteers • Company H, 63rd Regiment • (5th Regiment N.C. Cavalry) • N.C. Troops

Calvin was born in 1840 in Davie County. He was the son of John, a farmer, (1812, Davidson) and Martha Minor (1812, Davidson). Prior to the war Calvin lived in the Fulton District with the J.W. Baity family. He enlisted in Davie County at age 23, July 12, 1862, for the war. He was captured on the Weldon Railroad on August 21, 1864, and confined at Point Lookout, Maryland, where he remained until released after taking the Oath of Allegiance on June 5, 1865.

745. Minor, Henry
Private, Captain William E. Booe's Partisan Rangers • N.C. Volunteers • Company H, 63rd Regiment • (5th Regiment N.C. Cavalry) • N.C. Troops

Henry was born in 1831 in Davidson County. He worked as a farm laborer for William Wyatt in the Shady Grove District of Davie County and in 1859 he married Margaret Ann Carter. He enlisted in Davie County at age 31, on July 12, 1862, for the war. He was present or accounted for until "killed June 21, 1863, at Upperville, Virginia." Henry's name is listed on the Memorial Monument for the Davie County men who died in the Civil War, 1861–1865.

746. Minor, John
Private, Company B, 48th Regiment • N.C. Troops

John was born in 1838 in Davie County, the son of John (1812, Davidson) and Martha (1812, Davidson). He lived and farmed in Smith Grove prior to enlisting in Davie County at age 24 on March 24, 1862. He was reported in the hospital at Winchester, Virginia, in September–October, 1862. He was hospitalized at Danville, Virginia, on December 28, 1862, with remittent fever, but returned to duty on January 17, 1863. He was present or accounted for in February–June, 1863, and March–April, 1864. No further records.

747. Minor, Madison
Private, Captain William E. Booe's Partisan Rangers • N.C. Volunteers • Company H, 63rd Regiment • (5th Regiment N.C. Cavalry) • N.C. Troops

Madison was born in 1842 in Davie County. He was the son of John (1812, Davidson) and Martha (1812, Davidson). John was a farmer as was his son Madison, who was farming in Smith Grove in 1860. In 1862 Madison enlisted in Davie

County at age 19, on July 12, 1862, for the war. He was captured at Hanover Court House, Virginia, on May 31, 1864, and confined at Point Lookout, Maryland, until transferred to Elmira, New York, on July 12, 1864. He died at Elmira on November 14, 1864, of "chronic diarrhea." Madison's name is listed on the Memorial Monument for the Davie County men who died in the Civil War, 1861–1865.

748. Minor, Zerel
Private, Captain William E. Booe's Partisan Rangers • N.C. Volunteers • Company H, 63rd Regiment • (5th Regiment N.C. Cavalry) • N.C. Troops

Zerel was born in Davie County in 1837. He was the son of John (1812, Davidson) and Martha (1812, Davidson) who were farmers. In 1860 Zerel was a farmer in Smith Grove District where, at age 25, he enlisted on July 12, 1862, for the war. Zerel was captured on the Weldon Railroad on August 21, 1864, and confined at Point Lookout, Maryland, until paroled and was exchanged at Boulware's Wharf, James River, Virginia, on March 16, 1865. After the war, he returned to Davie County, Fulton District, where he married Ama Hendrix on December 8, 1870. Zerel and Ama would have three children: Johnnie (1870), George (1872) and Rebecca (1876). Zerel died on June 20, 1902. He is buried in Fork Baptist Church Cemetery.

749. Mock, Henry A.
Private, "Davie Greys" • Company F, 13th Regiment • (3rd Regiment, N.C. Volunteers) • N.C. Troops

Henry was born in 1831 in Davie County to George (1789, Surry) and Delila (1790, Caswell) Mock. In 1860 he was a farmer in the Mocksville District where he married Elizabeth C. (1841, North Carolina). They had two daughters: Emily C. (1857) and Pamella A. (1859). On March 26, 1863, at age 30, he enlisted in Davie County for the war. He deserted on April 29, 1863, and was reported as a deserter until he was reported in confinement in January–February, 1864, and in confinement through April 1864. He rejoined the company prior to May 6, 1864, when he allowed himself to be "captured purposely" at Wilderness, Virginia. He was confined at Point Lookout, Maryland, until transferred to Elmira, New York, July 25, 1864, where he died on March 8, 1865, of "chronic diarrhoea." Elizabeth's application for a widow's pension is on file in the State Archives, Raleigh, North Carolina. Henry's name is listed on the Memorial Monument for the Davie County men who died in the Civil War, 1861–1865.

750. Mock, W. G. (William)
Private, "Davie Sweep Stakes" • Company G, 4th Regiment • N.C. State Troops

William resided in Davie County and enlisted at Orange Court House, Virginia, March 15, 1864, for the war. He was captured at Fisher's Hill, Virginia, September 22–23, 1864, and confined at Point Lookout, Maryland, until exchanged October 30, 1864, or November 15, 1864. He was then captured at Petersburg, Virginia, April 3, 1865, and confined at Hart's Island, New York Harbor, until released June 19, 1865, after taking the Oath of Allegiance.

751. Monday (Munday), Isaac
Private, Company H, 57th Regiment • N.C. Troops

Isaac was born in 1843. He made his home with Wade and Rebecca Phelps Munday prior to enlisting for the war. In 1860 the family lived in the Liberty District of Davie County but Isaac enlisted in Rowan County at age 19, on July 4, 1862. He was reported present through February 28, 1863. He was wounded in the hand at Chancellorsville, Virginia, on May 4, 1863, and returned to duty prior to September 1, 1863. He was captured at Rappahannock Station, Virginia, on November 7, 1863, and confined at Point Lookout, Maryland, on November 11, 1863. Isaac died in the smallpox hospital at Point Lookout on or about January 25, 1864. Isaac's name is not presently listed on the Memorial Monument for the Davie County men who died in the Civil War, 1861–1865.

752. Monday (Munday), Wade C. (Casborn)
Private, Company D, 42nd Regiment • N.C. Troops • Captain William Howard's Company • N.C. Prison Guard

Wade married Rebecca Phelps (1841, Davie) on May 14, 1859, in Davie County. In 1860 they lived in Liberty District where he farmed prior to enlisting in Davie County on February 4, 1862, in company D of the 42nd Regiment. On May 1, 1862, he transferred to Captain Howard's Company. No further military information is presently available. Casborn and Rebecca settled in Jerusalem District where they continued to farm and raise their children: Mary (1860), William (1862) and John Calton (1864).

753. Monday (Munday), William
Private, "Davie Greys" • Company F, 13th Regiment • (3rd Regiment, N.C. Volunteers) • N.C. Troops

William was born in 1840. He resided in Davie County where he worked as a farmer. In 1860 he lived in the Liberty District, with W.C. and Rebecca Munday. At age 21, on April 26, 1861, he enlisted in Davie County. He was present or accounted for until wounded in the right side and back and captured at South Mountain, Maryland, September 14, 1862. He was confined at various Federal hospitals until confined at Fort McHenry, Maryland, on or about November 17, 1862. He was paroled and transferred to City Point, Virginia, where he was received November 21, 1862, for exchange. William rejoined the company prior to May 1, 1863. He was wounded at Chancellorsville, Virginia, May 1–3, 1863, and "Went into the fight when he could scarcely bear his gun from the effects of his wounds." He rejoined the company prior to July 1, 1863, and was present or accounted for through October 1864. However, he was reported absent sick or absent on detail during most of the period. He was captured in the hospital at Richmond, Virginia, on April 3, 1865, and was paroled on April 20, 1865.

754. Moore, Jehu
Private, Company F, 42nd Regiment • N.C. Troops

Jehu was born in North Carolina in 1845. He enlisted in Davie County on April 15, 1864, for the war. He was present or accounted for through October 1864. Jehu was paroled at Mocksville on June 3, 1865. In 1870 at age 25, he lived with the Nancy Clement family and worked as a farm laborer.

755. Moore, William A.
Musician, Company E, 42nd Regiment • N.C. Troops

William was born in 1829 in Davie County, the son of William (1810, Davie) and Sarah (1814, Davie) Moore. William worked with his father as a cooper prior to enlisting in Davie County at age 30, March 18, 1862. He mustered in as a Private and was promoted to Musician (Drummer) in July–August, 1863. He was present or accounted for through October 1864, and paroled at Mocksville on June 7, 1865. William married Mary A. (1845) and they had a daughter Sarah E. (1872).

756. Moose, William R.
Private, Company C, 48th Regiment • N.C. Troops • Company G, 4th Regiment • N.C. State Troops

William was born in 1842 in Iredell County where he resided as a farmer prior to enlisting in Iredell at age 20, March 1, 1862. He was reported present in September–October, 1862, wounded in the arm at Fredericksburg, Virginia, December 13, 1862, and returned to duty prior to March 1, 1863. He was present or accounted for in March–June, 1863. He transferred to Company G, 4th Regiment, N.C. State Troops, November 11, 1863, in exchange for Sergeant William P. Hanes. William R. was present or accounted for until wounded at Spotsylvania Court House, Virginia, May 19, 1864. He retired to the Invalid Corps and was assigned to duty at Salisbury, North Carolina, on January 17, 1865.

757. Morris, Edwin Simmons
Captain, Regiment Adjutant • 77th Regiment, 19th Division • N.C. Militia 1861–1865

Edwin was born February 24, 1825, in Virginia, to Eliza H. Fowler (1808, Virginia). His wife Anne E. was born in Halifax County, Virginia, on February 14, 1830. They moved to Davie County where Edwin was appointed First Lieutenant of Company J and then promoted to Captain where he served as Adjutant to the Regiment when the militia was activated. Their children were Benjamin (1857), Eliza O. (1859), Edwin H. (1860), Endora H. (1866), Ann C. (1868) and Lucian L. (1872). The family resided in the Jerusalem District where they farmed. Annie died on February 1, 1894, and Edwin died November 12, 1903. Both are buried in Liberty Baptist Church Cemetery.

758. Motley, M.M. (Madison)
Corporal, Company E, 42nd Regiment • N.C. Troops

Madison was born August 31, 1829, in Pittsylvania County, Virginia. He moved to Davie County where he farmed, married Martha A. (1831, North Carolina) and raised three daughters: Elizabeth (1859), Nancy (1863) and Martha (1866). Madison was a farmer prior to enlisting in Davie County on May 13, 1862, for the war. He mustered in as a Private. He was promoted to Corporal on February 29, 1864, and was present or accounted for until captured at or near Wise's Forks, Kinston, North Carolina, on March 10, 1865. He was confined at Point Lookout, Maryland, on March 16, 1865, and released there two months later after taking the Oath of Allegiance. (Company records dated February 1863 give his age as 34.) Madison returned to Davie County and resumed his life as a farmer in the Jerusalem District. He died on October 17, 1881, and is buried in Fork Baptist Church Cemetery.

759. Mullican, Lewis S.
Sergeant, "Davie Sweep Stakes" • Company G, 4th Regiment • N.C. State Troops

Lewis was born in 1838 to John (1812, Davidson) and Sarah (1805, Davie) Mullican. They lived in the Mocksville District where Lewis enlisted at age 23, June 4, 1861, for the war. He mustered in as a Corporal. He was wounded at Seven Pines, Virginia, May 31, 1862, rejoined the company and was promoted to Sergeant in November–December, 1862. He was wounded at Chancellorsville, Virginia, May 3, 1863, and reported absent wounded until retired to the Invalid Corps on or about February 28, 1865, by reason of "amputation of left arm, gunshot wound in right shoulder, dislocation of finger, and bayonet wounds of the right thigh."

760. Myers, Andrew L.
Private, Company G, 7th Regiment • Confederate Cavalry • Company D, 16th Battalion • N.C. Cavalry

Andrew transferred from Company G, 7th Regiment Confederate Cavalry to Company D, 16th Battalion N.C. Cavalry on July 11, 1864. He was captured at Fort Harrison, Virginia, September 30, 1864, and confined at Point Lookout, Maryland, until paroled and exchanged at Boulware's Wharf, James River, Virginia, on March 19, 1865.

761. Myers, Henry J.
Private, Company E, 42nd Regiment • N.C. Troops

Henry was born January 4, 1839, in Davie County to John (1801, Davie) and Elizabeth (1803, Davie) Myers. He lived and worked on his parents' farm prior to enlisting in Davie County at age 23, on March 18, 1862. He was present or accounted for through October 1864, and paroled at Mocksville on June 7, 1865. Henry returned home and married Nerva P. Massey on December 25, 1865. They had five children by 1880: Conrad (1868), William T. (1870), John U. (1871), Mary E. (1876) and Lelia C. (1879). Henry died at the age of 86. He is buried in Fork Baptist Church Cemetery. An application for a pension is on file at the State Archives, Raleigh, North Carolina.

762. Myers, James
Private, Company K, 30th Regiment • N.C. Troops

James was born in 1823 in Davie County. He, his wife Sarah (1828, Davidson) and their growing family lived and farmed in the Shady Grove District of Davie County prior to the war. At that time their children were Margaret (1852), Nancy Jane (1854), Mary (1856), Conrad (1859) and George (1861). James enlisted in Wake County at age 40 on July 9, 1863, for the war. He was present or accounted for until captured at Kelly's Ford, Virginia, November 7, 1863, and confined at Point Lookout, Maryland, November 11, 1863. He was paroled there on or about February 24, 1865, and transferred to Aiken's Landing, James River, Virginia, where he was received February 25–March 3, 1865, for exchange. Upon returning home to Davie County, James and his family lived and worked in the Fulton District. By 1880 the family had grown by four more children: James J. (1864), David (1866), Charles (1868) and Sarah Lou (1874). James's pension application is on file at the State Archives, Raleigh, North Carolina.

763. Myers, Jefferson C.
Private, Company G, 7th Regiment • Confederate Cavalry • Company D, 16th Battalion • N.C. Cavalry

Jefferson transferred from Company G, 7th Regiment Confederate Cavalry to Company D, 16th Battalion N.C. Cavalry on July 11, 1864. He was captured near Petersburg, Virginia, on October 27, 1864, and confined at Point Lookout, Maryland, where he remained until released after taking the Oath of Allegiance on May 12, 1865.

764. Myers, Jesse
Private, Company F, 22nd Regiment • N.C. Troops

Jesse enlisted at Camp Holmes on November 8, 1863, for the war. He was wounded in the thigh at Wilderness, Virginia, May 5, 1864. He was hospitalized at Staunton, Virginia, where he died on June 24, 1864, of wounds. Jesse's name is listed on the Memorial Monument for the Davie County men who died in the Civil War, 1861–1865.

765. Myers, Solomon Wesley
Private, Company E, 42nd Regiment • N.C. Troops

Solomon was born in 1833 in Davidson County. In 1850 at age 17, he lived and worked as a laborer in Davie County on the farm of Joseph M. Houser. On April 12, 1860, he married Sarah Ann Rabin (1839) and they made their home with

Sarah's mother, Mary Rabin (1815). He enlisted at age 35, on March 18, 1862, in Davie County. He was present or accounted for until captured at or near Wise's Forks, Kinston, North Carolina, on March 8, 1865, and was confined at Point Lookout, Maryland, on March 16, 1865. Solomon was released there on June 29, 1865, after taking the Oath of Allegiance.

766. Myers, William B.
Private, Company B, Carolina Rangers • 10th Virginia Cavalry Regiment

William was born in 1843. He enlisted in Davie County on October 29, 1861, at age 18. He was present or accounted for through December 31, 1864.

767. Myers, Zadock
Private, Company D, 42nd Regiment • N.C. Troops

Zadock was born in 1817 in Davie County. By 1850 he was married to Catherine (1818, Rowan) and was the father of John (1847). The following year he married Delphia Siddin on October 29, 1851. They lived in the Smith Grove District where he worked as a laborer. They had four children prior to the war: Mary J. (1854), William (1857), Mahala (1859) and Uriah (1861). Zadock enlisted in Rowan County on March 18, 1862. (Military records list his age as 21; age 45 is probably more nearly correct.) He was discharged prior to September 1, 1862, after providing a substitute. Following his return the family lived in the Fulton District where he farmed; however, by 1880 Adelphia, age 59, was listed as the sole head of household. She died in 1906 and is buried in Advance Methodist Church Cemetery.

768. Nail, Abraham M. (A.M.)
Sergeant, "Davie Greys" • Company F, 13th Regiment • (3rd Regiment, N.C. Volunteers) • N.C. Troops • Private, Company M, 7th Regiment • Confederate Cavalry • Company E, 16th Battalion • N.C. Cavalry

Abraham was born in 1826 in Davie County. He married Mary M. McGuire on December 24, 1851, in Mocksville where he worked as a cabinet maker. He made his home with R.F. and Maria Johnson prior to enlisting in Davie County at age 34, on April 26, 1861. He was appointed Sergeant on June 1, 1861, and was present or accounted for until he was discharged at Richmond, Virginia, on July 26, 1862, under the provisions of the Conscript Act. He apparently re-enlisted as a Private shortly afterward because he was transferred from Company M, 7th Regiment Confederate Cavalry to Company E, 16th Battalion N.C. Cavalry on July 11, 1864. He was present or accounted for through October 1, 1864, and paroled at Salisbury, North Carolina, in 1865.

769. Nail, Alexander S.
Private, Company B, Carolina Rangers • 10th Virginia Cavalry Regiment

Alexander was born November 11, 1822, in Davie County. He and his wife Margaret lived in the Town of Mocksville, with their children, where he worked as a laborer prior to enlisting at age 39, on October 29, 1861. He was present or accounted for until he was discharged for over-age on June 18, 1862. He returned home where he was employed as a tobacco factory worker. In 1880 he was a farmer. Their children were John (1850), Maria (1852), Abram M. (1854), Savannah (1859), Jesse (1861), Mary (1864) and Robert (1869). He later went to live in the home for disabled veterans. An application for a pension is on file at the State Archives, Raleigh, North Carolina. Alexander died on July 23, 1903, and is buried in Bethel United Methodist Church Cemetery.

770. Nail, Henry
Private, Company F, 42nd Regiment • N.C. Troops

Henry was born in 1835 in Davie County to Thomas (1810, Davie) and Barbary (1814, Davie) Nail. They lived and farmed in the Mocksville District of Davie County where Henry married Jincey Ann (1841) Wood on November 6, 1859. Two years later he enlisted in Davie County at age 27, on March 18, 1862. He was present or accounted for through December 10, 1864. Henry's brother Phillip also served in this company. Jincey and Henry had three children: Rufus (1863), Mary Lee (1864) and Minnie (1867). By 1870 however, Henry was no longer with the family. Jenny was "keeping house" with three small children. On May 4, 1876, Jennie [sic] A. Nail, age 30, married James M. Furcron, age 40, in Davie County. In 1880 James and "Jane" had a daughter, age 1, named Dovey. The family of six lived in the Mocksville District where James supported them by working as a shoe and boot maker.

771. Nail, Jasper H.Y.
Musician, "Davie Greys" • Company F, 13th Regiment • (3rd Regiment, N.C. Volunteers) • N.C. Troops

Jasper was born January 22, 1841, in Davie County. He made his home with Lucinda and

Lutisha Nail and worked as a farmer in the Mocksville area prior to enlisting in Davie County at age 19, on April 26, 1861. He mustered in as a Private, was appointed Musician on September 1, 1861, and was present or accounted for until paroled at Richmond, Virginia, on or about April 17, 1865. North Carolina pension records indicate that he was wounded in the left thigh at Malvern Hill, Virginia, in "June 1863." Jasper died on November 4, 1914. He is buried at Oak Grove United Methodist Church Cemetery.

772. Nail, John A.
Sergeant, "Davie Greys" • Company F, 13th Regiment • (3rd Regiment, N.C. Volunteers) • N.C. Troops

John was born in 1840. He resided in Davie County or Rowan County and was by occupation a farmer prior to enlisting in Davie County at age 21, on April 26, 1861. He mustered in as a Private and was promoted to Corporal on April 28, 1862. He was present or accounted for until he was captured at Sharpsburg, Maryland, on September 17, 1862. John was confined at Fort Delaware, Delaware, until he was transferred to Aiken's Landing, James River, Virginia, on October 2, 1862, for exchange. He was declared exchanged at Aiken's Landing on November 10, 1862, later rejoining the company in November–December, 1862, and was promoted to Sergeant prior to January 1, 1863. John was present or accounted for until wounded at Chancellorsville, Virginia, May 1–3, 1863. He rejoined the company prior to July 1–3, 1863, when he was wounded in the right shoulder and captured at Gettysburg, Pennsylvania. John was hospitalized at Chester, Pennsylvania, and was promoted to First Sergeant on September 1, 1863, while a prisoner of war. John was paroled at Chester and transferred to City Point, Virginia, where he was received on September 23, 1863, for exchange, later re-joining the company in March–April, 1864, and was reduced to the rank of Sergeant in May–June, 1864. He was present or accounted for until paroled at Appomattox Court House, Virginia, on April 9, 1865. John was paroled again at Salisbury, North Carolina, on July 8, 1865.

773. Nail, Philip A.
Private, "Davie Greys" • Company F, 13th Regiment • (3rd Regiment, N.C. Volunteers) • N.C. Troops

Philip was born in 1841 in Rowan County and resided in Davie County where he was a farmer prior to enlisting in Davie County at age 20, on August 6, 1861. He was present or accounted for until he died in the hospital at Richmond, Virginia, June 28, 1862, of "continued fever." Philip's name is listed on the Memorial Monument for the Davie County men who died in the Civil War, 1861–1865

774. Nail, Phillip
Private, Company F, 42nd Regiment • N.C. Troops

Phillip was born in Davie County in 1839 to Thomas (1810, Davie) and Barbary (1814, Davie) Nail. They lived and farmed in the Mocksville District of Davie County where Phillip enlisted at age 23, on March 18, 1862. He was present or accounted for through October 1864. Following the end of the war he returned to Davie County and to farming. On November 17, 1870, he married Susan Rose. Their daughter Mary E. was born in 1871. On December 28, 1873, Phillip married Mary Rose. (The wives were sisters.) Their daughter Alice C. was born in 1877, but Mary, Alice's mother died prior to 1880. Once again Phillip married, this time to Margaret E. (1861) Pennington, on January 23, 1883. During these turbulent years, Phillip continued to farm. He lived to the ripe old age of 93, dying in 1932. He is buried in Oak Grove United Methodist Church Cemetery where his tombstone lists his Civil War service. Phillip's brother Henry also served in this company.

775. Nash, B.R. (Berry R.)
Sergeant, Company E, 42nd Regiment • N.C. Troops

B.R. was born in 1846 in Davie County to John B. (1825, Virginia) and Nancy Harben (1825, Davie). John was a laborer in Smith Grove prior to enlisting in Davie County at age 26, on March 18, 1862. He mustered in as a Sergeant and was present or accounted for until he was appointed Musician on February 29, 1864, and transferred to the regimental band.

776. Naylor, Bat W. (Batson)
Private, Company E, 42nd Regiment • N.C. Troops

Bat was born in 1843 in Davie County to Batson S. (1812, Davie) and Ann (1812, Virginia) Naylor. Batson was a farmer and carpenter, and his son Bat was a laborer who lived in the Smith Grove District. At age 19, on March 18, 1862, Bat enlisted in Davie County. He was present or accounted for through October 1864. (The Salem *People's Press* of June 30, 1864, indicates he was wounded in action on June 1–15, 1864.)

777. Naylor, Benjamin T.
Third Lieutenant, Company E, 42nd Regiment • N.C. Troops

Benjamin was born in Davie County in 1840. He was the son of Batson S. (1812, Davie) and Ann R. (1812, Virginia) Naylor. On October 18, 1860, Benjamin and S.E. Brock were married. The couple lived in Smith Grove where Benjamin worked as a laborer prior to enlisting in Davie County for the war, on July 8, 1862. He mustered in as a Private and was promoted to Corporal on March 22, 1863. He was promoted to Sergeant on February 29, 1864, and appointed Third Lieutenant on October 14, 1864. He was present or accounted for through October 1864. Benjamin was paroled at Mocksville on June 8, 1865.

778. Naylor, John Ozmont
Private, Captain William E. Booe's Partisan Rangers • N.C. Volunteers • Company H, 63rd Regiment • (5th Regiment N.C. Cavalry) • N.C. Troops

John was born in Davie County in 1836, the son of Wm. A. (1813, Davie) and Elizabeth (1812, Davie). In 1860 John worked as a laborer and lived in Smith Grove with his parents. On February 10, 1861, he married Amanda Booe. He enlisted on July 10, 1862, at age 25, in Davie County for the war. He was present or accounted for through August 1864 on the company muster roll. John was reported in the hospital at Richmond, Virginia, in October 1864. He was paroled at Salisbury, North Carolina, in 1865. In 1870 he lived and farmed in the Mocksville area. He and Amanda were the parents of eight children: Mary C. (1861), John F. (1864), William Thomas (1867), Lela V. (1868), Sallie K. (1872), Nina B. (1875), Nola J. (1878) and Watson (1881).

779. Naylor, Little Berry
Second Lieutenant, Company K • 77th Regiment, 19th Division • N.C. Militia 1861–1865

Little Berry was born in 1832 in North Carolina to S.W. (1807, Virginia) and Mahetell [sic] (1811, North Carolina) Naylor. S.W. was a miller and a farmer in the Farmington District of Davie County. When the militia was activated, Little Berry was appointed to the rank of Second Lieutenant of Company K. No further mention is made of the family.

780. Naylor, S.T. (Samuel)
Private, Captain William E. Booe's Partisan Rangers • N.C. Volunteers • Company H, 63rd Regiment • (5th Regiment N.C. Cavalry) • N.C. Troops

Samuel was born in 1840 in Davie County to Samuel W. (1808, Davie or Virginia) and Mehetabel (1818, Davie) Naylor. His father was a miller, a machinist and a farmer in the Farmington District in 1860. Samuel married Elizabeth Virginia Chinn on January 28, 1861. He enlisted in Davie County at age 22, July 10, 1862, for the war. He mustered in as a Sergeant and was "reduced to ranks for cowardice August 1, 1863." He was present or accounted for through November 1864, and was paroled at Salisbury, North Carolina, in 1865.

781. Naylor, T.N. (Thomas)
Private, Company E, 42nd Regiment • N.C. Troops

Thomas was born in 1848 in Davie County, the son of Batson S. (1812, Davie) and Ann R. (1812, Virginia) Naylor. His father was a farmer and carpenter who resided in Smith Grove. Thomas had an older brother, Batson W., who also served in this company. Thomas enlisted in Davie County on October 1, 1864, for the war. He was paroled at Mocksville on June 8, 1865. After the war, Thomas settled in the Mocksville District and became a farmer. On February 8, 1877, he married Frances Feribee. They were the parents of a daughter, Minnie B. (1878). The 1880 census shows them farming and living in the Mocksville District.

Amanda Booe Naylor and John Ozment Naylor. John married Amanda Booe February 10, 1861, just days before the war began (Marie Roth).

T.N. (Thomas) Naylor (Brenda Bailey)

782. Newnam, H.L. (H.A. Newman)
Private, Captain William E. Booe's Partisan Rangers • N.C. Volunteers • Company H, 63rd Regiment • (5th Regiment N.C. Cavalry) • N.C. Troops

H.L. enlisted in Davie County at age 19, on July 13, 1862, for the war. He was present or accounted for until he died in the hospital at Wilson, North Carolina, April 22, 1863, of "febris typhoides." H.L.'s (H.A.) name is listed on the Memorial Monument for the Davie County men who died in the Civil War, 1861–1865.

783. Newnam (Newman), T.L.
Private, Captain William E. Booe's Partisan Rangers • N.C. Volunteers • Company H, 63rd Regiment • (5th Regiment N.C. Cavalry) • N.C. Troops

T.L. enlisted in Davie County at age 30, on July 14, 1862, for the war. His name was reported on a muster roll dated September 17, 1862. No further records.

784. Newnam (Newman), W.F.
Private, Captain William E. Booe's Partisan Rangers • N.C. Volunteers • Company H, 63rd Regiment • (5th Regiment N.C. Cavalry) • N.C. Troops

W.F. enlisted in Davie County on July 14, 1862, for the war. He was present or accounted for until he died in the hospital at Wilson, North Carolina, on April 16, 1863, of "febris typhoides." W.F.'s name is listed on the Memorial Monument for the Davie County men who died in the Civil War, 1861–1865.

785. Newnan, A.W.
Private, Company M, 7th Regiment • Confederate Cavalry • Company E, 16th Battalion • N.C. Cavalry

A.W. enlisted in Davie County September 3, 1862, with the rank of Private. He was transferred from Company M, 7th Regiment Confederate Cavalry to Company E, 16th Battalion N.C. Cavalry on July 11, 1864. He was present or accounted for through October 1, 1864, and two months later furloughed from the hospital at Richmond, Virginia, for sixty days, beginning December 3, 1864. He was paroled at Salisbury, North Carolina, on May 22, 1865.

786. Nichols, B.F. (Benjamin)
Second Lieutenant, Company G, 7th Regiment • Confederate Cavalry • Company D, 16th Battalion • N.C. Cavalry

In 1860 Benjamin lived with Robert and Elizabeth Sprouce in the Mocksville District of Davie County. Robert was a physician. Benjamin worked as an overseer prior to enlisting as a Second Lieutenant. He served in Company G, 7th Regiment until he was transferred to Company D, 16th Battalion on July 11, 1864. He was reported as absent on leave from February 28, 1865, on an inspection report dated February 28, 1865. He was later paroled in Salisbury, North Carolina, the same year. Ben returned to Davie County where he farmed in the Mocksville District. He married Ann Lathem on January 6, 1869; their children were Minnie (1870), John H. (1871), Maggie J. (1874) and Malvin (1878). He died on February 2, 1892, and is buried in Oak Grove United Methodist Church Cemetery.

787. Nolly, William H.
Private, Company B, Carolina Rangers • 10th Virginia Cavalry Regiment

William was born October 11, 1843. He enlisted in Davie County at age 17, on October 29, 1861. He was present until captured at Dinwiddie Court House, Virginia, on April 1, 1865. He was sent to Point Lookout, Maryland, where he was released June 15, 1865. He returned to the Jerusalem District of Davie County where he married Letitia Wagner on December 13, 1865. Jacob was born in 1867. William worked as a farmer until his death, April 15, 1905. He is buried in Liberty United Methodist Church Cemetery.

788. Norman, S. Alexander ("Sandy")
Private, Company E, 42nd Regiment • N.C. Troops

S. Alexander was born in 1836 in North Carolina. He married Caroline (1830, North Carolina) and they settled in the Farmington District of Davie County where he worked as a farm laborer. They had four children by 1860: Eliz. (1854), Nancy J. (1857), Sarah (1859) and Lucey C. (1860). "Sandy" enlisted in Davie County at age 26, on March 18, 1862. He was present or accounted for through March 12, 1865, and paroled at Greensboro, North Carolina, on June 3, 1865. He married a second time, on November 21, 1869, to Mary Wheeler. His name appears on the marriage record as "Alexander."

789. Oaks (Oakes), James P.
Second Lieutenant, Company A, 21st Regiment • N.C. Troops

James was born in 1837 in Davie County. He worked as a merchant in the Smith Grove area of Davie County prior to enlisting at age 20, on May 8, 1861. He mustered in as a Private but was quickly elected Third Lieutenant to rank from April 27, 1861. He was promoted to Second Lieutenant on May 25, 1862, and was present or accounted for until wounded at Sharpsburg, Maryland, September 17, 1862. He returned to duty prior to March 1, 1863, and was present or accounted for until he was reported absent wounded in September–October, 1864; however, the place and date were not reported. He retired to the Invalid Corps on March 13, 1865. James returned to Davie County. He and Catharine (1845) Howard were married on January 10, 1867. In 1870 James worked as a huckster in the Fulton District. He died in 1875, the same year of his daughter Maggie's birth. James is buried in Advance United Methodist Church Cemetery. Following James's death, Catharine and Maggie lived with Catharine's father, Henry G. Howard, a manufacturer, in Jerusalem Township.

790. O'Neal, William H.
Private, Company D, 42nd Regiment • N.C. Troops

William was born in 1844 in Davie County to Sarah (1812, Davie) O'Neal. He resided in Rowan County and enlisted in Rowan or Davie at age 25, January 30, 1862. He was present or accounted for until captured at or near Cold Harbor, Virginia, June 3, 1864. He was confined at Point Lookout, Maryland, June 11, 1864, and transferred to Elmira, New York, where he arrived on July 17, 1864. He was released there on July 3, 1865, after taking the Oath of Allegiance. Three months after returning home he married Mary Jane Tacket, October 12, 1865. In 1880 William and Jane lived with her parents, Samuel and Martha Tacket, in the Clarksville District where William worked as a laborer.

791. Orrell, David E.
Private, Company G, 5th Regiment • N.C. State Troops

David was born in 1839 in Davie County to Daniel (1801, Virginia) and Susannah (1799, Virginia) Orrel [sic]. They resided in the Smith Grove District where David worked as a laborer. He married Mary Ann Foster on January 5, 1860; he married Jane Barrow on May 11, 1862. On August 13, 1862, he enlisted in Northampton County at age 22, for the war. He deserted from camp near Fredericksburg, Virginia, December 26, 1862. Company muster roll dated November–December, 1863, states that he was "in arrest under charge of desertion." Company muster roll dated January–February, 1864, states he was "court-martialed for desertion — found guilty and sentenced to three years hard labor with a five pound ball and chain serving sentence in Salisbury, North Carolina." Reported in confinement at Salisbury through December 1864. David and Jane would have four children by 1880: Cornelia (1866), Cicero (1867), Lidia (1869) and Mary S. (1874). Records show that in 1870 David was listed as a farmer in the Fulton District and in 1880 as a distiller. He died on July 3, 1890, and is buried in Advance United Methodist Church Cemetery. There is an application for a widow's pension from Watauga County on file in the State Archives, Raleigh, North Carolina.

792. Orrell (Orel), Robert R.
Private, Company D, 42nd Regiment • N.C. Troops

Robert was born September 16, 1823, in Davie County. He married Nellie Call on August 29, 1843, in Davie County. They had a family of seven children prior to the war: twins Louis F. and Lazetta C. (1849), Henry (1851), Edger (1853), Daniel (1855), Nancy (1857) and Delia E. J. (1859). Robert resided in Davie County but enlisted in Rowan County at age 38, April 8, 1862. He was reported as a deserter who was under arrest in July–August, 1862. He was reported under arrest during November 1862–June 1863. He returned to duty prior to November 1, 1863, and was present or accounted for until hospitalized at Raleigh, North Carolina, on January 18, 1865, with erysipelas. He returned to duty on February 21, 1865. Following the war he returned to Davie County and settled in Fulton District where he farmed and five of the children attended school. Robert and Edgar farmed together in 1880. Four years later Robert died, May 31, 1884. He is buried in Advance United Methodist Church Cemetery.

793. Orrender (Orander), Charles R.
Private, Company A, 42nd Regiment • N.C. Troops

Charles was born in Virginia in 1845. He was the son of William Orrender, Sr. (1808, Virginia). Charles resided in Davie County and was by occupation a tobacconist prior to enlisting in Lenoir County at age 18, on October 4, 1863, for the war. He was present or accounted for until captured at or near Battery Anderson, near Fort Fisher, North Carolina, on December 25, 1864. He was confined at or near Fort Monroe, Virginia, on or about December 29, 1864. He was transferred to Point Lookout, Maryland, where he arrived on January 2, 1865. Charles was released at Point Lookout on May 14, 1865, after taking the Oath of Allegiance. In 1870 he was living in Fulton District and was a tobacco trader.

794. Owen, N. Richard
Private, Company B, Carolina Rangers • 10th Virginia Cavalry Regiment • "Davie Sweepstakes" • Company G, 4th N.C. Cavalry • Company A, 42nd Regiment • N.C. Troops

Noah (Richard) was born March 18, 1834, in Davidson County to William (1801, Davidson) and Catherine (1803, Davidson) Owen. Both he and his father were farmers. Richard married Mary K. Grainger on March 26, 1857, and they made their home in the Farmington District of Davie County where he enlisted in the 10th Virginia Cavalry on October 29, 1861, at age 27. He was present until wounded in the left hand and admitted to Richmond hospital on June 25, 1862. He was furloughed for 30 days on July 10, 1862, and then was absent without leave January and February, 1863. He was present until he was admitted to Richmond hospital on August 1, 1863, with chronic diarrhoea. He returned to duty on November 3, 1863, and was present until he again was absent without leave January 1–4, 1864. He was in attendance July 8, 1864, and then transferred to Company G, 4th North Carolina Cavalry on November 13, 1864. As a Private in Co. A, 42nd Regiment he was captured at or near Battery Anderson, near Fort Fisher, North Carolina, on December 25, 1864, and confined at or near Fort Monroe, Virginia, on or about December 27, 1864. He was transferred to Point Lookout, Maryland, where he arrived on January 2, 1865. Richard was released on June 29, 1865, after taking the Oath of Allegiance. In 1870 the family was living in the Farmington District where Richard was a farm laborer. Mary Katherine and Richard had nine children: Mary (1861), Jennie (1864), Barbara (1865), William (1866), Annie (1868), Charlie (1871), John (1873), Lulah (1876) and Thomas (1880). In 1880 the family continued to live in the Farmington District where Richard worked as a shoemaker. He died on April 21, 1895, and is buried in Smith Grove United Methodist Church Cemetery.

795. Owen, William H.
Private, "Davie Sweep Stakes" • Company G, 4th Regiment • N.C. State Troops

William was born in 1841 in Davidson County to John (1807, Davidson) Owen. He lived and worked as a laborer with Pleas. and Amanda Gaton in the Chinquepin District of Davie County prior to enlisting at age 20, July 1, 1861, for the war. Company muster rolls indicate he was killed at Gaines' Mill, Virginia, June 26, 1862; however, Federal medical records indicate that he died in the hospital at Point Lookout, Maryland, April 18, 1865, of "pneumonia." Records of the Federal Provost Marshal do not indicate that he was captured. No further records. William's name is listed on the Memorial Monument for the Davie County men who died in the Civil War, 1861–1865.

796. Owens, A.L.
Private, Company M, 7th Regiment • Confederate Cavalry • Company E, 16th Battalion • N.C. Cavalry

A.L. enlisted in Davie County September 3, 1862, with the rank of Private. He was transferred from Company M, 7th Regiment Confederate Cavalry to Company E, 16th Battalion N.C. Cavalry on July 11, 1864, while absent wounded. He died of wounds August 3, 1864. A.L.'s name is listed on the Memorial Monument for the Davie County men who died in the Civil War, 1861–1865.

797. Owens, Henry C. (Clay)
Private, Company D, 42nd Regiment • N.C. Troops

Henry was born in 1844 in Davidson

County to John (1807, Davidson) Owens. His father moved the family across the Yadkin River to Davie County where he worked as a "well-diger" and Henry worked as a laborer in the Chinquepin District. At age 23, Henry enlisted in Rowan County on March 4, 1862. He was present or accounted for through October 1864, and was paroled at Mocksville on June 3, 1865. He and Louisa Standly were married in Davie County on May 9, 1867. No further records.

798. Owens, Michael
Private, Company A, 42nd Regiment • N.C. Troops

Michael resided in Davie County and enlisted in Rowan County at age 19, March 6, 1862. He was present or accounted for until he deserted on August 23, 1863. He returned to duty on December 16, 1863. He was present or accounted for until captured at or near Battery Anderson, near Fort Fisher, North Carolina, on December 25, 1864. He was confined at or near Fort Monroe, Virginia, on or about December 27, 1864. Michael was transferred to Point Lookout, Maryland, where he arrived on January 2, 1865. He was released on June 29, 1865, after taking the Oath of Allegiance.

799. Pack, John
Captain, Company C • 77th Regiment, 19th Division • N.C. Militia 1861–1865

John was born in Davie County in 1820. He and his wife Aurena (Irene) (1823, Davie) farmed in Smith Grove prior to the war. When the militia was activated John was appointed Captain of Company C. After the war the family moved to Fulton District to farm. The children were Henry Giles (1844), William Harrison (1848), Osborn F. (1850) and Charles (1861).

800. Paris, Thomas M. Williams
First Lieutenant, Company M • 77th Regiment, 19th Division • N.C. Militia 1861–1865

Thomas was born in 1835 in North Carolina. He married Sarah E. Baity on April 28, 1858, in Davie County where they settled in Chinquepin District. He worked as a farmer, and when the militia was activated he was appointed First Lieutenant of Company M. In 1870 at age 35, Thomas was a "Minister of the Gospel." He and Sarah lived in the Clarksville District with their six children: Mary Bet (1859), Sarah H. (1861), John F. (1863), Nancy A. (1865), Silas W. (1866) and Wm. B. (1867).

801. Parish (Paris), Solomon
Private, "Davie Sweep Stakes" • Company G, 4th Regiment • N.C. State Troops

Solomon was born in 1833. He married Elizabeth Sasser July 20, 1859. They resided in the Mocksville District of Davie County where Solomon worked as a laborer and where he enlisted at age 28, June 4, 1861, for the war. He was present or accounted for until detailed for duty as a Provost Guard at Gordonsville, Virginia, August 15, 1863. He was reported absent on detail through August 1864, and paroled at Salisbury, North Carolina, in 1865. The exact date of parole was not reported.

802. Parish, Thomas
Private, Company D, 42nd Regiment • N.C. Troops

Thomas was born in Wake County in 1800. He was a shoemaker by trade. He resided in Davie County and was married to Elizabeth (1804, Davie). Thomas enlisted in either Davie or Rowan County at age 60, on or about March 27, 1862. He was present or accounted for until he deserted on August 19, 1863. There were six children in the household throughout the years, but it is unclear which were Thomas's and which, if any, were grandchildren: Laura (1844), Jane (1840), Marion (1859), Betsy (1862), Sally (1864) and Molly (1867). In 1870 the family had settled in the Calahaln District.

803. Parker, Childs A.
Private, Company E, 42nd Regiment • N.C. Troops

Childs was born in 1834 in Davie County to Shelby G. (1801, Davie) and Roena (1818, Rowan) Parker. His father worked as a wheelright [sic] and Childs was a cabinet maker. When he enlisted his occupation was given as "a mechanic." He married Mary Howard on December 14, 1854, and they were the parents of Sarah J. (1858) and Rebeca [sic] (1860) before the war began. The family lived in Fulton District prior to Childs's enlisting in Davie County at age 28, March 18, 1862. He was present or accounted for through October 1864, and paroled at Salisbury, North Carolina, on May 25, 1865. Upon his return home the family increased by three more children: DeWitt (1866), Marshall (1867) and Infant (1870). Sadly, when the 1870 census was taken, Mary was listed as head of the household and they resided in Jerusalem District.

804. Parker, Edward N.
Sergeant, "Davie Sweep Stakes" • Company G, 4th Regiment • N.C. State Troops

Edward was born in 1822. He lived with his mother Elizabeth in the Mocksville District of Davie County where he worked as a trader; in 1860 he lived in the B.W. Parker household prior to enlisting at age 39, June 5, 1861, for the war. He mustered in as a Private and was promoted to Sergeant on October 31, 1862. Six months later he was wounded in the right shoulder at Chancellorsville, Virginia, May 3, 1863. He was reported absent wounded until June 23, 1864, when he was detailed for duty in the hospital at Salisbury, North Carolina. On May 3, 1865, he was paroled at Greensboro, North Carolina, and returned home from the war where at the age of 50, he married Mary E. Emberson, 38, on March 11, 1873.

805. Parks, Mack
Private, Company E, 42nd Regiment • N.C. Troops

Mack was born in Davidson County in 1817. In 1850 at age 33, he married Sally (Sarah) who was also born in 1817 in Davidson County. He was the father of three girls: Elizabeth (1841), Rebecca (1844) and Etta (1846). A granddaughter, Sarah E. (1863) also lived with them. Mack was a lifelong farmer, living and working in the Fulton District. At the age of 46, on March 18, 1862, he enlisted in Davie County. He was present or accounted for until discharged on August 6, 1862. The reason he was discharged was not reported. (He may have served later as Private in Company A, 4th Regiment N.C. Senior Reserves.) He returned home to his work and family.

806. Parks, William
Private, Company E, 42nd Regiment • N.C. Troops

William was born in 1820 in Davidson County. In 1850 he lived with his wife Tabitha (1824, Davidson) and young daughter Sarah (1836) in Davie County where he worked as a farmer. After Tabitha's death on January 2, 1858, William married America Cope on June 29, 1858. He enlisted in Davie County on October 2, 1863, for the war. He was present or accounted for until captured at or near Cold Harbor, Virginia, on June 1–3, 1864, and confined to Point Lookout, Maryland, on June 11, 1864. He was transferred to Elmira, New York, where he arrived on July 17, 1864, and died there on September 27, 1864, of "chronic diarrhoea." America and William had two children prior to his death in 1864: Charles Parks (1861) and Ellen Parks (1863). Three years after William's death in 1864, America, at age 34, married George McDaniel on March 10, 1867. William Parks' children are listed in the 1870 census under the names of George and America McDaniel. William's name is listed on the Memorial Monument for the Davie County men who died in the Civil War, 1861–1865.

807. Parnell, Benjamin
First Lieutenant, Company A, 57th Regiment • N.C. Troops

Benjamin was born in 1828 in Johnston County. At age 21, he was a blacksmith and a resident of Davie County. On October 13, 1847, he and Susanna E. Hudson (1825, Davie) were married. Their son, John T., was born in Mocksville in 1848, where the family lived and worked. At age 34, Benjamin enlisted in Rowan County where he was appointed Second Lieutenant on July 4, 1862. He was reported in command of the company in September 1862–February 1863, and promoted to First Lieutenant on January 8, 1863. Benjamin resigned for reasons of health on April 10, 1863. His resignation was accepted on or about April 25, 1863. He then returned to Mocksville where he resumed his work as a blacksmith. Benjamin died on June 14, 1899, and is buried in Joppa Cemetery.

808. Parnell, J.W.
Private, Company G, 7th Regiment • Confederate Cavalry • Company D, 16th Battalion • N.C. Cavalry

J.W. enlisted in Davie County on September 3, 1862, with the rank of Private. He was transferred from Company G, 7th Regiment Confederate Cavalry to Company D, 16th Battalion N.C. Cavalry on July 11, 1864, while absent "detailed with artillery detachment." He remained absent detailed through August 1864. He was present or accounted for through October 1, 1864, and paroled at Greensboro, North Carolina, on May 13, 1865.

809. Parrass, J.S.
Private, Company G, 7th Regiment • Confederate Cavalry • Company D, 16th Battalion • N.C. Cavalry

J.S. enlisted in Davie County on September 3, 1862, with the rank of Private. He was transferred from Company G, 7th Regiment Confederate Cavalry to Company D, 16th Battalion N.C. Cavalry on July 11, 1864, while absent on detail as wagoner and teamster. He was absent on detail through August 1864, and present or accounted for through October 1864.

810. Parrish, W.P.
Private, Company M, 7th Regiment • Confederate Cavalry • Company E, 16th Battalion • N.C. Cavalry

W.P. was born in 1844 in North Carolina. At age 16 he worked in the Calahaln District as a laborer prior to enlisting. He transferred from Company M, 7th Regiment Confederate Cavalry, July 11, 1864, to Company E, 16th Battalion, where he was present or accounted for through October 1, 1864. He was paroled at Mocksville on June 9, 1865.

811. Parrish, Wesley W.
Private, Company A, 21st Regiment • N.C. Troops

Wesley resided in Davie County where he enlisted at age 29, on May 8, 1861. He was present or accounted for until he died in the hospital at Lynchburg, Virginia, on or about August 28, 1861, of disease. Wesley's name is not presently listed on the Memorial Monument for the Davie County men who died in the Civil War, 1861–1865.

812. Parrish, Willis G.
Private, Company A, 21st Regiment • N.C. Troops

Willis resided in Davie County where he enlisted at age 22, on May 8, 1861. He was present or accounted for until he died in the hospital at Front Royal, Virginia, on September 30, 1861, of disease. Willis's name is not presently listed on the Memorial Monument for the Davie County men who died in the Civil War, 1861–1865.

813. Peacock, George W.
Private, Company G, 7th Regiment • Confederate Cavalry • Company D, 16th Battalion • N.C. Cavalry

George enlisted in Davie County on September 3, 1862, with the rank of Private. He was transferred from Company G, 7th Regiment Confederate Cavalry to Company D, 16th Battalion N.C. Cavalry on July 11, 1864, while absent in confinement at Point Lookout, Maryland, as a prisoner of war. He was transferred to Elmira, New York, July 25, 1864, where he died of "chronic diarrhoea," January 8, 1865. George's name is listed on the Memorial Monument for the Davie County men who died in the Civil War, 1861–1865.

814. Pearson, Charles William
Company F, 9th Regiment N.C. Troops (1st Regiment N.C. Cavalry) • Captain, Company H, 63rd Regiment • (5th Regiment N.C. Cavalry) • N.C. Troops

Charles was born in 1842 in Davie County to Elizabith [sic] (1813, Davidson) Pearson. He transferred from Company F, Ninth Regiment N.C. State Troops (1st Regiment N.C. Cavalry) upon appointment to Third Lieutenant, March 2, 1863. He was promoted to second Lieutenant in September 1863, and was present or accounted for through August 1864. He was recommended for the ranks of First Lieutenant and Captain successively and passed examination before the Brigade Examining Board. On January 4, 1865, he was named Captain to rank from July 20, 1864, the date of Captain Booe's retirement. He was paroled at Salisbury, North Carolina, May 1, 1865.

815. Peebles, Aaron G.
Private, Company B, Carolina Rangers • Tenth Virginia Cavalry Regiment

Aaron was born on January 9, 1840, in Davie County, to Elizabeth (1806, Chatham) Peebles. His mother was a farmerist and Aaron was a student prior to the war. Their property had significant value along with an overseer to supervise the farm operation and the field hands who lived there. They were located in the Shady Grove District where Aaron enlisted on January 6, 1862, at age 22. He was present through May 6, 1862, and returned to duty from Richmond hospital August 18, 1862. He died of pneumonia in Richmond hospital on January 19, 1863. There is a grave in Peebles Family Cemetery with a tombstone that reads "Arron G. Peebles." Aaron's name is listed on the Memorial Monument for the Davie County men who died in the Civil War, 1861–1865.

816. Peebles (Peeples), John Headen
Captain, Company E, 42nd Regiment • N.C. Troops

John was born in 1836 in Davie County. He lived with his mother Elizabeth (1806, Chatham) and siblings on a large and apparently prosperous farm managed by an overseer and worked by slaves. By 1860 John had married M.E. Harris (Martha) and was the father of a growing family. They would have five children: Veroa (1857), Lucius (1858), Joseph G. (1860), William D. (1862) and Fanny (1870). They lived in the Smith Grove District of Davie County. On May 10, 1862, he was appointed First Lieutenant of this company.

He was present or accounted for until wounded in the left foot in battle at Camp Wingfield, near Edenton, North Carolina, on March 23, 1863. He was reported absent wounded through April 1864. He was promoted to Captain in March–April, 1864, and resigned on June 10, 1864, by reason of disability from wounds. His resignation was accepted on July 11, 1864. John and Martha maintained a farm in the Fulton District where they raised their children. John's application for a pension is on file at the State Archives, Raleigh, North Carolina.

817. Peebles, Nathanial Aaron
Captain, Company D • 77th Regiment, 19th Division • N.C. Militia 1861–1865

Nathanial was born in 1838 in Davie County to Drury and Elizabeth (1806, Chatham) Peebles. By 1850 his father had died and his mother managed their 800 acre farm and 32 slaves, along with her own six children. When the militia was activated Nathanial was appointed Captain of Company D. After the war he married M. Jane "Jenny" Lowe (1844, North Carolina). They farmed in Fulton District and later in Jerusalem District. Their children were Bessie (1869), Clara (1870), Mary (1872) and Cicero (1875). According to her tombstone, Jenny died on February 21, 1886.* Nathaniel's second marriage was to Bella M. (Julia) Chaffin on December 16, 1884, according to *Davie County Marriages* book. He died on May 3, 1904, and is buried in Peebles Family Cemetery. (*Date contradicts the date of Nathanial's second marriage.)

818. Pence, Henry
Private, Company G, 5th Regiment • N.C. State Troops

Henry was born in 1842 to Henry H. (1803, North Carolina) and Margaret (1822, North Carolina) Pence. They lived in the Calahaln District of Davie County where Henry worked as a laborer prior to enlisting in Northampton County, at age 20, August 13, 1862, for the war. He died in the hospital at Mount Jackson, Virginia, November 9, 1862, of "typhoid fever." Henry's name is not presently listed on the Memorial Monument for the Davie County men who died in the Civil War, 1861–1865.

819. Pennington, James
Corporal, Company G, 5th Regiment • N.C. State Troops

James was born in 1825 in North Carolina. In 1860 he worked as a farm laborer on the Robert Blackwell farm where he met Icyan Williams. He and Icy were married October 28, 1860; their first child, Betty, was born in 1861. On August 13, 1862, he enlisted in Northampton County, for the war. He mustered in as a Private and was promoted to Corporal on February 3, 1863. He was wounded in the left hip and captured at Gettysburg, Pennsylvania, July 1–4, 1863, where he was hospitalized until transferred to Fort McHenry, Maryland, on or about July 6, 1863. He was transferred to Fort Delaware, Delaware, July 7–12, 1863, and transferred to Point Lookout, Maryland, October 15–18, 1863. He was paroled there on February 18, 1865, and transferred to Boulware's Wharf, James River, Virginia, for exchange. He was reported present with a detachment of paroled and exchanged prisoners at Camp Lee, near Richmond, Virginia, February 27, 1865. He returned home to the Calahaln District of Davie County where he resumed family life. Four more children were added: Mary (1863), Robert (1865), Charles (1867) and Alice (1869). On December 26, 1878, James married Rebecca Campbell. Atlas was born the following year.

820. Penry, Boone T.
First Sergeant, "Davie Greys" • Company F, 13th Regiment(3rd Regiment, N.C. Volunteers) • N.C. Troops*

Boone was born in Davie County on May 25, 1832. He was the son of Boone and Mary B. Penry. Prior to enlisting in Davie County on August 6, 1861, he had been a student in the Mocksville District. He mustered in as a Private and was present or accounted for until hospitalized at Richmond, Virginia, June 13, 1862, with a gunshot wound of the foot; however, the place and date wounded were not reported. He returned to duty on or about September 2, 1862, and was promoted to Sergeant on December 6, 1862. On April 17, 1863, he was promoted to First Sergeant and was present or accounted for until killed at Chancellorsville, Virginia, May 3, 1863. He is buried at Center United Methodist Church Cemetery, along with his parents. His father's grave has the unique distinction of being the oldest grave in the cemetery. Boone's name is listed on the Memorial Monument for the Davie County men who died in the Civil War, 1861–1865.

821. Penry, Joel
Private, Captain William E. Booe's Partisan Rangers • N.C. Volunteers • Company H, 63rd Regiment • (5th Regiment N.C. Cavalry) • N.C. Troops

Joel was born in 1821 in Davie County, the son of Mary Penry (1788, Davie). He married Ursley (Ursula) Dwiggins (1821, Davie) on December 13, 1848, and their daughter Sarah M. was born in 1850. He was a farmer in the Mocksville District, where he enlisted on September 18, 1863, for the war. He was present or accounted for through October 1864. Joel was paroled at Salisbury, North Carolina, in 1865. In 1870 he farmed in the Calahaln area where he died on August 29, 1872. He is buried in Dwiggins Family Cemetery.

822. Penry, Thomas Smith
Second Lieutenant, Company F • 77th Regiment, 19th Division • N.C. Militia 1861–1865

Thomas was born in 1833 in Davie County. He worked as a farm laborer on the farm of James (1780, Davie) and Hannah (1779, Davie) Penery [sic], who were probably his grandparents. On December 28, 1853, Thomas married Nancy (1836, North Carolina) Kerfees and they established their home in the Mocksville District. When the militia was activated, Thomas was appointed Second Lieutenant of Company F. Following the war, he continued to farm and raise his nine children: Caleb B. (1858), John P. (1860), Charles (1862), Robert L. (1864), Mary E. (1866), William (1869), Sarah E. (1872), Lula J. (1874) and Lelia A. (1876). Thomas died on March 1, 1901, and is buried in Center United Methodist Church Cemetery.

823. Penry, William H.
Private, "Davie Greys" • Company F, 13th Regiment • (3rd Regiment, N.C. Volunteers) • N.C. Troops

William was born in 1836 in Davie County to John (1805, Davie) and Susannah (1808, Davie) Penry. He resided in Davie County and was by occupation a farmer prior to enlisting there at age 25, April 26, 1861. He was present or accounted for until captured at or near Frederick City, Maryland, September 10–12, 1862. He was confined at Fort Delaware, Delaware, until transferred to Aiken's Landing, James River, Virginia, October 2, 1862, for exchange. He was declared exchanged at Aiken's Landing on November 10, 1862, and rejoined the company prior to January 1, 1863, and was present or accounted for until he was killed at Gettysburg, Pennsylvania, July 1, 1863. William's name is listed on the Memorial Monument for the Davie County men who died in the Civil War, 1861–1865.

824. Perry, M.F.
Private, Company E, 42nd Regiment • N.C. Troops

M.F. was born in Davie County in 1845. He was the son of William H. (1819, Orange) and Mary (1824, Davie) Perry. Both M.F. and William Perry were life-long farmers in the Farmington District. On June 15, 1863, he enlisted in Davie County, for the war. He was present or accounted for until wounded in an unspecified action on August 18, 1864, and reported absent wounded through October 1864. He was hospitalized at Greensboro, North Carolina, on February 21, 1865, with intermittent fever and was transferred on February 23, 1865. M.F. was married to Louisa (1845), and their children were Annie (1872) and Clauzell (1877). They all lived in the Farmington District.

825. Perry, William
Private, "Davie Sweep Stakes" • Company G, 4th Regiment • N.C. State Troops

William was born in 1827. He was a shoemaker, married to Winney and the father of three children before 1860: Eliza J. (1847), John (1850) and Pleasant (1856). They lived in the Farmington District of Davie County where he enlisted at age 34, June 4, 1861, for the war. He was wounded at Seven Pines, Virginia, May 31, 1862, and reported absent wounded or absent without leave until he rejoined the company in November–December, 1863. He was wounded again, this time at Spotsylvania Court House, Virginia, on or about May 13, 1864, and died on May 13, 1864. Winnie's (Winney) application for a widow's pension is on file in the State Archives, Raleigh, North Carolina. William's name is listed on the Memorial Monument for the Davie County men who died in the Civil War, 1861–1865.

826. Perry, William Haywood
Captain, Company B • 77th Regiment, 19th Division • N.C. Militia 1861–1865

William was born in 1819 in Orange County to Nancy (1799, Orange) Perry. He married Mary Fulford (1824, Davie), June 29, 1843. They settled in the Farmington District where they farmed and raised their children: Martha (1844), Mathew (Nathan F.) (1845), James M. (1848), John (1850), Charlotte (1854), Josephine (1856) and Mary E. (1859). When the militia was activated, William was appointed Captain of Company B. His family continued to increase as four more children were born in the 1860s; they were Mollie (1860),

Sallie (1862), Vance (1864) and Charlie (1869). Perry died prior to 1880 and Mary, age 56 continued to farm with five children at home, with the older ones providing income working as a teacher, a dress maker and a farm laborer.

827. Phelps, Britton
Private, Company G, 7th Regiment • Confederate Cavalry • Company D, 16th Battalion • N.C. Cavalry

Britton was born in Davie County in 1842 to Jacob (1820, Davidson) and Ailcy (Alice Miller) Phelps. Britton enlisted in Davie County on September 3, 1862, with the rank of Private. He was transferred from Company G, 7th Regiment Confederate Cavalry to Company D, 16th Battalion N.C. Cavalry on July 11, 1864, while absent in confinement at Point Lookout, Maryland, as a prisoner of war. He died there of "chronic diarrhoea" on October 25, 1864. Britton's name is listed on the Memorial Monument for the Davie County men who died in the Civil War, 1861–1865.

828. Phelps, Charlie
Private, Company G, 7th Regiment • Confederate Cavalry • Company D, 16th Battalion • N.C. Cavalry

Charlie enlisted in Davie County on September 3, 1862, with the rank of Private. He was transferred from Company G, 7th Regiment Confederate Cavalry to Company D, 16th Battalion N.C. Cavalry on July 11, 1864, while absent in confinement at Point Lookout, Maryland, as a prisoner of war. He remained there until paroled and exchanged at Boulware's Wharf, James River, Virginia, March 16, 1865.

829. Phelps, Uriah Hunt
Lieutenant Colonel, 77th Regiment, 19th Division • N.C. Militia 1861–1865

Uriah was born in 1826 in Davidson County to Hiram (1798, Massachusetts) and Comfort (1786, Guilford) Clemmons Chaffin Phelps. In 1850 Uriah farmed with his father in the Shady Grove District of Davie County where they grew grain for their distillery business. Uriah's mother died in 1855; his father married Jane Orrell in 1856 and by 1860, Uriah had three small siblings in the house: Ida (1857), Seth H. (1858) and Arrilley F. (1859). When the militia formed he became second in command with the rank of Lieutenant Colonel.

830. Phillips, John W.
Private, Company G, 7th Regiment • Confederate Cavalry • Company D, 16th Battalion • N.C. Cavalry

John enlisted in Davie County on September 3, 1862, with the rank of Private. He transferred from Company G, 7th Regiment Confederate Cavalry on July 11, 1864, to Company D, 16th Battalion N.C. Cavalry. He was captured near Petersburg, Virginia, October 27, 1864, and confined at Point Lookout, Maryland, where he died of "dysentery acute" on June 10, 1865. John's name is listed on the Memorial Monument for the Davie County men who died in the Civil War, 1861–1865.

831. Phillips, L.F.
Private, Company G, 7th Regiment • Confederate Cavalry • Company D, 16th Battalion • N.C. Cavalry

L.F. transferred from Company G, 7th Regiment Confederate Cavalry to Company D, 16th Battalion N.C. Cavalry on July 11, 1864. He was captured at Fort Harrison, Virginia, on September 30, 1864, and confined at Point Lookout, Maryland, where he remained until paroled and exchanged at Boulware's Wharf, James River, Virginia, March 19, 1865.

832. Pigg, Hugh
Private, Company B, 46th Regiment • N.C. Troops

Hugh was born in Davie County in 1845 and resided in Rowan County where he was by occupation a farmer prior to enlisting in Rowan County at age 17, on March 22, 1862. He was discharged prior to September 1, 1862, by reason of being underage.

833. Plott, John
Private, Company D, 42nd Regiment • N.C. Troops

John was born January 1, 1822, and made his home in Davie County. He lived in the Shady Grove District where he worked as a blacksmith and where he married Elizabeth Ieames (1833) on July 4, 1859. John enlisted at age 40, on April 7, 1862. He was present or accounted for until captured at Cold Harbor, Virginia, on June 2, 1864, and was confined at Point Lookout, Maryland, on June 11, 1864. He was transferred to Elmira, New York, on July 12, 1864, paroled at Elmira on March 14, 1865, and received at Boulware's Wharf, James River, Virginia, on or about March 18, 1865, for exchange. In 1870 the family was living in Farmington District where John worked as a farmer and blacksmith. John and Elizabeth were the parents of eleven children: Mitchel M. (1856), James M. (1858), William A. (1860), Sarah (1862), Aaron (1864), Mary Ellen (1866), Ruth (1868), Clarisa A. (1869), Nancy (1871), John C. (1873) and Thomas (1875). John died in 1894 and is buried in Bethlehem United Methodist Church Cemetery.

834. Pool, Benjamin F. (Franklin)
Private, "Davie Greys" • Company F, 13th Regiment • (3rd Regiment, N.C. Volunteers) • N.C. Troops

Benjamin was born in 1840 in Randolph County. He resided in Davie County, Mocksville District, where he was a farmer prior to enlisting in Davie County at age 21, August 6, 1861. He was present or accounted for until he died in the hospital in Richmond, Virginia, August 5, 1862, of disease. He was married to Elizabeth (1841, North Carolina) and they had one son Anderson D. (1859). Elizabeth's pension application and subsequent correspondence are on file in the State Archives, Raleigh, North Carolina. Benjamin's name is listed on the Memorial Monument for the Davie County men who died in the Civil War, 1861–1865.

835. Pool, Randolph
Private, "Davie Greys" • Company F, 13th Regiment • (3rd Regiment, N.C. Volunteers) • N.C. Troops

Randolph was born in 1844. He resided in Davie County where he enlisted at age 23, August 6, 1861. He was present or accounted for until wounded in the left knee at Chancellorsville, Virginia, May 3, 1863. He rejoined the company prior to July 14, 1863, when he was captured at Falling Waters, Maryland. He was confined at Old Capitol Prison, Washington, D.C., until transferred to Point Lookout, Maryland, August 8, 1863. From there, he was transferred to Elmira, New York, August 16, 1864, where he was paroled on March 10, 1865, and transferred to Boulware's Wharf, James River, Virginia, March 15, 1865, for exchange. Randolph was paroled at Mocksville on June 9, 1865. On April 1, 1866, Randolph and Malona Blackwood were married in Davie County. They would have seven children by 1880: James (1866), Emma (1868), Lula M. (1872), John P. (1874), Thomas L. (1877), Lelia F. (1878) and Anna D. (1879). In 1880, at age 36, he was a "crippled farmer" living with his family in or near Mocksville. His application for a pension is on file at the State Archives, Raleigh, North Carolina.

836. Potts, A.J. (Andrew)
Private, Company E, 42nd Regiment • N.C. Troops

A.J. was the son of Jeremiah (1802, Davie) and Mary (1797, Davie) Potts. He was born in 1827 in Davie County where he worked as a farm laborer. On February 17, 1856, A.J. married Manerva Jarvis. They lived in the Smith Grove District, prior to his enlisting in Davie County at age 34, on March 18, 1862. He was present or accounted for through October 1864, and paroled at Mocksville on June 7, 1865. A.J. and Manerva's children were (Elizabeth?), Lucy (1857), Wm. B. (1859) and Franklin (1860). The family continued to live in the Fulton District. (Andrew was the brother of Francis and Peter who also served in this company.)

837. Potts (Pots), Calvin J.
Corporal, Company B, 46th Regiment • N.C. Troops

Calvin was born in 1832 in Davie County. At age 18, he lived with his mother, Elizabeth (1795, Maryland) Potts, and worked as a farmer. He married Emaline Carter, age 22, on March 30, 1853. She was the daughter of Nathaniel (1802, Cumberland) and Nancy (1808, Cumberland) Carter. Calvin and Emely had two sons: John Pots (1854) and James Pots (1857). In 1860, prior to enlisting, Calvin lived with the John Myers family in the Shady Grove District where he worked as a laborer, and Emely and their two sons lived with her mother, Nancy, in the Liberty District. Calvin enlisted in Rowan County at age 27, February 5, 1862. He mustered in as a Private and was present or accounted for until wounded at Fredericksburg, Virginia, December 13, 1862. He returned to duty prior to January 1, 1863. He was captured at the South Anna Bridge, near Richmond, Virginia, July 4, 1863. He was confined at Fort Monroe, Virginia, and paroled there on July 16, 1863. He was received at City Point, Virginia, July 17, 1863, for exchange. He returned to duty prior to November 1, 1863, and was promoted to Corporal February 1, 1864. He was wounded at Wilderness, Virginia, on or about May 5, 1864, and returned to duty prior to July 1, 1864. He was captured near Petersburg, Virginia, "on the night of 28 of July when he drove his musket into the ground and went over to the Federal lines." He was confined at Point Lookout, Maryland, August 5, 1864, then transferred to Elmira, New York, August 8, 1864, where he died on January 5, 1865, of "chronic diarrhoea."

Calvin's name is not presently listed on the Memorial Monument for the Davie County men who died in the Civil War, 1861–1865.

838. Potts, F.A., (Francis)
Private, Company E, 42nd Regiment • N.C. Troops

Francis was born in 1828 in Davie County to Jeremiah (1802, Davie) and Mary (1797, Davie) Potts. He was the brother of Andrew and Peter who also served in this company. Francis married Letitia Caton on February 3, 1853; their six children were George (1854), Sarah J. (1859), Archibald (1862), Charles (1866), Pleasant (Jackson?) (1868) and Edward (1870). He farmed in Shady Grove prior to enlisting in Davie County or at Camp French at age 34, on August 28, 1862, for the war. He was present or accounted for through October 1864, and paroled at Mocksville on June 6, 1865. Following the war, the family lived in the Fulton District where Frank continued to farm. He is buried in Advance United Methodist Church Cemetery with his tombstone attesting to his service in Company E of the 42nd Regiment. It does not, however, give the date of his death.

839. Potts, Hiram
Private, Company E, 42nd Regiment • N.C. Troops

Hiram was born in Davie County in 1835. His father was William (1805, Davie), who made his living as a cooper; his mother was Sarah (1815, Davie) Potts. He was the brother of Newberry Potts who also served in this company. Hiram married Mary J. Cope on November 13, 1860. The pair lived in the Liberty District where Hiram worked as a laborer until he enlisted on March 18, 1862, at age 26, in Davie County. He was present or accounted for through August 1862. Company records dated November–December, 1862, indicate that he was a prisoner of war; however, records of the Federal Provost Marshal do not substantiate that report. He returned to duty in January–February, 1863, and was present or accounted for through March 20, 1865. Hiram was paroled in Mocksville on June 3, 1865. By 1880 the family had moved from Jerusalem District and were farming in Fulton District. Hiram and Mary J. would have seven children by 1880: Mildred (1861), William (1865), Franklin (1867), Mary (1868), Sarah (1874), Sanford (1877) and Turner W. (1879).

840. Potts, Milton (Allen M.W.)
Private, Company A, 42nd Regiment • Captain William Howard's Company • N.C. Prison Guard • 1st Company A, Salisbury Prison Guard • "The Rough and Readys" • Company G, 66th Regiment • N.C. Troops

Milton was born in 1845 in Davie County to William L. (1805, Davie) and Sarah (1815, Davie) Alexander Potts. They lived in the Fulton District of Davie County where William worked as a cooper. Milton enlisted in Davidson County on November 26, 1861. He transferred to Captain William Howard's Company on or about May 1, 1862. He served as Private in 1st Company A before transferring to Company G of the 66th Regiment. He was reported present through October 13, 1864. He was captured near Kinston, North Carolina, on March 8, 1865, confined at Point Lookout, Maryland, March 16, 1865, and released at Point Lookout on June 16, 1865, after taking the Oath of Allegiance. Milton returned to Davie County where he married Rhoda Jane Wishon on November 14, 1867. Charles W. was born in 1869, followed by Daniel H. (1872), William L. (1874) and Lela R. (1877).

841. Potts, Newberry
Private, Company E, 42nd Regiment • N.C. Troops

Newberry was born November 28, 1843, in Davie County to William (1805, Davie) and Sarah (1815, Davie) Potts. His father was a cooper, and Newberry was a laborer. He was also the brother of Hiram Potts who served in this company. He worked in Fulton District prior to enlisting in Davie County at age 18, on March 25, 1862. He was present or accounted for through January 25, 1865. He was paroled at Salisbury, North Carolina, on June 5, 1865, and took the Oath of Allegiance there on June 27, 1865. He married Edie Ann Carter (1838) on January 21, 1868. Edie had a son, George Carter (1863), from a previous marriage. She and Newberry were the parents of Pleasant (1869), James H. (1870), Julie E. (1874) and Minnie (1876). Newberry's application for a Civil War pension is on file at the State Archives, Raleigh, North Carolina. He died on July 19, 1920, and is buried in Fork Baptist Church Cemetery.

842. Potts, Peter W.M.
Private, Company E, 42nd Regiment • N.C. Troops

Peter was born in 1840 in Davie County to Jeremiah (1802, Davie) and Mary (1797, Davie) Potts. His father was a farmer, and Peter was a laborer. He was also the brother of A.J. and Francis who served in this company. Peter lived in the Shady Grove area of Davie County with the Richard and Elizabeth Bailey family prior to enlisting at age 21, on March 18, 1862. He was present or accounted for until he died in the hospital at Weldon, North Carolina, on April 5, 1863, of "pneumonia." Peter's name is listed on the Memorial Monument for the Davie County men who died in the Civil War, 1861–1865.

843. Potts, William
Private, Company E, 42nd Regiment • N.C. Troops

William was born in 1829 in Davie County. He married Mary C. Potts on February 2, 1857. Their children were Em. R.E. (1858) and Amanda J. (1859). The family lived in the Smith Grove District where William supported his family by working as a farmer prior to enlisting at age 33, on March 18, 1862. He was present or accounted for until he died in the hospital at Petersburg, Virginia, on February 6, 1863, of "chronic diarrhoea." William's name is listed on the Memorial Monument for the Davie County men who died in the Civil War, 1861–1865.

844. Potts, William S.
Private, Company G, 7th Regiment • Confederate Cavalry • Company D, 16th Battalion • N.C. Cavalry

William enlisted in Davie County on September 3, 1862, with the rank of Private. He transferred from Company G, 7th Regiment Confederate Cavalry to Company D, 16th Battalion N.C. Cavalry on July 11, 1864. He was present or accounted for through October 1, 1864, and paroled at Salisbury, North Carolina, in 1865.

845. Powell, E.H. (Elias)
Private, Company M, 7th Regiment • Confederate Cavalry • Company E, 16th Battalion • N.C. Cavalry

Elias married Sarah Jane Cheshire on September 28, 1852, in Davie County. He enlisted in Davie County on September 3, 1862, with the rank of Private. He was transferred from Company M, 7th Regiment Confederate Cavalry to Company E, 16th Battalion, N.C. Cavalry on July 11, 1864, while absent on detail at General Hospital No. 2, Wilson, N.C. He was reported as absent on detail through December 1864. Elias lived to be 84 years old; he died on January 16, 1915, and is buried in Zion Chapel United Methodist Church Cemetery, formerly known as Hickory Grove Methodist Church.

846. Powell, William Hay
Private, Captain William E. Booe's Partisan Rangers • N.C. Volunteers • Company H, 63rd Regiment • (5th Regiment N.C. Cavalry) • N.C. Troops

William was born March 20, 1836, in Davie County. In the 1850s he lived with Garland and Sarah Anderson in the Calahaln District, where he worked as a farmer, prior to marrying Mary Emaline Robinson on May 5, 1859. Their daughter Rebecca was born in 1860, followed by James R. (1863), William M. (1866), Roberson L. (1871), Marshal T. (1875) and Mary L. (1877). William's sister Henretta also lived with them. He enlisted in Davie County on July 16, 1862, for the war, and was present or accounted for through February 1865. He returned home to Calahaln and resumed his life as a farmer. He died on September 22, 1907, and is buried in Center United Methodist Church Cemetery.

847. Prather, Alfred A.
Private, Company F, 42nd Regiment • N.C. Troops

Alfred enlisted in Davie County at age 21, March 18, 1862. He was present or accounted for until killed "in trench" near Petersburg, Virginia, September 15, 1864. Alfred's name is listed on the Memorial Monument for the Davie County men who died in the Civil War, 1861–1865.

848. Prather, Eli
Private, Company F, 42nd Regiment • N.C. Troops

Eli enlisted in Davie County on December 18, 1862, for the war. He was present or accounted for until he died in the hospital at Richmond, Virginia, September 13, 1864, of "febris typhoides." Eli's name is listed on the Memorial Monument for the Davie County men who died in the Civil War, 1861–1865.

849. Prewet (Pruett), N. (Nath)
Private, Captain William E. Booe's Partisan Rangers • N.C. Volunteers • Company H, 63rd Regiment • (5th Regiment N.C. Cavalry) • N.C. Troops

Nath was born in 1838 in North Carolina, the son of Abe (1801, North Carolina) Pruett. Prior to the war, Nath and his brothers helped their father farm in the Chinquepin District. Nath enlisted in Davie County on July 18, 1862, for the war. He was present or accounted for through October 1862. His brother Anderson also served in this company.

850. Pruett, Anderson
Private, Captain William E. Booe's Partisan Rangers • N.C. Volunteers • Company H, 63rd Regiment • (5th Regiment N.C. Cavalry) • N.C. Troops

Anderson was born in 1843 in North Carolina. He was the son of Abe Pruett (1801, North Carolina), a farmer in the Chinquepin District of Davie County. Anderson enlisted in Davie County on July 18, 1862, for the war. He deserted in April 1863, and was absent without leave through December 1863. The March and August muster rolls report him as "absent under guard—charge of desertion." He was paroled at Salisbury, North Carolina, in 1865. His brother Nath also served in this unit.

851. Queen, William
Private, Company E, 42nd Regiment • N.C. Troops

William was born in 1827 in Davie County. He married Melinda (1828, Davie) Mason on November 20, 1847. They had a son Augustus (1853). William married his second wife, Rebecca (1823, Davie) Gibson, on June 14, 1857; she was a widow with a young daughter, Prassie (1849). William and Rebecca would have four children: John (1858), Virginia (Caroline) (1861), Elizabeth (1864) and Lula (1867). William worked a shoemaker prior to the war. The place and date of his enlistment were not reported; he was paroled at Mocksville on June 7, 1865. William married for the third time on April 7, 1878, to Elizabeth A. (1844) Walker, who was a widow with a young son, Curtis Walker (1869). The family lived in the Fulton District where William worked as a farmer.

852. Raban, Jonathan
Private, Company E, 42nd Regiment • N.C. Troops

Jonathan was born in North Carolina in 1836. In 1860 he was a laborer in the Farmington District. On January 13, 1861, he married Mary Jane Garner (1841, Davie). At age 26, on March 18, 1862, Jonathan enlisted in Davie County. He was present or accounted for until wounded in the left arm at Bermuda Hundred, Virginia, on May 20, 1864. He was reported absent wounded through October 1864, and paroled at Mocksville on June 5, 1865. Mary Jane and Jonathan were the parents of two children: Franklin (1867) and John (1870). In 1870 the family lived in Jerusalem District where Jonathan made a living as a wagoner.

853. Raben, Samuel W.
Private, "Davie Greys" • Company F, 13th Regiment • (3rd Regiment, N.C. Volunteers) • N.C. Troops

Samuel was born in 1835. He resided in Davie County where he enlisted at age 26, August 6, 1861. He was present or accounted for until killed at Gaines' Mill, Virginia, June 27, 1862. Samuel's name is listed on the Memorial Monument for the Davie County men who died in the Civil War, 1861–1865.

854. Ratledge, D.J. (Daniel)
Private, Company M, 7th Regiment • Confederate Cavalry • Company E, 16th Battalion • N.C. Cavalry

Daniel was born in 1838 in Davie County. He worked as a farmer in the Calahaln District where he lived with his brother and sister-in-law, L.P. and Elizabeth E. Smith Ratledge, until he married Martha A. Haith on September 5, 1861. One year later he enlisted in Davie County, September 3, 1862, with the rank of Private. He was transferred from Company M, 7th Regiment Confederate Cavalry to Company E, 16th Battalion N.C. Cavalry on July 11, 1864. He was present or accounted for through October 1, 1864. He returned to his wife and children: Dora (1862), Emma (1866), John P. (1867), James H. (1870), Daniel A.D. (1874), Martial J. (1876), Nancy A. (1878) and Auther R. (1879). He died in 1892 and is buried in Zion Chapel United Methodist Church Cemetery (formerly known as Hickory Grove Methodist Church).

855. Ratledge, Isaac
Private, Company M. 7th Regiment • Confederate Cavalry • Company E, 16th Battalion • N.C. Cavalry

Isaac was born in 1834 in Davie County. He made his home with John and Lydia Smith of Ijames, prior to marrying Rebecca D. Moore on August 18, 1857. Isaac was a farmer before he enlisted in Davie County, September 3, 1862, as a Private. He was transferred from Company M, 7th Regiment Confederate Cavalry to Company E, 16th Battalion, N.C. Cavalry on July 11, 1864, while absent without leave. He was reported as such through October 1, 1864. No further records. His two children were James Lee (1861) and John B. (1871).

856. Ratledge, L.P. (Lorenzo)
Private, Company M, 7th Regiment • Confederate Cavalry • Company E, 16th Battalion • N.C. Cavalry

Lorenzo was born November 4, 1831. At age 18 he married Elizabeth E. Smith on May 28, 1850. They lived in Calahaln with their four children prior to the war: Thos. H. (1852), Isabela J.

(1854), James S. (1855) and John F. (1858). Elizabeth died on March 6, 1862. On September 3, 1862, Lorenzo enlisted in Davie County with the rank of Private. He was transferred from Company M, 7th Regiment Confederate Cavalry to Company E, 16th Battalion N.C. Cavalry on July 11, 1864. He was present or accounted for through October 1, 1864. He married Rebecca J. Stewart on May 31, 1865. Lorenzo continued to farm after the war, but by 1880 he was blind and disabled. He died on August 14, 1909.

857. Ratledge, W.H. (William)
Private, Company M, 7th Regiment • Confederate Cavalry • Company E, 16th Battalion • N.C. Cavalry

William was born October 2, 1840, in Davie County. He lived with John and Lydia Smith of Ijames until he enlisted September 3, 1862, with the rank of Private. He was transferred from Company M, 7th Regiment Confederate Cavalry to Company E, 16th Battalion N.C. Cavalry on July 11, 1864, with the rank of Sergeant. He was reduced to ranks by reason of his being absent without leave from August 16, 1864, to September 18, 1864. He was present or accounted for through October 1, 1864, and paroled at Salisbury, North Carolina, in 1865. He married Martha M. Chaffin on November 16, 1865. Their children were Willey L. (1868), John M. (1870), Sarah V. (1873) and Lulu M. (1876). William died on September 11, 1923, and is buried in Ijames Baptist Church Cemetery.

858. Ratts, Hiram C.
Private, Company F, 42nd Regiment • N.C. Troops

Hiram was born in 1825 in North Carolina. He married Elizabeth Clement on October 14, 1852. Their four children were Franklin (1853), Anne Eliza (1856), James B. (1859) and Henry (1861). Hiram enlisted in Davie County on April 18, 1863, for the war. He was present or accounted for through October 1864. After the war he returned home to Davie County where he lived until his death on March 3, 1893. Elizabeth died on July 21, 1918. Both are buried in Fork Baptist Church Cemetery.

859. Redwine, John F.
Private, Company E, 42nd Regiment • N.C. Troops

John F. was born in Rowan County on December 30, 1827. He resided in Davie County when he married Elizabeth Baily on February 11, 1850. They lived in the Liberty District prior to March 18, 1862, when John enlisted at age 35. He was present or accounted for until captured at or near Wise's Forks, Kinston, North Carolina, on March 10, 1865, confined at Point Lookout, Maryland, March 16, 1865, and released there on June 17, 1865, after taking the Oath of Allegiance. John and Elizabeth were the parents of three children: Martha J. (1852), DeWitt C. (1854) and William T. (1859). Following the war the family settled in the Fulton District where John continued to support them by farming. John's pension application is on file at the State Archives, Raleigh, North Carolina. John died on December 16, 1896. He is buried at Fork Baptist Church Cemetery. His tombstone reads "John F. Redwine, Rev."

860. Reid, W.E. (William)
Private, Company H, 23rd Regiment • N.C. Troops

William was born in 1836. He and his wife Susan (1833, North Carolina) were the parents of Mary J. (1857), Robert Lee (1867) and William (1868). William enlisted in Iredell County August 1, 1862, for the war. He was wounded in the left hand at Chancellorsville, Virginia, on or about May 2, 1863. He returned to duty on an unspecified date and was wounded in the spine at Spotsylvania Court House, Virginia, on May 12, 1864. William returned to duty prior to November 1, 1864. He was present or accounted for through December 1864, and was paroled at Salisbury, North Carolina, on June 24, 1865. He returned home to Jerusalem District and his family. William died in 1923 and is buried in Liberty United Methodist Church Cemetery.

861. Revis, John E.
Private, "Davie Sweep Stakes" • Company G, 4th Regiment • N.C. State Troops

John was born in 1842 in Davie County. He married Sarah Jane Whitaker on December 4, 1859. Records show them living in the Chinquepin District. John enlisted at age 19, June 4, 1861, for the war. He was admitted to the hospital in Richmond, Virginia, December 15, 1862, with a gunshot wound of the hand; however, the place and date he was wounded were not reported. He remained absent wounded until May 18, 1863, when he was reported absent without leave. He was apprehended prior to October 13, 1863, when he was confined at Castle Thunder Prison, Richmond, under charges of "stealing, firing upon citizens while passing along the road, threatening to burn citizens' houses and being a desperate character generally and a terror to the neighborhood in which he lived." His name appears on a court-martial record dated January 19, 1864. He was detailed as a guard in the hospital at Richmond on February 11, 1864, and was ordered transferred to the hospital in Salisbury, North Carolina, on April 9, 1864. He deserted to the enemy at Rosersville, Maryland, or at Middleton, Maryland, July 9, 1864, then was confined at Old Capitol Prison, Washington, D.C., until he was transferred to Elmira, New York, July 23, 1864. He was released at Elmira on May 29, 1865, after taking the Oath of Allegiance.

862. Rhidenhour, John W. (Ridenhour)
Private, "Davie Greys" • Company F, 13th Regiment • (3rd Regiment, N.C. Volunteers) • N.C. Troops

John was born in 1828. He married Crisia Cody on January 31, 1856, and by 1860, they were the parents of two boys: Luther C. (1858) and Geo. T. (1859). The family lived in the Fulton District of Davie County where John worked as a farmer. He then resided in Davidson County according to his military record, but he enlisted in Davie County at age 34, July 16, 1862, for the war. He was present or accounted for until wounded and captured at Gettysburg, Pennsylvania, July 1, 1863. He was hospitalized at Chester, Pennsylvania, where he died August 12, 1863, of "traumatic erysipelas." John's name is listed on the Memorial Monument for the Davie County men who died in the Civil War, 1861–1865.

863. Riblin, J.L. (Jacob)
Private, Captain William E. Booe's Partisan Rangers • N.C. Volunteers • Company H, 63rd Regiment • (5th Regiment N.C. Cavalry) • N.C. Troops

J.L. was born in 1831 in Davie County. By 1850 he had married Mary L., had a daughter, Nancy (1849) and was working to establish his farm. Prior to the war he married Sarah A. Beauchamp on March 16, 1859. Their children were Anderson J. (1860), Emma (1861), Virginia (1864), Ida F. (1866) and Charles (1868). J.L. enlisted in Davie County at age 32, July 14, 1862, for the war. He was captured near Madison Court House, Virginia, September 22, 1863, and confined at Old Capitol Prison, Washington, D.C., until transferred to Point Lookout, Maryland, September 26, 1863. He remained there until paroled and exchanged at City Point, Virginia, March 20, 1864. He was present or accounted for through February 1865, and paroled at Salisbury, North Carolina, a few months later.

864. Rice, Thomas D.
Private, Company B, Carolina Rangers • 10th Virginia Cavalry Regiment

Thomas enlisted in Davie County on September 12, 1863. He was present or accounted for until he was paroled at Salisbury, North Carolina, on June 9, 1865.

865. Rice, William A. (Albert)
Private, Company B, Carolina Rangers • 10th Virginia Cavalry Regiment

William was born in 1835 in North Carolina, to Joseph W. (1807, Davie) and Carmila (1814, Davie) Rice. They lived in the Mocksville District of Davie County where both William and his father farmed. He married Mary Foster on July 22, 1856, in Davie County. Their daughter Sarah E. was born in 1859. He enlisted in Davie County on March 11, 1862, at age 26. He was present or accounted for until he deserted to the enemy on April 12, 1865. He took the Oath of Allegiance and transportation furnished to Howard County, Indiana. W.A., M.F. and S.E. Rice (all born in N.C.) are found on the 1870 census in Crooked Creek, Boone County, Arkansas.

866. Rich, Isaac Oakes
Sergeant, Company E, 42nd Regiment • N.C. Troops

Isaac was born in Davie County in 1840. He was the son of Joseph (1811, Davie), a wagon maker, and Sarah (1802, Davie). He was a teacher prior to enlisting in Davie County at age 22, on March 18, 1862. He was mustered in as a Corporal and promoted to Sergeant in January–February, 1864. Isaac was present or accounted for through October 1864.

867. Rich, Nathaniel Green
Private, Captain William E. Booe's Partisan Rangers • N.C. Volunteers • Company H, 63rd Regiment • (5th Regiment N.C. Cavalry) • N.C. Troops

Nathaniel was born in 1832 in Davie County to John (1782, Davie) and Nancy (1791, Davie) Rich. He worked as a farmer and married Malinda (1831, North Carolina). Their children were Nancy E. (1853), Frank P. (1855), Manda G. (1856) and John R. (1858). Nathaniel enlisted in Davie County at age 30, on July 18, 1862, for the war. He was present or accounted for on company muster rolls through August 1864, being wounded in action on August 21, 1864, and admitted to the hospital at Petersburg, Virginia. He was transferred to the hospital at Danville, Virginia, on September 30, 1864, and furloughed for 30 days on October 6, 1864. He was paroled at Salisbury, North Carolina, in 1865.

868. Rich, Samuel Chase
Private, Company F, 42nd Regiment • N.C. Troops

Samuel was born in Davie County on October 5, 1845. He was the son of Isaac N. (1808, Davie) and Catharine (1820, Davie) Rich. He enlisted in Davie County on September 18, 1863, for the war. He was present or accounted for through October 1864, and was paroled at Greensboro, North Carolina, on May 1, 1865. On February 22, 1872, he married Elizabeth C. McMahan (1855, North Carolina). Their children were Joseph (1874) and Mattie (1876). In 1880 they continued to live and work in the Farmington District. Samuel died on May 4, 1900, and is buried at Eaton's Baptist Church Cemetery.

869. Rich, W.C.
Confederate States Navy

W.C. is one of two men identified as having served in the Confederate Navy from Davie County. His enlistment date was August 3, 1863, in Davie County.

870. Rich, W.G.
Private, Captain William E. Booe's Partisan Rangers • N.C. Volunteers • Company H, 63rd Regiment • (5th Regiment N.C. Cavalry) • N.C. Troops

W.G. enlisted in Davie County, on July 6, 1862, for the war. No further records.

871. Richardson, A.M. (Addison)
Private, Company M, 7th Regiment • Confederate Cavalry • Company E, 16th Battalion • N.C. Cavalry

Addison was born February 8, 1825, in Davie County. He married Sarah Jane Blaylock (July 13, 1826, Virginia) on November 10, 1842, and they settled in the Chinquepin District. He worked as a farmer prior to enlisting in Davie on June 3, 1863, as a Private. He was transferred from Company M, 7th Regiment Confederate Cavalry to Company E, 16th Battalion N.C. Cavalry on July 11, 1864. He was reported as absent without leave from August 16, 1864, through October 1, 1864. He was paroled in Salisbury, North Carolina, in 1865, and returned to Davie where he settled his family in the Clarksville District. The children were George W. (1843), Thomas Jasper (1846), Rachel (1849), Wm. Newton (1851), John W. (1853), Jesse M. (1856), Joel C. (1858), Cenith A. (1861) and Marshal Pinkney (1866). Addison died on April 20, 1907, and is buried in New Union United Methodist Church Cemetery. Sarah Jane died on September 4, 1915, and is also buried at New Union.

872. Richardson, David Columbus
Prison Guard

David was born February 24, 1818, in Davidson County. He married Mary Beck Ragsdale on August 12, 1841, in Davie County, where they apparently lived for the rest of their lives. As far as census listings go, David had the distinction of being the only "Hatter" in Davie County in 1850. (His present day descendants say they have documentation that he sold his hats to the military.) After that, however, he joined the legions of farmers in the county and apparently lived a more mundane life of raising crops and nine children: Nancy (1844), John (1849), Wm. G. (1851), Mary A. (1854), Martha J. (1855), Thomas C. (1856), Addison B. (1857), David (1866), and James A. (1870). His military service as a prison guard is documented in the *Roster of Confederate Soldiers* by Janet Hewitt, page 139 of Volume XIII, located in Rowan County Library. David died October 4, 1902, and is buried in New Union Methodist Church Cemetery.

873. Richardson, G.W. (George)
Private, Company M, 7th Regiment • Confederate Cavalry • Company E, 16th Battalion • N.C. Cavalry

George was born August 4, 1843, in Davie County to Addison M. (1825, Davie) and Sarah Jane Blaylock (1826, Virginia) Richardson. He lived in the Chinquepin District when he worked as a laborer prior to enlisting September 3, 1862, as a Private. He was transferred from Company M, 7th Regiment Confederate Cavalry to Company E, 16th Battalion N.C. Cavalry on July 11, 1864. He was reported as absent without leave from August 16, 1864, through October 1, 1864, and was paroled in Salisbury, North Carolina, in 1865. After the war George farmed in Calahaln, married Samantha Marlow on September 1, 1867, and raised three children: Jasper L. (1869), Lillian L. (1871) and Marion B. (1879). George died June 25, 1927, and is buried in Bear Creek Baptist Church Cemetery.

874. Riddle, T.C. (Thomas Calvin)
Private, Company D, 42nd Regiment • N.C. Troops

T.C. Riddle, wife Sophia and daughter (name unknown) (Ann Sheek).

T.C. was born July 31, 1825, to William and Nancy Slater (1791, Davie) Riddle. He married Susan Vogler on February 21, 1851; their children were Penelopy (1852), Fildean (1854), Leander (1857) and Louisa (1858). Susan died prior to 1860 and T.C. married Sophia Regina Buller in 1861. Prior to the war he and his family had lived with his mother in the Farmington District of Davie County. On September 28, 1863, T.C. enlisted in Lenoir County, North Carolina, for the war. He was 35. He was present or accounted for until hospitalized at Richmond, Virginia, on June 20, 1864, with gunshot wounds in both thighs. The place and date were not reported. He was absent wounded through October 1864, and paroled at Mocksville on June 7, 1865. For the rest of his life he would walk with two crutches. On his return trip home the train carried him to Lexington, North Carolina. Someone then transported him by wagon to the old Hampton Plantation between Lexington and Clemmons. In the meantime Sophia had borrowed a horse and wagon and raced to pick him up at the plantation and drive him back home to Davie County. Legend has it that the return trip was excruciating, especially being jostled in the wagon as it traveled over the miles of rough terrain. Sophia brought T.C. safely home and it wasn't long before they were the parents of Catherine (1865), Asbury (1867), John

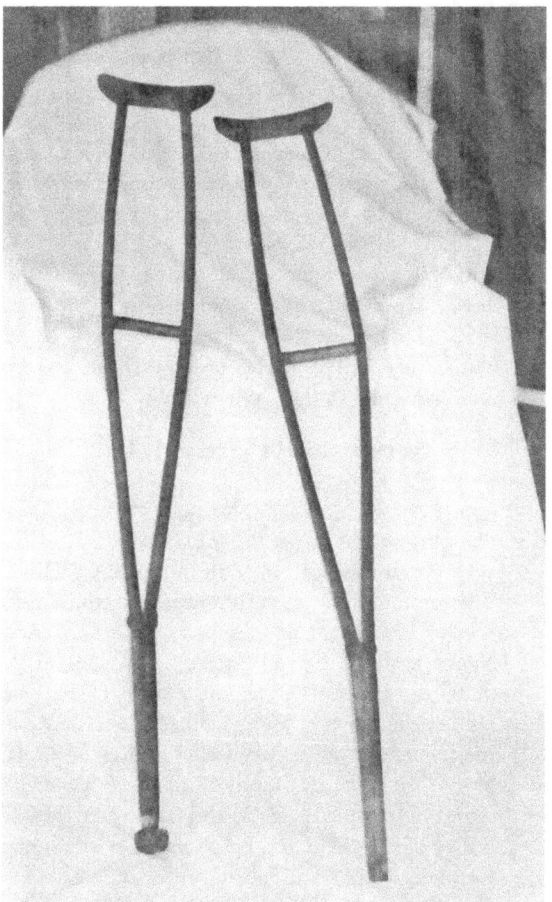

These crutches brought T.C. Riddle from the battlefield to the safety of his home in Davie County (Estelle Smith).

(1870), Emaline (1875), Adar [*sic*] (1879) and Mary (1883). Sophia died on May 31, 1892, and T.C. died on October 10, 1909. They are buried in Macedonia Moravian Church Cemetery.

875. Ridenhour, John M.
Private, Company E, 42nd Regiment • N.C. Troops

John was born in 1828 in North Carolina. He was a farmer in the Mocksville District in 1860. He and his wife Maria were the parents of five children when he enlisted for the war: Albert A. (1851), Laura L. (1853), Ellen F. (1855), Marian F. (1857) and Alice A. (1858). John enlisted at Hamilton, North Carolina, on April 8, 1863, for the war. He was present or accounted for until captured at or near Wise's Forks, Kinston, North Carolina, on March 10, 1865, confined at Point Lookout, Maryland, on March 16, 1865, and released at Point Lookout on May 14, 1865, after taking the Oath of Allegiance.

876. Ridenhour, Lasson
Private, "Davie Greys" • Company F, 13th Regiment • (3rd Regiment, N.C. Volunteers) • N.C. Troops

Lasson was born in 1835. He resided in Davie County and was by occupation a farmer prior to enlisting in Davie County at age 26, April 26, 1861. He was present or accounted for until he died in the hospital at Richmond, Virginia, July 2, 1862, of "typhoid fever." Lasson's name is listed on the Memorial Monument for the Davie County men who died in the Civil War, 1861–1865.

877. Roberson (Robertson), Hugh Emmerson
Second Lieutenant, Company Dm • 77th Regiment, 19th Division • N.C. Militia 1861–1865

Hugh was born in 1838 in North Carolina. When the militia was activated he was appointed Second Lieutenant of Company D. He married Nancy J. (1842, Davie) Sheets on November 11, 1860, and they settled in the Fulton District of Davie County where Hugh worked as a mill wright [sic]. There were six surviving children in 1880: Mary (1862), Laura (1864), Amanda (1866), Cicero (1869), Sallie L. (1872) and Chas. A.B. (1880). Nancy died in 1892 and Hugh married M. Nancy Cuthrell, age 35, on February 15, 1894. She apparently died shortly thereafter, because Hugh married Jennie Bell Smoot on May 20, 1897. Hugh then died in 1899 and is buried in Rose Cemetery.

878. Roberts, Paschal
Private, Company F, 42nd Regiment • N.C. Troops

Paschal was born in 1825 in Davie County to Mary (1799, Virginia) Roberds [sic]. Paschal farmed with his parents until he married Margaret Cartner (1826, North Carolina) in Davie County on April 1, 1851. Prior to the war, Paschal and Margaret, along with sons William W. (1852) and James C. (1860), lived and farmed in the Mocksville District. On December 18, 1862, Paschal enlisted there at age 37, for the war. He was present or accounted for through December 27, 1864. After the war the family lived in the Calahaln District where Mary J. (1866) and Sarah E. (1870) were born. William became a "cabinet workman" and Paschal and James farmed. Margaret died January 30, 1899. Paschal died January 24, 1907. They are buried at Salem United Methodist Church Cemetery.

879. Robertson, Thomas E.
Private, Company E, 42nd Regiment • N.C. Troops

Thomas was born September 1, 1839. He enlisted in Davie County at age 22, on or about March 11, 1862. He was present or accounted for through October 1864, and was paroled at Mocksville on June 5, 1865. Thomas was married to Bettie E. Robertson, and they were the parents of three boys: Johnnie (1870), Luther A. (1874) and George L. (1876). The family farmed in Fulton following the war. Thomas died June 11, 1919, and is buried in Advance United Methodist Church Cemetery.

880. Robinson, James F.
Private, Company B, Carolina Rangers • 10th Virginia Cavalry Regiment

James was born in 1840. He enlisted in Davie County on October 29, 1861, at age 21. His presence or absence was not stated through April 30, 1862. After that, he was present or accounted for until he was paroled in Salisbury, North Carolina, on May 15, 1865.

881. Roessler (Rosler), Julius
Captain, "Davie Greys" • Company F, 13th Regiment • (3rd Regiment, N.C. Volunteers) • N.C. Troops

Julius was born in 1827 in Prussia. At age 33, he was a merchant living in Mocksville, along with 16 others, in a hotel managed by H.R. and Elvira Austin. On May 5, 1861, he was elected First Lieutenant but was defeated for reelection when the regiment was reorganized on April 26, 1862. He rejoined the company on or about August 1, 1863, when he was elected First Lieutenant. He was present or accounted for until he was admitted to the hospital at Danville, Virginia, May 9, 1864, with a gunshot wound to the head; however, the place and date he was wounded were not reported. He rejoined the company prior to July 1, 1864, and was present or accounted for until paroled at Appomattox Court House, Virginia, April 9, 1865. Records of the Federal Provost Marshal indicate he was promoted to Captain in November 1864–April 1865.

882. Rose, Pompey S.
Private, "Davie Sweep Stakes" • Company G, 4th Regiment • N.C. State Troops

Pompey was born in 1837. He resided in Davie County where he enlisted at age 24, June 4, 1861, for the war. He was wounded at Gaines' Mill, Virginia, June 27, 1862. After seven months, he rejoined the company prior to February 5, 1863, and was present or accounted for until he was wounded at Spotsylvania Court House, Virginia, May 12, 1864. He was reported absent wounded through August 1864, but rejoined the company prior to April 3, 1865, when he was captured at Petersburg, Virginia. He was confined at Hart's Island, New York Harbor, until released June 19–20, 1865, after taking the Oath of Allegiance.

883. Rose, Samuel W.
Private, "Davie Sweep Stakes" • Company G, 4th Regiment • N.C. State Troops

Samuel was born in 1837 to Wilson (1809, Davie) and Mehida (Matilda?) (1810, Davie) Rose. They lived in the Mocksville District, where Samuel worked as a farmer prior to enlisting at age 24, June 4, 1861, for the war. He was admitted to the hospital at Richmond, Virginia, December 16, 1862, with a gunshot wound of the arm; however, the place and date he was wounded were not reported. He returned to duty January 6, 1863, and died in Davie County prior to May 12, 1863. The cause and exact date of death were not reported. Samuel's name is listed on the Memorial Monument for the Davie County men who died in the Civil War, 1861–1865.

884. Rotan (Rolan), Eli C.
Private, Company D, 42nd Regiment • N.C. Troops

Eli was born in 1841 in Davie County. He resided in Mocksville where he made his living as a painter; in 1860 he lived with J.S. Wright and his family. At age 21, on March 22, 1862, he enlisted in Rowan County. He was present or accounted for until discharged on August 10, 1862. The reason for the discharge is not known. He returned to Davie County where he married Eliza E. Graves, September 6, 1886, according to the book: *Davie County Marriages*. This date should probably be 1866. In the 1870 census Eli and Elizabeth, ages 29 and 27 respectively, lived in Jerusalem District where he made shoes and harnesses. In 1871 they had a son, James T. In 1880 Eli, by then crippled, continued his work and continued to live in the same district with his family.

885. Rudacil, H.F. (Hiram F.)
Private, "Davie Sweep Stakes" • Company G, 4th Regiment • N.C. State Troops

H.F. was born in 1838. He married Martha Ann Lyerly in Davie County on January 24, 1858. They lived in the Calahaln District where he worked as a farmer prior to enlisting at age 24, March 13, 1862, for the war. He was wounded in the arm at Chancellorsville, Virginia, May 3, 1863, and reported absent wounded until discharged on or about December 28, 1863, by reason of wounds. He returned home where he resumed his life as a farmer. By 1870 he and Martha were the parents of three children: Sanford A. (1866), Henry T. (1868) and Jane L. (1870).

886. Rudacil (Rudasill), John
Private, Company F, 42nd Regiment • N.C. Troops

John was born in 1817 in Rowan County. Prior to 1850, he married Lamira (Zemirah) who was born in 1818 in Iredell County. They lived and farmed in the Calahaln District of Davie County, where he enlisted at age 45, March 18, 1862. He was present or accounted for through October 1864.

887. Rudicil, Anderson
Private, Company G, 5th Regiment • N.C. State Troops

Anderson was born in 1834 in Davie County. He enlisted in Northampton County at age 28, August 13, 1862, for the war. He died in camp near Fredericksburg, Virginia, February 16, 1863, of "pneumonia." Anderson's name is not presently listed on the Memorial Monument for the Davie County men who died in the Civil War, 1861–1865.

888. Rusher, Edward A.
Second Lieutenant, Company D, 42nd Regiment • N.C. Troops

Edward was a resident of Rowan County when he enlisted in Davie County at age 30. He was appointed Third Lieutenant on or about February 4, 1862. He was promoted to Second Lieutenant on November 25, 1862. He was present or accounted for until hospitalized at Richmond, Virginia, August 2, 1864, with amputation of both legs as a result of gunshot wounds received near Petersburg, Virginia. The date he was wounded was not reported. He died at Richmond on August 7, 1864. Edward's name is not presently listed on the Memorial Monument for the Davie County men who died in the Civil War, 1861–1865.

889. Russell, Gideon F.
Private, Captain William E. Booe's Partisan Rangers • N.C. Volunteers • Company H, 63rd Regiment • (5th Regiment N.C. Cavalry) • N.C. Troops • Captain, W.M. McGregor's Company • Virginia Horse Artillery

Gideon was born in 1838 in North Carolina. He and his wife Nancy (1840, North Carolina) farmed in the Chinquepin District of Davie County prior to his enlisting in Davie County, July 18, 1862, for the war. He was present or accounted for until transferred to Captain W.M. McGregor's Company, Virginia Horse Artillery, September 24, 1864.

890. Ruth, William
Private, 1st Company A, Salisbury Prison Guard • "The Rough and Readys" • Company G, 66th Regiment • N.C. Troops

William previously served as Private in 1st Company A, Salisbury Prison Guard. He was transferred to Company G of the 66th Regiment on October 2, 1863. He was reported present through April 30, 1864. He was killed at Cold Harbor, Virginia, June 7, 1864. William's name is not presently listed on the Memorial Monument for the Davie County men who died in the Civil War, 1861–1865.

891. Sain, A.T. (Albert)
Private, Company G, 7th Regiment • Confederate Cavalry • Company D, 16th Battalion • N.C. Cavalry

Albert was born in 1825 in Davie County. He married Sarah E. Sain on April 28, 1849, and they lived in the Mocksville District with their children, Wiley (1851), Casper (1853) and Martha J. (1859). Albert was a farmer when he enlisted in Davie County on November 20, 1863, with the rank of Private. He transferred from Company G, 7th Regiment Confederate Cavalry to Company D, 16th Battalion N.C. Cavalry on July 11, 1864. He was present or accounted for through October 1, 1864. He survived the war, returned home and lived until December 1, 1881. He is buried in Sain Family Cemetery.

892. Sain, Andrew
Private, "Davie Greys" • Company F, 13th Regiment • (3rd Regiment, N.C. Volunteers) • N.C. Troops

Andrew was born in 1840 in Davie County to George (1803, Davie) and Lucinda (1806, Davie) Sain. They resided in Davie County where Andrew enlisted at age 21, August 6, 1861. He mustered in as a Private and was promoted to Corporal on September 1, 1863, but then was reduced to ranks in May–June, 1864. He was present or accounted for until paroled at Appomattox Court House, Virginia, April 9, 1865. Andrew resumed life in Davie where he farmed in the Mocksville District. He married twice. He first married Mary L. Furches, age 27, January 23, 1873; a daughter, Dorsey J. was born in 1874. Then, on December 9, 1875, Andrew married Eunice Davis. In 1880 Andrew and his family continued to farm in the Mocksville District.

893. Sain, Basil
Private, Company M, 7th Regiment • Confederate Cavalry • Company E, 16th Battalion • N.C. Cavalry

Basil was born in 1832 in Davie County to George (1803, Davie) and Lucinda (1806, Davie) Sain. He married Martha Dooling on January 19, 1854, and they moved to Mocksville District where George W. was born in 1858. When war began Basil enlisted in Davie County on September 3, 1862. He was transferred from Company M, 7th Regiment Confederate Cavalry into Company E, 16th Battalion N.C. Cavalry on July 11, 1864. He was present or accounted for through October 1, 1864.

894. Sain, Casper
Second Lieutenant, Company L • 77th Regiment, 19th Division • N.C. Militia 1861–1865

Casper was born November 5, 1829, in Davie County to George (1803, Davie) and Lucinda (1806, Davie) Sain. He farmed with his father and brothers until he became a grocery keeper. He married Ruth Holman (1841, North Carolina) on January 24, 1860; he was 29 and she was 19. She died June 10, 1863. When the militia was activated Casper was appointed Second Lieutenant of Company L. He returned to farming and in 1868, he married Jane Knox. She died in 1906 and is buried in Rose Cemetery. Casper died on December 13, 1909, and is buried in Sain Family Cemetery.

895. Sain, Cheshire
Third Lieutenant, "Davie Greys" • Company F, 13th Regiment • (3rd Regiment, N.C. Volunteers) • N.C. Troops

Cheshire was born on September 23, 1819, in Davie County. He worked as a farmer and a blacksmith. On November 16, 1840, he married Mary Elizabeth Booe (1823) and settled in the Shady Grove area. Their children were Eleanor A. (1842), William M. (1844), Casander (1846), James M. (1848), Sarah E.P. (1850), John P. (1853), Mary E. (1855), Albert F. (1859) and Corah (1861). On May 5, 1861, Cheshire was elected Third Lieutenant. He was present or accounted for until he was defeated for re-election when the regiment was reorganized on April 26, 1862. (He may have served later as Captain of Company A, 4th Regiment N.C. Senior Reserves.) He returned to family life and resumed his work in the Mocksville District of Davie. He died October 2, 1893, and is buried in Oak Grove United Methodist Church Cemetery.

896. Sain, Jacob
Private, "Davie Greys" • Company F, 13th Regiment • (3rd Regiment, N.C. Volunteers) • N.C. Troops

Jacob was born in 1841 in Davie County to George (1803, Davie) and Lucinda (1806, Davie) Sain. He was the brother of Andrew and Joseph who also served in this company. They resided in Davie County where Jacob worked as a farmer prior to enlisting in Davie County at age 20, April 26, 1861. He was present or accounted for until he died in the hospital at Richmond, Virginia, on or about August 4, 1862, of disease. Jacob's name is listed on the Memorial Monument for the Davie County men who died in the Civil War, 1861–1865.

897. Sain, John A.
Private, Company F, 42nd Regiment • N.C. Troops

John was born in Davie County on July 6, 1843, the son of John (1797, Davie) and Nancy (1816, Davie) Sain. John's parents were farmers living in the Mocksville District in 1860. He enlisted in Davie County at age 19, March 18, 1862. He was present or accounted for until hospitalized at Petersburg, Virginia, on May 20, 1864, with a gunshot wound of the left thigh. The place and date were not reported. In September–October, 1864, he returned to duty. He was paroled in Greensboro, North Carolina, on May 1, 1865. John married Margaret A. Davis (1844) on August 22, 1867. Their children were Willie (1868) and Charity J. (1877). In 1880 they resided in Fulton District where they were farmers. John died November 23, 1919. He is buried in Fork Baptist Church Cemetery.

898. Sain, Joseph
Private, "Davie Greys" • Company F, 13th Regiment • (3rd Regiment, N.C. Volunteers) • N.C. Troops

Joseph was born in 1838 in Davie County to George (1803, Davie) and Lucinda (1806, Davie) Sain. They resided in Davie County where Joseph worked as a miller prior to enlisting at age 23, April 26, 1861. He was present or accounted for until he died in the hospital or "on the road between Winchester and Staunton" on or about October 24, 1862, of disease. Joseph's name is listed on the Memorial Monument for the Davie County men who died in the Civil War, 1861–1865.

899. Sain, Nathan Anderson
Private, Company D, 42nd Regiment • Captain William Howard's Company • N.C. Prison Guard • 1st Company A, Salisbury Prison Guard • "The Rough and Readys" • Company G, 66th Regiment • N.C. Troops

Nathan was born in 1846 in Davie County to Giles (1824, Davie) and Lydia (1818, Davie) Taylor Sain. Nathan lived with J.N. and Mary E. Bivens in Mocksville prior to enlisting in Davie County with the rank of Private on or about January 25, 1862. He served in Company D of the 42nd before transferring to Captain William Howard's Company on or about May 1, 1862. He served as Private in 1st Company A until October 2, 1863, when he transferred to Company G of the 66th. He was present or accounted for through April 30, 1864. He was reported sick at home from July 30 through August 31, 1864. He returned to duty in September–October, 1864, and was paroled at Mocksville on June 2, 1865. In 1870 Nathan worked as a farm laborer and lived in the Fulton District with Emma Sain (1851, North Carolina) and Willie (1867).

900. Sain, Nimrod B.
Second Lieutenant, "Davie Greys" • Company F, 13th Regiment • (3rd Regiment, N.C. Volunteers) • N.C. Troops

Nimrod was born in 1829 in Davie County. At age 21 he lived alone. On January 14, 1851, he and Elizabeth Foster were married. Their children were Mary M. (1853), John C. (1854), Thos. A. (1855) and Margaret M. (1857). Nimrod was a carpenter prior to enlisting in Davie County at age 32, April 26, 1861. He was promoted to Sergeant from an unspecified rank on June 1, 1861, and then elected Second Lieutenant to rank from April 26, 1862. He was present or accounted for until wounded at Gettysburg, Pennsylvania, July 1, 1863. He rejoined the company in September–October, 1863, and was present or accounted for until he resigned on February 28, 1864, by reason of "chronic rheumatism." His resignation was accepted on March 11, 1864.

901. Sain (Sane), Thomas M.
Private, Company F, 42nd Regiment • N.C. Troops

Thomas was born in 1832 in North Carolina. He married Mary Jane Howell (1839, North Carolina) on July 9, 1856. Prior to the war, they farmed in the Chinquepin District of Davie County. Their two young children were John H. (1857) and Susan M. (1859). On March 24, 1862, at age 30, Thomas enlisted in Davie County. He mustered in as a Corporal and was reduced to ranks in May–June, 1863. He was present or accounted for through October 1864. He was paroled at Mocksville on June 7, 1865, and Thomas returned to his family and farming in the Farmington District. Seven more children were added: Annie (Lydia) (1865), Rosa (1868), Jacob (1869), Mary C. (1872), Joshua (1874), Sarah (1876) and Laura (1877).

902. Sain, William
Private, "Davie Greys" • Company F, 13th Regiment • (3rd Regiment, N.C. Volunteers) • N.C. Troops

William was born in 1834 in Davie County. He married Catherine Sain (1837, Davie) on January 17, 1854. They had two children: Junius Franklin (1855) and Ann (1861). They resided in the Mocksville District of Davie County where William worked as a farmer prior to enlisting at age 27, August 6, 1861. He was present or accounted for until he died in the hospital at Petersburg, Virginia, May 13, 1862, of disease. William's name is listed on the Memorial Monument for the Davie County men who died in the Civil War, 1861–1865.

Calvin Cowles Sanford (Hugh Larew)

903. Sanford, Calvin Cowles
Third Lieutenant, Company F, 42nd Regiment • N.C. Troops

Calvin was born October 15, 1843, in Davie County at County Line, to Amos B. and Mary Lunn (1803, Currituck) Sanford. He was a student in Farmington and Olin prior to enlisting in Davie County at age 18, on March 18,

Calvin C. Sanford Store (established 1867). Calvin C. Sanford and James Adams purchased this building from William L. and Rufus D. Brown when they moved to Winston-Salem. Not long afterward, John Adams died and Calvin was left with the full debt to pay. Then the building burned and there was no fire insurance (Hugh Larew).

Calvin Cowles Sanford family, circa 1909. Front row, left to right: John Cowles Sanford, Laura Sanford, Calvin Cowles Sanford, Mary Brown Sanford and Thomas Franklin Sanford; back row: Hugh Adams Sanford, Rufus Brown Sanford, Edwin Cowles Sanford, William Lafayette Sanford and Mary Louise Sanford (Hugh Larew).

1862. He mustered in as a Sergeant and was promoted to First Sergeant in May–June, 1863. He was appointed Third Lieutenant on December 4, 1863. He was present or accounted for until wounded in the arm at or near Bermuda Hundred, Virginia, on or about May 20, 1864. He returned to duty prior to September 1, 1864, and was present or accounted for through October 1864. He was paroled at Greensboro, North Carolina, on May 1, 1865. He returned to Mocksville and taught school for two years in Farmington before becoming a store clerk. For the next 62 years he would be one of the area's most successful and influential businessmen and his history would be inextricably tied with the history of Mocksville. He married Mary D. Brown on January 11, 1872; their children were William Lafayette (1872), Thomas Franklin (1874, Rufus Brown (1877), Edwin Cowles (1879), Laura (1881), Hugh Adams (1883), John Calvin (1886) and Mary Louise (1888). They were educated at UNC–Chapel Hill, Davidson College, UNC–Greensboro, Converse College and Fishburne Military Academy. Clark's *Regiments* states that "Lieutenant C.C. Sanford is a successful merchant in Mocksville and a most excellent citizen." He also served two terms as sheriff. He died on March 6, 1929, and is buried in Joppa Cemetery. According to his great-grandson, Hugh Larew, every business in town closed on the day of the funeral. (See two additional photographs on page 190.)

904. Seaford, J.D.
Private, Captain William E. Booe's Partisan Rangers • N.C. Volunteers • Company H, 63rd Regiment • (5th Regiment N.C. Cavalry) • N.C. Troops

J.D. was born in North Carolina on May 1, 1843. He was the son of Simeon (1815, North Car-

Top: Some of the Sanford family enjoying a pleasant summer afternoon. *Bottom:* C.C. Sanford and grandchildren (both: Hugh Larew).

olina) and Eliza Seaford (1815, North Carolina). In 1860 he was 17 years old, working as a farmer in Mocksville. He enlisted in Davie County at the age of 19, for the war, on July 16, 1862. J. D. was present or accounted for through February 1863, when he was reported as "absent on sick furlough." After the war, he lived in Calahaln and worked as a farmer, later becoming disabled. On January 4, 1881, he married Alice F. McDaniel (1860), and lived to be 83 years old. He died on

September 28, 1926, and is buried in Center United Methodist Church Cemetery.

905. Seaford, Peter
Private, Company G, 5th Regiment • N.C. State Troops

Peter was born in 1834 to Philip (1798, Rowan) and Elizabeth (1798, Rowan) Seaford. On October 19, 1858, he married Mary E. Turner (1835). A son, Charles W. was born in 1860. They resided in the Mocksville District where Peter worked as a farmer prior to enlisting in Northampton County at age 26, August 13, 1862, for the war. He was present or accounted for until captured at Gettysburg, Pennsylvania, July 1–2, 1863. He was confined at Fort McHenry, Maryland, and at Fort Delaware, Delaware, until transferred to Point Lookout, Maryland, on October 15–18, 1863. He died in the hospital at Point Lookout on October 20, 1863, of "scorbutus" (scurvy). Peter's name is not presently listed on the Memorial Monument for the Davie County men who died in the Civil War, 1861–1865.

906. Seaford, Solomon
Private, Company G, 5th Regiment • N.C. State Troops

Solomon was born in 1829 to Philip (1798, Rowan) and Elizabeth (1798, Rowan) Seaford. He married Mary A. Foster (1835, North Carolina) on April 12, 1854, and by 1860 they had become parents to three children: William A. (1855), Mary E. (1858) and Robert M. R. (1859). They resided in the Mocksville District where Solomon worked as a cooper prior to enlisting in Northampton County at age 33, August 13, 1862, for the war. He died at Winchester, Virginia, in October 1862. Cause of death was not reported. Solomon's name is not presently listed on the Memorial Monument for the Davie County men who died in the Civil War, 1861–1865.

907. Seagraves (Segraves), Jacob A.
Private, Company D, 42nd Regiment • N.C. Troops • Company C, 3rd Battalion • N.C. Light Artillery

Jacob A. was born in Davie County in 1837. He was the son of Jacob (1803, Wake) and Susannah (1800, Rowan) Segraves [*sic*]. At age 22, on March 12, 1862, he enlisted in Rowan County. He was present or accounted for until transferred to Company C, 3rd Battalion, N.C. Light Artillery, on October 28, 1863.

908. Seamon (Seamont), H. (Henry) R.
Private, Company H, 23rd Regiment • N.C. Troops

H.R. was born in Davie County in 1842 to John (1802, Cabarrus) and Mary (1802, Cabarrus) Seamon. In 1860 Henry lived with his parents in Calahaln where he and his father farmed. At age 18, on August 1, 1862, he enlisted in Iredell County for the war. He was present or accounted for until paroled at Appomattox Court House, Virginia, April 9, 1865.

909. Seamon, Losen (Lawson)
Private, Company F, 42nd Regiment • N.C. Troops

Losen Seamon was born in 1826 in North Carolina. On January 8, 1850, he married Angeline Pence (1832). He worked as a laborer prior to enlisting in Davie County on December 18, 1862, for the war. He died in the hospital at Weldon, North Carolina, on March 31, 1863, of disease. Losen and Angelina were the parents of five children: Henry A. (1850), Rachel E. (1852), Mary J. (1856), Emily A. (1858) and Cora B. (1861). Angelina's claim for a pension is on file in the State Archives, Raleigh, North Carolina. It reads in part that Lawson [*sic*] died "of disease, the particulars of which are unknown." Losen's name is listed on the Memorial Monument for the Davie County men who died in the Civil War, 1861–1865.

910. Setzer, M.Y. (Milford)
Sergeant, Company D, 42nd Regiment • N.C. Troops • Private, Company M, 7th Regiment • Confederate Cavalry • Company E, 16th Battalion • N.C. Cavalry

M.Y. was born in Davie County in 1841, to Andrew (1802, Rowan) and Temperance (1817, Davie) Setzer. Milford's father was a wagon maker. On or about January 19, 1862, he mustered in as a Sergeant. No further record in this regiment. However, on September 3, 1862, Milford enlisted in Davie County with the rank of Private. He was transferred from Company M, 7th Regiment Confederate Cavalry to Company E, 16th Battalion N.C. Cavalry on July 11, 1864. He was present or accounted for through October 1, 1864, and paroled in Salisbury, North Carolina, in 1865. He married Chloe E. Hilliard on February 2, 1865.

911. Shackleford, J. (John)
Private, Captain William E. Booe's Partisan Rangers • N.C. Volunteers • Company H, 63rd Regiment • (5th Regiment N.C. Cavalry) • N.C. Troops

John was born in 1843 in Virginia. In 1860 he made his home in the Fulton District with Tabner Shackleford (1837, Virginia), John Taylor (1838, Scotland) and Wm. Shackleford (1844, Virginia). All four men were tobacconists. John enlisted in Davie County on April 1, 1864, for the war. He died in the hospital at Richmond, Virginia, June 25, 1864, of "febris typhoides" and was buried in Hollywood Cemetery in that city. John's name is listed on the Memorial Monument for the Davie County men who died in the Civil War, 1861–1865.

912. Shadrick (Shaddock), David
Private, Company E, 42nd Regiment • N.C. Troops

David was born in 1832 in Stokes County, the son of Scion (1798, Chatham) and Syddia (1804, Chatham) Shadrick. His father was a farmer and David worked as a laborer. He married Manerva King on February 18, 1858; their three children were William (1856), Thomas W. (1858) and Martha (1863). David enlisted in Davie County at age 30, March 18, 1862. He was reported absent without leave in November–December, 1862, and in confinement during March–June, 1863. He returned to duty on July 16, 1863, and was present or accounted for until killed at Bermuda Hundred, Virginia, May 18, 1864. Manerva married Charles Rabin in Davie County on September 20, 1866. Their sons were John Rabin (1868) and Anderson (1874). Thomas and Martha Shadrick continued to live with their mother and stepfather in the Farmington District in 1880. David's name is listed on the Memorial Monument for the Davie County men who died in the Civil War, 1861–1865.

913. Shadrick, Isaac
Private, Company E, 42nd Regiment • N.C. Troops

Isaac was born in 1839 in North Carolina. He enlisted in Davie County at age 23, March 18, 1862. He was present or accounted for through October 1864. Isaac married Mary Jane King on April 19, 1866. She was born in North Carolina in 1840.

914. Shadrick (Shaddock), Sion (Scion)
Private, Company E, 42nd Regiment • N.C. Troops

Sion was born in 1840 in Stokes County, the son of Scion (1798, Chatham) and Syddia (1804, Chatham) Shadrick. He enlisted in Davie County at age 22, March 18, 1862. He was present or accounted for until he died in the hospital at Petersburg, Virginia, on or about November 18, 1862, of "pleuritis." Sion's name is listed on the Memorial Monument for the Davie County men who died in the Civil War, 1861–1865.

915. Shamel, S.N.
Private, Captain William E. Booe's Partisan Rangers • N.C. Volunteers • Company H, 63rd Regiment • (5th Regiment N.C. Cavalry) • N.C. Troops

S.N. was born in 1832 in Forsyth County. He was a farmer living in Farmington when he married Elizabeth (1836, North Carolina). Their son, William T., was born in 1856. S.N. enlisted in Davie County at age 30, on July 14, 1862, for the war. He was present or accounted for until discharged at Farmville, Virginia, on July 15, 1864, by reason of "parapligia of lower extremities." He was detailed to provost guard after being discharged.

916. Sharp, Samuel L.
Sergeant, "Davie Sweep Stakes" • Company G, 4th Regiment • N.C. State Troops

Samuel was born to Mary A. Sharp (1796, Davie) in 1839. At age 19, Samuel was a student living in the Shady Grove District of Davie County where he, his mother and sisters lived with W.R. Sharpe, physician, prior to Samuel's enlisting at age 22, June 4, 1861, for the war. He mustered in as a Private and was promoted to Sergeant prior to June 30, 1862, when he was admitted to the hospital at Richmond, Virginia, with a wound of the knee. The place and date wounded were not reported. No further records.

917. Shaw, Augustus
Private, "Davie Greys" • Company F, 13th Regiment • (3rd Regiment, N.C. Volunteers) • N.C. Troops

Augustus was born in 1832 in North Carolina. He married Sarah Jane Haith (1832) on March 24, 1853, in Davie County where they would have nine children: Mary L. (1854), Sarah P. (1855), Nancy C. (1858), Martha E. (1860), Lena S. (1865), John E. (1868), Thomas (1870), Millard F. (1874) and Margaret L. (1877). Augustus enlisted in Davie County at age 34, March 26, 1863, for the war. He deserted April 12, 1863. The family resided in the Clarksville District where Augustus worked as a farmer. He died in 1903. Both he and Sarah are buried in New Union United Methodist Church Cemetery.

918. Shaw, William
Private, "Davie Greys" • Company F, 13th Regiment • (3rd Regiment, N.C. Volunteers) • N.C. Troops

William was born in 1827. He resided in Davie County where he enlisted at age 36 on March 26, 1863, for the war. He deserted on

April 12, 1863, but was reported in confinement from September–October 1863, through February 1864. "Shot by order of court martial" on April 26, 1864. William's name is not presently listed on the Memorial Monument for the Davie County men who died in the Civil War, 1861–1865.

919. Sheek, Albert A.
Private, Company F, 13th Regiment • (3rd Regiment, N.C. Volunteers) • N.C. Troops

Albert was born in Davie County in 1844. He lived with Jacob (1796, Davie) and Sarah Sheek (1791). Albert enlisted in Davie County at age 17, June 18, 1861. He was present or accounted for until he was wounded near Richmond, Virginia, in March–June, 1862. He rejoined the company prior to November 1, 1862, but was discharged prior to January 1, 1863. The reason for the discharge was not reported. Albert and Cornelia G. Gilliam were married on February 24, 1864.

920. Sheek, Isaac
Private, "Davie Sweep Stakes" • Company G, 4th Regiment • N.C. State Troops

Isaac was born in 1841 to Daniel (1823, Davie) and Ann Anfield (1817, Davie) Sheek. He worked as a laborer in the Farmington District prior to enlisting at age 20, June 4, 1861, for the war. He was present or accounted for through June 1862. No further records.

921. Sheek, J.D.
Ordnance Sergeant, "Davie Sweep Stakes" • Company G, 4th Regiment • N.C. State Troops

J.D. enlisted in Davie County on June 4, 1861, for the war. He mustered in as a Sergeant and was present or accounted for until paroled at Appomattox Court House, Virginia, April 9, 1865. His rank was given on parole as Ordnance Sergeant.

922. Sheek, Leven Alexander
Private, Company E, Company K • 1st Junior Reserve Infantry Regiment • North Carolina

Leven was born in Davie County on April 5, 1847, to Richmond (1824, Davie) and Sarah Riddle (1829, Tennessee) Sheek. They lived in the Farmington District and supported themselves by farming. Leven was too young to enlist when war was declared but by the time he was 17 he qualified for conscription into the Junior Reserves and so on May 25, 1864, he became a Private in Company E, Company K, in the 1st Junior Reserve Infantry Regiment. He married Ellen Celia Allen (1848, Davie) on August 27, 1868; their children were Mollie (1870), Thomas (1872), John (1872) and William. Leven died May 13, 1936, and is buried in Macedonia Moravian Church Cemetery.

923. Sheets, George W.
Private, Company B, Carolina Rangers • 10th Virginia Cavalry Regiment

George was born in Davie County on February 22, 1839, to David J. (1815, Davie) and Manerva (1820, Davie) Howard Sheets. They lived in the Smith Grove District of Davie County where his father farmed and George was a laborer prior to his enlistment on October 29, 1861, at age 22. He was present or accounted for throughout his tour of duty. He was absent on detached service at Brigade Headquarters as a teamster from January–April, 1864, and again July–August, 1864. His last roll call of January 27, 1865, showed him present with no horse. No further military record. George married Susan Wyatte on September 15, 1864. They settled in Fulton District where they farmed and raised their family: Thomas M. (1867), William D. (1869), Mary J. (1871), George A. (1874), Noah (1876) and Junius (1879). George died February 23, 1915, and is buried in Fork Baptist Church Cemetery. His brother Thomas C. Sheets also served in this company.

924. Sheets (Sheeks), John
Private, "Davie Greys" • Company F, 13th Regiment • (3rd Regiment, N.C. Volunteers) • N.C. Troops

John was born in 1841. He resided in Davie County where he lived with James and Josephine S. Walker in Smith Grove. John was working as a laborer when he enlisted at age 21, in Davie County on August 6, 1861. He was present or accounted for until wounded and captured at Gettysburg, Pennsylvania, on July 1–5, 1863. John was confined at Fort Delaware, Delaware, until transferred to Point Lookout, Maryland, on October 15–18, 1863. He was released at Point Lookout on February 24, 1864, after taking the Oath of Allegiance and joining the U.S. Army. The unit to which he was assigned is not reported. John and Nancy Berryman were married on December 28, 1865. They became the parents of two sons: Dewit (1867) and Lewis (1869). In 1870 John was a house carpenter living in the Farmington District. On February 22, 1877, at age 36, he married Jane Loyed (1860).

925. Sheets, Thomas C.
Private, Company B, Carolina Rangers • 10th Virginia Cavalry Regiment

Thomas was born in 1845 in Davie County to David J. (1815, Davie) and Manerva (1820, Davie) Howard Sheets. They lived in the Smith Grove District where his father was a farmer and Thomas was a farmhand prior to his enlistment on August 30, 1863, at age 18. He was present or accounted for through July 8, 1864. He was wounded in action beginning May 1, 1864, through October 1, 1864, and issued clothing on October 31, and again on December 31, 1864. No further military records. Thomas returned to Davie County where he worked as a tobacco trader at age 24. He married Sarah T. Van Eaton (1848, North Carolina) on November 17, 1868. Their children were Charley (1866), Nathan (1870), George D. (1871), Hugh C. (1873), Milton C. (1876) and Joseph H. (1879). Thomas is listed in the 1890 Confederate Veterans Census. His brother George W. Sheets also served in this company. Thomas died November 7, 1930. He is buried in Advance United Methodist Church Cemetery.

926. Sheets, Wesley M.
Private, "Davie Sweep Stakes" • Company G, 4th Regiment • N.C. State Troops

Wesley was born on February 7, 1832. He was married to Mary Emiline (1838) Sheets and lived in the Farmington District with their three children prior to the war: Mary L. (1857), Jas. M. (1859) and Mildred M. (1860). Wesley enlisted at age 29, June 4, 1861, for the war. He was wounded at Seven Pines, Virginia, May 31, 1862. He rejoined the company prior to January 1, 1863, and was present or accounted for through August 1864. North Carolina pension records indicate he was wounded in the left arm at Winchester, Virginia, September 20, 1864. He returned home and at age 38 was farming in the Fulton District. Four more children were added to the family: Hugh E. (1869), Nancy J. (1871), Jacob (1874) and Minnie Lee (1878). Wesley died November 14, 1906; Mary Emiline died on October 1, 1911. Both Mary Emiline and Wesley are buried in the Advance Methodist Church Cemetery.

927. Shives, David Franklin
Private, Company D, 42nd Regiment • Company F, 42nd Regiment • N.C. Troops

David was born in Davie County in 1835 where he worked as a farmer in the Calahaln District. On December 28, 1856, he married Louisa J. Keesler [*sic*]. Two children were born prior to the war: Henry (1857) and Hamilton (Hampton) (1858). David enlisted in Company D in Davie County at age 26 on January 29, 1862. He transferred to Company F of this regiment in May–June, 1862. He was present or accounted for through November 21, 1864, and paroled at Mocksville on June 6, 1865. In the meantime, the family continued to increase: Mary (1862), Alice (1863), Mirier Duck (1864), Laura (1866) and Burton Lee (1869).

928. Shives, Giles M.
Private, "Davie Sweep Stakes" • Company G, 4th Regiment • N.C. State Troops

Giles was born in 1839 in Davie County to Daniel (1814, Cabarrus) and Jane (1817, Iredell) Shives. He married Elizabeth Jorden [*sic*] (1826), on November 18, 1857; Delia J. was born in 1858. They lived in the Shady Grove District where Giles farmed prior to enlisting at age 22, on June 4, 1861, for the war. He was reported "captured by the enemy" June 1, 1862; however, records of the Federal Provost Marshal do not substantiate this report. He was present or accounted for until paroled at Salisbury, North Carolina, in 1865. Exact date of parole was not reported. He served as a "pioneer" during much of the war.

929. Shives, James
Private, "Davie Sweep Stakes" • Company G, 4th Regiment • N.C. State Troops

James was born in 1840 in Davie County to Daniel (1814, Cabarrus) and Jane (1817, Iredell) Shives. He married Susan Jordan on November 29, 1857, in Davie County. They lived in the Mocksville District where he enlisted at age 24, March 6, 1862, for the war. He died "in camp" at or near Richmond, Virginia, June 27–28, 1862. One report states "cause of death not reported." Another report states that he died of disease. James's name is listed on the Memorial Monument for the Davie County men who died in the Civil War, 1861–1865.

930. Shives, Joseph P.
Private, "Davie Sweep Stakes" • Company G, 4th Regiment • N.C. State Troops

Joseph was born in 1844 in Davie County to Daniel (1814, Cabarrus) and Jane (1817, Iredell)

Shives. He worked as a farm laborer in the Mocksville District prior to enlisting at age 18, March 8, 1862, for the war. He was present or accounted for until killed at Spotsylvania Court House, Virginia, May 10, 1864. Joseph's name is listed on the Memorial Monument for the Davie County men who died in the Civil War, 1861–1865.

931. Shoemaker, Alfred C.
Private, Company E, 42nd Regiment • N.C. Troops

Alfred was born in 1829 in Iredell County. He married Nancy C. Cheshire Gowan (1820, Davie) on November 4, 1856. Each had been married previously and each had children. Their combined family eventually encompassed Richard W. (1844), Simon C. (1847), Martha E. (1849), Major N. (1852), George W. (1857), James F. (1860), Thomas J. (1864) and Rowan Gowan (1852). Alfred enlisted in Davie County at age 33, March 18, 1862. He was present or accounted for until wounded at or near Bermuda Hundred, Virginia, May 20, 1864. He reported absent wounded through October 1864. He retired to the Invalid Corps on December 19, 1864, and was paroled at Mocksville on June 3, 1865. He returned to his home in the Mocksville District but this time he was classified as a "crippled" farmer. He died on March 20, 1896, and is buried in Union Chapel United Methodist Church Cemetery.

932. Shores, Enoch
Private, Captain William E. Booe's Partisan Rangers • N.C. Volunteers • Company H, 63rd Regiment • (5th Regiment N.C. Cavalry) • N.C. Troops

Enoch was born in 1846. He enlisted in Davie County at age 16, on July 8, 1862, for the war as a substitute for Newton Spellman. His name was reported on the muster roll dated September 17, 1862. No further records.

933. Shores, H.
Private, Captain William E. Booe's Partisan Rangers • N.C. Volunteers • Company H, 63rd Regiment • (5th Regiment N.C. Cavalry) • N.C. Troops

H. enlisted in Davie County on April 15, 1863, for the war. He was captured near Middleburg, Virginia, June 19, 1863, and confined at Old Capitol Prison, Washington, D.C., until paroled and exchanged at City Point, Virginia, on June 30, 1863. He was present or accounted for until he "deserted July 1, 1863." He was reported as a deserter on muster rolls through August 1864.

934. Shores, S.O.
Private, Captain William E. Booe's Partisan Rangers • N.C. Volunteers • Company H, 63rd Regiment • (5th Regiment N.C. Cavalry) • N.C. Troops

S.O. enlisted in Davie County on July 16, 1862, for the war as a substitute for J. Spelman. He was present or accounted for through October 1862.

935. Shores, Wiley
Private, Captain William E. Booe's Partisan Rangers • N.C. Volunteers • Company H, 63rd Regiment • (5th Regiment N.C. Cavalry) • N.C. Troops

Wiley provided W.J. Barnes as his substitute.

936. Sidden, William
Private, Company E, 42nd Regiment • N.C. Troops

William was born in Davie County in 1824. He married Nancy (1832, Davie) Leone on March 18, 1850, and they lived in the Shady Grove District where William worked as a farmer prior to enlisting in Davie County on October 2, 1863, for the war. He was present or accounted for through February 23, 1865. The family resettled in the Fulton District where William and his five sons continued to farm. Nancy and William had six children: Haley Jane (1854), Thos. W. (1858), Edmond (1860), George (1863), Joseph Lee (1866) and Charles R. (1869).

937. Simerson, John H.
Private, Company M, 7th Regiment • Confederate Cavalry • Company E, 16th Battalion • N.C. Cavalry

John enlisted in Davie County on September 10, 1863, with the rank of Private. He was transferred from Company M, 7th Regiment, Confederate Cavalry to Company E, 16th Battalion N.C. Cavalry on July 11, 1864. He was present or accounted for through October 1, 1864, and paroled at Salisbury, North Carolina, May 20, 1865.

938. Simmons, Henry
Private, "Davie Greys" • Company F, 13th Regiment • (3rd Regiment, N.C. Volunteers) • N.C. Troops

Henry was born in 1835 to Jeremiah (1793, Virginia) and Sarah (1809, Virginia) Simmons. They resided in Davie County where Jeremiah worked as a carpenter and Henry was a laborer. He married Sousan (Ann) Foster December 16, 1860. Their daughter Mary was born in 1858. Henry enlisted in Davie County at age 23 on August 6, 1861. He was present or accounted for until he died at home in Davie County in September 1862. His name is listed on the Memorial Monument for the Davie County men who died in the Civil War, 1861–1865.

939. Sloan, William Henry
Private, Company D, 42nd Regiment • Company F, 42nd Regiment • N.C. Troops

William was born in 1845 in Davie County to Samuel (1818, Rowan) and Jane (1807, Davidson) Sloan. They resided in the Chinquepin District of Davie County where William enlisted at age 16, on January 30, 1862. He transferred to Company F of this regiment in May–June, 1862. He was present or accounted for through October 1864, and paroled at Mocksville on June 3, 1865. Following the war he returned to Davie County where he married Laura (1844, North Carolina) and raised his children: Willie (1867), Lillie (1870), Neally (1872), Charles (1874) and Mary (1879).

940. Smith, Alfred A.
Corporal, Company G, 7th Regiment • Confederate Cavalry • Company D, 16th Battalion • N.C. Cavalry

Alfred enlisted in Davie County on September 3, 1862, with the rank of Private. He was promoted to Corporal and transferred from Company G, 7th Regiment Confederate Cavalry to Company D, 16th Battalion N.C. Cavalry on July 11, 1864. He was present or accounted for through October 1, 1864.

941. Smith, Asbury
Private, Company F, 42nd Regiment • N.C. Troops

Asbury was born in 1841 in Davie County to Seamont (1811, Davie) and Mary Smith (1812, Davie). Seamont was a shoe-maker. Asbury enlisted in Petersburg, Virginia, on November 18, 1862, for the war. He was present or accounted for until he deserted on March 31, 1863. He was paroled at Mocksville on June 16, 1865. Asbury and Mary Ellen Beck (1850, North Carolina) were married on June 19, 1870. Their children were Robert N. (1870), Tabitha (1872), James R. (1874) and Mary L. (1877). In 1880 Asbury farmed in Calahaln with his wife and children.

942. Smith, Beal I.
First Lieutenant, "Davie Sweep Stakes" • Company G, 4th Regiment • N.C. State Troops

Beal was born June 16, 1829, to John Smith of Ijames (1799, Iredell) and Lydia (1806, Davie). He worked as a clerk in the Calahaln District where he enlisted at age 31, June 4, 1861, for the war. He mustered in as Sergeant, was promoted to First Sergeant in November–December 1862, and appointed Second Lieutenant to rank from February 14, 1863. He was wounded in his left leg at Chancellorsville, Virginia, May 3, 1863. After being appointed First Lieutenant on August 3, 1863, he was reported absent wounded through December 1863. Following his retirement to the Invalid Corps on July 22, 1864, he was assigned to duty at Gordonsville, Virginia. At age 48, Beal married Martha A. Spry, age 22, on August 30, 1878. By age 50 in 1880, he was the father of Osker B. (1877) and Duke L. (1879). He died February 16, 1895, and is buried at Center United Methodist Church Cemetery.

943. Smith, Doctor F.
Private, Company A, 42nd Regiment • N.C. Troops

Doctor resided in Davie County. The place and date of enlistment were not reported. He was captured at or near Battery Anderson near Fort Fisher, North Carolina, December 25, 1864. He was confined at or near Fort Monroe, Virginia, on or about December 27, 1864, and transferred to Point Lookout, Maryland, where he arrived on January 2, 1865. He was released at Point Lookout on June 20, 1865, after taking the Oath of Allegiance.

944. Smith, Elwood
Private, Company M, 7th Regiment • Confederate Cavalry • Company E, 16th Battalion • N.C. Cavalry

Elwood was transferred from Company M, 7th Regiment Confederate Cavalry to Company E, 16th Battalion N.C. Cavalry on July 11, 1864. He was present or accounted for through October 1, 1864.

945. Smith, Franklin A.
Private, "Davie Sweep Stakes" • Company G, 4th Regiment • N.C. State Troops

Franklin was born in 1841 in Davie County to Anderson W. (1820, Davie) and Mary Kerby (1822, Davie) Smith. They lived in the Mocksville District where he enlisted at age 20, June 4, 1861, for the war. He was reported absent without leave November 20, 1862, until November–December, 1863, when he was reported "in confinement." He was court-martialed on or about January 19, 1864, but rejoined the company prior to July 12, 1864, when he was captured near Washington, D.C. He was confined at Old Capitol Prison, Washington, until transferred to Elmira, New York, on July 23, 1864. After taking the Oath of Allegiance, he was released at Elmira on July 11, 1865.

946. Smith, James Douglas
Private, Company E, 42nd Regiment • N.C. Troops

James was born in Davie County in 1846. He was the son of James K. (1814, Davie) and Mary (1817, Davie) Smith. Prior to the war James worked as a laborer in the Farmington District. He enlisted for the war at age 17, April 15, 1864. James was present or accounted for through October 1864, and paroled at Mocksville on June 7, 1865. Nancy Leinbach and James Douglas were married on November 27, 1866. They were the parents of John, born 1867. James Douglas returned to the Farmington District and to farm work. He died on March 23, 1903, and is buried at Bethlehem United Methodist Church.

947. Smith, James W.
Private, "Davie Sweep Stakes" • Company G, 4th Regiment • N.C. State Troops

James was born in 1840 to Anderson (1820, Davie) and Mary (1822) Kerby Smith. He resided in Davie County where he enlisted at age 21, June 4, 1861, for the war. He was present or accounted for until wounded at Chancellorsville, Virginia, May 3, 1863. Company muster rolls indicate that he died June 1, 1863, of wounds; however, medical records indicate he was admitted to the hospital at Richmond, Virginia, July 13, 1863, with "chronic diarrhoea" and furloughed for 40 days on July 22, 1863.

948. Smith, Jonathan
Captain, Smith Grove Rifles • (Artillery Company Militia 1860–1861)

Captain Smith is mentioned in *History of Davie County* by James W. Wall, pp. 161–162. Captain Smith apparently commanded one of two militias in Davie County prior to the war. The other militia company was the Mocksville Rifles commanded by Colonel William F. Kelly and Major A.A. Harbin.

949. Smith, L.W.
Private, 1st Company A, Salisbury Prison Guard • "The Rough and Readys" • Company G, 66th Regiment • N.C. Troops

L.W. previously served as Private in 1st Company A, Salisbury Prison Guard. He was transferred to Company G of the 66th on October 2, 1863, while listed as a deserter. He reported for duty in November–December, 1863, and deserted on January 23, 1864.

950. Smith, Levi K.
Private, Company A, 42nd Regiment • N.C. Troops

Levi was born in 1825 in Davie County to Thomas and Nancy Smith. He was a farmer all his life. Levi married Mary A. Etchison on November 10, 1853. They resided in Davie County in the Farmington District. Levi enlisted in Rowan County at age 30, on March 31, 1862. He was present or accounted for until wounded at or near Cold Harbor, Virginia, on June 1–3, 1864. He returned to duty prior to July 1, 1864, and was captured at or near Battery Anderson, near Fort Fisher, North Carolina, December 25, 1864. He was confined at or near Fort Monroe, Virginia, December 27, 1864, and transferred to Point Lookout, Maryland, where he arrived on January 2, 1865. He was released on June 20, 1865, after taking the Oath of Allegiance. Levi and Mary were the parents of eight children: Jonathan (1857), Nathan (1861), Levi (1863), Mary A.

Levi Kitely Smith survived the Yankee prison at Point Lookout, Maryland. Although the armistice was signed April 9, 1865, he was held until June 20, 1865 (Estelle Smith).

(1866), Gibson A. (1869), Perlina (1873), Matilda (1876) and Emaline (1879). In 1870 and 1880 they were farming in Farmington.

951. Smith, S.A.
Private, Captain William E. Booe's Partisan Rangers • N.C. Volunteers • Company H, 63rd Regiment • (5th Regiment N.C. Cavalry) • N.C. Troops

S.A. was born in Davie County where he enlisted at age 23, July 15, 1862, for the war. He was present or accounted for on company muster rolls through October 1863, when he was reported with the remark: "Died of wounds received October 15, 1863." S.A.'s name is listed on the Memorial Monument for the Davie County men who died in the Civil War, 1861–1865.

952. Smith, S.L. (Samuel)
Private, Captain William E. Booe's Partisan Rangers • N.C. Volunteers • Company H, 63rd Regiment • (5th Regiment N.C. Cavalry) • N.C. Troops

Samuel was born in 1843 in North Carolina. He was the son of Levi G. (1817, Davie) and Elizabeth Amanda McMahan (1818, Davie) Smith. He was a laborer, living at home with his family in Farmington, when he enlisted in Davie County at age 19, July 15, 1862, for the war. He was captured near Hagerstown, Maryland, July 12, 1863, and confined at Point Lookout, Maryland, until paroled and exchanged at City Point, Virginia, March 20, 1864. He was present or accounted for through October 1864.

953. Smith, Samuel T.
Private, Company E, 42nd Regiment • N.C. Troops

Samuel was born in 1844 in Davie County, the son of Thomas A. (1823, Davie) who was a blacksmith, and Elizabeth (1826, Davie) Smith. Samuel was living in Farmington when he enlisted in Davie County at age 19, April 15, 1864, for the war. He was present or accounted for through December 7, 1864, and was paroled at Mocksville on June 7, 1865. (North Carolina pension records indicate he was wounded in the right arm at Petersburg, Virginia, in 1864.) Samuel returned to the Farmington District and on November 11, 1866, married Martha A. Hodges. They were the parents of four children: John R. (1868), Charlie (1871), Joseph (1877) and Elizabeth (1880). Samuel died on May 17, 1916, and is buried in Macedonia Moravian Church Cemetery.

954. Smith, W.H.H.
Private, Company D, 42nd Regiment • N.C. Troops

W.H.H. Smith resided in Davie County and enlisted at Petersburg, Virginia, at age 18, October 20, 1863, for the war. He was present or accounted for until captured at Cold Harbor, Virginia, June 3, 1864. He was confined at Point Lookout, Maryland, on June 11, 1864, and transferred to Elmira, New York, where he arrived on July 17, 1864. He was paroled at Elmira on March 2, 1865, and transferred to the James River, Virginia, for exchange. No further records.

955. Smith, William A.
Private, "Davie Greys" • Company F, 13th Regiment • (3rd Regiment, N.C. Volunteers) • N.C. Troops

William was born in 1837 in Davie County to Andrew (1807, Randolph) and Sarah (1815, Davie) Smith. In 1860 he was a farmer living in the Mocksville District, where on April 26, 1861, he enlisted at age 24. William mustered in as a Private and was appointed Musician on June 1, 1861. He was reduced to ranks in September–October, 1861, and was present or accounted for until killed at Gaines' Mill, Virginia, on June 27, 1862. William's name is listed on the Memorial Monument for the Davie County men who died in the Civil War, 1861–1865.

956. Smith, William D. (David)
Private, Captain William E. Booe's Partisan Rangers • N.C. Volunteers • Company H, 63rd Regiment • (5th Regiment N.C. Cavalry) • N.C. Troops

William was born on October 21, 1841, in North Carolina. He was the son of Levi G. (1817, Davie) and Elizabeth Amanda McMahan (1818, Davie) Smith. William worked as a laborer in Farmington. On April 3, 1862, William married Angeline Elizabeth Jones, then enlisted in Davie County at age 20, on July 15, 1862, for the war. He was present or accounted for through December 1864. After the war he returned home to Farmington. Angeline and William would have seven children: Julia E. (1863), Sarah A. (1866), Emma F. (1867), Janie (1870), Lydia (1872), Henry (1875) and Charlie (1879). William died February 17, 1922, and is buried in Bethlehem United Methodist Church Cemetery.

957. Smith, William H.
Private, Company B, Carolina Rangers • 10th Virginia Cavalry Regiment

William was born in 1832 in North Carolina. He lived in the Farmington District of Davie County where he worked as a farmer prior to enlisting there on October 29, 1861, at age 29. He was present or accounted for throughout his service. He was absent sick with a debility in a Charlottesville, Virginia, hospital on November 9, 1863; he returned to duty on November 20, 1863. He was present through August 1864, and was issued clothing on September 30 and on December 31, 1864. No further records.

958. Smith, William Harden
Private, Company F, 42nd Regiment • N.C. Troops

William was born on May 18, 1836, in North Carolina. He married Phebe James on December 24, 1856, in Davie County. Prior to 1880 they would have nine children: Rachel (1858), James (1861), Thomas (1863), Henry (1865), Morgan (1867), Mary (1870), Albert (1873), Sarah (1875) and Leonidas (1879). William enlisted in Davie County on March 27, 1862, at age 27. He was present or accounted for through June 1863. He deserted on an unspecified date but was under arrest on October 12, 1863. He remained in confinement during November 1863–October 1864. He was paroled at Mocksville on June 7, 1865. (North Carolina pension records indicate that he was wounded in the right hand near Kinston, North Carolina, on March 1, 1865.) He died on July 17, 1919. William is buried in Bethlehem United Methodist Church Cemetery. His tombstone lists his Civil War service.

959. Smith, William J.
Private, Company F, 42nd Regiment • N.C. Troops

William was born in 1835. He enlisted at Petersburg, Virginia, at age 27, on November 18, 1862, for the war. He was present or accounted for until he deserted on March 31, 1863. He was paroled at Mocksville on June 10, 1865. Both William and his wife Nancy are buried at New Union United Methodist Church Cemetery. Their stones read: William J. Smith, January 27, 1835/June 27, 1917; Nancy L. Smith, January 25, 1840/May 3, 1919.

960. Smith, William P.
Private, Company F, 42nd Regiment • N.C. Troops

William was born in 1846 in Davie County to Holden (1811, Davie) and Nancy (1812, Davie) Eaton Smith. The family lived in the Farmington District of Davie County where William enlisted on April 15, 1864, for the war. He was present or accounted for until he died in the hospital at Greensboro, North Carolina, on November 16, 1864, of pneumonia. William's name is listed on the Memorial Monument for the Davie County men who died in the Civil War, 1861–1865.

961. Smith, Zemerick N.
Private, Company M, 7th Regiment • Confederate Cavalry • Company E, 16th Battalion • N.C. Cavalry

Zemerick was transferred from Company M, 7th Regiment Confederate Cavalry to Company E, 16th Battalion N.C. Cavalry on July 11, 1864. He was present or accounted for through October 1, 1864, but was captured at Hatcher's Run, Virginia, April 1, 1865, just nine days before the war ended. He was confined at Hart's Island, New York Harbor, where he remained until transferred to DeCamp General Hospital, David's Island, N. Y. Harbor, April 29, 1865. He died in the hospital of "typhoid fever" May 5, 1865. Zemerick's name is listed on the Memorial Monument for the Davie County men who died in the Civil War, 1861–1865.

962. Smoot, Alexander
Private, Company F, 42nd Regiment • N.C. Troops

Alexander was born in 1840. He enlisted in Davie County at age 22, March 18, 1862. He was present or accounted for through October 1864.

963. Smoot, Daniel J.
Second Lieutenant, "Davie Sweep Stakes" • Company G, 4th Regiment • N.C. State Troops

Daniel was born in 1841 in Davie County to Samuel J. (1798, Virginia) and Rebecca (1820, Davie) Smoot. His father was a successful Davie County farmer in the Calahaln District. Daniel enlisted June 4, 1861, for the war. He mustered in as a Corporal and was appointed Second Lieutenant March 22, 1863. On May 3, 1863, he was wounded in the forehead at Chancellorsville, Virginia. He rejoined the company prior to September 1, 1863, and was present or accounted for until wounded in the leg at Spotsylvania Court House, Virginia, May 12, 1864. He died eight days later in the hospital at Richmond, Virginia, following the amputation of his leg. Daniel's name is listed on the Memorial Monument for the Davie County men who died in the Civil War, 1861–1865.

964. Smoot, John
Private, Company F, 42nd Regiment • N.C. Troops

John was born in Davie County in 1835. He worked as a laborer on the Robert Griffen farm in 1850. At the age of 27, he enlisted in Davie

County on March 18, 1862. He was present or accounted for through October 1864. John was paroled at Mocksville on June 5, 1865.

965. Smoot, Pinkney
Private, Company F, 42nd Regiment • N.C. Troops

Pinkney enlisted in Davie County on April 15, 1864, for the war. He was present or accounted for until he was hospitalized at Richmond, Virginia, on December 14, 1864, with "typhoid pneumonia." Pinkney died in the hospital at Richmond on December 18, 1864. Pinkney's name is listed on the Memorial Monument for the Davie County men who died in the Civil War, 1861–1865.

966. Smoot, Wilson D.
Private, Company F, 42nd Regiment • N.C. Troops

Wilson enlisted in Davie County on February 25, 1864, for the war. He was wounded at or near Bermuda Hundred, Virginia, May 20, 1864, and was hospitalized at Petersburg, Virginia, where he died on May 21, 1864, of his wounds. Wilson's name is listed on the Memorial Monument for the Davie County men who died in the Civil War, 1861–1865.

967. Snider, A.W.
Private, Company B, 57th Regiment • N.C. Troops

A.W. resided in Davie County and enlisted in Rowan County at age 18, July 4, 1862, for the war. He died in the hospital at Richmond, Virginia, on or about October 11, 1862, of "brain fever." A.W.'s name is not presently listed on the Memorial Monument for the Davie County men who died in the Civil War, 1861–1865.

968. Snyder, R.W.
Private, Company G, 7th Regiment • Confederate Cavalry • Company D, 16th Battalion • N.C. Cavalry

R.W. enlisted in Davie County on September 3, 1862, with the rank of Private. He was transferred from Company G, 7th Regiment Confederate Cavalry to Company D, 16th Battalion N.C. Cavalry on July 11, 1864, while absent in confinement at Point Lookout, Maryland, as a prisoner of war. He was paroled and exchanged at Boulware's Wharf and Cox's Wharf, James River, Virginia, on February 20–21, 1865.

969. Sparks, C.M. (Charles)
Private, Captain William E. Booe's Partisan Rangers • N.C. Volunteers • Company H, 63rd Regiment • (5th Regiment N.C. Cavalry) • N.C. Troops

Charles Sparks survived the war and lived out his life in this house (Mohney, *The Historic Architecture of Davie County*).

C.M. was born February 15, 1840, in Davie County, the son of Martha (1799, Virginia) Sparks. He farmed in Shady Grove where he married Sarah Jane Beauchamp on November 1, 1859. At age 22, on July 18, 1862, he enlisted in Davie County for the war. He was captured on the Weldon Railroad on August 21, 1864, and confined at Point Lookout, Maryland, until he was paroled and exchanged September 30, 1864. He was admitted to the hospital in Richmond, Virginia, on October 6, 1864, and transferred to Camp Lee, near Richmond, the next day. After the war the family moved to the Farmington District where they continued to farm. The children were Harrison (1861), Ida (1863), Sarah (Sally) (1864), Minnie (1867), Niner (1871), Joseph (1874) and Baxter (1878). Charles's mother Martha also lived with them. Charles died on October 6, 1907, and is buried in Bethlehem United Methodist Church Cemetery.

970. Sparks, John Harvey
Second Lieutenant, Company H • 77th Regiment, 19th Division • N.C. Militia 1861–1865

John was born in 1834 in Davie County to Martha E. (1799, Virginia) Sparks. His father had died prior to 1850, leaving Martha with a thriving farm, four children and eighteen slaves to manage. By 1860 John was a student, age 24 in the Smith Grove District of Davie County. He married Mary E. Howard on March 27, 1861, and was probably appointed Second Lieutenant of Company H around that time, or earlier. John and Mary would have two surviving children: Lula (1863) and James (1866). They moved to Fulton District where John supported his family as a miller/farmer. He died on May 1, 1881, and is buried in Advance United Methodist Church Cemetery.

971. Speas, W.H.
Private, Captain William E. Booe's Partisan Rangers • N.C. Volunteers • Company H, 63rd Regiment • (5th Regiment N.C. Cavalry) • N.C. Troops

W.H. enlisted in Davie County on April 15, 1863, for the war. He was wounded in action near Hagerstown, Maryland, on July 10–12, 1863, and died of wounds at Williamsport, Maryland. W.H.'s name is listed on the Memorial Monument for the Davie County men who died in the Civil War, 1861–1865.

972. Spellman, Newton
Private, Captain William E. Booe's Partisan Rangers • N.C. Volunteers • Company H, 63rd Regiment • (5th Regiment N.C. Cavalry) • N.C. Troops

Newton furnished Enoch Shores as his substitute.

973. Spelman, J.
Private, Captain William E. Booe's Partisan Rangers • N.C. Volunteers • Company H, 63rd Regiment • (5th Regiment N.C. Cavalry) • N.C. Troops

Furnished S.O. Shores as his substitute.

974. Spencer, O.H. (Oliver Hause)
Sergeant, Company E, 42nd Regiment • N.C. Troops

Oliver was born in 1836 in the Marlborough District of South Carolina. He married L. W. Carter in Davie County on November 7, 1860. Their first child, Elizabeth, was born in 1862, the year that Oliver enlisted. He was a farmer when he enlisted in Davie County at age 27, on April 29, 1862, for the war. He mustered in as a Sergeant but within two months had been reduced to ranks prior to July 1, 1862. On October 7, 1862, he was discharged by reason of "general debility and broken constitution following from measles and typhoid fever." He returned to his family in Jerusalem District where he supported them by farming. William was born in 1863 and Franklin was born in 1865. In 1880 the family were still together; Letitia kept house, Oliver farmed, Elizabeth D. taught school and the two boys were students. Oliver died on April 19, 1914, and is buried in Rose Cemetery, Mocksville.

975. Sport, William B.
Private, Company F, 42nd Regiment • N.C. Troops

William B. was born in 1836 in Davie County. He married Nancy Caroline Lazenby (1835) on December 1, 1859. In 1860 he and Nancy farmed in the Mocksville District where William enlisted in Davie County at age 26, on March 18, 1862. He was present or accounted for through October 1864. He was killed at Bentonville, North Carolina, in March 1865. William's name is listed on the Memorial Monument for the Davie County men who died in the Civil War, 1861–1865.

976. Spry, Berry (Asbury)
Private, Company E, 42nd Regiment • N.C. Troops

Berry was born in 1835 in Davie County. In 1860 he was a farmer in Smith Grove. On April 20, 1860, he and Nancy Myers (1842, North Carolina) were married. He enlisted in Davie County at age 27 on March 18, 1862. He was present or accounted for until he deserted on August 10, 1864. He was paroled at Mocksville on June 7, 1865. Nancy and Berry would have two daughters: Elizabeth (1866) and Mary D. (1869). Following the war Asbury supported his family by farming and distilling whiskey.

977. Spry, Calvin
Private, Company H, 57th Regiment • N.C. Troops

Calvin was born in North Carolina in 1834. He was a farmer-laborer who lived in the Fulton District of Davie County before the war. He and Mary Graves were married on September 15, 1859. At age 26, on July 4, 1862, in Davie County he enlisted for the war. He was reported absent without leave on September 10, 1862, but returned to duty on October 26, 1862. He was reported present through May 11, 1863, but was wounded in the knee and captured at Gettysburg, Pennsylvania, on July 2–3, 1863. He was hospitalized at Chester, Pennsylvania, and paroled there on or about August 17, 1863. Calvin was received at City Point, Virginia, on August 20, 1863, for exchange. He was reported absent without leave from December 15, 1863, through October 31, 1864. Calvin returned to duty in November–December, 1864. He was reported present in January–February, 1865, but was captured at Fort Stedman, Virginia, on March 25, 1865, and confined at Point Lookout, Maryland, on March 28, 1865. He was released at Point Lookout on June 19, 1865, after taking the Oath of Allegiance. Calvin and Mary were the parents of Sarah (1860), Margaret (1864), Infant (1867), Charles (1872), Camila (1876) and Noah (1879). After the war, the family settled in the Jerusalem District where Calvin returned to farming; they were still there in 1880. Calvin died in 1901 and is buried in Liberty United Methodist Church Cemetery.

978. Spry, John Giles
Private, Company F, 42nd Regiment • N.C. Troops

John was born in 1842 in Davie County. He was the son of John (1814, Davie) and Elizabeth (1813, Davie) Spry. They lived in the Smith Grove District. John enlisted in Davie County on January 12, 1864, and was present or accounted for until he deserted on June 13, 1864. He married Margy (1846) Graves on July 20, 1864. He was paroled at Salisbury, North Carolina, on May 23, 1865. They lived in Fulton District where daughter Nellie was born in 1868; by 1880 they lived in Jerusalem District where John was a shoemaker.

979. Spry, William
Private, Company D, 42nd Regiment • N.C. Troops

William enlisted in Davie County on or about January 25, 1862. No further records.

980. Stafford, J.M.
Private, Company G, 7th Regiment • Confederate Cavalry • Company D, 16th Battalion • N.C. Cavalry

J.M. was transferred from Company G, 7th Regiment Confederate Cavalry to Company D, 16th Battalion N.C. Cavalry on July 11, 1864. He was present or accounted for through October 1, 1864, and paroled at Appomattox Court House, Virginia, April 9, 1865.

981. Standerford, John
Private, Company G, 7th Regiment • Confederate Cavalry • Company D, 16th Battalion • N.C. Cavalry

John was transferred from Company G, 7th Regiment Confederate Cavalry to Company D, 16th Battalion N.C. Cavalry on July 11, 1864. He was present or accounted for through October 1, 1864, and paroled at Greensboro, North Carolina, on May 11, 1865.

982. Stanley, Jefferson J.
Private, Company D, 42nd Regiment • N.C. Troops

Jefferson was born on June 15, 1834, in Davie County to Nathan (1801, Davie) and Hannah (1801, Davie) Stanley. Nathan was a cooper and Jefferson worked as a laborer in the Chinquepin District. On March 11, 1860, Jefferson married Jane Swathlander; Mary E. was born in 1861. At age 25, on March 26, 1862, Jefferson enlisted in Rowan County. He was present or accounted for through October 1864, and paroled at Mocksville on June 3, 1865. He resumed family life and became a farmer in Clarksville. Two more children were born: Joseph W. (1867) and Sarah (1869). According to her tombstone, Elizabeth Jane died on March 31, 1906. Jefferson then married Martha, according to his tombstone. There is a problem, however. Martha's tombstone states that she died at age 28 on April 18, 1900. J. J. died on April 5, 1915. They are all buried at Bear Creek Baptist Church Cemetery.

983. Stanley, Nathan W. (Jr.)
Private, Company D, 42nd Regiment • N.C. Troops

Nathan was born in 1832 in Davie County, the son of Nathan Sr., a cooper, who was born in

1801 in Davie County, and Hannah, who was also born in Davie County in 1801. Nathan was the brother of Jefferson J. Stanley who also served in this company. In 1860 Nathan resided in Chinquepin where, on February 5, 1860, he married Sarah A. (S) Hall. Their daughter Elizabeth was born in 1861. On March 26, 1862, at age 23, Nathan enlisted in Rowan County. He was present or accounted for until he was captured near Richmond, Virginia, on October 7, 1864, and confined at Point Lookout, Maryland, on October 29, 1864. He died at Point Lookout on February 21, 1865, of "pneumonia." Nathan's name is listed on the Memorial Monument for the Davie County men who died in the Civil War, 1861–1865.

984. Steelman, George
Private, Captain William E. Booe's Partisan Rangers • N.C. Volunteers • Company H, 63rd Regiment • (5th Regiment N.C. Cavalry) • N.C. Troops

George was born in North Carolina in 1837. He married Sarah Jane Etchison (1839, North Carolina) on January 27, 1857, and they settled in the Farmington District of Davie County where he worked as a farmer. Their son Perry R. was born in 1857. George enlisted in Davie County on July 15, 1862, for the war. He was present or accounted for through October 1864. He was admitted to the hospital at Raleigh, North Carolina, on December 7, 1864, with "cirrhosis" and died on December 26, 1864. George's name is listed on the Memorial Monument for the Davie County men who died in the Civil War, 1861–1865.

985. Steelman, J.W.
Private, Captain William E. Booe's Partisan Rangers • N.C. Volunteers • Company H, 63rd Regiment • (5th Regiment N.C. Cavalry) • N.C. Troops

J.W. enlisted in Davie County at age 18, on July 15, 1862, for the war. He was wounded in action at Upperville, Virginia, June 21, 1863, and was present or accounted for through December 1864.

986. Stewart (Stuart), Daniel
Private, Company E, 42nd Regiment • N.C. Troops

Daniel was born in 1831 in Davie County, the son of Johannah Stewart (1802, Davie). He married Elizabeth Parks on November 16, 1854. Their three children were Wm. H. (1856), Jon F. (1858) and Eliza J. (1860). Daniel worked as a laborer in Fulton District prior to enlisting in Davie County at age 31, on March 18, 1862. He was present or accounted for until he died at Merry Hill, North Carolina, on March 22, 1863. The cause of death was not reported. Daniel was the brother of Spencer Stewart of this company. Daniel's name is listed on the Memorial Monument for the Davie County men who died in the Civil War, 1861–1865.

987. Stewart (Steward), Edward D.
Private, Company E, 42nd Regiment • N.C. Troops

Edward was born in 1835 in Davie County to Samuel (1795, Davie) and Rebecca (1805, Davie) Stewart. They farmed in the Fulton District. Edward married Elizabeth Potts on Novem-

Edward D. Stewart. According to an article in *The State*, "Uncle Ned" attributed his long life to "taking it easy" and to eating "collards, turnip greens, sweet potatoes, backbone and dumplings." He died at age 101 (Alvin Howard).

ber 14, 1861, just prior to enlisting in Davie County at age 25, on March 18, 1862. He was present or accounted for through October 1864, and paroled at Statesville on June 8, 1865. (North Carolina pension records indicate he was wounded in his right leg at Bermuda Hundred, Virginia, on an unspecified date.) Edward and Elizabeth had four children: Samuel (1864), Lula (1866), Ida (1868) and Sanford E. (1872). The family continued to farm in the Fulton District. Edward lived to be 101 years old; he died on December 29, 1936, and is buried in Fork Baptist Church Cemetery.

988. Stewart, Hezekiah
Private, Company F, 42nd Regiment • N.C. Troops

Hezekiah was born in 1832 in North Carolina. He married Rebecca (1835, North Carolina) and in 1860 they lived, along with their son Francis (1857), in the Chinquepin District. Hezekiah was a laborer when he enlisted in Davie County at age 30, March 18, 1862. He was present or accounted for until he died in the hospital at Lynchburg, Virginia, on August 1, 1862, of "febris typhoides." Hezekiah's name is listed on the Memorial Monument for the Davie County men who died in the Civil War, 1861–1865.

989. Stewart (Steward), Spencer
Private, Company E, 42nd Regiment • N.C. Troops

Spencer was the son of Johannah Stewart (1802, Davie). He was born in 1843 in Davie County. He was a laborer in the Fulton District in 1860, where he lived with the Coleman Foster family. At age 19, on March 18, 1862, he enlisted in Davie County, for the war. He was present or accounted for until he died in the hospital at Petersburg, Virginia, on January 8, 1863, of "dysentery." Spencer was the brother of Daniel Stewart, who also served in this company. Spencer's name is listed on the Memorial Monument for the Davie County men who died in the Civil War, 1861–1865.

990. Stewart, William
Private, Company E, 42nd Regiment • N.C. Troops

William was born in 1833 in North Carolina. He married Mary McDaniel (1840, North Carolina) on June 20, 1857. They lived in the Shady Grove District where he worked as a laborer. William enlisted in Davie County at age 29, on March 18, 1862. He was present or accounted for through October 1864, and paroled at Mocksville on June 7, 1865. (The Salem *People's Press* of June 30, 1864, indicates he was wounded in action June 1–15, 1864.) Their three children were Wm. F. (1863), Rebecca (1871) and Mollie (1875). He resumed his life in Davie County where he lived to be approximately 70 years of age. He is buried in Smith Grove United Methodist Church Cemetery.

991. Stonestreet, Jediah
Private, Company B, Carolina Rangers • 10th Virginia Cavalry Regiment

"Jeddi" was born circa 1822 in Davie County to Nancy Stonestreet (1795, Guilford). He worked as a laborer to support his mother prior to enlisting in Davie County on April 1, 1863. He served through August 1863; after that he was absent sick with "Hernia ing sing acdue" in Richmond hospital on September 11, 1863. He was furloughed for 35 days on September 16, 1863; absent sick through December 1863; absent without leave January–April 1, 1864, and July–August, 1864. He was dropped as a deserter with no date given. Jiddiah returned home to his wife Mary and their four children: William P. (1860), Margaret (1862), Ardella (1865) and Martha (1868). They resided in the Clarksville District where he worked as a farmer.

992. Stonestreet, John H.
Private, "Davie Greys" • Company F, 13th Regiment • (3rd Regiment, N.C. Volunteers) • N.C. Troops

John was born in 1836, the son of Welborne (1814, Davie) and Sarah (1815, Davie) Stonestreet. In 1860 he lived and worked as a laborer in the Mocksville District. On August 6, 1861, he enlisted at age 25, in Davie County. He was present or accounted for until wounded at Spotsylvania Court House, Virginia, on May 21, 1864. John rejoined the company in July–August, 1864, and was present or accounted for until paroled at Appomattox Court House, Virginia, on April 9, 1865. John married Emely C. Coon on October 16, 1866. They continued to reside in Davie County and both are buried in Center United Methodist Church Cemetery. John died November 26, 1911.

993. Stout, William Laranza
Private, Company E, 42nd Regiment • N.C. Troops

William was born in 1838 in Davidson County. In 1850 at age 12, he lived with John Heath and family. William was a farmer prior to enlisting in Davie County at age 24, on March 18,

1862. He was present or accounted for until discharged on June 17, 1863, by reason of "rheumatismus chronica and neuralgia."

994. Stroud, David (D.F.)
Private, Company F, 42nd Regiment • N.C. Troops

David was born in 1829. He married Sarah A. Rudisell on November 20, 1850. Their three children were Richard A. (1856), James T. (1858) and Henry G. (1860). David spent his life as a farmer in the Calahaln District except for his service in the army. He enlisted in Davie County at age 32, March 24, 1862. He was present or accounted for through October 1864. David married Nancy Caroline Lazenby Sport on November 2, 1871. He died on May 31, 1907, and is buried in Salem United Methodist Church Cemetery.

995. Stroud, Rich S.
Private, Company H, 23rd Regiment • N.C. Troops

Rich was born in North Carolina in 1836. He was the son of Andrew Stroud (1804–1894). Richard married Mary Jane Swisher in Davie County on January 15, 1856. They settled in a log farmhouse near his father's dwelling where they lived until Rich's death in 1923. Richard and Mary Jane had two children prior to the war: Newman E. (1857) and Laura E. (1860). He enlisted in Iredell County on September 5, 1862, for the war. Not long afterward he received a wound that would plague him the rest of his life. The military record states that he was present or accounted for until he was wounded in the neck and shoulder at Cedar Creek, Virginia, October 19, 1864. He was reported absent wounded through December 1864. (Pension records indicate he was shot in the back of the neck in North Carolina on November 14, 1863.) He returned to his home in Calahaln where he farmed and raised his family: Richard E. (1862), Jackson A. (1868), James M. (1871), Mary C. (1874) and Alice U. (1876). In 1880 prospects for the family, according to census information, indicated a rather grim situation: Richard was listed as a disabled farmer while Mary Jane was "keeping house/lying in," and the eldest son Richard was a laborer/disabled." They weathered the situation, however, with each of the three living a minimum of forty more years. Richard, the father, died on October 25, 1923, and is buried in Society Baptist Church Cemetery.

996. Stuart, J.G. (John)
Corporal, Company B, Carolina Rangers • 10th Virginia Cavalry Regiment

John was born on May 24, 1824, in Davie County to Elizabeth (1797, Davie) Stewart [*sic*]. He married Jane Myers on April 5, 1853. Their children were Martha A. (1850), Winfield Scott (1852), Adelia (1854), Comodore D. (1857) and Sam T. (1859). They lived in the Fulton District of Davie County where Giles farmed and where he enlisted on December 20, 1862, at age 38. Within two weeks he was absent sick for two months. He was present or accounted for on horse details after that, until paroled in Mocksville on June 9, 1865. J.G. is buried in the Stewart Family Cemetery. The date of his death conflicts with his military service, January 6, 1860 [*sic*]. Jane and the children continued to live in the Fulton District.

997. Sullivan, Patrick
Private, Company H, 57th Regiment • N.C. Troops

Patrick resided in Davie County and enlisted in Rowan County at age 28, on July 4, 1862,

Rich S. Stroud and wife, Mary Jane Swisher Stroud (Mohney, *The Historic Architecture of Davie County*).

for the war. He deserted at Richmond, Virginia, on August 13, 1862.

998. Summers, Greenberry
Private, Company M, 7th Regiment • Confederate Cavalry • Company E, 16th Battalion • N.C. Cavalry

Greenberry enlisted in Davie County on October 23, 1863, as a Private. He was transferred from Company M, 7th Regiment Confederate Cavalry to Company E, 16th Battalion N.C. Cavalry on July 11, 1864. He was present or accounted for through October 1, 1864.

999. Swaringen, Iva F.
Private, "Davie Sweep Stakes" • Company G, 4th Regiment • N.C. State Troops

Iva resided in Davie County when he enlisted at age 32, June 4, 1861, for the war. He was killed at Seven Pines, Virginia, May 31, 1862. Iva's name is listed on the Memorial Monument for the Davie County men who died in the Civil War, 1861–1865.

1000. Swaringen, Samuel T.
Private, Company H, 63rd Regiment • (5th Regiment N.C. Cavalry) • Private, "Davie Greys" • Company F, 13th Regiment • (3rd Regiment, N.C. Volunteers) • N.C. Troops

Samuel was born in 1831. He married Sarah C. Griffith on December 29, 1857, and they had two boys: Charles G. (1860) and Zadac V. (1861). Samuel enlisted in Davie County at age 30, July 15, 1862, for the war. He was present or accounted for until transferred to Company F, 13th Regiment, N.C. Troops (3rd Regiment, N.C. Volunteers) July 25, 1864. Upon transferring to Company F, 13th Regiment, Samuel either deserted or was captured at Point of Rocks, Virginia, August 13, 1864. He was confined at Fort Monroe, Virginia, until transferred to Point Lookout, Maryland, August 16, 1864. He was paroled at Point Lookout and transferred to Boulware's Wharf, James River, Virginia, where he was received March 19, 1865, for exchange. He died at age 59, on September 9, 1891. Samuel and Sarah were buried in Yadkin Valley Baptist Church Cemetery.

1001. Tacket, John G.
Private, Captain William E. Booe's Partisan Rangers • N.C. Volunteers • Company H, 63rd Regiment • (5th Regiment N.C. Cavalry) • N.C. Troops

John Tacket was born in 1841 in Davie County. He was the son of Samuel (1815, Stokes) and Nancy Gibson (1824, Davie) Tacket. Prior to the war, the family lived and farmed in the Smith Grove District of Davie County. John enlisted in Davie County on July 15, 1862, for the war. He was present or accounted for until he "deserted October 11, 1863." He was reported as "absent under guard for desertion" on March–April, 1864, muster roll and reported as a "deserter" on the July–August, 1864, muster roll. Federal Provost Martial records carry him as a "deserter" with the remark that he was "captured May 19, 1864." He was confined at Point Lookout, Maryland, until transferred to Elmira, New York, on July 3, 1864, where he died on April 28, 1865, of "variola" (smallpox). John's name is listed on the Memorial Monument for the Davie County men who died in the Civil War, 1861–1865.

1002. Taylor, Andrew Jackson
Private, 2nd Company B, 42nd Regiment • N.C. Troops

Andrew was born July 14, 1835, in Rowan County to Ashern and Piddie Sanders Taylor. He enlisted in Rowan County at age 25, on March 17, 1862, and three months later married Elizabeth Harris, June 9, in Davie County. His military record states that he was present or accounted for through October 1864. North Carolina records indicate that he was shot through the face at Bentonville in April 1865. He returned home to Davie County and Jerusalem District where he farmed to feed his increasing family. By 1880 there were six children in the household: Sarah (1865), Adelia (1868), Willie J. (1873), John H. T. (1875), Jesse F. (1877) and a son age three months. Their daughter Mary Taylor Howerton, was born on May 20, 1888, and lived her adult life in Cooleemee. Jack Taylor died in her home at 53 Duke Street, March 14, 1918. He is buried at Liberty United Methodist Church Cemetery.

1003. Taylor, G.M. (Greenburg)
Private, Company H, 57th Regiment • N.C. Troops

Greenburg was born in Davie County in 1825. In 1850 he was a laborer on a farm owned by James and Cassey Latham, until he moved to Smith Grove and lived with the J.B. Nash family. He worked as a carpenter until he enlisted in Rowan County at age 37, on July 4, 1862, as a substitute. He was hospitalized at Richmond, Virginia, on November 9, 1862. He died in the hospital at Richmond on November 27, 1862, of "febris typhoides." G.M.'s name is listed on the

Memorial Monument for the Davie County men who died in the Civil War, 1861–1865.

1004. Taylor, Giles
Private, Company F, 42nd Regiment • N.C. Troops

Giles was born in 1830 in North Carolina. He married Luanda Seamont (1828, North Carolina) on November 28, 1849. In 1860 he lived with his wife and three children in the Mocksville District. The children were Lutiska (1854), Elizabeth (1857) and Mary A. (1859). Giles enlisted in Davie County at age 32, on March 18, 1862. He was present or accounted for until wounded by a mortar shell at Petersburg, Virginia, on or about July 5, 1864. He was hospitalized at Petersburg where he died of his wounds on July 7, 1864. Giles's name is listed on the Memorial Monument for the Davie County men who died in the Civil War, 1861–1865.

1005. Taylor, John
Private, Company F, 42nd Regiment • N.C. Troops

John enlisted in Davie County at age 27, March 18, 1862. He was present or accounted for through October 1864. He was paroled at Mocksville on June 7, 1865.

1006. Taylor, John
Private, "Davie Sweep Stakes" • Company G, 4th Regiment • N.C. State Troops

John resided in Davie County where he enlisted at age 23, June 4, 1861, for the war. He was wounded at Seven Pines, Virginia on May 31, 1862, and reported absent wounded until discharged March 13, 1863.

1007. Taylor, Walter
Private, Captain William E. Booe's Partisan Rangers • N.C. Volunteers • Company H, 63rd Regiment • (5th Regiment N.C. Cavalry) • N.C. Troops

Walter was born on April 5, 1843, in North Carolina, the son of W. Taylor (1810, Scotland) and Catherine (1811, Scotland). In 1860 the family farmed in the Shady Grove District of Davie County, where Walter enlisted at age 19, on July 15, 1862, for the war. He was present or accounted for through October 1864. He returned home to marry Jennie Foot on September 24, 1868. Their children were Archie (1871), John (1872), Maggie (1875) and Charlie (1877). They farmed in the Farmington District and later in Calahaln. Walter died June 2, 1890, and is buried in Smith Grove United Methodist Church Cemetery.

1008. Taylor, Wiley M.
Sergeant, Company M, 7th Regiment • Confederate Cavalry • Company E, 16th Battalion • N.C. Cavalry

Wiley enlisted in Davie County September 3, 1862, with the rank of 5th Sergeant. He transferred from Company M, 7th Regiment Confederate Cavalry to Company E, 16th Battalion N.C. Cavalry on July 11, 1864, with the rank of Sergeant while absent sick in the hospital. He was reduced to ranks July–August, 1864, and reported as absent sick through October 1, 1864. No further records.

1009. Taylor, William M.
Sergeant, Company E, 42nd Regiment • N.C. Troops

William was born in 1840 in Scotland, the son of Walter (1810, Scotland) and Catherine (1811, Scotland) Taylor. The family settled in the Shady Grove District of Davie County where they farmed. William enlisted in Davie County at age 22, March 18, 1862. He mustered in as a Private, was promoted to Corporal on December 31, 1863, and promoted to Sergeant on July 31, 1864. He was present or accounted for until captured at or near Wise's Forks, Kinston, North Carolina, on March 10, 1865. He was confined at Point Lookout, Maryland, on March 16, 1865, and released there two months later on May 15, 1865, after taking the Oath of Allegiance. William returned to his family who had moved to Fulton District, where he worked as a huckster. He married Catherine Barneycastle in Davie County on December 15, 1872. His daughter Catherine was born in 1873. William died on July 28, 1877, and is buried in Bethlehem United Methodist Church Cemetery.

1010. Teague, William P.
Private, Company F, 42nd Regiment • Hospital Steward • Field and Staff, 66th Regiment • N.C. Troops

In 1860 William was a student who lived in the Farmington District of Davie County. He lived with the Dr. J. W. Wiseman family and later married Mary Jane Wiseman on November 21, 1861. He enlisted in Forsyth County on February 18, 1863, for the war. He was present or accounted for until appointed Hospital Steward and transferred to the Field and Staff of the 66th Regiment, on January 26, 1864. He was paroled at Greensboro, North Carolina, on May 17, 1865. William and Mary had at least one child. There is an infant grave in Eaton's Baptist Church Cemetery that reads, "Infant Teague," child of Dr. and

Mrs. W. J. Teague [sic], no date given for birth, died on July 20, 1865. No further information.

1011. Terrell, D.W.
Corporal, Company B, 57th Regiment • N.C. Troops

D.W. resided in Davie County and enlisted at age 30, on July 4, 1862, for the war. He mustered in as Corporal. He died at Port Royal, Virginia, on February 25, 1863. Cause of death is not reported. D.W's name is not presently listed on the Memorial Monument for the Davie County men who died in the Civil War, 1861–1865.

1012. Tharpe, J.T.
Private, Company E, 42nd Regiment • N.C. Troops

J.T. enlisted in Davie County on September 27, 1862, for the war. He was present or accounted for until he deserted on September 8, 1863.

1013. Thomas, Daniel W.
Private, Company E, 42nd Regiment • N.C. Troops

Daniel was the son of Elijah (1800, Davie) and Elizabeth (1806, Davie) Thomas. He was born in 1842 in Davie County where his father was a farmer. He lived in the Mocksville District prior to enlisting at age 20, on March 18, 1862, for the war. He was present or accounted for through October 1864, and paroled at Mocksville on June 6, 1865. Daniel married Mary A. Walker on February 28, 1869, and they settled in the Farmington District of Davie County. Mary and Daniel were the parents of two children: Evan (1871) and John (1880). Daniel was the brother of Emanuel S. Thomas who also served in this company. He was also the brother of Evan J. and John B. Thomas.

1014. Thomas, E.J. (Evan Jackson)
Sergeant, Company M, 7th Regiment • Confederate Cavalry • Company E, 16th Battalion • N.C. Cavalry

Evan was born on December 12, 1832, in Davie County to Elijah (1800, Davie) and Elizabith [sic] (1806, Davie) Thomas. Evan married Laura Rice on October 2, 1859, and they lived in the Mocksville District where he farmed prior to enlisting there September 3, 1862, with the rank of Private. E. J. was transferred from Company M, 7th Regiment Confederate Cavalry to Company E, 16th Battalion N.C. Cavalry on July 11, 1864, as a Private. However, he was appointed Sergeant July–August, 1864, and was present or accounted for through October 1, 1864. His children were

Evan J. Thomas, 1832–1889 (Josephine Anderson and Joel Reese, Iredell County Public Library).

Charley (1861), John (1862), Van (1866), Atlas (1868) and Laura (1870). He farmed in Calahaln District in 1870. He was the brother of three other soldiers: Daniel W., Emanuel S. and John B. Thomas. Evan died on April 19, 1889, and is buried in Mount Bethel United Methodist Church Cemetery in Harmony.

1015. Thomas, Emanuel S.
Private, Company E, 42nd Regiment • N.C. Troops

Emanuel resided in Davie County where he enlisted on March 18, 1862. He was the son of Elijah (1800, Davie) and Elizabeth (1806, Davie) Thomas. He was present or accounted for through April 1864; he died at home in Davie County prior to September 1, 1864, of "fever contracted in camp." (The Salem *People's Press* of June 30, 1864, indicates he was wounded in action on June 1–15, 1864.) Emanuel's name is listed on the Memorial Monument for the Davie County men who died in the Civil War, 1861–1865. He was the brother of Daniel W., Evan J. and John B. Thomas who also served in the war.

1016. Thomas, John B.
Private, "Davie Greys" • Company F, 13th Regiment • (3rd Regiment, N.C. Volunteers) • N.C. Troops

John was born in 1839 to Elijah (1800, Davie) and Elizabeth (1806, Davie) Thomas. He resided in Davie County where he worked as a farmer/laborer prior to enlisting in Davie County at age 22, April 26, 1861. He was the brother of fellow soldiers Daniel W., Evan J., and Emanuel S. Thomas. He was present or accounted for until he died at Ben's Church, near Smithfield, Virginia, on or about July 26, 1861, of disease. John's name is listed on the Memorial Monument for the Davie County men who died in the Civil War, 1861–1865.

1017. Thomason, Willy W.
Captain, Company H • 77th Regiment, 19th Division • N.C. Militia 1861–1865

Willy was born in 1830 in North Carolina. He married Virginia C. Cuthrell (1841, North Carolina) on October 28, 1858, and they settled in Smith Grove where he worked as a teacher. Their son Victor was born in 1860. When the militia was activated, Willy was appointed Captain of Company H.

1018. Thompson, John
Private, "Guilford Guards" • 2nd Company E, 2nd Regiment • N.C. State Troops

John was born on October 18, 1834, in Davie County. He was the son of Hannah Thompson who lived in Liberty Township. Prior to the war he was a farmer; at age 28, March 27, 1862, he enlisted for the war. He was wounded at Malvern Hill, Virginia, on July 1, 1862. Through October 1864 he was present or accounted for on company muster rolls. John was captured in the hospital at Richmond, Virginia, on April 3, 1865, and confined at Newport News, Virginia, until released after taking the Oath of Allegiance on June 30, 1865. He returned home to Davie County where he made a living as a farmer until his death on January 8, 1903, in Jerusalem Township. He is buried in Jerusalem Baptist Church Cemetery.

1019. Thompson, Jonas
Private, Company B, Carolina Rangers • 10th Virginia Cavalry Regiment

Jonas was born in 1844 in Davie County to Hannah (1805, Davie) Thompson. He enlisted in Davie on January 17, 1862, at age 18. He was present or accounted for until he was wounded in action. No further details.

1020. Thompson, Joseph
Private, Company M, 7th Regiment • Confederate Cavalry • Company E, 16th Battalion • N.C. Cavalry

Joseph enlisted in Davie County on September 10, 1863, as a Private. He was transferred from Company M, 7th Regiment Confederate Cavalry to Company E, 16th Battalion N.C. Cavalry on July 11, 1864. He was present or accounted for through October 1, 1864.

1021. Thompson, Rufus R.
Private, Company E, 42nd Regiment • N.C. Troops

Rufus R. Thompson married Elizabeth M. Nail on July 14, 1853, in Davie County. He enlisted in Davie County at age 36 on March 18, 1862, with the rank of Private. He was present or accounted for until he died in the hospital at Petersburg, Virginia, January 10, 1863, of "ascites." Rufus's name is listed on the Memorial Monument for the Davie County men who died in the Civil War, 1861–1865.

1022. Thompson, William Graham
Second Lieutenant, "Davie Greys" • Company F, 13th Regiment • (3rd Regiment, N.C. Volunteers) • N.C. Troops

William was born in 1842 in Rowan County. He was the son of William A. (1812, Rowan) and Elizabeth (1812, Rowan) Thompson. They resided in Davie County where they farmed. William G. enlisted in Davie County at age 19, April 26, 1861. He mustered in as a Private and was promoted to First Sergeant on April 28, 1862, then to Third Lieutenant on April 12, 1863. He was present or accounted for until wounded in the thigh at Chancellorsville, Virginia, May 3, 1863. He rejoined the company in March–April, 1864, and was promoted to Second Lieutenant. He was present or accounted for until paroled at Appomattox Court House, Virginia, April 9, 1865.

1023. Thorn, T.J.
Private, Company M, 7th Regiment • Confederate Cavalry • Company E, 16th Battalion • N.C. Cavalry

T.J. enlisted in Davie County on December 22, 1862, with the rank of Private. He was transferred from Company M, 7th Regiment Confederate Cavalry to Company E, 16th Battalion N.C. Cavalry, on July 11, 1864. He was present or accounted for through October 1, 1864.

1024. Thornton, George
Private, Company B, Carolina Rangers • 10th Virginia Cavalry Regiment

According to the date on his tombstone, George was born February 8, 1841. His parents were James (1815, Davie) and Martha (1817, Stokes) Thornton. They resided in the Mocksville District of Davie County where George was a student prior to enlisting; the place and date of enlistment are not given. His military record states only that he was issued clothing on December 13, 1864, and that he was paroled in Mocksville on June 9, 1865. He married Lourena (Louisa) Hege on December 24, 1867. Their sons were Alexander (1869) and Pleasant (1879). The family lived in Fulton District where George farmed but later moved to Shady Grove Township where in 1890 he was included in the Confederate Veterans Census. He died June 4, 1908, and is buried in Quaker Cemetery. The tombstone states that he was the husband of "Sarah J. Thornton."

1025. Todd, David
Private, Captain William E. Booe's Partisan Rangers • N.C. Volunteers • Company H, 63rd Regiment • (5th Regiment N.C. Cavalry) • N.C. Troops

David enlisted in Davie County at age 21, July 14, 1862, for the war. He was wounded in the left knee at Upperville, Virginia, on June 21, 1863, and admitted to the hospital at Richmond, Virginia, on July 18, 1863. He was present or accounted for through February 1865. No further information.

1026. Todd, William
Private, Captain William E. Booe's Partisan Rangers • N.C. Volunteers • Company H, 63rd Regiment • (5th Regiment N.C. Cavalry) • N.C. Troops

William enlisted in Davie County on July 18, 1862, for the war. He was present or accounted for through October 1862. No further information.

1027. Totten, John C., Jr.
Private, "Davie Greys" • Company F, 13th Regiment • (3rd Regiment, N.C. Volunteers) • Company A, 13th Regiment • (3rd Regiment, N.C. Volunteers) • N.C. Troops

John was born in 1835. He resided in Davie County or Caswell County and was by occupation a farmer prior to enlisting in Davie County at age 26, August 6, 1861. He was present or accounted for until captured at South Mountain, Maryland, September 14, 1862. He was confined at Fort Delaware, Delaware, until transferred to Aiken's Landing, James River, Virginia, October 2, 1862, for exchange and declared exchanged at Aiken's Landing on November 10, 1862. He was transferred to Company A of this regiment on December 15, 1862. He was present or accounted for until wounded in the leg at Gettysburg, Pennsylvania, on July 1–3, 1863. John died in the hospital at Danville, Virginia, on July 19, 1863, of "typhoid fever." John's name is not presently listed on the Memorial Monument for the Davie County men who died in the Civil War, 1861–1865.

1028. Travillion, Meekins (Mickeus)
Private, "Davie Sweep Stakes" • Company G, 4th Regiment • N.C. State Troops

Meekins was born in 1827 in Albemarle County, Virginia. He made his home with the Berry Foster family in the Smith Grove District. He enlisted in Davie County at age 34, June 4, 1861, for the war. He died at Guinea Station, Virginia, February 5–6, 1863, or "at home" on April 17, 1863. Cause of death was not reported. Meekins's name is listed on the Memorial Monument for the Davie County men who died in the Civil War, 1861–1865.

1029. Tucker, Daniel Seaborn
First Lieutenant, Company D • 77th Regiment, 19th Division • N.C. Militia 1861–1865

Daniel was born in 1832 in Davidson County. By 1850 he lived with his mother Mary (1806, Davidson) and his brother Frederick, age 13, in Davie County, where he supported the family by farming. He married Louisa Markland, his neighbor, on March 18, 1852. When the militia was activated, he was appointed First Lieutenant of Company D while living in the Smith Grove District. Following the war Daniel moved his growing family to Jerusalem District and then to Fulton. He and Louisa were the parents of seven children by 1880: Frederick P. (1855), Palena S. (1857), Calidonia (1859), Vance (1862), George (1865), William (1868) and Richard (1873). David died on October 27, 1893, and is buried in Advance United Methodist Church Cemetery.

1030. Tucker, Frederick M.
First Corporal, Company B, Carolina Rangers • 10th Virginia Cavalry Regiment

Frederick was born in 1837 in Davie County to Mary (1806, Davidson) Tucker. He worked as a trader in the Shady Grove District of Davie County where he enlisted on May 12, 1862, as a Private. He was promoted to Third Corporal; then promoted to First Corporal. He was present or accounted for, often leaving on horse detail to replace the horses that had been lost. He was wounded in action circa June 30, 1864, and absent sick with dysentery and typhoid fever in Richmond hospital on July 20, 1864. On August 30, 1864, he was furloughed to Fulton District for 40 days. No further record.

1031. Tucker, John
Private, Company B, 57th Regiment • N.C. Troops

John resided in Davie County and enlisted in Rowan County at age 32, on July 4, 1862, for the war. He was hospitalized at Richmond, Virginia, on October 25, 1862, with debility. He died in the hospital at Richmond on January 5, 1863, of "variola and pneumonia." John's name is not presently listed on the Memorial Monument for the Davie County men who died in the Civil War, 1861–1865.

1032. Tucker, Thomas D.
Private, Company B, 57th Regiment • N.C. Troops

Thomas resided in Davie County and enlisted in Rowan County at age 19, on July 4, 1862, for the war. He was reported present through October 31, 1862. Thomas was killed in Fredericksburg, Virginia, on December 13, 1862. Thomas's name is not presently listed on the Memorial Monument for the Davie County men who died in the Civil War, 1861–1865.

1033. Turner, Edmond D.
Private, "Davie Sweep Stakes" • Company G, 4th Regiment • N.C. State Troops

Edmond was born in 1841. He resided in Davie County where he enlisted at age 20, June 4, 1861, for the war. He was wounded in the right thigh and right arm at Seven Pines, Virginia, May 31, 1862. He married Coney L. Poplin, August 26, 1863. He was reported absent wounded through August 1864 and paroled at Mocksville on June 9, 1865. Edmond worked as a harness maker and Coney "kept house" for their growing family: Mary C. (1865), Carolina F. (1868), Henry M. (1869), William D. (1873) and Mittie E. (1879).

1034. Turner, Esquire
Private, Company F, 42nd Regiment • N.C. Troops

Esquire enlisted in Davie County on July 1, 1863, for the war. He was present or accounted for until wounded in the right knee in an unspecified action on July 3, 1864. He was hospitalized at Richmond, Virginia, where he died on August 8, 1864, of wounds. Esquire's name is listed on the Memorial Monument for the Davie County men who died in the Civil War, 1861–1865.

1035. Turner, George Washington
Private, Company F, 42nd Regiment • N.C. Troops

George was born in Davie County in 1831. He was the son of Alexander Turner (1793, Maryland) who was a mechanic and farmer. Prior to the war they resided in the Calahaln District where George married Adeline Gentle on October 11, 1860. He enlisted in Davie County at age 29, March 18, 1862. He was present or accounted for until he died in the hospital at Petersburg, Virginia, on or about October 9, 1862, of "diarrhoea." George's name is listed on the Memorial Monument for the Davie County men who died in the Civil War, 1861–1865.

1036. Turner, Henry
Private, "Davie Sweep Stakes" • Company G, 4th Regiment • N.C. State Troops

Henry was born in 1833. He married Martha C. (1842, North Carolina) and they lived in the Liberty District of Davie County where he worked as a ditcher prior to enlisting at age 28, June 4, 1861, for the war. He deserted July 18, 1861, but was reported "in confinement" from October 19, 1861, through December 1861. He was present or accounted for from April 30, 1862, until reported absent without leave through August 1864.

1037. Turner, J.A.
Private, Company M, 7th Regiment • Confederate Cavalry • Company E, 16th Battalion • N.C. Cavalry

J.A. was born in 1848 in Davie County. He was the son of Alexander (1792, Maryland) and Mary A. (1822, Cabarrus) Turner. Military records show that J.A. was transferred from Company M, 7th Regiment, on July 11, 1864, while absent in confinement at Point Lookout, Maryland, as a prisoner of war. J.A. died at Point Lookout, Maryland, of "phthisis" (tuberculosis) on February 13, 1865. J.A.'s name is listed on the Memorial Monument for the Davie County men who died in the Civil War, 1861–1865.

1038. Turner, Pinkney (Pinckney)
Private, "Davie Greys" • Company F, 13th Regiment • (3rd Regiment, N.C. Volunteers) • N.C. Troops

Pinkney was born November 30, 1838, in Davie County. He was the son of Alexander (1792, Maryland) Turner. In 1860 they lived in the Mocksville District of Davie County where Pinkney taught school. He enlisted at age 27, August 26, 1861, and was present or accounted for until captured at Falling Waters, Maryland, July 14, 1863. He was confined at Point Lookout, Maryland, until paroled and transferred at City Point,

Certificate of Release of Prisoner of War.

HEAD QUARTERS, POINT LOOKOUT, MD.

Provost Marshal's Office, June 21st, 1865.

I hereby Certify, That Pinckney Turner Prisoner of War, having this day taken the Oath of Allegiance to the UNITED STATES, as prescribed by the President in his proclamation of December 8th, 1863, is in conformity with instructions from the War Department, hereby released and discharged.

In witness whereof, I hereunto affix my official Signature and Stamp.

Maj. and Provost Marshal.

United States of America.

I, Pinckney Turner, of the County of Davie, State of NC, do solemnly swear that I will support, protect, and defend the Constitution and Government of the United States against all enemies, whether domestic or foreign; that I will bear true faith, allegiance, and loyalty to the same, any ordinance, resolution, or laws of any State, Convention, or Legislature, to the contrary notwithstanding; and further, that I will faithfully perform all the duties which may be required of me by the laws of the United States; and I take this oath freely and voluntarily, without any mental reservation or evasion whatever.

P. Turner

Subscribed and sworn to before me, this twenty first day of June A. D. 1865.

Maj. and Provost Marshal.

The above-named has fair complexion, black hair, and blue eyes; and is 5 feet 10 inches high.

Top: Pinkney Turner's Certificate of Release from Prison (Davie County Public Library). *Bottom:* Pinkney Turner's Oath of Allegiance (Davie County Public Library).

Virginia, where he was received March 6, 1864, for exchange. He was reported absent without leave until he rejoined the company in July–August, 1864, and was present or accounted for until captured at Appomattox, Virginia, April 6, 1865. He was confined at Point Lookout, Maryland, until released on June 21, 1865, after taking the Oath of Allegiance. By 1870 Pinkney had resumed his life in Davie County where he lived and taught in Calahaln. He and Sallie S. Brown were married on October 18, 1871; their daughter Hettie was born in 1876. Pinkney died on July 7, 1927. He is buried in Turner Family Cemetery.

1039. Turrentine (Terrentine), William F.
Private, Company A, 57th Regiment • N.C. Troops

William was born in 1830 in Davie County. He married Hannah C. (1832, North Carolina) Foster on October 31, 1850; their children were James (1852), Lucy J. (1854), John F. (1858) and Margaret (1860). William worked as an overseer in the Mocksville District prior to enlisting at age 32, on July 4, 1862, in Rowan County for the war. He was killed at Fredericksburg, Virginia, on December 13, 1862. William's name is listed on the Memorial Monument for the Davie County men who died in the Civil War, 1861–1865.

1040. Tutarno (Tutterow), A.P.
Private, Company M, 7th Regiment • Confederate Cavalry • Company E, 16th Battalion • N.C. Cavalry

A.P. was born in North Carolina on September 6, 1830. He worked as a farmer in the Chinquepin District prior to enlisting in Davie County, September 3, 1862, with the rank of Private. He transferred from Company M, 7th Regiment Confederate Cavalry to Company E, 16th Battalion N.C. Cavalry on July 11, 1864. He was present or accounted for through October 1, 1864, and paroled at Salisbury, North Carolina, in 1865. He and Nancy M. Parish were married November 27, 1856. He died January 14, 1914, and is buried in New Union United Methodist Church Cemetery. His tombstone indicates that he was "Reverend."

1041. Tutarow (Tutterow), Thomas P.
Private, Company M, 7th Regiment • Confederate Cavalry • Company E, 16th Battalion • N.C. Cavalry

T.P. enlisted in Davie County on September 3, 1862, with the rank of Private. He was transferred from Company M, 7th Regiment Confederate Cavalry to Company E, 16th Battalion N.C. Cavalry on July 11, 1864, while absent in confinement at Point Lookout, Maryland, as a prisoner of war. He was transferred to Elmira, New York, August 15, 1864, where he died on January 23, 1865, of "pneumonia." Thomas's name is listed on the Memorial Monument for the Davie County men who died in the Civil War, 1861–1865.

1042. Tutrow (Tutterow), Thomas J.
Private, Company B, Carolina Rangers • 10th Virginia Cavalry Regiment

Thomas was born in 1842 in Davie County to Jacob (1813, Davie) and Caroline (1813, Iredell) Tutterow. His father was a blacksmith and Thomas was a farmer in the Calahaln District where he enlisted on November 8, 1861, at age 18. He married Mary Ann Chaffin/Hunter on March 13, 1862. He then was present or accounted for until he was wounded in action, his leg being amputated, before October 1, 1864. He died of "tetanus trauma" in Kittrell Springs, North Carolina, on October 2, 1864, and is buried there. Thomas's name is listed on the Memorial Monument for the Davie County men who died in the Civil War, 1861–1865.

1043. Tuttarow (Tutorow) (Tuterow), George W.
Private, Company F, 13th Regiment • (3rd Regiment, N.C. Volunteers) • N.C. Troops

George was born in 1840, the son of Jacob (1813, Davie) and Caroline (1813, Iredell) Tutarow. He lived in Calahaln with his parents and worked as a blacksmith prior to enlisting at age 20, April 26, 1861, in Davie County. He was present or accounted for until wounded near Richmond, Virginia, in March–June, 1862. The battle in which he was wounded was not reported. George rejoined the company in November–December, 1862, and was present or accounted for until wounded at Chancellorsville, Virginia, on May 3, 1863. He rejoined the company in January–February, 1864, and was present or accounted for until paroled at Appomattox Court House, Virginia, on April 9, 1865. After the war, George returned to Calahaln and to his blacksmith occupation. He and Mary E. Watts were married soon after and they came parents of five children: Almeda C. (1873), Sarah A. (1874), Thomas W. (1877), William L. (1878) and John W. (7 months). George died in 1899 and is buried in Center United Methodist Church Cemetery.

1044. Tutterow (Tuttarow), John V. (B.)
Private, "Davie Greys" • Company F, 13th Regiment • (3rd Regiment, N.C. Volunteers) • N.C. Troops

John was born April 5, 1839, in Davie County, the son of Jacob (1813, Davie) and Caroline (Catharine) (1813, Iredell) Tutterow. They lived and worked in the Calahaln District where John was a farmer and his father was a "smith." On August 6, 1861, at age 21, he enlisted in Davie County. He was present or accounted for until wounded in the left ankle at Gettysburg, Pennsylvania, July 1, 1863. He rejoined the company in March–April, 1864, and was present or accounted for until wounded in the right lung at Spotsylvania Court House, Virginia, May 10, 1864. After rejoining the company in July–August, 1864, he was present or accounted for until captured near Petersburg, Virginia, March 25, 1865, and confined at Point Lookout, Maryland, until released on June 21, 1865, after taking the Oath of Allegiance. John returned to Davie County where he farmed. He married Martha J. Warren Kerfeese on December 10, 1867. Four years later Martha died, leaving a son, John L. Kerfeese (1859) from her previous marriage, and another son, Austin Hall Tutterow (1868), the son of Martha and John V. On February 25, 1875, John V. married Margaret A. (Louise M.) Foster and in 1879 their daughter Meaky J. was born. John died on December 20, 1923, and is buried in Center United Methodist Church Cemetery.

1045. Tutterow, William Nelson
Private, Company F, 42nd Regiment • N.C. Troops

William was born in 1843 in Davie County. He was the son of David B. (1813, Davie) and Mary (1815, Davie) Tuterow [sic]. In 1860 the family farmed in the Mocksville District of Davie County where on March 18, 1862, William enlisted at age 19. He was present or accounted for until wounded in the right thigh in an unspecified action on June 10, 1864. He was hospitalized at Farmville, Virginia. He returned to duty in September–October, 1864, and was paroled at Mocksville on June 5, 1865. William married Nancy L. Richardson on December 20, 1866; their son David was born in 1868. William died on March 20, 1869. He is buried in Center United Methodist Church Cemetery. In 1870 Nancy and her small son had returned to her parents' home (David C. and Mary B. Richardson), where Nancy served as a "domestic servant" to the family of ten members.

1046. Tutterow, William W.
Private, Company F, 42nd Regiment • N.C. Troops

William was born February 19, 1819, in Davie County to David (1790, Davie) and Ruth (1790, Davie) Tutterow. They farmed in the Mocksville District where William enlisted at age 42, on March 24, 1862. He was present or accounted for until discharged on October 24, 1862, by reason of "general debility, dyspepsia and mental imbecility." He returned to Davie County where he lived and farmed in the Calahaln District. In 1880 William and his sister Lieusendy were living with his ninety-year-old father. William died on May 23, 1897. He is buried in Center United Methodist Church Cemetery.

1047. Tysinger (Teringer), Henry H.
Private, Company E, 42nd Regiment • N.C. Troops

Henry was born in Randolph County circa 1841, the son of Peter (1821, North Carolina) and Frances (1820, North Carolina) Teringer (Tysinger). They farmed in Fulton District in Davie County where Henry enlisted at age 19, March 18, 1862. He was present or accounted for through April 1864. He died in the hospital near Petersburg, Virginia, prior to September 1, 1864. The cause of death was not reported. Both Henry and his brother William served in this company and both men died. Henry's name is listed on the Memorial Monument for the Davie County men who died in the Civil War, 1861–1865.

1048. Tysinger (Teringer), William
Sergeant, Company E, 42nd Regiment • N.C. Troops

William was born in 1842 in North Carolina, to Peter (1821, North Carolina) and Frances (1820, North Carolina) Teringer (Tysinger). William lived with his family in Fulton District where he helped his father farm. William enlisted in Davie County at age 18, on March 18, 1862. He mustered in as a Private and was promoted to Sergeant prior to July 1, 1862. He was present or accounted for until he died in the hospital at Petersburg, Virginia, on September 19, 1862, of "febris continua." Both William and his brother Henry served in this company and both men died. William's name is listed on the Memorial Monument for the Davie County men who died in the Civil War, 1861–1865.

1049. Van Eaton, Barton R.
Private, Company B, Carolina Rangers • 10th Virginia Cavalry Regiment

Barton was born in 1842 in Davie County to John (1793, Davie) and Lydia (1803, Rowan) Van Eaton. His father was a prosperous farmer in the Farmington District and Barton was a farmhand when he enlisted in Davie County on October 29, 1861, at age 18. He was present or accounted for. He was absent in the Richmond hospital on September 1, 1862, furloughed for 40 days September 17, 1862, and sick in the Lynchburg hospital May 8, 1863. He surrendered at Appomattox Court House on April 9, 1865.

1050. Van Eaton, F.M.
Private, Company A, 57th Regiment • N.C. Troops

F.M. was born in Davie County in 1838. He resided in Davie County and was a farmer before enlisting in Rowan County for the war, at age 24, on July 4, 1862. He was reported present or accounted for through October 31, 1863, but was captured at Rappahannock Station, Virginia, on November 7, 1863. He was sent to Washington, D.C., then confined at Point Lookout, Maryland, on November 11, 1863, and was paroled there on March 16, 1864. He was received at City Point, Virginia, on March 20, 1864, for exchange. He returned to duty subsequent to April 30, 1864, but was captured at Winchester, Virginia, on July 20, 1864. He was confined at Camp Chase, Ohio, on July 28, 1864, and paroled there on or about March 2, 1865. He was received at Boulware's and Cox's Wharves on the James River, Virginia, on March 10–12, 1865, for exchange. No further records.

1051. Van Eaton, James M.
Private, Company F, 42nd Regiment • N.C. Troops

James was born in Davie County in 1836. He was the son of John (1793, Davie) and Lydia (1803, Rowan) Van Eaton. James married Susan R. Ferebee, February 7, 1861, and they settled in the Farmington District of Davie County where he enlisted at age 26, March 25, 1862. He was mustered in as a Corporal but was reduced to ranks in May–June, 1863. He was present or accounted for until he was wounded by a "fragment of a mortar shell inflicting a severe wound on the left side of the head and tearing the left ear off," near Petersburg, Virginia, on or about July 5, 1864. He was hospitalized at Richmond, Virginia, where he died on July 18, 1864, of wounds. James's name is listed on the Memorial Monument for the Davie County men who died in the Civil War, 1861–1865. (He is listed on the Memorial as "James M. Van.")

1052. Van Eaton, McDonald
Private, Company B, Carolina Rangers • 10th Virginia Cavalry Regiment

McDonald was born in 1843 in Davie County to Abraham (1806, Davie) and Cloe (1815, Davie) Van Eaton. He was a farmer in the Mocksville District of Davie County when he enlisted in Company C, 2nd N.C. Cavalry, Iredell County on June 29, 1861, at age 28. He transferred to Company B, 10th Virginia Cavalry on February 1, 1863. He was present or accounted for through 1864. No further record. He returned to Davie County where he married Malinda Wagner on November 8, 1865. He received a pension in Boone County, Arkansas, and he died on March 29, 1909.

1053. Van Eaton, Richard T.
Private, Company H, 57th Regiment • N.C. Troops

Richard was born in 1836. He resided in Davie County where he lived with Mumford and Temperance Bean. In 1860 Richard was living in Liberty District where he worked as a carpenter and where he married Mary C. Holman on October 30, 1860. He enlisted in Rowan County at age 25, on July 4, 1862, for the war. He was present or accounted for through February 28, 1865. He surrendered at Appomattox Court House, Virginia, on April 9, 1865. He was "a most gallant soldier" (Clark's *Regiments* Vol. III, p. 428). Their children were: Sarah (1863), Alice C. (1862), John Lee (1867), Willie F. (1871) and Mattie J. (1877). Richard died on August 30, 1925, and is buried in Bethel United Methodist Church Cemetery.

1054. Van Zant (Vancham), Enoch C.
Private, Company H, 57th Regiment • N.C. Troops

Enoch was born in North Carolina in 1835. He resided in Davie County where he worked as a farmer and was married to Sarah (1841, North Carolina). They lived and farmed in the Mocksville District where at age 27, on July 4, 1862, he enlisted for the war. He was reported absent sick on August 25 and September 26, 1862. He returned to duty prior to November 1, 1862. He was reported at home on sick furlough in November–December, 1862. He returned to duty in January–February, 1863, then was reported absent without leave on May 17–October 31, 1863. He returned to duty in November–December, 1863.

Enoch was reported on detail at Kinston, North Carolina, as a blacksmith in March 1864–February 1865. He survived the war.

1055. Veach, William E.
Private, Company H, 57th Regiment • N.C. Troops

William was born in Davie County in 1844. He was the son of William (1812, Davie) and Elizabeth (1816, Davie). At age 18, William enlisted in Davie County for the war on July 4, 1862. He was hospitalized at Richmond, Virginia, on November 9, 1862, then furloughed for 30 days on December 8, 1862. He returned to duty in January–February, 1863. William was hospitalized again at Danville, Virginia, on June 18, 1863, with intermittent fever and transferred to Salisbury, North Carolina, on June 25, 1863. After returning to duty prior to September 1, 1863, he was captured at Rappahannock Station, Virginia, on November 7, 1863. William was confined at Point Lookout, Maryland, May 3, 1864. He was received at Aiken's Landing, James River, Virginia, on May 8, 1864, for exchange. On December 2, 1864, he was reported absent without leave. On May 19, 1865, he was paroled at Salisbury, North Carolina. William married Sarah Ann Foster on January 17, 1867. By 1880 they had four children: Mary E. (1868), Sarah J. (1872), Annie B. (1877) and Willie Mc (1880). In 1880 they were living and farming in Jerusalem District. William is buried in Liberty United Methodist Church Cemetery. His tombstone reads: William E. Veach, Company H, 57th Inf. CSA, no dates given.

1056. Verher (Vesler), Peter
Private, Company F, 13th Regiment • (3rd Regiment, N.C. Volunteers) • N.C. Troops

Peter enlisted at Camp Holmes on January 11, 1864, for the war. He was present or accounted for until wounded at Wilderness, Virginia, May 5, 1864. He died in September–October, 1864, of wounds. The place of death was not reported. Peter's name is listed on the Memorial Monument for the Davie County men who died in the Civil War, 1861–1865. His name is listed as Peter Vesler.

1057. Verner, Hardy
Private, Company M, 7th Regiment • Confederate Cavalry • Company E, 16th Battalion • N.C. Cavalry

Hardy enlisted in Davie County on September 3, 1862, with the rank of Private. He was transferred from Company M, 7th Regiment Confederate Cavalry to Company E, 16th Battalion N.C. Cavalry on July 11, 1864, while absent in confinement at Point Lookout, Maryland, as a prisoner of war. He remained at Point Lookout until paroled and exchanged at Varina, Virginia, September 22, 1864. He and his wife Emily had one daughter prior to the war: Margaret S. Verner, December 2, 1857. All three are buried at New Union United Methodist Church Cemetery.

1058. Vinagum, Daniel V.
Private, Company F, 13th Regiment • (3rd Regiment, N.C. Volunteers) • N.C. Troops

Daniel resided in Davie County and was by occupation a tailor prior to enlisting in Davie County at age 21, on April 26, 1861. He was present or accounted for until wounded at South Mountain, Maryland, September 14, 1862. He was reported on detail as a teamster from October 25, 1862, through October 1863. He rejoined the company in November–December, 1863, and was present or accounted for until wounded at or near Petersburg, Virginia, on June 22, 1864. He rejoined the company in September–October, 1864, and was present or accounted for until paroled at Appomattox Court House, Virginia, on April 9, 1865.

1059. Vinagum (Venagmes), Thomas V.
Private, "Davie Greys" • Company F, 13th Regiment • (3rd Regiment, N.C. Volunteers) • N.C. Troops

Thomas was born in 1838 in South Carolina. He married Catharine Jones on December 25, 1859, in Davie County where he worked as a tobacconist in the Liberty District. Thomas and Catharine had one son, Henry (1861); Thomas enlisted at age 22, April 26, 1861, in Davie County. He was present or accounted for until wounded at Gettysburg, Pennsylvania, on July 1, 1863, and died in the hospital at Staunton, Virginia, August 28, 1863, of wounds. The Roll of Honor indicates that he "distinguished himself as a scout in several hard fought battles." Thomas's name is listed on the Memorial Monument for the Davie County men who died in the Civil War, 1861–1865.

1060. Vogler, John Emory
Private, Company G, 7th Regiment • Confederate Cavalry • Company D, 16th Battalion • N.C. Cavalry

John enlisted in Davie County on September 3, 1862, with the rank of Private. He was transferred from Company G, 7th Regiment Confederate Cavalry to Company D, 16th Battalion N.C. Cavalry on July 11, 1864. He was captured at Fort Harrison, Virginia, on September 30, 1864, and confined at Point Lookout, Maryland. No further records.

1061. Vogler, Mathew D.
Private, Company G, 7th Regiment • Confederate Cavalry • Company D, 16th Battalion • N.C. Cavalry

Mathew enlisted in Davie County on September 3, 1862, with the rank of Private. He was transferred from Company G, 7th Regiment Confederate Cavalry to Company D, 16th Battalion N.C. Cavalry on July 11, 1864. He was present accounted for through October 1, 1864.

1062. Von Eaton, John I.
Sergeant, "Davie Greys" • Company F, 13th Regiment • (3rd Regiment, N.C. Volunteers) • N.C. Troops

John was born in Davie County in 1838, the son of Abraham (1806, Davie) and Cloe (1815, Davie) Von Eaton. He resided as a farmer in the Liberty District in 1860. At age 22, he enlisted in Davie County on April 26, 1861. John was mustered in as Sergeant. He was present or accounted for until "killed by the accidental discharge of his own gun" near Orange Court House, Virginia, on November 29, 1862. John's name is listed on the Memorial Monument for the Davie County men who died in the Civil War, 1861–1865.

1063. Von Eaton, Samuel P.
Private, "Davie Greys" • Company F, 13th Regiment • (3rd Regiment, N.C. Volunteers) • N.C. Troops

Samuel lived in Davie County where he was born in 1824 to John (1793, Davie) and Lydia (1803, Rowan) Von Eaton. He was a student living at home with his parents in Farmington on June 18, 1861, when he enlisted for the war. He was present or accounted for until he died in the hospital at Richmond, Virginia, on July 1, 1862, of "continued fever." Samuel's name is listed on the Memorial Monument for the Davie County men who died in the Civil War, 1861–1865.

1064. Wadkins, William H. (Henderson)
Private, Co. E, 42nd Regiment • N.C. Troops

William was born in Davidson County in 1836. He resided in the Liberty District where he made a living working as a laborer-farmer; he was married to Sarah (1835, North Carolina). On March 18, 1862, at age 26, he enlisted in Davie County. William was present or accounted for through October 1864. He was paroled at Salisbury, North Carolina, on May 22, 1865. He returned home where the family worked at farming in the Jerusalem District. William and Sarah were the parents of six children: Margaret (1856), DeWitt(1858), Ellen (1859), Turner (1865), Thomas (1868) and Cora (1871).

1065. Waggoner (Wagner), David
Private, Company F, 42nd Regiment • N.C. Troops

David was born in 1819 in Davidson County. In 1850 he, his wife Anna (1824, Granville), and two children John (1843, Stokes) and Catharine (1848, Davie) were living in Davie County where David worked as a laborer. (Marriage records show that David married Hanevic Orrell on August 26, 1854. This date probably should read 1844.) In 1860 the family lived in Shady Grove District where David worked as a carpenter. Emma had been born in 1858 and David had married Summerfield (1837, North Carolina). David enlisted in Davie County at age 43, March 24, 1862. He was present or accounted for through October 1864. He was paroled at Mocksville on June 9, 1865. By 1870 three more children had been born: Fannie (1861), Mary (1866) and David (1870). The family lived in the Fulton District where David, at age 49, continued to farm. David's son John H. also served in this company.

1066. Waggoner (Wagner), John H.
Corporal, Company F, 42nd Regiment • N.C. Troops

John was born in Stokes County in 1843. He was the son of David (1819, Davidson) and Anna (1824, Granville) Orrell Waggoner. In 1860 the family was living in the Shady Grove District where John worked as a laborer. He enlisted in Davie County at age 19, on March 18, 1862. He was mustered in as a Private, and promoted to Corporal in May–June, 1863. He was present or accounted for until killed near Bermuda Hundred, Virginia, on May 20, 1864. John and his father David served in this company and regiment. John's name is listed on the Memorial Monument for the Davie County men who died in the Civil War, 1861–1865.

1067. Wagner, Henry M., Jr.
Second Corporal, Company B, Carolina Rangers • 10th Virginia Cavalry Regiment

Henry was born in 1841 in Davie County to

William (1776, Cabarrus) and Catherine (1813, Cabarrus) Wagner. They lived in the Fulton District of Davie County where his father farmed and Henry worked as a laborer prior to enlisting on October 29, 1861, at age 20. He had a rather checkered military tour of duty. Initially he followed the routine of being present or being accounted for on detached duty, and was appointed Third Corporal on March 1, 1863. He was then present two months and absent sick two months, and was promoted to Second Corporal. He was present September–October, 1863, then lost his horse. He was reduced to Private on October 31, 1863, detailed to Lee's Brigade January–February, 1864, absent in arrest March–April, 1864, and a prisoner in state prison July–August, 1864. No further record.

1068. Wagner, Henry M., Sr.
Private, Company B, Carolina Rangers • 10th Virginia Cavalry Regiment

Henry was born in 1839 in Davie County to John (1814, Cabarrus) and Mary (1814, Cabarrus) Wagner. His father was a farmer and Henry was a laborer in the Fulton District of Davie County where he enlisted October 29, 1861, at age 22. He was present through April 30, 1862. On October 22, 1862, he was captured at Hedgesville, West Virginia, and sent to Fort McHenry, Maryland, where he was exchanged on November 10, 1862. Again he was present or his absences were accounted for. He was sick with typhoid fever in a Richmond hospital on June 24, 1864, and returned to duty on August 3, 1864, but became sick again through August 31, 1864. He was present through January 27, 1865, and was paroled at Salisbury, North Carolina, in May 1865. Henry received a pension in Boone County, Arkansas. He died on October 11, 1921.

1069. Wagner, Jacob
Private, "Davie Sweep Stakes" • Company G, 4th Regiment • N.C. State Troops

Jacob was born in 1837, probably in Cabarrus County. He married Mary Gabbard (1827, Davie) on March 26, 1850, in Davie County where they resided when he enlisted at age 24, June 4, 1861, for the war. He was wounded at Gaines' Mill, Virginia, June 27, 1862. He rejoined the company prior to September 27, 1862, when he was confined at Old Capitol Prison, Washington, D.C. The place and date of capture were not reported. He was exchanged prior to October 8, 1862, and present or accounted for until wounded at Chancellorsville, Virginia, May 3, 1863, where he died, May 4–5, 1863, of wounds. Application and correspondence regarding his pension are on file at the State Archives, Raleigh, North Carolina, and also at Davie County Public Library in Mocksville. Jacob's name is listed on the Memorial Monument for the Davie County men who died in the Civil War, 1861–1865.

1070. Wagner, W.R. (William)
Private, "Davie Sweep Stakes" • Company G, 4th Regiment • N.C. State Troops

William was born in 1833 in Davie County. He enlisted at age 27, March 8, 1862, for the war. He was killed at Seven Pines, Virginia, May 31, 1862. W.R.'s name is listed on the Memorial Monument for the Davie County men who died in the Civil War, 1861–1865.

1071. Wagoner (Wagner), William
Private, Company E, 42nd Regiment • N.C. Troops

William was born in 1829 in Cabarrus County, the son of William (1776, Cabarrus) and Catherine (1813, Cabarrus) Wagner. He married Mary Jane Howard on November 22, 1853, and they lived in the Liberty District of Davie County where he enlisted in Davie County at age 33, on March 18, 1862. William was present or accounted for until wounded in the right side of the neck in an unspecified action on September 6, 1864. He was hospitalized at Richmond, Virginia, and furloughed for sixty days on September 24, 1864. No further records. William and Mary Jane were the parents of three girls: Mary C. (1853), Martha M. (1855) and Frances H. (1860). By 1880 they were living in the Jerusalem District where they lived and farmed with their daughter and son-in-law, Martha and Michael Swink.

1072. Walker, George Washington
Corporal, Company F, 42nd Regiment • N.C. Troops

George was born in North Carolina in 1836. He was a farmer in Davie County in the Calahaln District, where he married Liddi E. Martin on January 19, 1858. They had three children: Laura E. (1858), James D. (1861) and Martha L. (1863). George enlisted in Davie County at age 26, March 18, 1862. He mustered in as a Private and was promoted to Corporal in May–June, 1863. He was present or accounted for until wounded in the left thigh at or near Bermuda Hundred, Virginia, in May 1864. He returned to duty prior to September 1, 1864, was captured at or near Wise's Forks, Kinston, North Carolina, on March 10, 1865, confined at Point Lookout, Maryland, March 16, 1865, and released there on June 21, 1865, after taking the Oath of Allegiance. George returned to Calahaln and his family. He married Mary J. (1857) Fulcher on December 23, 1879.

1073. Walker, Henry G.
Sergeant, Company D, 42nd Regiment • N.C. Troops

Henry was born in 1841 in Davie County. In the 1850 census he resided with Mary Walker, Sarah and his brother and sisters. At age 19 he was a farm laborer living with Jacob and Sarah Sheek in the Mocksville District. At age 23 on January 31, 1862, he enlisted in Davie County. Henry was mustered in as a Private, then promoted to Corporal prior to July 1, 1862. He was promoted to Sergeant in September–December, 1862. Henry was present or accounted for until captured at Cold Harbor, Virginia, on June 1–3, 1864, and confined at Point Lookout, Maryland, July 11, 1864. He was transferred to Elmira, New York, where he arrived on July 17, 1864. Henry died at Elmira on January 1, 1865, of "pneumonia." Henry's name is listed on the Memorial Monument for the Davie County men who died in the Civil War, 1861–1865.

1074. Walker, James
Private, Company E, 42nd Regiment • N.C. Troops

James was born in Davie County on January 26, 1833, the son of Sarah Walker. In his early years he was a farmer in the Smith Grove District. He married Sarah P. Rich (1837) on January 3, 1859. On March 18, 1862, at age 27, he enlisted in Davie County. He was present or accounted for through October 1864, and was paroled at Mocksville on June 7, 1865. Sarah and James were the parents of three children: Sarah E. (1860), Isaac (1866) and Mary (1868). They made their home in the Farmington District, where James died February 18, 1872. He is buried in the Walker Family Cemetery.

1075. Walker, John W.
Corporal, Company D, 42nd Regiment • Captain William Howard's Company • N.C. Prison Guard • Third Lieutenant, 1st Company A • Salisbury Prison Guard • Third Lieutenant, "The Rough and Readys" • Company G, 66th Regiment • N.C. Troops

John was born in Davie County on November 3, 1839, to Vincent (1816, Davie) and Delpha (1821, Davie) Walker. He worked as a laborer in the Mocksville District prior to enlisting on February 2, 1862. On or about May 1, 1862, he transferred from Company D, 42nd Regiment, to

James Walker owned this home and land in 1858. After his safe return home from the war, he lived here until his death (Mohney, *The Historic Architecture of Davie County*).

Captain William Howard's Company, N.C. Prison Guard, with the rank of Corporal. He was serving as Third Lieutenant of 1st Company A, Salisbury Prison Guard when he transferred to Company G, 66th Regiment on October 2, 1863. He was reported present through April 30, 1864, but was hospitalized at Richmond, Virginia, July 24, 1864, with chronic diarrhoea and then a week later was furloughed for sixty days. He remained absent sick through October 31, 1864. He died on November 12, 1864. The place and cause of death are not given, but one source reported that he died of pneumonia on duty. He is buried at Center United Methodist Church Cemetery. John's name is not presently listed on the Memorial Monument for the Davie County men who died in the Civil War, 1861–1865.

1076. Walker, John W.
Private, Company E, 42nd Regiment • N.C. Troops

John was born on August 16, 1844, in Davie County. He was one of eleven children born to William (1797, Davie) and Anna (1870, Davie) Walker. They lived in the Shady Grove area of Davie County where William was a cooper and John was a laborer prior to the war. John enlisted in Davie County at age 19, January 19, 1863, for the war. He was present or accounted for through October 1864. He returned home where he married Jane Taylor on April 12, 1868. Six children followed: Catharine (1868), Charlie (1871), John A. (1872), Jenner R. (1874), Vance (1876) and Norah (1879). Jane died on August 25, 1886, and John married Martha Hanes, age 23, on March 1, 1888. He died on November 11, 1920; Martha died February 22, 1926. All three are buried in Bethlehem United Methodist Church Cemetery.

1077. Walker, R.A.
Private, Company G, 7th Regiment • Confederate Cavalry • Company D, 16th Battalion • N.C. Cavalry

R.A. enlisted in Davie County on September 3, 1862, with the rank of Private. He was transferred from Company G, 7th Regiment Confederate Cavalry to Company D, 16th Battalion N.C. Cavalry on July 11, 1864, while absent "detailed with artillery." He was absent on detail through August 1864, and present or accounted for through October 1, 1864.

1078. Walker, William
Private, Company E, 42nd Regiment • N.C. Troops

William was born April 17, 1839. He enlisted in Davie County at age 22, on March 18, 1862. He was present or accounted for through October 1864. He was paroled at Mocksville on June 7, 1865. (North Carolina pension records indicate he was wounded in the head at Bermuda Hundred, Virginia, on an unspecified date.) Despite his injury William lived until March 5, 1910. He is buried in Smith Grove United Methodist Church Cemetery.

1079. Walker, William A.
Private, Company H, 57th Regiment • N.C. Troops

William was born in 1843 in Davie County. He was the son of Vincent (1816, Davie) and Delpha (Delvia) (1821, Davie). He worked in the Mocksville District as a laborer, and at age 19, he enlisted in Rowan County on July 4, 1862, for the war. He was reported present through May 11, 1863, but was reported absent without leave on June 29 and July 2, 1863. William was captured by the enemy at or near Fairfield or Chambersburg, Pennsylvania, on July 5, 1863. He was hospitalized at Harrisburg, Pennsylvania, on August 4, 1863, with pneumonia. He was transferred to the hospital at Baltimore, Maryland, on August 14, 1863. He was confined at Fort McHenry, Maryland, on September 12, 1863, and transferred to Point Lookout, Maryland, on September 15, 1863, where he died in the hospital on December 6, 1863, of "chronic diarrhoea." William's name is not presently listed on the Memorial Monument for the Davie County men who died in the Civil War, 1861–1865.

1080. Walker, William E.
Private, Company E, 42nd Regiment • N.C. Troops

William was born in 1845 in Davidson County to Elliott (1818, Davie) and Malinda (1815, Davie) Walker. His father was a shoemaker and William was a laborer in Farmington District when William enlisted at age 17, March 18, 1862. He was present or accounted for until he deserted in February–April, 1863. Following the war William married Amey F. Brock on February 26, 1866.

1081. Wall, William
Second Lieutenant, Company J • 77th Regiment, 19th Division • N.C. Militia 1861–1865

William could not be specifically identified because there were several young men with the same name who could have qualified.

1082. Wallace, Daniel C.
Private, "Davie Greys" • Company F, 13th Regiment • (3rd Regiment, N.C. Volunteers) • N.C. Troops

Daniel was born in 1830 in Virginia. In 1860 he and his wife Caroline O. (1842, North Carolina) lived in the Mocksville District of Davie County where he worked as a tobacconist prior to enlisting at age 30, April 26, 1861. He was present or accounted for until wounded near Richmond, Virginia, in March–June, 1862. He rejoined the company prior to November 1, 1862, and was present or accounted for until wounded at Gettysburg, Pennsylvania, July 5, 1863. He died in Pennsylvania, July 7–8, 1863, of wounds. Daniel's name is listed on the Memorial Monument for the Davie County men who died in the Civil War, 1861–1865.

1083. Walls, John
Private, Company D, 42nd Regiment • Private, Company F, 42nd Regiment • N.C. Troops

John was born in 1845. He resided in Mecklenburg County before moving to Davie County. He worked as a laborer at age 15 while he and his younger brother Robert Walls, age 10, lived in the Mocksville District with the John Jordan family. John Walls enlisted in Davie County at age 17, February 2, 1862. He was present or accounted for until transferred to Company F of this regiment in May–June, 1862. He was present or accounted for in Company F of this regiment through October 1864.

1084. Walls, Montraville
Private, "Davie Sweep Stakes" • Company G, 4th Regiment • N.C. State Troops

Montraville was born in 1842. In 1860 he made his home in the Mocksville District with Gurney and Casena Jordan prior to enlisting at age 18, June 4, 1861, for the war. He was wounded in the left hand at Seven Pines, Virginia, May 31, 1862, and was absent wounded until discharged on June 9, 1863, or June 15, 1863, by reason of loss of use of the left hand. He returned to Davie County where he married Sarah Elizabeth Sain on January 8, 1871.

1085. Ward, Frank B.
First Lieutenant • Captain William E. Booe's Partisan Rangers • N.C. Volunteers • Company H, 63rd Regiment • (5th Regiment N.C. Cavalry) • N.C. Troops

Frank was born in 1833 in Davie County. He was the son of W. J. and Mary (1803, Davie) Ward. On October 25, 1855, he married Lydia M. Bowden; Mary B. was born in 1858. They resided in the Farmington District of Davie County where he farmed prior to enlisting at age 29, July 15, 1862, for the war. He was appointed 3rd Lieutenant to rank from September 1, 1862, and promoted to Second Lieutenant to rank from

Frank B. Ward lived in this house until his death on May 15, 1907. Although the house appears to be of more recent vintage, it is actually a two-story log house (Mohney, *The Historic Architecture of Davie County*).

Frank B. Ward was retired to the Invalid Corps after being wounded at Middleburg, Virginia (Ann Sheek).

December 20, 1862. On February 4, 1863, he was promoted to First Lieutenant. Shortly thereafter he was wounded at Middleburg, Virginia, and furloughed for thirty days on July 20, 1863. Because of wounds received at Middleburgh he was retired to the Invalid Corps. During the war years Frank and Lydia increased their family by three more children: Martha (1861), John T. (1863) and Manerva (1864), followed by Edna V. (1869) and Laura (1875). After Lydia's death in 1890, Frank married Virginia Churchill, age 26, on February 3, 1892. He died on May 15, 1907, and is buried in Bethlehem United Methodist Church Cemetery.

1086. Ward, William P.
Private, Company D, 42nd Regiment • N.C. Troops

William was born in 1825 in North Carolina. He worked as a farmer in the Farmington District of Davie County where he married Mary E. Smith (1841, North Carolina) on May 29, 1856. Their children were Ada C. (1858), Louisa V. (1860), John W. (1862), Martha E. (1864) and Lelia (1868). William enlisted in Rowan County at age 37, March 24, 1862. He was present or accounted for through October 1864, and paroled at Mocksville on June 7, 1865. He returned to his life in Farmington. However, his wife Mary Elizabeth died February 7, 1873. On November 4, 1875, he married Catharine Bailey, and in 1880 the family lived in the Fulton District. William died on April 5, 1905. He is buried in Macedonia Moravian Church Cemetery.

1087. Warner, C.J.
Private, Company G, 7th Regiment • Confederate Cavalry • Company D, 16th Battalion • N.C. Cavalry

C.J. enlisted in Davie County on September 3, 1862, with the rank of Private. He was transferred from Company G, 7th Regiment Confederate Cavalry to Company D, 16th Battalion N.C. Cavalry on July 11, 1864. He was captured at Fort Harrison, Virginia, September 30, 1864, and confined at Point Lookout, Maryland, where he died of "chronic diarrhoea" on December 31, 1864. C.J.'s name is listed on the Memorial Monument for the Davie County men who died in the Civil War, 1861–1865.

1088. Warner, H.W.
Private, Company G, 7th Regiment • Confederate Cavalry • Company D, 16th Battalion • N.C. Cavalry

H.W. enlisted in Davie County on September 3, 1862, with the rank of Private. He was transferred from Company G, 7th Regiment Confederate Cavalry to Company D, 16th Battalion N.C. Cavalry on July 11, 1864, while absent in confinement at Point Lookout, Maryland, as a prisoner of war. He was transferred to Elmira, New York, on August 15, 1864, where he remained until released after taking the Oath of Allegiance on June 23, 1865.

1089. Warner, J.A.
Private, Company G, 7th Regiment • Confederate Cavalry • Company D, 16th Battalion • N.C. Cavalry

J.A. enlisted in Davie County on September 3, 1862. He was transferred from Company G, 7th Regiment Confederate Cavalry to Company D, 16th Battalion N.C. Cavalry on July 11, 1864. He was present or accounted for through October 1, 1864.

1090. Warren, William C.
Private, Captain William E. Booe's Partisan Rangers • N.C. Volunteers • Company H, 63rd Regiment • (5th Regiment N.C. Cavalry) • N.C. Troops

William was born in North Carolina in

1833. In 1860 he was a farmer in the Mocksville District. On December 27, 1856, he married Rebecca Jane Hendren (1840, North Carolina). A daughter Sarah A.F. was born in 1858. William enlisted in Davie County at age 30, on July 15, 1862, for the war. He was detailed as a nurse on May–June, 1863, through August 1863. William died in the hospital at Richmond, Virginia, on June 25, 1864, of disease. William's name is listed on the Memorial Monument for the Davie County men who died in the Civil War, 1861–1865.

1091. Watkins, Aquilla
Private, Company G, 7th Regiment • Confederate Cavalry • Company D, 16th Battalion • N.C. Cavalry

Aquilla enlisted in Davie County on December 7, 1862, with the rank of Private. He was transferred from Company G, 7th Regiment Confederate Cavalry to Company D, 16th Battalion N.C. Cavalry on July 11, 1864. He was captured at Fort Harrison, Virginia, on September 30, 1864, and confined at Point Lookout, Maryland, until released after taking the Oath of Allegiance on June 21, 1865.

1092. Watkins, Henry
Private, Company G, 7th Regiment • Confederate Cavalry • Company D, 16th Battalion • N.C. Cavalry

Henry transferred from Company G, 7th Regiment Confederate Cavalry to Company D, 16th Battalion N.C. Cavalry on July 11, 1864. He was present or accounted for through October 1, 1864, as "detailed to issue forage."

1093. Welch, Daniel B.
Corporal, Company M, 7th Regiment • Confederate Cavalry • Company E, 16th Battalion • N.C. Cavalry

Daniel enlisted in Davie County and was promoted to Corporal. He was transferred from Company M, 7th Regiment Confederate Cavalry to Company E, 16th Battalion N.C. Cavalry, on July 11, 1864. He was present or accounted for through October 1, 1864.

1094. Welch, Elijah A.
Private, Company G, 7th Regiment • Confederate Cavalry • Company D, 16th Battalion • N.C. Cavalry

Elijah transferred from Company G, 7th Regiment Confederate Cavalry to Company D, 16th Battalion N.C. Cavalry on July 11, 1864. He was captured at Fort Harrison, Virginia, on September 30, 1864, and confined to Point Lookout, Maryland, where he died of "consumption" on December 13, 1864. Elijah's name is listed on the Memorial Monument for the Davie County men who died in the Civil War, 1861–1865.

1095. Welch, John A.
Second Lieutenant, Company M, 7th Regiment • Confederate Cavalry • Company E, 16th Battalion • N.C. Cavalry

John was born in Davie County in 1830. In 1850 he worked as a clerk and made his home with John P. and Mary Gowan. He enlisted in Davie County and was commissioned Second Lieutenant in 1862. He was transferred from Company M, 7th Regiment Confederate Cavalry on July 11, 1864, to Company E, 16th Battalion N.C. Cavalry. He was wounded in his left ankle and admitted to the hospital at Richmond, Virginia, October 29, 1864, where he died on November 15, 1864. John's name is listed on the Memorial Monument for the Davie County men who died in the Civil War, 1861–1865.

1096. Welch, Wesley
Private, Company G, 7th Regiment • Confederate Cavalry • Company D, 16th Battalion • N.C. Cavalry

Wesley was transferred from Company G, 7th Regiment Confederate Cavalry to Company D, 16th Battalion N.C. Cavalry on July 11, 1864. He was present or accounted for through October 1, 1864.

1097. Wellman, M.
Private, Company F, 42nd Regiment • N.C. Troops

The place and date of enlistment were not reported. He was paroled at Greensboro, North Carolina, on May 1, 1865, and paroled again at Mocksville on June 7, 1865.

1098. West, Anderson Wiley
Second Lieutenant, Company B • 77th Regiment, 19th Division m• N.C. Militia 1861–1865

Anderson was born in 1838 in Davie County to John and Nancy West. They lived in the Farmington District where Anderson was appointed Second Lieutenant of Company B. He married Amanda (1847, North Carolina) and continued to farm to feed his growing family. Their children were John Chalmus (1868), Wm. A. (1869), Luther (1871), George (1874), Jenny (1877) and Wesley (1879). A.W. West died on March 31, 1916, and is buried in Bethlehem United Methodist Church Cemetery. (See photograh on page 224.)

1099. West, Jiles (Giles)
Private, "Davie Greys" • Company F, 13th Regiment • (3rd Regiment, N.C. Volunteers) • N.C. Troops

Anderson West and his wife Amanda settled here after the war (Mohney, *The Historic Architecture of Davie County*).

Giles West returned to his father's home after the war. He and his wife Nancy raised their children here (Mohney, *The Historic Architecture of Davie County*).

Jiles was born in 1836 in Davie County to John (1797, Davie) and Nancy (1814, Surry) West. In 1860 he lived with his father and brothers in the Farmington area of Davie County where he enlisted on July 16, 1862, for the war. He was present or accounted for until furloughed for sixty days from hospital in Richmond, Virginia, on December 14, 1864. He was paroled at Mocksville on June 9, 1865. He married Nancy E. Bowden on September 16, 1869; they lived with his father, age 72, and worked with him on his farm while they proceeded to raise five children: Lula (1872), John (1874), Mary A. (1876), Julia (1877) and Lilla (1878). Jiles died on March 3, 1905, and is buried in Bethlehem United Methodist Church Cemetery.

1100. Wheeler, Lemuel B.
Private, Company E, 42nd Regiment • N.C. Troops

Lemuel was born in 1838 in Davie County. He was the son of David R. (1801, Guilford) and Asneth (1806, Virginia) Wheeler. He resided in Davie County where he enlisted at age 22, on March 18, 1862. He was present or accounted for through December 9, 1864, and was captured in the hospital in Richmond, Virginia, on April 3, 1865. Lemuel was transferred to Newport News, Virginia, on April 23, 1865, and was released at Newport News on June 30, 1865, after taking the Oath of Allegiance.

1101. Whitaker, Alfred
Private, "Davie Greys" • Company F, 13th Regiment • (3rd Regiment, N.C. Volunteers) • N.C. Troops

Alfred was born in 1843 in Davie County. He had a twin brother, Thomas. They lived with Jesse (1790, Davie) and Hassey (1820, Iredell) Whitaker in 1850, but at age 17 in 1860, Alfred lived with the C.S. Anderson family in the Calahaln District and worked as a farm laborer. He enlisted in Davie County at age 18, April 26, 1861. He was present or accounted for until killed in a skirmish on the Potomac River on September 5, 1862. Alfred's name is listed on the Memorial Monument for the Davie County men who died in the Civil War, 1861–1865.

1102. Whitaker, Noah
Private, "Davie Greys" • Company F, 13th Regiment • (3rd Regiment, N.C. Volunteers) • N.C. Troops

Noah was born in 1827 in Davie County. In 1850 at age 20, he lived with the Richard and Elizabeth Nail family and worked as an apprentice. In 1860 he was living in Calahaln and working as a house carpenter. On April 26, 1861, at age 34, he enlisted in Davie County. He was present or accounted for until discharged on July 26, 1862, under the provisions of the Conscription Act. Noah was married to Amanda, age 20, prior to 1860.

1103. White, Michael
Private, "Davie Greys" • Company F, 13th Regiment • (3rd Regiment, N.C. Volunteers) • N.C. Troops

Michael was born in "Wadford" County, Ireland, in 1831, and resided in Davie County where he was by occupation a farmer or laborer prior to enlisting in Davie County at age 30, on April 26, 1861. He was present or accounted for until discharged on August 12, 1862, by reason of being an "unnaturalized foreigner."

1104. Whitlock, John H.
Private, "Davie Sweep Stakes" • Company G, 4th Regiment • N.C. State Troops

John was born in 1831 to Thomas (1800, Surry) and Temperance (1805, Davie) Whitlock. They resided in the Chinquepin District of Davie County where John worked as a laborer prior to enlisting at age 30, July 2, 1861, for the war. He was present or accounted for until wounded in the right hand at Spotsylvania Court House, Virginia, May 19, 1864, and his right hand was amputated. He retired to the Invalid Corps on November 30, 1864, or January 2, 1865, and paroled at Salisbury, North Carolina, in 1865. The exact date of parole is not reported. John returned to the Clarksville District of Davie County where he married L. Jane Hill, February 12, 1865. By 1870 they were the parents of Robert Lee (Tommy) (6 months). The 1880 census lists them as farming in the Farmington District.

1105. Whitlock, Thomas F.
Private, "Davie Sweep Stakes" • Company G, 4th Regiment • N.C. State Troops

Thomas was born in 1837 to Thomas (1800, Surry) and Temperance (1805, Davie) Whitlock. They resided in the Chinquepin District of Davie County prior to Thomas's enlisting at age 24, July 1, 1861, for the war. He was wounded at Seven Pines, Virginia, May 31, 1862. He died on June 16, 1862. The place of death was not reported. Thomas's name is listed on the Memorial Monument for the Davie County men who died in the Civil War, 1861–1865.

1106. Whitman, Phillips N.
Private, Company G, 7th Regiment • Confederate Cavalry • Company D, 16th Battalion • N.C. Cavalry

Phillips was transferred from Company G, 7th Regiment Confederate Cavalry to Company D, 16th Battalion N.C. Cavalry on July 11, 1864, and while absent "detailed with artillery." He was wounded in his left arm on August 18, 1864, and furloughed from the hospital at Petersburg, Virginia, for sixty days on August 25, 1864. He was present or accounted for through October 1, 1864, on company muster rolls.

1107. Wilkerson, Mark
Private, "Davie Sweep Stakes" • Company G, 4th Regiment • N.C. State Troops

Mark was born in 1842. He resided in Davie County where he enlisted at age 20, March 13, 1862, for the war. He died on or about June 10, 1862. The company muster rolls indicate that he was "supposed to have died in some hospital, Richmond, Virginia." Cause of death was not reported. Mark's name is listed on the Memorial Monument for the Davie County men who died in the Civil War, 1861–1865.

1108. Williams, Beauford B.
Sergeant, "Davie Sweep Stakes" • Company G, 4th Regiment • N.C. State Troops

Beauford was born in 1839. His father was Francis Williams (1800, Virginia), a physician. Beauford worked as a clerk and made his home with the J.M. Johnson family in the town of Mocksville where he enlisted at age 22, June 5, 1861, for the war. He mustered in as a Sergeant. He died at Camp Pickens, near Manassas, Virginia, September 24, 1861. Cause of death was not reported. Beauford is buried in the Dr. Francis Rush Williams Family Cemetery in the Farmington Township. His tombstone reads: "Killed at a Civil War Battle." Beauford's name is listed on the Memorial Monument for the Davie County men who died in the Civil War, 1861–1865.

1109. Williams, D.L.
Private, Company E, 42nd Regiment • N.C. Troops

D.L. was born in Cabarrus County in 1831. He was the son of Jacob (1800, Cabarrus) and Leah (1804, Cabarrus) Williams according to the 1850 census of Davie County. Daniel was a farmer in 1850. In 1860 he was living in Fulton and working as a carpenter. He and Emily E. Rice were married on January 12, 1862. Daniel enlisted for the war on July 22, 1862, in Davie County. He was present or accounted for through October 1864; however, he was reported absent on detail as a shoemaker during most of that period. Daniel and Emily were the parents of four children: Douglas (1864), Oliver L. (1866), Lula (Camilla) (1869) and Cicero (1872). Daniel died on March 29, 1915, and is buried in Bethlehem United Methodist Church Cemetery.

1110. Williams, Daniel M.
Corporal, "Davie Greys" • Company F, 13th Regiment • (3rd Regiment, N.C. Volunteers) • N.C. Troops

Daniel was born in 1841 in Davie County, the son of Jacob (1800, Cabarrus) and Leah (1804, Cabarrus) Williams. In 1860 Daniel lived in Fulton District where he worked as a clerk. On April 26, 1861, he enlisted in Davie County. He mustered in as a Private and was present or accounted for until wounded and captured at Gettysburg, Pennsylvania, on July 1–4, 1863. Daniel was hospitalized at Davids Island, New York Harbor, until paroled and transferred to City Point, Virginia, where he was received on September 16, 1863, for exchange. He rejoined the company in March–April, 1864, and was promoted to Corporal on May 1, 1864. He was present or accounted for until captured at Wilderness, Virginia, on May 6, 1864. He was confined at Point Lookout, Maryland, until transferred to Elmira, New York, on August 10, 1864. He was paroled at Elmira and transferred to James River, Virginia, on February 20, 1865, for exchange, then hospitalized at Richmond, Virginia, until furloughed for thirty days on March 13, 1865. He was paroled at Salisbury, North Carolina, on May 23, 1865, and took the Oath of Allegiance on July 7, 1865. Daniel married Amanda Haneline on January 11, 1866. They settled in the Fulton District and worked as farmers in 1870 and 1880. Daniel and Amanda were the parents of six children: Sarah (1867), Jacob (1869), Jesse Lee (1871), Maggie (1873), Jennie (1875) and Amanda (1880). Daniel died on May 30, 1934 and is buried in Fork Baptist Church Cemetery.

1111. Williams, F.
Private, Captain William E. Booe's Partisan Rangers • N.C. Volunteers • Company H, 63rd Regiment • (5th Regiment N.C. Cavalry) • N.C. Troops

He enlisted in Davie County on April 1, 1864, for the war. He was present or accounted for through August 1864, when he was reported as "absent wounded, furloughed." No further information.

1112. Williams, Franklin
Captain, "Davie Greys" • Company F, 13th Regiment • (3rd Regiment, N.C. Volunteers) • N.C. Troops

Franklin was born in 1838 to J. Ishmael (1803, Cabarrus) and Margaret (1860, Cabarrus) Williams. At age 23, Franklin taught school in Smith Grove prior to enlisting for the war in Davie County. He mustered in as a Private and was elected First Lieutenant to rank from April 26, 1862. He was present or accounted for until wounded at Fredericksburg, Virginia, on or about December 13, 1862. After rejoining the company prior to January 1, 1863, he was promoted to Captain on June 5, 1863. He was present or accounted for until wounded in the left leg and captured at Gettysburg on or about July 1, 1863. Franklin was hospitalized at various Federal hospitals until transferred to Johnson's Island, Ohio, where he arrived on December 9, 1863. Then he was confined at various Federal prisons until transferred from Point Lookout, Maryland, to Cox's Wharf, James River, Virginia, where he was received on October 15, 1864, for exchange. He was reported absent wounded through October 1864.

1113. Williams, Henry
Private, Company M, 7th Regiment • Confederate Cavalry • Company E, 16th Battalion • N.C. Cavalry

Henry was born in Davie County in 1829. He married Nancy (1829, Davidson) and they had four children prior to the war: Richard F. (1848), Peter (1849), John M. (1855) and Jas. M. (1858). They lived in Smith Grove where Henry farmed before he enlisted in Davie County with the rank of Private on September 18, 1863. He was transferred from Company M, 7th Regiment Confederate Cavalry to Company E, 16th Battalion N.C. Cavalry, on July 11, 1864. He was present or accounted for through October 1, 1864, and paroled at Salisbury, North Carolina, in 1865.

1114. Williams, Jacob W.
Corporal, Company E, 42nd Regiment • N.C. Troops

Jacob was born in 1830 in Cabarrus County, the son of Jacob (1800, Cabarrus) and Leah (1804, Cabarrus) Williams. He was also the brother of Daniel Lawson Williams who served in this company. Jacob was a farmer when he married Elizabeth Dwyre on January 27, 1853, in Davie County. A daughter, Sarah, was born in 1855. They lived in the Farmington District prior to the war. Jacob enlisted in Davie County at age 32, March 18, 1862. He mustered in as a Corporal and died in the hospital at Lynchburg, Virginia, on July 20, 1862, of "typhoid fever." Jacob's name is listed on the Memorial Monument for the Davie County men who died in the Civil War, 1861–1865.

1115. Williams, James
Private, Captain William E. Booe's Partisan Rangers • N.C. Volunteers • Company H, 63rd Regiment • (5th Regiment N.C. Cavalry) • N.C. Troops

James was born in 1837. He enlisted in Davie County at age 25, July 15, 1862, for the war. He was wounded in action at Upperville, Virginia, on June 21, 1863, and was present or accounted for through October 1864. He is buried in Smith Grove United Methodist Church Cemetery. No dates are given.

James Williams family, from left to right: Sally, Beulah, John, Bet, Charlie, James (seated) and Ellen (Ann H. Boger).

1116. Williams, John
Corporal, Company E, 42nd Regiment • N.C. Troops

John was born in 1841 in Davie County, the son of Martin (1817, Davie) and Charity (1822, Davie) Williams. His father was a farmer and John was a laborer in the Farmington District prior to the war. John enlisted in Davie County at age 21, on March 18, 1862. He mustered in as a Private, was promoted to Corporal in January–February, 1863, and died in the hospital at Weldon, North Carolina, on or about February 22, 1863, of "intermittent fever." John's name is listed on the Memorial Monument for the Davie County men who died in the Civil War, 1861–1865.

1117. Williams, John Rufus
First Lieutenant, Company C • 77th Regiment, 19th Division • N.C. Militia, 1861–1865

John was born December 21, 1828, in Cabarrus to Jacob (1800, Cabarrus) and Leah (1804, Cabarrus) Williams. By 1850 his parents had moved their family of eleven children to Davie County where they farmed. John married Elizabeth Foster on October 20, 1853, and became a merchant in Fulton District and then a farmer and tobacco manufacturer. When the militia was activated he was appointed First Lieutenant of Company C. He and Elizabeth were the parents of Jno. R. (1854) and Chalmus (1858). John's tombstone at Fork Baptist Church Cemetery reads "John Rufus Williams, Born in Cabarrus County, died in Davie County, December 21, 1828–July 31, 1915."

1118. Williams, Milton
Private, Company F, 42nd Regiment • N.C. Troops

Milton was born in Davie County in 1839. He was the son of James (1807, Davidson) Williams. In 1860 at age 21, Milton lived with J.W. and Anie L. Clifford in the Chinquepin District. He married Rachel E. Clifford on December 18, 1860. He was a farmer prior to enlisting in Davie County at age 23, March 18, 1862. He was present or accounted for until captured at or near Wise's Forks, Kinston, North Carolina, on March 10, 1865. He was confined at Point Lookout, Maryland, on March 16, 1865, and released there on May 15, 1865, after taking the Oath of Allegiance.

1119. Williams, Neil Henry Calvin
Second Lieutenant, Company C • 77th Regiment, 19th Division • N.C. Militia 1861–1865

Neil was born in 1835 in Cabarrus County to Jacob (1800, Cabarrus) and Leah (1804, Cabarrus) Williams. At age 24, he married Sarah J. Foster on July 5, 1859. She gave birth to Charles and died on May 11, 1860. When the militia was activated Neil was appointed Second Lieutenant of Company C. Also during that time he married Sarah E. Rice on July 28, 1861, and little Charlie had a mother again. Two more children were born: Sarah (1862) and Robert (1864). Neil supported his family by farming and trading tobacco. He died on August 4, 1924, and is buried in Bethel United Methodist Church Cemetery.

1120. Williams, Richard M.
Private, "Davie Sweep Stakes" • Company G, 4th Regiment • N.C. State Troops

Richard M. was born in 1833. His father was Francis Williams (1800, Virginia), a physician. Richard worked as a farmer on his father's farm in the Farmington District prior to enlisting at age 27 on June 4, 1861, for the war. He was wounded in the groin at Seven Pines, Virginia, May 31, 1862. He rejoined the company in July–December, 1862, and was present or accounted for until admitted to the hospital at Richmond, Virginia, February 27, 1865, with "rheumatism." He was captured in the hospital at Richmond on April 3, 1865, and confined at Libby Prison, Richmond. He was transferred to Newport News, Virginia, on April 23, 1865. Final disposition was not reported. By 1870 Richard was living in the Farmington District where he worked as a carpenter. On November 16, 1879, he married Julia A. James. Both are buried at Bethlehem United Methodist Church Cemetery. Julia died on May 31, 1900; R.M. died on January 9, 1927.

1121. Williams, Rush Francis
Second Lieutenant, Company B • 77th Regiment, 19th Division • N.C. Militia 1861–1865

Rush F. was born in 1835 in Davie County to Dr. Francis Williams (1800, Virginia). They resided in Farmington where Rush served as a physician in 1860, at age 24. When the militia was activated, he was appointed Second Lieutenant of Company B. He married Mary F. March on May 27, 1862, and died only six years later, on July 20, 1868. He is buried in the Dr. Francis Rush Williams Family Cemetery.

1122. Williams, William
Private, Company M, 7th Regiment • Confederate Cavalry • Company E, 16th Battalion • N.C. Cavalry

William enlisted in Davie County on October 2, 1863, with the rank of Private. He was transferred from Company M, 7th Regiment Confederate Cavalry to Company E, 16th Battalion N.C. Cavalry, on July 11, 1864, while absent in confinement at Elmira, New York, as a prisoner of war. He died at Elmira of "chronic diarrhoea" October 1, 1864. William's name is listed on the Memorial Monument for the Davie County men who died in the Civil War, 1861–1865.

1123. Williams, William
First Lieutenant • Captain William E. Booe's Partisan Rangers • N.C. Volunteers • Company H, 63rd Regiment • (5th Regiment N.C. Cavalry) • N.C. Troops

William enlisted in Davie County on July 15, 1862, for the war. He was appointed to First Lieutenant to rank from September 1862. He submitted his resignation January 22, 1863, by reason of "disability" and it was officially accepted February 4, 1863.

1124. Willson, William C.
Second Lieutenant, Company F, 42nd Regiment • N.C. Troops

William was appointed Second Lieutenant on or about March 21, 1862. He was present or accounted for until he was wounded in the shoulder and back at or near Camp Wingfield near Edenton, North Carolina, on or about March 23, 1863. He was reported absent wounded until November 13, 1863, when he resigned by reason of "partial paralysis of both arms" as a result of wounds. His resignation was accepted on November 21, 1863.

1125. Wilson, J.W. (James)
Private, Captain William E. Booe's Partisan Rangers • N.C. Volunteers • Company H, 63rd Regiment • (5th Regiment N.C. Cavalry) • N.C. Troops

James was born in 1835 in North Carolina. He was married to Nancy C. (Camomile) (1843, North Carolina). Their children were Patrick H. (1858), Sarah E. (1860), Henry W. (1863), John T. (1865), George H. (1867) and Louisa Catherine (1869). They lived in the Liberty District of Davie County. He was issued clothing on July 23, September 5, October 17 and November 30, 1864. He was paroled at Salisbury, North Carolina, on June 5, 1865, and returned to Davie County where he worked as a carpenter and farmer in Jerusalem District.

1126. Wilson, James W.
Private, Captain William E. Booe's Partisan Rangers • N.C. Volunteers • Company H, 63rd Regiment • (5th Regiment N.C. Cavalry) • N.C. Troops

James enlisted in Davie County on July 18, 1862, for the war. He mustered in as Corporal and was reduced to ranks August 1, 1863. He was captured near Madison Court House, Virginia, on September 22, 1863, and confined at Old Capitol Prison, Washington, D.C., until transferred to Point Lookout, Maryland, September 26, 1863. He was paroled at Point Lookout and exchanged at City Point, Virginia, on March 15, 1864. He was present or accounted for through August 1864 and paroled at Salisbury, North Carolina, on May 16, 1865.

1127. Wilson (Willson), John M.
Private, Company D, 42nd Regiment • Captain William Howard's Company • N.C. Prison Guard • N.C. Troops

John was born in 1827 in Davidson County. In 1850 he made his home with the Elizabeth Nesbit family in Davie County where he worked as a laborer. He married Mary A. Snider on December 3, 1859, and they settled in the Liberty District where he worked as a carpenter prior to enlisting with the rank of Private in Davie County on January 31, 1862. He was transferred to Captain William Howard's Company on or about May 1, 1862. Following the war, he married Catherine C. Austin on February 12, 1867.

1128. Wilson, W.W. (William)
Private, Company M, 7th Regiment • Confederate Cavalry • Company E, 16th Battalion • N.C. Cavalry

William was born in 1826 in Warren County. He married Melony (1832, Davie) Cheshire, on October 23, 1848, and they lived in the Mocksville District before he enlisted. Their children were Mary (1849), Sarah O. (1852), Alice M. (1852), Wm. T. (1856), Margaret (1856), John W. (1857) and Fanny M. (1861). William enlisted in Davie County on December 20, 1862. He was transferred from Company M, 7th Regiment Confederate Cavalry to Company E, 16th Battalion N.C. Cavalry on July 11, 1864. He was present or accounted for through October 1, 1864. He was paroled at Appomattox Court House, Virginia, April 9, 1865.

1129. Wiseman, Alfred W.
Assistant Surgeon, Field and Staff • 7th Regiment • N.C. State Troops

Alfred was born in 1834. He resided in the Liberty District of Davie County where he served as a doctor prior to enlisting at age 27. He was appointed assistant surgeon on April 17, 1862, to rank from February 13, 1862. He was present or accounted for until captured at Sharpsburg, Maryland, on September 19, 1862, after being left behind to attend the wounded. He was paroled and transferred to Aiken's Landing, James River, Virginia, where he was received November 2, 1862, for exchange. On November 10, 1862, he was declared exchanged at Aiken's Landing, and then declared present or accounted for until he resigned on or about January 7, 1863, by reason of "ill health." He returned home and resumed his medical practice in the Jerusalem District of Davie County. He was married to Sarah Greenberry Waddell; they had a son William Alfred (1884) who died in 1885. Dr. Wiseman died in 1907 and Sarah died in 1924. All are buried in the Tatum Family Cemetery which is now a part of the Jerusalem Baptist Church Cemetery.

1130. Wiseman, Joseph W.
First Lieutenant, Company F, 42nd Regiment • N.C. Troops • Assistant Surgeon, Field and Staff • 42nd Regiment • N.C. Troops

Joseph was born in 1826 to Nancy Owens (1791) Wiseman. He married Alphonsine S. Douthit on November 18, 1857. They resided in the Farmington District where he served as a physician prior to enlisting. On March 21, 1862, he was appointed Second Lieutenant three days after the company was raised and enlisted at Mocksville on March 18, 1862. He was present or accounted for until he resigned on June 22, 1863. No reason was given for his resignation. He later served as assistant surgeon of this regiment. He survived the war and resumed his life in Farmington. Alphonsine died in 1890 and he married Ellen L. Conrad. They remained in Farmington until they passed away.

1131. Wiseman, William W.
First Sergeant, Company F, 42nd Regiment • N.C. Troops

William was born in 1845 in Davie County. He was the son of Richard O. (1816, Davidson) and Gracey (1820, Davie) Wiseman. They lived in the Farmington District where William was a student and his father farmed. William enlisted in Davie County at age 17, on April 21, 1862, for the war. He mustered in as a Sergeant and was promoted to First Sergeant on December 4, 1863. He was present or accounted for through December 19, 1864, and paroled at Greensboro, North Carolina, on May 1, 1865.

1132. Wood, Carter
Private, Company B, Carolina Rangers • 10th Virginia Cavalry Regiment

Carter was born in 1843 in Davie County to William (1801, Virginia) and Margaret (1815, Surry) Wood. They resided in the Farmington District where Carter worked as a laborer prior to enlisting in Davie County on October 29, 1861, at age 18. He was present or accounted for, with diarrhoea and/or pneumonia sending him to the hospital in Richmond on January 23, 1863, Danville hospital on March 12, 1863 and Richmond hospital again on March 26, 1864. He returned to duty following each bout of illness. His last military entry was December 31, 1864, for receiving clothing. He returned to Davie County and by 1870 was a farm hand working for the Bhannson [sic] family in Farmington. He married Nancy Hill on December 30, 1874. Carter is buried in Wesley Chapel United Methodist Church Cemetery. His tombstone states that he was born January 22, 1832, and died on March 15, 1915.

1133. Wood, Henry J. (P.)
Private, Captain William E. Booe's Partisan Rangers • N.C. Volunteers • Company H, 63rd Regiment • (5th Regiment N.C. Cavalry) • N.C. Troops

Henry was born in Davie County in 1838 to Lucinda Wood (1805, Davie). In 1850 he lived with the Jonathon Miller family and worked as a farmer. He lived in the Farmington District when, on October 14, 1858, Henry and Sarah J. Smith (1838, North Carolina) were married . He enlisted on July 15, 1862, in Davie County for the war. He was reported on May–June, 1863, muster roll as "captured June 21 at Upperville, Virginia," and reported as "present" on September–October, 1863, Muster roll. No Federal Provost Marshal records relative to his capture or release were found. He was present or accounted for through December 1864, and sent to the hospital in January 1865 with disease. He died in July 1865. There were three children living in the household: Mary L. (1859), James F. (1862) and Sam'l B. (1867). In 1870 Sarah, a widow, was living in the Farmington District. Henry's name is listed on the Memorial Monument for the Davie County men who died in the Civil War, 1861–1865.

1134. Wood, Ira
Private, "Davie Sweep Stakes" • Company G, 4th Regiment • N.C. State Troops

Ira was born in 1839 to William (1801, Virginia) and Margaret (1815, Surry) Wood. He lived in the Farmington District where he worked as a laborer prior to enlisting at age 22, June 5, 1861, for the war. He deserted on July 18, 1861, but was arrested in Davie County on July 28, 1861. He was reported "in confinement in Regimental guard house" from August 7, 1861, through October 1861. He was court-martialed and sentenced to imprisonment for two months. He died on or about April 29, 1862. Place and cause of death were not reported. Ira's name is listed on the Memorial Monument for the Davie County men who died in the Civil War, 1861–1865.

1135. Wright, Amos
Private, Company A, 42nd Regiment • N.C. Troops

Amos was born in 1845. He resided in Davidson County and enlisted in New Hanover County at age 18, October 20, 1863, for the war. He was present or accounted for until captured at or near Battery Anderson, near Fort Fisher, North Carolina, on December 25, 1864. He was confined at or near Fort Monroe, Virginia, on or about December 27, 1864, and transferred to Point Lookout, Maryland, where he arrived on January 2, 1865. He was released on June 17, 1865, after taking the Oath of Allegiance. (North Carolina pension records indicate he was wounded in the shoulder at Cold Harbor, Virginia, in May 1864.) He married Margaret E. Powell on March 28, 1867, in Davie County, but is not listed in the Davie census. He died in 1932, according to his tombstone in Legion Memorial Park Cemetery in Cooleemee.

1136. Wright, John L.
Sergeant, Company D, 42nd Regiment • Captain William Howard's Company • N.C. Prison Guard

John was born in 1816. He and his wife Mary M. had three children prior to the war: Ellen (1854), Alice (1856) and George W. (1859). John enlisted in Davie County on or about January 19, 1862. His promotion record was not reported. He was transferred to Captain William Howard's Company on or about May 1, 1862. Following the war, the family lived in the Mocksville District of Davie County where John worked as a buggy repairman and two more children were born: Henry (1865) and Robert Lee (1867).

1137. Wyatt, W.H.
Private, Captain William E. Booe's Partisan Rangers • N.C. Volunteers • Company H, 63rd Regiment • (5th Regiment N.C. Cavalry) • N.C. Troops

W.H. was born on May 30, 1833. He was the son of William (1802, Davie) and Susan (1806, Davie) Wyatt. In 1860 he was a farmer living in the Mocksville District and married to Maloney (Margaret) Ellen Brinegar. He enlisted in Davie County at age 29, on July 12, 1862, for the war. W.H. was present or accounted for through October 1862. He settled in Fulton District in 1870; he and Maloney were the parents of two children: Hiram O. (1867) and Junius P. (1873). He died on February 20, 1905, and is buried in Fork Baptist Church Cemetery.

1138. Wynn, Cope H.
Private, Captain William E. Booe's Partisan Rangers • N.C. Volunteers • Company H, 63rd Regiment • (5th Regiment N.C. Cavalry) • N.C. Troops

Cope enlisted in Davie County on May 1, 1863, for the war. He was wounded in the right arm at Upperville, Virginia, and captured on June 22, 1863. He was admitted to Lincoln U.S. Army General Hospital, Washington, D.C., on June 24, 1863, and sent to Old Capitol Prison, Washington, D.C., on August 16, 1863, and from there to Point Lookout, Maryland, on August 23, 1863. He remained at Point Lookout until paroled and exchanged at City Point, Virginia, on March 20, 1864. He was present or accounted for until he retired to the Invalid Corps on October 25, 1864, and was assigned to light duty on November 15, 1864. No further information.

1139. Yates, Albert A.
Private, Company G, 7th Regiment • Confederate Cavalry • Company D, 16th Battalion • N.C. Cavalry

Albert enlisted in Davie County on September 3, 1862, with the rank of Private. In 1880 Albert Yates lived and worked in Jerusalem Township in Davie County as a carpenter.

1140. Yates, Timothy
Private, Company G, 7th Regiment • Confederate Cavalry • Company D, 16th Battalion • N.C. Cavalry

Timothy enlisted in Davie County on September 3, 1862, with the rank of Private. He was transferred from Company G, 7th Regiment Confederate Cavalry to Company D, 16th Battalion N.C. Cavalry on July 11, 1864. He was present or accounted for through October 1, 1864.

1141. Zimmerman, G.W.
Sergeant, Captain William E. Booe's Partisan Rangers • N.C. Volunteers • Company H, 63rd Regiment • (5th Regiment N.C. Cavalry) • N.C. Troops

G.W. enlisted in Davie County at age 23, on July 8, 1862, for the war. He mustered in as Corporal and was appointed Sergeant on August 1, 1863. He was present or accounted for through February 1865.

1142. Zimmerman, Jackson
Private, Company B, Carolina Rangers • 10th Virginia Cavalry Regiment

Jackson was born in 1840 in Davidson County to Thomas (1803, Stokes) and Susan (1804, Davidson) Zimmerman. They farmed in the Shady Grove District of Davie County where Jackson enlisted on May12, 1862. He was present or accounted for until he was paroled at Mocksville, on June 9, 1865. He married Emly [sic] Bailey on April 7, 1867, and Georgianna was born in 1868. Emily died and Jackson hired Sarah Saterfield as a domestic servant; Sarah also had a daughter, Cora (Coreah), who was born in 1868. Jackson and Sarah soon married and became the parents of Cornelia A. (1876) and Bettie (1879). They lived in Fulton District where Jackson supported his family by farming. He is listed in the Confederate Veterans Census of 1890. He died on March 24, 1894, and is buried in Elbaville United Methodist Church Cemetery. His brother Thomas also served in this company.

1143. Zimmerman, Thomas
Private, Company B, Carolina Rangers • 10th Virginia Cavalry Regiment

Thomas was born in 1837 in Davidson County to Thomas (1803, Stokes) and Susan (1804, Davidson) Zimmerman. They farmed in the Shady Grove District of Davie County where Thomas enlisted on October 29, 1861, at age 21. He was listed present through April 30, 1862, but died of typhoid fever in a Lynchburg hospital on February 26, 1863. His personal effects consisted of "$110.00 and sundries." Thomas's name is listed on the Memorial Monument for the Davie County men who died in the Civil War, 1861–1865.

* * *

Some soldiers were not located when we did our research, but information about them has been provided to us by their family members. These soldiers served with the Junior or Senior Reserves, the 9th Battalion and/or in the medical field. Some of them were:

1144. Glasscock, James Lafayette
9th Battalion, Junior Reserves • Confederate States Army

His assigned duty was to "guard the sugar" on the train at Salisbury, North Carolina.

His father also served.

James Lafayette Glasscock (1848–1937) (Jane Tutterow)

1145. Glasscock, Thomas Napoleon
Davis Company, N.C. Home Guard • Confederate States Army

1146. Hendricks, George W.
Company F, 9th Battalion

George served in Company F, 9th Battalion from 1864–1865. (See photograph on page 233.)

1147. Kimbrough, Marmaduke D.
Assistant Surgeon • Forsyth County Militia

Marmaduke was born in Yadkin County to John Young and Amy Joiner Kimbrough on June 2, 1838. He attended the University Medical College in Philadelphia, and graduated with a M.D. degree. He began his medical practice in Brookstown and served as assistant surgeon during the Civil War. He married Sarah E. Brock of Farmington on May 14, 1861, and eventually

George W. Hendricks (1846–1908) (Charles W. Hendricks)

Marmaduke D. Kimbrough

moved to Mocksville where he continued his medical practice. Dr. and Mrs. Kimbrough were the parents of ten children: Camilla Frances, Mary L., Chalmers L., Sally B., Julia Rena, Joseph William, John Armitt, Algin Lezora, Alexander M. and Puryear Ramsey. Dr. Kimbrough served as Chairman of the Davie County Republicans Committee from 1882 until 1896, and also served as the chairman of the Congressional and Judicial District Committee. He died November 26, 1910, and is buried in Smith Grove United Methodist Church Cemetery.

Appendix 1: Company Rosters

2nd Company E, 2nd Regiment, N.C. State Troops

Fraley, John T.	Second Lieutenant
Hobson, James M.	First Lieutenant
Hobson, John M.	Second Lieutenant
Fraley, Milas J.	Private
Thompson, John	Private

Company C, 4th Regiment

Anderson, Andrew J.	Sergeant

Company G, 4th Regiment

Kelly, Samuel A.	Captain
Kelly, William Frohock	Captain
Brown, Rufus D.	Second Lieutenant
Brown, Thomas J.	Second Lieutenant
Cain, Daniel J.	Second Lieutenant
Davis, Samuel C.	Second Lieutenant
Guffy, Carson A.	Second Lieutenant
Jones, William B.	Second Lieutenant
Smith, Beal I.	First Lieutenant
Smoot, Daniel J.	Second Lieutenant
Allen, Isaac	Private
Athan, Asbury	Private
Austin, Green B.	Musician
Austin, James	Private
Austin, John	Private
Austin, William	Private
Bagarly, John F.	Private
Bailey, _____	Private
Baker, Thomas J.	Private
Barlow, John J.	Private
Beachamp, John W.	Private
Beck, Little	Private
Beck, William H.	Private
Beck, William P.	Private
Beeman, Richmond S.	Private
Beeman, T.A.	Private
Bentley, A.	Private
Berryman, Alfred S.	Private
Blackwelder, Daniel E.	Private
Bowden, John O.	Private
Burk, James W.	Sergeant
Cain, Anderson H.	Private
Cain, William G.	Private
Campbell, Thomas B.	Private
Carter, William C.	Private
Chaffin, Alexander W.	Private
Chaffin, Nathan M.D.	Private
Charles, John N.	Private
Clary, James	Private
Clary, William	Private
Cook, James	Private
Cranfield, J. H.	Private
Cranfield, Jackson Lewis	Private
Cranfield, James L.	Private
Cranfill, Gideon	Private
Cranfill, Jonathan	Private
Cunningham, F.M.	Private
Cunningham, George H.	Private
Cunningham, Rubin	Private
Cunningham, Samuel M.	Private
Cunningham, Thomas	Private
Davis, Samuel A.	Private
Davis, Samuel G.	Private
Davis, Silas	Private
Davis, William	Private
Dismuks, Richard L.	Sergeant
Douthit, Edward J.	Private
Dowdy, James	Private
Etcherson, James W.	Private
Farrington, Romulus	Private
Foster, John W.	Musician
Furches, John M.	Private
Gaither, William H.	Private
Guffy, Samuel M.	Private
Hagie, Davidson	Private
Hall, Ferdinand E.	Corporal
Hall, Henry H.	Private
Hanes, Harrison H.	Private
Hanes, Jacob H.	Corporal
Hanes, William P.	Sergeant
Haskins, James F.	Private
Hendricks, William A.	Private
Hightower, Anderson E.	Private
Hill, David F.	Private
Ijames, Henry H.	Private

Appendix 1

Ijames, John F.	Private
Ijames, John W.	Private
James, J.F.	Private
James, J.W.	Private
Jones, Samuel A.	Private
Jordan, Eli	Private
Jordan, Gurney	Private
Jordan, Jonathan	Private
Jordan, William C.	Private
Keith, C.C.	Private
Kelly, John	Private
King, L.B.	Private
Lane, John H.	Private
Lane, William A.	Private
Latham, Jeremiah M.	Private
Lynch, William	Private
McCrackin, William A.	Private
McDaniel, Nathan	Private
McElroy, William J.	Private
Martin, Benjamin J.	Private
Mock, W. G.	Private
Moose, William R.	Private
Mullican, Lewis S.	Sergeant
Owen, William H.	Private
Parish, Solomon	Private
Parker, Edward N.	Private
Perry, William	Sergeant
Revis, John E.	Private
Rose, Pompey S.	Private
Rose, Samuel W.	Private
Rudacil, H. F.	Private
Sharp, Samuel L.	Sergeant
Sheek, Isaac	Private
Sheek, J.D.	Ordnance Sergeant
Sheets, Wesley M.	Private
Shives, Giles M.	Private
Shives, James	Private
Shives, Joseph P.	Private
Smith, Franklin A.	Private
Smith, James W.	Private
Swaringen, Iva F.	Private
Taylor, John	Private
Travillion, Meekins C.	Private
Turner, Edmond D.	Private
Turner, Henry	Private
Vogler, John E.	Private
Wagner, Jacob	Private
Wagner, W.R.	Private
Walls, Montraville	Private
Whitlock, John H.	Private
Whitlock, Thomas F.	Private
Wilkerson, Mark	Private
Williams, Beauford B.	Sergeant
Williams, Richard	Private
Wise, Henry A.	Private
Wood, Ira	Private

Company E, 4th Regiment, N.C. State Troops

Hendrix, John H.	Private
Baity, William J.	Private

Company G, 5th Regiment

Baity, William J.	Corporal
Call, John	Private
Cheshire, John A.	Private
Cheshire, Richard B.	Private
Clifford, Joseph C.	Private
Clifford, William G.	Private
Codie, Godfrey	Private
Collette, Robert W.	Private
Dixon, William	Private
Evans, William	Private
Foster, A.F.	Private
Fray, Benjamin	Private
Frost, Calvin	Private
Gaither, Wiley	Private
Granger, M.L.	Private
Graves, Jacob B.	Private
Grimes, William A.	Private
Hartman, Enoch	Private
Hendrix, John H.	Private
Holdman, Thomas	Private
Horn, Levi (Louis) G.	Private
Ijams, James M.	Private
Jones, Matthew	Private
McDaniel, W.H.	Private
Orrell, David E.	Private
Pence, Henry	Private
Pennington, James	Corporal
Rudicil, Anderson	Private
Seaford, Peter	Private
Seaford, Solomon	Private

Field and Staff, 7th Regiment Infantry

Wiseman, Alfred W.	Assistant Surgeon

Company F, 7th Regiment Infantry

Fry, William	Corporal
Haire, Perry	Corporal

Company I, 9th Regiment

Lookabill, William H.	Private

Company F, 13th Regiment

Clement, Jesse A.	Captain
Foster, George	Captain
Roessler, Julius	Captain

Williams, Franklin	Captain	Ijams, James D.	Sergeant
Clement, Wiley A.	Second Lieutenant	Ijams, Matthew N.	Corporal
Driver, John E.	Second Lieutenant	Kurfees, Caleb W.	Private
Sain, Cheshire	Third Lieutenant	Kurfees, Franklin J.	Private
Sain, Nimrod B.	Second Lieutenant	Kurfees, Zedock C.	Private
Thompson, William Graham	Second Lieutenant	Lassiter, Ethadra W.	Private
Allen, James P.	Private	Leach, David	Private
Allen, Mathew A.	Private	Leach, John	Sergeant
Anderson, Charles S.	Private	Leach, John W.	Private
Baity, Thomas B.	Private	Leonard, Emanuel	Private
Beck, William	Private	Little, Robert A.	Private
Bell, N.R.	Private	McArter, Thomas	Private
Bessent, Daniel D.	Private	McClenan, Mathew A.	Corporal
Blackwood, John B.	Private	McDonald, James	Private
Boles, James D.	Private	McGuire, William F.	Sergeant
Booe, George W.	Sergeant	Madra, William H.	Private
Booe, George W.	Private	Marlin, John L.	Private
Boyd, James S.	Private	Martin, David W.	Private
Brinegar, John	Private	Mason, Grief G.	Corporal
Burton, Daniel P.	Private	May, Urban C.	Private
Burton, Noel E.	Private	Miller, James W.	Private
Butler, Thomas S.	Private	Mock, Henry A.	Private
Campbell, George W.	Private	Monday, William	Private
Cartner, James F.	Private	Nail, Abraham M.	Sergeant
Chandler, Solomon	Private	Nail, Jasper H.Y.	Musician
Chaplin, Alexander	Private	Nail, John A.	Sergeant
Click, Daniel W.	Private	Nail, Philip A.	Private
Cloninger, Alonzo	Private	Penry, Boone T.	First Sergeant
Danner, Eli	Private	Penry, William H.	Private
Davis, Franklin	Private	Pool, Benjamin F.	Private
Daywalt, Alfred J.	Private	Pool, Randolph	Private
Dedman, Thomas H.	Private	Raben, Samuel W.	Private
Dingler, James	Private	Rhidenhour, John W.	Private
Divire, Daniel	Corporal	Ridenhour, Anderson J.	Private
Dobbins, Alfred M.C.	Private	Ridenhour, Losson	Private
Eccles, John C.	Private	Sain, Andrew	Private
Ellis, Thomas N.	Private	Sain, Jacob	Private
Ellison, Donalson	Private	Sain, Joseph	Private
Fletcher, Mathew	Private	Sain, William	Private
Foster, Henry	Private	Shaw, Augustus	Private
Foster, Henry C.	Sergeant	Shaw, William	Private
Foster, Jacob	Private	Sheek, Albert A.	Private
Foster, Samuel	Private	Sheets, John	Private
Furches, Samuel W.	Private	Simmons, Henry	Private
Furches, Thomas W.	Private	Smith, William A.	Private
Gatton, Franklin	Private	Stonestreet, John H.	Private
Gatton, Harrison	Private	Swaringen, Samuel T.	Private
Graves, John W.	Private	Thomas, John B.	Private
Harris, John W.	Private	Totten, John C., Jr.	Private
Harrison, Richard	Private	Turner, Pinkney	Private
Hendren, Arthur N.	First Sergeant	Tuttarow, George W.	Private
Hendrix, Jehu	Private	Tutterow, John V.	Private
Hepler, Benjamin F.	Private	Verber, Peter	Private
Hinkle, George W.	Private	Vinagum, Daniel V.	Private
Hobbs, Julius	Sergeant	Vinagum, Thomas V.	Private
Hodges, Joseph	Private	Von Eaton, John I.	Sergeant
Holt, Robert A.	Private	Von Eaton, Samuel P.	Private
House, John W.	Private	Wallace, Daniel C.	Private
Howard, Harrison H.	Corporal	West, Jiles	Private
Hunter, John W.	Private	Whitaker, Alfred	Private

Whitaker, Noah — Private
White, Michael — Private
Williams, Daniel M. — Corporal

Company B, 15th Regiment

Coon, Benjamin G. — Second Lieutenant

Company D, 16th Battalion, N.C. Cavalry

(formerly Company G, 7th Regiment Confederate Cavalry)

Clement, Jesse A. — Captain
Gaither, L.G. — First Lieutenant
Harper, C.E. — Third Lieutenant
Nichols, B.F. — Second Lieutenant
Adams, John Q. — Private
Barrouth, Henry F. — Private
Binkley, J.W. — Private
Black, Daniel — Private
Black, Samuel F. — Private
Blackburn, James A. — Private
Blackburn, John — Private
Boner, Jacob — Private
Bowers, Eli W. — Private
Boyer, John — Private
Brandon, Thomas — Private
Brandon, W.F. — Private
Brewer, Hubbard — Private
Call, Will H. — Sergeant
Caudell, F. Marion — Private
Cline, Henry — Private
Conner, J.C. — Private
Crews, William P. — Private
Ellis, Ezekiel P. — Private
Foster, Samuel — Private
Gullet, William — Private
Harper, George W. — Private
Harper, John L. — Sergeant
Harper, John R. — Private
Hauser, Philip A. — Private
Hauser, Wiley — Private
Holder, A.A. — Private
Holder, Jacob — Private
Holder, Sowell — Private
Idol, A. Jackson — Corporal
Jones, Emory W. — Private
Jones, W. Albert — Private
Latham, Samuel B. — Sergeant
Ledford, John A. — Private
McBride, John A. — Private
McKaughan, Isiah S. — Private
McKaughan, J.H. — Sergeant
McKaughan, Richard H. — Private
McKaughan, William J. — Corporal
Miller, John R. — Private
Millraney, J.H. — Private
Myers, Andrew L. — Private
Myers, Jefferson C. — Private
Parnell, J.W. — Private
Parrass, J.S. — Private
Peacock, George W. — Private
Phelps, Britton — Private
Phelps, Charlie — Private
Phillips, John W. — Private
Phillips, L.F. — Private
Potts, William S. — Private
Sain, A.T. — Private
Smith, Alfred — Corporal
Snyder, R.W. — Private
Stafford, J.M. — Private
Standerford, John — Private
Vogler, John Emory — Private
Vogler, Matthew — Private
Walker, R.A. — Private
Warner, C.J. — Private
Warner, H.W. — Private
Warner, J.A. — Private
Watkins, Aquilla — Private
Watkins, Henry — Private
Welch, Elijah A. — Private
Welch, Wesley — Private
Whitman, Phillip N. — Private

Company E, 16th Battalion, N.C. Cavalry

(formerly Company M, 7th Regiment Confederate Cavalry)

Clement, Baxter Clegg — Captain
Johnson, S.W. — First Lieutenant
Welch, John A. — Second Lieutenant
Allen, J.F. — Private
Allen, William W. — Private
Bailey, H.H. — Private
Barneycastle, Jabus A. — Private
Beck, A.M. — Private
Beck, J.P. — Corporal
Beck, St. Leger — Private
Bingham, G.M. — Sergeant
Burgess, Thomas — Private
Call, David — Corporal
Call, Henry — Sergeant
Call, Nathan F. — Private
Cheshire, F.A. — Private
Clement, Jesse Lee — Private
Clifford, A.M. — Private
Davis, William E. — Private
Dwire, John H. — Private
Dyson, William L. — Private
Ellis, James M. — Private
Ellis, Wiley Jones — Private
Foster, Archibald — Private
Foster, John — Private
Furches, John M. — Private
Furches, Thomas G. — Private
Furches, William F. — Sergeant

Gaither, David	Private
Gaither, Greenberry	Private
Gaither, Z.L.	Private
Gullet, William	Private
Hanes, Pleasant Henderson	Private
Hargrave, John H.	Private
Jones, John	Private
Long, L.W.	Private
Lowery, D.L.	Private
Lowery, John T.T.	First Sergeant
March, H. Giles	Private
Martin, Giles	Private
McClamrock, Julius Lawrence	Private
McClamrock, Lucius Milton	Private
McDaniel, George	Private
McDaniel, William	Private
Nail, A.M.	Private
Newnan, A.W.	Private
Owens, A.L.	Private
Parrish, W.P.	Private
Powell, Elias H.	Private
Ratledge, D.J.	Private
Ratledge, Isaac	Private
Ratledge, L.P.	Private
Ratledge, William H.	Private
Richardson, A.M.	Private
Richardson, George W.	Private
Sain, Basil	Private
Setser, M.Y.	Private
Simerson, John H.	Private
Smith, Elwood	Private
Smith, Zimereck N.	Private
Summers, Greenberry	Private
Taylor, Wiley M.	Private
Thomas, E.J.	Sergeant
Thompson, Joseph	Private
Thorn, T.J.	Private
Turner, J.A.	Private
Tutarow, Thomas P.	Private
Tutorow, A.P.	Private
Verner, Hardy	Private
Welch, Daniel B.	Corporal
Williams, Henry	Private
Williams, William	Private
Wilson, W.W.	Private

Company L, 17th Regiment (2nd Organization)

Cartner, John	Private

Company A, 21st Regiment

Oaks, James P.	Second Lieutenant
Miller, John A.	Private
Parrish, Wesley W.	Private
Parrish, Willis G.	Private

Company B, 21st Regiment (11th Regiment N.C. Volunteers)

Anderson, A.A.	Sergeant
Anderson, A.A.	Private

Field and Staff Company A, 1st Battalion N.C. Sharpshooters

Anderson, A.A.	Sergeant Major

Company H, 23rd Regiment

Johnson, B.S.	Private
Reid, W.E.	Private
Seamon, H.R.	Private
Stroud, Rich S.	Private

Company K, 30th Regiment

Myers, James	Private

Field and Staff, 42nd Regiment

Brown, John Edmunds	Colonel
Brown, Thomas J.	Major
Brown, William Carter	Surgeon
Wiseman, Joseph W.	Assistant Surgeon
Anderson, Edwin M.	Sergeant Major
Dwire, H.X.	Quartermaster Sergeant
Clouse, L.A.	Musician
Craver, David Lindsey	Musician
Dulin, William M.	Musician

Company A, 42nd Regiment

Cope, John	Private
Deadman, James R.	Private
Ellis, William A.	Private
Kindley, J.D.	Private
Orrender, Charles R.	Private
Owens, Michael	Private
Owens, N. Richard	Private
Potts, Milton	Private
Smith, Doctor F.	Private
Smith, Levi K.	Private

2nd Company B, 42nd Regiment

Cloninger, Alonzo	Private
Hamilton, William M.	Private
House, David A.	Private
House, John W.	Private
Taylor, A. Jackson	Private

Company D, 42nd Regiment

Foster, A.M.	Third Lieutenant
Rusher, Edward A.	Second Lieutenant
Allen, Peter	Private

Appendix 1

Austin, James C.	Private
Baxter, John W.	Sergeant
Brindle, Robert R.	Private
Brown, William	Private
Burgis, John M.	Private
Carter, Abraham	Private
Carter, William	Private
Casey, Ephraim C.	Private
Cope, Andrew	Private
Cornatser, Jacob C.	Private
Daniel, William Harrison	Private
Eaton, Joseph C.	Private
Ellis, William R.	Private
Etchison, Giles B.	Private
Foster, Azanah L.	Private
Foster, James A.	Private
Foster, James M.	Private
Foster, Jesse N.	Private
Foster, John E.	Private
Foster, Samuel L.	Private
Foster, Samuel Mc.	Private
Gatton, James	Private
Gentle, Jordan M.	Private
Graves, Andrew	Private
Graves, Daniel	Private
Griffin, William T.	Sergeant
Holder, William	Private
Hood, William	Private
Howard, Robert	Private
Jacobs, John	Private
James, John R.	Private
James, W. Asberry	Private
Jenkins, Addison	Private
Jones, Martin	Private
Leonard, Jesse	Private
Livengood, Daniel G.	Private
Livengood, John N.	Private
Martin, James C.	Private
May, William F.	Private
Monday, Wade C.	Private
Myers, Zadock	Private
O'Neal, William H.	Private
Orrell, Robert R.	Private
Owens, Henry C.	Private
Parish, Thomas	Private
Plott, John	Private
Riddle, T.C.	Private
Rotan, Eli C.	Private
Sain, Nathan	Private
Seagraves, Jacob A.	Private
Setzer, Milford R.	Sergeant
Shives, David Franklin	Private
Sloan, William Henry	Private
Smith, W.H.H.	Private
Spry, William	Private
Stanley, Jefferson J.	Private
Stanly, Nathan W.	Private
Walker, Henry G.	Sergeant
Walker, John W.	Corporal
Walls, John	Private
Ward, William P.	Private
Wilson, John M.	Private
Wright, John L.	Sergeant

Company E, 42nd Regiment

Brown, Thomas J.	Major
Hanes, Spencer Joseph	Captain
Peebles, John Headen	Captain
Anderson, Edwin M.	Third Lieutenant
Brock, James V.	Third Lieutenant
Ellis, William J.	First Lieutenant
Naylor, Benjamin T.	Third Lieutenant
Adams, W.	Private
Allen, Abram T.	Private
Armsworthy, J.C.	Private
Austin, Asberry	Sergeant
Bailey, John K.	Corporal
Baker, Thomas J.	Private
Barlow, Wiley	Private
Barneycastle, James	Private
Barneycastle, P.F.	Private
Binkley, James H.	Private
Brinkley, James	Private
Brock, Richard E.	First Sergeant
Brogden, John W.	Private
Call, Murphy G.	Private
Canter, Pleasant H.	Private
Canter, William M.	Private
Caton, Green	Private
Caton, Orrell	Private
Chaffin, Charles Stanley	Private
Chambers, Martin	Private
Chambers, Peter	Private
Chaplain, John	Private
Click, Michael	Private
Clouse, L.A.	Sergeant
Cook, George B.	Private
Cope, William G.	Private
Cranfield, William H.	Private
Cuthrell, James N.	Private
Daniels, William	Private
Daniels, William L.	Private
Daniels, Wilson W.	Private
Dulin, William M.	Sergeant
Dwire, H.X.	First Sergeant
Etcherson, Alexander H.	Private
Foote, L.R.	Private
Foster, Benjamin L.	Private
Foster, Coleman	Private
Foster, Franklin A.	Musician
Foster, James H.W.	Private
Foster, Robert	Private
Foster, Thomas	Private
Foster, William H.	Private
Foster, William M.	Private
Fry, Albert W.	Private
Fry, James	Private
Gabard, William	Private
Garwood, David T.	Private

Garwood, L.B.	Private	Naylor, Bat W.	Private
Garwood, Robert	Private	Naylor, T.N.	Private
Gheen, William	Private	Norman, S. Alexander	Private
Gowan, Richard W.	Private	Parker, Childs A.	Private
Gowen, Simeon C.	Private	Parks, Mack	Private
Granger, James M.	Private	Parks, William	Private
Graves, Albert N.	Private	Perry, M.F.	Private
Graves, George F.	Private	Potts, A.J.	Private
Graves, Jeremiah	Private	Potts, F.A.	Private
Graves, John Ellis	Private	Potts, Hiram	Private
Graves, John Franklin	Private	Potts, Newberry	Private
Graves, Nathan	Private	Potts, Peter W.M.	Private
Graves, William H.	Private	Potts, William	Private
Green, George E.	Corporal	Queen, William	Private
Hammond, Bryant W.	Private	Raban, Jonathan	Private
Hanes, George A.	Private	Redwine, John F.	Private
Harbin, James H.	Private	Rich, Isaac Oakes	Sergeant
Helfer, A.Y.	Private	Ridenhour, John M.	Private
Helfer, Pleasant E.	Private	Robertson, Thomas E.	Private
Helfer, S.F.	Private	Shadrick, David	Private
Hellard, William	Private	Shadrick, Isaac	Private
Hendricks, Nalke	Private	Shadrick, Sion	Private
Hendrix, Stephen	Private	Shoemaker, Alfred C.	Private
Hendrix, W.G.	Private	Sidden, William	Private
Holder, Hosea L.	Private	Smith, James Douglas	Private
Howard, Morgan G.	Private	Smith, Samuel T.	Private
Howard, Nathan	Private	Spencer, O.H.	Private
Howard, Philip G.	Private	Spry, Berry	Private
Howard, Wilson	Private	Stewart, Daniel	Private
James, Thomas A.	Private	Stewart, Edward D.	Private
Johnson, General W.	Private	Stewart, Spencer	Private
Keller, Joseph	Private	Stewart, William	Private
King, Anderson	Private	Stout, William Loranza	Private
King, Calvin	Private	Taylor, William M.	Sergeant
King, William A.	Private	Tharpe, J.T.	Private
Lagle, Henry E.	Private	Thomas, Daniel W.	Private
Langley, Pleasant	Private	Thomas, E.S.	Private
Lard, George W.	Private	Thompson, Rufus R.	Private
Lard, Levi	Private	Tysinger, Henry H.	Private
Lard, Samuel	Private	Tysinger, William M.	Sergeant
Lashmit, John W.	Private	Wadkins, William H.	Private
Linster, McAfee	Private	Wagoner, William	Private
Livengood, Dan E.	Private	Walker, James	Private
Lyons, Richard J.	Private	Walker, John W.	Private
McDaniel, Elias	Private	Walker, William	Private
McDaniel, George W.	Private	Walker, William E.	Private
McDaniel, Nace	Private	Ward, S.S.	Private
Manning, Benjamin F.	Private	Wheeler, Lemuel B.	Private
Marshall, George W.	Private	Williams, D.L.	Private
Massey, Daniel W.	Private	Williams, Jacob W.	Corporal
Massey, Thomas G.	Private	Williams, John	Corporal
Miller, Jacob C.	Private		
Miller, John E.	Private		
Miller, John F.	Private		
Miller, John H.	Private		
Moore, William A.	Musician		
Motley, M.M.	Corporal		
Myers, Henry J.	Private		
Myers, Solomon Wesley	Private		
Nash, B.R.	Sergeant		

Company F, 42nd Regiment

Clement, Wiley A.	Captain
Bailey, William Hall	Second Lieutenant
Clement, John H.	First Lieutenant
Sanford, Calvin Cowles	Third Lieutenant
Willson, William C.	Second Lieutenant
Wiseman, Joseph W.	First Lieutenant

Appendix 1

Anderton, William D.	Private
Bailey, Henry L.	Private
Baity, George W.	Private
Berryman, James M.	Private
Boger, Moses	Private
Boger, Paul	Private
Bolds, James L.	Private
Booe, Marshall N.	Private
Booe, William M.	Private
Bowles, B.F.	Private
Bowles, G.W.	Private
Bracken, John W.	Private
Bracken, William H.	Private
Cain, Daniel H.	Private
Cain, William F.	Private
Campbell, Benjamin Frank	Private
Charles, Francis W.	Private
Charles, William F.	Private
Clark, Edward M.	Sergeant
Clifford, Franklin A.	Private
Clifford, John H.	Private
Collett, Ezekiel	Private
Cranfield, Hanes	Private
Cranfield, Henry	Private
Craver, David Lindsey	Private
Danner, Samuel	Private
Dayvault, Solomon M.	Private
Dayvault, William M.	Sergeant
Deadman, James R.	Private
Deadman, Thomas H.	Private
Drake, William D.	Private
Etchison, W.C. Perry	Private
Evans, Thomas	Private
Ferribee, Thomas M.	Private
Foster, Albert N.	Private
Foster, John M.	Private
Frost, James D.	Private
Gaither, Zadock L.	Private
Gatton, Pleasant	Private
Granger, James F.	Private
Granger, John P.	Private
Granger, W. Burton	Private
Gray, Thomas	Private
Grimes, Noah B.	Corporal
Hoose, William	Private
Horn, Enoch	Private
Horn, John J.	Private
Horn, William Pinkney	Private
Horne, Stephen W.	Sergeant
Howard, Cornelius	Private
Howard, Joseph	Private
Howard, Samuel B.	Private
Howell, Alexander Charles	Private
Hunter, Henry H.	Private
Hunter, Samuel	Private
Inscore, Lewis	Private
Jarvis, Jonathan	Private
Johnson, Baker A.	Private
Johnson, William G.	Corporal
Jones, Ebed	Private
Keller, John D.	Private
Kerfees, John Peter	Private
Kesler, Henry P.	Private
Kesler, M.F.	Private
Kesler, William Richard	Private
Lapish, George	Private
Lapish, John A.	Private
Latham, David Hampton	Private
Latham, James M., Sr.	Private
Lazenby, John Tilman	Private
Leach, James Franklin	Private
Linville, John F.	Private
McDaniel, Alfred A.	Private
McDaniel, Benjamin L.	Private
McGill, John A.	Private
McGuire, Timothy	Private
Marlow, George Washington	Private
Miller, James W.	Private
Moore, Jehu	Private
Nail, Henry	Private
Nail, Phillip	Private
Prather, Alfred A.	Private
Prather, Eli	Private
Ratts, Hiram C.	Private
Rich, Samuel Chase	Private
Roberts, Paschal	Private
Rudicil, John	Private
Sain, John A.	Private
Sain, Thomas M.	Private
Seamon, Losen	Private
Shives, David Franklin	Private
Sloan, William Henry	Private
Smith, Asbury	Private
Smith, William Harden	Private
Smith, William J.	Private
Smith, William P.	Private
Smoot, Alexander	Private
Smoot, John	Private
Smoot, Pinkney	Private
Smoot, Wilson D.	Private
Sport, William B.	Private
Spry, John Giles	Private
Stewart, Hezekiah	Private
Stroud, David	Private
Taylor, Giles	Private
Taylor, John	Private
Turner, Esquire	Private
Turner, George Washington	Private
Tutterow, William Nelson	Private
Tutterow, William W.	Private
Van Eaton, James M.	Private
Waggoner, David	Private
Waggoner, John H.	Corporal
Walker, George Washington	Corporal
Walls, John	Private
Wellman, M.	Private
Williams, Milton	Private
Wiseman, William W.	First Sergeant

Company A, 46th Regiment
Holeman, James S.   Private

Company B, 46th Regiment
Harris, Williamson G.   Private
Pigg, Hugh   Private
Potts, Calvin J.   Corporal

Company B, 48th Regiment
Anderson, John T.   Private
Hanes, John H.   Sergeant
Minor, John   Private

Company C, 48th Regiment
Moose, William R.   Private

Company D, 53rd Regiment
Longworth, Samuel   Private

Company A, 57th Regiment
Parnell, Benjamin   First Lieutenant
Baity, J.W.   Private
Beck, Henry   Private
Beck, J.W.   Private
Brock, J.W.   Corporal
Cope, Frederick T.   Private
Etchison, C.H.   Private
Furches, Lewis Alexander   Private
Grant, A.T.   Private
Hellard, Joe   Private
Hellard, Thomas   Private
Keller, Fraley Thomas   Private
Kluttz, Green C.   Private
Little, Daniel M.   Private
Turrentine, William F.   Private
Van Eaton, F.M.   Private

Company B, 57th Regiment
Ferrell, E.L.   Private
Snider, A.W.   Private
Terrell, D.W.   Corporal
Tucker, John   Private
Tucker, Thomas D.   Private

Company H, 57th Regiment
Brinkley, John F.   Sergeant
Call, Henry G.   Private
Deadman, James Anderson   Private
Foster, Andrew J.   Private
Gaither, George W.   Private
Gaither, James M.   Private
Gullett, Joseph T.   Private
Hill, George W.   Private
Holman, J.B.   Private
Kepley, Burgess   Private
Leonard, Jacob   Private
McDaniel, John G.   Private
Monday, Isaac   Private
Spry, Calvin   Private
Sullivan, Patrick   Private
Taylor, G.M.   Private
Van Eaton, Richard T.   Private
Van Zant, Enoch C.   Private
Veach, William E.   Private
Walker, William A.   Private

Company K, 57th Regiment
Douthit, J.M.   Private
Kluttz, Green C.   Private

Company H, 63rd Regiment
Booe, William E.   Captain
Pearson, Charles William   Captain
Campbell, Arthur N.   First Lieutenant
Howell, John C., Sr.   Second Lieutenant
Howell, Joseph H.   Second Lieutenant
Ward, Frank B.   First Lieutenant
Williams, William   First Lieutenant
Albea, William   Sergeant
Allen, A.C.   Private
Allen, B.R.   Private
Arnold, Thomas L.   Buglar
Bailey, Lemuel Johnston   Private
Bailey, Thomas   Private
Baity, F.A.   Corporal
Baity, G.A.   Private
Barnes, W.J.   Private
Barnhart, George E.   Private
Beeman, T.A.   Private
Booe, G.W.   Private
Booe, William H.   Private
Bowden, S.W.   Private
Bracken, Thomas H.   Private
Brackin, John   Private
Brandon, J.C.   Private
Brandon, Joshua   Private
Brandon, W.A.   Private
Brinegar, M.   Private
Brock, L.E.   Private
Brown, T. Frank   Private
Byerly, Hiram   Corporal
Cain, John L.   Private
Carter, J.H.   Private
Casey, E. Perry   Private
Caton, B.F.W.   Private
Chaplin, Jesse   Private
Clark, L.   Private
Click, W.H.   Private
Conrad, P.J.   Private
Cuthrell, George W.   Private

Appendix 1

Dedman, D.M.	Private
Dedman, W.A.	Private
Dwiggens, D.H.	Private
Dwiggens, James Patterson	Private
Eaton, B.F.	Private
Eaton, J.C.	Private
Ellis, E.F.	Private
Etcherson, Edmund	Private
Faircloth, J.D.	Private
Ferebee, S.	Private
Ferebee, W.H.	Corporal
Fleming, S.F.	Sergeant
Foard, John B.	Private
Foster, H.W.	Private
Foster, K.R.	Private
Foster, William M.	Private
Frost, J.F.	Private
Fry, George W.	Private
Gaugh, John	Private
Hartman, G.A.	Private
Hanes, John P.	Private
Hendrix, C.	Private
Hendrix, F.M.	Private
Hightower, Anderson E.	Private
Hill, B.	Private
Hobson, W. Henry	Private
Hodges, John D.	Private
Holman, J.	Private
Holman, Jacob B.	Private
Horn, Thomas	Private
Howard, B.S.	Private
Howard, Joseph Bryant	Private
Howard, Samuel B.	Private
Hutchins, Andrew J.	Private
Ijames, B.G.	Private
Ijames, B.R.	Private
Jackson, Daniel H.	Private
James, Julius	Private
Jones, Henry T.	Private
Kees, John	Private
Kerfuse, J.R.	Private
Lakey, Ellis	Private
Langley, C.A.	Private
Lassiter, J.	Private
Lewis, William	Private
Lunn, John T.	Private
Madison, Harrison	Private
May, F.L.	Private
McClammar, R.	Private
McClammer, M.	Private
McClannan, J.W.	Private
McClannon, W.H.	Private
Miller, Henry	Private
Minor, C.	Private
Minor, Henry	Private
Minor, Madison	Private
Minor, Zerel	Private
Naylor, J.O.	Private
Naylor, S.T.	Private
Newnam, H.L.	Private
Newnam, T.L.	Private
Newnam, W.F.	Private
Penry, Joel	Private
Powell, William Hay	Private
Prewet, N.	Private
Pruett, Anderson	Private
Riblin, J.L.	Private
Rich, Nathaniel Greene	Private
Rich, W.G.	Private
Russell, Gideon F.	Private
Seaford, J.D.	Private
Shackleford, J.	Private
Shamel, S.N.	Private
Shores, Enoch	Private
Shores, H.	Private
Shores, S.O.	Private
Shores, Wiley	Private
Smith, S.A.	Private
Smith, S.L.	Private
Smith, William D.	Private
Sparks, C.M.	Private
Speas, W.H.	Private
Spellman, Newton	Private
Spelman, J.	Private
Steelman, George	Private
Steelman, J.W.	Private
Steelman, Jackson	Private
Swaringen, Samuel T.	Private
Tacket, John G.	Private
Taylor, Walter	Private
Todd, David	Private
Todd, William	Private
Warren, William C.	Private
Williams, F.	Private
Williams, James	Private
Wilson, J.W.	Private
Wilson, James W.	Private
Wood, Henry J.	Private
Wyatt, W.H.	Private
Wynn, Cope H.	Private
Zimmerman, G.W.	Sergeant

Field and Staff, 66th Regiment

Griffin, Samuel C.	Musician
Hall, George W.	Musician

Company G, 66th Regiment

Walker, John W.	Third Lieutenant
Austin, James C.	Musician
Baxter, John W.	Corporal
Brown, Burton	Private
Brown, William	Sergeant
Burton, James M.	Sergeant
Cain, Patrick H.	Private
Carter, Abram H.	Private
Carter, William	Private
Foster, Jesse N	Private
Fraley, John H.	Private

Gobble, Henry C.	Private
Graves, Daniel	Private
Griffin, Noah J.	Private
Griffin, Samuel C.	Musician
Griffin, William T.	Sergeant
Hunt, Henry H.	Private
Hunt, John W.	Private
Leslie, F.M.	Private
Marlin, Joel P.	Corporal
Martin, James C.	Private
Miller, James L.	Private
Potts, Milton	Private
Ruth, William	Private
Sain, Nathan Anderson	Private
Smith, L.W.	Private

Davie County Militia, 77th Regiment, 19th Division

Harbin, Allen Alexander	Colonel
Phelps, Uriah Hunt	Lieutenant Colonel
Bryan, Dr. Talliafero Jay	Major
Little, Samuel Winfield	Major
Booe, Alexander Martin	Captain
Brown, William Carter	Captain
Clouse, William	Captain
Crump, James Adderson	Captain
Daniel, Wilson C.	Captain
Hendron, Denton	Captain
Kinyoun, David Williams	Captain
Lunn, Benjamin Franklin	Captain
Mason, Franklin	Captain
McGuire, James	Captain
Morris, Edwin Simmons	Captain
Pack, John	Captain
Peebles, Nathanial Aaron	Captain
Perry, William Haywood	Captain
Thomason, Willy W.	Captain
Anderson, John	First Lieutenant
Brown, William L.	First Lieutenant
Cain, Richard Franklin	First Lieutenant
Chaffin, Martin Rowan	First Lieutenant
Clark, William Albea	First Lieutenant
Dyson, David Linsey	First Lieutenant
Griffith, Charles Franklin	First Lieutenant
Hobson, Samuel Morehead	First Lieutenant
Isaley, Jesse E.	First Lieutenant
Johnson, James Mullis	First Lieutenant, Regiment Assistant Commissary
Jones, Wifey A.G.	First Lieutenant
Kelly, Albert Calvin	First Lieutenant
Kelly, James Addison	First Lieutenant, Regiment Assistant Quartermaster
Morris, Edwin Simmons	First Lieutenant
Paris, Thomas Williams	First Lieutenant
Tucker, Daniel Seaborn	First Lieutenant
Williams, John Rufus	First Lieutenant
Anderson, Charles Jefferson	Second Lieutenant
Brock, Richard Emmerson	Second Lieutenant
Cain, Casper	Second Lieutenant
Carter, Darius	Second Lieutenant
Carter, William Anderson	Second Lieutenant
Chick, John Nicholas	Second Lieutenant
Cook, Lemuel Blick	Second Lieutenant
Crump, Pleasant John	Second Lieutenant
Deadman, Haley	Second Lieutenant
Eckerson, Andrew Eno	Second Lieutenant
Felker, George	Second Lieutenant
Frost, Ebernaza	Second Lieutenant
Holman, Henry Clay	Second Lieutenant
Lee, Henry Jackson	Second Lieutenant
Lenard, Mathias	Second Lieutenant
Markland, Matthew	Second Lieutenant
Martin, Pleasant Rowan	Second Lieutenant
Naylor, Little Berry	Second Lieutenant
Penry, Thomas Smith	Second Lieutenant
Robeson, Hugh Emmerson	Second Lieutenant
Sain, Casper	Second Lieutenant
Sparkes, John Harvey	Second Lieutenant
Wall, William	Second Lieutenant
West, Anderson Wiley	Second Lieutenant
Williams, Neil Henry Calvin	Second Lieutenant
Williams, Rush Francis	Second Lieutenant

Company E, Company K, 1st Junior Reserve Infantry Regiment North Carolina

Sheek, Leven Alexander	Private

Company B, Carolina Rangers, 10th Virginia Cavalry Regiment

Clement, William Bailey (Dart)	Major
Bingham, Gustavus Adolphus	First Lieutenant
Brock, Noah Monroe	First Lieutenant
Adams, John F.	Private
Atham, Horatio	Third Corporal
Bailey, Nathan A.	Private
Bailey, William A.	Private
Baity, Wiley	Private
Bowles, Benjamin T.	Private
Bowles, Erwin L.	Private
Bowles, William J.	Private
Brewbaker, Richard P.	Private
Brock, J.N. (James)	Private
Brock, Thomas M.	Private
Brock, William F.	First Corporal
Call, Burke (Birch)	Private
Caton, Alfred (Alpha)	Private
Cope, P. Jacob	Private
Davis, Joseph N.	Private
Deaver, Nathan	Private
Ellis, Nathaniel B.	Fourth Corporal

Appendix 1

Ellis, Wiley R.	Private
Etchison, Shadrach M.	Second Corporal
Ferebee, Joseph H.	Private
Foster, Anderson	Private
Foster, Anderson E.	Private
Foster, Henry	Private
Foster, John B.	Fourth Sergeant
Foster, John M.	Private
Foster, Richmond Henry	Private
Fraley, Henry L.	Private
Frost, William A.	Private
Garwood, Lewis B. (Burton)	Private
Heinrich, George	First Sergeant
Hellard, William Henry	Private
Hendricks, James M.	Third Corporal
Hendricks, Jesse A.	Private
Hendricks, William	Private
Jones, Thomas J.	Private
Livingood, David	Private
Logan, Isaac	Private
McClammoch, John	Private
Miller, Henry	Private
Myers, William B.	Private
Nail, Alexander S.	Private
Nolly, William H.	Private
Owen, N. Richard	Private
Peebles, Aaron G.	Private
Rice, Thomas D.	Private
Rice, William A. (Albert)	Private
Robinson, James F.	Private
Sheets, George W.	Private
Sheets, Thomas C.	Private
Smith, William H.	Private
Stonestreet, Jediah	Private
Stuart, J.G.	Corporal
Thompson, Jonas	Private
Thornton, George	Private
Tucker, Frederick M.	First Corporal
Tutrow (Tutterow), Thomas J.	Private
Van Eaton, Barton R.	Private
Van Eaton, McDonald	Private
Wagner, Jr. Henry M.	Second Corporal
Wagner, Sr. Henry M.	Private
Wood, Carter	Private
Zimmerman, Jackson	Private
Zimmerman, Thomas	Private

20th Regiment, Tennessee Volunteers

Austin, Ephriam A.

Appendix 2: Townships Covered in the Censuses

Note: Until 1836 Davie County was part of Rowan County.

1790 Rowan County Townships in Present-day Davie County

Townships not listed on census

1800 Rowan County Townships in Present-day Davie County

Salisbury

1810 Rowan County Townships in Present-day Davie County

Carolina
Lexington
Not Stated
Salisbury

1820 Rowan County Townships in Present-day Davie County

Salisbury
Yadkin
Lexington

1830 Rowan County Townships in Present-day Davie County

Townships not listed on census

1840 Davie County Townships

Townships not listed on census

1850 Davie County Townships

Townships not listed on census

1860 Davie County Townships

Chinquapin
Farmington
Fulton
Hunting Creek
Liberty
Mocksville
Shady Grove
Smith Grove

1870 Davie County Townships

Calahaln
Clarksville
Farmington
Fulton
Jerusalem
Mocksville

1880 Davie County Townships

Calahaln
Clarksville
Farmington
Fulton
Jerusalem
Mocksville
Smith Grove

1890 Davie County Townships

Most of census information was destroyed in fire in Washington

1900 Davie County Townships

Calahaln
Clarksville
Farmington
Fulton

Appendix 2

Jerusalem
Mocksville
Shady Grove

1910 Davie County Townships
Calahaln
Clarksville
Farmington
Fulton
Jerusalem
Mocksville
Shady Grove

1920 Davie County Townships
Calahaln
Clarksville
Farmington
Fulton
Jerusalem
Mocksville
Shady Grove

1930 Davie County Townships
Advance
Calahaln

Clarksville
Farmington
Fulton
Jerusalem
Mocksville
Shady Grove

Number of Soldiers from Each Township

Calahaln	91
Chinquepin	65
Clarksville	34
Farmington	164
Fulton	143
Hunting Creek	2
Jerusalem	68
Liberty	51
Mocksville	10
Shady Grove	47
Smith Grove	95
Unidentified	373
TOTAL	**1143**

Appendix 3:
Burial Sites of Davie County Confederate Soldiers

Advance Baptist Church Cemetery

Location: From Highway 158, travel Highway 801 south to Advance. Cemetery is on the right side of highway past the railroad.
    Massey, Thomas G.

Advance United Methodist Church Cemetery

Location: From Highway 158, travel Highway 801 south to Advance. Cemetery is on the left just past the railroad.
    Bailey, William A.
    Carter, J.H.
    Caton, Alfred (Alpha)
    Caton, Orrell
    Chambers, Peter
    Garwood (Garrawood), David T.
    Green, George E.
    Hartman, Enoch
    Howard, Joseph
    Jones, Wifey (Wiley) A.G.
    Myers, Zadock
    Oaks (Oakes), James P.
    Orrell, David E.
    Orrell (Orel), Robert R.
    Potts, F.A. (Francis)
    Robertson, Thomas E.
    Sheets, Thomas C.
    Sheets, Wesley M.
    Sparks, John Harvey
    Tucker, Daniel Seaborn

Anderson Family Cemetery

Location: Located in a heavily wooded knoll south of Charles Anderson House in Calahaln.
    Anderson, A.A. (Albert Alexander)
    Anderson, Andrew Jackson
    Anderson, Charles Jefferson

Bear Creek Baptist Church Cemetery

Location: Take Highway 601 North from Mocksville to Liberty Church Road, turn left and travel to Bear Creek Road, turn left again and the church will be on the right.
    Bowles, William J.
    Cain, William G.
    Cartner, John
    Cunningham, Samuel M.
    Danner, Frederick (M.)
    Foote, L.R. (Luther)
    Frost, J.F.
    Holeman (Holman), James S.
    Little, Dr. Samuel Winfield
    Richardson, G.W. (George)
    Stanley, Jefferson J.

Bethel United Methodist Church Cemetery

Location: From North Main Street, Mocksville, turn right on Milling Road to Bethel Church Road; turn right and church will be on the right opposite Crown Wood Furniture Plant.
    Foster, George
    Foster, Samuel
    Nail, Alexander S.
    Van Eaton, Richard T.
    Williams, Neil Henry Calvin

Bethlehem United Methodist Church Cemetery

Location: From Mocksville, travel Highway 158 to Redland Road, turn left, cross over Interstate 40; church is on the left.
    Bowden, S.W.
    Faircloth, J.D. (Jacob)
    Foster, William M.
    Howard, B.S. (Benjamin)

James, W. (William Asberry)
McElroy, William J.
Plott, John
Smith, James Douglas
Smith, William D. (David)
Smith, William Harden
Sparks, C.M. (Charles)
Taylor, William M.
Walker, John W.
Ward, Frank B.
West, Anderson Wiley
West, Jiles (Giles)
Williams, D.L.
Williams, Richard M.

Booe-Hunter-Powell Family Cemetery

Location: This small overgrown family cemetery is located on the side of Danner Road; north of Holman Crossroads on Highway 601 North.
Graves, John W. (H.)

Center United Methodist Church Cemetery

Location: Located approximately four and one-half miles west of Mocksville on Highway 64 just past Interstate 40.
Bailey, Henry L.
Bolds (Boles) (Bowles), James L.
Casey, E. Perry
Dwiggins, D.H.
Dwiggins, James Patterson
Gowen, Simeon C.
Granger, W. Burton
Horn, Enoch
Ijames, B.G. (Basil) (Boswell)
Ijames, B.R. (Beal)
Ijams (Ijames), James D.
Keller, Joseph
Kerfees, John Peter
Kerfuse, J.R. (James)
Kurfees (Kerfoose) (Chalmus), Zedock C.
Leach, David
Penry, Boone T.
Penry, Thomas Smith
Powell, William Hay
Seaford, J.D.
Smith, Beal I.
Stonestreet, John H.
Tuttarow (Tutorow) (Tuterow), George W.
Tutterow (Tuttarow), John V. (B.)
Tutterow, William Nelson
Tutterow, William W.
Walker, John W.

Chestnut Grove United Methodist Church Cemetery

Location: Located at 3240 Highway 601, north of Mocksville.
Bracken, John W.
Clement Family Cemetery
Location: Located on Eaton Street in Mocksville.
Clement, Baxter Clegg
Clement, Jesse A.
Clement, Jesse Lee
Clement, John H. (Henry)
Clement, Wiley Adam
Clement, William Bailey (Dart)

Concord United Methodist Church Cemetery

Location: From Mocksville, travel Highway 601 south four miles to Deadmon Road; turn left, go to Highway 801 south; turn right and cemetery is on the left.
Barnhart, George E. (Ephraim)
Butler, Thomas S.
Divire (Dwire), Daniel
Foster, Andrew
Foster, Jesse N.
Hodges, John D.

Cornatzer Baptist Church Cemetery

Location: 609 Cornatzer Road, Advance, North Carolina.
Cornatser (Cornatzer), Jacob C.

Cornatzer United Methodist Church Cemetery

Location: Travel Highway 64 east from Mocksville to Cornatzer Road; turn left; cemetery is three miles on the right.
McDaniel, Elias

Crump Family Cemetery

Location: Located on Cherry Hill Road, SR 1819, on Singleton Land.
Crump, James Adderson
Crump, Pleasant John

Dwiggins Family Cemetery

Location: One mile south of Center United Methodist Church, which is four miles west of Mocksville, on Highway 64.
Penry, Joel

Eaton's Baptist Church Cemetery

Location: Travel Highway 601 north past William R. Davie School, turn right on Richie Road; cemetery is at the end of the road.

Cain, James H.
Collett, Ezekiel
Collette, Benjamin F.
Etchison, C.H. (Caswell)
Frost, Eberneza (Ebenezer)
Furches, John M.
Furches, Lewis Alexander
Furches, Thomas W. (H.)
Furches, W.F. (William)
Howell, John C.
Hunter, John W.
McClammar, R. (Robert Reece)
Rich, Samuel Chase

Elbaville United Methodist Church Cemetery

Location: 2595 N.C. Highway 801 South, Advance.

Byerly, Hiram
Ellis, Wiley R.
Markland (Marklin), Matthew
Zimmerman, Jackson

Ellis Family Cemetery

Location: Take Highway 801 to People's Creek Road on Neely property. Entry through farm gate at sharpest angle of this road coming from Elbaville United Methodist Church.

Ellis, William R.

Farmington Community Cemetery

Location: Travel Highway 158 to Farmington Road, turn left, drive across Highway 801; on left at the Methodist Church.

Bahnson, Charles F.
Brock, Richard Emmerson
Brock, Thomas M.
Harding, Green Berry (Patterson)
Hartman, G.A.
Horne, Stephen W.
Johnson, James Mullis
Johnson, William Gaston

Fork Baptist Church Cemetery

Location: 3140 Highway 64 east from Mocksville.

Bailey, Benjamin (Berry)
Carter, Abraham (Abram H.)
Chaplin, Alexander (James)
Cope, P. Jacob
Foster, A.M.
Foster, Albert N.
Foster, Coleman
Foster, John E.
Foster, Samuel L.
Foster, William H.
Graves, George F.
Hendrix, N.G. (Ningey)
Lard (Laird), Levi (Levy)
McDaniel, George W.
Minor, Zerel
Motley, M.M. (Madison)
Myers, Henry J.
Potts, Newberry
Ratts, Hiram C.
Redwine, John F.
Sain, John A.
Sheets, George W.
Stewart (Steward), Edward D.
Williams, Daniel M.
Williams, John Rufus
Wyatt, W.H.

Foster Family Cemetery

Location: Located off Highway 601 North on Madison Road. Go past houses on left, in field of hedgerow, follow to edge of woods. No access road.

Foster, Henry

Frost Family Cemetery

Location: Drive Highway 601 north to Holman Cross Roads, turn right on Cana Road to Woodward Road. Cemetery is about 100 feet from Woodward Road on the right.

Frost, William A.

Fulton United Methodist Church Cemetery

Location: 5500 Highway 801 South, Advance.

Fry, George W.
Hanes (Hains), George A.
Hanes, Jacob H.
Hanes, John H.
Hanes (Hains), Spencer Joseph

Hendricks Family Cemetery

Location: The cemetery is located on a slight rise one hundred yards west of the Dutchman's Creek bridge on Highway 601 North.

Hendrix, F.M. (Francis Monroe)

Hobson Family Cemetery

Location: Drive Highway 601 south from Mocksville to Pleasant Acres Drive. Cemetery is about one hundred yards from the end of the drive.

Hobson, John M.
Hobson, Samuel Morehead
Hobson, W. Henry

Ijames Baptist Church Cemetery

Location: Travel Highway 64 west from Mocksville to Sheffield Road; turn right. Church is on the right, on corner of Ijames Church Road and Sheffield Road.
    Ratledge, W.H. (William)

Jerusalem Baptist Church Cemetery

Location: Church is on east side of Highway 601 South approximately seven miles from Mocksville. Cemetery is on both sides of the road.
    Beck, Henry
    Bessent, Daniel D.
    Charles, John N. (Newton)
    Livengood, Dan E.
    Thompson, John

Joppa Cemetery

Location: Highway 601 North (Yadkinville Road) in Mocksville on the right. Next to Squire Boone Shopping Center.
    Austin, Ephraim A.
    Austin, James C. (Clinton)
    Brown, Burton
    Deaver, Nathan
    Gaither, William H.
    Griffin (Griffon), William T.
    Harbin, Allen Alexander
    Jones, William B.
    Kelly, Albert Calvin
    Kelly, James Addison
    Kelly, William Frohock
    McGuire, James
    Parnell, Benjamin
    Sanford, Calvin Cowles

Legion Memorial Park Cemetery

Location: Located on Highway 801 at Cooleemee, North Carolina.
    Cope, John
    House, John W.
    Wright, Amos

Liberty Baptist Church Cemetery

Location: Highway 601 north of Mocksville, approximately five miles, turn left on Liberty Church Road. Church is approximately five miles on the left.
    Morris, Edwin Simmons

Liberty United Methodist Church Cemetery

Location: Highway 601 South from Mocksville, turn right on Gladstone Road.
    Daniel, Wilson C.
    Dedman, W.A.
    Granger, James F.
    Graves, Albert N.
    Graves, Jeremiah
    Hendron (Hendren), Denton
    Marlin, Joel P.
    Nolly, William H.
    Spry, Calvin
    Taylor, Andrew Jackson
    Veach, William E.

Macedonia Moravian Church Cemetery

Location: From intersection of Highways 158 and 801, drive north on 801 approximately three miles towards Farmington. Cemetery is on the right, next to the church.
    Allen, Peter
    Cook, Lemuel Blick
    Griffith, Charles Franklin
    Hall, Ferdinand E. (Eugene)
    Hall, Henry H. (F.)
    Lee, Henry Jackson
    Miller, John E.
    Riddle, T.C. (Thomas Calvin)
    Sheek, Leven Alexander
    Smith, Samuel T.
    Ward, William P.

Mount Bethel United Methodist Church Cemetery

514 Mount Bethel Road, Harmony, North Carolina
Location: Highway 64 West from Mocksville to Highway 901. Bear right on 901 and go approximately 2.2 miles to Rimrock Road. Turn left, go approximately 2.5 miles to end of road and turn left on Mount Bethel Road. Church is on the right.
    Thomas, E.J. (Evan Jackson)

New Union United Methodist Church Cemetery

Location: Highway 64 West from Mocksville to Sheffield Road. Turn right, go approximately 5 miles, church is on the left.
    Foster, William M.
    Richardson, Addison M.
    Richardson, David Columbus
    Shaw, Augustus
    Smith, William J.
    Tutarno (Tutterow), A.P.
    Verner, Hardy

Oak Grove United Methodist Church Cemetery

Location: Approximately two miles east of Mocksville on Highway 158 at corner of Oak Grove Church Road.

Bowles, G.W.
Gaither, George W.
Gaither, James M.
McClamrock, Lucius Milton
Nail, Jasper H.Y.
Nail, Phillip
Nichols, B.F. (Benjamin)
Sain, Cheshire

Oakwood Cemetery, Raleigh, North Carolina

Location: 701 Oakwood Avenue, Raleigh, North Carolina.
Adams, John F.

Oakwood Cemetery, Statesville, North Carolina

Location: 114 Oakwood Road, Statesville, North Carolina
Anderson, Dr. John

Olive Branch Cemetery

Location: Highway 158 to Farmington Road; turn left and travel approximately five miles. Cemetery is on a knoll on the left side of the road.
Brock, J.N.
Brock, L.E.
Clark, William Albea
Lunn, Benjamin Franklin

Peebles Family Cemetery

Location: Highway 801 South from Advance, turn left on People's Creek Road at Elbaville Church. Cemetery is on private land on site overlooking Yadkin River.
Peebles, Aaron G.
Peebles, Nathanial Aaron

Quaker Cemetery

Location: Highway 64 East to Garwood Road, turn left. Cemetery is on private land on left side of the road.
Thornton, George

Rose Cemetery

Location: Cemetery Street, Mocksville, North Carolina.
Bailey, Thomas
Bailey, William Hall
Booe, Alexander Martin
Brown, Dr. William Carter
Chaffin, Martin Rowan
Etchison, W.C. Perry

Gaither, Lemuel G.
Grant, A.T.
Roberson (Robertson), Hugh Emmerson
Spencer, O.H. (Oliver Hause)

Sain Family Cemetery

Location: Highway 158 East from Mocksville to Sain Road, turn right; go ¼ mile to pull-off on right side of road. Cemetery is ½ mile down a path in the woods.
Sain, A.T. (Albert)
Sain, Casper

St. Matthews Lutheran Church Cemetery

Location: Highway 64 West from Mocksville to Davie Academy Road, turn left. Church is on the right.
Dayvault (Daywalt), Solomon M.
Daywalt, Alfred J. (Alford Davalt)
Felker, George

Salem United Methodist Church Cemetery

Location: Drive Highway 64 west from Mocksville approximately eight miles to Davie Academy Road; turn left, drive two miles and cross the Interstate 40 bridge; turn left on Salem Church Road.
Dyson, David Linsey
Foster, John M.
Kesler, M.F. (Madison)
Lapish, John A.
Lowery, D.L. (Dabney)
Martin, James C.
McDaniel (McDannel), Benjamin L. (Lewis)
Roberts, Paschal
Stroud, David (D.F.)

Smith Grove United Methodist Church Cemetery

Location: 3492 Highway 158 East, from Mocksville, North Carolina.
Allen, B.R.
Call, Murphy G.
Clouse, L.A.
Ellis, Thomas Nelson
Ellis, William A.
Foster, Benjamin L.
Hanes, Harrison Henry
Haskins (Hoskins), James F.
Hendrix, C. (William Coston)
Howard, Joseph Bryant
Howard, Samuel B.
Martin, Giles (John G.)
McClammer (McCamroch), M. (James Martin)

McClammoch, John
Miller, Jacob C.
Miller, James W.
Owen, N. Richard
Stewart, William
Taylor, Walter
Walker, William
Williams, James

Society Baptist Church Cemetery

Location: Highway 64 West from Mocksville, to Society Church Road, turn right; church is on the left.
Gray, Thomas
Guffy, Samuel M.
Holman, J.B.
Horn, William Pinkney
Mason, Franklin
Stroud, Rich S.

Stewart Family Cemetery

Location: Highway 801 South, one mile past Fulton Methodist Church. Cemetery is ¾ mile off highway on private property.
Stuart, J.G.

Tatum Family Cemetery

Location: This is now a part of the Jerusalem Baptist Church Cemetery, which is located on Highway 601 South approximately seven miles from Mocksville.
Deadman, Haley
Wiseman, Alfred W.

Turner Family Cemetery

Location: Located off Jericho Road in the woods on private property, ¼ mile east of the corner of Jericho and Buck Seaford Road.
Turner, Pinkney (Pinckney)

Union Chapel United Methodist Church Cemetery

Location: Four miles north of Mocksville on Highway 601.
Boger, Paul
Cheshire, John A.
Holman, Henry Clay
Shoemaker, Alfred C.

Walker Family Cemetery

Location: On Dulin Road, off Highway 158 East from Mocksville.
Walker, James

Wesley Chapel United Methodist Church Cemetery

Location: Off N.C. Highway 801 North in Pino area.
Ferebee, W.H. (William)
Foster, Franklin (Francis) A.
Hutchins, Andrew J.
Lakey, Ellis
Latham, James M., Sr.
McClannan (Clanen), J.W. (John)
McClannon, W.H. (William
Wood, Carter

Williams, Dr. Francis Rush Family Cemetery

Location: This family burying ground is located on Cedar Creek Road west of Farmington in Farmington Township.
Williams, Beauford B.
Williams, Rush Francis

Yadkin Valley Baptist Church Cemetery

Location: Highway 158 East from Mocksville, turn left on Highway 801 North to right on Yadkin Valley Road. Church is approximately three miles on right.
Swaringen, Samuel T.

Zion Chapel United Methodist Church Cemetery

Location: Highway 64 West from Mocksville, to right on Sheffield Road. Pass Cleary's Crossroads, New Union UMC buildings on right, cemetery on left.
Beck, A.M. (Andrew)
Beck, St. Leger
Kesler, William Richard
Lowery, John T.T.
Powell, E.H. (Elias)
Ratledge, D.J. (Daniel)

Appendix 4:
Mocksville Monument Names of Men Who Died in the Civil War

Located on Court Square, Mocksville, North Carolina. References are to entry numbers.

Adams, W. 3
Allen, A.C. 5
Allen, Isaac 8
Anderson, Charles S. 16
Anderton, William D. 20
Athan, Asbury 24
Austin, James 29
Austin, John 31
Austin, William 33
Bailey, Lemuel J. 40
Baity, Thomas B. 50

Barlow, John J. 55
Beauchamp, John W. 64
Beck, William 71
Beeman, Richard S. 74
Bell, N.R. 76
Bentley, A. 77
Berryman, James M. 79
Bessant (Bessent), Daniel D. 80
Black, Daniel L. 85
Blackburn, John 88
Blackwelder, Daniel E. 89

Memorial Monument (Marie Roth)

Appendix 4

Boger, Moses 91
Bowden, John O. 104
Bowden, Matthew (no information available)
Boyd, James S. 113
Brewer, Hubbard 124
Brindle, Robert R. 125
Brinegar, M. 126
Briniger, John 127
Brock, John W. Clark 131
Brock, Levin E. 133
Brock, Thomas M. 136
Brock, William F. 137
Cain, Anderson H. 156
Cain, Daniel H. 157
Cain, Daniel J. 158
Cain, William F. 163
Call, Henry G. 168
Carter, William C. 184
Cartner, James F. 185
Chaffin, Alexander W. 193
Chaffin, Nathan M.D. 196
Chandler, Solomon 199
Chaplin, Jesse 201
Chaplin, Solomon (no information available)
Charles, William F. 205
Cheshire, Johnathan W. 208
Church, William 211
Clary, James 215
Click, Daniel W. 223
Cloninger, Alonzo 232
Conrad, P.J. 240
Cook, James 242
Cope, Andrew 245
Cope, William G. 249
Cornatzer, Nathan B. (no information available)
Correll, David H. (no information available)
Cranfield, Hanes 251
Cranfield, Jackson Lewis 253
Cranfield, James L. 254
Cranfill, Gideon 256
Cunningham, F.M. 262
Cunningham, George 263
Cunningham, Thomas 266
Davis, Franklin 274
Dayvault, Solomon M. 282
Debnam (Deadman), James A. 286
Dedmon, D.M. 291
Dismuks, Richard L. 293
Dixon, Henry (no information available)
Dowdy, James 299
Drake, William D. 300
Eaton, J.C. 310
Eccles, John C. 311
Ellis, E.F. 313
Ellis, James M. 315
Ellis, Nathaniel B. 316
Ellis, William R. 322
Ellis, Willy Jones 318
Ellison, Donalson 323
Etcherson, James W. 326

Etchison, Shadrach M. 329
Ferebee, Joseph C.
Ferebee, S. 337
Foster, Azanah L. 352
Foster, James A. 362
Foster, James H.W. 363
Foster, John E. 368
Foster, Robert 374
Foster, Samuel L. 377
Foster, Thomas 379
Frost, William A. 392
Fry, Albert W. 393
Furches, Thomas W. 401
Gaither, William H. 410
Garwood, Robert 414
Gatton, Franklin 415
Gatton, James 417
Gatton, Pleasant 418
Granger, James M. 427
Graves, John Ellis 438
Green, George E. 445
Grimes, Noah B. 450
Hall, Ferdinand L. 459
Hall, Henry H. 461
Hanes, George A. 464
Hanes, Jack H. (no information available)
Hanes, Jacob H. 466
Harper, John A. 479
Helfer, S.F. 491
Hendrix, Stephen 506
Hepler, Benjamin F. 510
Hill, David F. 513
Hill, George W. 514
Hillard (Hellard), J. 492
Hobbs (Hobb), Julius 516
Hodges, Joseph 522
Holder, Hosea L. 524
Holder, Jacob 525
Holman, Jacob B. 532
Hoose, William 535
Horn, John J. 537
Horn, Lewis G. 538
Howard, Harrison H. 547
Howard, Nathan 550
Ijames, Henry H. 568
Ijames, John W. 570
Jackson, Daniel H. 575
Jacobs, John 576
James, J.F. 577
James, J.W. 578
James, Thomas A. 581
Jarvis, Jonathan 583
Johnson, S.W. 589
Jones, Henry T. 593
Jones, James Madison (no information available)
Jones, Samuel A. 598
Jordan, Gurney 604
Jordan, Jonathan 605
Kees, John 607
Kesler, Henry P. 619

Mocksville Monument Names

King, Anderson 623
King, L.B. 625
Kurfees, Caleb W. 629
Kurfees, Franklin J. 630
Laird (Lard), George W. 640
Lane, William A. 635
Latham, Jeremiah M. 648
Leach, James Franklin 652
Leach, John W. 654
Leonard, Emanuel 658
Leonard, Jesse 660
Little, D.M. 665
Little, Robert A. 666
Livengood, Christian (no information available)
Logan, Isaac 672
Lunn, John T. 679
Lynch, William A. 680
Madra, William H. 683
Marlin, John L. 688
Marshall, George W. 690
Martin, Benjamin J. 691
Martin, David W. 692
Mason, Grief G. 697
McBride, John A. 703
McCarter, Thomas 704
McClenan, Matthew A. 712
McCracken, William A. 713
McDaniel, Mace 720
McDonald, James 724
Minor, Henry 745
Minor, Madison 747
Mock, Henry A. 749
Myers, Jesse 764
Nail, Philip A. 773
Newnam, H.A. 782
Newnam, W.F. 784
Owen, William H. 795
Owens, A.L. 796
Parks, William 806
Peacock, George W. 813
Peebles, Aaron G. 815
Penry, Boone T. 820
Penry, William H. 823
Perry, William 825
Phelps, Britton 827
Phillips, John W. 830
Pool, Benjamin F. 834
Potts, Peter W.M. 842
Potts, William 843
Prather, Alfred A. 847
Prather, Eli 848
Raben, Samuel W. 853
Ridenhour, Anderson J. (no information available)
Ridenhour (Rhidenhour), John W. 862
Ridenhour, Losson 876
Rose, Samuel W. 883
Sain, Jacob 896
Sain, Joseph 898
Sain, William 902
Seamon, Losson 909

Shackleford, J. 911
Shadrick, David 912
Shadrick, Sion 914
Shives, James 929
Shives, Joseph P. 930
Simmons, Henry 938
Smith, S.A. 951
Smith, William A. 955
Smith, William P. 960
Smith, Zimmereck N. 961
Smoot, Daniel J. 963
Smoot, Pinkney 965
Smoot, Wilson D. 966
Speas, W.H. 971
Sport, William B. 975
Stanly (Stanley), Nathan W. 983
Steelman, George 984
Stewart, Daniel 986
Stewart, Hezekiah 988
Stewart, Spencer 989
Swaringen, Iva F. 999
Tacket, John G. 1001
Taylor, G.M. 1003
Taylor, Giles 1004
Thomas, E.S. 1015
Thomas, John B. 1016
Thompson, Rufus A. 1021
Travillion, Meekins C. 1028
Turner, Esquire 1034
Turner, George W. 1035
Turner, J.A. 1037
Turrentine, William F. 1039
Tutterow (Tutrow), Thomas J. 1042
Tutterow (Tutarow), Thomas P. 1041
Tysinger, Henry H. 1047
Tysinger, William M. 1048
Van (Van Eaton), James M. 1051
Vesler (Verher), Peter 1056
Vinagum, Thomas V. 1059
Von Eaton, John I. 1062
Von Eaton, Samuel P. 1063
Waggoner, John H. 1066
Wagner, Jacob 1069
Wagner, W.R. 1070
Walker, Henry G. 1073
Wallace, Daniel C. 1082
Warner, C.J. 1087
Warren, William C. 1090
Welch, Elijah A. 1094
Welch, John A. 1095
Whitaker, Alfred 1101
Whitlock, Thomas F. 1105
Wilkerson, Mark 1107
Williams, Beauford B. 1108
Williams, Jacob W. 1114
Williams, John 1116
Williams, William 1122
Wood, Henry J. 1133
Wood, Ira 1134
Zimmerman, Thomas 1143

Appendix 5:
Men Who Died in the Civil War Not on the Mocksville Monument

Located on Court Square, Mocksville, North Carolina. References are to entry numbers.

Anderson, Andrew Jackson 14
Anderson, John T. 19
Austin, Ephraim A. 27
Baity, J.W. 48
Baity, William J. 52
Baxter, John W. 63
Brinkley, John F. 129
Brown, William 144
Brown, Dr. William Carter 146
Burton, James M. 153
Call, John 169
Carter, William 182
Cheshire, Richard (Richmond) B. 209
Clifford, Joseph C. 229
Clifford, William C. 230
Codie (Cody), Godfrey 235
Collette, Robert W. 238
Dixon (Dixson), William 294
Douthit, J.M. 298
Evans, William 332
Foster, A. (Anderson) F. 345
Fraley, John T. 385
Fraley, Milas J. 386
Fray (Frey), Benjamin F. 387
Frost, Calvin E. 388
Gaither, Wiley 409
Granger, Moses Lee 429
Graves, Daniel 434

Graves, Jacob B. 436
Grimes, William A. 451
Gullet, Joseph Thomas 454
Haire, Perry 457
Hellard (Hilliard), Thomas 493
Holdman (Holman), Thomas 528
Kluttz, Green C. 628
Leach, John 653
Longworth, Samuel 674
Monday (Munday), Isaac 751
Parrish, Wesley W. 811
Parrish, Willis G. 812
Pence, Henry 818
Potts (Pots), Calvin J. 837
Rudicil, Anderson 887
Rusher, Edward A. 888
Ruth, William 890
Seaford, Peter 905
Seaford, Solomon 906
Shaw, William 918
Snider, A.W. 967
Terrell, D.W. 1011
Totten, John C., Jr. 1027
Tucker, John 1031
Tucker, Thomas D. 1032
Walker, John W. 1075
Walker, William A. 1079

Bibliography

Major Reference Centers

State Archives, Raleigh, N.C.

Davie County Public Library, Mocksville, N.C.

In addition to the traditional reference materials in the Davie County Library, there are over four hundred pages of recently acquired copies of applications for Civil War pensions, lists of pension applicants, letters concerning qualifications and correspondence concerning family members.

Newspapers

Davie County did not have its own newspaper until fifteen years after the Civil War ended in 1865. *The People's Press* of Salem, N.C., 1851–1892, remained in operation throughout the war reporting news of deaths and injuries of soldiers from the area.

Public Documents

Federal Census of Davidson County, N.C.: 1850, 1860, 1870, 1880

Federal Census of Davie County:
    1850 by Forsyth County Genealogical Society
    1860 by Nancy K. Murphy and Everette G. Sain
    1870 by Nancy K. Murphy and Everette G. Sain
    1880 by Nancy K. Murphy and Everette G. Sain

Davie County Marriages 1836–1900
    Includes Bride's Index. Compiled for the Davie County Historical and Genealogical Society by Nancy K. Murphy
    Davie County Cemeteries Volume I, A-K and Volume II, L-Z. Compiled by the Davie County Historical and Genealogical Society, Mocksville, N.C.
    Marriage Records of Davidson County, N.C. 1822–1880 Volume I. Compiled by Marie L. Hinson, 1992

Published Works

Almasy, Sandra Lee. *North Carolina 1890 Civil War Veterans Census*. Joliet, Ill.: Kensington Glen Publishing, 1990.

Barrow, Charles Kelley, J.H. Segars and R.B. Rosenburg, eds. *Forgotten Confederates: An Anthology about Black Southerners*. Journal of Confederate History series, vol. XIV. Atlanta, GA: Southern Heritage Press, 1995.

Bradley, Stephen E., Jr. (abstracted by). *North Carolina Confederate Home Guard Examinations 1863–1864*. Keysville, VA: 1993.

_____, ed. *North Carolina Confederate Military Officers Roster*. Wilmington, N.C.: Broadfoot, 1992.

Casstevens, Frances H. *The Civil War and Yadkin County*. Jefferson, N.C.: McFarland, 1997.

Clark, Walter, ed. *Histories of the Several Regiments and Battalions from North Carolina in the Great War 1861–1865*. Written by members of the Respective Commands. 5 volumes. Raleigh, N.C.: E.M. Uzzell, 1901.

Cook, Gerald Wilson. *The Last Tarheel Militia 1861–1865*. Winston-Salem, N.C.: G.W. Cook, 1987.

Davis, William C. *The Commanders of the Civil War*. London: Salamander Books, 1999.

Driver, Robert J. *10th Virginia Cavalry*. Lynchburg, VA: H.E. Howard, 1982.

Hairston, Peter W. *The Cooleemee Plantation and Its People*. Winston-Salem, N.C.: Hunter, 1986.

The Heritage of Davidson County. Winston-Salem, N.C.: Hunter, 1982.

The Heritage of Davie County. Waynesville, N.C.: Walsworth, 1997.

The Heritage of Rowan County. Charlotte, N.C.: Delmar, 1991.

Hewitt, Janet. *North Carolina Roster of Confederate Soldiers 1861–1865, Volume III*. Wilmington, N.C.: Broadfoot, 1999.

Jordan, W.T., Louis Manarin and Matthew Brown. *North Carolina Troops 1861–1865: A Roster*. Raleigh: N.C. Department of Cultural Resources, Division of History and Archives, 1988.

Marsh, C.C. *Official Records of the Union and Confederate Navies in the War of the Rebellion*. Series II, vol. I. Washington, D.C.: Government Printing Office, 1921.

Mohney, Kirk Franklin. *The Historic Architecture of Davie County, North Carolina*. Winston-Salem, N.C.: Winston Printing, 1986.

Moore, John W., ed. *Roster of N.C. Troops in the War Between the States*. 4 volumes. Raleigh, N.C.: Edwards and Broughton, 1882.

Tompkins, Robert M., ed. *Death Notices from the*

People's Press [Salem, N.C.] *1851–1892*. Winston-Salem, N.C.: Forsyth County Genealogical Society, 1997.

Wall, James W. *History of Davie County*. Mocksville, N.C.: Davie County Historical Publishing Assoc., 1969.

Watford, Christopher M., ed. *The Civil War in North Carolina: Soldiers' and Civilians' Letters and Diaries, 1861–1865; Volume 1: The Piedmont*. Jefferson, N.C.: McFarland, 2003.

_____. *The Civil War Roster of Davidson County, North Carolina*. Jefferson, N.C.: McFarland, 2001.

Index

References are to entry numbers in the Roster
except when preceded by *p* indicating a page number.

Adams, John F. 1
Adams, John Q. 2
Adams, W. (William) 3
Aiken's Landing, James River, Virginia 46, 48, 129, 400, 401, 457, 573, 603, 679, 762, 772, 823, 1027, 1055, 1129
Albea, William 4
Alexander, Margaret J. 623
Alexander, Nancy M. 56
Alexander, Zilvia (Zilpha) 639
Allen, A.C. 5
Allen, Abram T. 6
Allen, B.R. 7
Allen, Dorcas A. 7
Allen, Eliza 364
Allen, Ellen Celia 922
Allen, Isaac 8
Allen, J.F. 9
Allen, James P. 10
Allen, Margaret J. 739
Allen, Peter 11
Allen, Rebecca 11
Allen, S.J. 255
Allen, William W. 12
Anderson, A.A. (Albert Alexander) 13
Anderson, Andrew Jackson 14
Anderson, Charles Jefferson 15
Anderson, Charles S. 16
Anderson, Delia 176
Anderson, Edwin M. 17
Anderson, Elizabeth C. 15
Anderson, Dr. John 18
Anderson, John T. 19
Anderson, Julia Ellen 18
Anderson, Martha M. 17
Anderson, Mary Frances 13
Anderson, Mary Jane 568
Anderson, Nancy 16
Anderson, Tobitha Olivia 18
Anderton, William D. 20
Antietam, Maryland *p*4, 222
Appomattox Court House, Virginia *p*3, 13, 24, 34, 75, 81, 134, 152, 172, 216, 219, 222, 257, 265, 284, 294, 358, 360, 398, 402, 416, 443, 452, 469, 471, 508, 515, 523, 529, 571, 582, 585, 631, 772, 881, 892, 908, 921, 980, 992, 1022, 1038, 1043, 1049, 1053, 1058, 1128
Armsworthy, J.C. 21
Arnold, Thomas L. 22
Atham, Horatio 23
Atham, Mary 23
Athan, Asbury 24
Athan, Mary Polly 24
Austin, Asberry 25
Austin, Barbara C. 30
Austin, C. 26
Austin, Catherine 28
Austin, Catherine C. 1127
Austin, Cornelia (Nealey A.) 245
Austin, Elizabeth J. 25
Austin, Ephraim A. 27
Austin, Green B. 28
Austin, James 29
Austin, James C. (Clinton) 30
Austin, John 31
Austin, Mary E. 612
Austin, R.M. (Richard) 32
Austin, William 33

Bagarly, John F. 34
Bahnson, Charles F. 35
Bahnson, Jane Amanda 35
Bailey, Anna 43
Bailey, Benjamin (Berry) 36
Bailey, Catherine 1086
Bailey, Emily 1143
Bailey, H.H. 37
Bailey, Henry L. 38
Bailey, Jessie 42
Bailey, John K. 39
Bailey, Lemuel Johnston 40
Bailey, M.A. 39
Bailey, Mary Elizabeth 189
Bailey, Nancy 38, 494
Bailey, Nathan A. 41
Bailey, P. Jane 43
Bailey, Thomas 42
Bailey, William A. 43
Bailey, William Hall 44

Baily, Elizabeth 859
Baitey, Lydia M. 163
Baity (Beaty), Abigail 47
Baity, Amanda J. 66
Baity, Eliza 45
Baity, F.A. (Francis) 45
Baity, G.A. (George Alex) 46
Baity (Beaty), George W. 47
Baity, J.S. (Jane) (Jenetta) 46
Baity, J.W. 48
Baity, James D. 49
Baity, Margaret I. (Isabella) 84
Baity, Mary 48
Baity, Sarah C. 49
Baity, Sarah E. 800
Baity, Sarah Elisabeth 52
Baity (Beatty), Thomas B. 50
Baity, Wiley 51
Baity, William J. 52
Baker, Elizabeth 54
Baker, Margaret E. 53
Baker, Thomas J. 53
Baker, Thomas J. (Jefferson) 54
Baltimore, Maryland 53, 154, 521, 1079
Banks, Mary Ann 442
Barber, Lina 217
Barlow, John J. 55
Barlow, Nancy M. 56
Barlow, Sarah 55
Barlow, Wiley 56
Barnes, W.J. 57
Barneycastle, Catherine 1009
Barneycastle, Jabus A. 58
Barneycastle, James 59
Barneycastle, Louisa Elizabeth 706
Barneycastle, P.F. (Pleasant Franklin) 60
Barnhardt, Elizabeth S. 61
Barnhart, George E. (Ephraim) 61
Barrouth, Henry F. 62
Barrow, Jane 791
Baxter, John W. 63
Beaty, Abigail *see* Baity, Abigail

Index

Beaty, George W. *see* Baity, George W.
Beatty, Thomas B. *see* Baity, Thomas B.
Beauchamp, Elizabeth Jane 325
Beauchamp, John W. 64
Beauchamp, Mary E. 64
Beauchamp, Nancy Elizabeth 483
Beauchamp, Sarah A. 863
Beauchamp, Sarah Jane 969
Beck, A.M. (Andrew) 65
Beck, Amanda J. 66
Beck, Annie M. 69
Beck, Elizabeth 70
Beck, Henry 66
Beck, J.P. 67
Beck, J.W. (John) 68
Beck, Juley 65
Beck, Little W. 69
Beck, Margaret M.A. 72
Beck, Mary 872
Beck, Mary Ellen 941
Beck, Nancy Melinda 284
Beck, Rachel 73
Beck, St. Leger 70
Beck, Sarah A. 70
Beck, Sarah E.J. 68
Beck, William 71
Beck, William H. 72
Beck, William P. 73
Beeman, Richmond S. 74
Beeman, T.A. (Thomas) 75
Bell, N.R. 76
Bently, A. (Abner) 77
Bently, Mary J. 77
Bentonville *p*4
Berryman, Alfred S. 78
Berryman, James M. 79
Berryman, Nancy 924
Bessent, Daniel D. 80
Bessent, Sarah (Sallie) 204
Bingham, G.M. (George) 81
Bingham, Gustavus Adolphus 82
Binkley, J.W. 83
Binkley, James H. 84
Binkley, Margaret I. (Isabella) 84
Black, Daniel L. 85
Black, Samuel F. 86
Blackburn, James A. 87.
Blackburn, John 88
Blackwelder, Daniel E. 89
Blackwelder, Margaret E. 53
Blackwell, Julia Ellen 18
Blackwell, Mary T. 676
Blackwood, John B. 90
Blackwood, Malona 835
Blackwood, Mariah (Ann M.) 90
Blaylock, Sarah Jane 871
Boger, Jane 92
Boger, Moses 91
Boger, Paul 92
Boger, Sarah M. 91

Boger, Vira 92
Boid, Melinda 629
Bolds (Boles) (Bowles), James L. 93
Bolds (Boles) (Bowles), Jusha (Jerusha) 93
Boles (Bowles), James D. 94
Boles, James L. *see* Bolds, James L.
Boles, Jusha *see* Bolds, Jusha
Boles (Bowles), Martha E. 94
Boner, Jacob 95
Booe, Alexander Martin 96
Booe, Amanda 778
Booe, (Nancy) Emaline 102
Booe, G.W. 97
Booe, George W. 98, 99
Booe, Jane 101
Booe, Marshall N. (Ney) 100
Booe, Mary Elizabeth 895
Booe, Rebecca 441
Booe, Ruth Ann 356
Booe, Sarah Anne J. 96
Booe, William E. 101
Booe, William H. 102
Booe, William M. 103
Boulware's Wharf, James River, Virginia 62, 118, 121, 122, 225, 338, 375, 405, 572, 618, 659, 729, 748, 760, 819, 828, 831, 833, 835, 968, 1000, 1050
Bowden, Clearissy 105
Bowden, Jennetta 105
Bowden, John O. 104
Bowden, Lydia M. 1085
Bowden, Nancy E. 1099
Bowden, S.W (Shadrick) 105
Bowers, Eli W. 106
Bowles, Amanda E. 108
Bowles, B.F. 107
Bowles, Benjamin T. 108
Bowles, Clementine 110
Bowles, Eliza 109
Bowles, Erwin L. 109
Bowles, G.W. 110
Bowles, James D. *see* Boles, James D.
Bowles, James L. *see* Bolds, James L.
Bowles, Jusha *see* Bolds, Jusha
Bowles, Lucy Ann 425
Bowles, Margaret T. 705
Boles, Martha E. *see* Boles, Martha E.
Bowles, Mary 107
Bowles, Prudence 111
Bowles, William J. 111
Boyd, James S. (Sam'l) 112
Boyer, John 113
Bracken, E.J. 116
Bracken, Elizabeth C. 114
Bracken, John W. 114
Bracken, Mary 114

Bracken, Nancy Jane 115
Bracken, Sarah A. 115
Bracken, Thomas H. 115
Bracken, William H. 116
Brackin, Ellen Elizabeth 117
Brackin, John 117
Brackin, Sallie (Sarah) 117
Bradford, Ellen 553
Branden, W.F. 118
Brandon, J.C. 119
Brandon, Joshua 120
Brandon, Thomas 121
Brandon, W.A. 122
Brewbaker, Richard P. 123
Brewer, Hubbard L. 124
Brindle (Brintle), Nancy 125
Brindle (Brintle), Robert R. 125
Brinager, John *see* Briniger, John
Brinegan, John *see* Briniger, John
Brinegar, M. 126
Brinegar, Maloney (Margaret) Ellen 1137
Brinegar, Sarah 492
Briniger (Brinager) (Brinegan), John 127
Brinkley, James 128
Brinkley, John F. 129
Brinkley, Margaret J. 129
Brintle, Nancy *see* Brindle, Nancy
Brintle, Robert R. *see* Brindle, Robert R.
Brock, C. Brunt (Buley) (Bulah) 136
Brock, Emeline F. 195
Brock, Emily 134
Brock, J.N. (James) 130
Brock, J.W. 131
Brock, James V. 132
Brock, L.E. (Levin) 133
Brock, Margaret A. 130
Brock, Martha J. 137
Brock, Mary A. 135
Brock, Noah Monroe 134
Brock, Richard Emmerson 135
Brock, S.E. 777
Brock, Sarah E. 1147
Brock, Sarah L. 131
Brock, Thomas M. 136
Brock, William F. 137
Brogden, John W. 138
Brogden, Mary 138
Brown, Ann P. 146
Brown, Burton 139
Brown, Delphine 143
Brown, Dovie A. 566
Brown, Emma J. 472
Brown, Hetty C. 139
Brown, J. Frank 140
Brown, John Edmunds 141
Brown, Mary D. 903
Brown, Mary Eliza 147

Brown, Rufus D. 142
Brown, Sallie S. 1038
Brown, Sally I. 142
Brown, Thomas J. (Jeff) 143
Brown, William 144, 145
Brown, Dr. William Carter 146
Brown, William L. 147
Brunt, Pheebee E. 341
Bryan, Leila Imogene 615
Bryan, Margaret T. 148
Bryan, Dr. Talliafero Jay 148
Buley, C. Brunt 136
Buller, Sophia Regina 874
Bullybough, Caroline 552
Burgess, John M. *see* Burgis, John M.
Burgess, Thomas 149
Burgis (Burgess), John M. 150
Burk, James W. 151
Burkeville, Virginia 73
Burton, Agnes 153
Burton, Daniel P. 152
Burton, James M. 153
Burton, Mary 579
Burton, Nancy T. 152
Butler, Ann Mariah 345
Butler, Lucy Jane 154
Butler, Q.P. (Quintilla) 608
Butler, Thomas S. 154
Byerly, Eliza 155
Byerly, Hiram 155

Cain, Adeline 157
Cain, Amanda A. 671
Cain, Anderson H. 156
Cain, Betty 164
Cain, C.M. (Catherine Martha) 668
Cain, Daniel H. 157
Cain, Daniel J. 158
Cain, E.L (Elizabeth) 689
Cain, Elizabeth 159
Cain, James H. (Harrison) 159
Cain, John L. 160
Cain, Leonora S. 162
Cain, Lydia M. 163
Cain, Nancy J. 344
Cain, Patrick A. 161
Cain, Richard (Richmond) F. 162
Cain, Sarah 160
Cain, William F. 163
Cain, William G. 164
Calahaln District 13, 14, 15, 16, 18, 38, 65, 70, 73, 90, 92, 103, 112, 176, 185, 187, 265, 284, 303, 307, 332, 335, 370, 404, 406, 415, 416, 429, 444, 452, 462, 509, 515, 536, 537, 538, 540, 566, 567, 571, 573, 585, 608, 609, 617, 619, 620, 629, 631, 636, 637, 650, 654, 676, 677, 694, 696, 714, 715, 728, 802, 810, 818, 819, 821, 846, 854, 856, 873, 878, 885, 886, 904, 908, 927, 941, 942, 963, 994, 995, 1007, 1014, 1035, 1038, 1042, 1043, 1044, 1046, 1072, 1101, 1102
Caldwell, Fanny 458
Call, Burke (Birch) 165
Call, David 166
Call, Elizabeth 166
Call, Henry 167
Call, Henry G. 168
Call, John 169
Call, Marie L. 448
Call, Martha E. 170
Call, Mary 165, 171
Call, Mary Jane 554
Call, Matilda 552
Call, Minerva 354
Call, Murphy G. 170
Call, Nathan F. 171
Call, Nellie 792
Call, Sallie E. 170
Call, Sarah A. 169
Call, W.H. (Will) 172
Campbell, Arthur N. (Neely) 173
Campbell, Benjamin Frank 174
Campbell, Delia 176
Campbell, Easter H. 538
Campbell, George W. 175
Campbell, Jane E. 176
Campbell, Margaret C. 409
Campbell, Rachal 529
Campbell, Sarah Ann 175
Campbell, Thomas B. 176
Cansas, Elizabeth 248
Canter (Carter), Francis 177
Canter (Carter), Pleasant H. 177
Canter, William Anderson *see* Carter, William Anderson
Canter, William M. 178
Carter, Abraham (Abram H.) 179
Carter, Amanda 181
Carter, Ann P. 146
Carter, Darius (Davis) 180
Carter, Edie Ann 841
Carter, Elizabeth 368
Carter, Emaline 837
Carter, Emily E. 179
Carter, Francis *see* Canter, Francis
Carter, J.H. (Hinson) 181
Carter, Jane 511
Carter, L.W. (Letitia) 974
Carter, Margaret Ann 745
Carter, Nancy Ann 179
Carter, Pleasant H. *see* Canter, Pleasant H.
Carter, Sarah Ann 180
Carter, William 182
Carter (Canter), William Anderson 183
Carter, William C. 184
Cartner, Emily 186
Cartner, James F. 185
Cartner, John 186
Cartner, Margaret 878
Cartner, Martha M. 186
Casey, Camila 187
Casey, E. Perry 187
Casey, Eliza Jane 188
Casey, Elizabeth 429
Casey, Ephraim C. 188
Caton, Alfred (Alpha) 189
Caton, Green (Greenberry) 190
Caton, Letitia 838
Caton, Mary 191
Caton, Mary Elizabeth 189
Caton, Orrell 191
Caton, Sallie (Sarah) 190
Caton, Sarah 191
Catton, Amanda E. 322
Caudle, Candice 375
Caudle, F. Marion 192
Chaffin, Alexander W. 193
Chaffin, Bella M. (Julia) 817
Chaffin, Charles Stanley 194
Chaffin, Elvira 193
Chaffin, Emeline F. 195
Chaffin, Martha M. 857
Chaffin, Martin Rowan 195
Chaffin, Mary Ann 1042
Chaffin, Mary Frances 195
Chaffin, Nathan M.D. 196
Chalmus, Mariah E. *see* Kurfees, Mariah E.
Chalmus, Zedock C. *see* Kurfees, Zedock C.
Chambers, Martin 197
Chambers, Peter 198
Chambers, Sallie (Sarah) 190
Chancellorsville, Virginia 64, 69, 80, 98, 151, 154, 168, 207, 215, 232, 238, 262, 265, 271, 279, 280, 317, 360, 399, 401, 410, 415, 416, 459, 500, 510, 517, 518, 522, 547, 562, 571, 614, 631, 651, 653, 665, 666, 691, 713, 724, 729, 751, 753, 759, 772, 804, 820, 835, 860, 885, 942, 947, 963, 1022, 1043, 1069
Chandler, Solomon 199
Chaplin, Alexander (James) 200
Chaplin, Jesse 201
Chaplin, John 202
Chaplin, Mary Ann 200
Charles, Francis W. 203
Charles, John N. (Newton) 204
Charles, Sarah (Sallie) 204
Charles, William F. 205
Cheshire, F.A. (Francis) 206
Cheshire, John A. 207
Cheshire, Jonathan Wesley 208
Cheshire, Martha M. 17
Cheshire, Mary J. 207
Cheshire, Melony 1128

Index

Cheshire, Nancy C. 931
Cheshire, Paulina 208
Cheshire, Richard (Richmond) B. 209
Chick (Click), John Nicholas 210
Chicomohomony, Battle of 14
Chinn, Elizabeth Virginia 780
Chinn, Margaret A. 130
Chinn, Mary Eliza 147
Chinquepin District 20, 50, 54, 114, 116, 138, 156, 157, 163, 186, 188, 193, 206, 227, 228, 229, 230, 241, 242, 251, 253, 257, 277, 312, 344, 357, 389, 390, 411, 418, 422, 463, 489, 491, 502, 512, 559, 562, 568, 572, 575, 591, 627, 628, 667, 670, 702, 795, 797, 800, 849, 850, 861, 871, 873, 889, 901, 939, 982, 983, 988, 1040, 1104, 1105, 1118
Church, William 211
Churchill, Virginia 1085
City Point, Virginia 68, 69, 97, 105, 119, 133, 154, 168, 187, 237, 246, 339, 394, 419, 480, 502, 504, 515, 520, 521, 533, 558, 573, 633, 753, 772, 837, 863, 933, 952, 977, 1038, 1050, 1110, 1126, 1138
Clanen, J.W. (John) see McClannan, J.W. (John)
Clanen, Martha C. see McClannan, Martha C.
Clark, Cornelia V. 214
Clark, Edward M. 212
Clark, L. (Louis) 213
Clark, Nancy E. 214
Clark, William Albea 214
Clarksville District 54, 111, 114, 115, 164, 188, 227, 236, 237, 241, 265, 272, 312, 330, 344, 389, 390, 392, 399, 404, 441, 502, 529, 530, 562, 627, 647, 790, 800, 871, 917, 982, 991, 1104
Clary, Amanda A. 274
Clary, James 215
Clary, William 216
Clement, Baxter Clegg 217
Clement, Elizabeth 858
Clement, Jesse A. 218
Clement, Jesse Lee 219
Clement, John H. (Henry) 220
Clement, Lettie 219
Clement, Lina 217
Clement, Mary Emily 220
Clement, Mary J. 470
Clement, Mattie K. 222
Clement, Melinda 218
Clement, Nancy Cornelia 221
Clement, Sarah Anne J. 96
Clement, Wiley Adam 221

Clement, William Bailey (Dart) 222
Click, Daniel W. 223
Click, Elizabeth A. 285
Click, John Nicholas see Chick, John Nicholas
Click, Martha A. 287
Click, Michael 224
Click, Millie J. 224
Click, Sarah C. 224
Click, W.H. 225
Clifford, A.M. 226
Clifford, Franklin A. 227
Clifford, John H. 228
Clifford, Joseph C. 229
Clifford, Louesa Ellen 227
Clifford, Martha E. 226
Clifford, Rachel E. 1118
Clifford, Sarah M. 238
Clifford, Simantha M. 411
Clifford, William C. 230
Cline, Henry 231
Cloninger, Alonzo 232
Clouse, Ann M. 233
Clouse, L.A. 233
Clouse, Lou C. 467
Clouse, Nancy 234
Clouse, William 234
Codie (Cody), Godfrey 235
Cody, Godfrey see Codie, Godfrey
Cody, Crisia 862
Cold Harbor, Virginia 79, 222, 280, 379, 426, 434, 439, 464, 510, 652, 674, 698, 790, 806, 833, 890, 950, 954, 1073, 1135
Colette, Abigail 47
Collett, Ezekiel 236
Collett, Sarah L. 236
Collette, Benjamin F. 237
Collette, Robert W. 238
Collette, Sally 237
Collette, Sarah M. 238
Confederate Soldiers' Home, Raleigh 1
Conner, J.C. 239
Conrad, Ellen L. 1130
Conrad, P.J. (Phillip) 240
Conrad, Susan 240
Cook, George B. 241
Cook, James 242
Cook, Lemuel Blick 243
Cook, Martha 241
Cook, Susannah 243
Coon, Benjamin G. 244
Coon, Camila 187
Coon, Emely C. 992
Coon, Mary E. 571
Coon, Matilda J. 567
Cope, America 806
Cope, Andrew 245
Cope, Cornelia (Nealey A.) 245
Cope, Elizabeth 248

Cope, Frederick T. 246
Cope, John 247
Cope, Mary 246
Cope, Mary J. 246, 839
Cope, P. Jacob 248
Cope, William G. 249
Cornatser (Cornatzer), Jacob C. 250
Cornatser (Cornatzer), Lucinda (Cynthia) 250
Cornatzer, Camilla (Carmela) (Comila) 358
Cornatzer, Eliza 716
Cornatzer, Jacob C. see Cornatser, Jacob C.
Cornatzer, Lucinda see Cornatser, Lucinda
Cox's Wharf, James River, Virginia 216, 327, 729, 968, 1112
Cranfield, Hanes 251
Cranfield, Henry 252
Cranfield, Jackson Lewis (Louis) 253
Cranfield, James L. 254
Cranfield, Martha 702
Cranfield, S.J. 255
Cranfield, William H. 255
Cranfill, Gideon 256
Cranfill, Jonathan 257
Craver, David Lindsey 258
Crews, William P. 259
Crump, Elizabeth 260
Crump, James Adderson 260
Crump, Pleasant John 261
Cunningham, Elviney 265
Cunningham, F.M. (Francis) 262
Cunningham, George H. 263
Cunningham, Margaret 262
Cunningham, Nancy 264
Cunningham, Rubin W. 264
Cunningham, Samuel M. 265
Cunningham, Thomas M. 266
Curant, Suan T. 696
Cuthrell, James N. 267
Cuthrell, M. Nancy 877
Cuthrell, Nancy 267
Cuthrell, Virginia C. 1017

Daner, Mary 534
Daniel, Jane 268
Daniel, Mary 269
Daniel, Sarah C. 224
Daniel, William Harrison 268
Daniel, Wilson C. 269
Daniels (Dannel), William L. 270
Dannel, William L. see Daniels, William L.
Danner, Delia 271
Danner, Eli 271
Danner, Elizabeth, 272
Danner, Frederick (M) 272
Danner, Nancy Emaline 273
Danner, Rebecca 11

Danner, Samuel 273
Davis, Amanda A. 274
Davis, Eliza Jane 279
Davis, Eunice 892
Davis, Franklin (J.F.) 274
Davis, Joseph N. 275
Davis, Margaret A. 897
Davis, Margaret C. 423
Davis, Mercer J. 276
Davis, Peneller 280
Davis, Samuel A. 277
Davis, Samuel C. 278
Davis, Sarah 277
Davis, Silas 279
Davis, Susan 277
Davis, William 280
Davis, William E. 281

Davalt, Rebecca P. *see* Dayvault, Rebecca P.
Davalt, William M. *see* Dayvault, William M.
Davalt, Vashti M. *see* Daywalt, Vashti
Dayvault (Daywalt), Mary L. 282
Dayvault, (Davalt), Rebecca P. 283
Dayvault (Daywalt), Solomon M. 282
Dayvault, (Davalt), William M. 283
Daywalt, Alfred J. (Alford Davalt) 284
Daywalt, Mary L. *see* Dayvault, Mary L.
Daywalt, Nancy Melinda 284
Daywalt, Solomon M. *see* Dayvault, Solomon M.
Daywalt (Davalt), Vashti M. 284
Deadman, Eliza C. 288
Deadman, Elizabeth A. 285
Deadman, Haley 285
Deadman (Debnam), James Anderson 286
Deadman, James R. 287
Deadman, Martha A. 287
Deadman (Debnam), Pauline 286
Deadman, Thomas H. 288
Deaver, Ader 289
Deaver, Nathan 289
Debnam, James Anderson *see* Deadman, James Anderson
Debnam, Pauline *see* Deadman, Pauline
Dedman, Anna 290
Dedman, Lucy Jane 154
Dedman, W.A. 290
Dedmon, D.M. (Daniel) 291
Dingler, James 292
Dingler, Mary A. 292
Dismuks, Richard L. 293

Divire (Dwire), Daniel 294
Divire (Dwire), Hettie 294
Dixon (Dixson), Rebecca 295
Dixon (Dixson), William 295
Dixson, Rebecca *see* Dixon, Rebecca
Dixson, William *see* Dixon, William
Dobbins, Alfred M.C. 296
Dooling, Martha 893
Doudy, James *see* Dowdy, James
Doudy, Mary *see* Dowdy, Mary
Douthit, Alphonsine S. 1130
Douthit, Edward J. 297
Douthit, J.M. 298
Douthit, Martha F. 297
Dowdy (Doudy), James 299
Dowdy (Doudy), Mary 299
Drake, Catharine 300
Drake, Nancy C. 599
Drake, William D. 300
Driver, Amanda A. 301
Driver, John E. 301
Dulin, William M. 302
Dwiggins, D.H. 303
Dwiggins, James Patterson 304
Dwiggins, Louisa 303
Dwiggins, Sarah P. 304
Dwiggins, Susan 240
Dwiggins, Ursley (Ursula) 821
Dwire, Daniel *see* Divire, Daniel
Dwire, H.X. (Henry) 305
Dwire, Hettie *see* Divire, Hettie
Dwire (Dwyer), John F. 306
Dwire, Mary M. 305
Dwire, Sarah A. 350
Dwyer, John F. *see* Dwire, John F.
Dwyre, Elizabeth 1114
Dyson, David Linsey 307
Dyson, Elizabeth 444
Dyson, Emeline (Ruthy E.) 307
Dyson, W.L. (William) 308

Earnest, Mary 269
Eaton, B.F. (Benjamin) 309
Eaton, J.C. 310
Eaton, Lucinda 309
Eaton, Maria Tabitha 389
Eaton, Martha T. 398
Eaton, Mary 48
Eccles, Jane E. 727
Eccles (Eckles), John C. 311
Eckerson (Etchisson), Andrew Eno 312
Eckerson (Etchisson), Mary 312
Eckles, John C. *see* Eccles, John C.
Ellis, Amanda E. 322
Ellis, Dorothy A. 321
Ellis, E.F. (Enoch) 313
Ellis, Ezekiel P. 314
Ellis, Frances 318

Ellis, Hannah 320
Ellis, James M. 315
Ellis, Martha E. 170
Ellis, Mary C. 317
Ellis, Nathaniel B. 316
Ellis, Salie F. 319
Ellis, Thomas Nelson 317
Ellis, Wiley Jones 318
Ellis, Wiley R. 319
Ellis, William A. 320
Ellis, William J. 321
Ellis, William R. 322
Ellison, Donalson 323
Elmira, New York 49, 57, 85, 86, 122, 126, 230, 238, 297, 311, 314, 318, 338, 379, 436, 439, 525, 532, 547, 608, 618, 638, 698, 709, 721, 747, 749, 790, 806, 813, 833, 835, 837, 861, 945, 954, 1001, 1041, 1073, 1088, 1110, 1122
Elum, Elizabeth F. 585
Emberson, Mary E. 804
Etcherson (Etchisson), Alexander H. 324
Etcherson, Edmond (Edward) 325
Etcherson, Elizabeth Jane 325
Etcherson (Etchisson), James W. 326
Etcherson (Etchisson), Martha A.C. 324
Etcheson, Susan 527
Etchison, C.H. (Caswell) 327
Etchison, Elizabeth 484
Etchison, Giles B. 328
Etchison, Lou (Louisa C.) 327
Etchison, Lydia 582
Etchison, Mary A. 950
Etchison, Nancy L. 330
Etchison, Perlina K. 329
Etchison, Sarah 328
Etchison, Sarah Jane 984
Etchison, Shadrach M. 329
Etchison, W.C. Perry 330
Etchisson, Alexander H. *see* Etcherson, Alexander H.
Etchisson, Andrew Eno *see* Eckerson, Andrew Eno
Etchisson, James W. *see* Etcherson, James W.
Etchisson, Martha A.C. *see* Etcherson, Martha A.C.
Etchisson, Mary *see* Eckerson, Mary
Evans, Elizabeth 331
Evans, Mary 332
Evans, Thomas 331
Evans, William 332

Faircloth, Bettie Bell 333
Faircloth, J.D. (Jacob) 333
Faircloth, Mary 333

Index

Farmington District 8, 10, 11, 23, 35, 39, 46, 55, 56, 90, 107, 108, 116, 130, 132, 133, 134, 135, 136, 137, 170, 177, 181, 188, 214, 215, 233, 234, 243, 245, 272, 273, 277, 295, 297, 299, 305, 306, 309, 310, 313, 324, 325, 327, 328, 329, 331, 333, 336, 338, 340, 355, 364, 371, 387, 397, 398, 400, 401, 402, 428, 438, 449, 450, 459, 461, 465, 468, 469, 473, 474, 484, 485, 500, 522, 527, 534, 539, 541, 544, 548, 550, 552, 556, 564, 576, 579, 580, 582, 588, 590, 615, 633, 638, 639, 645, 646, 647, 656, 664, 672, 677, 678, 679, 683, 693, 705, 706, 707, 710, 711, 712, 726, 738, 739, 779, 780, 788, 794, 824, 825, 826, 833, 852, 868, 874, 901, 912, 915, 920, 922, 924, 926, 946, 950, 952, 953, 956, 957, 960, 969, 984, 1007, 1010, 1013, 1049, 1051, 1063, 1074, 1080, 1085, 1086, 1098, 1099, 1104, 1108, 1114, 1116, 1120, 1121, 1130, 1131, 1132, 1133, 1134, 1147
Farmville, Virginia 66, 915, 1045
Farrington, Romulus 334
Feezer, Amanda 435
Felker, George 335
Felker, Leah 335
Felker, Sarah E. 335
Ferebee, Joseph H. 336
Ferebee, Lou (Louisa C.) 327
Ferebee, Martha J. 137
Ferebee, Mary A. 338
Ferebee, Nancy E. 647
Ferebee, Paulina M. 564
Ferebee, S. (Samuel T.) 337
Ferebee, Susan R. 1051
Ferebee, W.H. (William) 338
Feribee, Frances 781
Ferrell, E.L. 339
Ferribee, Sarah R. 340
Ferribee, Thomas M. 340
Fleming, Pheebee E. 341
Fleming, S.F. 341
Fletcher, Mathew 342
Foard, John B. 343
Foot, Jennie 1007
Foote, L.R. (Luther) 344
Foote, Nancy J. 344
Fort Delaware, Delaware 2, 131, 168, 216, 399, 454, 462, 476, 517, 572, 603, 614, 675, 722, 772, 819, 823, 905, 924, 1027
Fort Fisher, Wilmington, North Carolina p3, 18, 39, 54, 255, 320, 446, 462, 793, 794, 798, 943, 950, 1135

Fort Harrison 62, 88, 118, 375, 479, 649, 742, 760, 831, 1060, 1087, 1091, 1094
Fort McHenry 572, 753, 819, 905, 1068, 1079
Fort Monroe, Virginia 41, 320, 462, 525, 793, 794, 798, 837, 943, 950, 1000, 1135
Fort Wool, Virginia 413, 488
Foster, A. (Anderson) F. 345
Foster, A.M. (Azariah) 346
Foster, Albert N. 347
Foster, Anderson 348
Foster, Anderson E. 349
Foster, Andrew J. 350
Foster, Ann Mariah 345
Foster, Archibald 351
Foster, Azanah L. 352
Foster, Benjamin L. 353
Foster, Camilla (Carmela) (Comila) 358
Foster, Candice 375
Foster, Catherine 361
Foster, Coleman 354
Foster, E. (Louiser) 642
Foster, Eliza 347, 349, 364
Foster, Eliza C. 288
Foster, Elizabeth 368, 900, 1117
Foster, Ellen 367
Foster, Emeline 353, 381
Foster, Fanny 373
Foster, Franklin (Francis) A. 355
Foster, George 356
Foster, H.W. (Henderson) 357
Foster, Hannah C. 1039
Foster, Henry 358, 359
Foster, Henry C. 360
Foster, Jacob 361
Foster, James A. 362
Foster, James H.W. 363
Foster, James M. 364
Foster, (Nancy) Jane 427
Foster, Jesse N. 365
Foster, John 366
Foster, John B. 367
Foster, John E. 368
Foster, John M. 369, 370
Foster, John W. 371
Foster, Julie E. 370
Foster, K.R. (Kerr) 372
Foster, L.J. 709
Foster, Laurena (Louvenia) 503
Foster, Loueza V. 357
Foster, Lydia 381
Foster, Margaret 412
Foster, Margaret A. 1044
Foster, Martha 380
Foster, Mary 355, 865
Foster, Mary A. 360, 376, 575, 906
Foster, Mary Ann 791
Foster, Mary Ann M. 365
Foster, Mary Emily 220

Foster, Mary J. 246
Foster, Minerva 354
Foster, Nancy 435
Foster, Nancy E. 465
Foster, Richmond Henry 373
Foster, Robert 374
Foster, Ruth Ann 356
Foster, Samuel 375, 376
Foster, Samuel L. 377
Foster, Samuel Mc. 378
Foster, Sarah A. 350
Foster, Sarah Ann 549, 1055
Foster, Sarah C. 346
Foster, Sarah Ellen 708
Foster, Sarah J. 1119
Foster, Sousan (Ann) 938
Foster, Susannah F. 641
Foster, Thomas 379
Foster, William H. 380
Foster, William M. 381, 382
Fraley, Amanda Jane 383
Fraley, Henry L. 383
Fraley, John H. 384
Fraley, John T. 385
Fraley, Milas J. 386
Fray (Frey), Benjamin F. 387
Fredericksburg, Virginia p4, 69, 80, 222, 246, 296, 332, 361, 386, 396, 398, 440, 457, 474, 483, 522, 615, 625, 628, 721, 756, 791, 837, 887, 1032, 1039, 1112
Frey, Benjamin F. see Fray, Benjamin F.
Frost, Calvin E. 388
Frost, Eberneza (Ebenezer) 389
Frost, Elizabeth 159
Frost, Elizabeth Cordelia 390
Frost, J.F. (James) 390
Frost, James D. (Commissary Sergeant) 391
Frost, Maria Tabitha 389
Frost, William A. 392
Fry, Albert W. 393
Fry, George W. 394
Fry, James 395
Fry, Roxana 394
Fry, William 396
Fulcher, Mary J. 1072
Fulford, Mary 826
Fulton District 6, 19, 29, 31, 33, 43, 48, 61, 78, 84, 127, 131, 146, 152, 153, 154, 155, 166, 167, 168, 171, 179, 180, 190, 191, 196, 197, 198, 199, 200, 202, 248, 250, 294, 301, 306, 319, 333, 347, 349, 350, 354, 358, 359, 360, 367, 372, 373, 374, 375, 380, 384, 385, 386, 394, 403, 412, 413, 425, 426, 432, 443, 464, 466, 467, 470, 483, 495, 496, 503, 505, 516, 545, 546, 548, 553, 554, 555, 587, 601,

634, 635, 639, 641, 642, 658, 659, 660, 668, 685, 686, 699, 716, 718, 744, 748, 762, 767, 789, 791, 792, 793, 799, 803, 805, 816, 817, 836, 838, 839, 840, 841, 851, 859, 862, 877, 879, 897, 899, 911, 923, 926, 936, 970, 977, 978, 986, 987, 989, 996, 1009, 1024, 1029, 1030, 1047, 1048, 1065, 1067, 1068, 1086, 1109, 1110, 1117, 1137, 1142
Furches, John M. 397
Furches, Lewis Alexander 398
Furches, Lou 402
Furches, Martha T. 398
Furches, Mary Ann 398
Furches, Mary L. 399, 892
Furches, Nancy E. 214
Furches, Samuel W. 399
Furches, Susan M. 677
Furches, Thomas G. 400
Furches, Thomas W. (H.) 401
Furches, W.F. (William) 402

Gabard, William 403
Gabbard, Mary 1069
Gaines' Mill, Virginia 90, 112, 137, 222, 265, 360, 376, 464, 474, 683, 692, 795, 853, 882, 955, 1069
Gaither, David 404
Gaither, George W. 405
Gaither, Greenberry 406
Gaither, James M. 407
Gaither, Lemuel G. 408
Gaither, Margaret 262
Gaither, Margaret C. 409
Gaither, Mary A. 405
Gaither, Mary E. 406
Gaither, Nancy 264
Gaither, Sallie L. 408
Gaither, Simantha M. 411
Gaither, Wiley 409
Gaither, William H. 410
Gaither, Zadock L. 411
Garner, Mary Jane 852
Garrawood, David T. *see* Garwood, David T.
Garrawood, Jane *see* Garwood, Jane
Garwood (Garrawood), David T. 412
Garwood, Emily E. 179
Garwood (Garrawood), Jane 412
Garwood, Lewis B. (Burton) 413
Garwood, Margaret 412
Garwood, Mary 413, 414
Garwood, Mary E. 412
Garwood, Robert 414
Garwood, Sarah Ann 180
Gatton, Amanda 418
Gatton, Amanda A. 301

Gatton, Franklin 415
Gatton, Harrison 416
Gatton, James 417
Gatton, Pleasant 418
Gatton, Temperance F. 416
Gaugh, John 419
Gentle, Adeline 1035
Gentle, Jordan M. 420
Gettysburg, Pennsylvania *p*4, 131, 216, 222, 229, 237, 263, 284, 295, 454, 458, 474, 480, 493, 504, 515, 533, 572, 658, 701, 719, 722, 724, 729, 772, 819, 823, 862, 900, 905, 924, 977, 1027, 1044, 1059, 1082, 1110, 1112
Ghean, William *see* Gheen, William
Gheen (Ghean), William 421
Gibbs, Mary A. 485
Gibbs, Sally I. 142
Gibson, Rebecca 851
Glascock, Elvira 193
Glasscock, Abner 422
Glasscock, James Lafayette 1144
Glasscock, Martha M. 628
Glasscock, Thomas Napoleon 1145
Gobble, Henry C. 423
Gobble, Margaret C. 423
Godbey, Mary 312
Godby, Sarah E.J. 68
Gordon, Mary Cline 441
Gordonsville, Virginia 33, 76, 415, 466, 602, 801, 942
Gowan, Barbara C. 30
Gowan, Lucy Ann 425
Gowan, Nancy C. 931
Gowan, Richard W. 424
Gowen, Simeon C. 425
Gowens, Martha E. 94
Grainger, Mary K. 794
Granger, Catherine 426
Granger, Elizabeth 429
Granger, (Nancy) Emaline 102, 273
Granger, James F. 426
Granger, James M. 427
Granger, (Nancy) Jane 427
Granger, John Peter 428
Granger, M.L. (Moses Lee) 429
Granger, Mary 332
Granger, Mary E. 428
Granger, Mary F. 430
Granger, W. Burton 430
Grant, A.T. 431
Grant, Rebecca 431
Graves, Albert N. 432
Graves, Amanda 435
Graves, Andrew J. 433
Graves, Daniel 434
Graves, Eliza E. 884
Graves, Elizabeth C. 114

Graves, Ethel (Ellen) 438
Graves, George F. 435
Graves, Jacob B. 436
Graves, Jeremiah 437
Graves, John Ellis 438
Graves, John Franklin 439
Graves, John W. (H.) 440
Graves, Lucinda 439
Graves, Margaret 437
Graves, Margie 978
Graves, Marja I. 434
Graves, Mary 114, 977
Graves, Mary Ann 442
Graves, Mary Cline 441
Graves, Mary Elizabeth 437
Graves, Nancy 435
Graves, Nathan 441
Graves, (Mary) Polly 437
Graves, Rebecca 441
Graves, S.E. 559
Graves, Sarah C. 439
Graves, William H. 442
Gray, Caroline 707
Gray, Elizabeth 444
Gray, G.F. (George F.) 443
Gray, Thomas 444
Green, E.J. 116
Green, George E. 445
Green, M. (Mellina) 651
Greensboro, North Carolina 1, 44, 93, 106, 128, 141, 143, 179, 190, 212, 220, 221, 267, 305, 321, 396, 421, 473, 541, 559, 590, 731, 733, 738, 788, 804, 808, 824, 868, 897, 903, 960, 981, 1010, 1097, 1131
Griffin, Margaret 446
Griffin (Griffon), Marie L. 448
Griffin, Noah J. (G.) 446
Griffin, Samuel C. 447
Griffin (Griffon), William T. 448
Griffith, Charles Franklin 449
Griffith, Sarah 449
Griffith, Sarah C. 1000
Griffon, Marie L. *see* Griffin, Marie L.
Griffon, William T. *see* Griffin, William T.
Grimes, Noah B. 450
Grimes, Sarah 489
Grimes, Sarah L. 236
Grimes, Temperance F. 416
Grimes, William A. 451
Guffy, Carson A. 452
Guffy, Samuel M. 453
Gullet, Anne (Anna) 640
Gullet, Joseph T. (Thomas) 454
Gullet, Luvenia 716
Gullet, William 455

Hagerstown, Maryland 97, 119, 133, 187, 310, 337, 419, 502, 521, 558, 952, 971

Index

Hagie (Hajhe) (Hagy), Davidson 456
Hagy, Davidson *see* Hagie, Davidson
Haire, Perry 457
Hairston, Columbia Lafayette 458
Hairston, Fanny 458
Hairston, Peter Wilson 458
Haith, Martha A. 854
Haith, Sarah Jane 917
Hajhe, Davidson *see* Hagie, Davidson
Hall, Delphine 143
Hall, Ferdinand E. (Eugene) 459
Hall, George W. 460
Hall, Henry H. (F.) 461
Hall, Jessie 42
Hall, Mary C. 575
Hall, Rebecca C. 460
Hall, Sarah A. 983
Hamilton, Catherine 462
Hamilton, William M. 462
Hammond (Hammons), Bryant W. (Briant) 463
Hammond (Hammons), Rachel 463
Hammons, Bryant W. *see* Hammond, Bryant W.
Hammons, Rachel *see* Hammond, Rachel
Hains, George A. *see* Hanes, George A.
Hains, Mary J. *see* Hanes, Mary J.
Hains, Spencer Joseph *see* Hanes, Spencer Joseph
Haneline, Amanda 1110
Hanes (Hains), George A. 464
Hanes, Harrison Henry 465
Hanes, Hester Ann 468
Hanes, Jacob H. 466
Hanes, John H. 467
Hanes, John P. 468
Hanes, Lou C. 467
Hanes, Martha 1076
Hanes (Hains), Mary J. 470
Hanes, Mary M. 305
Hanes, Nancy 465
Hanes, Nancy E. 465
Hanes, Pleasant Henderson 469
Hanes, Sallie E. 471
Hanes (Hains), Spencer Joseph 470
Hanes, William P. 471
Hanover Junction, Virginia 94, 334
Harbin, Allen Alexander 472
Harbin, Emma J. 472
Harbin, James H. 473
Harding, Elizabeth 474
Harding, Green Berry (Patterson) 474

Hargrave, John H. 475
Harper, C.E. (Cannon) 476
Harper, George W. 477
Harper, J.L. (John) 478
Harper, John R. 479
Harpers Ferry *p*4
Harris, Ann 480
Harris, Betty 164
Harris, Elizabeth 1002
Harris, Fanny E. 671
Harris, John W. 480
Harris, Lucinda 481
Harris, M.E. (Martha) 816
Harris, Mary A. 481
Harris, Sarah 481
Harris, Williamson G. 481
Harrison, Jane 482
Harrison, Richard 482
Hartman, Elizabeth 484
Hartman, Enoch 483
Hartman, G.A. (George) 484
Hartman, Jennetta 105
Hartman, Nancy Elizabeth 483
Hartman, Sarah A. 484
Haskins (Hoskins), James F. 485
Haskins (Hoskins), Mary 485
Hauser, Philip A. 486
Hauser, Wiley 487
Hayse, Sarah A. 618
Hearne, Elizabeth 260
Hege, Lourena 1024
Heinrich, George 488
Helfer, A.Y. (Amos Young) 489
Helfer, M.E. 489
Helfer, Pleasant E. 490
Helfer, Rebecca A. 489
Helfer, S.F. (Samuel) 491
Helfer, Sarah 489
Helfer, Susan 490
Hellard, Joe 492
Hellard (Hillard), Nancy 494
Hellard, Sarah 492
Hellard (Hillard), Thomas 493
Hellard (Hillard), William 494
Hellard, William Henry 495
Hendren, Arthur N. (Neely) 508
Hendren, Denton *see* Hendron, Denton
Hendren, Rebecca Jane 1090
Hendren, Sarah Ann (Sallie) 508
Hendricks, George W. 1146
Hendricks, James M. 496
Hendricks, Jesse A. 497
Hendricks, Lucy J. 496
Hendricks, Mahala 500
Hendricks, Mariah C. 497
Hendricks, Mary A. 292
Hendricks, Nalke 498
Hendricks, William 499
Hendricks, William A. 500
Hendrix, Ama 748
Hendrix, C. (William Coston) 501

Hendrix, Elizabeth J. 505
Hendrix, F.M. (Francis Monroe) 502
Hendrix, Jehu (John) 503
Hendrix, John H. 504
Hendrix, Laurena (Louvenia) 503
Hendrix, Martha A/J 502
Hendrix, Mary A. 360
Hendrix, Mary E. 501
Hendrix, N.G. (Ningey) 505
Hendrix, Sarah 328
Hendrix, Stephen 506
Hendrix, W.G. (Walter) (Walker) 507
Hendron (Hendren), Denton 509
Hendron, Sarah Ann 509
Hepler, Benjamin F. 510
Hightower, Anderson E. 511
Hightower, Jane 511
Hill, B. (Benton) 512
Hill, David Franklin 513
Hill, George W. 514
Hill, J.S. (Jane) (Jenetta) 46
Hill, L. Jane 1104
Hill, Lutisha 514
Hill, Mary A. 338
Hill, Nancy 1132
Hillard, Catherine 28
Hillard, (Mary) Polly 437
Hillard, Nancy *see* Hellard, Nancy
Hillard, Thomas *see* Hellard, Thomas
Hillard, William *see* Hellard, William
Hilliard, Chloe E. 910
Hines, Martha 241
Hinkle, George W. 515
Hinkle, Mary A. 515
Hobb, Julius (Junius) 516
Hobson, E.O. (Ossie) 520
Hobson, James M. 517
Hobson, John M. 518
Hobson, Samuel Morehead 519
Hobson, W. Henry 520
Hodges, Jane 522
Hodges, John D. 521
Hodges, Joseph 522
Hodges, Martha A. 953
Hodges, Sallie A. 521
Holder, A.A. 523
Holder, Hosea L. 524
Holder, Jacob 525
Holder, Sowell 526
Holder, Susan 527
Holder, William 527
Holdman (Holman), Sarah F. 528
Holdman (Holman), Thomas 528

Holeman (Holman), James S. 529
Holeman (Holman), Rachal 529
Holman, Heneretta L. 532
Holman, Henry Clay 530
Holman, J.B. 531
Holman, James S. *see* Holeman, James S.
Holman, Jacob B. 532
Holman, Jane 101
Holman, Mary C. 1053
Holman, Rachal *see* Holeman, Rachal
Holman, Ruth 894
Holman, Sarah E. 530
Holman, Sarah F. *see* Holdman, Sarah F.
Holman, Thomas *see* Holdman, Thomas
Holmes, Mary 165
Holmes, Rebecca A. 489
Holt, Robert A. 533
Hood, Mary 534
Hood, William 534
Hoose (House), William (J.W.?) 535
Horn, Easter H. 538
Horn, Elizabeth 540
Horn, Enoch 536
Horn, John J. 537
Horn, Levi (Louis) G.(iles) 538
Horn, Mary 539
Horn, Rebecca N. 536
Horn, Sarah R. 340
Horn, Thomas 539
Horn, William Pinkney 540
Horne, Stephen W. 541
Horne, Temperance 541
Hoskins, Eliza B.D. 601
Hoskins, James F. *see* Haskins, James F.
Hoskins, Mary *see* Haskins, Mary
House, David A. 542
House, Elizabeth 543
House, John W. 543
House, Mary 542
House, William (J.W.?) *see* Hoose, William (J.W.?)
Howard, B.S. (Benjamin) 544
Howard, Catherine 789
Howard, Caroline 552
Howard, Cornelius 546
Howard, Eliza 548
Howard, Ellen 553
Howard, Harrison H. (Henry) 547
Howard, Joseph 548
Howard, Joseph Bryant 545
Howard, Loucinda 546
Howard, Martha Matilda 544
Howard, Mary 545, 555, 803
Howard, Mary E. 970

Howard, Mary Jane 554, 1071
Howard, Matilda 552
Howard, Minerva L. (Louisa) 699
Howard, Morgan G. 549
Howard, Nancy E. 544
Howard, Nathan 550
Howard, Philip G. 551
Howard, Robert 552
Howard, Samuel B. 553, 554
Howard, Sarah 550
Howard, Sarah Ann 549
Howard, Wilson 555
Howell, Alexander Charles 556
Howell, Ester E. 557
Howell, Jane C. 627
Howell, John C. 557
Howell, Joseph H. 558
Howell, Lou 402
Howell, Mary A. 135
Howell, Mary Jane 901
Howell, Rebecca C. 460
Hudson, Susanna E. 807
Hunt (Hunter), Henry H. 559, 561
Hunt, John W. 560, 562
Hunt (Hunter), S.E. 559
Hunter, Henry H. *see* Hunt, Henry H.
Hunter, Mary Ann 1042
Hunter, Mary E. 562
Hunter, S.E. *see* Hunt, S.E.
Hunter, Sally 237
Hunter, Samuel 563
Hunting Creek District 282, 283
Hutchins, Andrew J. 564
Hutchins, Paulina M. 564

Idol, A. Jackson 565
Ieames, Elizabeth 833
Ijames, B.G. (Basil) (Boswell) 566
Ijames, B.R. (Beal) 567
Ijames, Dovie A. 566
Ijames (Ijmes) (Ijams), Henry H. 568
Ijames, James D. *see* Ijams, James D.
Ijames, John F. 569
Ijames, John W. 570
Ijames (Ijmes) (Ijams), Mary Jane 568
Ijames, Mary E. *see* Ijams, Mary E.
Ijames, Matilda J. 567
Ijams, Henry H. *see* Ijames, Henry H.
Ijams (Ijames), James D. 571
Ijams, James M. 572
Ijams (Ijames), Mary E. 571
Ijams, Mary Jane *see* Ijames, Mary Jane
Ijams, Matthew N. 573

Ijmes, Henry H. *see* Ijames, Henry H.
Ijmes, Mary Jane *see* Ijames, Mary Jane
Inscore, Lewis 574
Inscore, Margaret E. 574

Jackson, Daniel H. 575
Jackson, Martha C. 710
Jackson, Mary C. 575
Jacobs, (Gacop), John 576
James, J.F. (James) 577
James, J.W. 578
James, John R. 579
James, Julia A. 1120
James, Julius 580
James, Lydia 582
James, Martha Matilda 544
James, Mary 579
James, Nancy E. 544
James, Phebe 958
James, Sarah A. 580
James, Thomas A. 581
James, W. (William) Asberry 582
Jarvis, Jonathan 583
Jarvis, Manerva 836
Jarvis, Mary 107
Jarvis, Rachel 583
Jarvis, Sarah Ann 583
Jenkins, Addison 584
Jerusalem District 48, 61, 66, 80, 94, 114, 138, 152, 154, 204, 224, 260, 268, 285, 287, 290, 346, 350, 365, 376, 423, 426, 432, 435, 442, 462, 480, 508, 515, 519, 520, 542, 566, 567, 571, 596, 603, 608, 612, 614, 615, 616, 622, 632, 668, 671, 752, 757, 758, 787, 789, 803, 817, 839, 852, 860, 884, 974, 977, 978, 1002, 1018, 1029, 1055, 1064, 1071, 1125, 1129, 1139
Johnson, B.S. (Burton) 585
Johnson, Baker A. 586
Johnson, Elizabeth F. 585
Johnson, Ellen 586
Johnson, Emma C. 590
Johnson, James Mullis 588
Johnson, Jane Amanda 35
Johnson, Nancy Ann 179
Johnson, Rachel Ann 588
Johnson, S.W. (Samuel) 589
Johnson, Sarah 588
Johnson, Temperance 587
Johnson, General W. 587
Johnson, William Gaston 590
Johnston, Edy 614
Jones, Angeline Elizabeth 956
Jones, Caroline 596
Jones, Catherine 1059
Jones, Ebed 591
Jones, Eliza B.D. 601

Index

Jones, Emory W. 592
Jones, Henry T. 593
Jones, John 594
Jones, Madison 595
Jones, Mariah C. 497
Jones, Martin 596
Jones, Matthew (Mathew) 597
Jones, Nancy C. 599
Jones, Sallie E. 471
Jones, Samuel A. 598
Jones, Thomas J. 599
Jones, W. Albert 600
Jones, Wifey A.G. 601
Jones, William B. 602
Jordan, Eli 603
Jordan, Gurney 604
Jordan, Jane 603
Jordan, Jonathan 605
Jordan, Sarah 606
Jordan, Susan 929
Jordan, William C. 606
Jorden, Elizabeth 928
Junior Reserves 922

Kees, John 607
Keesler, Louisa J. 927
Keller, Fraley Thomas 608
Keller, John D. 609
Keller, Joseph 610
Keller, Mariah E. 631
Keller, Mary 269, 715
Keller, Mehetable 610
Keller, Q.P. Quintilla 608
Keller, Rebecah E. 609
Kelly, Albert Calvin 611
Kelly, Edy 614
Kelly, James Addison 612
Kelly, John 613
Kelly, Leila Imogene 615
Kelly, Margaret C. 614
Kelly, Mary E. 612
Kelly, Samuel A. (Abner) 614
Kelly, William Frohock 615
Kenly, Elizabeth S. 61
Kepley, Burgess (Burgeons) 616
Kepley, Mary Jane 616
Kerfeece, Caleb W. *see* Kurfees, Caleb W.
Kerfeece, Melinda *see* Kurfees, Melinda
Kerfees, John Peter 617
Kerfees, Mary 617
Kerfees, Nancy 822
Kerfeese, Franklin J. *see* Kurfees, Franklin J.
Kerfeese, Martha J. 1044
Kerfeese, Martha J. *see* Kurfees, Martha J.
Kerfoose, Caleb W. *see* Kurfees, Caleb W.
Kerfoose, Franklin J. *see* Kurfees, Franklin J.

Kerfoose, Mariah E. *see* Kurfees, Mariah E.
Kerfoose, Martha J. *see* Kurfees, Martha J.
Kerfoose, Melinda *see* Kurfees, Melinda
Kerfoose, Zedock C. *see* Kurfees, Zedock C.
Kerfuse, J.R. (James) 618
Kerfuse, Sarah A. 618
Kerry, Mariah Jane 698
Kesler, Henry P. 619
Kesler, M.F. (Madison) 620
Kesler, Nancy Louisa 621
Kesler, William Richard 621
Kimbrough, Marmaduke D. 1147
Kimbrough, Sarah E. 1147
Kindley, J.D. 622
Kindley, Louisa 622
King, Anderson 623
King, Calvin 624
King, Francis 177
King, L.B. 625
King, Manerva 912
King, Margaret J. 623
King, Mary Jane 913
King, Sarah 623
King, William A. 626
Kinymon, David Williams *see* Kinyoun, David Wiliams
Kinymon, Jane C. *see* Kinyoun, Jane C.
Kinyon, David Williams *see* Kinyoun, David Williams
Kinyon, Jane C. *see* Kinyoun, Jane C.
Kinyoun (Kinyon) (Kinymon), David Williams 627
Kinyoun (Kinyon) (Kinymon), Jane C. 627
Kluttz, Green C. 628
Kluttz, Martha M. 628
Knox, John 894
Kurfees (Kerfeece) (Kerfoose), Caleb W. 629
Kurfees (Kerfoose) (Kerfeese), Franklin J. 630
Kurfees (Kerfoose) (Chalmus), Mariah E. 631
Kurfees (Kerfoose) (Kerfeese), Martha J. 630
Kurfees (Kerfeece) (Kerfoose), Melinda 629
Kurfees, Sarah 160
Kurfees (Kerfoose) (Chalmus), Zedock C. 631

Lagle, Henry E. 632
Lagle, Jane 268
Lagle, Sarah 632
Laird, Anne *see* Lard, Anne
Laird, E. *see* Lard, E.

Laird, George W. *see* Lard, George W.
Laird, Levi *see* Lard, Levi
Laird, Martha M. 380
Laird, Samuel *see* Lard, Samuel
Laird, Susannah F. *see* Lard, Susannah F.
Lakey, Elizabeth 633
Lakey, Ellis 633
Lane, John H. 634
Lane, William A. 635
Langley, C.A. 638
Langley, Melinda 638
Langley, Pleasant 639
Langley, Zilvia (Zilpha) 639
Lapish, Elizabeth 636
Lapish, George 636
Lapish, (Margaret) Jane 637
Lapish, John A. 637
Lapish, Julia Ann 636
Lapish, Pelina A. 636
Lapish, Sarah 637
Lard, Amanda 181
Lard (Laird), Anne (Anna) 640
Lard (Laird), E. (Louiser) 642
Lard (Laird), George W. 640
Lard (Laird), Levi (Levy) 641
Lard (Laird), Samuel 642
Lard (Laird), Susannah F. 641
Lashmit, John W. 643
Lassiter, Ethadra W. 644
Lassiter, J. (Jesse) 645
Lassiter, Martha J. 645
Latham, David Hampton 646
Latham, Elizabeth Ann 646
Latham, James M., Sr. 647
Latham, Jeremiah M. 648
Latham, Nancy E. 647
Latham, Samuel B. 649
Lathem, Ann 786
Lazenby, Catherine S. 650
Lazenby, John Tilman 650
Lazenby, Nancy Caroline 975, 994
Leach, Catharine 300
Leach, David 651
Leach, James Franklin 652
Leach, John 653
Leach, John W. 654
Leach, M. (Mellina) 651
Leach, Mary F. 430, 653
Leach, Rebecah E. 609
Leach, Sarah P. 304
Ledford, John A. 655
Lee, Elizabeth 656
Lee, Henry Jackson 656
Lee, Martha A.C. 324
Leinbach, Nancy 946
Lenard, Ellen 657
Lenard, Mathias 657
Leonard, Christina 659, 660
Leonard (Lenard), Emanuel 658
Leonard, Jacob 659

Leonard, Jesse 660
Leone, Nancy 936
Leslie (Lesley), F. (Franklin) M. 661
Lesley, F.M. *see* Leslie, F.M.
Lewis, William 662
Liberty District 34, 66, 80, 213, 221, 224, 235, 246, 249, 261, 268, 286, 288, 290, 291, 343, 346, 349, 365, 435, 481, 494, 497, 499, 518, 519, 520, 521, 535, 543, 549, 551, 616, 632, 665, 666, 671, 751, 752, 753, 837, 839, 859, 1018, 1036, 1053, 1059, 1062, 1064, 1071, 1125, 1127, 1129
Lindsay, Lettie 219
Linster, McAfee 663
Linville, John F. 664
Linville, Rebecca 664
Little, Daniel M. 665
Little, Robert A. 666
Little, Dr. Samuel Winfield 667
Livengood, C.M. (Catherine Martha) 668
Livengood, Dan E. 668
Livengood, Daniel G. 669
Livengood, Eliza Jane 188
Livengood, John N. 670
Livengood, Mary S. 670
Livingood, Amanda A. 671
Livingood, David 671
Livingood, Fannie E. 671
Locke, Sarah Ann 175
Logan, Isaac 672
Long, L.W. 673
Longwirth, Temperance 541
Longworth, Samuel 674
Lookabill, William H. 675
Lowe, M. Jane 817
Lowery, D.L. (Dabney) 676
Lowery, John T.T. 677
Lowery, Mary T. 676
Lowery, Susan M. 677
Lowry, Nancy 38
Loyed, Jane 924
Luckey, Margaret T. 148
Lunn, Benjamin Franklin 678
Lunn, John T. 679
Lunn, Louisa J. 678
Lunn, Melvina R. 678
Lyerly, Martha Ann 885
Lynch, William 680
Lyons, Richard J. 681

Maddre, William H. *see* Madra, William H.
Madison, Harrison 682
Madison Court House, Virginia 40, 57, 201, 338, 638, 863, 1126
Madra (Maddre) (Mady), William H. 683

Mady, William H. *see* Madra, William H.
Manassas, Virginia *p*4, 8, 13, 34, 184, 196, 216, 222, 461, 485, 1108
Manning, Benjamin F. 684
March, Delitha 685
March, Elizabeth Luticia 685
March, H. Giles 685
March, Mary F. 1121
Markland (Marklin), Ann 686
Markland, Louisa 1029
Markland (Marklin), Matthew 686
Marklin, Ann *see* Markland, Ann
Marklin, Matthew *see* Markland, Matthew
Marler, E.L. *see* Marlow, E.L.
Marler, George Washington *see* Marlow, George Washington
Marlin, Joel P. 687
Marlin, John L. 688
Marlow (Marler), E.L. (Elizabeth) 689
Marlow (Marler), George Washington 689
Marlow, Samantha 873
Marshall (Marshel), George W. (Wesley) 690
Marshel, George W. *see* Marshall, George W.
Martin, Benjamin J. 691
Martin, David W. (William) 692
Martin, Emeline (Ruthy E.) 307
Martin, Giles (John G.) 693
Martin, James C. 694
Martin, Liddi E. 1072
Martin, Mary A. 695
Martin, Mattie K. 222
Martin, Mehetabel 693
Martin, Pleasant Rowan 695
Martinsville, Virginia 74
Mason, Drucilla 696
Mason, Ethel (Ellen) 438
Mason, Franklin 696
Mason, Grief G. (P.) 697
Mason, Lucinda 481
Mason, Melinda 851
Mason, Suan T. 696
Massey, Daniel (David) 698
Massey, Mariah Jane 698
Massey, Minerva L. (Louisa) 699
Massey, Nerva P. 761
Massey, Susanah 698
Massey, Thomas G. 699
May, F.L. 700
May, Martha 702
May, Urban C. 701
May, William F. 702
McBride, J.A. (John) 703
McCarter, Thomas 704
McClamma, Sarah Ellen *see* McClamrock, Sarah Ellen

McClammar, Margaret T. 705
McClammar, R. (Robert Reece) 705
McClammer (McClamroch), Louisa Elizabeth 706
McClammer (McClamroch), M. (James Martin) 706
McClammoch, Caroline 707
McClammoch, John 707
McClamroch, Louisa Elizabeth *see* McClammer, Louisa Elizabeth
McClamroch, M. *see* McClammer, M. (James Martin)
McClamrock (McClamma), Julius Lawrence 708
McClamrock, L.J. 709
McClamrock, Lucius Milton 709
McClamrock, Mary C. 317
McClamrock (McClamma), Sarah Ellen 708
McClanen, Mathew A. *see* McClenan, Mathew A.
McClannan (Clanen), J.W. (John) 710
McClannan (Clanen), Martha C. 710
McClannon, Mary Frances 195
McClannon, Sarah A. 711
McClannon, W.H. (William) 711
McClenan (McClanen), Mathew A. 712
McCracken, William A. 713
McDaniel, Alfred A. 714
McDaniel, Alice F. 904
McDaniel (McDannel), Benjamin L. (Lewis) 715
McDaniel, Elias 716
McDaniel, Eliza 716
McDaniel, Ellen Elizabeth 117
McDaniel, George 717
McDaniel, George W. 718
McDaniel (McDannel), John G. 719
McDaniel, Luvenia 716
McDaniel, M. America 718
McDaniel, Mary 246, 990
McDaniel (McDannel), Mary 715
McDaniel, Nace 720
McDaniel, Nathan 721
McDaniel, Sarah 714
McDaniel, W.H. (William Howard) 722
McDaniel, William 723
McDannel, John G. *see* McDaniel, John G.
McDannel, Mary *see* McDaniel, Mary
McDonald, James 724
McElroy, Rachel C. 725
McElroy, William J. 725
McGill, John A. 726
McGill, Sallie 726

Index

McGuire, Eliza Ann 728
McGuire, James 727
McGuire, Jane E. 727
McGuire, Mary M. 768
McGuire, Safrona J. 729
McGuire, Timothy 728
McGuire, William F. 729
McKaughan, Isiah S. 730
McKaughan, J.H. 731
McKaughan, Richard H. 732
McKaughan, William J. 733
McMahan, Elizabeth C. 868
Miller, Allice 741
Miller, Bulah W. 738
Miller, Emma C. 590
Miller, Henry 734, 735
Miller, Jacob C. 736
Miller, James L. 737
Miller, James W. 738
Miller, John E. 739
Miller, John F. 740
Miller, John H. 741
Miller, John R. 742
Miller, Louisa J. 678
Miller, M.E. 489
Miller, Mary E. 64
Miller, Margaret J. 739
Miller, Polly 736
Millraney, J.H. 743
Minor, Ama 748
Minor, C. (Calvin) 744
Minor, Henry 745
Minor, John 746
Minor, Madison 747
Minor, Margaret Ann 745
Minor, Zerel 748
Mock, Elizabeth C. 749
Mock, Henry A. 749
Mock, Susannah Sheek 243
Mock, W.G. (William) 750
Mocksville District 17, 25, 27, 28, 38, 40, 42, 44, 47, 59, 63, 65, 70, 81, 91, 92, 93, 100, 101, 108, 110, 111, 115, 117, 129, 139, 147, 148, 149, 150, 159, 162, 175, 194, 207, 209, 216, 219, 222, 226, 236, 237, 238, 248, 260, 264, 266, 269, 270, 274, 289, 292, 295, 300, 303, 304, 315, 317, 326, 328, 348, 353, 356, 360, 361, 376, 388, 405, 407, 425, 428, 430, 434, 439, 440, 441, 442, 446, 447, 448, 465, 468, 472, 474, 481, 506, 508, 509, 511, 515, 528, 529, 533, 552, 559, 574, 588, 589, 596, 597, 598, 602, 604, 608, 609, 610, 611, 612, 614, 617, 618, 631, 648, 649, 651, 652, 661, 681, 691, 692, 693, 695, 705, 707, 708, 709, 727, 729, 736, 741, 749, 759, 768, 769, 770, 771, 774, 778, 781, 786, 801, 804, 807, 820, 821, 822, 834, 865, 875, 878, 883, 884, 891, 892, 893, 895, 897, 899, 902, 903, 904, 905, 906, 929, 930, 931, 945, 955, 975, 992, 1004, 1013, 1014, 1024, 1038, 1039, 1044, 1046, 1052, 1054, 1073, 1075, 1079, 1082, 1083, 1084, 1090, 1108, 1128, 1136, 1137, 1147
Monday (Munday), Isaac 751
Monday (Munday), Rebecca 752
Monday (Munday), Wade C. (Casborn) 752
Monday (Munday), William 753
Moore, Jehu 754
Moore, Mary A. 755
Moore, Rebecca D. 855
Moore, William A. 755
Moose, William R. 756
Morris, Anne E. 757
Morris, E.O. (Ossie) 520
Morris, Edwin Simmons 757
Motley, M.M. (Madison) 758
Motley, Martha A. 758
Motley, Nancy T. 152
Mullican, Lewis S. 759
Munday, Isaac *see* Monday, Isaac
Munday, Rebecca *see* Monday, Rebecca
Munday, Wade C. (Casborn) *see* Monday, Wade C. (Casborn)
Munday, William *see* Monday, William
Myers, Andrew L. 760
Myers, Catherine 767
Myers, Delphia 767
Myers, Henry J. 761
Myers, James 762
Myers, Jane 996
Myers, Jefferson C. 763
Myers, Jesse 764
Myers, Nancy 976
Myers, Nerva P. 761
Myers, Sarah 762
Myers, Sarah Ann 765
Myers, Solomon Wesley 765
Myers, William B. 766
Myers, Zadock 767

Nail, Abraham M. (A.M.) 768
Nail, Alexander S. 769
Nail, Elizabeth M. 1021
Nail, Henry 770
Nail, Jasper H. Y. 771
Nail, Jincey Ann (Jenny) (Jane) 770
Nail, John A. 772
Nail, Margaret 769
Nail, Margaret E. 774
Nail, Mary 774
Nail, Mary M. 768
Nail, Melinda 218
Nail, Philip A. 773
Nail, Phillip 774
Nail, Susan 774
Nash, B.R. (Berry R.) 775
Naylor, Amanda 778
Naylor, Ann M. 233
Naylor, Bat W. (Batson) 776
Naylor, Benjamin T. 777
Naylor, Elizabeth J. 25
Naylor, Elizabeth Virginia 780
Naylor, Ester E. 557
Naylor, Frances 781
Naylor, John Ozmont 778
Naylor, Little Berry 779
Naylor, S.E. 777
Naylor, S.T. (Samuel) 780
Naylor, T.N. (Thomas) 781
Neely, Paulina 208
Nelson, Ader 289
Newman, H.A. *see* Newnam, H.L.
Newman, T.L. *see* Newnam, T.L.
Newman, W.F. *see* Newnam, W.F.
Newnam, H.L. (H.A. Newman) 782
Newnam (Newman), T.L. 783
Newnam (Newman), W.F. 784
Newnan, A.W. 785
Newport News, Virginia 73, 164, 1018, 1100, 1120
Nichols, Ann 786
Nichols, B.F. (Benjamin) 786
Nolly, Letitia 787
Nolly, William H. 787
Norman, Caroline 788
Norman, Mary 788
Norman, S. Alexander ("Sandy") 788

Oakes, Catherine *see* Oaks, Catherine
Oakes, James P. *see* Oaks, James P.
Oakes, Rachel C. 725
Oaks (Oakes), Catherine 789
Oaks (Oakes), James P. 789
O'Neal, Mary Jane 790
O'Neal, William H. 790
Orander, Charles R. *see* Orrender, Charles R.
Orel, Nellie *see* Orrell, Nellie
Orel, Robert R. *see* Orrell, Robert R.
Orrel, Susanah 698
Orrell, A. 369
Orrell, David E. 791
Orrell, Hanevic 1065
Orrell, Jane 791
Orrell, Mary Ann 791
Orrell (Orel), Nellie 792
Orrell (Orel), Robert R. 792

Orrender (Orander), Charles R. 793
Otrich, Margaret J. 129
Owen, Mary K. 794
Owen, N. Richard 794
Owen, Rachel 583
Owen, William H. 795
Owens, A.L. 796
Owens, Elizabeth 540
Owens, Henry C. (Clay) 797
Owens, Louisa 797
Owens, Mary 555
Owens, Michael 798
Owens, Sarah F. 528

Pack, Aurena (Irene) 799
Pack, John 799
Painter, Sarah Ann 583
Paris, Elizabeth *see* Parish, Elizabeth
Paris, Sarah E. 800
Paris, Solomon *see* Parish, Solomon
Paris, Thomas M. Williams 800
Parish (Paris), Elizabeth 70, 801, 802
Parish, Nancy M. 1040
Parish (Paris), Solomon 801
Parish, Thomas 802
Parker, Childs A. 803
Parker, Edward N. 804
Parker, Jane 603
Parker, Mary 803
Parker, Mary Ann M. 365
Parker, Mary E. 804
Parker, Nancy Cornelia 221
Parker, Nancy L. 330
Parker, Rebecca 431
Parks, America 806
Parks, Eliza 347
Parks, Elizabeth 986
Parks, M. America 718
Parks, Mack 805
Parks, Sally (Sarah) 805
Parks, Tabitha 806
Parks, William 806
Parnell, Benjamin 807
Parnell, J.W. 808
Parnell, Susanna E. 807
Parrass, J.S. 809
Parrish, W.P. 810
Parrish, Wesley W. 811
Parrish, Willis G. 812
Peacock, George W. 813
Pearson, Charles William 814
Peebles, Aaron G. 815
Peebles, Bella M. 817
Peebles (Peeples), John Headen 816
Peebles, M. Jane 817
Peebles (Peeples), M.E. (Martha) 816
Peebles, Nathanial Aaron 817

Peeples, John Headen *see* Peebles, John Headen
Peeples, M.E. (Martha) *see* Peebles, M.E. (Martha)
Pence, Angeline 909
Pence, Henry 818
Pennington, Icyan 819
Pennington, James 819
Pennington, Margaret E. 774
Penny, Sarah 623
Penry, Boone T. 820
Penry, Joel 821
Penry, Nancy 16, 822
Penry, Thomas Smith 822
Penry, Ursley (Ursula) 821
Penry, William H. 823
Perry, Eliza Jane 279
Perry, Louisa 824
Perry, M.F. 824
Perry, Martha F. 297
Perry, Mary 826
Perry, William 825
Perry, William Haywood 826
Perry, Winnie 825
Petersburg, Virginia *p*4, 59, 91, 146, 168, 174, 178, 197, 203, 217, 270, 271, 282, 289, 318, 362, 393, 406, 421, 424, 440, 448, 470, 486, 518, 524, 535, 542, 550, 553, 576, 603, 610, 637, 639, 640, 660, 664, 674, 750, 763, 830, 837, 843, 847, 867, 882, 888, 897, 902, 914, 941, 953, 954, 959, 966, 989, 1004, 1021, 1035, 1044, 1047, 1048, 1051, 1058, 1106
Phelps, Britton 827
Phelps, Charlie 828
Phelps, P. Jane 43
Phelps, Rebecca 752
Phelps, Uriah Hunt 829
Phillips, John W. 830
Phillips, L.F. 831
Pigg, Hugh 832
Plains Station, Virginia 8
Plott, Clearissy 105
Plott, Elizabeth 833
Plott, John 833
Poindexter, Mary Frances 13
Point Lookout, Maryland 2, 9, 11, 38, 39, 40, 46, 49, 53, 54, 56, 57, 62, 68, 71, 85, 86, 88, 92, 94, 97, 98, 107, 110, 118, 119, 121, 122, 126, 129, 131, 133, 145, 154, 170, 176, 187, 201, 203, 216, 225, 227, 230, 238, 246, 255, 268, 273, 287, 288, 297, 310, 311, 314, 315, 317, 319, 320, 327, 328, 338, 339, 342, 347, 350, 361, 370, 375, 379, 383, 405, 406, 407, 419, 431, 432, 436, 439, 444, 446, 454, 477, 479, 486, 488, 498, 502,
503, 504, 507, 517, 521, 525, 532, 547, 558, 572, 573, 579, 591, 620, 638, 649, 659, 664, 679, 700, 701, 702, 709, 715, 722, 729, 742, 744, 747, 748, 749, 750, 751, 758, 760, 762, 763, 765, 787, 790, 793, 794, 795, 798, 806, 813, 819, 827, 828, 830, 831, 833, 835, 837, 840, 859, 863, 875, 905, 924, 943, 950, 952, 954, 968, 969, 977, 983, 1000, 1001, 1009, 1037, 1038, 1041, 1044, 1050, 1055, 1057, 1060, 1072, 1073, 1079, 1087, 1088, 1091, 1094, 1110, 1112, 1118, 1126, 1135, 1138
Pool, Benjamin F. (Franklin) 834
Pool, Elizabeth 834
Pool, Malona 835
Pool, Randolph 835
Poplin, Coney L. 1033
Pots, Calvin J. *see* Potts, Calvin J.
Potts, A.J. (Andrew) 836
Potts (Pots), Calvin J. 837
Potts, Delitha 685
Potts, Edie Ann 841
Potts, Elizabeth 987
Potts, Emaline 837
Potts, Emeline 381
Potts, F.A. (Francis) 838
Potts, Hiram 839
Potts, Letitia 838
Potts, Manerva 836
Potts, Mary C. 843
Potts, Mary J. 839
Potts, Milton (Allen M.W.) 840
Potts, Newberry 841
Potts, Peter W.M. 842
Potts, Rhoda Jane 840
Potts, William 843
Potts, William S. 844
Powell, E.H. (Elias) 845
Powell, Heneretta L. 532
Powell, Margaret E. 1135
Powell, Mary Emaline 846
Powell, William Hay 846
Prather, Alfred A. 847
Prather, Eli 848
Prather, Vashti M. 284
Prewet (Pruett), N. (Nath) 849
Pruett, Anderson 850
Pruett, N. (Nath) *see* Prewet, N. (Nath)

Queen, Elizabeth A. 851
Queen, Melinda 851
Queen, Rebecca 851
Queen, William 851

Raban, Jonathan 852
Raban, Mary Jane 852
Raben, Samuel W. 853

Index

Rabin, Sarah Ann 765
Ragsdale, Mary 872
Rappahannock Station, Virginia 68, 129, 246, 327, 339, 751, 1050, 1055
Ratledge, D.J. (Daniel) 854
Ratledge, Elizabeth E. 856
Ratledge, Isaac 855
Ratledge, L.P. (Lorenzo) 856
Ratledge, Martha A. 854
Ratledge, Martha M. 857
Ratledge, Rebecca D. 855
Ratledge, Rebecca J. 856
Ratledge, W.H. (William) 857
Ratts, Elizabeth 858
Ratts, Hiram C. 858
Reavis, Elizabeth 272
Reavis, Elviney 265
Redman, Martha A/J 502
Redwine, Elizabeth 859
Redwine, John F. 859
Reid, Susan 860
Reid, W.E. (William) 860
Revis, Ellen 586
Revis, John E. 861
Revis, Nancy Jane 115
Revis, Rachel 463
Revis, Sarah Jane 861
Rhidenhour, Crisia 862
Rhidenhour, John W. (Ridenhour) 862
Riblin, J.L. (Jacob) 863
Riblin, Mary L. 863
Riblin, Sarah A. 863
Rice, Emily E. 1109
Rice, Laura 1014
Rice, Mary 865
Rice, Sarah E. 1119
Rice, Thomas D. 864
Rice, William A. (Albert) 865
Rich, Elizabeth C. 868
Rich, Isaac Oakes 866
Rich, Malinda 867
Rich, Nathaniel Green 867
Rich, Samuel Chase 868
Rich, Sarah A. 580
Rich, Sarah P. 1074
Rich, W.C. 869
Rich, W.G. 870
Richardson, A.M. (Addison) 871
Richardson, David Columbus 872
Richardson, G.W. (George) 873
Richardson, Hettie 295
Richardson, Mary 872
Richardson, Nancy L. 1045
Richardson, Nancy Louisa 621
Richardson, Samantha 873
Richardson, Sarah Jane 871
Richmond, Virginia 3, 16, 24, 30, 31, 45, 48, 50, 63, 66, 77, 86, 94, 108, 115, 121, 125, 127, 129, 130, 131, 137, 139, 145, 164, 168, 174, 185, 199, 207, 211, 223, 262, 265, 266, 272, 274, 275, 279, 286, 289, 298, 309, 314, 323, 327, 331, 336, 350, 359, 361, 363, 370, 392, 393, 398, 405, 407, 413, 420, 445, 448, 454, 456, 469, 474, 492, 514, 528, 538, 545, 559, 568, 577, 583, 598, 599, 602, 606, 608, 616, 621, 625, 628, 629, 635, 653, 659, 666, 672, 687, 688, 698, 704, 712, 713, 719, 720, 721, 735, 737, 753, 768, 771, 773, 778, 785, 794, 815, 819, 820, 834, 837, 848, 861, 874, 876, 883, 888, 896, 911, 916, 919, 922, 929, 947, 963, 965, 967, 969, 983, 991, 997, 1003, 1018, 1025, 1030, 1031, 1034, 1049, 1051, 1055, 1063, 1068, 1071, 1075, 1082, 1090, 1095, 1099, 1100, 1107, 1110, 1120, 1132
Riddle, Sophia Regina 874
Riddle, Susan 874
Riddle, T.C. (Thomas Calvin) 874
Ridenhour, John M. 875
Ridenhour, Lasson 876
Ridenhour, Maria 875
Riley, Emeline 353
Rinshaw, Sarah Ann 509
Roberson (Robertson), Hugh Emmerson 877
Roberson (Robertson), M. Nancy 877
Roberson (Robertson), Nancy J. 877
Roberts, Eliza Ann 728
Roberts, Margaret 878
Roberts, Mary 617
Roberts, Paschal 878
Robertson, Bettie E. 879
Robertson, Elizabeth Ann 646
Robertson, Hugh Emmerson *see* Roberson, Hugh Emerson
Robertson, M. Nancy *see* Roberson, M. Nancy
Robertson, Nancy J. *see* Roberson, Nancy J.
Robertson, Thomas E. 879
Robinson, James F. 880
Robinson, Mary Emaline 846
Roessler (Rosler), Julius 881
Rolan, Eli C. *see* Rotan, Eli C.
Rose, Mary 774
Rose, Pompey S. 882
Rose, Samuel W. 883
Rose, Susan 774
Rosler, Julius *see* Roessler, Julius
Rotan (Rolan), Eli C. 884
Rotan, Eliza E. 884
Rudacil, H.F. (Hiram F.) 885
Rudacil (Rudasill), John 886
Rudacil (Rudasill), Lamira (Zemirah) 886
Rudacil, Martha Ann 885
Rudicil, Anderson 887
Rudisell, Sarah 994
Rudasill, John *see* Rudacil, John
Rudasill, Lamira (Zemirah) *see* Rudacil, Lamira (Zemirah)
Rusher, Edward A. 888
Russel, Margaret M.A. 72
Russell, Gideon F. 889
Russell, Nancy 889
Ruth, William 890

Saferit, Leah 335
Safret, Mary L. 282
Sain, A.T. (Albert) 891
Sain, Amanda Jane 383
Sain, Andrew 892
Sain, Basil 893
Sain, Casper 894
Sain, Catherine 361, 902
Sain, Cheshire 895
Sain, Elizabeth 900
Sain, Emma 899
Sain, Eunice 892
Sain, Jacob 896
Sain, Jane 894
Sain, John A. 897
Sain, Joseph 898
Sain, Margaret A. 897
Sain, Martha 893
Sain, Mary Elizabeth 895
Sain (Sane), Mary Jane 901
Sain, Mary L. 892
Sain, Nathan Anderson 899
Sain, Nimrod B. 900
Sain, Ruth 894
Sain, Sarah E. 891
Sain, Sarah Elizabeth 1084
Sain (Sane), Thomas M. 901
Sain, William 902
Salisbury, North Carolina *p*4, 7, 30, 51, 53, 61, 63, 65, 66, 67, 70, 94, 97, 102, 103, 105, 108, 109, 117, 133, 145, 152, 153, 161, 166, 167, 171, 179, 181, 182, 187, 192, 207, 222, 224, 228, 237, 246, 247, 264, 269, 271, 279, 280, 290, 303, 308, 309, 325, 343, 346, 348, 349, 351, 354, 355, 359, 365, 370, 373, 381, 382, 384, 390, 404, 408, 411, 412, 413, 423, 426, 434, 435, 437, 439, 442, 446, 447, 448, 454, 458, 481, 494, 495, 520, 542, 543, 549, 551, 552, 559, 562, 564, 567, 572, 573, 594, 596, 597, 622, 632, 633, 634, 649, 659, 661, 663, 665, 687, 694, 710, 717, 719, 723, 737, 739, 756, 768, 772, 778, 780,

785, 786, 791, 801, 803, 804, 814, 821, 840, 841, 844, 850, 857, 860, 861, 863, 864, 867, 871, 873, 880, 890, 899, 910, 928, 937, 949, 978, 1040, 1055, 1064, 1068, 1075, 1104, 1110, 1113, 1125, 1126, 1144
Sanders, Sallie E. 170
Sane, Mary Jane *see* Sain, Mary Jane
Sane, Thomas M. *see* Sain, Thomas M.
Sanford, Calvin Cowles 903
Sanford, Mary D. 903
Sasser, Elizabeth 801
Saterfield, Sarah 1142
Seaford, Alice F. 904
Seaford, Catherine S. 650
Seaford, J.D. 904
Seaford, Mary A. 515, 906
Seaford, Mary E. 905
Seaford, Peter 905
Seaford, Solomon 906
Seagraves (Segraves), Jacob A. 907
Seamon, Angeline 909
Seamon (Seamont), H. (Henry) R. 908
Seamon, Losen (Lawson) 909
Seamont, H. (Henry) *see* Seamon, H. (Henry)
Seamont, Luanda 1004
Segraves, Jacob A. *see* Seagraves, Jacob A.
Setzer, Chloe E. 910
Setzer, M.Y. (Milford) 910
Seven Pines, Virginia *p*4, 14, 33, 55, 64, 72, 104, 156, 158, 164, 193, 204, 222, 242, 293, 297, 299, 456, 459, 465, 568, 598, 603, 605, 635, 713, 759, 825, 926, 999, 1006, 1033, 1070, 1084, 1105, 1120
Shackleford, J. (John) 911
Shaddock, David *see* Shadrick, David
Shaddock, Manerva *see* Shadrick, Manerva
Shaddock, Sion (Scion) *see* Shadrick, Sion (Scion)
Shadrick (Shaddock), David 912
Shadrick, Isaac 913
Shadrick (Shaddock), Manerva 912
Shadrick, Mary Jane 913
Shadrick (Shaddock), Sion (Scion) 914
Shady Grove District 41, 43, 165, 181, 189, 191, 197, 198, 280, 302, 364, 394, 456, 466, 467, 469, 471, 507, 530, 623, 624, 691, 698, 716, 745, 762, 815, 829, 833, 837, 838, 842, 895,
916, 928, 936, 969, 990, 1007, 1009, 1024, 1030, 1065, 1066, 1076, 1142, 1143
Shamel, Elizabeth 915
Shamel, S.N. 915
Sharp, Samuel L. 916
Sharpe, Elizabeth C. 15
Shaver, Roxana 394
Shaw, Augustus 917
Shaw, Sarah Jane 917
Shaw, William 918
Sheek, Albert A. 919
Sheek, Ellen Celia 922
Sheek, Isaac 920
Sheek, J.D. 921
Sheek, Leven Alexander 922
Sheek, Susannah 243
Sheeks, Jane *see* Sheets, Jane
Sheeks, John *see* Sheets, John
Sheeks, Nancy *see* Sheets, Nancy
Sheets, George W. 923
Sheets (Sheeks), Jane 924
Sheets (Sheeks), John 924
Sheets, Mary E. 412
Sheets, Mary Emiline 926
Sheets (Sheeks), Nancy 924
Sheets, Nancy J. 877
Sheets, Sarah T. 925
Sheets, Susan 923
Sheets, Thomas C. 925
Sheets, Wesley M. 926
Shives, Catherine 426
Shives, David Franklin 927
Shives, Elizabeth 636, 928
Shives, Giles M. 928
Shives, James 929
Shives, Joseph P. 930
Shives, Louisa J. 927
Shives, Sarah 606
Shives, Susan 929
Shoemaker, Alfred C. 931
Shoemaker, Nancy C. 931
Shores, Enoch 932
Shores, H. 933
Shores, S.O. 934
Shores, Wiley 935
Sidden, Nancy 936
Sidden, William 936
Siddin, Delphia 767
Simerson, John H. 937
Simmons, Henry 938
Simmons, Sousan (Ann) 938
Slater, Delia 271
Sloan, Laura 939
Sloan, William Henry 939
Smith, Alfred A. 940
Smith, Angeline Elizabeth 956
Smith, Asbury 941
Smith, Beal I. 942
Smith, Bulah W. 738
Smith, Elizabeth E. 856
Smith, Elwood 944
Smith, Doctor F. 943
Smith, Franklin A. 945
Smith, James Douglas 946
Smith, James W. 947
Smith, Jonathan 948
Smith, L.W. 949
Smith, Levi K. 950
Smith, Lucinda 439
Smith, M.A. 39
Smith, Martha A. 942, 953
Smith, Martha M. 186
Smith, Mary 333
Smith, Mary A. 950
Smith, Mary E. 562, 1086
Smith, Mary Ellen 941
Smith, Melvina R. 678
Smith, Nancy 946, 959
Smith, Perlina K. 329
Smith, Phebe 958
Smith, Rachel Ann 588
Smith, S.A. 951
Smith, S.L. (Samuel) 952
Smith, Samuel T. 953
Smith, Sarah A. 70
Smith, Sarah J. 1133
Smith, W.H.H. 954
Smith, William A. 955
Smith, William D. (David) 956
Smith, William H. 957
Smith, William Harden 958
Smith, William J. 959
Smith, William P. 960
Smith, Zemerick N. 961
Smith Grove District 7, 25, 39, 43, 46, 49, 51, 52, 64, 77, 84, 104, 105, 109, 126, 166, 169, 170, 177, 225, 233, 250, 316, 317, 318, 319, 320, 322, 325, 353, 370, 427, 438, 445, 465, 485, 500, 501, 503, 504, 527, 544, 545, 548, 554, 579, 581, 583, 625, 643, 657, 681, 686, 693, 699, 706, 707, 734, 736, 738, 746, 747, 748, 767, 775, 776, 777, 778, 781, 789, 791, 794, 799, 816, 836, 843, 923, 924, 925, 948, 970, 976, 978, 990, 1001, 1003, 1007, 1017, 1028, 1029, 1074, 1078, 1112, 1113, 1115, 1147
Smoot, Alexander 962
Smoot, Daniel J. 963
Smoot, John 964
Smoot, Pinkney 965
Smoot, Rebecca P. 283
Smoot, Wilson D. 966
Snider, A.W. 967
Snider, Mary A. 1127
Snider, Millie J. 224
Snider, Sarah C. 346
Snyder, R.W. 968
South Mountain, Maryland 98, 630, 738, 753, 1027, 1058
Sparks, C.M. (Charles) 969

Index

Sparks, John Harvey 970
Sparks, Mary E. 970
Sparks, Sarah Jane 969
Speas, W.H. 971
Spellman, Newton 972
Spelman, J. 973
Spencer, L.W. (Letitia) 974
Spencer, O.H. (Oliver Hause) 974
Sport, Nancy Caroline 975
Sport, William B. 975
Spotsylvania Court House, Virginia 36, 49, 52, 89, 98, 230, 235, 238, 279, 297, 385, 409, 436, 466, 517, 597, 614, 756, 825, 860, 882, 930, 963, 992, 1044, 1104
Spry, Berry (Asbury) 976
Spry, Calvin 977
Spry, John Giles 978
Spry, Margie 978
Spry, Martha A. 942
Spry, Mary 977
Spry, Nancy 976
Spry, William 979
Sprye, Jane 482
Stafford, J.M. 980
Standerford, John 981
Standly, Louisa 797
Stanley, Jane 982
Stanley, Jefferson J. 982
Stanley, Nathan W. (Jr.) 983
Stanley, Sallie (Sarah) 117
Stanley, Sarah A. 983
Steelman, Adeline 157
Steelman, Elizabeth 474
Steelman, George 984
Steelman, J.W. 985
Steelman, Sarah Jane 984
Steward, Edward D. *see* Stewart, Edward E.
Steward, Elizabeth *see* Stewart, Elizabeth
Steward, Spencer *see* Stewart, Spencer
Stewart (Stuart), Daniel 986
Stewart (Steward), Edward D. 987
Stewart (Stuart), Elizabeth 986
Stewart (Steward), Elizabeth 987
Stewart, Elizabeth Luticia 685
Stewart, Hezekiah 988
Stewart, Mary 990
Stewart, Rebecca 988
Stewart, Rebecca J. 856
Stewart (Steward), Spencer 989
Stewart, William 990
Stone, Mary S. 670
Stonestreet, Emely C. 992
Stonestreet, Jediah 991
Stonestreet, John H. 992
Stonestreet, Marja I. 434
Stonestreet, Mary 991

Stonestreet, Mary J. 207
Stout, William Laranza 993
Stroud, David (D. F.) 994
Stroud, Mary Jane 995
Stroud, Nancy Caroline 994
Stroud, Rich S. 995
Stroud, Sarah 994
Stuart, Columbia Lafayette 458
Stuart, Daniel *see* Stewart, Daniel
Stuart, Elizabeth *see* Stewart, Elizabeth
Stuart, J.G. (John) 996
Stuart, Jane 996
Sullivan, Patrick 997
Summers, Greenberry 998
Sutherland's Station, Virginia 71
Sutton, Margaret 437
Swaringen, Iva F. 999
Swaringen, Samuel T. 1000
Swaringen, Sarah C. 1000
Swathlander, Jane 982
Swisher, Mary Jane 995

Tacket, John G. 1001
Tacket, Mary Jane 790
Tanner, Rebecca 11
Tatum, Lucinda 309
Taylor, Andrew Jackson 1002
Taylor, Catherine 1009
Taylor, Elizabeth 1002
Taylor, G.M. (Greenburg) 1003
Taylor, Giles 1004
Taylor, Jane 92, 1076
Taylor, Jennie 1007
Taylor, John 1005, 1006
Taylor, Leonora S. 162
Taylor, Luanda 1004
Taylor, Vira 92
Taylor, Walter 1007
Taylor, Wiley M. 1008
Taylor, William M. 1009
Teague, Mary Jane 1010
Teague, William P. 1010
Teringer, Henry H. *see* Tysinger, Henry H.
Teringer, William *see* Tysinger, William
Terrell, D.W. 1011
Terrentine, Hannah C. *see* Turrentine, Hannah C.
Terrentine, William F. *see* Turrentine, William F.
Tharpe, J.T. 1012
Thomas, Daniel W. 1013
Thomas, E.J. (Evan Jackson) 1014
Thomas, Emanuel S. 1015
Thomas, (Margaret) Jane 637
Thomas, John B. 1016
Thomas, Juley 65
Thomas, Laura 1014
Thomas, Mary A. 1013
Thomason, Virginia C. 1017

Thomason, Willy W. 1017
Thompson, Catherine 462
Thompson, Elizabeth M. 1021
Thompson, John 1018
Thompson, Jonas 1019
Thompson, Joseph 1020
Thompson, Rufus R. 1021
Thompson, Sallie A. 521
Thompson, William Graham 1022
Thorn, T.J. 1023
Thornton, Georg 1024
Thornton, Lourena (Louisa) 1024
Todd, David 1025
Todd, William 1026
Totten, John C., Jr. 1027
Travillion, Meekins (Mickeus) 1028
Tucker, Daniel Seaborn 1029
Tucker, Frederick M. 1030
Tucker, John 1031
Tucker, Louisa 1029
Tucker, Thomas D. 1032
Turner, Adeline 1035
Turner, Coney L. 1033
Turner, Edmond D. 1033
Turner, Esquire 1034
Turner, George Washington 1035
Turner, Henry 1036
Turner, J.A. 1037
Turner, Julia Ann 636
Turner, Martha C. 1036
Turner, Mary E. 905
Turner, Pinkney (Pinckney) 1038
Turner, Sallie S. 1038
Turner, Tobitha Olivia 18
Turrentine (Terrentine), Hannah C. 1039
Turrentine, Sarah 632
Turrentine (Terrentine), William F. 1039
Tutarno (Tutterow), A.P. 1040
Tutarno (Tutterow), Nancy M. 1040
Tutarow (Tutterow), Thomas P. 1041
Tuterow, George W. *see* Tuttarow, George W.
Tuterow, Mary E. *see* Tuttarow, Mary E.
Tutirow, Mariah (Ann M.) 90
Tutorow, George W. *see* Tuttarow, George W.
Tutorow, Mary E. *see* Tuttarow, Mary E.
Tutrow (Tutterow), Mary Ann 1042
Tutrow (Tutterow), Thomas J. 1042
Tuttarow (Tutorow) (Tuterow), George W. 1043
Tuttarow, John V. (B.) *see* Tuterow, John V. (B.)

Tuttarow, Margaret A. *see* Tutterow, Margaret A.
Tuttarow, Martha J. *see* Tutterow, Martha J.
Tutterow (Tutorow) (Tuterow), Mary E. 1043
Tutterow, A.P. *see* Tutarno, A.P.
Tutterow (Tuttarow), John V. (B.) 1044
Tutterow (Tuttarow), Margaret A. 1044
Tutterow (Tuttarow), Martha J. 1044
Tutterow, Mary Ann *see* Tutrow, Mary Ann
Tutterow, Nancy L. 1045
Tutterow, Nancy Louisa Richardson 621
Tutterow, Nancy M. *see* Tutarno, Nancy M.
Tutterow, Rebecca N. 536
Tutterow, Sarah M. 91
Tutterow, Thomas J. *see* Tutrow, Thomas J.
Tutterow, Thomas P. *see* Tutarow, Thomas P.
Tutterow, William Nelson 1045
Tutterow, William W. 1046
Tysinger, Bettie Bell 333
Tysinger (Teringer), Henry H. 1047
Tysinger (Teringer), William 1048
Tyson, Sarah Elisabeth 52

Upperville, Virginia 45, 101, 105, 115, 123, 213, 394, 520, 593, 607, 633, 735, 745, 985, 1025, 1115, 1133, 1138

Vancham, Enoch C. *see* Van Zant, Enoch C.
Vancham, Sarah *see* Van Zant, Sarah
Van Eaton, Barton R. 1049
Van Eaton, F.M. 1050
Van Eaton, James M. 1051
Van Eaton, Malinda 1052
Van Eaton, Mary C. 1053
Van Eaton, McDonald 1052
Van Eaton, Pauline 286
Van Eaton, Richard T. 1053
Van Eaton, Sarah T. 925
Van Eaton, Susan R. 1051
Van Zant (Vancham), Enoch C. 1054
Van Zant (Vancham), Sarah 1054
Veach, Jane 412
Veach, Sarah Ann 1055
Veach, William E. 1055
Venagmes, Catharine *see* Vinagum, Catharine

Venagmes, Thomas V. *see* Vinagum, Thomas V.
Venus Point, Savannah River, Georgia 2, 9, 53, 57, 638, 700
Verher (Vesler), Peter 1056
Verner, Emily 1057
Verner, Hardy 1057
Vesler, Peter *see* Verher, Peter
Vinagum (Venagmes), Catharine 1059
Vinagum, Daniel V. 1058
Vinagum (Venagmes), Thomas V. 1059
Vogler, John Emory 1060
Vogler, Mathew D. 1061
Vogler, Susan 874
Von Eaton, John I. 1062
Von Eaton, Samuel P. 1063

Waddell, Sarah Greenberry 1129
Wadkins, Sarah 1064
Wadkins, William H. (Henderson) 1064
Waggoner (Wagner), Anna 1065
Waggoner (Wagner), David 1065
Waggoner (Wagner), Hanevic 1065
Waggoner (Wagner), John H. 1066
Waggoner (Wagner), Summerfield 1065
Wagner, Anna *see* Waggoner, Anna
Wagner, Christina C. 659
Wagner, David *see* Waggoner, David
Wagner, Hanevic *see* Waggoner, Hanevic
Wagner, Jacob 1069
Wagner, John H. *see* Wagoner, John H.
Wagner, Henry M., Jr. 1067
Wagner, Henry M., Sr. 1068
Wagner, Letitia 787
Wagner, Malinda 1052
Wagner, Mary 1069
Wagner, Mary Jane *see* Wagoner, Mary Jane
Wagner, Summerfield *see* Waggoner, Summerfield
Wagner, W.R. (William) 1070
Wagner, William *see* Wagoner, William
Wagoner, Ann 480
Wagoner (Wagner), Mary Jane 1071
Wagoner (Wagner), William 1071
Walker, Elizabeth A. 851
Walker, George Washington 1072
Walker, Henry G. 1073
Walker, James 1074
Walker, Jane 1076
Walker, John W. 1075, 1076

Walker, Liddi E. 1072
Walker, Martha 1076
Walker, Mary A. 1013
Walker, Mary J. 1072
Walker, R.A. 1077
Walker, Sarah P. 1074
Walker, William 1078
Walker, William A. 1079
Walker, William E. 1080
Wall, William 1081
Wallace, Daniel C. 1082
Walls, John 1083
Walls, Mary 414
Walls, Montraville 1084
Walls, Sarah Elizabeth 1084
Ward, Catherine 1086
Ward, Frank B. 1085
Ward, Lydia M. 1085
Ward, Mary E. 1086
Ward, Sarah E. 530
Ward, Sarah L. 131
Ward, Virginia 1085
Ward, William P. 1086
Warner, C.J. 1087
Warner, H.W. 1088
Warner, J.A. 1089
Warren, M. (Mellina) 651
Warren, Martha J. 630, 1044
Warren, Mary F. 653
Warren, Rebecca Jane 1090
Warren, Safrona J. 729
Warren, Sarah Ann (Sallie) 508
Warren, William C. 1090
Washington, D.C. 40, 57, 69, 105, 201, 338, 394, 401, 518, 520, 573, 608, 633, 638, 679, 700, 721, 835, 861, 863, 933, 945, 1069, 1126, 1138
Watkins, Aquilla 1091
Watkins, Henry 1092
Watts, Mary E. 1043
Welch, Daniel B. 1093
Welch, Elijah A. 1094
Welch, John A. 1095
Welch, Wesley 1096
Wellman, M. 1097
Wellman, Mehetabel 693
Wellmon, Mary E. 428
West, Amanda 1098
West, Anderson Wiley 1098
West, Jiles (Giles) 1099
West, Nancy E. 1099
Wheeler, Lemuel B. 1100
Wheeler, Mary 788
Whitaker, Alfred 1101
Whitaker, Amanda 1102
Whitaker, Noah 1102
Whitaker, Rachel 73
Whitaker, Sarah Jane 861
White, Michael 1103
White, Sarah A. 711
White Oak Swamp, Virginia 41, 413, 488

Index

Whitlock, John H. 1104
Whitlock, L. Jane 1104
Whitlock, Thomas F. 1105
Whitman, Phillips N. 1106
Wilkerson, Mark 1107
Williams, Amanda 1110
Williams, Beauford B. 1108
Williams, Cornelia V. 214
Williams, D.L. 1109
Williams, Daniel M. 1110
Williams, Elizabeth 1114, 1117
Williams, Elizabeth J. 505
Williams, Emily E. 1109
Williams, F. 1111
Williams, Franklin 1112
Williams, Henry 1113
Williams, Icyan 819
Williams, Jacob W. 1114
Williams, James 1115
Williams, John 1116
Williams, John Rufus 1117
Williams, Julia A. 1120
Williams, Mary E. 501
Williams, Mary F. 1121
Williams, Milton 1118
Williams, Nancy 465, 1113
Williams, Neil Henry Calvin 1119
Williams, Pelina A. 636
Williams, Rachel E. 1118
Williams, Richard M. 1120
Williams, Rush Francis 1121
Williams, Sarah 714
Williams, Sarah A. 484
Williams, Sarah E. 1119
Williams, Sarah J. 1119
Williams, William 1122, 1123
Williamsburg p4
Willson, Allice 741
Willson, Catherine C. *see* Wilson, Catherine C.
Willson, John M. *see* Wilson, John M.
Willson, Mary A. *see* Wilson, Mary A.
Willson, William C. 1124
Wilson (Willson), Catherine C. 1127
Wilson, J.W. (James) 1125
Wilson, James W. 1126
Wilson (Willson), John M. 1127
Wilson (Willson), Mary A. 405, 1127
Wilson, Melony 1128
Wilson, Nancy C. (Camomile) 1125
Wilson, W.W. (William) 1128
Winchester, Virginia p1, 24, 53, 253, 256, 339, 504, 614, 674, 746, 898, 906, 926, 1050
Wiseman, Alfred W. 1129
Wiseman, Alphonsine S. 1130
Wiseman, Ellen L. 1130
Wiseman, Joseph W. 1130
Wiseman, Louesa Ellen 227
Wiseman, Mary Jane 1010
Wiseman, Sarah Greenberry 1129
Wiseman, William W. 1131
Wise's Forks, Kinston, North Carolina 11, 38, 56, 92, 107, 110, 170, 203, 227, 268, 273, 287, 288, 328, 340, 347, 432, 444, 498, 507, 579, 591, 620, 623, 664, 702, 715, 758, 765, 859, 875, 1009, 1072, 1118
Wishawn, Sarah C. 439
Wishon, Rhoda Jane 840
Wood, Carter 1132
Wood, Henry J. (P.) 1133
Wood, Ira 1134
Wood, Jincey Ann (Jenny) (Jane) 770
Wood, Mary 191
Wood, Nancy 1132
Wood, Sarah 191
Wood, Sarah J. 1133
Wright, Amos 1135
Wright, John L. 1136
Wright, Margaret E. 1135
Wright, Mary M. 1136
Wyatt, Maloney (Margaret) Ellen 1137
Wyatt, Mary A. 695
Wyatt, W.H. 1137
Wyatte, Susan 923
Wynn, Cope H. 1138

Yates, Albert A. 1139
Yates, Timothy 1140
Young, Hester Ann 468

Zimmerman, Ann 686
Zimmerman, Emly 1142
Zimmerman, G.W. 1141
Zimmerman, Jackson 1142
Zimmerman, Sarah 1142
Zimmerman, Thomas 1143

www.ingramcontent.com/pod-product-compliance
Lightning Source LLC
Chambersburg PA
CBHW081544300426
44116CB00015B/2750